P9-CAG-305

Introduction to Programming Using

VISUAL BASIC 6.0

An Integrated Visual/Procedural Approach
Second Edition

Gary Bronson

Fairleigh Dickinson University

Scott/Jones Inc.
P.O. Box 696,
El Granada, California 94018
Voice: 650-726-2436
Facsimile: 650-726-4693
e-mail: scotjones2@aol.com
Web page: //www.scottjonespub.com

ISBN 1-57676-031-6

Introduction to Programming Using Visual Basic 6.0:
An Integrated Visual/Procedural Approach, Second Edition
Gary Bronson

Copyright © 1999 by Scott/Jones, Inc.
All rights reserved. No part of this book may be reproduced or transmitted in
any form without written permission of the publisher.

ISBN: 1-57676-031-6

Text Design and Composition: Cecelia Morales
Cover Design: Bill Ulch, Art Central
Copyediting: Cathy Baehler
Book Manufacturing: Bawden Printing, Inc.

Scott/Jones Publishing Company
Publisher: Richard Jones
Sponsoring Editorial Group: Richard Jones and Cathy Glenn
Production Management: Heather Bennett
Marketing & Sales: Barbara Masek, Lynne McCormick, Hazel Dunlap, Donna Cross, Michelle Windell
Business Operations: Chuck Paetzke, Michelle Robelet, Cathy Glenn, Michelle Windell

9 0 1   X Y Z

A Word About Trademarks

All product names identified in this book are trademarks or registered trademarks of their respective companies. We have used the names in an editorial
fashion only, and to the benefit of the trademark owner, with no intention of
infringing the trademark.ActiveX , Microsoft, Visual Basic, Windows, and Word
are trademarks of Microsoft Corporation. DEC, VAX, and VMX are trademarks
of Digital Equipment Corporation. IBM and Lotus are trademarks of
International Business Machines. INTEL is a trademark of Intel Corporation.
WordPerfect is a trademark of Corel Corporation.

Additional Titles of Interest from Scott/Jones

Computing with Java
by Art Gittleman

Starting Out with C++
by Tony Gaddis

Problem Solving with C
by Jacqueline A. Jones and Keith Harrow

Assembly Language for the IBM PC, Second Edition
QuickStart in C++
by William B. Jones

Advanced Visual Basic 6, Second Edition
by Kip Irvine

C by Discovery, Second Edition
by L. S. Foster

The DOS 6 Coursebook
The Visual Basic 6 Coursebook Fourth Edition
by Forest Lin

Visual Basic with Business Applications, Second Edition
by Mark Simkin

The Access Guidebook
Concise Guide to Access for Office 97
by Maggie Trigg and Phyllis Dobson

The Windows 98 Textbook, Standard Edition
The Windows 98 Textbook, Extended Edition
A Short Course in Windows 98
by Stewart Venit

Contents

Part Two: Data Structures and Storage

CHAPTER 8

Structured Data   383

CHAPTER 9

Accessing Databases   443

Part Three: Additional Capabilities

Preface

Visual Basic® has emerged as the preeminent programming language for Microsoft Windows® based applications. A major reason for this is that Visual Basic® provides a rather complete set of visual objects, such as Command buttons, Labels, Text boxes, and Picture boxes, that can easily be assembled into a working graphical user interface (GUI—pronounced Gooeey) and integrated into a Windows® operating system environment. From both a teaching and learning viewpoint, Visual Basic requires familiarity with three elements, only one of which is common to traditional programming languages such as Basic, Pascal, and C. These are

- The new visual objects required in creating a Windows-based graphical user interface;
- The new concept of event-based programming, where the user, rather than the programmer, determines the sequence of operations that is to be executed; and
- The traditional concept of procedural program code.

The major objective of both the first and second editions of this text-book is to introduce each of these elements, within the context of sound programming principles, in a manner that is accessible to the beginning programmer.

Change from Version 5.0 to Version 6.0

The most noticeable, but certainly not the most extensive change to this second edition, has been the change in Visual Basic itself—from Version 5.0 to Version 6.0. From the standpoint of an introductory text, the actual language features affected by this version change are actually rather minimal. The significant change, however, is in the new Version 6.0 interactive development interface (IDE), the environment within which students will develop their Visual Basic applications and the subject of Chapter Two. Here the changes are noticeable. Version 6.0 is visually very different from Version 5.0. Because the development environment is the first place students encounter Visual Basic, it is very important that the description of this new interface match what the students will actually see.

Additional Changes To This Edition

Once the decision was made to come out with a new edition, two extensive changes that were anticipated, were included. The first of these changes is the inclusion of a **real-world, multi-form commercial application** that uses all of the language features described in the text. This project, which is keyed to the language features presented in each chapter, is presented as an optional series of focus sections to provide a detailed look at how an actual business system would be developed. Starting with the construction of a main menu form, and using rapid application prototyping techniques, a fully developed business system having a Splash screen and About dialogs is designed and implemented, segment by segment. To avoid the problem of forcing adopters to follow the project's topic development, the project is not used to introduce topics; rather, it is used to illustrate concepts previously covered in a given chapter. Thus, you can use the project in a number of ways to support your particular course by emphasizing selected techniques, omitting the project altogether, or using it in its entirety.

The second change has been to include **end-of-chapter programming projects**. These exercises, which range from the simple to the challenging, are in addition to the end-of-section problems that were also provided in the prior edition.

Finally, although less dramatic in their scope, a number of **new pedagogical features** and material has been incorporated into this new edition. These include introduction of Hungarian notation, introduction of Task Trigger List (TTL) tables, and a set of new Tips from the Pros boxes that highlight practical programming techniques.

The basic requirement of this second edition, however, remains the same as the first edition: that all topics be presented in a clear, unambiguous, and accessible manner to beginning students. Toward this end, the central elements of the first edition remain essentially unchanged in the second edition. Thus, all of the topics, examples, explanations, and figures in the first edition, except for being updated to Version 6.0, will be found in this edition.

Prerequisites

In using this text no prerequisites are assumed. A short Chapter 1 briefly presents computer literacy material for those who need this background. The large numbers of examples and exercises used in the text are drawn from everyday experience and business fields. Thus, an instructor may choose applications and select a topic presentation that matches students' experience for a particular course emphasis.

Distinctive Features

Writing Style

I firmly believe that for a textbook to be useful it must provide a clearly defined supporting role to the leading role of the professor. Once the professor sets the stage, however, the textbook must encourage, nurture, and assist the student in acquiring and owning the material presented in class. To do this, the text must be written in a manner that makes sense to the student. Thus, first and foremost, I feel that the writing style used to convey the concepts presented is the most important and distinctive aspect of any text.

Flexibility

To be an effective teaching resource, this text is meant to provide a flexible tool that each professor can use in a variety of ways, depending on how many programming concepts and programming techniques are to be introduced in a single course, and when each is to be introduced. This is accomplished by partitioning the text into three parts and providing Knowing About sections at the end of each chapter.

Part I

Excluding Chapter 1, which offers basic computer literacy material, Part I covers the fundamental visual and procedural elements of Visual Basic. While this basic groundwork is being laid, much of the enrichment material presented in the Knowing About sections can be introduced as desired. For example, the material on Forms Design (Section 3.9) and Creating Menu Systems (Section 11.8) can be introduced almost any time after Chapter 3. In addition, many professors find that student interest is heightened by introducing the animation and graphics material in Chapter 11 immediately after the introductory material in Chapter 2.

Parts II and III

Once Part I is completed, the material in Parts II and III can be covered in any order. For example, in a more traditional introduction to programming course, Part I would be followed by Chapter 8. However, if a requirement is that the course must emphasize database applications, Part I could just as easily be followed by Chapter 9. In a third instance, if the course is to have a more theoretical slant, Part I can be immediately followed by Chapter 12. In each of these cases, a "pick-and-choose" approach to the Looking Further sections can be applied as these topics are appropriate to the overall course structure and emphasis. Thus, regardless of what the decision is, this book provides a flexible means of customizing a course around the central core topics presented in Part I. This flexibility of topic introduction is illustrated by the following topic dependency chart.

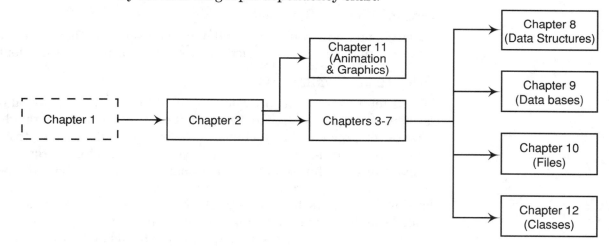

Software Engineering

Although this is primarily an introductory Visual Basic text, as opposed to a CS1 introductory programming book, the text is meant to familiarize students with the fundamentals of software engineering, from both a procedural and an object-oriented viewpoint. This process begins in Section 1.2 with the formal introduction of the software development cycle and is a thread maintained throughout the text. In some instances, this conceptual material can be skipped. For example, a course could omit Chapter 1 entirely and begin with Chapter 2. Similarly, in a strictly language-oriented course, the introductory section on repetition statements (Section 8.1), which presents the concepts of both pre- and posttest loops, might be omitted. The same is true of the database theory presented in Section 9.1. In most cases, however, the more general programming aspects are interwoven within the text's main language component precisely because the text is meant to both introduce and strengthen the why as well as the how.

Program Testing

Every single Visual Basic program in this text has been successfully entered and executed using Microsoft Visual Basic Version 6.0. A source diskette of all programs is included with the text. This will permit students to both experiment and extend the existing programs and more easily modify them as required in a number of end-of-section exercises.

Pedagogical Features

To facilitate the goal of making Visual Basic accessible in a first-level course, the following pedagogical features have been incorporated into the text.

End-of-Section Exercises

Almost every section in the book contains numerous and diverse skill-builder and programming exercises. In addition, solutions to selected odd-numbered exercises are provided on the disk included with the text.

End-of-Chapter Exercises

A completely new set of end-of-chapter programming projects has been provided. These projects range from the simple to the more complex, and thus provide a spectrum of more challenging assignments then those provided in the end-of-section exercises.

End-of-Chapter Self Test

Each chapter now contains an end-of-chapter self test. These test items were taken from the existing instructional resources provided to all adopters.

RAD Focus Sections

These ten new sections provide a detailed look at how an actual business system would be developed. The actual practice of applying rapid application development (RAD) techniques to developing the system, from a main menu for a multi-form commercial system, to developing real-life operational data entry forms and informational forms, such as Splash screens and About dialogs, are presented. Although each section applies specific material developed in the text to the application, the application is meant to illustrate both the need for and application of known techniques. Thus, specific sections can be covered or not, as it fits the needs of your class, or the project as a whole can be used as the central element in the course.

Case Studies

A set of seven case studies that mirror the development of the Focus case is provided. These can be used as semester projects for either individual or group assignment. If assigned as a group project, each member of the group should be responsible for various subsections of the project, with the group as a whole responsible for designing the main menu and interface requirements.

Tips From the Pros

These shaded boxes present useful technical points, programming tips, and programming tricks of a more practical nature that are known and used by professional programmers.

Pseudocode Descriptions

Pseudocode is stressed throughout the text. Flowchart symbols are presented, but are used only in illustrating flow-of-control constructs.

Common Programming Errors and Chapter Review

Each chapter ends with a section on common programming errors and a review of the main topics covered in that chapter.

Knowing About Sections

Given the many different emphases that can be applied in teaching Visual Basic, a number of basic and enrichment topics have been included. These sections range from such basic material as using the Help facility to additional topics, such as defining error types and using the Wizards. The purpose of these sections is to provide flexibility as to the choice of which topics to present and the timing of when to present them.

Programmers Notes

These shaded boxes are meant primarily as a reference for commonly used tasks, such as creating a new project, saving a project, and successfully navigating through the integrated development environment (IDE), the Programmers Notes are also used to highlight programming techniques and provide additional concept material.

Appendices and Supplements

An expanded set of appendices is provided. These include appendices on keywords, operator precedence, ANSI codes, additional controls, Object Linking and Embedding (OLE), and solutions to selected odd-numbered exercises. In addition, the Student Disk packaged with this text includes source code to all applications presented in the text, as well as the source code for the Rotech Systems project. The code for this project is contained within ten folders that mirror the progressive development of the completed application. Lastly, an executable version of the completed Rotech application, as well as executable versions of selected end-of-chapter programming projects, is also provided on the disk.

The second edition is also improved by the following supplements: **Solutions To All Even Numbered Exercises** are provided by Brooks Hollar, from James Madison University, and are available to adopters from the publisher. **Powerpoint Slides** are available to adopters; these were created by Catherine Wyman from DeVry Institute of Technology. **Updated and Expanded Test Items,** also provided by Professor Wyman, are available from the publisher to adopters of this text. Some of these test items repeat the self test items at the end of each chapter, for those professors who wish to administer the same test to students, to measure improvements over time. **Animated Tutorials** also accompany this text, and are provided by the publisher and Carol Peterson from South Plains College to adopters for free distribution to students.

An Expanded Set of Tutorials are provided for sale to departments. These are an excellent resource for any lab, and/or for any distance education classes on Visual Basic. Lastly, by agreement with Microsoft Press, the publisher has made the **Working Model of Visual Basic 6.0,** available on CD, for adoption with this book.

Acknowledgments

This book began as an idea. It became a reality only due to the encouragement, skills, and efforts supplied by many people. I would like to acknowledge their contribution. First, I would like to thank Richard Jones, my editor at Scott/Jones Publishing Company. In addition to his continuous faith and encouragement, his ideas and partnership were instrumental in creating this text. In addition, I would like to express my gratitude to the following individual reviewers.

For the First Edition

Ben Acton
Montgomery College

Dennis Benincasa
Macomb Community College

Sid Brounstein
Montgomery College

Jan Buttermore
Riverside Community College

John Hay
Valencia Community College

Lee Hunt
Collin County Community College

Harold Kollmeier
Franklin Pierce College

Mark Lattanzi
James Madison University

Hseuh-Ming Tommy Lu
Delaware Technical College

Matt McCaskill
Brevard Community College

Jim Moore
Indiana University-Purdue
    University

George Novacky
University of Pittsburgh

Merrill Parker
Chattanooga State Technical
    Community College

Margaret Anne Pierce
Georgia Southern University

James L. Richards
Bemidji State University

Ethel Schuster
Simmons College

Jeffrey Scott
Blackhawk Technical College

John Sharlow
Eastern Connecticut State
    University

Robert Signorile
Boston College

B.J. Sineath
Forsyth Technical Community
    College

Milton Smith
Texas Tech University

Marianne Stefanski
Triton College

Cherie Stevens
South Florida Community College

Sharon Stewart
Howard Community College

Ken Strukel
Hibbing Community College

Melinda White
Santa Fe Community College

For the Second Edition

Eraj Basnayake
Gainesville College

Madeline Baugher
SW Oklahoma State University

Jeffrey Kent
Los Angeles Valley College

Michael Koepp
Everett Community College

Annette Lagemann
James Madison University

Steve Liddle
Brigham Young University

Joe Loomis
College of San Mateo

Scott McLeod
Riverside Community College

Dion Melton
Texas State University

Frank L. Myers
Cabrillo College

Merrill Parker
Chattanooga State Technical
    Community College

Leonard R. Smith
Aquinas College

Martha Tilmann
College of San Mateo

Catherine Wyman
DeVry Institute

Jim Adams
Lloyd Lewis
Dave Hammer
Student reviewers from DeVry
    Institute

Each of these individuals supplied extremely detailed and constructive reviews of both the original manuscript and a number of revisions. Their suggestions, attention to detail, and comments were extraordinarily helpful to me as the manuscript evolved and matured through the editorial process.

Once the review process was completed, the task of turning the final manuscript into a textbook depended on many people other than myself. For this I especially want to thank the production editor, Heather Bennett, the copyeditor and proofreader, Cathy Baehler, and the compositor, Cecelia Morales. The dedication of these people was incredible and very important to me. I am also very appreciative of the suggestions and work of the promotion manager at Scott/Jones, Hazel Dunlap.

Special acknowledgment goes to Mark Lattanzi, of James Madison University, who graciously supplied the material that formed both the Laboratory Exercises for the first edition and part of the Programming Projects for the second edition. This set of projects was further expanded and enhanced by the contributions of Merrill Parker, of Chattanooga State Technical Community College. Additionally, Cherie Stevens of South Florida Community College provided valuable insight and suggestions into various topics used throughout the text, in both editions. Special thanks also goes to Janie Schwark, Academic Product Manager of Developer Tools, at Microsoft, for providing invaluable support and product information. Additionally, the help and meticulous attention to detail provided by both Lindsay Minnaar and Lea Mullikin, two of my students at Fairleigh Dickinson University, in the preparation of the index, is greatly appreciated.

I would also like to gratefully acknowledge the encouragement and support of Fairleigh Dickinson University. Specifically, this includes the positive academic climate provided by the university and the direct encouragement and support of my dean, Dr. Paul Lerman; associate dean, Dr. Ron Heim; and my chairperson, Dr. Joel Harmon. Without their support, this text could not have been written.

Finally, I deeply appreciate the patience, understanding, and love provided by my friend, wife, and partner, Rochelle.

Gary Bronson
1999

Dedicated to Rochelle, Matthew, Jeremy, and David

Part One
Fundamentals

Introduction to Computers and Programming

1

1.1 Introduction to Programming

A computer, such as the modern notebook shown in Figure 1-1, is a machine made of physical components that are collectively referred to as *hardware*. In this regard, a computer is the same as any other machine composed of physical elements, such as an automobile or lawn mower. Like these other machines, a computer must be turned on and then driven, or controlled, to do the task it was meant to do. How this gets done is what distinguishes computers from other types of machinery.

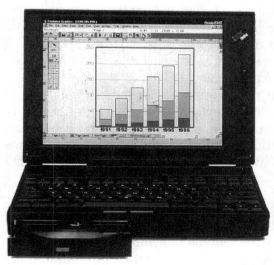

In an automobile, for example, control is provided by the driver, who sits inside of and directs the car. In a computer, the driver is a set of instructions, called a *program*. More formally, a computer program is defined as a self-contained set of instructions used to operate a computer to produce a specific result. Another term for a program or set of programs is *software*, and we will use both terms interchangeably throughout the text.

Historically, the first recorded attempt at creating a general purpose calculating machine controlled by externally supplied instructions was by Charles Babbage in England, in 1822. The set of instructions for this machine, which Babbage called an analytical engine, was developed by Ada Byron, the daughter of the poet, Lord Byron. Thus, Ada Byron is sometimes considered the world's first programmer.

Although Babbage's machine was not successfully built in his lifetime, the first practical realization of his idea was achieved in 1946 with the

Figure 1-1
An IBM ThinkPad Notebook
Computer

3

Figure 1-2
Charles Babbage's Analytical
Engine

ENIAC (Electrical Numerical Integrator and Computer) at the University of Pennsylvania in 1946. ENIAC, which was based on work done previously by Dr. John V. Atanasoff and Clifford Berry at Iowa State University in 1937, was not a stored program computer with instructions directing its operation inside the machine. Rather, ENIAC depended on externally connected wires to direct its operation. This meant that reprogramming ENIAC to alter its operation required changing the external wiring.

The final goal of storing both the raw data and the instructions directing its manipulation within the computer's memory was realized in 1949 at the University of Cambridge. Here the EDSAC (Electronic Delayed Storage Automatic Computer) became the first commercially produced computer to permit instructions stored inside the computer's memory to direct and control the machine's operation. With EDSAC, the theory of a computer program as a stored sequence of instructions, to be executed in order, became a reality that made modern computing possible.

First and Second Generation (Low-Level) Languages

Once the goal of a stored program was achieved, the era of programming languages began. The instructions used in EDSAC initiated the first generation of such languages, which were also referred to as *machine languages*. These languages consist of a sequence of instructions represented as binary numbers such as

```
11000000 00000001 00000010
11110000 00000010 00000011
```

Each new computer type, even including modern desktop and notebook computers, can only be operated by a machine-language program that is compatible with the computer's internal processing hardware. The difference in the processing hardware of early computers, such as IBM, Univac, and Sperry-Rand, meant that each manufacturer had its own machine language. This same situation is still present today and explains why machine-language programs that operate on Intel-based machines, such as IBM personal computers (PCs), cannot run on Motorola-based Sun computers or Apple Macintoshes. As you might expect, it is very tedious and time consuming to write machine-language programs.

One of the first advances in programming was the replacement of machine-language binary codes with abbreviated words, such as ADD, SUB, and MUL, to indicate the desired operation, and both decimal numbers and labels to indicate the location of the data. For example, using these words and decimal values, the previous two machine-language instructions might be written:

```
ADD 1, 2
MUL 2, 3
```

Programming languages that use this type of symbolic notation are referred to as *assembly languages*. Assembly languages formally comprise the *second generation* of computer languages. Since computers can only execute machine-language programs, the set of instructions contained within an assembly-language program must be translated into machine language

Figure 1-3
Assembly Programs Must be Translated

before it can be executed on a computer (Figure 1-3). Translator programs that translate assembly-language programs into machine-language programs are known as *assemblers*.

Both first-generation machine languages and second-generation assembly languages are referred to as *low-level languages*. Low-level languages are, by definition, machine dependent, in that programs written in a low-level language can only be run on a particular type of computer. This is because low-level languages all use instructions that are directly tied to specific processing hardware. Such programs do, however, permit using special features of a particular computer and generally execute at the fastest possible levels.

Third and Fourth Generation (High-Level) Languages

With the commercial introduction of the FORTRAN[1] in 1957, the third generation of languages began. This new generation of computer languages initiated the era of high-level languages. The term *high level* refers to the fact that the programs written in these languages can be translated to run on a variety of computer types, unlike the low-level languages that are restricted to a particular computer type. If a high-level program is going to be run on an IBM computer, for example, a translator program would produce an IBM machine-language program for execution. Similarly, if the program were to be run on another type of computer, an appropriate specific translator would be used. We are still in the era of high-level languages. Figure 1-4 illustrates the relationship and evolution of programming languages. As shown, both third- and fourth-generation languages are considered high-level languages. Additionally, as illustrated, third generation languages include both procedure-oriented and object-oriented languages.

Figure 1-4
The Evolution of Programming Languages

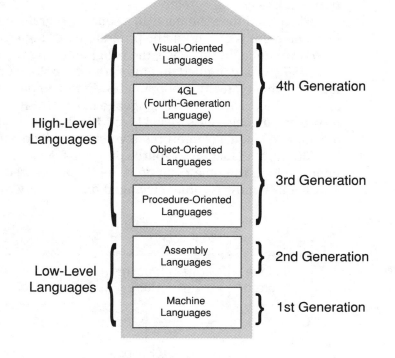

---

[1]FORTRAN is an acronym for FORMula TRANslation.

Procedure-Oriented Languages

Third generation languages, which began with FORTRAN, grew rapidly to include COBOL, BASIC, Pascal, and C. All of these languages are procedure-oriented languages. The term *procedure-oriented* reflects the fact that these languages allow programmers to concentrate on the procedures they are using to solve a problem without regard for the specific hardware that will ultimately run the program. Unlike low-level languages that permitted only one mathematical operation per instruction, a single procedural language instruction can permit many such operations to be performed. For example, an instruction in a procedure-oriented high-level language to add two numbers and multiply the result by a third number could appear as

```
answer = (first + second) * third
```

Typically, a group of such statements are combined together to create a logically consistent set of instructions, called a procedure, that is used to produce one specific result. A complete program is then composed of multiple procedures that together fulfill a desired programming objective.

Until the early 1980s, all new programming languages were predominately high-level procedure-oriented languages. Programs written in these languages are typically produced by following the steps shown in Figure 1-5. Here the programmer first plans what the program will do. The required instructions are then entered into the computer using a text-editing program and stored together as a file, which is referred to as the *source program* or *source file*. The source program is then translated into machine language by a translator program and subsequently run on a computer. The final machine-language program is referred to as an *executable program*, or *executable*, for short.

Translation into a machine-language program is accomplished in two ways. When each statement in a high-level language source program is translated individually and executed immediately, the programming language is referred to as an *interpreted language*, and the program doing the translation is called an *interpreter*.

When all of the statements in a source program are translated before any one statement is executed, the programming language used is called a *compiled language*. In this case, the program doing the translation is called a *compiler*. Both compiled and interpreted versions of a language can exist, although one typically predominates. For example, although compiled versions of the original BASIC language exist, BASIC is predominately an interpreted language, as is Visual Basic. Similarly, although C is predominately a compiled language, interpreted versions of C do exist.

Although all high-level source programs must still be translated into machine code to run on a computer, the steps required to produce a program (shown in Figure 1-5) have changed dramatically over the last few years,

Figure 1-5
Traditional Procedural
Programming Steps to Create a
Program

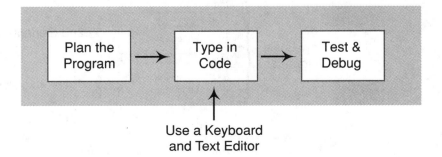

Plan the Program → Type in Code → Test & Debug

Use a Keyboard
and Text Editor

with the introduction of a new type of high-level languages. Languages of this new type are referred to as both *object-oriented* and *event-driven*.

Object-Oriented Languages

Although high-level languages represented a major advancement over their low-level counterparts, the procedural aspect of high-level languages did pose some problems. One of these was the difficulty of reusing procedural programs for new or similar applications without extensive revision, retesting, and revalidation. The second and more fundamental reason for disenchantment with procedural-based programming was its incompatibility with graphical screens and windowed applications. Programming multiple windows on the same graphical screen is virtually impossible using standard procedural programming techniques.

The reason for this is that the major procedural languages were developed before the advent of graphical user interfaces. Because the standard input and output devices prior to the 1980s all used character-based text, such as that produced by a standard keyboard and printer, procedural languages were geared to the input, processing, and output of text characters and not to the creation of graphical images such as those shown in Figure 1-6. At a minimum, a new way of constructing and then interacting with such images was required.

The solution to producing programs that efficiently manipulate graphical screens and provide reusable windowing code was found in artificial intelligence and simulation programming techniques. Artificial intelligence offered extensive research on geometrical object specification and recognition. Simulation provided considerable background in representing items as objects with well-defined interactions between them. This object-based paradigm[2] fitted well in a graphical windowed environment, where each window could be specified as a self-contained object.

An object is also well suited to a programming representation because it can be specified by two basic characteristics: a current *state*, which defines how the object appears at the moment, and a *behavior*, which defines how the object reacts to external inputs. To make this more meaningful, consider the screen image reproduced in Figure 1-7.

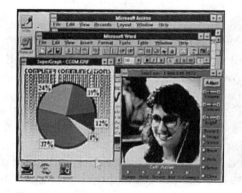

Figure 1-6
A Multi-windowed Screen

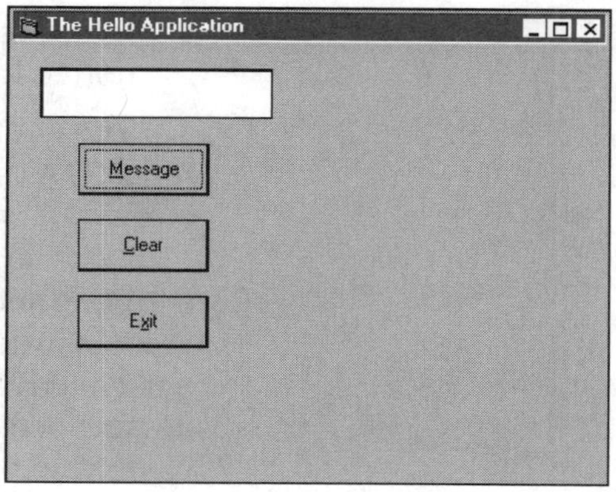

Figure 1-7
The Screen Image of an Executing Visual Basic Program

---

[2]A paradigm is a way of thinking about or doing something.

Figure 1-7 was produced by a very simple Visual Basic Program—one, in fact, that we will write in the next chapter. This screen is an example of a graphical user interface (GUI, pronounced "goo-eey"); it provides a graphical way for the user to interact with the program. Examining Figure 1-7 a bit closer reveals that it contains five objects, four of which the user can interact with directly. The first object is the window itself, which includes the caption (or title), The Hello Application, and three buttons, the Close, Maximize, and Minimize buttons in the top right corner.

Within the window illustrated in Figure 1-7 are four basic objects: three Command buttons and one Text box. Each of the Command buttons has its own caption, Message , Clear, and Exit, respectively. The Text box currently contains no text. In object-oriented terms, the three Command buttons and the single Text box are objects that have been placed on a form when the program was being designed and developed. When the program is run, producing the image shown in Figure 1-7, the form becomes a window. Each object in the window is defined by a set of properties that determine where and how that object appears. The most obvious properties of the Command buttons are their position on the screen and their captions; each of these properties was set by the programmer.

Events

The most noticeable difference between procedure-based and object-based programs is the manner in which the user interacts with a running program. Take another look at Figure 1-7. Here the user has a number of options. He or she can choose to click on any of the internal Command buttons, in any sequence, or on one of the buttons on the top line of the window itself. For the moment, let us only concern ourselves with the three Command buttons labeled Message, Clear, and Exit. Selecting any one of these buttons constitutes an event. As a practical matter, a user-initiated event can be triggered in one of the following three ways:

- By placing the mouse pointer over a Command button and clicking the left mouse button (clicking means pushing and releasing the left mouse button),

- By simultaneously holding down the ALT key and pressing one of the underlined letters (this is called "activating a hot key"), or

- By pressing the TAB key until the desired button is highlighted with a dotted line and then pressing the ENTER key.

The control that is highlighted with the dotted line is said "to have the focus." (As shown in Figure 1-7 the Message button has the focus, so pressing ENTER will activate this control.)

Once an event is triggered by a user, which in this case is done by simply selecting and activating one of the three button controls in the window, program instructions take over. If the programmer has written instructions for a user-activated event, some processing will take place; otherwise, no processing occurs. For the program shown on Figure 1-7,there are three events Command button, the message "Hello There World!" is displayed in the Text box. Clicking on the Clear Command button clears the text area of the Text box, while clicking on the Exit Command button results in a beep and termination of the program.

Notice that the sequence of events, that is, which actions are taken and in what order, is controlled by the user. The user can click any one of three

Command buttons, in any order, or even run a different Windows program while the Visual Basic program is executing. This user determination of which event will take place next, as the program is running, is quite a different approach than the traditional procedure-based programming paradigm. In a procedure-based program, the decisions as to which actions can be taken and in what order are controlled by the programmer when the program is being designed.

Unfortunately, an event-based user graphical interface such as that illustrated in Figure 1-7 does not eliminate the need for all procedural code. The programmer must still provide the code to appropriately process the events triggered by the user. From a design standpoint then, the construction of an object-based program proceeds using the steps shown in Figure 1-8.

The revolutionary aspect of programming languages such as Visual Basic is that they provide a basic set of objects that can be placed on a form while a program is being developed. This is done within an integrated design environment that makes creating the graphical interface quite easy. Thus, in using Visual Basic, the programmer does not have to be concerned either with writing the code for producing the graphical objects or with recognizing when certain events, such as "the mouse was clicked on the Command button," actually occur. Once the desired objects are selected and placed on the form, Visual Basic takes care of creating the object and recognizing appropriate object events. Programming languages that permit the programmer to manipulate graphical objects directly, without requiring the programmer to provide the necessary code to support selected objects and their interface, are sometimes referred to as Visual Languages. Visual Basic is an example of a Visual Language. Using such a language, however, still requires programmer responsibility for

1. Initially selecting and placing objects on a form when the program is being developed; and

2. Writing and including procedural code to correctly process events that can be triggered by a user's interaction with the program's objects when the program is run.

An example of a classic object-oriented language, without the visual programming interface, is C++. The visual language equivalent of C++ is Visual C++. One of the major differences between Visual Basic and Visual C++ is that Visual Basic provides the ability to place existing objects into a program, while Visual C++ also provides the ability to create new objects.

Finally, sitting between object-oriented languages and visual languages in Figure 1-4 is a group of languages referred to as *4GLs*. These are the initial fourth-generation languages (hence, 4GL) that permit users to access and

Figure 1-8

The Steps in Developing an Object-Based Program

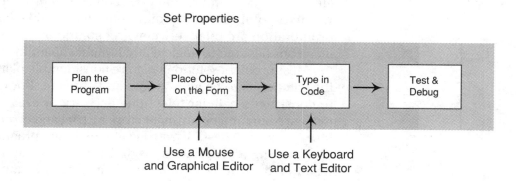

format information without writing any procedural code. For example, in a 4GL, both a programmer and user can type the following English-like command to produce a formatted report with the desired information:

List the name, starting date, and salary for all employees who have more than 20 years of service

In a 4GL, this request for information causes the program to produce the actual code for satisfying the request without any programmer intervention. Since a similar type of operation occurs in visual languages, where the code for each object is automatically generated by simply placing an object on a form, visual languages such as Visual Basic are sometimes also classified as 4GLs.

Exercises 1.1

1. Define the following terms:
   a. first-generation language
   b. second-generation language
   c. third-generation language
   d. fourth-generation language
   e. high-level language
   f. low-level language
   g. machine language
   h. assembly language
   i. assembler
   j. interpreter
   k. compiler
   l. object
   m. event
   n. graphical user interface
   o. procedure-oriented language
   p. object-oriented language

2. Describe the accomplishments of the following people:
   a. Charles Babbage
   b. Ada Byron

3. a. Describe the difference between high and low-level languages.
   b. Describe the difference between procedure-oriented and object-oriented languages.

4. Describe the similarities and differences between procedure and object-oriented languages.

5. a. To be classified as a fourth-generation language (4GL), the language must provide a specific capability. What is this capability?
   b. Must a 4GL provide the ability to create event-driven programs?

1.2 Problem Solution and Software Development

Problem solving has become a way of life in modern society because as society has become more complex, so have its problems. Issues such as solid waste disposal, global warming, international finance, pollution, and nuclear proliferation are relatively new, yet solutions to these problems now challenge our best technological and human capabilities.

Most problem solutions require considerable planning and forethought if the solution is to be appropriate and efficient. For example, imagine trying to construct a cellular telephone network or create an inventory management system for a department store by trial and error. Such a solution would be expensive at best, disastrous at worst, and practically impossible.

Creating a program is no different, because a program is a solution developed for a particular problem. First you must determine what the problem is and what method will be used to solve it. Each field of study has its own name for the systematic approach to solving problems. In science and engineering the approach is referred to as the *scientific method*, while in quantitative analysis, it is called the *systems approach*.

The technique used by professional software developers for understanding the problem that is being solved and for creating an effective and appropriate software solution is called the *software development procedure*. This procedure, as illustrated in Figure 1-9, consists of three overlapping phases:

- Development and Design,
- Documentation, and
- Maintenance.

As a discipline, *software engineering* is concerned with creating readable, efficient, reliable, and maintainable programs and systems, and uses the software development procedure to achieve this goal.

Phase I: Development and Design

This phase begins with either a statement of a problem or a specific request for a program, which is referred to as a *program requirement*. Once a problem has been stated or a specific request for a program solution has been made, the development and design phase begins. This phase consists of the four well-defined steps illustrated in Figure 1-10 and summarized below.

Figure 1-9

The Three Phases of Program Development

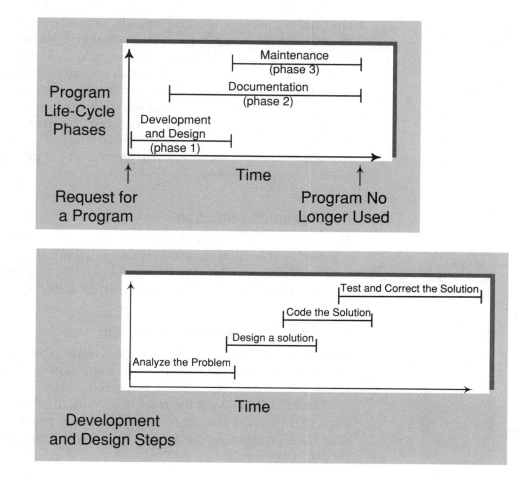

Figure 1-10

The Development and Design Steps

1. Analyze the Problem

This step ensures that we clearly define and understand the problem. The determination that the problem is clearly defined is only made when the person doing the analysis understands what outputs are required and what inputs will be needed. To accomplish this, the analyst must have an understanding of how inputs can be used to produce the desired output. For example, assume that you receive the following assignment:

> We need a program to provide information about student grades.
>
> —Management

A simple analysis reveals that it is not a well-defined problem because we do not know exactly what output information is required. Therefore, it would be a major mistake to begin immediately writing a program to solve it. To clarify and define the problem statement your first step should be to ask "Management" to define exactly what information is needed (the outputs) and what data will be provided (the inputs). If it is unclear how to obtain the required outputs from the given inputs, a more in-depth analysis may be required. This typically means obtaining more background information about the problem or application. It also frequently entails doing one or more hand calculations to ensure that you understand the inputs and how they must be combined to achieve the desired output.

2. Develop a Solution

In this step, we determine and select a solution for the problem. An acceptable and complete solution is typically refined from the preliminary solution identified in the analysis step. This solution must be checked to ensure that it correctly produces the desired outputs, typically by doing one or more hand calculations, if they were not already done in the analysis step.

Sometimes the selected solution is quite easy, and sometimes it is quite complex. For example, the solution to determining the dollar value of the change in one's pocket or determining the area of a rectangle is quite simple and consists of a simple calculation. The construction of an inventory tracking and control system for a department, however, is clearly more complex.

3. Program the Solution

This step, which is also referred to as implementing the solution, consists of translating the solution into a usable application. In Visual Basic, it means constructing a graphical user interface (GUI) and providing the necessary computer instructions, which are referred to as *code*.

4. Test and Correct the Application

As its name suggests, this step requires testing the completed application to ensure that it does, in fact, provide a solution to the problem. Any errors found during the tests must be corrected.

Listed in Table 1-1 is the relative amount of effort typically expended on each of these four development and design steps in large commercial programming projects. As this listing demonstrates, programming is not the major effort in this phase.

Table 1-1	
Step	**Effort**
Analyze the Problem	10%
Develop a Solution	20%
Program the Solution	20%
Test the Application	50%

Many new programmers have trouble because they spend the majority of their time writing the program, without spending sufficient time understanding the problem or designing an appropriate solution. In this regard, it is worthwhile to remember the programming proverb: "It is impossible to construct a successful application for a problem that is not fully understood." A somewhat equivalent and equally valuable proverb is "The sooner you start programming an application, the longer it usually takes to complete."

Phase II: Documentation

In practice, most programmers forget many of the details of their own programs a few months after they have finished working on them. If they or other programmers must subsequently make modifications to a program, much valuable time can be lost figuring out just how the original program works. Good documentation prevents this from happening.

For every problem solution, there are five elements in complete documentation:

1. Initial Application Description,
2. Description of Modification and Changes,
3. Well-Commented Code Listing,
4. Sample Test Runs, and
5. A User's Manual.

The documentation phase formally begins in the design phase and continues into the maintenance phase.

Phase III: Maintenance

Maintenance includes the correction of newly found errors and the addition of new features and modifications to existing applications. Figure 1-11 illustrates the relative proportion of time spent on maintenance as compared to development and design of a typical program.

Using the data provided in Figure 1-11, we see that the maintenance of existing programs currently accounts for approximately 75 percent of all programming costs. Students generally find this strange because they are accustomed to solving one problem and moving on to a different one. Commercial and scientific fields, however, do not operate this way. In these fields, one application or idea is typically built on a previous one, and may require months or years of work. This is especially true in programming. Once an application is written, which may take weeks or months, maintenance may continue for years as new features are needed. Advances in technology such as communication, networking, fiber optics, and new graphical displays constantly demand updated software products.

How easily a program can be maintained (corrected, modified, or enhanced) is related to the ease with which the program can be read and understood, which is directly related to the quality of its development and design.

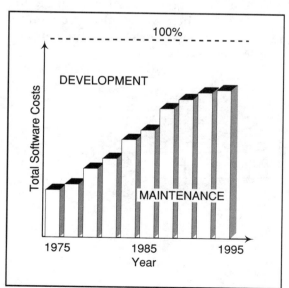

Figure 1-11

Maintenance Is the Predominant Software Cost

A Closer Look at Phase I

Because the majority of this text is concerned with Phase I of the software development procedure, we elaborate further on the four steps required for this phase. The use of these steps forms the central focus of our work in creating useful programming solutions.

Step 1: Analyze the Problem

Countless hours have been spent writing computer programs that either have never been used or have caused considerable animosity between programmer and user because the programmer did not produce what the user needed or expected. Successful programmers understand and avoid this by ensuring that the problem is clearly defined. This is the first step in creating an application and the most important, because it determines the specifications for a final solution. If the requirements are not fully and completely understood before programming begins, the results are almost always disastrous.

Imagine designing and building a house without fully understanding the architect's specifications. After the house is completed, the architect tells you that a bathroom is required on the first floor, where you have built a wall between the kitchen and the dining room. In addition, that particular wall is one of the main support walls for the house and contains numerous pipes and electrical cables. In this case, adding one bathroom requires a rather major modification to the basic structure of the house.

Experienced programmers understand the importance of analyzing and understanding a program's requirements before programming the solution. Most have, in the past, constructed programs that later had to be entirely dismantled and redone. The following exercise should give you a sense of this experience.

Figure 1-12 illustrates the outlines of six individual shapes from a classic children's puzzle. Assume that as one or more shapes are given, starting with shapes A and B, an easy-to-describe figure must be constructed.

Typically, shapes A and B are initially arranged to obtain a square, as illustrated in Figure 1-13. Next, when shape C is considered, it is usually combined with the existing square to form a rectangle, as illustrated in Figure 1-14. Then, when pieces D and E are added, they are usually arranged to form another rectangle, which is placed alongside the existing rectangle to form a square, as shown in Figure 1-15.

Figure 1-12

Six Individual Shapes

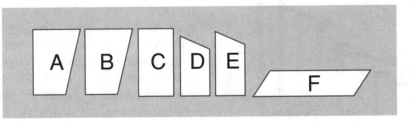

Figure 1-13

Typical First Figure

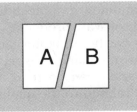

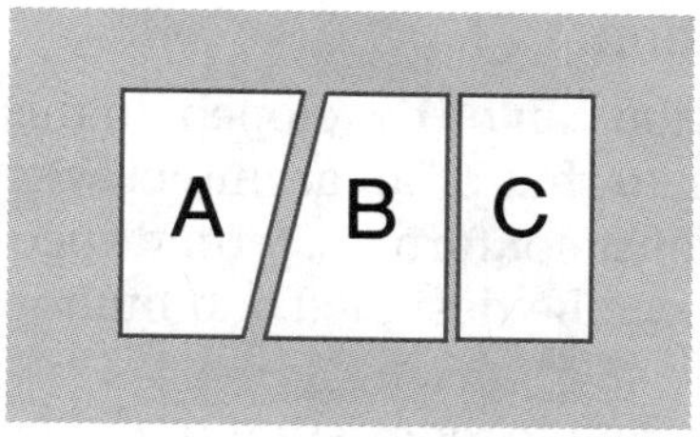

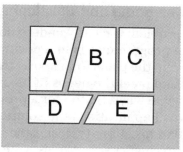

Figure 1-14
Typical Second Figure

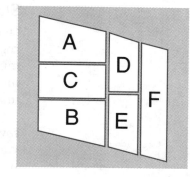

Figure 1-15
Typical Third Figure

Figure 1-16
The Last Piece

The process of adding new pieces onto the existing structure is identical to constructing a program and then adding to it as each subsequent requirement is understood, rather than completely analyzing the problem before undertaking to solve it. The problem arises when the program is almost finished and a requirement is added that does not fit easily into the established pattern. For example, assume that the last shape (shape F—see Figure 1-16) must now be added. This last piece does not fit into the existing pattern that has been constructed. In order to include this piece with the others, the pattern must be completely dismantled and restructured.

Unfortunately, many programmers structure their programs in the same sequential manner used to construct Figure 1-15. Rather than taking the time to understand the complete set of requirements, new programmers frequently start designing a solution based on understanding only a small subset of the total requirements. Then, when a subsequent requirement does not fit the existing program structure, the programmer is forced to dismantle and restructure either parts or all of the application.

Now, let's approach the problem of creating a figure from another view. If we started by arranging the first set of pieces as a parallelogram, all the pieces could be included in the final figure, as illustrated in Figure 1-16.

It is worthwhile observing that the piece that caused us to dismantle the first figure (Figure 1-15) actually sets the pattern for the final figure illustrated in Figure 1-17. This is often the case with programming requirements. The requirement that seems to be the least clear is frequently the one that determines the main interrelationships of the program. It is worthwhile to include and understand all the known requirements before beginning a solution. In sum, before any solution is attempted the analysis step must be completed.

The person performing the analysis must initially take a broad perspective, see all of the pieces, and understand the main purpose of what the program or system is meant to achieve. The key to success here, which ultimately determines the success of the final program, is to determine the main purpose of the system as seen by the person or organization making the request. For large applications, the analysis is usually conducted by a systems analyst. For smaller applications, the analysis is typically performed by the programmer.

Regardless of how the analysis is done, or by whom, at its conclusion there should be a clear understanding of

- What the system or program must do,
- What reports or outputs must be produced, and
- What inputs are required to create the desired outputs.

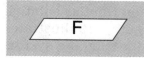

Figure 1-17
Including All the Pieces

Step 2: Designing and Developing a Solution

Once the problem is clearly understood, a solution can be developed. In this regard the programmer is in a position similar to that of an architect who must draw up the plans for a house: the house must conform to certain specifications and meet the needs of its owner but can be designed and built in many possible ways. So too for a program.

For small applications the solution may be simple, consisting of only a few calculations. More typically, the initial solution must be refined and organized into smaller subsystems, with specifications for how the subsystems will interface with each other. To achieve this goal, describing the solution starts at the highest level (top-most) requirement and proceeds downwards through the parts that must be constructed to achieve this requirement. To make this more meaningful, consider that a computer program is required to track the number of parts in inventory. The required output for this program is a description of all parts carried in inventory and the number of units of each item in stock; the given inputs are the initial inventory quantity of each part, the number of items sold, the number of items returned, and the number of items purchased.

For these specifications, a designer could initially organize the requirements for the program into the three sections illustrated in Figure 1-18. This is called a *first-level structure diagram*, because it represents the first overall structure of the program selected by the designer.

Once an initial structure is developed, it is refined until the tasks indicated in the boxes are completely defined. For example, both the data entry and report subsections shown in Figure 1-18 would be further refined as follows: the data entry section certainly must include provisions for entering the data. Since it is the system designer's responsibility to plan for contingencies and human error, provisions must also be made for changing incorrect data after an entry has been made and for deleting a previously entered value altogether. Similar subdivisions for the report section can also be made. Figure 1-19 illustrates a second-level structure diagram for an inventory tracking system that includes these further refinements.

The process of refining a solution continues until the smallest requirement is included within the solution. Notice that the design produces a tree-

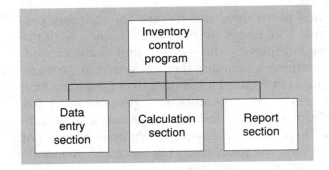

Figure 1-18
First-Level Structure Diagram

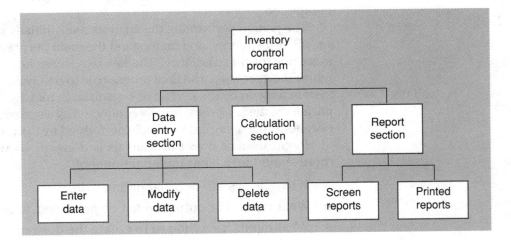

Figure 1-19
Second-Level Refinement
Structure Diagram

like structure where the levels branch out as we move from the top of the structure to the bottom. When the design is complete, each task designated in a box is typically coded with separate sets of instructions that are executed as they are called upon by tasks higher up in the structure.

Step 3: Program the Solution

Programming the solution involves translating the chosen design solution into a computer program. In Visual Basic this means creating all of the necessary graphical user interfaces and providing procedural code. If the analysis and solution steps have been correctly performed, this step becomes rather mechanical in nature.

In a well-designed program, the statements making up the procedural code will conform to certain well-defined patterns, or structures that have been defined in the solution step. These structures consist of the following types:

1. Sequence,
2. Selection,
3. Iteration, and
4. Invocation.

Sequence defines the order in which instructions within each event procedure are executed by the program. The specification of which instruction comes first, which comes second, and so on, is essential if the procedure is to achieve a well-defined purpose.

Selection provides the capability to make a choice between different operations, depending on the result of some condition. For example, the value of a number can be checked before a division is performed. If the number is not zero, it can be used as the denominator of a division operation, otherwise the division will not be performed and the user will be issued a warning message.

Repetition, which is also referred to as looping and iteration, allows the same operation to be repeated based on the value of a condition. For example, grades might be repeatedly entered and added until a negative grade is entered. In this case the entry of a negative grade is the condition that signifies the end of the repetitive input and addition of grades. At that point, the calculation of an average for all the grades entered could be performed.

Invocation involves invoking, or summoning into action, a set of procedural code as it is needed. For example, in response to a user-initiated action, such as clicking a button, an event procedure is called into action, or invoked.

Step 4: Test and Correct the Solution

The purpose of testing is to verify that a program works correctly and actually fulfills its requirements. In theory, testing would reveal all existing program errors (in computer terminology, a program error is called a *bug*[3]). In practice, this would require checking all possible combinations of statement

---

[3]The derivation of this term is rather interesting. When a program stopped running on the MARK I, at Harvard University in September 1945, Grace Hopper traced the malfunction to a dead insect that had gotten into the electrical circuits. She recorded the incident in her logbook at 15:45 hours as "Relay #70. . . . (moth) in relay. First actual case of bug being found."

execution. Because of the time and effort required, this is usually an impossible goal (we illustrate why in Section 5.8).

Since exhaustive testing is not feasible for most programs, different philosophies and methods of testing have evolved. At its most basic level, however, testing requires a conscious effort to ensure that a program works correctly and produces meaningful results. This means that careful thought must be given to what the test is meant to achieve and the data that will be used in it. If testing reveals an error (bug), the process of debugging, which includes locating, correcting, and verifying the correction, can be initiated. It is important to realize that although testing may reveal the presence of an error, it does not necessarily guarantee the absence of one. Thus, the fact that a test revealed one bug does not prove that another one is not lurking somewhere else in the program.

Backup

Although not part of the formal design and development process, it is critical to make and keep backup copies of your work at each step of the programming process. This becomes your recovery of last resort in the event of an unforeseen system crash or an unexpected loss of your original work.

Exercises 1.2

1. a. List and describe the four steps required in the development and design stage of an application.
   b. In addition to development and design stage, what are the other two stages required in producing a program and why are they required?

2. A note from your department head, Ms. R. Karp says:

   > Solve our inventory problems.
   > —R. Karp

   a. What should be your first task?
   b. How would you accomplish this task?
   c. Assuming everyone cooperates, how long do you think it would take to complete this task?

3. Program development is only one phase in the overall software development procedure. Assume that documentation and maintenance require 60 percent of the software effort in designing a system, and using Table 1-2, determine the amount of effort required for initial program coding as a percentage of total software effort.

4. Many people requesting a program or system for the first time consider programming to be the most important aspect of program development. They feel that they know what they need and think that the programmer can begin programming with minimal time spent in analysis. As a programmer, what pitfalls can you envision in working with such people?

5. Many first-time computer users try to contract with programmers for a fixed fee (total amount to be paid is fixed in advance). What is the advantage to the user in having this arrangement? What is the advantage to the programmer in having this arrangement? What are some disadvantages to both user and programmer?

6. Many programmers prefer to work on an hourly rate basis. Why do you think this is so? Under what conditions would it be advantageous for a programmer to give a client a fixed price for the programming effort?

7. Experienced users generally want a clearly written statement of programming work to be done, including a complete description of what the program will do, delivery dates, payment schedules, and testing requirements. What is the advantage to the user in requiring this? What is the advantage to a programmer in working under this arrangement? What disadvantages does this arrangement have for both user and programmer?

8. Assume that a computer store makes, on average, 15 sales per day. Assuming that the store is open six days a week and that each sale requires an average of 100 characters, determine the minimum storage that the system must have to keep all sales records for a two year period.

9. Assume that you are creating a sales recording system for a client. Each sale input to the system requires that the operator type in a description of the item sold, the name and address of the firm buying the item, the value of the item, and a code for the person making the trade. This information consists of a maximum of 300 characters. Estimate the time it would take for an average typist to input 200 sales. (**Hint**: To solve this problem you must make an assumption about the number of words per minute that an average typist can type and the average number of characters per word.)

10. Most commercial printers for personal computers can print at a speed of 165 characters per second. Using such a printer, determine the time it would take to print out a complete list of 10,000 records. Assume that each record consists of 300 characters.

1.3 ▶ Introduction to Modularity

One key feature of a well-designed program is its modular structure. In programming, the term *structure* has two interrelated meanings. The first refers to the program's overall construction, which is the topic of this section. The second refers to the form used to carry out individual tasks within a program, which is the topic of Chapters 5 and 6. In relation to the first meaning, programs whose structure consists of interrelated screens and tasks, arranged in a logical and easily understandable order to form an integrated and complete unit, are referred to as *modular programs*. Not surprisingly, it has been found that modular programs are noticeably easier to develop, correct, and modify than programs constructed otherwise. This is because modular programs permit each screen and its associated procedural code to be tested and modified without disturbing other modules and procedural code in the application.

In a modular application each part of the application is designed and developed to perform a clearly defined and specific function. For example, the first screen presented to a user might include a company logo and a choice of buttons that will activate other screens, as shown in Figure 1-20.

Figure 1-20
A Sample Opening Screen

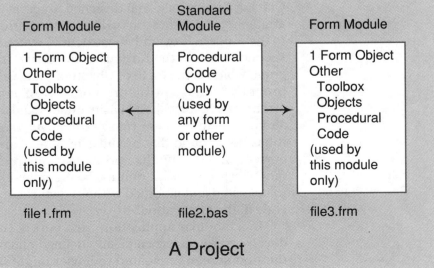

Depending on which button the user clicks, either another screen will appear or some specific task will be accomplished. Each subsequent screen or task would also be designed to produce a clearly understandable and useful result.

Not surprisingly, the segments used to construct a modular application are referred to as *modules*. In Visual Basic modules that contain both the visual parts of a program, that is, the screens seen by a user and the code associated with objects on the screen, are called *form modules*. For each screen in your Visual Basic application, you will have one form module. Thus, if your program has five screens, for example, it will contain five form modules. Each form module is given a unique name and is stored in Version 6.0 as an individual ASCII text file with the extension suffix .frm.

The procedural code that performs actual data processing tasks is most commonly executed in program units called *procedures* and *functions*. Most user-written procedures are stored directly within form modules because they contain the code associated with objects, such as buttons, that are on a screen. Procedural code that will be used by more than one form module, however, must be stored in special code-only modules. Two types of code-only modules exist, *standard* and *class modules*. Figure 1-21 illustrates the interrelationships for an application consisting of two screens and one standard module. As shown, each screen is stored using its own form module, which also contains procedures and functions that can only be used by the screen described in the module. Code that is to be shared between the two screens is stored on the standard module. Initially, we will concentrate on

Figure 1-21
An Application with Three Modules

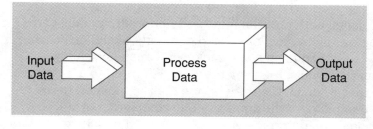

Figure 1-22
A Procedural Unit Accepts Data, Operates on the Data, and Produces a Result

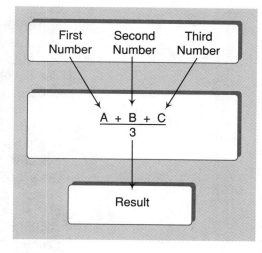

Figure 1-23
A Procedural Unit That Averages Three Numbers

single-screen applications that, by definition, are stored in a single form module.

Procedural Code

Functions and procedures, both of which contain Visual Basic language instructions, are essentially small procedural program units in their own right that must be capable of receiving data, operating on the data, and producing a result (see Figure 1-22). Typically, a function or procedure performs a single and limited task required by the larger application of which it is a part. We shall learn and use both of these unit types in our work, with initial emphasis on procedures.

It is useful to think of both types of program units, functions and procedures, as small machines that transform the data they receive into a finished product. For example, Figure 1-23 illustrates a program unit that accepts three numbers, computes their average, and displays the result.

All procedures have the same structure, which is described in detail in Section 2.3.

A particular type of procedure, one that we will be working with extensively, is an *event procedure*. This is a procedure called into operation, by either a system- or user-initiated event (see Section 1.1), such as the clicking of the mouse or the loading of a screen.

In Visual Basic, event procedures are designated solely by their event names and are described in detail in Section 2.3.

Exercises 1.3

1. Describe what information is contained in a form module.
2. Describe the relationship between the information contained in a form module and that contained in a standard module.
3. List two types of programming units that are used to contain procedural code.
4. What is an event procedure?
5. Assuming that cmdMessage is the name of a button on a screen, determine what events cause the following procedures to execute:

   a. `Private Sub cmdMessage_Click()`
   b. `Private Sub cmdMessage_DblClick()`

Note: Most projects, both programming and nonprogramming, can usually be structured into smaller subtasks or units of activity, each of which can be assigned to an individual user screen or window. The development of each screen can often be delegated to a different person, so that when all the screens and their associated tasks are finished and integrated, the application is complete. For Exercises 7 through 10, determine a set of screens and tasks that could be used for the application. Be aware that there are many possible solutions for each exercise. The only requirement is that the set of screens and their associated tasks, when taken together, complete the required application. The purpose of these exercises is to have you consider the different ways applications can be structured. Although there is no one correct solution to each problem, there are incorrect solutions and solutions that are better than others. An incorrect solution is one that does not fully solve the problem. One solution is better than another if it more clearly or easily allows a user to operate the application.

6. An inventory application needs to be written that must provide for inputting product data, such as where in the warehouse the product is located and its quantity, for deducting amounts when a product is shipped, and for generating reports, such as quantity on hand and quantity sold for all products.

7. A calculation program needs to be written that determines the area of a rectangle.

8. A billing application needs to be written that provides the user with three options: one is to enter the items that are to be billed, one to list all the bills prepared on any given day, and one to list the twenty most recently billed amounts to any given customer.

9. a. A national medical testing laboratory desires a computer system to prepare its test results. The system must be capable of creating each day's results. Additionally, the laboratory wants the ability to retrieve and output a printed report of all results that meet certain criteria; for example, all results obtained for a particular doctor, or all results obtained for hospitals in a particular state. Determine three or four major screens into which this system could be separated.

   b. Suppose someone enters incorrect data for a particular test result, a fact which is discovered after the data has been entered and stored by the system. What additional screen and processing are needed to correct this problem? Discuss why this capability might or might not be required by most applications.

   c. Assume that a user can alter or change data that has been incorrectly entered and stored. Discuss the need for including an "audit trail" that would allow for a later reconstruction of the changes made, when they were made, and who made them.

1.4 ► Algorithms

Before the body of any event procedure is written, the programmer must clearly understand what data he or she needs to use, the desired result, and the steps required to produce this result. This procedure or solution is an algorithm. More precisely, an *algorithm* is a step-by-step sequence of instructions that must terminate and describes how data is processed to produce desired outputs.

Only after we clearly understand the data we will be using and select an algorithm (the specific steps required to produce the desired result) can any coding begin. Seen in this light, writing an event procedure is simply translating a selected algorithm into a language the computer can use.

To illustrate an algorithm, we shall consider a simple problem. Assume a procedure that must calculate the sum of all whole numbers from 1 through 100. Figure 1-24 illustrates three methods we could use to find the required sum. Each method constitutes an algorithm.

Clearly, most people would not bother to list the possible alternatives in a detailed step-by-step manner, as we have done here, and then select one of the algorithms to solve the problem. But then, most people do not think algorithmically; they think intuitively. For example, if you had to change a flat tire on your car, you would not think of all the steps required, you would simply change the tire or call someone else to do the job. This is an example of intuitive thinking.

Unfortunately, computers do not respond to intuitive commands. A general statement such as "add the numbers from 1 to 100" means nothing to a computer, because the computer can only respond to algorithmic commands

Figure 1-24

Summing the Numbers 1 through 100

Method 1. Columns: Arrange the numbers from 1 to 100 in a column and add them.

```
      1
      2
      3
      4
      .
      .
      .
     98
     99
   +100
   ─────
   5050
```

Method 2. Groups: Arrange the numbers in convenient groups that sum 100. Multiply the number of groups by 100 and add in any unused numbers.

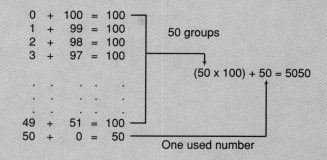

```
 0  +  100  =  100 ─┐
 1  +   99  =  100  │
 2  +   98  =  100  │  50 groups
 3  +   97  =  100  │
                    │      (50 x 100) + 50 = 5050
 .     .       .    │
 .     .       .    │
49  +   51  =  100 ─┘
50  +    0  =   50 ──── One used number
```

Method 3. Formula: Use the formula

$$Sum = \frac{n(a + b)}{2}$$

where

n = number of terms to be added
a = first number to be added (1)
b = last number to be added (100)

$$Sum = \frac{100(1+100)}{2} = 5050$$

written in an acceptable language such as Visual Basic. To program a computer successfully, you must clearly understand this difference between algorithmic and intuitive commands. You cannot tell a computer to change a tire or to add the numbers from 1 through 100. Instead, you must give the computer a detailed step-by-step set of instructions that, collectively, forms an algorithm. For example, the set of instructions

```
Set n equal to 100
Set a = 1
Set b equal to 100
Calculate sum = n(a + b)
                -------
                  2
Print the sum
```

constitutes a detailed method, or algorithm, for determining the sum of the numbers from 1 through 100. Notice that these instructions are not a Visual Basic procedure. Unlike a procedure, which must be written in a language the computer can respond to, an algorithm can be written or described in various ways. When English-like phrases are used to describe the algorithm (the processing steps), as in this example, the description is called *pseudocode*. When mathematical equations are used, the description is called a *formula*. When diagrams that employ the symbols shown in Figure 1-25 are used, the description is referred to as a *flowchart*. Figure 1-26 illustrates the use of these symbols in depicting an algorithm for determining the average of three numbers.

Figure 1-25
Flowchart Symbols

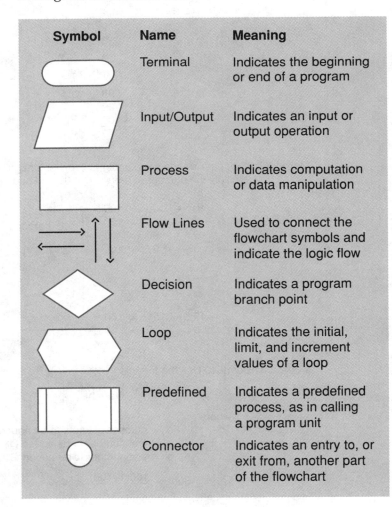

Symbol	Name	Meaning
	Terminal	Indicates the beginning or end of a program
	Input/Output	Indicates an input or output operation
	Process	Indicates computation or data manipulation
	Flow Lines	Used to connect the flowchart symbols and indicate the logic flow
	Decision	Indicates a program branch point
	Loop	Indicates the initial, limit, and increment values of a loop
	Predefined	Indicates a predefined process, as in calling a program unit
	Connector	Indicates an entry to, or exit from, another part of the flowchart

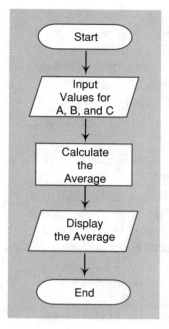

Figure 1-26
Flowchart for Calculating the
Average of Three Numbers

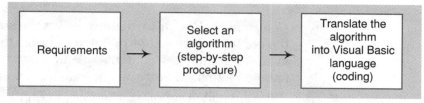

Figure 1-27
Coding an Algorithm

Because flowcharts are cumbersome to revise and can easily support unstructured programming practices, they have fallen out of favor with professional programmers, while the use of pseudocode to express the logic of algorithms has gained acceptance. An example of pseudocode for describing the steps needed to compute the average of three numbers is

Input the three numbers into the computer's memory
Calculate the average by adding the numbers and dividing the sum by three
Display the average

Only after an algorithm has been selected and the programmer understands the required steps can the algorithm be written using computer-language statements. The writing process is called *coding* the algorithm, which is the third step in our program development procedure (see Figure 1-27).

Exercises 1.4

1 Determine a step-by-step procedure (list the steps) to do the following tasks. (**Note**: There is no one single correct answer for each of these tasks. The exercise is designed to give you practice in converting intuitive-type commands into equivalent algorithms and making the shift between the thought processes involved in the two types of thinking.)

    a. Fix a flat tire.
    b. Make a telephone call.
    c. Go to the store and purchase a loaf of bread.
    d. Roast a turkey.

2 a. Determine the six possible step-by-step procedures (list the steps) to paint the flower shown in Figure 1-28, with the restriction that each color must be completed before a new color can be started. (**Hint**: one of the algorithms is *Use Yellow first, Green second, Black last.*)

    b. Which of the six painting algorithms (series of steps) is best if we are limited to using one paintbrush and that we know there is no turpentine to clean the brush.

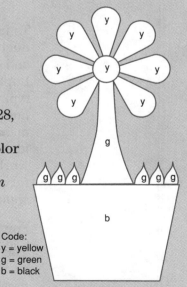

Code:
y = yellow
g = green
b = black

Figure 1-28
A Simple Paint-by-Number Figure

3 Determine and write an algorithm (list the steps) to interchange the contents of two cups of liquid. Assume that a third cup is available to hold the contents of either cup temporarily. Each cup should be rinsed before any new liquid is poured into it.

4 Write a detailed set of instructions, in English, to calculate the dollar amount of money in a piggybank that contains h half-dollars, q quarters, n nickels, d dimes, and p pennies.

5 Write a set of detailed, step-by-step instructions, in English, to find the smallest number in a group of three integers.

6 a. Write a set of detailed, step-by-step instructions, in English, to calculate the change remaining from a dollar after a purchase is made. Assume that the cost of goods purchased is less than a dollar. The change received should consist of the smallest number of coins possible.

   b. Repeat Exercise 6a but assume the change is to be given only in pennies.

7 a. Write an algorithm to locate the first occurrence of the name *JONES* in a list of names arranged in random order.

   b. Discuss how you could improve your algorithm for Exercise 7a. if the list of names was arranged in alphabetical order.

9 Write an algorithm to determine the total occurrences of the letter *e* in any sentence.

10 Determine and write an algorithm to sort four numbers into ascending (from lowest to highest) order.

1.5 ▶ Focus on Program Design and Implementation:[4]

The Rotech Case and Rapid Application Prototyping

To facilitate the transition from learning Visual Basic fundamentals to producing real-world applications, an actual business application is designed and constructed in this continuing series of Focus on Program Design and Implementation sections. Specifically, we will use rapid application prototyping, a method introduced at the end of this Focus section, to produce a multi-screen business system. To make the design and implementation meaningful, we will concentrate on a specific business application. The ideas presented, however, have general applicability to the majority of real-world systems you will encounter as a professional programmer. To reinforce these ideas, a series of business projects is given, one of which you should design and implement using the techniques presented.

Forms

The vast majority of commercial systems are transaction-oriented, where a *transaction* is defined as a logical unit of work. For example, purchasing an item from a store constitutes a transaction. Adding or delivering a product from inventory is a transaction. Sending an item in the mail is a transaction,

---

[4]The Focus sections present a specific, on-going case study that may be omitted without affecting the subject continuity.

Figure 1-29
A Sample Order-Entry Form

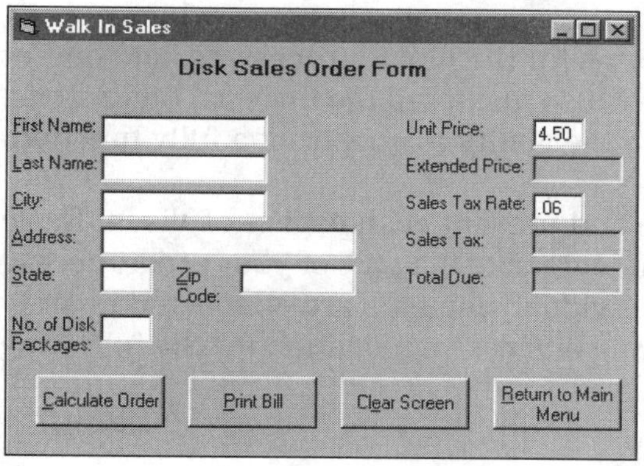

Figure 1-30
A Sample Main Menu Screen

and so on. Transactions that require a user to enter data at the terminal are handled by forms.

A **form** is a computer screen that is the interface for a user to enter data or to request information from the system and for displaying screen reports. For example, Figure 1-29 shows a form for user-entered order information.

Once data is entered into a form, an application will perform one or more tasks using the data, such as:

- Saving the data into a transactions file. For example, storing the data for each sale of merchandise into a file.

- Updating another file. For example, deducting a sale from the amount of inventory stored in an inventory file.

- Performing a calculation. For example, computing the total of a bill, including sales tax, for items purchased.

- Preparing a report. For example, printing a bill for items purchased, or providing a summary list of sales made in each sales region.

Additionally, commercial systems usually perform more than one data entry function. For example, a system might have one form for recording sales, one form for entering returns, one form for maintaining a customer list, one form for maintaining a sales force list, one form for maintaining a list of inventory items, and another form for selecting reports.

A general design approach for a multi-form system is to begin the application with a main-menu screen that lists the application's capabilities. This menu screen, a sample of which is shown in Figure 1-30, allows the user to select which part of the application they wish to work with. For example, by selecting the Walk Ins button shown in Figure 1-30, the user would be presented with Figure 1-29's order entry form.

To understand the forms required for a fully functioning business system requires knowledge of the following items:

1. The requirements of the system, which means what the system should accomplish.

2. How to design a data entry form (input).

3. How to perform calculations (processing).

4. How to construct reports that are displayed on the screen and those that produce hard-copy printed documents (output).

5. How to construct a main menu screen and connect it to the other forms in the system.

6. How to construct and maintain data files needed by the application.

The two most important items in this list are the first and last. The first, because you cannot build a useful system unless you clearly understand what the system is meant to accomplish. Without fully understanding this first item, you cannot use the other items in a positive way. The last item is equally important, because the majority of business systems deal with maintaining data stored as data files. These include adding transactions to a transactions file, maintaining a file of inventory items, maintaining a list of customer names and addresses, and maintaining a list of sales representatives. If the correct data is not stored somewhere that is available to the system, the other elements cannot be used to add data to the files, process the data, or create the desired output reports.

The remaining items in the list are really competency elements. They represent the tools that a programmer must have to correctly maintain data files and produce applications that meet the specified requirements. The first eight chapters of this text deal with these competency items, which consist of understanding how to design forms for the input, processing, and output of information. Only when you have also mastered the material on databases in Chapter 9 will you really have the ability to construct a fully functional business system.

The text is designed to isolate and present each aspect of Visual Basic in a way that you can understand it and make it a part of your programming tool kit. To illustrate how these individual elements are connected in practice, we will also construct a working business application for the following business case:

Rotech Systems, Inc., is a direct-mail firm that is in the business of warehousing products and distributing them in response to various promotional offers made to the public. For example, the special offers made on cereal boxes, where you must send in your name and address, a given number of IPC codes, and a shipping and handling fee to receive the offered item, are all handled by direct-mail firms. Similarly, computer disk manufacturers frequently make offers that you can receive a free set of disks by sending in the same type of data. These types of offers, as well as the ones you see on television for CD and tape sets, are all handled by direct-mail firms.

In our particular case, Rotech receives the responses by mail, enters the name and address of the person responding, the type and quantity of each item requested, and prepares a packing slip so that the items can be picked from inventory, packaged, and sent off. It is also Rotech's responsibility to maintain an up-to-date inventory record by keeping track of all product deliveries into inventory and disbursements made in response to a specific offer. For now we will consider that the offer is for a package of 10 diskettes. Additionally, the disk manufacturer has asked Rotech to accommodate any walk-in customers. These customers, referred to as walk-ins for short, are people who walk in to Rotech's offices and wish to purchase one or more of the promotional items. Due to goodwill considerations, the diskette manufacturer does not want to turn these people away, and has given Rotech permission to sell disk packages to these commercial customers for $4.50 for each package of 10 diskettes. For these sales a bill, which includes a 6% state sales tax, must be calculated and printed.

As their in-house programmer, you have been given the task to design and build a program to handle this application.

It its most general form, this application contains all of the elements you will encounter in the majority of your professional programming work. Let's see what these elements are, and how one goes about constructing a working system that correctly and successfully handles these elements.

Program Elements

The central feature of most commercial systems is the maintenance of a base of data. The data is stored in a file and is commonly referred to as both a data file and a database (the term database is actually a more encompassing term and is explained in detail in Chapter 9). Data, either stored in a separate data file or as an integral part of an application, is further subdivided into two types: static and dynamic.

TIPS FROM THE PROS

Developing Commercial Applications

When developing commercial applications, you will mainly be involved in constructing multi-form systems that interface with data stored in one or more data files. This is because almost all applications, except for very simple calculation programs, deal with extensive amounts of data and must perform many separate business functions. These functions include order-entry, invoice preparation, accounts receivable, accounts payable, maintenance of inventory, etc. In practice, one or more screens are allocated to performing each of these tasks.

By far the easiest to build and the most user-impressive aspect of this type of application is the menu system. This is the part of the system that tells the user what choices are available and provides a means of navigating between different parts of the system. The most difficult aspects of building a commercial system are constructing the databases and the user-interface that permits storing data into, retrieving data from, and processing the data within the database. In between these two extremes are a whole range of competency items that include screen design, performing calculations, correctly formatting output data, and preparing detailed printed reports.

Static data contains data that is relatively static, which means that the data does not change much from day-to-day. Thus, although static data must be maintained by additions, deletions, and modifications, there are relatively few such operations that are applied to this type of data on a daily basis. *Dynamic data*, on the other hand, is data that changes on a frequent basis, with changes made to it on almost a daily basis.

In our particular application, the product list constitutes the static data. Although there is only one item we are dealing with, the specifics of the 10-diskette package could change, or another item could be added to the offer.

Unlike the product list, the inventory file, which consists of how much of each product is in stock, changes daily. This is due to both the receipt of product, which, by itself, is relatively static, and the dispersal of product to the offer's responders. This is a dynamic situation because responses occur on a daily basis. We will also want to keep track of each responder, and for this purpose we will need a transactions data file. This file will consist of the name and address of each responder, and the product type and quantity requested. For now, however, do not be concerned with the details of each file, but begin to see the bigger picture, which is that most commercial systems contain two types of data—both static and dynamic, and that much of this data is stored in data files.

Next, every system must generate a series of reports, which is the output produced by the system. Reports are categorized as either screen or printed reports. A *screen report* is a report that generates its information on a screen, while a *printed report* generates a hard copy on a printer. Typically, a screen report provides a quick response to a single question. For example, in our application, such a report might be used to answer the question "How many packages of diskettes were requested last month from New Jersey." A printed report for our system includes a packing slip for each request. It could also include a monthly summary of how many diskette packages were distributed in each of the fifty states.

Most systems must also do some calculations. The calculations can vary from simple additions and subtractions of quantities to and from inventory, to more moderate calculations of invoices for goods sold, to sophisticated statistical analysis of seasonal fluctuations in product demand. In this category,

Figure 1-31
Components of a Typical Business System

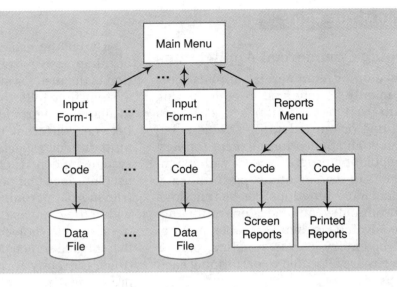

the Rotech application needs to make relatively minor calculations, which constitute adding to and subtracting from the quantity of product held in inventory, as well as calculating invoices for all walk-in sales.[5]

Finally, the last item that each system must provide is a series of forms that are used by the operator for entering all requests and producing all reports. This is the system's visual interface. Access to these forms will be provided by a menu system, which gives the operator a visual means of selecting a desired form and moving between forms. Figure 1-31 illustrates how these system elements are related within a typical commercial system and how an application's interface elements and code are linked to accomplish specific tasks.

In this text we will present each menu choice as a button, such as those shown in both Figures 1-30 and 1-32 (an alternate method, using a menu bar, is presented in Section 11.5). When a user selects a menu item by clicking on the desired button , another form appears. On this next form, which can be one of many, the user may then enter additional data and/or request that a certain task be completed.

Systems Analysis and Design

The traditional method of designing an application, prior to the introduction of visual languages such as Visual Basic, was always to start with a detailed

Figure 1-32
Another Main Menu Screen

Rotech Systems, Inc.

Order Entry

Accounts Payable

Accounts Receivable

Exit

Version 1.0

---

[5]In strict business terms, an **invoice** is a direct request for payment while a **bill** is simply a notification statement of money owed for goods or services provided.

systems analysis. This detailed analysis, which is also required with Visual Basic, but later in the development cycle, defines exactly what the system must accomplish by clearly specifying:

● What reports or outputs the system must produce
● What inputs are required to produce the desired output
● The number of users the system has to accommodate
● The average number of transactions that must be processed in a given time period, usually per hour or per day
● The maximum number of transactions that must be processed in a given time period, usually, per hour or per day
● The type of data that has to be stored by the system
● The maximum amount of data the system is required to store
● Backup procedures in case the system crashes (that is, fails)
● Security procedures for gaining access to the system
● Interface requirements with other systems

The first questions that need to be asked when doing an analysis should always involve finding out the motivation of the person making the request and his/her expectations for the program. For example, such questions as "What is the main problem you are having with your present system?" and "What are the main tasks that the new system must fulfill?" are ways of eliciting very useful and necessary information from the requester. Additional questions include, "If you could make a wish list for everything you want from the system, what would it be?" Later, the wish list can be ranked by those items that are essential, those that are very useful but not essential, and those that would be nice to have but could be omitted, if necessary, due to cost, equipment, or time constraints.

These questions are always asked so that the analyst can see the request from the requester's perspective. Frequently a simple initial request for a program conceals a raft of expectations that are not initially verbalized. It is the job of the analyst to uncover these expectations before the system is assembled. The analysis is completed when the objectives of the system or program have been understood, and all of the algorithms for completing each task are fully known.

Rapid Application Prototyping

Due to the ease with which visual interfaces can be constructed and modified, a more recent approach to designing an application is to start implementing a system before the systems analysis has been completed. This newer approach is referred to as *rapid application prototyping*, and is the development approach we will use in this text for our Rotech System project. It consists of the following procedure:

1. Gain a cursory understanding of the data used and the reports required by the system.

2. Construct a menu system that can be tested by the user—initially selecting a menu item will only bring up a blank form that performs no processing.

3. Complete each form, which includes any input, processing, output or calling of additional forms, and modify the menu system as you gain a complete understanding of the data , input, reporting requirements, and processing tasks.

In this rapid prototyping procedure, the user becomes an integral part of the development process. As you show the user the menu system, she or he can tell you if you have correctly captured all of the required tasks. As you fully understand the data and reporting requirements, you add functionality to the menu and each form, so that a selection ultimately leads to completing a desired task rather than bringing up a blank form. In this manner you get valuable user feedback on the menu's completeness and the ease of using each form, and modify elements of the application based on this feedback.

The advantage of rapid application prototyping is that you get both user buy-in and ownership, in addition to getting early warning alerts of anything the user either doesn't like about the system or elements of the system that are not operating as they should. Users that are actively involved in the design of the system, how it looks, how it works, and how it evolves, tend to take real ownership of the system, have a vested interest in seeing that the system succeeds, and tend to alert you to potential pitfalls early in the development cycle. Since *the success of a system is directly related to a user's perceived ease of use of both menus and data-entry forms*, and also to their perception that the system is accomplishing what they expect it to accomplish, it behooves you, as an applications programmer, to get the user involved early. Make special note of the word *perceived* here. Even if your system is operationally correct and really can accomplish what it is supposed to accomplish, if the user does not perceive it to be easy to use and functionally successful, your system will be judged unsuccessful. This may seem terribly unfair, but it is a major element of how business systems are judged.

To begin a rapid application prototype development you initially present the user with the first menu screen that they will see when the application is run. This menu is easily constructed using the techniques presented in the next chapter, and one is constructed for the Rotech application in Chapter 2's Program Planning and Implementation Focus section.

Task Trigger List (TTL) Tables

One of the first elements used in developing an application and constructing a main menu is a table that lists the tasks required by the system and the events that will "trigger" (that is, activate) each task. This table, referred to as a Task Trigger List (TTL) table, initially contains only the major tasks that your system must accomplish. As your understanding of the system develops, additional tasks are added to the list. When you have completed the system's design, the TTL table will contain all of the tasks performed by the system and the events by which each task is executed. Table 1-2 contains an initial TTL table for our Rotech Systems application.

Table 1-2 Initial Rotech Systems TTL Table		
Form: Main Menu		**Trigger**
Task	**Object**	**Event**
Enter Inventory Receipts		
Enter & Process a Mail-in Response		
Enter & Process a Walk-in Request		
Produce Reports		
Exit the System		

Notice that Table 1-2 essentially lists items that would be included in a first-level structure diagram, but has omitted both the objects and events used to trigger each task. Each task in this initial TTL table will be triggered by clicking a button contained on the main menu screen. Thus, the *objects* used to activate the tasks in the initial TTL list will be a set of buttons, and the specific *event* that triggers execution of a task will be the clicking of an appropriate button. In the next Focus section you will have the necessary information for completing Table 1-2 using correct object and event names. The completed initial table is then used to construct a working main menu.

Programming Projects

Note: For each selected project do the following:

- Define what constitutes the static and dynamic data
- List the data that you think should be stored in its own data file
- List the information that should be included with each transaction
- Construct an initial TTL table (list only the tasks, not the form, objects, or events)

Also note that your instructor may assign one of these projects as a semester project. In that case, you will be required to construct a suitable application using the development procedure presented for the Rotech Systems case in subsequent Focus sections.

Case Study 1

You have been asked to construct a billing system for a local lawyer. The billing system is meant to produce an invoice for the number of hours that the lawyer has spent for the client. The lawyer does not have many clients, and is content to enter in the name, address, and past due amount, for each client. Currently, the lawyer charges $100 for each hour of time spent.

Case Study 2

You have been asked by a local oil company to construct a notification system for its customers. The system is meant to produce an invoice that both notifies a customer that a delivery of oil was made, the amount of oil that was delivered, and the total bill for the most recent delivery. The company currently has 500 customers that it supplies with home heating oil, whose current retail price is $1.25 per gallon.

Case Study 3

You have been asked to construct a point-of-sale system for a local bookstore. The store currently has an inventory of 400 books that are described by an ISBN number, author, title, quantity in stock, and quantity on order. Your system must calculate a bill, including sales tax, when books are purchased, and deduct the number of books purchased in each sale from inventory. Additionally, the system must add to inventory when a shipment of books comes in or a book is returned.

Case Study 4

You have been asked to design a billing system for a local newspaper delivery service. The service delivers the local morning newspaper and has three rates: $2.50

per week for weekday delivery, $1.50 for Sunday delivery, and $3.50 for customers that get both weekday and Sunday delivery. Currently, the news delivery service has 200 customers.

Case Study 5

You have been asked to construct a system for a local dry-cleaning company. The dry-cleaning company currently serves about 600 active customers. The company provides dry cleaning for pants, shirts, blouses, dresses, suits, and outercoats at prices of $3.00, $1.50, $2.50, $4.00, $5.00, and $10.00, respectively.

Case Study 6

You have been asked to construct a billing system for a local psychologist. The psychologist's practice consists of seeing patients either individually or in groups. The psychologist charges $100 a session for individual therapy and $35 a session for group therapy. Currently the psychologist has an active patient list of 25 patients.

Case Study 7

A small municipal bond trading firm maintains a list of approximately 100 municipal bonds that it owns as part of its bond inventory. A bond is described by a 10-digit CUSIP number, an issuer's name, a maturity date, a coupon rate, and a price. The firm deals with approximately 100 other bond firms. Your system must record each bond purchase and sale. The firm has, on average, 30 transactions a day. Each transaction must record the salesperson, the firm bought from or sold to, the amount of bonds in the transaction, the type of transaction (purchase or sale), the price of the bond, the quantity of bonds transacted, and the CUSIP number of the bond. Currently the firm has five sales people.

1.6 ▸ Knowing About: Computer Hardware[6]

All computers, from large supercomputers costing millions of dollars to smaller desktop personal computers, must perform a minimum set of functions and provide the capability to

1. Accept input;
2. Display output;
3. Store information in a logically consistent format (traditionally binary);
4. Perform arithmetic and logic operations on either the input or stored data; and
5. Monitor, control, and direct the overall operation and sequencing of the system.

Figure 1-33 illustrates the computer hardware components that support these capabilities. These physical components are collectively referred to as *hardware*.

---

[6]This section can be omitted with no loss of subject continuity.

Figure 1-33
Basic Hardware Units of a
Computer

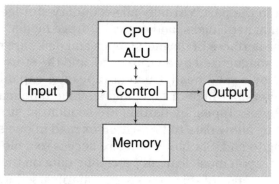

Memory Unit

This unit stores information in a logically consistent format. Typically, both instructions and data are stored in memory, usually in separate and distinct areas.

Each computer contains memory of two fundamental types: RAM and ROM. *RAM*, which is an acronym for *Random Access Memory*, is usually volatile, which means that whatever is stored there is lost when the computer's power is turned off. Your programs and data are stored in RAM while you are using the computer. The size of a computer's RAM memory is usually specified in terms of how many bytes of RAM are available to the user. Most personal computer (PC) memories currently consist of between one and 32 million bytes. A million bytes is called a megabyte, or MB, for short.

ROM, which is an acronym for *Read Only Memory*, contains fundamental instructions that cannot be lost or changed by the casual computer user. These instructions include those necessary for loading anything else into the machine when it is first turned on and any other instructions that need to be permanently accessible when the computer is turned on. ROM is *nonvolatile*; its contents are not lost when the power goes off.

Control Unit

The control unit directs and monitors the overall operation of the computer. It keeps track of where in memory the next instruction resides, issues the signals needed to both read data from and write data to other units in the system, and executes all instructions.

Arithmetic and Logic Unit (ALU)

The ALU performs all the arithmetic and logic functions—addition, subtraction, comparison, and so forth—provided by the system.

Input/Output (I/O) Unit

This unit provides access to and from the computer. It is the interface to which peripheral devices such as keyboards, cathode ray screens, and printers are attached.

Secondary Storage

Because RAM memory in large quantities is still relatively expensive and volatile, it is not practical as a permanent storage area for programs and data. Secondary or auxiliary storage devices are used for this purpose. Although data has been stored on punched cards, paper tape, and other media in the past, virtually all secondary storage is now done on magnetic tape, magnetic disks, and optical storage media.

The surfaces of magnetic tapes and disks are coated with a material that can be magnetized by a write head, and the stored magnetic field can be detected by a read head. Current tapes are capable of storing thousands of characters per inch of tape, and a single tape may store up to hundreds of megabytes. Tapes, by nature, are sequential storage media, which means that they allow data to be written or read in one sequential stream from beginning to end. Should you desire access to a block of data in the middle of the tape, you must scan all preceding data on the tape to find the block you want. Because of this tapes are primarily used for mass backup of the data stored on large-capacity disk drives.

A more convenient method of rapidly accessing stored data is provided by a *direct access storage device (DASD)*, where any one file or program can be written or read independent of its position on the storage medium. The most popular DASD in recent years has been the magnetic disk. A *magnetic hard disk* consists of either a single rigid platter or several platters that spin together on a common spindle. A movable access arm positions the read/write heads over, but not quite touching, the recordable surfaces.

Another common magnetic disk storage device is the removable *floppy diskette*. Currently, the most popular sizes for these are 3.5 inches and 5.25 inches in diameter, with capacities of 1.2 and 1.44 megabytes, respectively.

In optical media, data is stored by using laser light to change the reflective surface properties of a single removable diskette similar or identical to an audio compact disk. The disk is called a *CD-ROM* and is capable of storing several thousand megabytes.[7] Although the majority of CD-ROMs are currently read-only devices, methods are coming into use that permit the user to record, erase, and reuse optical disks in the same manner as a very high capacity magnetic disk.

Hardware Evolution

In the first commercially available computers of the 1950s, all hardware units were built using relays and vacuum tubes. The resulting computers were extremely large pieces of equipment, capable of making thousands of calculations per second, and costing millions of dollars. With the introduction of transistors in the 1960s, both the size and cost of computer hardware were reduced. The transistor was approximately one-twentieth the size of its vacuum tube counterpart. The transistors' small size allowed manufacturers to combine the ALU with the control unit. This combined unit is called the *central processing unit (CPU)*. The combination of the ALU and control units into one CPU made sense because a majority of control signals generated by a program are directed to the ALU in response to arithmetic and logic instructions within the program. Combining the ALU with the control unit simplified this interface and provided improved processing speed.

The mid-1960s saw the introduction of integrated circuits (ICs), which resulted in still another significant reduction in the space required to produce a CPU. Initially, integrated circuits were manufactured with up to 100 transistors on a single one-centimeter-square chip of silicon. Such devices are referred to as small-scale integrated (SSI) circuits.

Current versions of these chips contain from hundreds of thousands to over a million transistors and are referred to as very large scale integrated

---

[7]A thousand megabytes is referred to as a gigabyte.

Figure 1-34
VLSI Chip Connections for a Desktop Computer

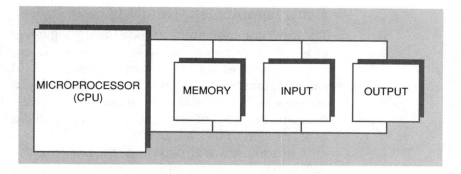

(VLSI) chips. VLSI chip technology has provided the means of transforming the giant computers of the 1950s into today's desktop models. The individual units required to form a computer (CPU, memory, and I/O) are now all manufactured on individual VLSI chips, respectively, and the single-chip CPU is referred to as a *microprocessor*. Figure 1-34 illustrates how these chips are connected internally within current personal computers, such as IBM-PCs.

Concurrent with the remarkable reduction in computer hardware size has been an equally dramatic decrease in cost and increase in processing speeds. Equivalent computer hardware that cost over a million dollars in 1950 can now be purchased for less than five hundred dollars. If the same reductions occurred in the automobile industry, for example, a Rolls-Royce could now be purchased for ten dollars! The processing speeds of current computers have also increased by a factor of a thousand over their 1950s predecessors; the computational speeds of current machines are now measured in both millions of instructions per second (MIPS) and billions of instructions per second (BIPS).

Bits and Bytes

It would have been very convenient if a computer stored numbers and letters inside its memory and arithmetic and logic units the way that people do. The number *126*, for example, would then be stored as 126, and the letter *A* stored as the letter A. Unfortunately, this is not the case.

The smallest and most basic data item in a computer is called a bit. Physically, a bit is really a switch that can be either open or closed. By convention, the open and closed positions of each switch are represented as a 0 and a 1, respectively.

A single bit that can represent the values 0 and 1, by itself, has limited usefulness. All computers, therefore, group a set number of bits together, both for storage and transmission. The grouping of eight bits to form a larger unit is an almost universal computer standard. Such groups are commonly referred to as bytes. A single byte consisting of eight bits, where each bit is either a 0 or 1, can represent any one of 256 distinct patterns. These consist of the pattern 00000000 (all eight switches open) to the pattern 11111111 (all eight switches closed), and all possible combinations of 0s and 1s in between. Each of these patterns can be used to represent either a letter of the alphabet; other single characters, such as a dollar sign, comma, etc.; a single digit; or numbers containing more than one digit. The patterns of 0s and 1s used to represent letters, single digits, and other single characters are called *character codes* (one such code, called the ANSI code, is presented in Section 3.1). The patterns used to store numbers are called *number codes*, one of which is presented below.

Two's Complement Numbers

The most common number code for storing integer values inside a computer is called the *two's complement* representation. Using this code, the integer equivalent of any bit pattern, such as 10001101, is easy to determine and can be found for either positive or negative integers, with no change in the conversion method. For convenience we will assume byte-sized bit patterns consisting of a set of eight bits each, although the procedure carries directly over to larger bit patterns.

The easiest way to determine the integer represented by each bit pattern is first to construct a simple device called a value box. Figure 1-35 illustrates such a box for a single byte. Mathematically, each value in the box illustrated in Figure 1-35 represents an increasing power of two. Since two's complement numbers must be capable of representing both positive and negative integers, the leftmost position, in addition to having the largest absolute magnitude, also has a negative sign.

Conversion of any binary number, for example 10001101, simply requires inserting the bit pattern in the value box and adding the values having ones under them. Thus, as illustrated in Figure 1-36, the bit pattern 10001101 represents the integer number –115.

The value box can also be used in reverse, to convert a base 10 integer number into its equivalent binary bit pattern. Some conversions, in fact, can be made by inspection. For example, the base 10 number –125 is obtained by adding 3 to –128. Thus, the binary representation of –125 is 10000011, which equals –128 + 2 + 1. Similarly, the two's complement representation of the number 40 is 00101000, which is 32 plus 8.

Although the value box conversion method is deceptively simple, the method is directly related to the underlying mathematical basis of two's complement binary numbers. The original name of the two's complement code was the weighted-sign code, which correlates directly to the value box. As the name *weighted sign* implies, each bit position has a weight, or value, of two raised to a power and a sign. The signs of all bits except the leftmost bit are positive and the sign of the leftmost bit is negative.

In reviewing the value box, it is evident that any two's complement binary number with a leading 1 represents a negative number, and any bit pattern with a leading 0 represents a positive number. Using the value box it is easy to determine the largest positive and negative values it can store. The greatest negative value that can be stored in a single byte is the decimal number –128, which has the bit pattern 10000000. Any other nonzero bit will simply add a positive amount to the number. A positive number must have a 0 as its leftmost bit. From this you can see that the largest positive eight-bit two's complement number is 01111111 or 127.

Words

One or more bytes may themselves be grouped into larger units, called *words*, which facilitate faster and more extensive data access. For example,

Figure 1-35
An Eight-Bit Value Box

–128	64	32	16	8	4	2	1

Figure 1-36
Converting 10001101 to a Base 10 Number

–128	64	32	16	8	4	2	1
1	0	0	0	1	1	0	1

–128 + 0 + 0 + 0 + 8 + 4 + 0 + 1 = –115

retrieving a word consisting of four bytes from a computer's memory results in more information than that obtained by retrieving a word consisting of a single byte. Such a retrieval is also considerably faster than four individual byte retrievals. This increase in speed and capacity, however, is achieved by an increase in the computer's cost and complexity.

Early personal computers, such as the Apple IIe and Commodore machines, internally stored and transmitted words consisting of single bytes. AT&T 6300 and IBM-PC/XTs use word sizes consisting of two bytes, while Digital Equipment, Data General, and Prime minicomputers store and process words consisting of four bytes each. Supercomputers, such as the CRAY-1 and Control Data 7000, use six- and eight-byte words, respectively.

The number of bytes in a word determines the maximum and minimum values that can be represented by that word. Table 1-3 lists these values for one-, two-, and four-byte words (each of the values listed can be derived using 8-, 16-, and 32-bit value boxes, respectively).

Table 1-3 Integer Values and Word Size

Word	Maximum Integer Value	Minimum Integer Value
1 Byte	127	–128
2 Bytes	32,767	–32,768
4 Bytes	2,147,483,647	–2,147,483,648

In addition to representing integer values, computers must also store and transmit numbers containing decimal points, which are mathematically referred to as real numbers. The codes used for real numbers are more complex than those used for integers, but still depend on a two's complement type of representation.

1.7 Common Programming Errors and Problems

The most common errors associated with the material presented in this chapter are:

1. A major programming error made by most beginning programmers is the rush to create and run an application before fully understanding what is required, including the algorithms that will be used to produce the desired result. A symptom of this haste to get a program entered into the computer is the lack of any documentation or even a program outline. Many problems can be caught just by checking the selected algorithm written in pseudocode.

2. A second major error is not backing up a program. Almost all new programmers make this mistake until they lose a program that has taken considerable time to code.

3. The third error made by many new programmers is not understanding that computers respond only to explicitly defined algorithms. Telling a computer to add a group of numbers is quite different than telling a friend to add the numbers. The computer must be given, in a programming language, the precise instructions for performing any operation.

1.8 ▶ Chapter Review

Key Terms

algorithm
analysis
assembler

assembly language
coding
compiler

development and design
documentation
hardware

Summary

1. The first recorded attempt at creating a self-operating computational machine was by Charles Babbage in 1822.

2. The ENIAC (Electrical Numerical Integrator and Computer) was the first working digital computer. It became operational in 1946 and depended on externally connected wires to direct its operation. The internal design of ENIAC was based on work done previously by Dr. John V. Atanasoff and Clifford Berry at Iowa State University in 1937.

3. The EDSAC (Electronic Delayed Storage Automatic Computer) became the first commercially produced computer to permit instructions stored inside the computer's memory to direct and control the machine's operation. Prior to this computers used external wiring to direct their operation.

4. Programming languages come in a variety of forms and types. Machine-language programs contain the binary codes that can be executed by a computer. Assembly languages permit the use of symbolic names for mathematical operations and memory addresses. Machine and assembly languages are referred to as *low-level languages*.

5. *High-level languages* are written using instructions that resemble a natural language, such as English, and can be run on a variety of computer types. Compiler languages require a compiler to translate the program into machine code, while interpreter languages require an interpreter to do the translation.

6. *Procedure-oriented* languages consist of a series of procedures that direct the operation of a computer.

7. *Object-oriented* languages permit the use of objects within a program. Each object is defined by its properties, such as size and color.

8. *Event-based* programs execute program code depending on what events occur, which in turn depends on what the user does.

9. GUIs are graphical user interfaces that provide the user with objects that recognize events, such as clicking a mouse.

10. An *algorithm* is a step-by-step sequence of instructions that describes how a computation is to be performed.

Test Yourself—Short Answer

1. A set of instructions to tell the computer what to do is called a _____.

2. An example of a *high-level* language is _____.

3. All high-level languages must be translated into _____ before they can be executed on the computer.

4. A programming language that is translated into executable code, line by line, *as it is executed* is called an _____ language.

5. A programming language that translates all of the code into executable statements *before* any execution takes place is called a _____ language.

6. The editor that is used in creating a graphical interface is a _____ editor.

7. The phase of software development that accounts for more than 75% of overall system cost for the majority of systems is _____ of the system.

8. The four steps required in the development and design phase of a program are _____, _____, _____, and _____.

9. Of the four steps required in the development and design phase of a program , the step that requires the most effort in large commercial systems is _____.

10. The visual parts of a Visual Basic program are stored in _____ modules.

Introduction to Visual Basic

In this chapter we begin our journey into learning both the fundamentals of programming and Visual Basic. First we examine the two elements required by every practical Visual Basic program: the screens and instructions seen by the user and the "behind the scenes" processing done by the program. We then present the basic design windows that you must be familiar with to produce such programs. Finally, we show you how to use these design windows to create the graphical user interface, or GUI, and then add processing instructions.

2.1 Elements of a Visual Basic Application

Visual Basic was initially introduced in 1991 as the first programming language that directly supported programmable graphical user interfaces using language supplied objects. Version 2.0 appeared in 1992, followed by Version 3.0 in 1993. Version 4.0, introduced in 1995, provided the additional capability of creating user-defined objects, and unlike earlier versions that created 16-bit machine code (see Section 1.7), each edition of Version 4 allowed the creation of 32-bit code.[1] Thus, Visual Basic 4 applications could achieve a Windows 95 look and feel.

On March 19, 1997, Microsoft announced the commercial introduction of Version 5.0. The major enhancements provided by this version were an improved design environment, an improved debugging environment, and the introduction of ActiveX support. From a practical standpoint, the term ActiveX has a number of different meanings (see Appendix F). Fundamentally, however, ActiveX is a programming technology that permits cross

---

[1] The Professional and Enterprise editions also permitted the construction of 16-bit code, while the Standard edition could only produce 32-bit code.

use of any ActiveX component by any programming language that supports the technology. This means that an ActiveX component created in Visual Basic can be used within a C++ environment that supports ActiveX. Additionally, complete ActiveX programs can be transferred across the Internet and executed by different computers connected to the Internet. Like earlier versions, Version 5.0 also permits integration and control of Microsoft Excel, Access, and Word applications directly from within a Visual Basic program.

Visual Basic Version 6.0, introduced in 1998, comes in three commercial editions, named the Student Edition, Professional Edition, and Enterprise Edition. This newest version, except for a number of advanced features, re-designed development screens, and an improved Help facility, retains all of the basic features common to Version 5.0. Essentially, we will be describing the Professional Edition, but will point out the differences between this and the other editions as we proceed. Henceforth, when the term Visual Basic Version 6.0 is used in the text, it will describe the common features of the Student, Professional, and Enterprise editions only.

From a programming viewpoint Visual Basic Version 6.0 is an object-based programming language that consists of two fundamental parts, a visual part and a language part.[2] The visual part of the language consists of a set of objects, while the language part consists of a high-level procedural programming language.

The two elements of the language, the visual part and the programming language part, are used together to create applications. An *application* is simply a Visual Basic program that can be run under the Windows operating system. The term application is frequently used in preference to the word program for two reasons: one, it is the term selected by Microsoft to designate any program that can be run under its Windows Operating System (all versions) and two, it is used to avoid confusion with older procedural programs that consist entirely of a language element. For our purposes we can express the elements of a Visual Basic application this way:

```
Visual Basic Application = Object-Based Visual Part + Procedural-Based Language Part
```

Thus, learning to create Visual Basic applications requires being very familiar with both elements, visual and language.

The Visual Element

From a user's standpoint, the visual part of an application is provided by the window. This is the graphical interface that allows the user to see the inputs and outputs provided by the application. This user interface is referred to as the *graphical user interface* (GUI). From a programmer's perspective the graphical user interface is constructed from a set of objects placed on a form when the program is being developed. For example, consider Figure

---

[2]An object-oriented programming language is one that not only uses objects but provides the additional ability to create new object types from existing types, using features called inheritance and polymorphism. Prior to Version 4.0, Visual Basic did not provide the ability to create new object types, and the term object-based effectively denoted that the language was a consumer, or user of objects, rather than a creator of them. Although Versions 4.0, 5.0, and 6.0 do provide the ability to create new object types, since they do not provide a true inheritance feature, they cannot be classified as object-oriented and are instead, still referred to as object-based languages.

Figure 2-1
A User's View of an Application

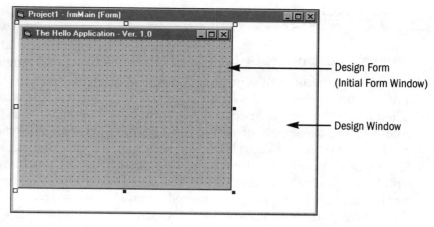

Design Form
(Initial Form Window)

Design Window

Figure 2-2
The Design Form on Which Figure 2-1 Is Based

2-1, which shows how a particular application would look to the user. From a programmer's viewpoint, the application shown in Figure 2-1 is based on the design form shown in Figure 2-2.

On this form, which is itself a Visual Basic object, the programmer can place various objects. When an application is run the form becomes a window that provides the background for the various objects placed on the form by the programmer. The objects on the window become the controls used to direct program events. Let's take a moment to look at the objects provided in common by all three Visual Basic editions. When Visual Basic is started one of the windows that it supplies is called the object toolbox. The standard object toolbox, which is provided by all three editions of Visual Basic and is illustrated in Figure 2-3, contains the objects we will use in constructing each graphical user interface.

Figure 2-3
The Standard Object Toolbox

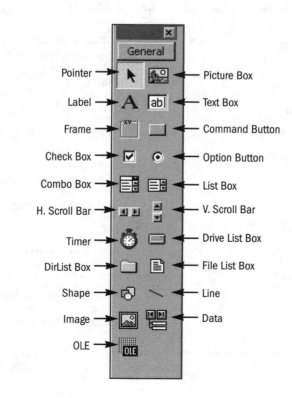

Pointer — Picture Box

Label — Text Box

Frame — Command Button

Check Box — Option Button

Combo Box — List Box

H. Scroll Bar — V. Scroll Bar

Timer — Drive List Box

DirList Box — File List Box

Shape — Line

Image — Data

OLE

PROGRAMMERS NOTES

Forms and Controls

A *form* is a container upon which controls are placed during the design of an application. When an application is executed, the form becomes either a window or dialog box. Forms can be of two types, SDI or MDI. The acronym SDI stands for Single Document Interface, which means that only one window at a time can be displayed by an application. SDI applications can have multiple windows, but only one window at a time can be viewed by a user.

The acronym MDI refers to Multiple Document Interface, which means the application consists of a single "parent" or main window that can contain multiple "child" or internal windows. For example, the Notepad application supplied with the Windows operating system is an SDI application, while Excel and Access are both MDI applications.

A *control* is an object that can be placed on a form, and has its own set of recognized properties, methods, and events. Controls are used to receive user input, display output, and trigger event procedures.

Surprisingly, a majority of applications can be constructed using a minimal set of the objects provided by the standard object toolbox. This minimal set consists of the Label, Text box, Picture, and Command button objects. The next set of objects frequently found in applications include the Check box, Option button, List box, and Combo box. Finally, the Timer and Image box can be used for constructing interesting moving images across the window. Table 2-1 lists these object types and describes what each object is used for. It is the purpose of the remaining sections of the text to more thoroughly introduce you to all of the objects in the toolbox, with special emphasis on the three objects (Label, Text box, and Command button) that you will use in almost every application you develop.

In addition to the basic set of controls provided in the standard toolbox by all three Visual Basic editions, an extended set of controls is provided

Table 2-1 Fundamental Object Types and Their Uses

Object Type	Use
Label	Create text that a user cannot directly change.
Text Box	Enter or display data.
Picture Box	Display text or graphics.
Command Button (also called a push-button)	Initiate an action, such as a display or calculation.
Check Box	Select one option from two mutually exclusive options.
Option Button (also called a radio-button)	Select one option from a group of mutually exclusive options.
List Box	Display a list of items from which one can be selected.
Combo Box	Display a list of items from which one can be selected, plus permit users to type the value of the desired item.
Image	Display a text or graphics with fewer options than a Picture box.
Timer	Create a timer to automatically initiate program actions.

within each edition. These added controls, which were referred to as OCXs in Version 4, are referred to as ActiveX controls in Versions 5 and 6.[3] Specifically, the Student, Professional, and Enterprise editions provide additional ActiveX controls, that can be included within the object toolbox. For a greater number of objects, either for special purpose applications or to enhance standard applications, third-party ActiveX controls can be purchased.[4]

Don't be overwhelmed by all of the available controls. At a minimum you will always have the objects provided by the standard toolbox available to you, and these are the ones we will be working with. Once you learn how to place the standard control objects on a form you will also understand how to place the additional objects, because every object used in a Visual Basic application, whether it is selected from a standard, extended, or third party object toolbox, is placed on a form in the same simple manner. Similarly, each and every object contains two basic characteristics: properties and methods.

An object's *properties* define its state, which is simply how the object appears on the screen. For example, the properties of a Text box include the location of the Text box on the form, the color of the box (the background color), the color that text will be displayed in the box (the foreground color), and whether it is read-only or can also be written to by the user.

Methods are pre-defined procedures that are supplied with the object for performing specific tasks. For example, you can use a method to move an object to a different location or change its size.

Additionally, each object recognizes certain actions. For example, a Command button recognizes when the mouse pointer is pointing to it and the left mouse button is clicked. These types of actions, as we have seen, are referred to as *events*. In our example we would say that the Command button recognizes the mouse-click event. Once an event is activated, however, we must write our own procedures to do something in response to the event. This is where the language element of Visual Basic comes into play.

The Language Element

Before the advent of graphical user interfaces, computer programs consisted entirely of a sequence of instructions, and programming was the process of writing these instructions in a language that the computer could respond to. The set of instructions and rules that could be used to construct a program was called a programming language. Frequently, the word *code* was used to designate the instructions contained within a program. With the advent of graphical user interfaces the need for code (program instructions) has not gone away—rather it forms the basis for responding to the events taking place on the GUI. Figure 2-4 illustrates the interaction between an event and program code.

As illustrated in Figure 2-4, an event, such as clicking the mouse on a Command button, sets in motion a sequence of occurrences. If code has

---

[3]The term OCX comes from the fact that each such control is stored in a separate file that has an `.ocx` extension. The terms ActiveX control and OCX control are effectively synonyms.

[4]The term *third-party* stems from the following: The first party is considered the supplier of the Visual Basic package (Microsoft, Borland, etc.). The second party is the applications developer (the programmer). The third party is the supplier of any additional software or tools used in the application.

Figure 2-4
An Event "Triggers" the Initiaion of
a Procedure

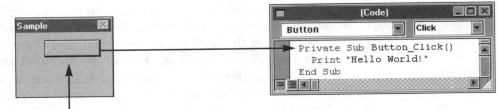

An event such as clicking on this button . . .   . . . causes this code to execute.

been written for the event, the code is executed, otherwise the event is ig-nored. This is, of course, the essence of graphical user interfaces and event-driven applications—the selection of which code is executed depends on what events occur, which ultimately depends on what the user does. The code, however, must still be written by the programmer.

The Visual Basic programming language is a high-level language that supports all of the procedural programming features found in most other modern languages. These include statements to perform calculations, as well as statements that permit repetitive instruction execution, and state-ments to select between two or more alternatives.

With these basics in mind, it is now time to create our first Visual Basic application. In the next section we introduce the Visual Basic programming environment and create an application that uses a single object, the form it-self. We will then add additional objects and code to create a more complete Visual Basic application.

Exercises 2.1

1. List the two elements of a Visual Basic Application.
2. What is the purpose of a GUI and what elements does a user see in a GUI?
3. What does a Visual Basic toolbox provide?
4. Name and describe the use of the four most commonly used toolbox objects.
5. When an application is run, what does a design form become?
6. What gets executed when an event occurs?

2.2 Getting Started in Visual Basic

It's now time to begin designing and developing Visual Basic programs. To do this you will have to bring up the opening Visual Basic screen and un-derstand the basic elements of the Visual Basic development environment. To bring up the opening Visual Basic screen either double-click on the Visual Basic icon (see Figure 2-5), which is typically located within the Visual Basic Group, or, if you have a shortcut to Visual Basic on the desktop, double-click on this icon.

When you first launch the Professional edition of Visual Basic, the New Project dialog box shown in Figure 2-6 will appear. This dialog consists of three tabs, named New, Existing, and Recent, respectively. Clicking on the Existing tab brings up a standard Windows 95 file Dialog box, which permits

Figure 2-5
The Visual Basic Icon within the
Visual Basic Group

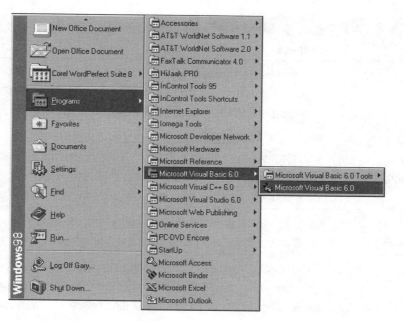

Figure 2-6
The Professional Edition's New
Project Dialog

Most Recently Used Projects Tab

Saved Projects Tab

New Projects Tab

Projects Type Icons

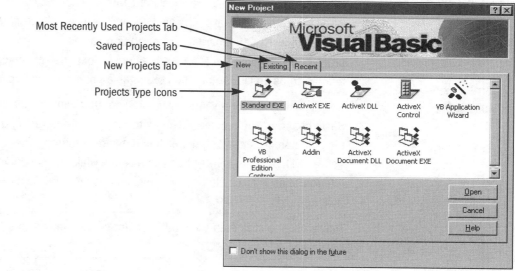

you to retrieve a previously saved Visual Basic program. Clicking on the
Recent tab permits you to chose from a list of the most recently accessed
Visual Basic programs.[5] The New tab, which is shown in Figure 2-6, provides
you with a choice of nine project types, which are listed in Table 2-2 (*page
50*). In this text we will primarily be concerned with the first three project
types listed in this table.

The major similarities and differences between the three Visual Basic
editions can be discerned by viewing their New Project dialogs. As shown
in Figure 2-7, the Student Edition provides only the first three project types
listed in Table 2-2. The Enterprise Edition provides the same nine project
types as the Professional Edition. The only difference within these project
types is that the Enterprise Edition provides an additional ActiveX control,

---

[5] Currently, the maximum size of this list is 99 items.

Table 2-2 The Professional Edition's Nine Available Project Types

Project Type	Purpose
1 Standard EXE	This provides a standard toolbox (see Figure 2-3), which is common to all three Visual Basic editions and is used to create a standard Visual Basic program. Since the 21 controls provided in the standard toolbox are built-in controls, this toolbox loads at the highest speed possible.
2 VB Professional Edition Controls	This provides the standard toolbox's built-in controls plus additional ActiveX controls that can be automatically added into the toolbox. Since ActiveX controls are stored as external files, selecting this option takes more time for the toolbox to load.[6]
3 VB Application Wizard	This provides a skeleton program containing the essential elements that can then be used as the foundation for a completed program.
4 ActiveX Controls	This provides the means of creating additional ActiveX controls, similar to the ones that are provided in the VB Professional Edition. These new controls can be used in a Visual Basic program or any programming language that supports ActiveX technology (see Section 10.8 for instructions to create an ActiveX control).
5 ActiveX EXE	This is used to create a Visual Basic program that can be called from another Visual Basic program, but always runs as a separate executable program. The program that calls the ActiveX EXE program is referred to as a *client*, while the called ActiveX EXE program is referred to as a *server*. In prior versions the server ActiveX program was referred to as an OLE Automation executable program (see Appendix F).
6 ActiveX DLL	This is used to create a Visual Basic program that can be called from another Visual Basic program, but becomes linked into the calling program and always runs as part of the same process in which the calling program is running. The program that calls the ActiveX DLL program is referred to as a *client*, while the called ActiveX DLL program is referred to as a *server*. In prior versions this was referred to as an OLE Automation DLL (see Appendix F).
7 ActiveX Document EXE	This is used to create an executable program that can be run as an Internet Web page document.
8 Document DLL	This is used to create a dynamically linked program that can be run as an Internet Web page document.
9 Addin	This provides the ability to include any ActiveX EXE and DLL program (Document or non-Document) that alters the design environment provided by Visual Basic.

Figure 2-7
The Learning Edition's New Project Dialog

Figure 2-8
The Enterprise Edition's New Project Dialog

---

[6] By default, the additional controls are stored with an `.ocx` extension in the Windows/System directory.

named the Remote Data Object (RDO) control, that can be used for remote data access. Additionally, the Enterprise Edition provides support for reduced instruction set computers (RISC), and comes with three additional CD-ROMs that contain programs for building structured query language (SQL—pronounced both as S-Q-L and Sequel) servers, source code managers, visual database tools, and development tools for developing and testing multi-platform based programs.

Initially, and throughout most of this textbook, we will select the Standard EXE project type from the New Project dialog shown in Figures 2-6 through 2-8. Making this selection will bring up the Integrated Development Environment or IDE, which has the development screen shown in Figure 2-9. Don't be upset if you do not see all of the windows shown in this figure, because we will shortly show you how to produce the desired development screen.

The five windows shown in Figure 2-9 are, as marked, the Toolbox window, the Initial Form window, the Project window, the Properties window, and the Form Layout window. Additionally, directly under the Title bar at the top of the figure, are a Menu bar and a Toolbar, which should not be confused with the Toolbox window. Table 2-3 (*page 52*) provides a description of these components. Before examining each component in depth, it will be useful to consider the Integrated Development Environment (IDE) as a whole and how it uses standard Windows 95 keyboard and mouse techniques.

The IDE as a Windows Workspace

The IDE (pronounced as both I-D-E, and IDEE) is an acronym for the Integrated Development Environment. It consists of three main components, which are the form and module development section, a code editor, and a debugger. In the normal course of developing a Visual Basic program, you will use each of these components. Initially, however, we will work with IDE's form and module development section, which is the screen shown in Figure 2-9. This screen is a typical Windows 98 MDI window. The term MDI is an acronym for Multiple Document Interface, which means the window consists of a single "parent" or main window that can contain multiple "child" (internal) windows. This is the same type of interface presented by both Excel and Access, each of which is an example of an MDI application.

Figure 2-9
The Integrated Development Environment's Initial Screen

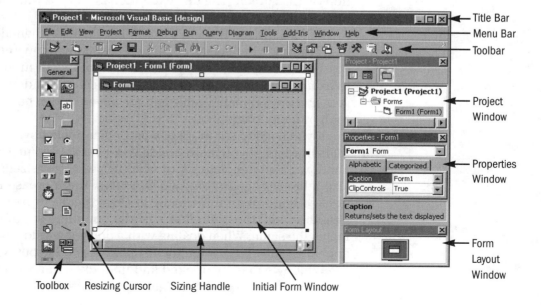

Table 2.3 Initial Development Screen Components

Component	Description
Title Bar	The colored bar at the top edge of a window that contains the window's name.
Menu Bar	Contains the names of the menus that can be used with the currently active window. The menu bar can be modified but cannot be deleted from the screen.
Toolbar	Contains icons, also called buttons, that provide quick access to commonly used Menu Bar commands. Clicking a Toolbar button carries out the designated action represented by that button.
Toolbox	Contains a set of objects that can be placed on a Form window to produce a graphical user interface (GUI).
Initial Form	The form upon which controls are placed to produce a graphical user interface (GUI). By default, this form becomes the first window that is displayed when a program is executed. This default can be changed by selecting the Properties item within the Project submenu.
Properties	Lists the property settings for the selected form or control and permits changes to each setting to be made. Properties, which are characteristics of an object, such as its size, name, and color can be viewed and altered either from an alphabetical or category listing.
Project	Displays a hierarchical list of projects and all of the items contained in a project. Also referred to as both the Project Resource Window and the Project Explorer.
Form Layout	Provides a visual means of setting the Initial Form window's position on the screen when a program is executed.

As a Windows-based application, each child window within the overall parent window, as well as the parent window itself, can be resized and closed in the same manner as all Windows 98 windows. Thus, to close a window you can double-click on the X in the upper right-hand corner of each window. Similarly, each window can be resized by first moving the mouse pointer to a window's border. Then, when the pointer changes to a double-headed arrow, click and drag the border in the desired direction. With one exception, each window can be moved by simply clicking the mouse within the window's Title bar, and then dragging the window to the desired position on the screen. The one exception is when a window is docked onto another window.

In Visual Basic Version 6.0, windows can be aligned and attached to other windows, which ensures that each such window remains visible and accessible. This alignment and attachment of two or more windows is referred to as *docking*. It is extremely useful because windows that are docked together always remain visible and are never hidden behind any other window, tool, or menu bar.

If you need to see more of a particular docked window, simply resize one of its borders. If you resize a side border that is common to all of the docked windows, the complete set of windows will be resized; otherwise, if you resize a border separating two windows, the increase in size of one of the docked windows will be made at the expense of its immediately attached neighbor, and the overall size of the complete set of docked windows remains the same. When dealing with a docked window border, the cursor will appear as shown between the Properties and Layout windows in Figure 2-9.

Windows may by docked and undocked in a variety of ways. The simplest method is to click the right mouse button within a selected window (as

(a)

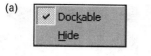

(b)

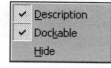

Figure 2-10
Context Sensitive Menus
Illustrating the Dockable Property

with all windows, a window is selected by clicking within it, in which case its Title bar typically changes color from gray to blue), which will bring up a menu similar to the one shown in Figures 2-10a and 2-10b. Menus that are displayed using the right mouse button are referred to as both *context menus* and *context sensitive menus*, because what is displayed by the menu depends on (i.e., is sensitive to) the context in which the menu is activated. Practically, this means that the displayed menu depends on which window is active and where in a particular window the right mouse is clicked.[7] For example, the context menu shown in Figure 2-10a was obtained by clicking the right mouse button on the Title bar of the Properties window shown in Figure 2-9, while the menu shown in Figure 2-10b was obtained by right-clicking within the Properties window itself. As shown in both figures, the Dockable item has been checked, indicating that the window is in a dockable state. Simply clicking on this item will deselect it, and permit the window to be moved about the screen independent of any other window. In general, a context menu simply provides shortcuts to frequently performed actions for the designated portion of a window in which the menu is activated.

A more comprehensive manner of both selecting and determining the set of dockable windows is to use the Menu bar (see Figure 2-11). Initially, in fact, the Menu bar is the most important item on the screen, because you can use it to tailor the IDE environment to your particular needs and liking. This includes bringing up any of the windows that are missing from the screen, adding controls to the toolbar, or making specific windows dockable and undockable.

For example, you can both determine which windows are dockable and then make your selections by using the Options item from within the Menu bar's Tools submenu (see Figure 2-12). This will bring up the Options dialog. By selecting the Docking tab, as shown in Figure 2-13, you can easily check all of the windows that you want to be docked.

More commonly, you will use the Menu bar when you have finished working on a current program and want to start a completely new program. In this case you would choose the File item from menu bar, which will bring up the File submenu illustrated in Figure 2-14. From this menu you can save the current project using the Save Project option and then click on the New Project command and a New Project dialog will appear. To access an existing program you can also use the Menu bar File item, except you would then select the Open Project command to reopen a previously saved program.

Figure 2-11
Visual Basic's Menu Bar

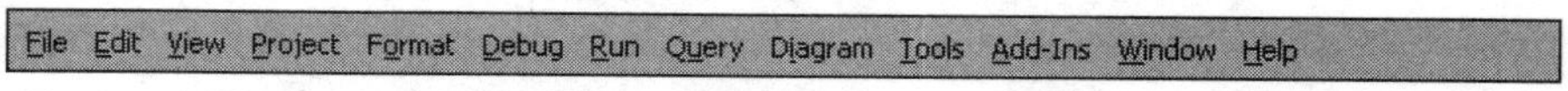

File   Edit   View   Project   Format   Debug   Run   Query   Diagram   Tools   Add-Ins   Window   Help

Figure 2-12
The Tools Submenu

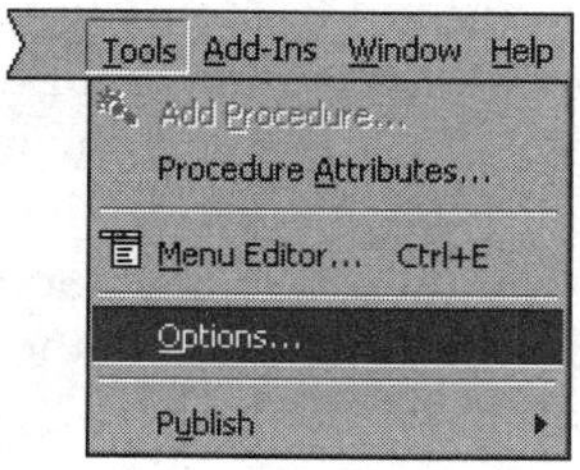

```
Tools   Add-Ins   Window   Help
  Add Procedure...
  Procedure Attributes...
  Menu Editor...   Ctrl+E
  Options...
  Publish                 ▶
```

---

[7]More correctly, context sensitive menus are activated by the *secondary mouse button*, which is usually the right button. The *primary mouse button*, which is typically the left button, is the button configured for Windows' click and double-click operations.

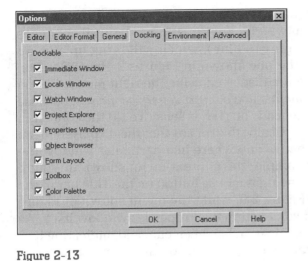

Figure 2-13
The Options Dialog

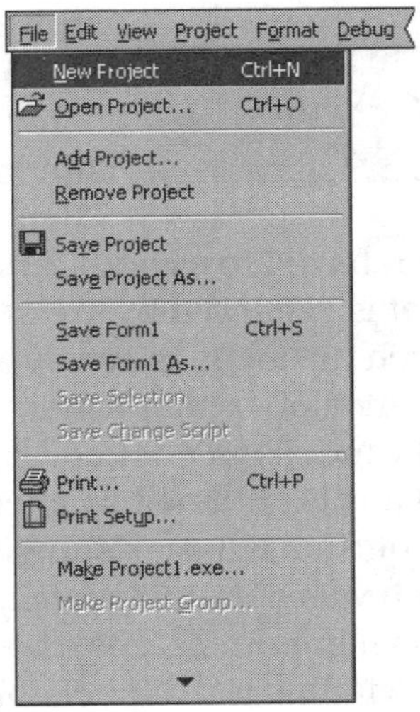

Figure 2-14
The File Submenu

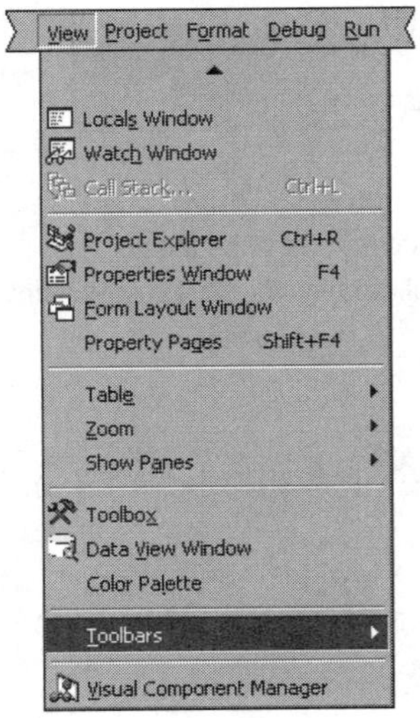

Figure 2-15
The View Submenu

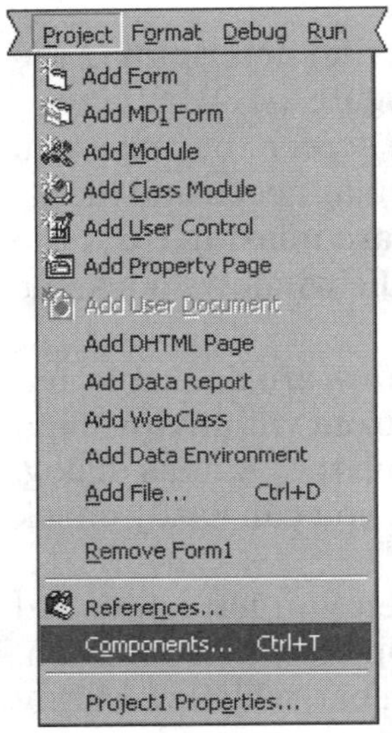

Figure 2-16
The Project Submenu

Similarly, these two options can also be activated by clicking on the first and second icons, respectively, on the Toolbar located immediately under the Menu bar.

Once a program has been opened, you can always use the Menu bar's View item to display any windows you need. For example, if either the Properties or Toolbox windows are not visible on the development screen, select the View item from the Menu bar. This will bring up the View submenu illustrated in Figure 2-15. From this submenu click on either the Properties or Toolbars items to bring up the desired window. Notice in Figure 2-15 that all of Visual Basic's windows are listed in the View submenu.

In a similar manner, you use the Menu bar to add or delete any of the ActiveX controls provided with your edition to the Toolbox. To do this, select the Components item from the Project menu, as shown in Figure 2-16. Selecting the Components item will bring up a component selection dialog, from which you can check the desired additional controls that you want added to the toolbox.

Having taken a quick tour through how the Menu bar is used to configure the development screen provided by Visual Basic, make sure that you begin with the initial development screen shown in Figure 2-17, which is the same as Figure 2-9 with the Form Layout window closed. We choose to close this window for the convenience of having more room to display the Properties window. If any additional windows appear on the screen, close them by clicking the window's close button (the box with the X in the upper right corner); the window does not have to be active to do this.

Notice that the caption within the top title bar of the screen shown in Figure 2-17 contains the words Microsoft Visual Basic [design]. The word [design] in the top Title bar caption is important because it tells us that we are in the design phase of a Visual Basic program. It is in this phase that every Visual Basic application is designed and developed. At any point within our development we can run the program and see how it will looks to the user.

Once the basic design windows are available, creating a Visual Basic application in the design phase requires the following three steps:

1. Create the graphical user interface (GUI).

2. Set the properties of each object on the interface.

3. Write the code.

Figure 2-17
The Basic Development Screen

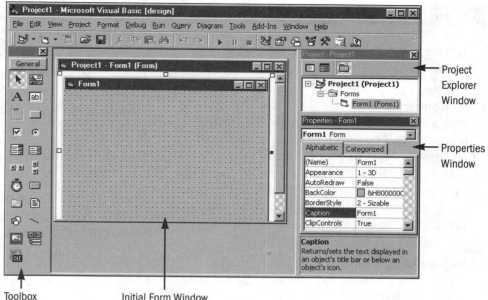

Toolbox   Initial Form Window

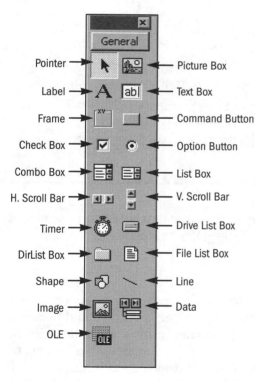

Figure 2-18
The Standard Object Toolbox

The foundation of creating the graphical user interface (Step 1) is the Initial Form window. It is on this design form that we place various objects to produce the interface that we want our users to see when the program is executed. When the program is run, the design form becomes a window and the objects that we place on the design form become visual controls that are used to input data, display output, and activate events. The objects that we can place on the design form are contained within the Toolbox shown in Figure 2-13. For convenience, this standard object Toolbox, which was previously introduced in Section 2.1, is reproduced as Figure 2-18.[8]

Again, don't be confused by the available objects. Simply realize that Visual Basic provides a basic set of object types that can be selected to produce a graphical user interface. It is the purpose of the remaining sections of this book to explain, in detail, what these objects represent and how to design a Visual Basic application using them. To give you an idea of how simple it is to design such an interface, however, move the mouse pointer to the Command button object on the Toolbox (this is the third object shown in Figure 2-18's right-hand column). Notice that a boxed label, called a ToolTip, pops up with the text `CommandButton`.[9] Here, the ToolTip simply provides the name of the pointed to icon. Now double-click the Command button icon. Notice that a Command button object appears on the form. Placing any object from the Toolbox onto a

---

[8]By default, all of the Toolbox's control objects are placed within the **General** tab. By right-clicking on this tab a context-sensitive menu will appear that provides the means of creating additional Toolbox tabs. Since you can copy objects between tabs (or use the mouse to drag and drop objects between tabs), you can use these additional tabs to customize your Toolbox. Thus, for example, you might keep your most commonly used controls within the **General** tab window, all controls connected with database applications on another tab, etc.

[9]By default, Visual Basic displays ToolTips. This feature, however, can be turned on or off from within the **General** tab of the Tools menu Options item.

PROGRAMMERS NOTES

Bringing Up the Basic Design Windows

To create a Visual Basic Program you will need the following three windows: the Toolbox window for selecting objects, a Form window for placing objects, and a Properties window for altering an object's properties. In addition, you should initially have the Project window visible. If any of these windows are in the background, you may click on them to activate and bring them to the foreground, or you may use the following procedures:

For a Form window:
For a new project, first select File from the Menu bar and then select New Project from the submenu (or use the hot-key sequence ALT+F, then N). This will bring up a new Form window.

For an existing project, select File from the menu bar and then select Open Project from the submenu (or use the hot-key sequence ALT+F, then O). This will bring up a Project window. Then, either

- Double-click on the Form icon to view the existing form, or
- Select the Object submenu item from the View menu bar item, or

- Press the SHIFT and F7 (SHIFT+F7) keys at the same time.

For a Toolbox window:
To either activate an existing Toolbox window or bring one up, if it is not on the screen, either:

- Select View and then Toolbox , or
- Use the hot-key sequence ALT+V and then press the X key (ALT+V / X).

For a Properties window:
To activate an existing Properties window or bring one up, if it is not on the screen, either:

- Select View and then Properties Window, or
- Use the hot-key sequence ALT+V, and then press the W key (ALT+V / W), or
- Press the F4 function key.

For a Project window:
To activate an existing Properties window or bring one up, if it is not on the screen, either:

- Select View and then Project Explorer, or
- Use the hot-key sequence ALT+V and then press the P key (ALT+V / P), or
- Press the Ctrl and R keys (CTRL +R) at the same time.

form is this simple. For now, however, click on the newly created Command button within the form and press the DELETE key to remove it.

Setting an Object's Properties

As we have already discovered, all objects have properties. These define where on the form the object will appear (the object's vertical and horizontal position relative to the upper left hand corner of the form), the color of the object, its size, and various other attributes. To gain an understanding of these properties, we will now examine the most basic object in Visual Basic, which is the form itself. Like any other object, the form has properties that define how it will appear as a window when the program is run. As an introduction to the ease with which properties are set, we will first explore these form properties. To do this make sure you have a basic design screen (see Figure 2-17).

Now activate the Properties window by clicking on it. The Properties window, which should appear as shown in Figure 2-19, is used for setting and viewing an object's properties. Using the appropriate tab, properties can be viewed either alphabetically, as is the case in Figure 2-19, or by category. In the alphabetical list however, the **Name** property is always listed first. This is done strictly for convenience, for the name of each control should

Figure 2-19
The Properties Window

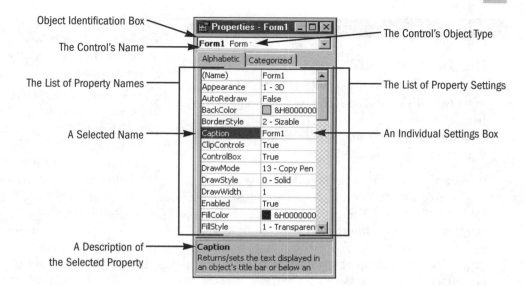

Object Identification Box

The Control's Name

The List of Property Names

A Selected Name

A Description of
the Selected Property

The Control's Object Type

The List of Property Settings

An Individual Settings Box

be changed for every control that is placed on a form. In the categorical list, individual properties are grouped according to appearance, font, position, behavior, etc.

No matter which tab is used, the first box within a Properties window is the *Object Identification box*, located immediately under the window's Title bar. This box lists the name of the object and its object type. In Figure 2-19 the name of the form is Form1 and its type is Form.

The two columns within the Properties window identify individual object properties. The column on the left is the properties list, which provides the names of all the properties of the object named in the object box. The column to the right is the settings list, which provides the current value assigned to the property on the left. A currently selected property is highlighted. For example, the **Caption** property is highlighted in Figure 2-19. The value assigned to a highlighted property can be changed directly in the property settings list.

Take a moment now and, using the keyboard arrows, move down the Properties window. Observe that each property is highlighted as it is selected, and that the description of the highlighted property is displayed in the description box at the bottom of the window.[10] Now move back until the **Name** property at the top of the alphabetical list is highlighted, as shown in Figure 2-20. The name Form1, shown in the figure, is the default name Visual Basic gives to the first form object provided for a new program. If a second form were used, it would be given the default name Form2, the third form would be named Form3, and so on.

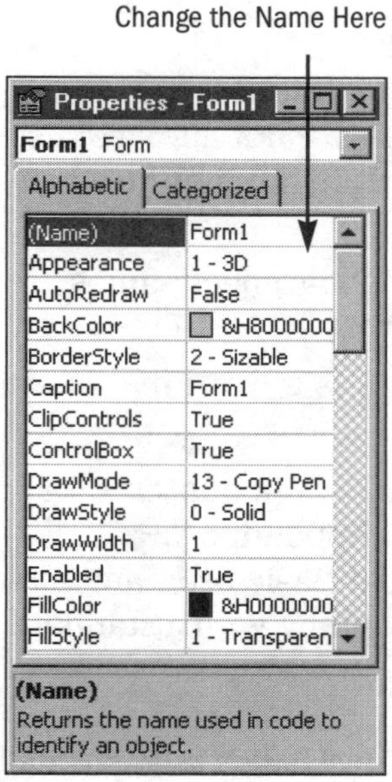

Change the Name Here

Figure 2-20
Setting the Name Property

The Name Property

There is nothing inherently wrong with keeping the default name that Visual Basic provides for each form and object you use. Good programming practice, however, dictates that all form and other object names be more descriptive and convey some idea about what the object is used for. The names permissible for all objects, of which a form is one, are also used to name oth-

---

[10] The description box can be toggled on or off by clicking the right mouse button from within the Properties window. This will produce the context sensitive menu previously shown in Figure 2-10b.

PROGRAMMERS NOTES

The Properties Window

The Properties window is where you set an object's initial properties. These are the properties the object will exhibit when the application is first run. They can be altered later, using procedural code.

To Activate the Properties Window:

To activate a particular object's Properties window, first click on the object to select it, and then press the F4 function key. For a new project, first select File from the menu bar and then select New Project from the submenu You can also Select View and then Properties Window (or use the hot-key sequence ALT+V, then W). This will activate the Properties window for the currently active object. Once the Properties window is active, clicking the down-facing arrowhead to the right of the object identification box (immediately under the Title bar) will activate a drop-down list that can be used to select any form object, including the form itself.

To Move to a Specific Property:

First make sure that the Properties window is active. To quickly move through the Properties window, press the CTRL and SHIFT keys together with the first letter of the desired property. This will move you directly to the next property beginning with this letter. For example, pressing the CTRL, SHIFT, and F4 key together will place you directly on the Caption property. Continuing with this sequence will cycle you through all the properties beginning with C. This sequence can also be used in place of the F4 function key to activate the Properties window.

At any time you can cursor up or down through the properties by using the up and down arrow keys or simply clicking on the desired property with the mouse.

---

er elements in the Visual Basic programming language, and are collectively referred to as *identifiers*. Identifiers can be made up of any combination of letters, digits, or underscores (_) selected according to the following rules:

1. The first character of an identifier must be a letter.

2. Only letters, digits or underscores may follow the initial letter. Blank spaces, special characters, and punctuation marks are not allowed; use the underscore or capital letters to separate words in an identifier consisting of multiple words.

3. An identifier can be no longer than 255 characters, but object names are limited to a maximum of only 127 characters.

4. An identifier should not be a keyword. (A *keyword* is a word that is set aside by the language for a special purpose.[11]

Table 2-4 contains a list of Visual Basic's most commonly encountered keywords and a complete list of keywords is provided in Appendix A.[12]

Using these rules the convention followed by Visual Basic programmers is to provide forms and other objects with a name beginning with a standard

---

[11]Unlike those in most other programming languages, not all of Visual Basic's keywords are restricted. A *restricted* keyword, which is referred to in other languages as a *reserved* word, is a Visual Basic keyword that is set aside by the language for a specific purpose and can only be used for that purpose. Examples of restricted keywords are **If**, **Else**, and **Loop**. The keyword **Click**, for example, is not restricted. In general, it is good programming practice to use keywords, restricted or not, only for their intended purpose.

[12]Although each keyword is capitalized, Visual Basic is case insensitive. A *case insensitive* language does not differentiate between uppercase and lowercase letters. Thus, the keyword **Sub**, for example, can be typed as sub, SUB, or sUB. Visual Basic will recognize each of these spellings and automatically convert all of them to the keyword **Sub.**

Table 2-4   Common Keywords

Boolean	Date	For	LostFocus	Property	Sub
Byte	DblClick	GotFocus	MouseDown	Public	Switch
Call	Dim	If	MouseMove	Rem	Then
Case	Do	Integer	MouseUp	Single	Variant
Click	Double	Let	Me	Static	Wend
Const	Else	Lxong	Next	Stop	While
Currency	End	Loop	Object	String	

three letter prefix to identify the object type, followed by a descriptive name for the specific object. The standard three letter prefix used for all forms is frm (Appendix B contains the complete list of prefixes used for all of the object types provided in the Toolbox window). Additionally, in this text we will use the descriptive name Main to describe the first form used in each Visual Basic Program we create. Thus, our first form will always be given the name frmMain. To assign this name to our current form, do the following:

If the Name property is not already highlighted, either click on the name property, arrow to this property in the Properties window, or press the CTRL, SHIFT, and N keys at the same time. (This is a fast way to get to the first property name beginning in N. Continuing this combination of key strokes will cycle you through all the property names beginning in N. This shortcut can be used with any other letter). Change the name to frmMain by directly typing in the settings list to the right of the **Name** property. The name change takes effect when you either press the ENTER key, move to another property, or activate another object.

The Caption Property

While a form's name property is important to the programmer when developing an application, it is the form's **Caption** property that is important to

---

PROGRAMMERS NOTES

The Form Layout Window

The Form Layout window is used to place the initial form at its desired position on the screen each time an application is executed. By clicking inside the form contained within the Form Layout window's monitor screen, and then dragging the resulting four-headed arrow, you can visually set the initial form's startup position. From a properties standpoint, what is being set is the form's **Top** and **Left** property values, which can also be set manually from within the Properties window. The Form Layout window is especially useful if your application uses two or more forms, because you can use the window to visually arrange the forms onscreen exactly as you want them to appear when the application is executed. This window can also be used to preview form window locations at varying monitor resolutions.

To activate an existing Form Layout window or bring one up, if it is not on the screen, either

● Select <u>V</u>iew and then Form Layout window, or

● Use the hot-key sequence ALT+V and then press the F key (ALT+V / F).

the user when a program is run. This is because it is the caption that the user sees within the a window's Title bar when an application is executing.

To change the **Caption** property select this property from the Properties window. To do this, make sure the Properties window is selected and try the shortcut method of pressing the [SHIFT], [CTRL], and [C] keys at the same time. This will take you to the first property name beginning in a C, which happens to be the **Caption** property (continued pressing of this key combination will simply cycle you through all property names beginning with the letter C). Now change the caption to read

```
The Hello Application - Version 1 (pgm2-1).
```

Notice that as you type the caption in the settings box, it automatically appears both in the settings section of the Properties window and directly on the Title bar of the form itself. If the caption is larger than the space shown in the settings box, as is the case in Figure 2-21, the caption will scroll as you type it in. When you have changed the caption, the design screen should appear as shown in Figure 2-21.

Before we leave the Properties window to run our application, let's take a moment more to see how properties that have restricted values can also be changed.

Both the **Name** and **Caption** properties were changed by simply typing in new values. Certain properties, however, have a fixed set of available values. For example, the **Appearance** property, which determines whether the object will appear flat or raised can only have the values 0-Flat or 1-3D. Similarly, the **FontName** property, which determines the type of font used for an object's displayed text, such as its caption, can only be selected from a list of available fonts. Likewise, the **BackColor** and **ForeColor** Properties, which determine the background color and the color of text displayed in the foreground, can only be selected from a predefined pallet of colors. When one of these properties is selected either a down-facing arrowhead property button (▼) or an ellipsis (…) property button will appear to the right of the selected setting. Clicking on this button will show you the available settings. A selection is then made by clicking on the desired value. In the case of colors, a palette of available colors is displayed, and clicking on a color sets the numerical code for the chosen color as the property's value.

Figure 2-21
The Design Screen after the Caption Change

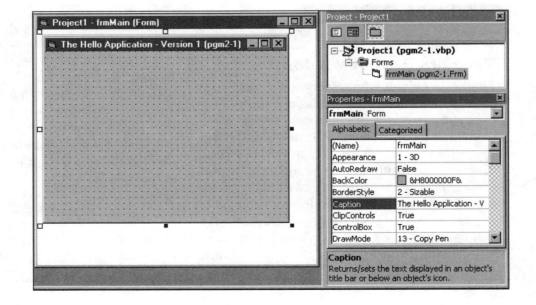

The Project Window

The Project window, which is also referred to as the *Project Resource window* and the *Project Explorer* displays a hierarchical list of projects and all of the current items contained in a project, as shown in Figure 2-22. As files are added or removed from a project, Visual Basic will reflect all of your changes within the displayed hierarchical tree.

The hierarchical tree uses the same folder tree structure found in Windows 95, which means that you can expand and contract tree sections by clicking on plus (+) and minus (–) symbols, respectively. As always, sections of the tree that are hidden from view due to the size of the window can be displayed using the attached scroll bars.

The Project window is extremely useful in providing a visual picture of what files are in a project and in providing a rapid means of accessing, copying, and deleting files associated with a project. For example, if a form object is not displayed on the design screen, you can make it visible by double-clicking on the desired form object from within the hierarchical tree. In a similar manner you can expand a folder, or bring up both code and visible objects by clicking on one of the three icons shown in Figure 2-22. You can also use standard windows drag-and-drop techniques to copy files between folders shown within the Project window. We will have much more to say about the Project window later in this chapter where we will use it to recall saved projects.

For now, however, two further items relating to the Project window are worth noting. First, the names given to each project added to the Project window are, by default selected as follows: the first project in the window is named `Project1`, the second project is named `Project2`, and so on. These names can be changed by either selecting the General tab from within the Properties option of the Project submenu, or selecting the Properties option from the context menu that is displayed by right-clicking on a project item within the Project window. In this text we will only use the Project window to work on one project at a time, and will always accept the default name (Project1). Having two or more projects visible at the same time is useful when debugging multiple projects that interface with one another, such as a client/server application (see Appendix F).

Finally, it is worth noting that the first two items in the View menu, Code and Object, have the same icons displayed in the Project window shown in Figure 2-22. Thus, both code and objects can be displayed by using either the View menu or the Project window.

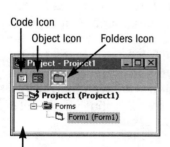

Code Icon

Object Icon   Folders Icon

Hierarchical Tree Structure

Figure 2-22

Running an Application

At any time during program development you can run your program using one of the following four methods:

1. Select the Run Menu and select Start.
2. Use the hot-key sequence [ALT]+[R], then press the [S] key.
3. Press the [F5] function key.
4. Click the Run button on the Menu toolbar at the top of screen.

If you do this now for Program 2-1, the program will appear as shown in Figure 2-23.

Notice that when the program is run, the form becomes a standard window. Thus, even though we have not placed any object on our form or added any code to our program, we can manipulate the window using standard

Figure 2-23

The Form as a Window When the Application Is Run

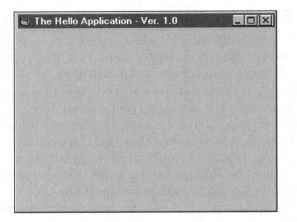

window techniques. Thus, you can click on the Maximize or Minimize buttons, move or resize the window, and close the application by clicking on the Close (X) button.

A nice feature of Visual Basic is that you can run your program at any point within its development process. This permits you to check both the look of the graphical user interface and the operation of any code that you write, while the program is being developed, rather than at the end of the design. As you write more involved programs it is a good idea to get into the habit of checking program features, by running the program, as the features are added.

To clearly distinguish between when a program is being developed and when it is being executed, Visual Basic uses the terms design time and run time. *Design time* is defined as the time when a Visual Basic application is being developed. During design time, objects are placed on a form, their initial properties are set, and program code is written. *Run time* is defined as the time a program is running. During run time, each form becomes a window, and the windows and controls respond to events, such as a mouse-click, by invoking the appropriate procedural code. Run time can be initiated directly from design time by pressing the F5 function key (or by any of the other methods listed in the accompanying Programmers' Notes on Running an Application). Although in this section we have changed object properties at design time, we will see in Section 2.4 that an object's properties can also be changed at run time.

Saving and Recalling a Project

In the next section we will add three Command buttons and one Text box to our form. Then, in Section 2.4, we will complete our application by adding

---

PROGRAMMERS NOTES

Running an Application

While creating a Visual Basic application, you can run the application at any time using any of the following procedures:

1. Select the Run Menu and select Start.

2. Use the hot-key sequence ALT+R, then press the S key (ALT+R/S).

3. Press the F5 function key.

4. Click on the run icon (the icon with the right-facing arrow head) on the Toolbar. (If the Toolbar is not visible, select it from the View menu.)

When you have completed your development and want to make a stand-alone executable version of the application that can be launched by clicking on its icon from within a Windows 98 program group, use the procedure presented in Appendix G.

program code. Before doing so, however, let's make sure you can save and then retrieve the work completed so far.

Unlike our current program, which consists of a single form module, a program can consist of many form modules, additional modules containing program code, and third-party supplied objects. A *form module* contains the data for a single form, information for each object placed on the form (in this case there are none), all event code related to these objects, and any general code related to the form as a whole. A *code module* contains procedural code (no objects) that will be shared between two or more form modules. This is the reason a separate project file, with its own name, is used. The project file keeps track of all form modules, and any additional code and object modules.

It is important to understand that *the information contained in each module is saved as an individual file*. Thus, if a project consisted of four individual forms, the application as a whole would be saved using one separate file for each form and an additional project file to save general information about the project as a whole. In our case the application will be saved using two files, one for the initial form and one for the project as a whole.

To save an application, first select the File menu and then select Save Project. At this point a dialog box similar to the one illustrated in Figure 2-24 will appear.

In response to the Save File dialog box illustrated in Figure 2-24, verify the folder where you want the form saved and enter the name of the file that will be used to save the form. In this case use the file name pgm2-1, which is the name of the file we used to store this form on the enclosed source-code diskette, or any other valid file name you prefer. After completing the input data for the Save File dialog box, press the OK Command button. Doing so will create a file named pgm2-1.frm (the extension suffix .frm is automatically provided by Visual Basic) to be stored within the named folder and cause the Save As Project dialog box illustrated in Figure 2-25 to appear.

For this project, type in the name pgm2-1 (the name we used to store the project file on the diskette packaged with this text) as the project file's name, or any other valid file name, and press the OK Command button. Doing this will save the project information in a file named pgm2-1.vbp in the named folder. Again the extension suffix .vbp is automatically appended by Visual Basic.[13] Thus, you will now have saved two files—one named pgm2-1.frm,

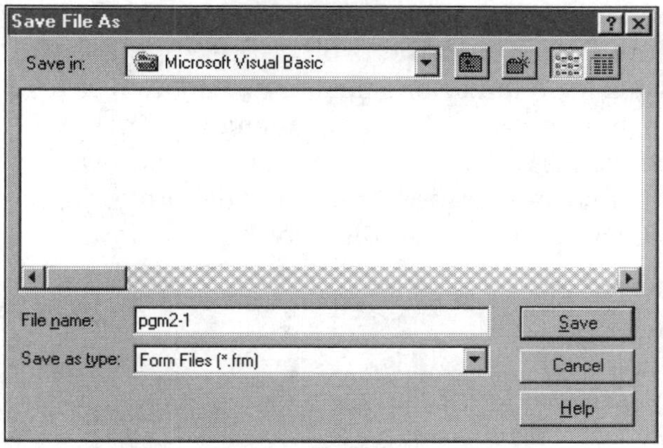

Figure 2-24
The Save File Dialog Box

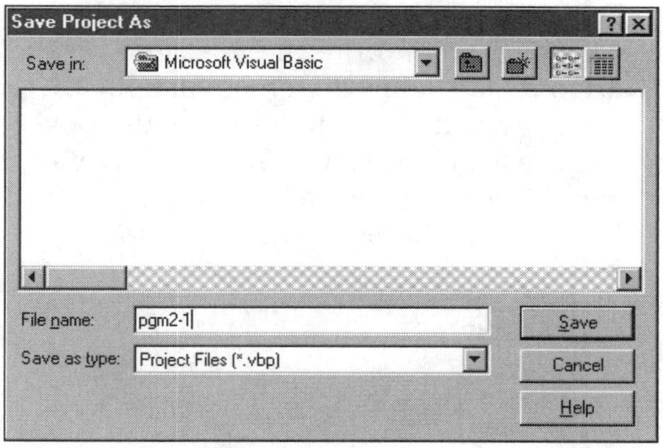

Figure 2-25
The Save Project As Dialog Box

---

[13]Prior to Version 4.0, project files were automatically saved with a .mak extension.

PROGRAMMERS NOTES

Understanding VB's File Structure

Here is a typical problem encountered by students who work with multiple computers. They create a VB application using a C drive folder on their work or home computer, copy the files to an A drive disk, and bring the disk to school. Using the school's computer, the application won't load correctly.

The quickest solution to this problem is to save each project (both the project file and all form files) on an A disk, no matter which computer you use. Then, no matter which machine you switch to, either the one at home, work, or school, your application will load correctly.

Another solution is to understand how VB actually locates each file in an application, and adjust the storage of each file accordingly. Every project, no matter how complicated, contains a single project file that is stored with a .vbp extension. Additionally, each form in the project is saved in a file with a .frm extension. Both of these file types are ASCII text files, so they can be read and modified using any ASCII editor. However, *you should not attempt to edit any of these files unless you are knowledgeable in viewing and editing text files.* Certainly, if you are unsure of your capabilities, make a copy of any file before you edit it, and do not edit any file unless you are knowledgeable about the DOS directory structure.

The easiest editor to use in order to view project and form files is the editor supplied with DOS, and available with each DOS window that is opened in both Windows 95 and 98. For example, if the name of your .vbp file is project1.vbp and the file is stored on the A drive disk, typing the command `edit a:project1.vbp` will bring up this file in the DOS editor. The file name can also be entered after the editor is activated, which is done by typing the word `edit` at the DOS prompt.

The actual file name under which each form and the project's overall definition is stored are the names listed in parentheses the Project Explorer Window. The first important relationship between the .vbp project definition file and all form files is this: *the project file is the single file that is initially loaded by Visual Basic, and it is the project file that tells VB where to locate all form files.* Within the project definition file there is a single line, one for each form, that tells VB the location and name of each form file. The second important relationship is this: *within each form file there are two lines that identify the form's object name,* such as frmMain, for example. These relationships are shown in the figure below.

In reviewing the figure note that the path name listed in the project file can be either an absolute or relative path name. Also note that the name in the two lines shown in the form file is the object name that is displayed in both the Name property setting box and listed in the Project Explorer Window.

Once you understand the relationships shown in the figure, you can always check where each form file should be located by checking its location within the project file; or you can alter a form file's location by changing its location in the project file, and then making sure that the form file is actually stored at the designated location. Similarly, you can change a form's object name by changing the name in the two lines shown in the figure. As we will see later, this provides a very convenient way of making a duplicate copy of an existing form.

When you save a form within VB, the name and location of the text file describing the form is updated within the project file. If you first save a form under one file name, and then save it using another file name (using the Save As command), both files will exist, but only the last file name and location are kept in the project file using a single line like the one shown below.

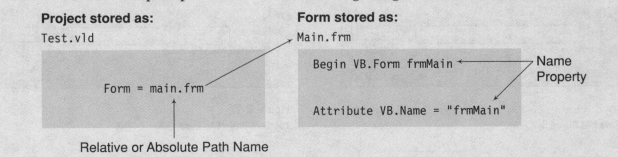

Project stored as:

`Test.vld`

`Form = main.frm`

Relative or Absolute Path Name

Form stored as:

`Main.frm`

`Begin VB.Form frmMain` ← Name Property

`Attribute VB.Name = "frmMain"`

Figure 2-26
The Open Project Dialog Box

Figure 2-26
The Open Project Dialog Box

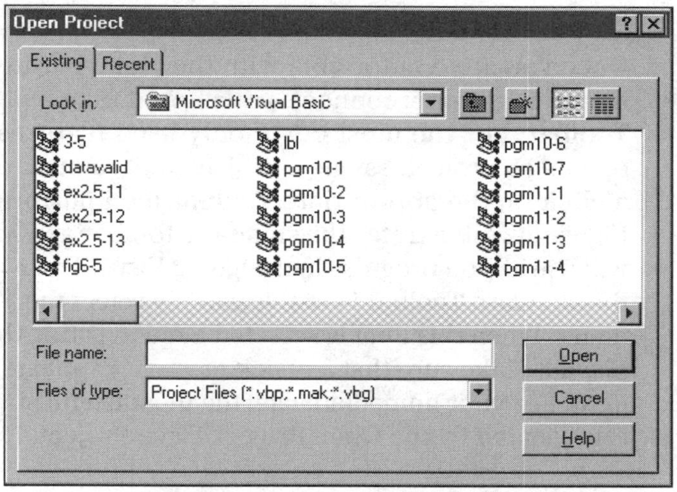

that contains all information related to the form, including the form itself, any objects placed on the form, and any code connected with these objects or the form, and a second file named pgm2-1.vbp, which contains information about the project as a whole. This second file lists all of the forms (in this case there is only one) and other modules (in this case there are none) that make up the complete project. Both of these files are automatically created in Version 5.0 as ASCII text files that can be examined using an ASCII text editor or displayed using the DOS TYPE command.

To retrieve a project, select Open Project from the File menu, at which point an Open Project dialog box similar to the one shown in Figure 2-26 is displayed. As shown in this figure, you can either select an existing project using the Existing tab, or select a recently accessed project using the Recent tab. These two tabs provide the same information displayed by the equivalent New Project dialog tabs when Visual Basic is first launched (see Figures 2-6 to 2-8 on pages 49–50). From either of these tabs, choose the desired project, which in our case is named pgm2-1.vbp. When you make your selection a design screen similar to the one previously shown as Figures 2-9 and 2-17 will appear.

If the design screen opened by Visual Basic does not display the Initial Form window, either double-click on the Form icon within the Project Explorer window or select this icon and click on the Object icon (see Figure 2-22). Notice that the Project Explorer window has a Code icon (again, see Figure 2-22). Clicking on this button produces the last basic design window that we will need, which is the Code window. We will make use of this window in the next section. For now, save the project and close the Visual Basic application.

Figure 2-27
Visual Basic's Standard Toolbar

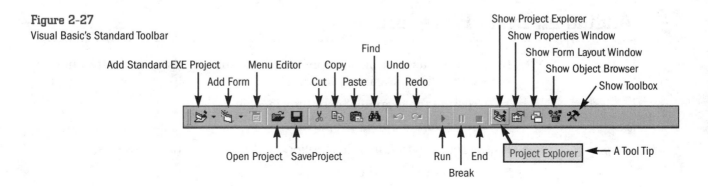

Using the Toolbar

Once you are comfortable with the Menu bar items and can see how they operate and interconnect, you should take a closer look at the standard Toolbar. For the most commonly used features of Visual Basic, such as opening a project, saving a project, and running or stopping an application, a click on the appropriate Toolbar icon performs the desired operation. Figure 2-27 illustrates the standard Toolbar and identifies the icons that you will use as you progress in designing Visual Basic applications. To make sure the standard Toolbar is visible, simply select the Toolbar item from the View menu. When this item is selected a menu listing the available toolbars is displayed. Make sure that a check mark (✓) appears to the left of the Standard item. For your immediate use, the most useful standard Toolbar buttons are represented by the Open Project, Save Project, Run, and End icons.

Exercises 2.2

1. Describe the difference between design time and run time.

2. a. What are the three windows that should be visible during an application's design?
   b. What are the steps for bringing up each of the windows listed in your answer to Exercise 2a?
   c. In addition to the three basic design windows, what two additional windows may also be visible on the design screen?

3. What two form properties should be changed for every application?

4. What does a form become during run time?

5. List the steps for creating a Visual Basic application.

6. a. List the rules that must be followed when naming a Visual Basic object.
   b. What is the three-letter prefix that should be used in every form's name?

7. Determine the number of properties that a form object has. (**Hint**: activate a form's Property window and count the properties.)

8. a. Design a Visual Basic application that consists of a single form with the caption Test Form. The form should have no Minimize button and no Maximize button, but should contain a Close button. (**Hint**: locate these properties in the Properties window and change their values from *True* to *False*).
   b. Run the application you designed in Exercise 8a.

9. By looking at the screen how can you tell whether an application is in design-time or run-time mode?

2.3 ▶ Adding an Event Procedure

In the previous section we completed the first two steps required in constructing a Visual Basic application:

1. Creating the graphical user interface, and
2. Setting initial object properties.

It now remains to finish the application by completing the third step:

3. Adding procedural code.

Figure 2-28
The Structure of an Event
Procedure

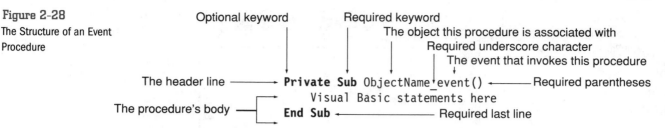

At this point our simple application, pgm2-1, produces a blank window when it is executed. If you click anywhere on the window, nothing happens. This is because no event procedures have been included for the form. We will complete this application by providing a mouse-click event procedure that displays a message whenever the application is running and the mouse is clicked anywhere on the application's window.

In a well-designed program each procedure consists of a set of instructions necessary to complete a well-defined task. Although a procedure can be initiated in a variety of ways, a procedure that is executed (that is called into action, or *invoked)* when an event occurs is referred to as either an *event procedure* or *event handler* (the terms are synonymous). The general structure of an event procedure is illustrated in Figure 2-28.

The first line of a procedure is always a header line. A *header line* begins with the optional keyword **Private**[14] and must contain the keyword **Sub** (this comes from the word Subprogram, the name of procedures in earlier versions of Basic), the name of the procedure and a set of parentheses. For event procedures the name must consist of an object identification, an underscore character, (_), and a valid event for the object. If the object is the form itself, the object name Form is used. For example, the header line Private Sub Form_Click() denotes an event procedure that will be activated when the mouse is clicked on the form. As was previously described in Section 1.3, the parentheses at the end of a header line are used for transmitting data to and from the procedure when it is invoked. Data transmitted in this fashion are referred to as *arguments* of the procedure. A set of parentheses with no intervening spaces, such as (), denotes that no data will be transmitted as arguments when the procedure is executed. The last line of each procedure consists of the keywords **End Sub**.

Statements following the program header line, up to and including the **End Sub** statement, as illustrated on Figure 2-28, are collectively referred to as a procedural unit's body. The *body* of the procedure determines what the unit does. Every Visual Basic statement must conform to certain rules, which collectively are called the language's *syntax*. Typically, each statement in the unit's body resides on a line by itself, although a single statement can continue across a maximum of 10 lines.[15] Multiple statements are allowed in Visual Basic but must be separated by colons (:).

For a form's mouse-click event, the required procedure's structure is

```
Private Sub Form_Click()
    Visual Basic statements in here
End Sub
```

The first and last lines of a procedure, consisting of the header line and terminating body line **End Sub**, are referred to as the procedure's *template*.

---

[14]The significance of the keyword **Private** is explained in Chapter 7.

[15]To continue a statement on the next line requires terminating the current line with a space followed by an underscore character (_).

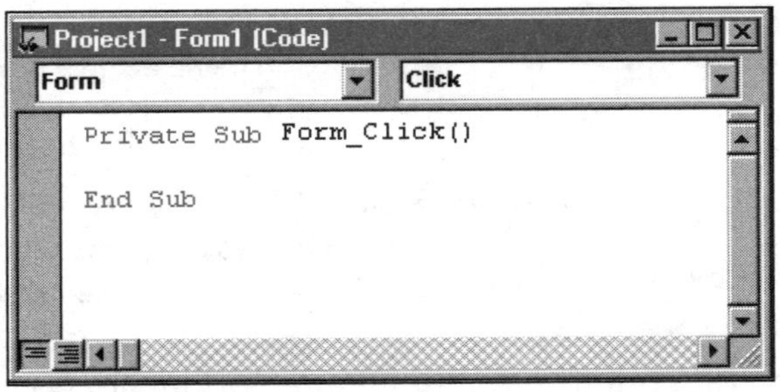

Figure 2-29
The Code Window, Showing a Click
Event Procedure Template

```
Project1 - Form1 (Code)
Form                          Click
    Private Sub Form_Click()

    End Sub
```

As shown in Figure 2-29, event procedure templates need not be manually typed because they are automatically provided in Visual Basic's Code window.

Before activating the Code window, we need to decide what Visual Basic statements will be included in the body of our event procedure. In this section we present two ways for easily displaying an output message: the **MsgBox** statement and the **Print** method.

The MsgBox Statement

Visual Basic provides over 200 different statements and built-in functions for constructing event procedures. The first statement we will use is the **MsgBox** statement.[16] The name of this statement is derived from the term Message Box, and its purpose is to display a box on the window with a user supplied message inside. For example, the boxes illustrated in Figure 2-30 were all created using the **MsgBox** statement. The general form of a **MsgBox** statement is

```
MsgBox "message", type, "title"
```

Although numerous types of pre-defined message boxes are available, for now we will limit ourselves to the four types listed in Table 2-5.

Table 2-5	MsgBox Types	
Type	**Icon**	**Example**
vbExclamation	Exclamation Point	Figure 2-30a
vbQuestion	Question Mark	Figure 2-30b
vbInformation	The Letter I	Figure 2-30c
vbCritical	The Letter X	Figure 2-30d

For example, the statement

```
MsgBox "Hello World!",vbExclamation, "Sample"
```

produced the message box shown in Figure 2-30a. Notice that the message Hello World! is included within the box, and the title at the top of the box is Sample. The exclamation icon included within the box is produced by the **vbExclamation** type used in the statement. (**vbExclamation** is a symbolic constant provided by Visual Basic, which is described in detail in Section 4.3). The icons shown in Figures 2-30b through 2-30d are **vbQuestion**,

---

[16] Strictly speaking, the MsgBox statement is a Visual Basic 3.0 statement that is supported in Version 6.0. After variables are introduced in Section 3.2, which will enable us to handle a function's return value, we will always use a MsgBox() function instead of a MsgBox statement.

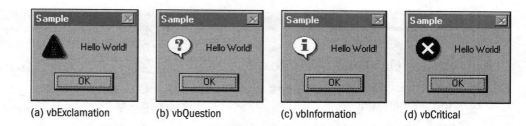

(a) vbExclamation   (b) vbQuestion   (c) vbInformation   (d) vbCritical

Figure 2-30
Message Boxes

vbInformation, and **vbCritical** types, respectively. Thus, Figure 2-30b was produced by the statement

```
MsgBox "Hello World!", vbQuestion, "Sample".
```

The message boxes shown in Figure 2-30 are all special cases of a more general type of box referred to as dialog boxes. A *dialog box* is any box that appears which requires the user to supply additional information to complete a task. In the case of the message boxes illustrated in Figure 2-30, the required additional information is simply that the user must either click the OK box or push the Enter key to permit the application to continue.

Messages, such as those displayed in message boxes, are called *strings* in Visual Basic. A *string* consists of a string of characters made up of letters, numbers, and special characters, such as the exclamation point. The beginning and end of a string of characters are marked by double quotes ("string in here").

Except for messages within double quotes and certain specific cases that will be noted as they occur, Visual Basic ignores all white space, where *white space* refers to any combination of blank spaces and tabs. Therefore, blank spaces may be freely inserted within a statement to improve its appearance. For example, both of the following statements produce the same result when typed.

```
MsgBox "Hello World!", vbExclamation,  "Sample"
MsgBox "Hello World!",vbExclamation,"Sample"
```

Now let's attach a **MsgBox** statement to our form so that the statement will be executed when the mouse is clicked. The required procedure is

```
Private Sub Form_Click()
    MsgBox "Hello World!", vbExclamation, "Sample"
End Sub
```

To enter this code, first make sure that you are in design mode and have a form named frmMain showing on the screen, as illustrated in Figure 2-31.

Figure 2-31
The frmMain Form at Design Time

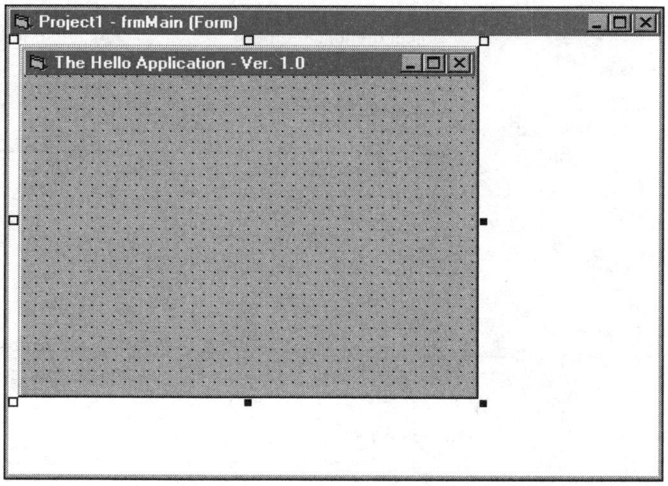

PROGRAMMERS NOTES

Activating the Code Window

To activate the Code window, use one of the following procedures:

1. If the Code window is visible, click on it.

2. Double-click anywhere on the design form.

3. Select the <u>C</u>ode item from the <u>V</u>iew menu.

4. Press the F7 key.

5. Select the <u>C</u>ode icon from the Project window.

To bring up the Code window, do any one of the following:

- If the Code window is visible, click on it.
- Double-click anywhere on the Form window.
- Select the <u>C</u>ode option from the <u>V</u>iew menu.
- Press the F7 function key anywhere on the design form.
- Select the Code icon from the Project window.

Any of these actions will bring up the Code window shown in Figure 2-32. The title of the Code window is frmMain; the object identification box should display Form and the procedure identification box should display Load. This indicates that the current object is the Form and the event procedure is Load. Notice that a template for the Form_Load procedure is automatically supplied within the Code window. The two buttons at the bottom of Figure 2-32, are new with Version 5.0. Pressing the Procedure View button activates the option where only one procedure at a time can be viewed, which was the default provided in all versions prior to 5.0. Pressing the Module View button displays all procedures and declarations that have been written, with each procedure separated by a line. When the Code window is not large enough to display either all procedures or even all of a single procedure, the scroll bars can be used to bring in sections of code within the visible window area.

When you have the Code window shown in Figure 2-32 visible, click on the down facing arrowhead (▼) to the right of the procedure identification box. This will produce the window shown in Figure 2-33. Here the dropdown list can be scrolled to provide all of the events associated with the selected object.

Figure 2-32
The Code Window

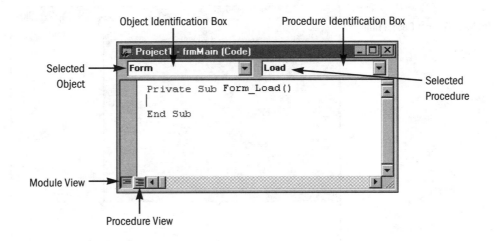

Figure 2-33
The List of Events Associated with a Form

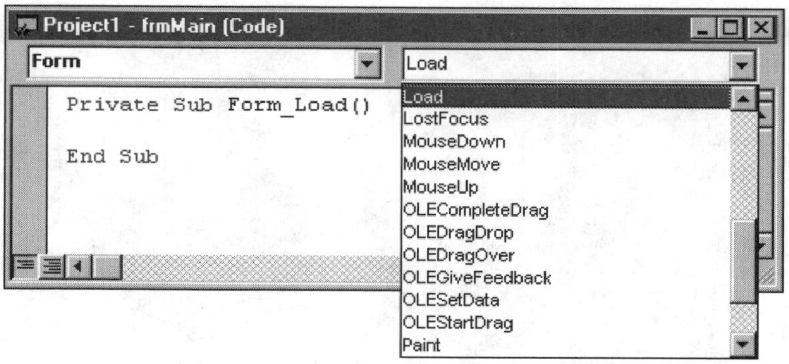

To select the **Click** procedure do any of the following:

- Use the list's scroll bar until the word **Click** is visible, and then click on this keyword.

- Use the up-arrow cursor key to highlight the word **Click**, and press ENTER.

- Press the CTRL+SHIFT+C keys together to move directly to **Click**, and press ENTER.

Any of these actions will make the Code window appear as shown in Figure 2-34.

Notice in Figure 2-34 that the Module View button has been selected (lower left-hand side of the figure). This selection has the effect of showing all code associated with the form, with lines used to separate code sections. For now, ignore the first line of code, Option Explicit, which is explained in Section 3-2. Clicking on the Procedure View button effectively hides this code by making only the **Click** event procedure immediately visible.

When you have gotten the Code window to look like the one shown in Figure 2-34, type in the line

```
MsgBox "Hello World!", vbExclamation, "Sample"
```

between the header line Private Sub Form_Click() and the terminating line End Sub that are automatically entered in the Code window. When this is completed, the procedure should be

```
Private Sub Form_Click()
  MsgBox "Hello World!", vbExclamation, "Sample"
End Sub
```

Notice that we have indented the single Visual Basic statement using two spaces. Although this is not required, indentation is a sign of good programming practice. Here it permits the statements within the procedure to be easily identified.

Figure 2-34
The Code Window for the
Form_Click Event Procedure

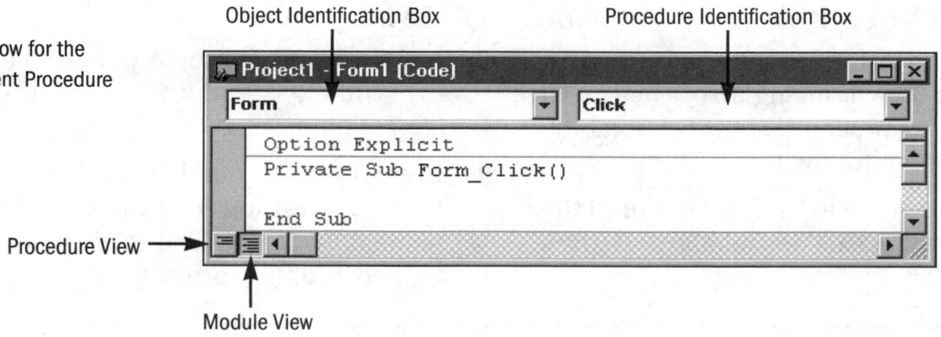

Object Identification Box   Procedure Identification Box

Procedure View

Module View

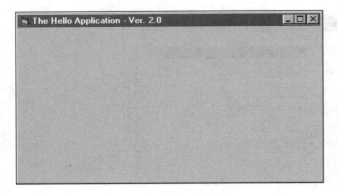

Figure 2-35
The Initial Run-Time Application Window

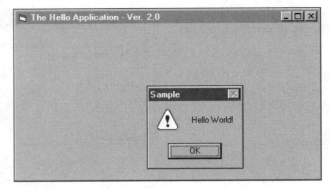

Figure 2-36
The Effect of the Mouse Click Event

Our event procedure is now complete and you can close the Code and Project windows. When you run the program, the application should appear as shown in Figure 2-35. Clicking anywhere on the window will create the window shown in Figure 2-36. To remove the message box, press either the escape ⌷ESC⌷ or ⌷ENTER⌷ key, or click on the OK Command button. Save the application by naming the form file pgm2-2.frm and the project file pgm2-2.Vbp.

Correcting Errors

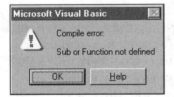

Figure 2-37a
Notification of an Error

If you incorrectly type the message box statement in your procedure, the code window with this procedure will automatically be displayed with the incorrect statement highlighted when the program is run. For example, if you inadvertently spell **MsgBox** as MsgBx, the window shown in Figure 2-37a will appear when you click the mouse (assuming both the project and form files were saved using the file name pgm2-2). If you then click OK in the message box (or press ⌷ENTER⌷), the caption at the top of the window will change from

```
pgm2-2 - Microsoft Visual Basic [run]
```

to

```
pgm2-2 - Microsoft Visual Basic [break]
```

and the Code window will be activated as shown in Figure 2-37b for making code changes. As shown, in this figure, the invalid MsgBx keyword is high-lighted and the header line of the procedure containing the invalid line of code is both highlighted and pointed to by an arrow in the left margin of the

PROGRAMMERS NOTES

Selecting a Procedure from the Code Window

To select a procedure from the Code window, first click on the down-facing arrow head (▼) at the right of the procedure identification box. Then use one of the following:

1. Use the drop-down list's scroll bar until the desired event name is visible and then click it.

2. Use the arrow cursor keys until the desired event name is highlighted and then press ⌷ENTER⌷.

3. Press the ⌷CTRL⌷ and ⌷SHIFT⌷ keys together with the first letter of the desired event's name until the desired event name is high-lighted and then press ⌷ENTER⌷.

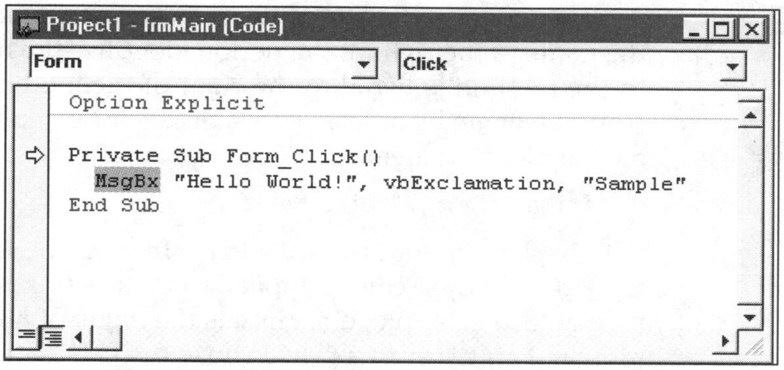

Figure 2-37b

Identification of the Invalid
Statement and its Procedure

```
Project1 - frmMain (Code)                          _ □ ×
Form                    ▼    Click                       ▼
    Option Explicit

⇨   Private Sub Form_Click()
        MsgBx "Hello World!", vbExclamation, "Sample"
    End Sub
```

Code window. Once the correction is made you can change back to run mode by pressing F7, clicking the Toolbar's Run icon, or using the Run menu item.

The Print Method

Currently you have been introduced to objects, their properties, and events. The last item you will need to be familiar with is an object's methods. A *method* is a built-in procedure that is an integral part of an object, like a property, but is used to perform a specific action on the object.

Two such methods that are connected to a form object are named **Print** and **Cls**. The **Print** method, as its name suggests, is a method that prints data provided to it, onto an object. For example, if the message "Hello World!" is given to a **Print** method that is attached to a form, this message will be printed (displayed) on the window generated by the form. The general syntax of the **Print** method is

```
Object-name.Print output-list
```

PROGRAMMERS NOTES

Code Editor Options

The editor provided with Visual Basic 6.0 provides a number of options that are very useful when you are entering code into the Code window. These include:

Color Coded Instructions:

The Visual Basic Editor displays procedural code in a variety of user-selected colors. By default, the following color selections are used:

- Keywords—Blue
- Comments—Green
- Errors—Red
- Other Text—Black

These default colors can be changed from within the Editor Format tab in the Tools' menu Option dialog box.

Completing a Word:

Once you have entered enough characters for Visual Basic to identify a word, you can have the Editor complete the word. This option can be activated by pressing the CTRL+SPACEBAR keys or by selecting it from the context menu that is displayed when the right-mouse button is clicked from inside the Code window.

Quick Syntax Information:

If you are trying to complete a statement, such as a MsgBox statement, and forget the required syntax, you can ask the editor to provide it. This option can be activated by pressing the CTRL+I keys, by selecting the Auto Quick Info from within the Editor tab in the Tools' menu Option dialog box, or by selecting it from the context menu that is displayed when the right-mouse button is clicked from inside the Code window.

The name to the left of the required period identifies the object, while the name to the right of the period identifies the method. Any data provided to the method is listed to the right of the method name, and is separated from the name by at least one space. For example, if `frmMain` is the name of a form, the statement

```
frmMain.Print "Hello World!"
```

will display the message "Hello World!" on the form. In addition to forms, the **Print** method can be applied to Picture boxes, Debug windows, and the printer. For example, if `picShow` is the name of a Picture box, the statement `picShow.Print "Here I am"` will cause the text `Here I am` to be displayed in the Picture box.

A useful option to using the **Print** method is that, if the object name is omitted, the display will always default to the current form. Thus, the statements

```
frmMain.Print "Hello World!" and Print "Hello World!"
```

are equivalent. In this text we will always use the shorter statement, so remember when you see it, and know that in using it we are printing to a form.

To see how this statement is used in practice, simply replace the MsgBox statement in the form's click event procedure with a **Print** statement so that the procedure is

```
Private Sub Form_Click()
 Print " Hello World!"
End Sub
```

When you run the program and click on the mouse now, the application window shown in Figure 2-38 will appear.

Although the form's click-event procedure displays only a single message, we can add additional **Print** statements within the procedure to display more than one message. See if you can read the following click-event procedure and determine what it does.

```
Private Sub Form_Click()
    Print "    Welcome to the Guess a Number Game Program"
    Print "I will think of a number between 1 and 100"
    Print "    You will have seven tries to guess the number"
    Print "After each guess I will tell you if you were "
    Print "    Either high, low, or guessed the correct number"
    Print "Have fun and good luck"
End Sub
```

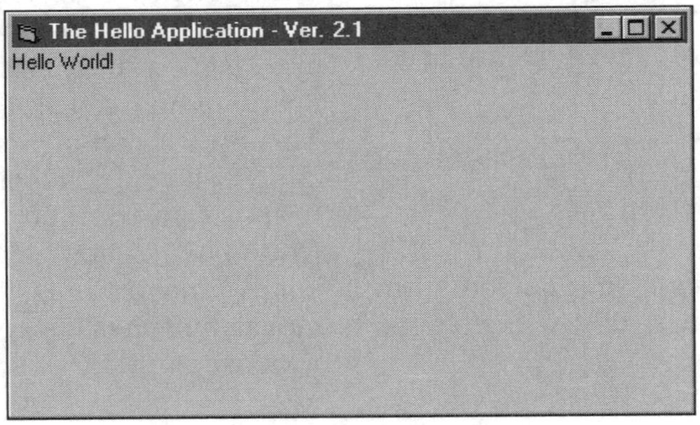

Figure 2-38

An Application Using the Print Method

When this click event is activated, the following will be displayed on the form:

```
    Welcome to the Guess a Number Game Program
I will think of a number between 1 and 100
    You will have seven tries to guess the number
After each guess I will tell you if you were
    Either high, low, or guessed the correct number
Have fun and good luck
```

As you might have guessed, each **Print** statement in the event procedure subroutine causes a new line to be displayed. Since the procedure has six **Print** statements, six individual lines are produced. In each case the message in the **Print** statement is displayed exactly as it appears within the enclosing double quotes, including spaces. Thus, the leading spaces in the first, third, and fifth messages are retained in the displayed output.

Also notice the sequence in which the statements in the event procedure are executed. The procedure begins with the header line and continues sequentially, statement by statement, until the **End Sub** statement is encountered. The statements within the body of this procedure are executed sequentially, with each **Print** statement producing a single line of output.

Altering the placement of any of the **Print** statements in the event procedure automatically alters the display on the form. For example, if the statements in the procedure are written in the order shown below,

```
Private Sub Form_Click()
    Print "Have fun and good luck"
    Print "I will think of a number between 1 and 100"
    Print "    You will have seven tries to guess the number"
    Print "After each guess I will tell you if you were "
    Print "    Either high, low, or guessed the correct number"
    Print "    Welcome to the Guess a Number Game Program"
End Sub
```

the following sequence of messages would be produced:

```
Have fun and good luck
I will think of a number between 1 and 100
    You will have seven tries to guess the number
After each guess I will tell you if you were
    Either high, low, or guessed the correct number
    Welcome to the Guess a Number Game Program
```

Although this set of messages has used only letters, this is not required in Visual Basic. Messages can contain any characters, including lowercase letters, percent signs (%), ampersands (&), exclamation points (!), and any other symbol supported by Visual Basic. All of these characters are allowed within messages because Visual Basic attributes no significance to them, other than to store and display the characters exactly as they appear in the message. Messages can even include double quotes by using two double quotes in succession. For example, the message "They said ""Hello"" to me" produces the output:

```
They said "Hello" to me
```

Finally, it is possible to use the **Print** statements with no output. For example, the statement

```
Print
```

causes a blank line to be displayed. Thus, the sequence of statements

```
Print "The greeting of the day"
Print
Print "for January 1st is"
Print
Print "Happy New Year!"
```

causes the following double spaced screen display:

```
The greeting of the day

for January 1st is

Happy New Year!
```

As we have seen, when no object name is used, the **Print** method defaults to the current form, which permitted us to use the abbreviated statement,

```
Print "Hello World!"
```

in place of the longer statement, `frmMain.print "Hello World!"`. Another style you may also encounter is the use of the question mark in place of the keyword **Print**, which saves having to type in the whole word **Print**. For example, each of the following statements produces the same effect in displaying the message `Hello World!` on the window named frmMain:

```
Print "Hello World!"
? "Hello World!"
frmMain.Print "Hello World!"
frmMain.? "Hello World!"
```

Certainly, if a lot of typing is involved in a program or you are trying to quickly test the effect of a **Print** statement, the question mark is advantageous. When the question mark is typed in the Code Window it is automatically converted to the word **Print** by the Visual Basic editor when you press the ENTER key or move to another line. In this text, however, we will always type the method name, **Print**, and only include an object name if we are not printing to the form. Thus, when you see the **Print** keyword by itself, you will know we are referring to the form.

The Cls Method

Notice that each time you generate the click event in our latest version of the Hello Application (which is stored on the enclosed diskette as `Pgm2-2a`) by clicking the mouse on the run-time window, the message `Hello World!`, shown in Figure 2-38, is printed again. For example, if you click the mouse five times, the message appears five times. This is because each click is a unique event that triggers the **Print** method.

At this stage you might want to provide a user with a way of clearing the window. Fortunately, a method named **Cls** exists for removing all data displayed by the **Print** method. For example, to clear the form named `frmMain`, the statement `Cls` can be used. If we attach this statement to the double-click mouse event (use the Code window), the event procedure becomes:

```
Private Sub Form_DblClick()
  Cls
End Sub
```

Now when you run your application each mouse click will display the message `Hello World!` and each double-click will clear the window of all printed messages. In addition to forms, the **Cls** method can be applied to other objects, such as Picture boxes and the Debug windows. When applied to these other objects, the **Cls** method must be preceded by the object's name. For example, if `picShow` is the name of a Picture box object, the statement `picShow.Cls` is required to clear the Picture box. When no object name is provided the **Cls** method refers to the current window. As with the **Print** method, however, a form name may also be used. Thus, in our application where the form's name is `frmMain`, the statements `Cls` and `frmMain.Cls` are equivalent, and both clear the window of any printed messages.

Exercises 2.3

1. Define the following terms:
   a. event procedure   c. method   e. argument
   b. dialog box   d. header line   f. template

2. a. What window do you use to enter the code for an event procedure?
   b. List two ways of activating the window you listed as the answer for Exercise 2a.

3. a. Assume that you have created a project with a form named `frmMain` that contains two Command buttons named `cmdButton1` and `cmdButton2`. Write the header line that is required for each object's click-event procedures.
   b. Write the template that will be supplied by Visual Basic for the `cmdButton1` click-event procedure.

4. Using the Code window determine how many event procedures are associated with a form.

5. Design and run the application presented in this section using the **MsgBox** statement in the form's click-event procedure.

6. a. Design and run the application presented in this section using the **Print** method in the form's click event procedure and the **Cls** method in the form's double-click event procedure.
   b. For the project designed in Exercise 6a. change the form's **Font** property to **MS Serif** in a 12-point size. Do this by first selecting the **Font** property and then click on the ellipsis (…) to the right of the settings box. Also change the form's **ForeColor** property to red. Do this by selecting the **ForeColor** property, clicking on the down arrow head (▼) to the right of the setting box, and then clicking on the red box. Now run the application.

7. Design and run a Visual Basic application that uses the **Print** method to print your name on one line, your street address on a second line, and your city, state, and zip code on a third line of the window when you click the mouse. (**Hint**: you will need three **Print** method statements in your event procedure.)

8. Design and run a Visual Basic application that prints the following verse in a window when a user clicks the mouse. By double-clicking the mouse the verse should be cleared from the window.

```
Computers, computers everywhere
    as far as I can see
I really, really like these things,
    Oh joy, O joy for me!
```

2.4 Adding Controls

Although the application presented in the previous section is useful in introducing the basic design-time windows needed for developing Visual Basic applications, it is not a very useful application in itself. To make it such we will have to add additional objects and event procedures to the form. Adding objects to the form creates the final graphical interface that the user will see and interact with when the program is run. Adding event procedures to the objects then brings them "alive," so that when they are selected something actually happens. In this section we present the basic method of placing objects on a form, and in the next section we will attach specific event procedures to these objects.

Objects placed on a form are formally referred to as *controls*. The controls consist of the objects that are selected from the Toolbox and placed on the form. Placing objects on a form is quite simple, and the same method is used for all objects. Thus, after placing one object on the form you have learned the method for placing any Toolbox object on a form.

The simplest procedure is to double-click on the desired toolbox object. This causes an object of the selected type to be automatically placed on the form. Once this is done you can change its size and position, and set any additional properties, such as its name, caption, or color. These later properties are modified from within the Properties window, and determine how the object appears when it is first displayed during run time.

By far the most commonly used Toolbox objects are the Command button, Text box, Label, and Picture box. For our second application we will use the first two of these object types, the Command button and Text box, to create the design-time interface shown in Figure 2-39.

To start our third project either select <u>N</u>ew Project from the <u>F</u>ile menu or press the ALT+F keys followed by the N key ((ALT)+F/N). Then change the **Name** property of the form to frmMain and change its **Caption** property to The Hello Application.

Adding a Command Button

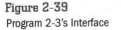

To place a Command button on the form, double-click on the Command button icon. This icon is the second icon in the toolbox's right column and consists of a rectangle with rounded corners. Double-clicking on this icon causes a Command button with eight small squares, referred to as *sizing handles*, to be placed in the middle of the form, as shown in Figure 2-40. The fact that the sizing handles are showing indicates that the object is *active*,

Figure 2-39
Program 2-3's Interface

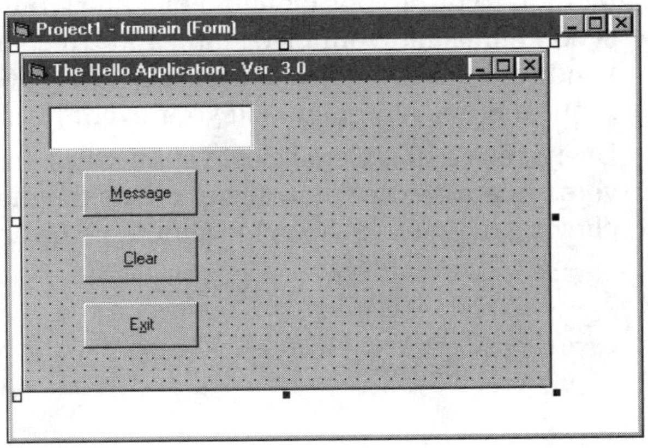

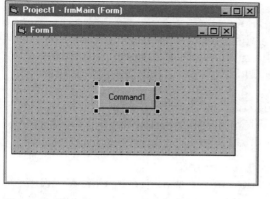

Figure 2-40
The First Command Button Placed on the Form

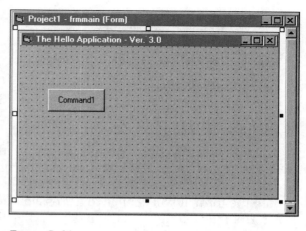

Figure 2-41
The Final Placement of the First Command Button

which means that it can be moved, resized, and have its other properties changed. Only one object can be active at a time. To deactivate the currently active object, use the mouse to click anywhere outside of it. Clicking on another object will activate this other object, while clicking on an area of the form where no object is located activates the form object itself.

The active object, which should now be the Command button just placed on the form, can be moved by placing the mouse pointer anywhere inside the object (but not on the sizing handles), holding down the mouse's left button, and dragging the object to its desired new position. Do this now and place this first Command button in the position of the Message button shown in Figure 2-39. Your form should now look like the one shown in Figure 2-41.

Once you have successfully placed the first Command button on the form, either use the same procedure to place two more Command buttons in the positions shown in Figure 2-42, or use the alternative procedure given in the Programmers' Notes box on page 79. Included in this box are additional procedures for resizing, moving, and deleting an object.

Adding a Text Box

Text boxes can be used for both entering data and displaying results. In our current application we will use a Text box for displaying a message when one of the form's Command buttons is clicked.

Figure 2-42
Placement of Three Command
Buttons on the Form

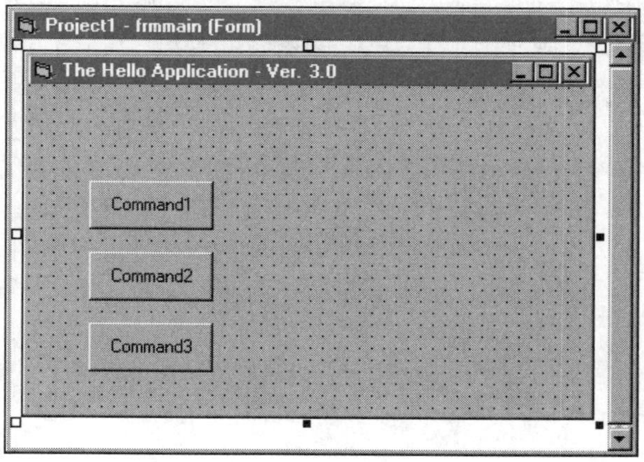

PROGRAMMERS NOTES

Creating and Deleting Objects

To Add an Object:
Double-click on the desired object in the Toolbox. Doing this places a pre-sized object on the form.

Or, click on the desired object in the Toolbox and then move the mouse pointer onto the form. When the mouse pointer moves onto the form, it will change to a crosshair cursor. Hold the left mouse button down when the crosshairs are in the desired position for any corner of the object and drag the mouse diagonally away from this corner, in any direction, to generate the opposite corner. When the object is the desired size, release the left mouse button.

To Resize an Object:
Activate the object by clicking inside of it. Place the mouse pointer on one of the sizing handles. This will cause the mouse pointer to change to a double-sided arrow (↔) Hold the left mouse button down and move the mouse in the direction of either arrow head. Release the mouse button when the desired size is reached.

To Move an Object:
Whether the object is active or not, place the mouse pointer inside of the object and hold down the left mouse button. Drag the object to the desired position and then release the mouse button.

To Delete an Object:
Activate the object by clicking inside of it, and then press the DEL key.

The Text box icon is the second icon in the toolbox's first column. A Text box object is placed on a form in the same way we placed the three Command button objects: that is, by simply double-clicking on the Text box icon. If you happen to double-click the wrong icon, simply activate it and press the DEL key to remove it. Once you have placed a Text box on the form, move and resize it so it appears as shown in Figure 2-43.

Setting the Initial Object Properties

At this point we have assembled all of the form controls that are required for our application. We still need to change the names of these objects from their default names and set the captions of the Command buttons to those previously shown in Figure 2-39. After that, we can add the code so that each Command button performs its designated task when it is clicked. So let's change the initial properties of our four objects to make them appear as shown in Figure 2-39. Table 2-6 lists the desired property settings for each object, including the form.

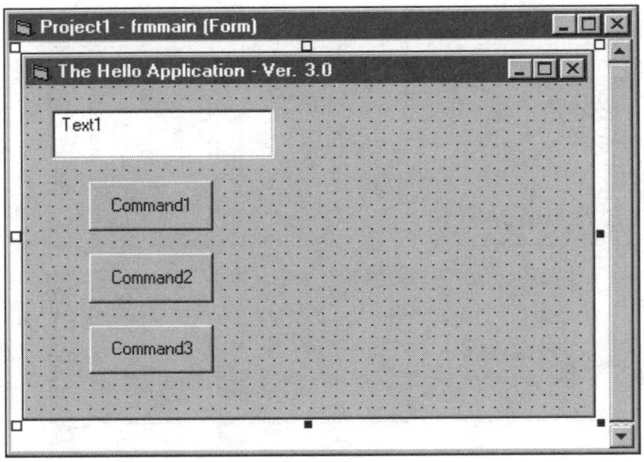

Figure 2-43
Placement of the Text Box

Table 2-6   Program 2-3's Initial Property Settings

Object	Property	Setting
Form1	Name	frmMain
	Caption	The Hello Program - Ver. 3.0
Command1	Name	cmdMessage
	Caption	&Message
Command2	Name	cmdClear
	Caption	&Clear
Command3	Name	cmdExit
	Caption	E&xit
Text1	Name	txtDisplay
	Text	(blank)

Before we set the properties listed in Table 2-6, two comments are in order. The first concerns the ampersand (&) symbol included in the captions of all of the Command buttons. This symbol should be typed exactly as shown. Its visual effect is to cause the character immediately following it to be underlined. Its operational effect is to create an *accelerator key*. An accelerator key, which is also referred to as a *hot-key sequence* (or hot key, for short), is simply a keyboard short cut for a user to make a selection. When used with a Command button it permits the user to activate that button by simultaneously pressing the [ALT] key with the underlined letter key, rather than by clicking with the mouse or by first selecting the Command button and then pressing the [ENTER] key.

The second comment concerns the **Text** property and its setting, which is the last entry in Table 2-6. Unlike Command buttons, Text boxes do not have captions. They do, however, have a property called **Text**. The setting of this property determines what text will be displayed in the Text box. As shown in Figure 2-43 the initial data shown in the Text box is Text1, which is the default value for this property. The term (blank) means that we will set this value to a blank.

Also note that, although we are setting the initial properties for all of the objects at the same time, this is not necessary. We are doing so here to show the various settings in one place. In practice we could just as easily have set each object's properties immediately after it was placed on the form.

Recall from the Programmers' Notes box on page 58 that a Properties window can be activated in a variety of ways: by pressing the [F4] function key or by selecting Properties from the View menu (which can also be obtained by the hot-key sequence [ALT]+[V], followed by [W]). Now, however, we have four objects on the design screen, which include the form, three Command buttons, and a Text box. To select the properties for a particular object, you can use any of the options listed in the Programmers' Notes box on page 58.

The simplest method is to first activate the desired object by clicking on it, and then press either the [F4] function key or the hot-key sequence, [CTRL]+[SHIFT] + the first letter of the desired property. For example, if a Command button is active, pressing [CTRL]+[SHIFT]+[N] will place the cursor at the **Name** property for the activated control. Because an object is automatically activated just after it is placed on a form, these two methods are particularly useful for immediately changing the object's properties. This

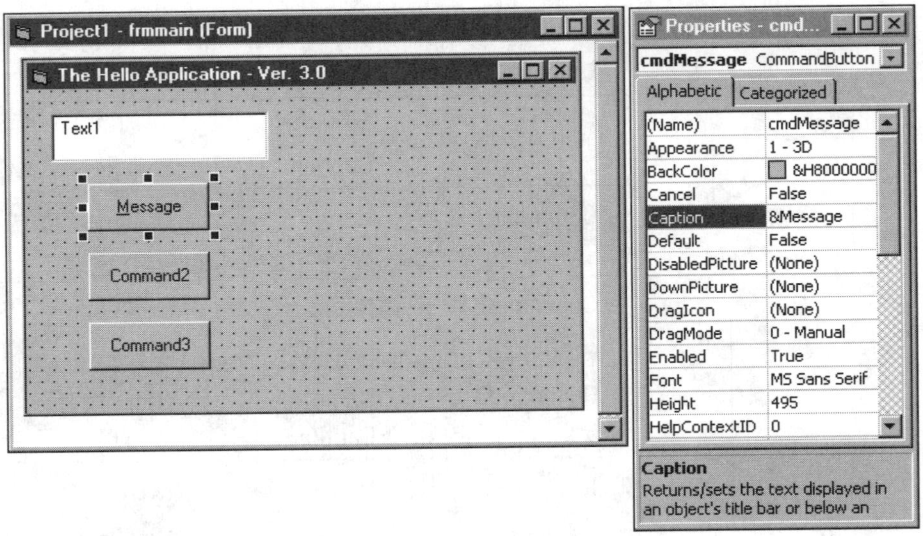

Figure 2-44
Changing Properties Settings

sequence of adding an object and immediately changing its properties is preferred by many programmers.

An alternative method is to bring up the Properties window for the currently active object, no matter what it is, and then click on the downward facing arrowhead key (▼) to the right of the object's name (see Figure 2-44). The drop-down list that appears contains the names of all objects associated with the form. Clicking on the desired object name in the list both activates the desired object and brings up its Properties window. This method is particularly handy when changing the properties of a group of objects, by sequencing through them after all objects have been placed on the form. Using either of these methods, alter the initial properties to those listed in Table 2-6.

At this stage, you should have the design screen shown in Figure 2-44. Within the context of a complete program development we have achieved the first two steps in our three-step process:

1. Create the graphical user interface.
2. Set the properties of each object on the interface.

We will complete the third and final step of writing the code in the next section. Before doing so, however, run the application by pressing the F5 function key. Although clicking on any of the Command buttons produces no effect (precisely because we have not yet attached any code to these buttons), we can use the application to introduce two important concepts connected with any form: focus and tab sequence.

Looking at the Focus and Tab Sequence

When an application is run and a user is looking at the form, only one of the form's controls will have *input focus*, or focus, for short. The control with focus is the object that will be affected by pressing a key or clicking the mouse. For example, when a Command button has the focus, its caption will be surrounded by a dotted rectangle, as shown in Figure 2-45. Similarly, when a Text box has the focus, a solid cursor appears on the box, indicating that the user can type in data.

An object can only receive focus if it is capable of responding to user input either through the keyboard or mouse. Thus, such controls as labels, lines, and rectangles can never receive the focus. In order to actually get the focus a control must have its **Enabled**, **Visible**, and **TabStop** properties set

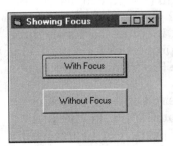

Figure 2-45
A Command Button With Focus
and Without Focus

PROGRAMMERS NOTES

Activating the Properties Window for a Specific Object

1. Activate the object by clicking on it, and then press the F4 function key.

2. Activate the object by clicking on it, and then press CTRL+SHIFT + the first letter of property you want to change.

3. Activate the Properties window for the currently selected object or form, whatever it may be, either by pressing the F4 key or selecting the Properties option from the Windows menu (ALT+V / W). Then change to the desired object from within the Properties window. Do this by clicking on the underlined down-arrow to the right of the object's name and then selecting the desired object from the drop-down list.

to **True**. By enabling an object you permit it to respond to user-generated events, such as pressing a key or clicking a mouse, while the **Visible** property determines whether an object will actually be visible on the window during run time (it is always available for view during design time). A **True TabStop** setting forces a tab stop for the object, while a **False** value causes the object to be skipped over in the tab stop sequence. As the default settings for all three properties is **True**, they do not usually have to be checked for normal tab operation. A control capable of receiving focus, such as a Command button, can get the focus in one of three ways:

1. A user clicks the mouse directly on the object.
2. A user presses the tab key until the object gets the focus.
3. The code activates the focus.

To see how the first method operates, press the F5 function key to execute the Hello Program (pgm2-3). Once the program is executing, click on any of the form objects. As you do, notice how the focus shifts. If any object does not respond, go back to the design stage and make sure that the object's **Enabled** property is set to **True**. Now press the tab key a few times and see how the focus shifts from control to control. The sequence in which the focus shifts from control to control as the tab key is pressed is called the *tab sequence*. This sequence is initially determined by the order in which controls are placed on the form. For example, assume you first create Command buttons named cmdCom1, cmdCom2, and cmdCom3, respectively, and then create a Text box named txtText1. When the application is run, the cmdCom1 button will have the focus. As you press the Tab key, focus will shift to the cmdCom2 button, then to the cmdCom3 button, and finally to the Text box. Thus, the tab sequence is cmdCom1 to cmdCom2 to cmdCom3 to txtText1. (This assumes that each control has its **Enabled**, **Visible**, and **TabStop** properties all set to **True**, which permits the object to receive focus.)

The default tab order obtained as a result of placing controls on the form can be altered by modifying an object's **TabIndex** value. Initially, the first control placed on a form is assigned a **TabIndex** value of 0, the second object is assigned a **TabIndex** value of 1, and so on. Controls that do not have a **TabIndex** property, such as lines and rectangles, are not assigned a **TabIndex** value. To change the tab order you simply have to change an object's **TabIndex** value and Visual Basic will renumber the remaining objects in a logical order. For example, if you have six objects on the form with **TabIndex** values from 0 to 5, and change the object with value 3 to a value of 0, the objects with initial values of 0, 1, and 2 will have their values automatically changed to 1, 2, and 3, respectively. Similarly, if you change the object with a **TabIndex** value of 2 to 5, the objects with initial values of 3, 4, and 5 will all have their values automatically reduced by one. Thus, the sequence from one object to another remains the same for all objects, except for the insertion or deletion of the altered object. If, however, you ever get confused, simply reset the complete sequence in the desired order by manually starting with a **TabIndex** value of 0 and then assigning values in the desired order. A control whose **TabStop** property has been set to **False** maintains its **TabIndex** value, but is simply skipped for the next object in the tab sequence.

The Format Menu Option[17]

The Format menu option provides the ability to align and move selected controls as a unit, as well as lock controls and make selected controls the same size. This is a great help in constructing a consistent look on a form that contains numerous controls. In this section we will see how this menu option is used.

As a specific example using the Format menu, consider Figure 2-46, which shows two command controls on a design form. To both align and make both controls the same size, the first operation that you must perform is to select the desired controls. This can be done by clicking on the form and dragging the resulting dotted line to enclose all of the controls you wish to format, as is illustrated on the figure, or by holding the Shift key down and clicking on the desired controls.

Once you have selected the desired controls for formatting, the last selected object will appear with solid grab handles. For example, in Figure 2-47 this is the lower Command control. The solid grab handles designate the control that is the *defining control*. It is this control that sets the pattern for both sizing and aligning the other selected controls. If this control is not the defining control you want, simply select another by clicking on it.

Having selected the desired defining control, click on the Format menu bar item and then select the desired format option. For example, Figure 2-48 illustrates the selection for making all controls within the dotted lines the same size. Within this submenu, you have the choice of making either the width, height, or both dimensions of all controls equal to the defining control's respective dimensions. The choice shown in this figure sets all selected controls equal in both width and height to the defining control.

In addition to sizing controls, you may also want to align a group of controls within a form. Figure 2-49 illustrates the options provided for the Align

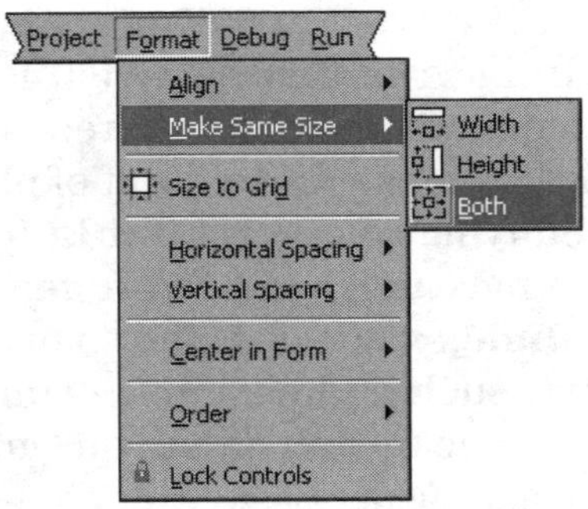

Figure 2-46
Preparing Two Controls for Formatting

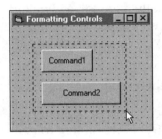

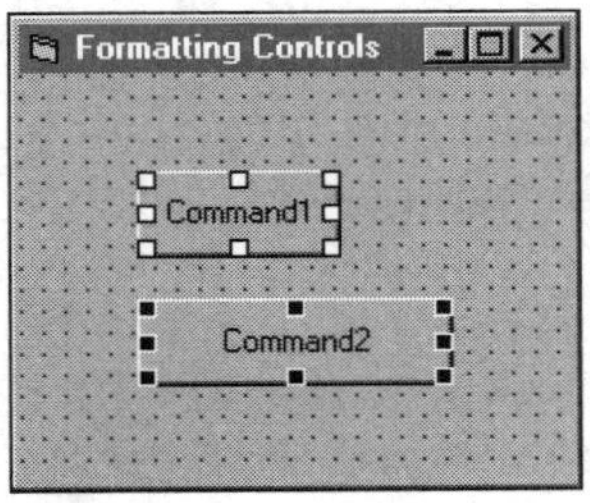

Figure 2-47
Locating the Defining Control

Figure 2-48
Making Controls the Same Size

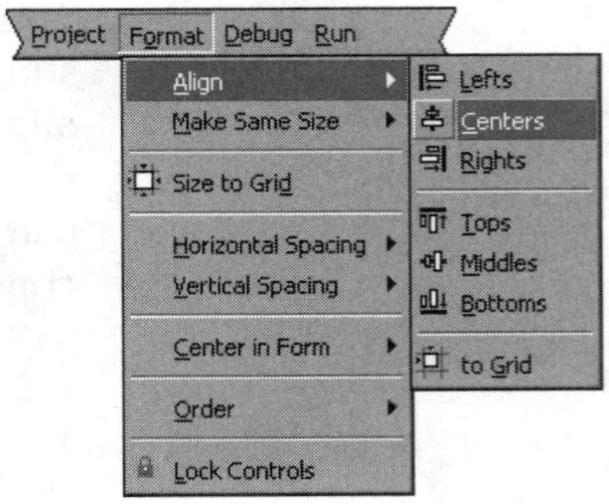

Figure 2-49
Aligning Controls to the Defining Control

---

[17]This topic may be omitted on first reading with no loss of subject continuity.

submenu. As shown, controls may be aligned in seven different ways, the first six of which are aligned relative to the position of the defining control. Choosing anyone of these first six options will move all other selected controls in relation to the defining control; the position of the defining control *is not* altered.

An additional and very useful feature of the format selection process is that all selected controls can be moved as a unit. This is accomplished by clicking within one of the selected controls and dragging the control. As the control is dragged, all other selected controls will move, as a group, while maintaining their relative positions to each other.

Finally, as shown in Figures 2-48 and 2-49, the Format menu provides a number of other format choices, all of which are rather self-evident in their effect, except perhaps for the Lock Control. This control locks all controls on the form in their current positions and prevents you from inadvertently moving them once you have placed them in their desired positions. Since this control works on a form-by-form basis, only controls on the currently active form are locked, and controls on other forms are unaffected.

Label, Line, and Picture Box Controls

Three controls that are easy to set up and are extremely useful for creating visual cues on a form are the Label, Line, and Picture box controls. Figure 2-50 shows where each of these controls is located on the Standard Object Toolbox.

The Label Control

Labels are used to provide the user with information. As such, they appear as headings within a form or next to a control to let user know the control's purpose. For example, in Figure 2-51, the heading `Disk Order Sales Form` is a label. Additionally, the text located to the left of each Text box is also a label. As the text within a Command button is provided by the button's **Caption** property, Command buttons rarely have labels associated with them.

Creating a label is very simple; all that is required is selecting the Label icon from the toolbox and setting both its **Caption** and **Font** properties. By definition, a label is a read-only control that cannot be changed by a user directly. The text displayed by a label is determined by its **Caption** property, which can be set at design time or at run time under program control. The **Caption** property's text value is displayed using the information provided by the Font property. For example, Figure 2-52 shows the **Font** property's setting box as it appears when the **Font** property was selected for the heading used in Figure 2-51. In particular, notice the **Caption** property at the top of

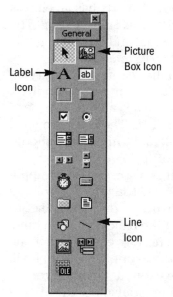

Figure 2-50
Locating the Label, Line and Picture Box Controls

Figure 2-51
A Form with Labels

Walk In Sales	
Disk Sales Order Form	

First Name: [   ] Unit Price: [4.50]
Last Name: [   ] Extended Price: [   ]
City: [   ] Sales Tax Rate: [.06]
Address: [   ] Sales Tax: [   ]
State: [   ] Zip Code: [   ] Total Due: [   ]
No. of Disk Packages: [   ]

[Calculate Order] [Print Bill] [Clear Screen] [Return to Main Menu]

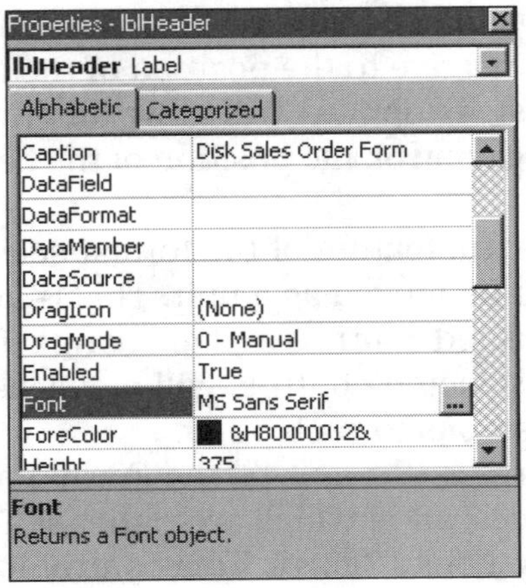

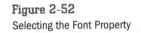

Figure 2-52
Selecting the Font Property

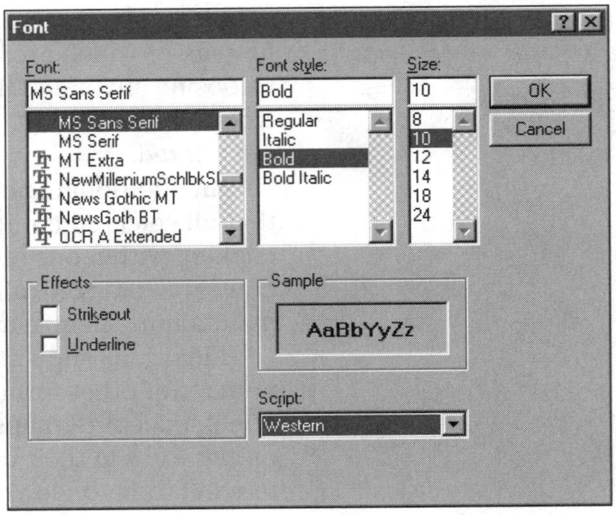

Figure 2-53
The Font Dialog Box

Figure 2-52, and then notice that the highlighted **Font** property has an ellipsis box (the box with the three dots) to the right of the MS Sans Serif setting. The ellipsis box appears when the **Font** property is selected, and clicking on this box causes the **Font** dialog box shown in Figure 2-53 to appear.

It is in the **Font** dialog box that you set the label caption's font type, style, and size. The size is in points, where there are 72 points to an inch. Notice that the label used as a heading in Figure 2-51 uses an MS Sans Serif font type and is displayed in bold with a point size of 10. The type size used for all of the other labels is 8 points, which is the default. In no case should you use a point size smaller than 6 points on any form.

Although it is the label's **Caption** property that is displayed on an application's interface, two additional useful properties in setting the caption are the AutoSize and **WordWrap** properties. If the **AutoSize** property is set to False, you must manually adjust the physical size of the Label at design time, using the sizing handles to fit the caption. It is generally easier to set the **AutoSize** property to **True**. Then, as you type in the caption, the Label will automatically expand its width to the right to fit the caption. If you prefer the Label to expand downwards to fit a caption, you must also set the **Word-Wrap** property to **True**. This forces the left and right sides to remain fixed and the caption to word wrap down as it is entered. Note, however, that the **WordWrap** property, which essentially changes the direction of the automatic expansion from the right to the bottom of the label, only takes effect if automatic expansion is activated by setting the **AutoSize** property to **True**.

The Line Control

Lines can be used to help users focus on specific areas of the screen and group related data within a defined screen area. The Line control is available directly from the toolbox, and if you double click on the Line tool, a default line is placed on the form. Each end of this line can be dragged to resize the line and place it in its desired position. Alternatively, by single clicking on the Line control and then clicking and holding the mouse within a form or object, you will set one end of the line. The second end of the line is established by dragging the mouse to the desired point. No matter how the line is initially established, it can always be resized by moving either or both end

Figure 2-54
The Line Control

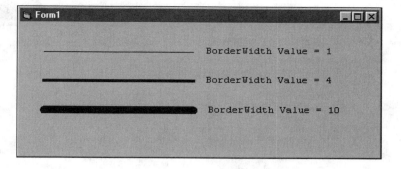

points. Additionally, you can alter the line's width, color, and style using the line's **BorderWidth**, **BorderColor**, and **BorderStyle** properties, respectively. Figure 2-54 illustrates three solid style Line controls with **Border-Width** values of 1, 4, and 10.

The Picture Box Control

A picture box is very similar to a Text box, with one important difference: unlike a Text box, which can be used for both input and output, a Picture box can only be used for output. In addition to being used for the output of text, however, a Picture box can also be used for displaying pictures, which are more commonly referred to as images.

The use of a Picture box for displaying text is presented in Section 3.1. Here, we show how to use a Picture box to display an image. The use of an Image control for displaying images is presented in Section 11.1.

Figure 2-55 shows the same image displayed in two Picture boxes. The only difference in the presentation is the setting of the Picture box's **BorderStyle** property. In the top figure the **BorderStyle** is set to Fixed Single, which is the default, while in the lower figure this setting has been changed to None.

A Picture Box control is placed on a form in the same manner as all other controls—by selecting the control from the Toolbox and placing it on the form. The Picture box so placed, however, will contain no image. The types of images that can be placed within a Picture box include bitmaps (files stored with either a .BMP or .DIB extension), icons (files stored with a .ICO extension), and metafiles (files stored with either a .WMF or .EMF extension).[18] To place an image within a Picture box you must select the **Picture** property and then click on the ellipsis box shown in Figure 2-56. Doing so produces the Load Picture dialog shown in Figure 2-57. It is from this dialog

Figure 2-55
Two Picture Boxes

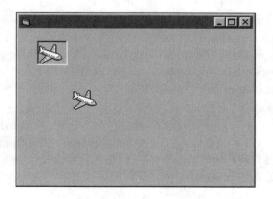

---

[18]A more complete description of each type of file is provided in Table 11-1.

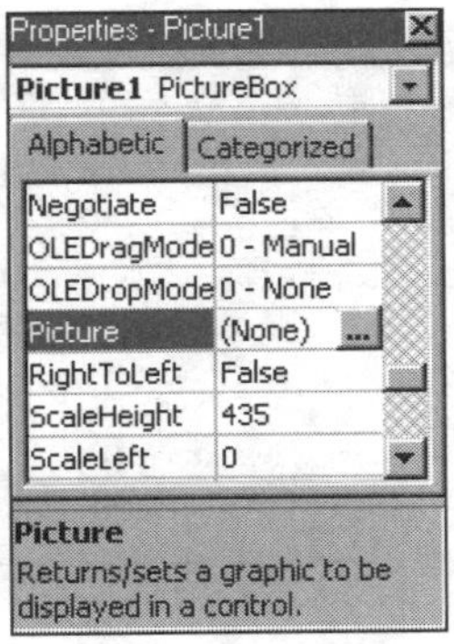

Figure 2-56
The Picture Property Setting

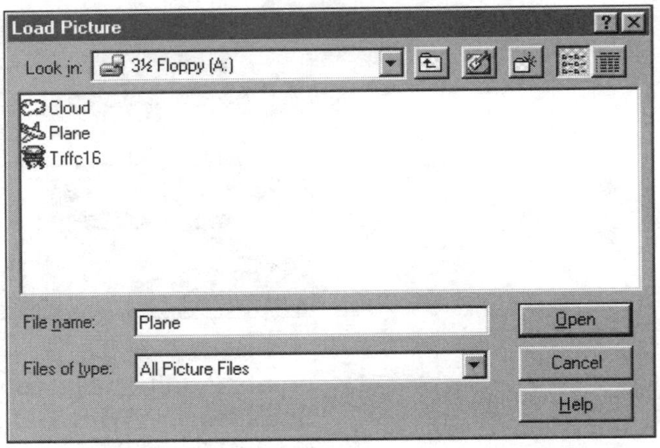

Figure 2-57
The Load Picture Dialog

that you select the location and image to be set as the **Picture** property; it is this image that is then displayed.

Exercises **2.4**

1 Determine how many initial properties can be set for a Command button. (**Hint**: Activate the Code window for a form that has a Command button and count the available procedures.)

2 Determine how many initial properties can be set for a Text box control.

3 Determine if a Label has a **Caption** or a **TabStop** property.

4 What is the difference between the **Name** and **Caption** properties?

5 How is a hot (accelerator) key created for a Command button?

6 Create a Command button named cmdInput having a **Caption** setting of Values.

7 Create a Command button named cmdDisplay having the **Caption** setting of Display.

8 Assume that one Command button has a **Caption** setting of Message, and a second Command button has a **Caption** setting of Display. Determine what happens when the hot-key sequence [ALT]+[A] is pressed twice. Do this by creating the two Command buttons and running the program.

9 Create a Text box named txtOne that has a red foreground color and a blue background color. The initial text displayed in the box should be Welcome to Visual Basic. (**Hint**: Use the **ForeColor** and **BackColor** properties; click on the ellipses (...) to bring up the available colors.)

10 Create a Text box named txtTwo that has a blue foreground color and a gray background color. The initial text displayed in the box should be High-Level Language. (**Hint**: Use the **ForeColor** and **BackColor** properties—click on the ellipses (...) to bring up the available colors.)

11 What are the three ways that an object can receive focus?

12. To receive focus in the tab sequence, what three properties must be set to **True**?

13. a. Create a graphical user interface that contains two Command buttons and two Text boxes. The names of these controls should be cmdOne, cmdTwo, txtFirst, and txtSecond. Set the tab sequence so that tab control goes from txtFirst to txtSecond to cmdOne to cmdTwo.

    b. For the tab sequence established in Exercise 13a., set the **TabStop** property of cmdOne to **False** and determine how the tab sequence is affected. What was the effect on the other objects' **TabIndex** values?

    c. For the tab sequence established in Exercise 13a., set the **TabStop** property of cmdOne to **True** and its **Visible** property to **False**. What is the run-time tab sequence now? Did these changes affect any object's **TabIndex** Values?

    d. For the tab sequence established in Exercise 13a., set the **TabStop** property of cmdOne to **True**, its **Visible** property to **True**, and its **Enabled** property to **False**. What is the run-time tab sequence now? Did these changes affect any object's **TabIndex** values?

    e. Change the tab sequence so that focus starts on txtFirst, and then goes to cmdOne, txtSecond, and finally cmdTwo. For this sequence what are the values of each object's **TabIndex** property?

14. a. Does setting a Command control's **TabStop** property to **False** ensure that it cannot receive focus?

    b. Does setting a Text box control's **TabStop** property to **False** ensure that it cannot receive focus?

For exercises 15–18 create the interfaces shown in each figure.

15.
Changing Fonts

Courier

Times Roman

Exit

16.
Calculating a Julian Date

Month   Day   Year

The Julian Date is:

Exit

17.
Colors

Hello World!

Foreground Color:

Black   Red   Green

Background Color:

White   Gray   Blue

Exit

18.
True and False

Enter a Saying: True

The number of true sayings is: False

The number of false sayings is:

Exit

2.5 ▶ Adding Event Procedures

Now that we have added four objects to Program 2-3 (The Hello Application, Ver. 3.0, shown in Figure 2-44 on page 82), we will need to supply these objects with event code. Although each object can have many events associated with it, one of the most commonly used events is the clicking of a Command button. For our Hello Application we will initially create three such mouse-click event handlers, each of which will be activated by clicking on one of the three Command buttons. Two of these event handlers will be used to change the text displayed in the Text box, and the last will be used to exit the program.

To change an object's property value while a program is running, a statement having the form

```
Object.Property = value
```

is used. The term to the left of the equal sign identifies the desired object and property. For example, `cmdMessage.Caption` refers to the **Caption** property of the control named `cmdMessage`, and `txtDisplay.Text` refers to the **Text** property of the control named `txtDisplay`, and `lblHeader.Caption` refers to the **Caption** property of the `lblHeader` control. The period between the object's name and its property is required. The value to the right of the equal sign provides the new setting for the designated property. For example, the statement `lblPrompt.Visible = False` sets the **Visible** property of the `cmdMessage` control to **False**. This has the effect of erasing the label from the screen. Similarly, the statement `lblHeader.Caption = "Sales Order Screen"` causes the text `Sales Order Screen` to be displayed as the label's caption.

For our program we want to display the text `Hello World!` when the Command button named `cmdMessage` is clicked. This requires the statement

```
txtDisplay.Text = "Hello World!"
```

to be executed for the click event of the `cmdMessage` control. Notice that this statement will change a property of one object, the Text box, using an event handler associated with another object, a Command button. Now let's attach this code to the `cmdMessage` button so that it is activated when this control is clicked. The required event procedure code is

```
Private Sub cmdMessage_Click()
    txtDisplay.Text = "Hello World!"
End Sub
```

To enter this code, double-click on the `cmdMessage` control. (Make sure you have the design form illustrated in Figure 2-39 on the screen.) This will bring up the Code window shown in Figure 2-58. As always, the template for the desired event is automatically supplied for you, requiring you to complete the procedure's body with your own code. You might also notice that the keywords **Private**, **Sub**, and **End** are displayed in a different color than the procedure's name.[19]

The object identification box should display `cmdMessage` and the procedure identification box should display `Click`. This indicates that the current object is the `cmdMessage` control and that the procedure we are working on

---

[19] Typically, the color for keywords (automatically supplied when a keyword is typed) is blue. This Keyword Text property can, however, be changed by selecting it within the Editor tab of the Options submenu in the Tools menu.

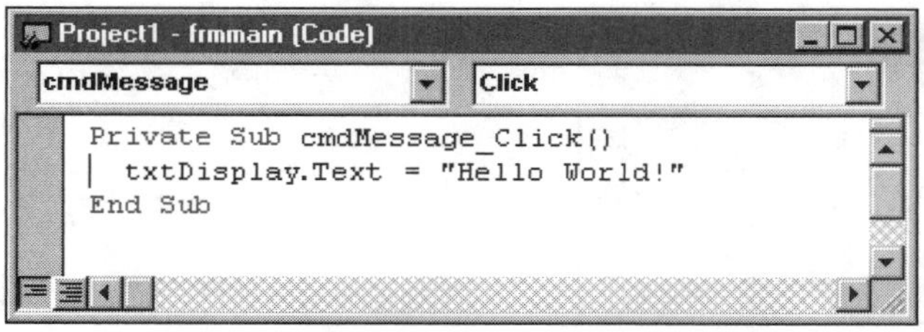

Figure 2-58
The Code Window

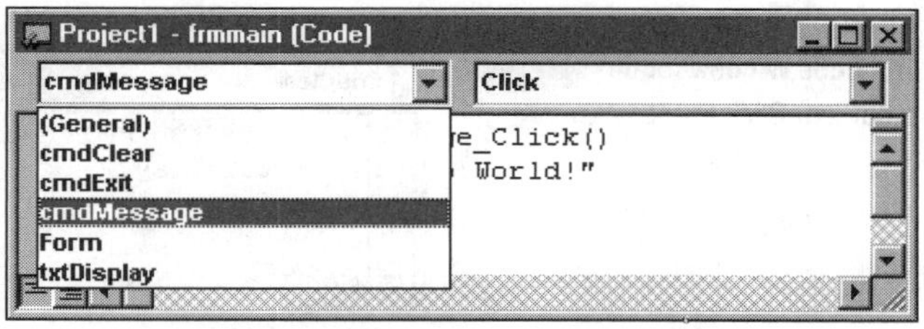

Figure 2-59
The Code Window Object List

is for the **Click** event. If either of these boxes do not contain the correct data, click on the down-facing arrow head to the right of the box and then select the desired object and procedure. Note that when you click on the arrow head to the right of the object identification box, a drop-down list appears as shown in Figure 2-59, which lists all of the form's objects, including the form itself, and the term **(General)**. **General** procedures are those that can be invoked by any and all of the form's procedures. To create a general procedure you must write your own procedure header line and body, which is the topic of Chapter 7.

When the Code window looks like the one shown in Figure 2-58, type in the line

```
txtDisplay.Text = "Hello World!"
```

between the header line, `Private Sub cmdMessage_Click()`, and the terminating `End Sub` line, so that the complete procedure appears as

```
Private Sub cmdMessage_Click()
  txtDisplay.Text = "Hello World!"
End Sub
```

Notice that we have indented the statement using two spaces. A space has also been placed around the equal sign. This is not required but is included for readability.

After your procedure is completed, press the F5 function key to run the program. When the program is running activate the `cmdMessage` control by clicking on it with the mouse, tabbing to it and pressing the ENTER key, or using the hot-key combination ALT+M. When any one of these actions is done, your screen should appear as shown in Figure 2-60.

Being able to run and test an event handler immediately after you have written it, rather than having to check each feature after the whole application is completed, is one of the nice features of Visual Basic. You should get into the habit of doing this as you develop your own programs.

Figure 2-60
The Interface Produced by Clicking
the Message Button

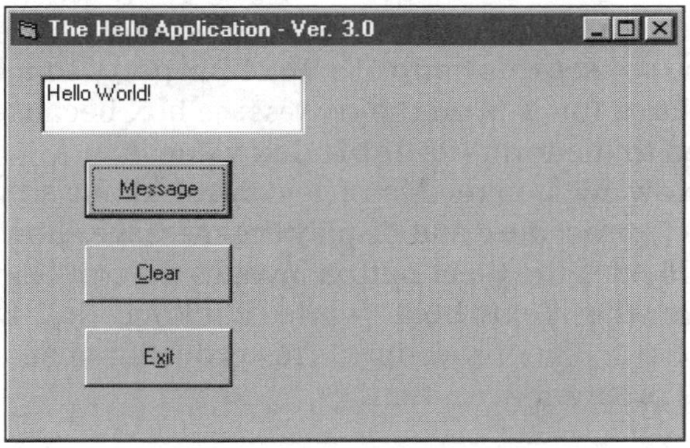

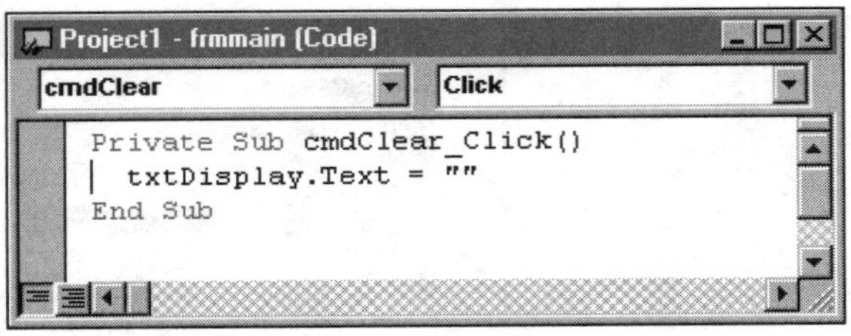

Figure 2-61

The Code Window for the
cmdClear Click Event

```
Project1 - frmmain (Code)                    _ □ ×
cmdClear              ▼    Click                    ▼
    Private Sub cmdClear_Click()
│     txtDisplay.Text = ""
    End Sub
```

Now let's finish this application by attaching event code to the **Click** events of the remaining two Command buttons, and then fixing a minor problem with the Text box control.

Bring up the Code window for the cmdClear button by double-clicking on this control after you have terminated program execution and are back in design mode. When the Code window looks like the one shown in Figure 2-61, add the single line

```
txtDisplay.Text = ""
```

between the procedure's header and terminating lines.

When this is completed, the procedure should be

```
Private Sub cmdClear_Click()
    txtDisplay.Text = ""
End Sub
```

The string "", with no spaces, is called the *empty string*. This string consists of no characters. Setting the **Text** property of the Text box to this string value will have the effect of clearing the Text box of all text. Note that a value such as "   ", which consists of one or more blank spaces, will also clear the Text box. A string with one or more blank spaces, however, is not an empty string, which is defined as a string having *no* characters.

When this procedure is completed, use the arrow to the right of the object identification box in the Code window to switch to the cmdExit control. (You can, of course, also double-click on the cmdExit control to bring up the Code window.) The event procedure for this event should be

```
Private Sub cmdExit_Click()
    Beep
    End
End Sub
```

Beep is an instruction that causes the computer to make a short beeping sound, while the keyword **End** terminates an application.

You are now ready to run the application by pressing the F5 function key. Running the application should initially produce the window shown in Figure 2-62. Notice that when the program is first run, focus is on the cmdMessage button and the Text box is empty. The empty Text box occurs because we set this control's **Text** property to a blank during design time. Similarly, focus is on the cmdMessage box because this was the first control added to the form (its **TabIndex** value is 0).

Now click on the Message control. Doing so will activate the cmdMessage Click() procedure and display the message shown in Figure 2-63.

Clicking the Clear button invokes the cmdClear_Click() procedure, which clears the Text box, while clicking the Exit button invokes the cmdExit_Click() procedure. This procedure causes a short beep and terminates program execution.

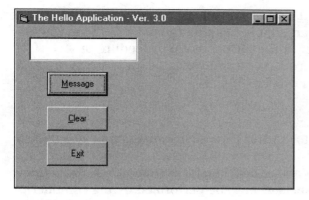

Figure 2-62
The Initial Run-Time Window

Figure 2-63
The Run-Time Window after the Message Button Is Clicked

Comments

Comments are explanatory remarks made within a program. When used carefully, comments can be very helpful in clarifying what a complete program is about, what a specific group of statements is meant to accomplish, or what one line is intended to do.

Comments are indicated by using either the apostrophe or the keyword **Rem**, which is short for Remark.

For example,

```
Rem this is a comment
' this is a comment
' this program calculates a square root
```

are all comment lines.

Comments, with one exception, can be placed anywhere within a program and have no effect on program execution. Visual Basic ignores all comments—they are there strictly for the convenience of anyone reading the program. The one exception is that comments cannot be included at the end of a statement that is itself continued on the next line.

A comment can always be written either on a line by itself or on the same line as a program statement that is not continued on the next line. When written on a line by itself, either an apostrophe or the keyword **Rem** may be used. When a comment is written on the same line as a program statement, the comment must begin with an apostrophe. In all cases a comment only extends to the end of the line it is written on. For example, the following event procedure illustrates the use of comments.

```
Rem This is the click event procedure associated with the Exit Command button
Private Sub cmdExit_Click()    ' this is the header line
    Beep ' this causes a short beep
    End  ' this ends the application
End Sub
```

In no case can a comment extend for more than one line. If you need to create multiline comments, each line must begin with either an apostrophe or the **Rem** keyword.

Typically, many comments are required when using nonstructured programming languages. These comments are necessary to clarify the purpose of either the program itself or individual sections and lines of code within the program. In Visual Basic, the program's inherent modular structure is intended to make the program readable, making the use of extensive comments unnecessary. However, if the purpose of a procedure or any of its statements is still not clear from its structure, name, or context, include comments where clarification is needed.

Statement Categories

You will have many statements at your disposal in constructing Visual Basic event procedures. All statements, however, belong to one of two broad categories: executable statements and nonexecutable statements. An *executable statement* causes some specific action to be performed by the compiler or interpreter. For example, a **MsgBox** statement or a statement that tells the computer to add or subtract a number is an executable statement. A *nonexecutable* statement is a statement that describes some feature of either the program or its data but does not cause the computer to perform any action. An example of a nonexecutable statement is a comment statement. As the various Visual Basic statements are introduced in the upcoming sections, we will point out which ones are executable and which are nonexecutable.

A Closer Look at the Text Box Control

Text boxes form a major part of almost all Visual Basic Programs, because they can be used for both input and output purposes. For example, run Program 2-3 (see Figure 2-62) again, but this time click on the Text box. Notice that a cursor appears in the Text box. At this point, you can type in any text you like, directly from the keyboard. The text you enter will stay in the box until you click on one of the Command buttons, which will either change the text to Hello World!, clear the box of all text, or terminate the program.

Since we have constructed the program essentially to use the Text box for output display purposes only, we would like to alter the operation of the Text box so that a user cannot enter data into the box. To do this we will set the box's **Click** event to immediately set focus on one of the Command buttons. The following procedure accomplishes this:

```
Private Sub txtDisplay_Click()
    cmdMessage.SetFocus
End Sub
```

PROGRAMMERS NOTES

Using the Object Browser window

To activate the Object Browser window:

- Select Object Browser from the View menu

or

- Press the F2 function key.

To activate a Code window from the Object Browser Window:

- Double-click on the desired object in the Classes box.

- Double-click on the desired event procedure in the Members box.

To cycle through each event code procedure in a Code window:

- Press the CTRL+↓ keys

or

- Press the CTRL+↑ keys.

Figure 2-64
The Code Window

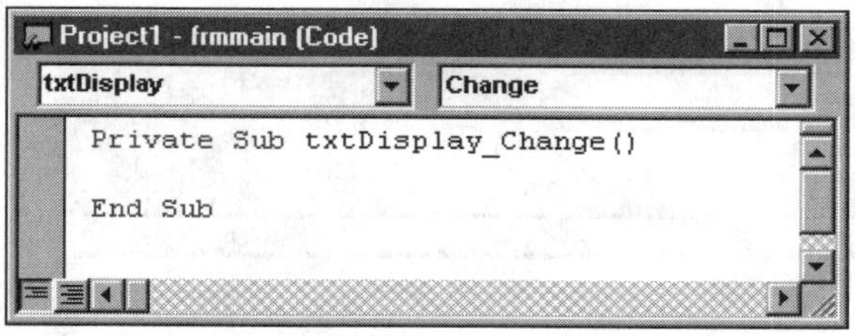

Enter this procedure now in the Text box's Code window. When you first bring up the Code window, for the Text box object (either press the SHIFT+F4 keys or use the <u>V</u>iew menu), the Code window may appear as shown in Figure 2-64. If this happens, click on the arrow to the right of the procedure identification box and select the **Click** event.

SetFocus, like **Print**, is a method. In this case, **SetFocus** is a method that sets the focus on its object.[20] Thus, when a user clicks on the Text box, it will trigger the txtDisplay_Click() procedure which in turn will call the cmdMessage **SetFocus** method. This method will set the focus on the <u>M</u>essage Command button.

Before leaving the Text box, two additional features should be mentioned. First, it is worthwhile noting that when you initially entered characters into the box, before we deactivated it for input, the entered characters were actually accepted as a string of text. This is always true of a Text box—all data entered or displayed is considered a string. As we will see in the next chapter, when we want to use a Text box to input a number, such as 12356, we will have to check carefully that a string representing an invalid number, such as 123a56, is not inadvertently entered. This type of validation is necessary because the Text box does not filter out unwanted characters from an input or displayed string. Finally, since we are only using the Text box for output, we could have used a Picture box instead. Picture boxes are very similar to Text boxes, except they cannot be used for input. Although we will use Picture boxes in the future for output-only display, we introduced the Text box here because it is one of the most widely used control objects.

Viewing All Your Procedures at Once

As you add controls and event procedures to an application, it becomes increasingly convenient to be able to get a listing of all the procedures and controls in a central place. Such a listing is possible using the Object Browser. This browser is obtained either by selecting <u>O</u>bject Browser from the <u>V</u>iew menu or by pressing the F2 function key anywhere during design time. Figure 2-65 shows the Object Browser window for pgm2-3.

Notice that the **Classes** box contains a list of modules, which in our case includes frmMain and the **Members** box contains a list of all methods and procedures currently available. In addition, procedures for which code has been written are highlighted in bold.

To view or edit any single event procedure, simply double-click on the desired procedure in the box. Once any Code window is active you can sequentially cycle through each event procedure by pressing the CTRL and ↓ keys together. This will cause the next procedure to be displayed. To reverse

---

[20]An alternative solution is to set the Locked property of the Text box to True. With this property set to True, the Text box is locked from receiving any input and effectively becomes a read-only box. It still, however, can be clicked on and receive focus.

Figure 2-65
The Object Browser Window

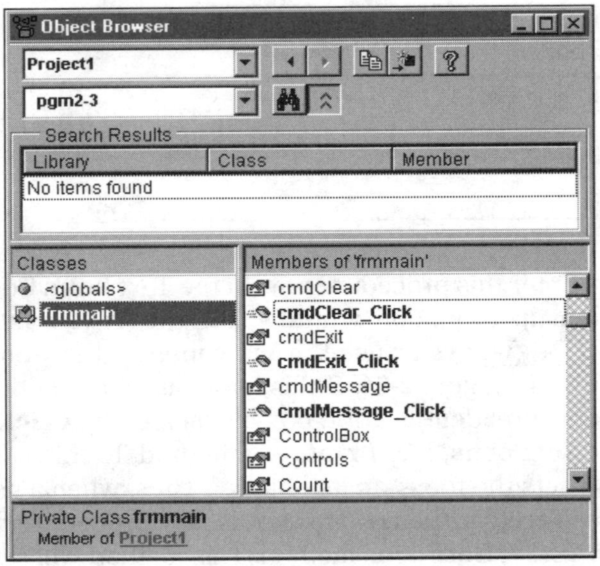

the sequence, simply press the [CTRL] and [↑] keys. These are the hot-key combinations for Next Procedure and Previous Procedure, respectively, from the Code window.

Exercises 2.5

1. a. Determine the number of events that can be associated with a Command button. (**Hint**: create a Command button and use the Code window to view its various events.)
   b. List the event names for each event that can be associated with a Command button.
2. Repeat Exercise 1a. for a Text box.
3. Repeat Exercise 1a. for a Label
4. Repeat Exercise 1a. for a Picture box.
5. List the objects and the events that the following procedures refer to:
   a. `Private Sub cmdDisplay_Click()`
   b. `Private Sub cmdBold_LostFocus()`
   c. `Private Sub txtInput_GotFocus()`
   d. `Private Sub txtOutput_LostFocus()`
6. Using the following correspondence:

Event Name	Event
Click	Click
DblClick	Double-click
GotFocus	Got-focus
LostFocus	Lost-focus

   a. Write the header line for the Double-click event associated with a Label control named `lblFirstName`.
   b. Write the header line for the Click event associated with a Picture box named `picID`.
   c. Write the header line for the Lost-focus event of a Text box named `txtLastName`.
   d. Write the header line for the Got-focus event of a Text box named `txtAddress`.

7 Write instructions that will display the following message in a Text box named `txtTest`:

a. `Welcome to Visual Basic`   d. `4 * 5 is 20`

b. `Now is the time`   e. `Vacation is Near`

c. `12345`

8 Determine the event associated with the Command button `cmdDisplay` and what is displayed in the Text box named `txtOut`, for each of the following procedures:

a.
```
Private Sub cmdDisplay_Click()
    txtOut.Text = "As time goes by"
End Sub
```

b.
```
Private Sub cmdDisplay_GotFocus()
    txtOut.Text = "456"
End Sub
```

c.
```
Private Sub cmdDisplay_LostFocus()
    txtOut.Text = "Play it again Sam"
End Sub
```

d.
```
Private Sub cmdDisplay_GotFocus()
    txtOut.Text = "           "
End Sub
```

9 a. Four properties that can be set for a Text box are named **FontBold**, **FontItalic**, **FontName**, and **FontSize**. What do you think these properties control?

b. What display do you think the following procedure produces when the Command button `cmdOne` is clicked?

```
Private Sub cmdOne_Click()
    txtOut.FontName = "Courier"
    txtOut.FontSize = 14
    txtOut.FontBold = True
    txtOut.FontItalic = True
    txtOut.Text = "COMPUTERS"
End Sub
```

10 Enter and run the Program 2-1.

For exercises 11 through 13, create the given interface and initial properties. Then complete the application by writing code to produce the stated task.

11

Object	Property	Setting
Form	Name	frmMain
	Caption	Messages
Command Button	Name	cmdGood
	Caption	&Good
Command Button	Name	cmdBad
	Caption	&Bad
Text Box	Name	txtMessage
	Text	(blank)

When a user clicks the <u>G</u>ood button, the message `Today is a good day!` should appear in the Text box, and when the <u>B</u>ad button is clicked, the message `I'm having a bad day today!` should be displayed.

⑫

Changing Fonts		
This is a test		
System		
Garamond		
Terminal		

Object	Property	Setting
Form	Name	frmMain
	Caption	Changing Fonts
Text Box	Name	txtDisplay
	Caption	This is a test
Command	Name	cmdSystem
Button	Caption	&System
Command	Name	cmdGaramond
Button	Caption	&Garamond
Command	Name	cmdTerminal
Button	Caption	&Terminal

When the first Command button is clicked, the text in the Text box should change to a System font, when the second Command button is clicked, the text should change to a Garamond font (if your system does not have a Garamond font, select a font that you do have available), and when the third Command button is clicked, the text should change to a Terminal font. (**Hint**: the statement txtDisplay.FontName = "System" will change the text in the Text box to a System font.)

⑬

Typeface		
This is a test		
Bold		
Italic		

Object	Property	Setting
Form	Name	frmMain
	Caption	Typeface
Command	Name	cmdBold
Button	Caption	&Bold
Command2	Name	cmdItalic
Button	Caption	&Italic
Text box	Name	txtDisplay
	Text	This is a test

By clicking on the Text box, the user should be able to enter any desired text in nonboldface and nonitalic font. When the user clicks on the Bold button, the text in the Text box should change to boldface, and when the user clicks on the Italic button, the text should change to italic. (**Hint**: Setting the Text property **FontBold** to **True** changes the font to boldface, while a **False** value removes boldface. Similarly, a **True** value for the property **FontItalic** sets italic and a **False** value removes it. The removal of bold and italic should be accomplished when the Text box gets the focus.)

⑭ Write a Visual Basic application having three Command buttons and one Text box that is initially blank. Clicking the first Command button should produce the message See no evil. Clicking the second Command button should produce the message Hear no evil, and clicking the third Command button should produce the message Speak no evil in the Text box.

⑮ Write a Visual Basic Program having four Command buttons and one Text box with the initial message Hello World. When the user clicks the first Command button, the message should change to bold. Clicking the second button should change the text to a nonbold state. Similarly, clicking the third Command button should italicize the Text box message, and clicking the fourth Command button should ensure that the message is not italicized. (**Hint**: See Exercise 13.)

2.6 ▶ Focus on Program Design and Implementation:

Creating a Main Menu[21]

Most commercial applications perform multiple tasks, with each task typically assigned its own form. For example, one form might be used for entering an order, a second form for entering the receipt of merchandise into inventory, and a third form used to specify information needed to create a report.

Although each additional form can be easily added to an existing project using the techniques presented later in this section, there is the added requirement for activating each form in a controlled and user-friendly manner. As a practical matter, this activation can be accomplished using an initial main menu form that is displayed as the application's opening window. This menu of choices provides the user with a summary of what the application can do, and is created as either a set of Command buttons or as a Menu bar. Here, we show how to rapidly prototype a main menu consisting of Command buttons, using the Rotech Systems case (see Section 1.5) as an example. The procedure for constructing a Menu bar is presented in Section 11.5.

Command Button Main Menus

The underlying principle used in creating a main menu screen is that a user can easily shift from one form to a second form by pressing a Command button. How this works for two screens is illustrated in Figure 2-66. Here, pressing the Command button shown on the Main Menu form causes the 2nd form to be displayed. Similarly, pressing the 2nd form's Command button redisplays the Main Menu form.

The flip-flopping between screens that is provided by the scheme shown in Figure a can be easily extended to produce a main menu screen, a sample of which is shown in Figure 2-66. For this screen there would be four additional screens, with each screen displayed by clicking one of the

Figure 2-66
Flip-Flopping between Two Screens

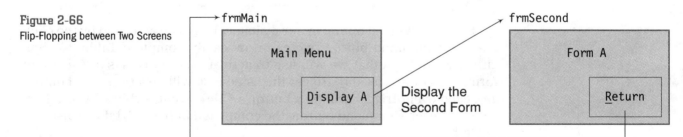

Figure 2-67
A Sample Main Menu Screen

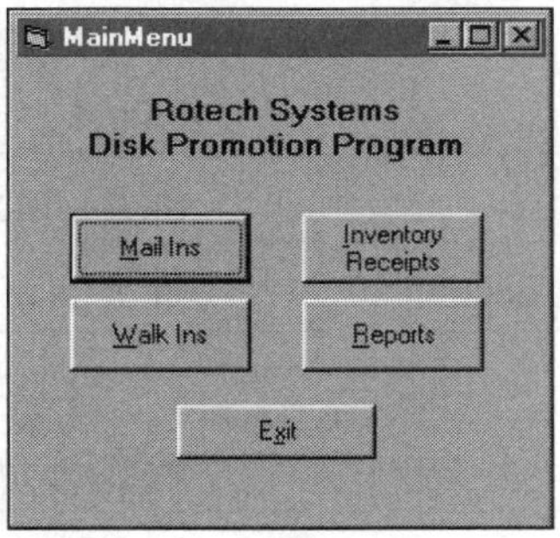

---

[21]This section can be omitted with no loss of subject continuity.

Command buttons on the main menu. In a completed application each additional screen is different, but each screen would have a Return button, like the one shown in Figure 2-66, to redisplay the main menu screen.

The menu options shown in this figure would be provided as the first operational form presented to the user. The term *operational form* means that the form is used to directly interface with the operational part of the system to perform a task, unlike an information form. *Information forms* are purely passive forms that provide information about the application, and which, if not included with the system, would not stop the system from performing its intended functions. Examples of information forms are an opening splash screen, which contains general advertising information that is displayed for a few seconds before the first operational form is presented, an About Box, which provides information about the application, such as author, copyright holder, and version number, and Help windows, which provide assistance on how to use various application features.

An application's initial main menu screen is constructed from the information contained in the system's initial TTL table. Specifically, we will construct the Rotech Systems main menu to provide access to the tasks listed in the TTL table developed in Section 1.5, and reproduced for convenience as Table 2-7.

Table 2-7 The Initial Rotech Systems TTL Table		
Form:	**Trigger**	
Task	**Object**	**Event**
Enter Inventory Receipts		
Enter & Process a Mail-in Response		
Enter & Process a Walk-in Request		
Produce Reports		
Exit the System		

Since each menu option in our main menu is to be activated by the clicking of a Command button, we can now easily complete Table 2-7. Specifically, the form that we will use to activate these tasks is a Main Menu form, each object used to trigger the listed task will be a Command button, and each event trigger will be a button's **Click** event. Arbitrarily assigning names to each Command button, the completed initial TTL table is listed as Table 2-8.

Table 2-8 The Completed Initial Rotech Systems TTL Table		
Form: Main Menu	**Trigger**	
Task	**Object**	**Event**
Enter Inventory Receipts	cmdInvRec	Click
Enter & Process a Mail-in Response	cmdMailin	Click
Enter & Process a Walk-in Request	cmdWalkin	Click
Produce Reports	cmdReport	Click
Exit the System	cmdExit	Click

TIPS FROM THE PROS

Creating a Main Menu

The development of a menu system is quite easy, provides one of the most visually impressive functioning parts of a system, and actually demands the least in terms of programming competency. The trick in developing a menu is to follow these steps:

1. Make the opening application's form a Main Menu form, which is a form that contains Command buttons used to display other forms.

2. Initially, add a single new form to the project, which ultimately will be replaced by an operational form. (Later on, additional new forms will be added, one for each operational form required by the project.)

3. Provide the new form with a Command button having a caption such as Return to Main Menu Form. This button is referred to as the Return button.

4. Attach two lines of code to the new form's Return button's Click event.

   These two lines of code appear as:

```
Me.Hide      ' this is a valid statement
frmMain.Show ' replace frmMain with any
             ' valid form name
```

The first code line is an instruction to hide the current form from view, while the second line displays the frmMain form. Thus, if the Main Menu form is named frmMain, the statement frmMain.Show displays the Main Menu form when the Return button is pressed. In general, each new form will have more than one Command button. One button, however, should always return the user directly to the Main Menu.

5. Attach two similar lines of code to each Main Menu Command button used to display a new form. These lines of code take the form:

```
Me.Hide        ' this is a valid statement
frmDesired.Show ' replace frmDesired
               ' with any valid form
               ' name
```

Initially, all Main Menu buttons will be used to display the same form added in Step 2. The reason for using the Hide method rather than the Unload statement, is based on the assumption that we will be returning to each form many times; so we try to keep each form in memory to minimize loading times.

For most forms, the time that a form is loaded is both noticeable and annoying to users. For example, when a form stored on the A disk drive is first loaded, you can actually see the load occur. To reduce this, most systems explicitly load as many forms as possible (which depends on available memory) early on, and then use the Hide and Show methods to hide and display forms as needed. In the absence of an explicit Load statement, the first Show method will perform a load prior to displaying a form.

Using the information in Table 2-8 tells us that, operationally, our main menu will consist of five Command buttons, with each button's **Click** event used to display another form. Specifically, clicking on the cmdInvRec button will activate an operational form for entering inventory receipts, clicking on the cmdMailin button will activate an operational form for entering an order for the promotional 10-diskette pack, clicking on the cmdWalkin button will activate an operational form for entering a walk in order, clicking on the cmdReport button will activate an operational form for producing reports, and clicking on the cmdExit button will terminate program execution. Using this information, and adding an information label to the Main Menu form, we construct Table 2-9, which is the initial Main Menu properties table.

Figure 2-68 illustrates a form having the properties described by Table 2-9. Specifically, we have chosen to group the two buttons associated with order entry (Mail Ins and Walk Ins) in one column, aligned the two remaining buttons in a second column, and centered the Exit button below and

Table 2-9   The Rotech Systems Main Menu Properties Table

Object	Property	Setting
Form	Name	frmMain
	Caption	Main Menu
Command button	Name	cmdMailins
	Caption	&Mail Ins
	TabIndex	0
Command button	Name	cmdWalkins
	Caption	&Walk Ins
	TabIndex	1
Command button	Name	cmdInvRec
	Caption	&Inventory Receipts
	TabIndex	2
Command button	Name	cmdReports
	Caption	&Reports
	TabIndex	3
Command button	Name	cmdExit
	Caption	E&xit
	TabIndex	4
Label	Name	lblHeader
	Caption	Rotech Systems Disk Promotion Program
	Font	MS Sans Serif, Bold, Size = 10

between the two columns. If there were an even number of Command buttons we could have aligned them vertically into two columns, including the Exit button as the last button in the second column, and made all the buttons the same size. Figures 2-69 and 2-70 show two alternatives to Figure 2-68. In each case, the size and placement of each button is programer determined, with the only overriding design consideration at this point being that the size of each command button within a grouping should be the same, and that the buttons should align in a visually pleasing manner. Although we will give a number of form design guidelines in Section 3.6, the basic rule is to produce a functionally useful form that is dignified and not ornate. The design and colors of your form should always be appropriate to the business whose application you are producing.

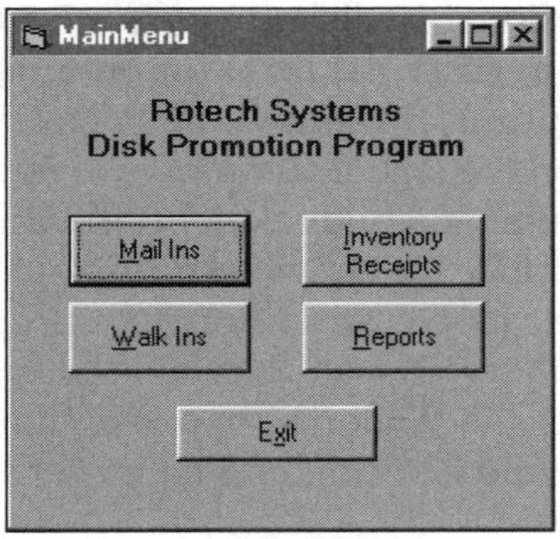

Figure 2-68
Rotech's Initial Main Menu Form

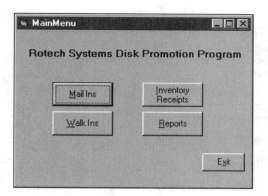

Figure 2-69
A Possible Main Menu Layout

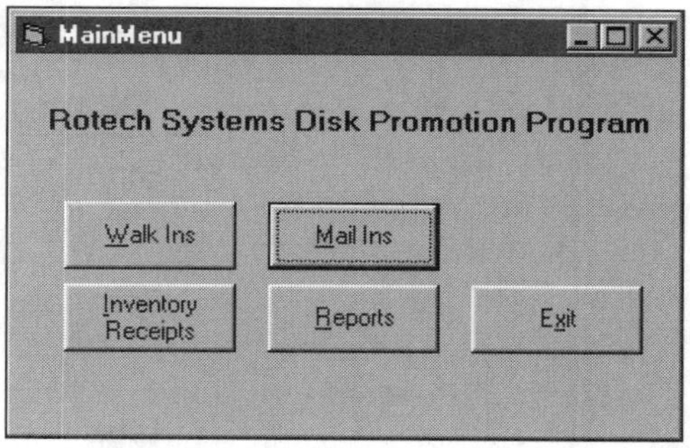

Figure 2-70
Another Main Menu Layout

As a functional matter for our particular application, since the majority of times a user will be interacting with the Mail Ins button, which deals with the system's most dynamic data, we have given this object the initial input focus. Thus, by simply pressing the Enter key, a user will activate the most commonly used button in the menu. The tab sequence then ensures a smooth transition that drives the focus from the Mail Ins button down the first column to the top of the second column of buttons, which is the Inventory Receipts button, and then down this column, over to the Exit button and back to the top of the first column.

In reviewing Figure 2-68, notice that the window both furnishes information about the application and provides a current list of available choices as a sequence of Command buttons. We now need to add additional forms and provide the code so that pressing any of the buttons except the Exit button unloads the current Main Menu form and displays the new form appropriate to the selected menu choice, while pressing the Exit button performs the normal operation of ending program execution.

Adding a Second Form

At this stage in our application's development we have neither sufficient understanding of the system's requirements nor sufficient knowledge of Visual Basic to construct a meaningful form to carry out the tasks indicated by the Main Menu. We can, however, easily add a second form, which is shown in Figure 2-71, to indicate that the form is under development. Notice that this second form contains a label and a command button, which are the same types of objects included in our Main Menu form. The properties for this second form are listed in Table 2-10. Since this form performs the single task of returning to the Main Menu form, a TTL table listing this single task is not created.

Figure 2-71
The Project's "Under Development"
Form

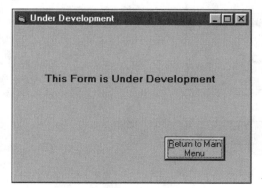

Table 2-10 The "Under Development" Form's Properties Table

Object	Property	Setting
Form	Name	frmStub
	Caption	Under Development
Command button	Name	cmdReturn
	Caption	&Return to Main Menu
Label	Name	lblReturn
	Caption	This Form is Under Development
	Font	MS Sans Serif, Bold, Size = 10

To add this second form to our project, either select the Add Form item from the Project menu, as shown in Figure 2-72, or press the Add Form button on the Standard Toolbar, as shown in Figure 2-73. Both of these choices will bring up the Add Form dialog shown in Figure 2-74, from which you should select the Form icon under the New tab. This will add the second form to the Project Explorer Window, as shown in Figure 2-75. Once you have generated this new form, configure it with the objects and properties listed in Table 2-10.

The form you have just created is an example of a stub form. The functional use of a **stub form** is simply to see that an event is correctly activated. In our particular case, it will be used to test the operation of the Main Menu to correctly display a second form and provide a return back to the Main Menu from the newly developed form. To do this, we now have to add the code that correctly shows and hides forms from the user's view.

Loading and Unloading Forms

The Visual Basic statements and methods provided for displaying and hiding forms from a user's view are listed in Table 2-11. The purpose of the Load and Unload statements are to explicitly load and unload a form into and out

Figure 2-72
Adding a Second Form Using the
Project Menu

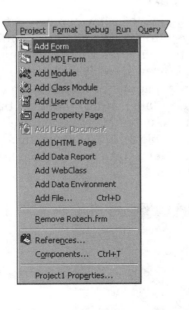

```
Project  Format  Debug  Run  Query
  Add Form
  Add MDI Form
  Add Module
  Add Class Module
  Add User Control
  Add Property Page
  Add User Document
  Add DHTML Page
  Add Data Report
  Add WebClass
  Add Data Environment
  Add File...        Ctrl+D
  Remove Rotech.frm
  References...
  Components...   Ctrl+T
  Project1 Properties...
```

Figure 2-73
Adding a Second Form Using a
Toolbar Button

Add Form Button

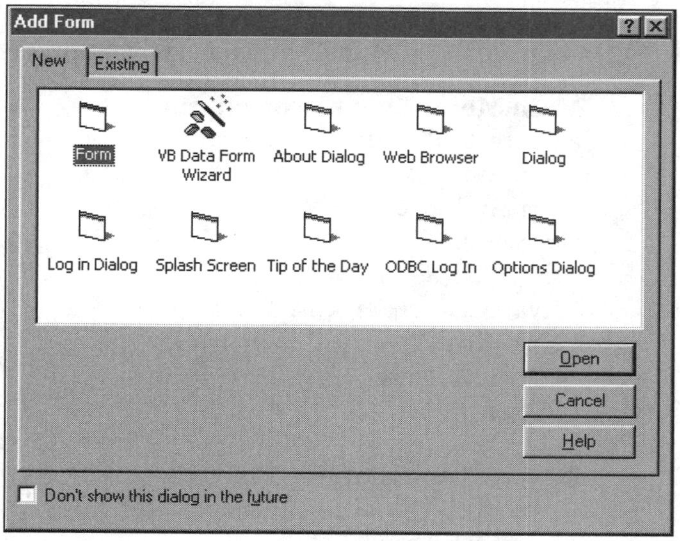

Figure 2-74
The Add Form Dialog Box

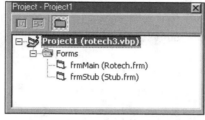

Figure 2-75
The Project Explorer Window
Showing Two Forms

of the computer's memory. When a project is first executed, the default is to automatically load and display the project's opening form. Other forms must then be loaded into memory before they can be displayed, and no longer needed forms should be unloaded, to conserve memory space.

Table 2-11 Form Display Statements and Methods

Instruction	Type	Syntax	Example	Description
Load	Statement	Load form-name	Load frmStub	Loads a form into memory. Used to initially load a form without immediately displaying it.
Unload	Statement	Unload form-name	Unload frmMain	Unloads a form from memory. Used to free memory space.
Show	Method	form-name.Show	frmStub.Show	Displays a form. If the form is not already loaded, a Load is performed before the form is displayed.
Hide	Method	form-name.Hide	frmMain.Hide	Hides a form, but does not unload it.
Refresh	Method	object-name.Refresh	frmMain.Refresh	Forces a complete redisplay of a form or other control. This ensures that all graphical elements are redrawn (see Chapter 11).

Using the statements and methods listed in Table 2-11, we can easily write event procedures to unload the Main Menu form and load and display the `Under Development` stub form when any Main Menu button, except the E<u>x</u>it button, is pressed. The required event procedure codes are:

Main Menu Event Procedures

```
Private Sub cmdMailins_Click()
    Me.Hide
    frmStub.Show
End Sub


Private Sub cmdWalkins_Click()
    Me.Hide
    frmStub.Show
End Sub

Private Sub cmdInvrec_Click()
    Me.Hide
    frmStub.Show
End Sub

Private Sub cmdReports_Click()
    Me.Hide
    frmStub.Show
End Sub

Private Sub cmdExit_Click()
    Beep
    End
End Sub
```

Each of these **Click** event procedures causes the `frmMain` form to be hidden and the `frmStub` form to be displayed whenever any Main Menu button is pressed, except for the E<u>x</u>it button.[21] The code for the stub form's return button's **Click** event is:

```
Private Sub cmdReturn_Click()
    Me.Hide        ' can be replaced with frmStub.Hide
    frmMain.Show
End Sub
```

That is, the <u>R</u>eturn button simply hides the current stub form and displays the initial `frmMain` window. The advantage of using a stub form is that it permits us to run a complete application that does not yet meet all of its final requirements. As each successive form is developed, the display of the stub form can be replaced with a display of the desired form. This incremental, or stepwise, refinement of the program is an extremely powerful development technique used by professional programmers. Another advantage to this rapid application prototyping technique is that, as new features are required, additional Command buttons can be easily added to the Main Menu form.

One modification that can be made to our Main Menu form is to have each button call a single, centrally placed, general-purpose procedure that

---

[21] An alternative to the `Me.Hide` statement is `frmMain.Hide`, which explicitly names the form to be hidden. Two other statements that will both hide and unload the form are `Unload Me`, which causes the current form, whatever it is named, to be unloaded, and the statement `Unload frmMain`, which explicitly names the form to be unloaded.

would then make the choice of which form to unload and display based on the button pressed. We consider this approach in Chapter 7 after both selection statements and general-purpose procedures are presented. You will encounter both the current technique and the general-purpose procedure technique in practice, and which one you adopt for your programs is more a matter of style than substance.

Note: *The Rotech Systems project, as it exists at the end of this section, can be found on the Student Disk in the* rotech2 *folder as* project rotech2.vbp.

Exercises 2.6

1. Implement the two screens and the relationship between the two forms previously shown in Figure 2-66. Thus, when a user presses the single button on the form with the label Main Menu, the screen labeled Form A should appear, and when the Return button on Form A is pressed, the form labeled Main Menu should appear.

2. a. Implement the three screens and the relationship shown in the accompanying figure. The Main Menu form should have a single Command button that displays Form A. Form A should have two Command buttons; one to return to the Main Menu and one to display Form B. Form B should also have two buttons, one to return control to Form A and one to return control directly to the Main Menu.

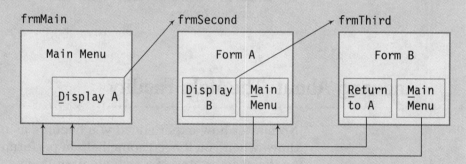

   b. Add a fourth form with the label Form C to the project created for Exercise 4a. This form is to be displayed using a Command button on form B. For this case, how many Command buttons should Form B contain for controlling the display of forms? Notice that when forms are chained together in the manner shown, there are at most three Command buttons; one button to "back-up" one level and return to the immediately preceding screen, one button to return directly to the Main Menu, and a third button to call the next form in the chain. For multilevel forms it is also convenient to provide a "hot key", such as the F10 function key that can be used on all forms to return directly to the Main Menu form and a second "hot key", such as the F9 function key that always redisplays the preceding form. (Creating this type of "hot key" is presented in Section 6.7.)

3. Either create the menu system developed in this section or locate and load the project from the Student Disk (project rotech2.vbp in the rotech2 folder).

4   a.   Add a new form, with the following properties, to the Rotech project:

Object	Property	Setting
Form	Name	frmWalkins
	Caption	Walk In Processing Form
Command button	Name	cmdReturn
	Caption	&Return to Main Menu
Label	Name	lblReturn
	Caption	This Form is Under Development
	Font	MS Sans Serif, Bold, Size = 10

This new form's Command button should return control to the Main Menu form when the button is clicked

b.   Modify the Main Menu <u>W</u>alk In button's **Click** event so that it displays the form you created in Exercise 4a, rather than displaying the frmStub form.

5   **CASE STUDY**

For your selected case project (see project specifications at the end of Section 1.5) complete the project's initial TTL Table and then create a working Main Menu that corresponds to the data in the completed table. Additionally, add an Under Development stub form to the project and verify that a user can successfully cycle between forms.

2.7 ▶ Knowing About: The Help Facility

No matter how experienced you become using Visual Basic, there will be times when you'll need some help in performing a particular task, looking up the exact syntax of a statement, or finding the parameters required by a built-in function. For these tasks, as well as locating numerous technical articles, you can use Visual Basic's online help facility. With Version 6.0 the online help consists of the complete MSDN (for Microsoft Developer Network) Library, which is supplied on two CD ROMS. Prior to Version 6.0, the MSDN Library only came with a paid subscription to the Microsoft Developer Network, which is a service targeted at sophisticated applications developers. The complete MSDN Library now doubles as the online help facility. It is an extremely powerful programming aid that contains a treasure trove of documentation, reference material, technical articles, and sample code.

To access the online help, select either the <u>C</u>ontents, <u>S</u>earch, or <u>I</u>ndex options from the <u>H</u>elp menu, as shown in Figure 2-76. When any of these options is selected, one of the screens shown as Figure 2-77, Figure 2-78, or Figure 2-79, will be displayed.

If the screen shown in Figure 2-77 is displayed, you do not have access to the online help and must install the MSDN Library before proceeding. The screen shown in Figure 2-78 simply requires you to locate and insert the second MSDN CD ROM disk into the CD ROM drive, at which point the main online help window shown in Figure 2-79 will appear. Notice that this main online help window is divided into two panes.

Figure 2-76
The Help Menu Options

Figure 2-77
The Online Help is Not Installed

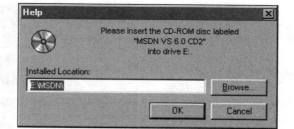

Figure 2-78
The Second CD ROM is Required

Figure 2-79
The Main Online Help Window

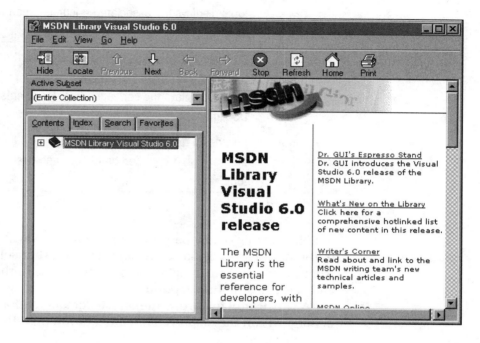

The left pane, which is referred to as the Navigation pane, contains the four tabs labeled <u>C</u>ontents, <u>I</u>ndex, <u>S</u>earch, and Favori<u>t</u>es. Each of these tabs provides a different way of accessing information from the online help, as summarized in Table 2-12. The right section, which is the Documentation pane, displays all information retrieved from the Library.

As shown in Figure 2-79, the <u>C</u>ontents tab, because it is on top of the other tabs, is the currently active tab. This arrangement occurred because the <u>C</u>ontents option was selected from the <u>H</u>elp menu (see Figure 2-76). If either the <u>I</u>ndex or <u>S</u>earch options had been selected, the same main online help window would appear, except that the respective <u>I</u>ndex or <u>S</u>earch tab would be active. No matter which tab is currently active, however, you can switch from one tab to another by clicking on the desired tab.

The Contents Tab

The Contents tab provides a means of browsing through all of the available reference material and technical articles contained within the MSDN Library. Essentially, this tab provides a table of contents of all of the material in the library, and displays the topics using the same folder tree structure found in Windows 95 and 98. For example, if you expand the single topic shown in Figure 2-79 by clicking on the plus sign box [+], and then expand the Visual Basic Documentation topic, you will see the tree shown in Figure 2-80. The information provided in the documentation pane was displayed by

Table 2-12   The Online Help Tabs

Tab	Description
Contents	Displays a Table of Contents for the online documentation. This table can be expanded to display individual topic titles; double-clicking a title displays the associated documentation in the Documentation pane.
Index	Provides both a general index of topics and a Text box for user entry of a specific topic. Entry of a topic causes focus to shift to the closest matching topic within the general index. Double clicking on an index topic displays the associated documentation in the Documentation pane.
Search	Provides a means of entering a search word or phrase. All topics matching the entered word(s) are displayed in a List box. Clicking on a topic displays the corresponding documentation in the Documentation pane.
Favorites	Provides a means of storing the name and location of a documentation topic that can then be directly accessed by clicking on the saved topic name.

double-clicking on the page highlighted in the Navigation pane. A hard copy of the displayed page is easily obtained by either selecting the <u>P</u>rint option from the <u>F</u>ile menu or right-clicking the mouse in the Documentation pane and selecting the Print option.

A very useful feature of the online documentation are the hyperlinks embedded within the displayed documentation text. By positioning the mouse on underlined text and clicking, the referenced text will be displayed. This permits you to rapidly jump from topic to topic, all while staying within the Documentation pane.

Figure 2-80

Using the Contents Tab

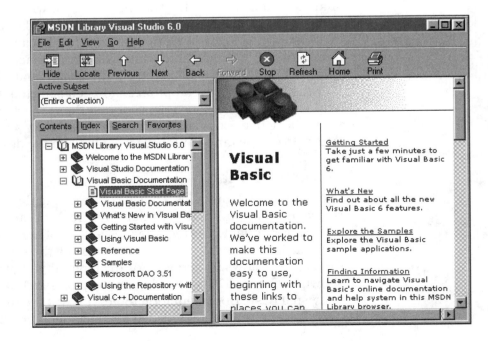

Figure 2-81
The Activated Index Tab

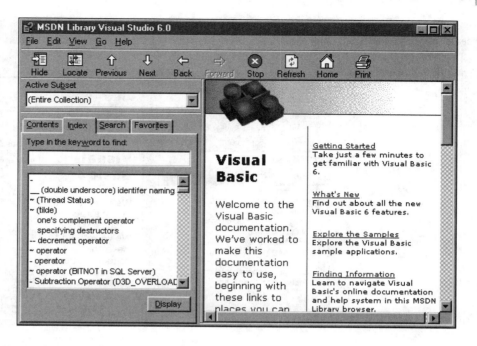

The Index Tab

For actual online help, as opposed to locating reference material or browsing for technical articles, the most useful of the tabs shown in Figure 2-79 is the Index tab. When you select this tab, the main online window illustrated in Figure 2-81 is displayed.

As shown in Figure 2-81, the Index tab is on top of the other tabs, which makes it the active tab. This tab operates much like an index in a book, with one major improvement. In a book, after looking up the desired topic, you must manually turn to the referenced page or pages. In the online help facility this look up and display is automatic, once you indicate the desired topic. Selection of the topic is accomplished by double-clicking on an item within the list of topics contained in the List box (this is the box located at the bottom of the tab). To locate a topic you can either type the topic's name within the tab's keyword Text box, which causes the item to be highlighted in the List box, or use the scroll bar at the right of the List box and manually move to the desired item.

For example, in Figure 2-82, the topic Print Method has been typed in the keyword Text box, and the List box entry for this topic has been selected. As each letter is typed in the Text box, the selected entry in the List box changes to match the input letters as closely as possible. In this case, since there are multiple library entries for the highlighted topic, if you double-click on the highlighted topic or press the Display Command button, the Multiple Topics dialog box shown in Figure 2-83 appears. Either by highlighting a desired topic in the Multiple Topics dialog box and clicking the Display button, or by double-clicking on the desired item directly in the List box, the documentation for the selected topic is displayed in the Documentation area. Figure 2-84 illustrates the documentation for the item highlighted in Figure 2-83.

A handy feature of the online help facility is that once you have selected and displayed the desired topic you can easily generate a hard copy of the information. This is accomplished by either selecting the Print item from either the File menu button at the top of the MSDN Library window, or by using the context menu provided by clicking the right-mouse button from within the displayed information.

Figure 2-82
The Index Tab with a Typed Entry

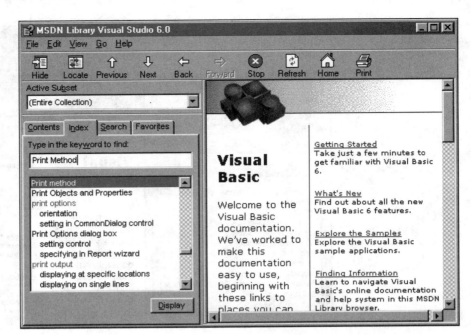

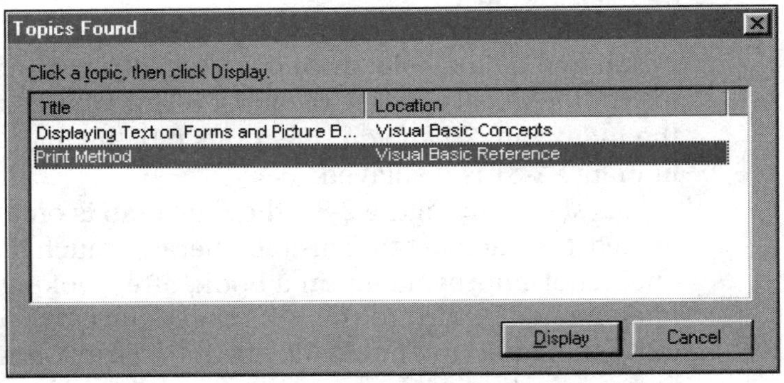

Figure 2-83
The Multiple Topics Dialog Box

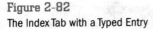

Figure 2-84
The Documentation Display

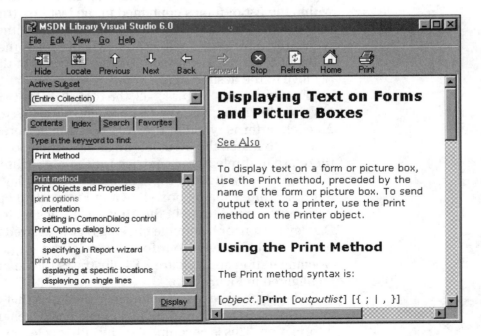

The Search Tab

The Search tab, which is shown as the active tab in Figure 2-85, permits searching either the complete MSDN Library, or sections of it, for the words entered into the tab's Text box. In creating a search phrase, you should enclose a phrase within double quotes and make use of boolean operators to limit the search. For example, using the current MSDN Library at the time when this book was written, a list of 63 topics was generated for the phrase "Named Constant", when the List Topics Command button shown in Figure 2-85 was pressed. The double quotes tells the search to look for the words Named Constant together. If the double quotes are omitted, the search finds all occurrences of either the word Named or Constant, and turns up 500 matches. This larger list was generated by locating every occurrence of either the word Named or Constant. The documentation shown in the figure was displayed by clicking on the third topic listed in the List box.

The Favorites Tab

Frequently, while navigating through the online help, you will locate one or more references and articles that you would like to explore in more detail at some later time. Many times the article will have been located by following a circuitous route through hyperlinks contained within the documentation itself. To mark such a topic for later retrieval, first click the Favorites tab. When this tab is active, the currently displayed topic is automatically entered in the Current topic Text box, as illustrated in Figure 2-86.

To add the current topic to the favorites list, press the Add button. If you want to rename the displayed topic, you can enter a new name in the Current topic text box before clicking the Add button; the new name will still refer to the displayed topic in the documentation pane. You then can retrieve the article at any future time by opening the Favorites tab and clicking on the desired entry.

Figure 2-85
Using the Search Tab

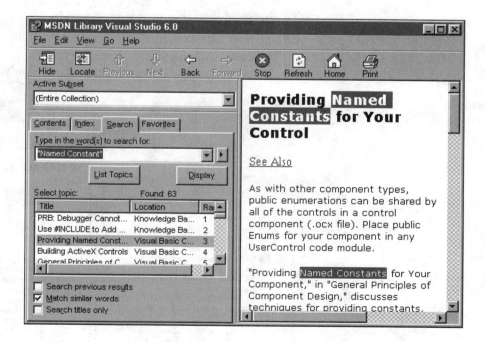

Figure 2-86
The Favorites Tab

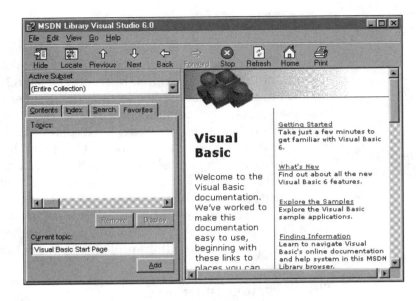

Exercises 2.7

1. Using the online help facility, locate the Welcome to Visual Basic page illustrated in Figure 2-87.

2. Using the online help facility, locate the Visual Basic Concepts page illustrated in Figure 2-88.

3. a. Using the Contents tab, and expanding the online documentation folder tree to look like that shown in Figure 2-89, display the illustrated documentation page.

   b. Obtain a hard copy printout of the documentation page displayed for Exercise 3a.

4. a. Using the Index tab, locate the documentation for the topic MsgBox Constants.

   b. Print out the documentation page located for Exercise 4a and compare it to the constants listed in Appendix E in this book.

5. a. Starting with screen shown in Figure 2-90, and expanding the Technical Articles topic, locate a technical article of your choosing. (*Note:* to obtain this screen you will have to alter the

Figure 2-87
Figure for Exercise 1.

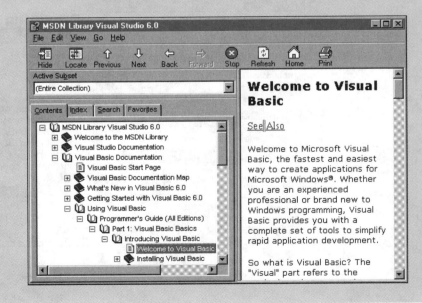

Figure 2-88

Figure for Exercise 2.

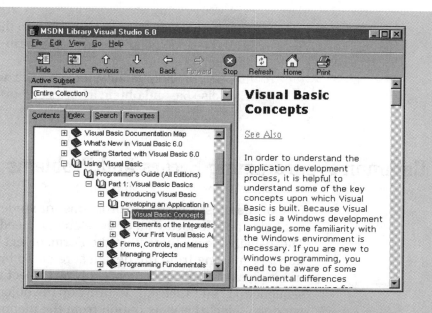

Figure 2-89

The CheckBox Documentation Page

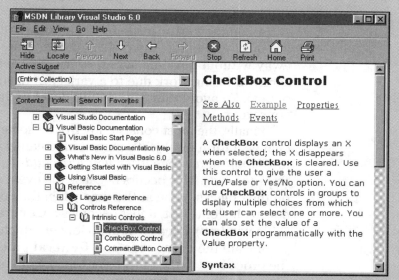

Figure 2-90

Figure for Exercise 5a.

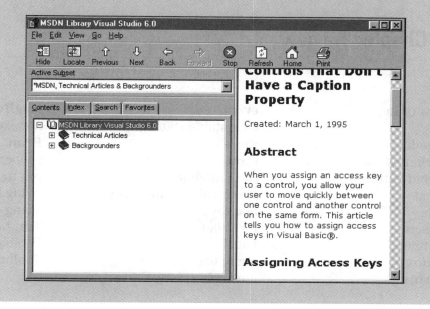

text in the Active Subset Text box to that shown in the figure.) Add the selected article to the Favorites list and close the help facility.

b. Reopen the help facility, locate the article that you saved in Exercise 5a, and obtain a hard copy print out of the article.

2.8 Common Programming Errors and Problems

One of the most frustrating problems for students learning Visual Basic is not being able to locate all of the elements needed to create an application. This usually means that either the Form, object Toolbox, or Properties window are missing from the design screen. To bring up the Form, either retrieve an existing project or select New Project from the File menu (hot-key sequence ALT+F, then N). To bring up the object Toolbox or the Properties window, select the View option from the menu bar and then select the desired window.

A common error made by beginning programmers is forgetting to save a project at periodic intervals at design time. Although you can usually get away without periodic saves, every experienced programmer knows the agony of losing work due to a variety of mistakes or an unexpected power outage. To avoid this, you should develop the habit of periodically saving your work.

Finally, the most consistently troublesome error occurs when you do not change a form or object's name immediately when you begin working with it. *Changing a name after you have added event code detaches the object from the code.* This occurs because the event code procedure name is based on the object's name at the time when the code is entered. The event-code doesn't become lost, it just becomes a **General** procedure (accessed via the Code window), because it is no longer attached to an existing object. After you locate the event code as a **General** procedure, you can either rename the procedure to the object's new name or copy and paste the code into the new object's event template.

2.9 Chapter Review

Key Terms

accelerator key	event	**MsgBox**
Cls	executable statement	nonexecutable statement
code module	focus	**Print**
Code window	form	properties
Command button	form module	run time
comment	graphical user interface	sizing handles
controls	hot key	string
design screen	identifier	Text box
design time	Label	Toolbar
dialog box	menu bar	Toolbox
empty string	methods	

Summary

1. In an object-based language the programmer uses pre-existing object types, while an object-oriented language permits creation of new object types and provides features called inheritance and polymorphism. Although Visual Basic does provide the means of creating new objects, since it does not provide a true inheritance feature, it is still classified as an object-based language.

2. Event-based programs execute program code depending on what events occur, which depends on what the user does.

3. GUIs are graphical user interfaces that provide the user with objects that recognize events, such as clicking a mouse.

4. An *application* is any program that can be run under a Windows Operating System.

5. The term *design time* refers to the period of time when a Visual Basic application is being developed.

6. The term *run time* refers to the period of time when an application is executing.

7. A Visual Basic program consists of a visual part and a language part. The visual part is provided by the objects used in the design of the graphical user interface, while the language part consists of procedural code.

8. The basic steps in developing a Visual Basic program are
   a. Create the graphical user interface.
   b. Set the properties of each object on the interface.
   c. Write procedural code.

9. A form is used during design time to create a graphical user interface for a Visual Basic application. At run time the form becomes a window.

10. The most commonly placed objects on a form are Command buttons, Labels, Text boxes, and Picture boxes.

11. Each object placed on a form has a **Name** property. Form names should begin with the prefix `frm`, Text boxes should be given a name beginning in `txt`, and Command buttons a name beginning in `cmd`.

12. Identifiers must be chosen according to the following rules:
   a. The first character of the name must be a letter.
   b. Only letters, digits or underscores may follow the initial letter. Blank spaces, special characters, and punctuation marks are not allowed; use the underscore or capital letters to separate words in an identifier consisting of multiple words.
   c. An identifier can be no longer than 255 characters in Versions 4.0, 5.0, and 6.0 (40 in Version 3.0). Object names are limited to 127 characters.
   d. An identifier should not be a keyword.

Test Yourself—Short Answer

1. A Visual Basic programmer works with the application in two modes, run time and _____.

2. The letters GUI are an acronym for _____.

3. There are two basic parts to a Visual Basic application, they are:

   _____

   _____

4. At run time, a form becomes a _____.

5. Using the right-click mouse button will produce a _____.

6. List the three design steps required in creating a Visual Basic application.

7. What is the difference between the **Name** property and the **Caption** property?

8. Write a Visual Basic statement to clear the contents of a Text box named txtText1.

9. Write a Visual Basic statement to clear a form.

10. Write a Visual Basic statement to place the words "**Welcome to Visual Basic**" in a text box named txtWelcome.

Programming Projects

Note: On all programming projects that you hand in, include your name (or an identification code, if you have been assigned one), and the project number in the lower left hand corner of the form.

1. a. Create the run-time interface shown in Figure 2-91. The application should display the message "My first Program" when the first Command button is clicked, and the message "Isn't this neat?!?" when the second Command button is clicked. Both messages should be in Ms Sans Serif, 18 point, Bold fonts. (An executable version of this program can be found on the student disk as firstpgm.exe)

   b. (Extra Challenge) Make the label appear randomly on the form by using the intrinsic function RND, the form's Width and Height properties, and the label's Left property.

2. Create the form shown in Figure 2-92 that displays a label with the caption text equal to Hello World. The form should have four Command buttons. One button should have the caption Invisible, and when this button is pressed the Hello World caption should become invisible but should have no effect on any other label. A second button, with the caption New Message, should make the Hello World caption invisible and display the text This is a New Message. Both messages should be in MS Sans

Figure 2-91

Figure 2-92

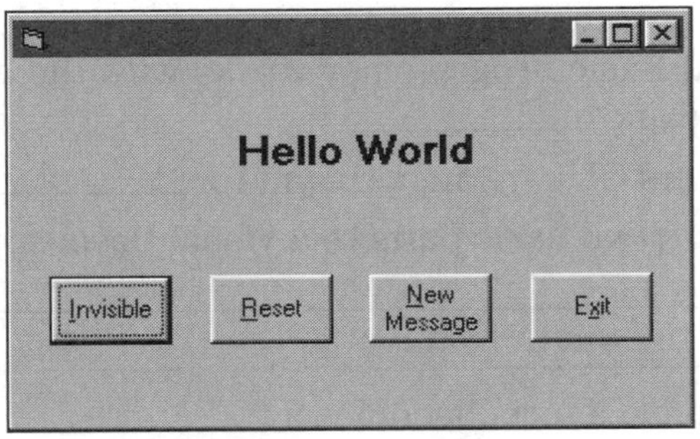

Serif, 14 point, bold fonts. The third button, with the caption Reset, should make the Hello World caption reappear. Finally, an Exit button should terminate the program.

3. a. Create the form shown in Figure 2-93 (a retirement party form). This form has the following properties.

     i. The title—RETIREMENT PARTY—was created with the MS Serif font, is 18 points in size, and is center aligned.

     ii. The lines are created with the line tool.

     iii. The individual rows are set to MS Sans Serif, the default.

     iv. The RSVP line was done with the Script font and 18 points. Additionally, the form should have an Exit Command button and Print Command button added to it. Do not add any event code to the PRINT button, so that when it is pressed, nothing will happen (you will add the event code to this button in Chapter 4).

  b. (Extra Challenge) Add the firecracker and checkmark images shown in Figure 2-94, using picture boxes. These images, named Misc39a.ico and Checkmrk.ico, can be found on the VB6.0 CDRom in the Common\Graphics\Icons\Misc folder.

Figure 2-93

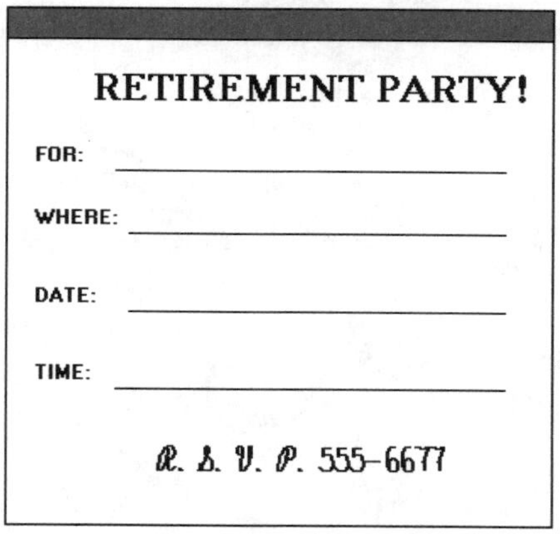

Figure 2-94

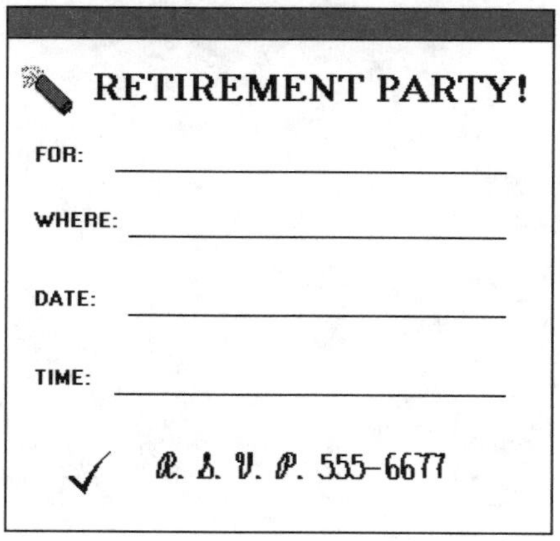

Data and Operations

Visual Basic programs can process different types of data in different ways. For example, calculating a company's income tax requires mathematical computations on numerical data, while sorting a list of names requires comparison operations using alphabetic data. In this chapter we introduce Visual Basic's elementary data types and the procedural operations that can be performed on them, with emphasis on numerical and string data.

3.1 ▸ Data Values and Arithmetic Operations

Visual Basic distinguishes between a number of fundamental types of data, such as integers, real numbers, character strings, boolean, date, currency, and so on. Table 3-1 lists all of the fundamental types recognized in Version 6.0, including their storage size and range of values (if you are unfamiliar with the concept of a byte, review Section 1.6). In this section we introduce the numerical, string, and boolean types. The remaining types are introduced in later sections.

Integer Values

An integer value in Visual Basic is any positive or negative number without a decimal point. Examples of valid integer values are

6   −12   +35   1000   186   −25821   +42

As these examples illustrate, integer constants, which are frequently referred to as integer numbers, or integers, for short, may either be signed (have a leading + or − sign) or unsigned (no leading + or − sign). No commas, decimal points, or special symbols, such as the dollar sign, are allowed. Examples of invalid integer constants are

$187.62   3,532   4.   8,634,941   2,371.98   +7.0

An integer constant can be any integer value between –32768, which is the smallest (most negative) value, to +32767, which is the largest (most positive) value. These values are defined by the 2-byte storage size required for all integers.[1]

Sometimes, larger integer numbers are required than those supported by the memory allocations shown in Table 3-1. For example, many financial applications use dates, such as 7/12/96. Notice in Table 3-1 that Visual Basic's Date type provides eight bytes of storage for each date, which is large enough to store both a date and a time. If a program must use and store many dates, where the time is not needed, the dates can be stored in a simple manner using integers. This is done by converting each date into an integer number representing the number of days from the turn of the last century (1/1/1900). This scheme makes it possible to store and sort dates, using a single integer number for each date. Unfortunately, for dates after 1987, the number of days from the turn of the last century is larger than the maximum value of 32,767 allowed for an integer.

Table 3-1 Fundamental Visual Basic Data Types

Type	Bytes of Storage	Range of Values
Byte	1	0 to 255
Integer	2	–32768 to 32767
Long	4	–2,147,483,648 to 2,147,483,647
Single	4	–3.402823E38 to –1.401298E-45 and +1.401298E-45 to +3.402823E38
Double	8	–1.79769313486232E308 to –4.94065645841247E-324 and +4.94065645841247E-324 to +1.79769313486232E308
String	1 per character	0 to approximately 65,500 characters (0 to 2E32 on 32-bit systems)
Boolean	2	True or False
Currency	8	–922337203685477.5808 to +922337203685477.5807
Date	8	January 1, 100 to December 31, 9999 (also includes space for the time as hours, minutes, and seconds)
Object	4	Any object reference
Variant (with numbers)	16	Any numeric value up to a Double
Variant (with characters)	22+1 per character	0 to approximately 2 billion

---

[1] It is interesting to note that in all cases the magnitude of the most negative integer allowed is always one more than the magnitude of the most positive integer. This is due to the method most commonly used to represent integers, called the two's complement representation. For an explanation of the two's complement representation, see Section 1.6.

To accommodate real application requirements such as this, Visual Basic provides for long integer values, which are referred to as Longs. A Long integer provides only four bytes of storage and can store integer values ranging from approximately –2 billion to +2 billion.

Floating Point Values

A floating point value, which is also called a real number, is any signed or unsigned number having a decimal point. Examples of floating point values are

+10.625   5.   –6.2   3251.92   0.0   0.33   –6.67   +2.

Notice that the numbers 5., 0.0, and +2. are classified as floating point numbers, while the same numbers written without a decimal point (5, 0, +2) would be integer values. As with integer values, special symbols, such as the dollar sign and the comma, are not permitted in real numbers. Examples of invalid real numbers are

5,326.25   24   123   6,459 $10.29

Visual Basic supports two different categories of floating point numbers: single and double. The name *single* is derived from the term *single-precision number* and *double* from *double-precision number*. The difference between these two types of numbers is the amount of storage allocated for each type. Visual Basic requires a double-precision number to use twice the amount of storage as that of a single-precision number. In practice this means that a single-precision constant in Visual Basic retains six decimal digits to the right of the decimal point and double-precision constants retain fourteen digits.

Exponential Notation

Floating point numbers can be written in exponential notation, which is similar to scientific notation and is commonly used to express both very large and very small numbers in a compact form. The following examples illustrate how numbers with decimals can be expressed in exponential and scientific notation.

Decimal Notation	Exponential Notation	Scientific Notation
1625.	1.625E3	1.625×10^3
63421.	6.3421E4	6.3421×10^4
.00731	7.31E-3	7.31×10^{-3}
.000625	6.25E-4	6.25×10^{-4}

In exponential notation, the letter *E* stands for exponent. The number following the *E* represents a power of 10 and indicates the number of places the decimal point should be moved to obtain the standard decimal value. The decimal point is moved to the right if the number after the *E* is positive, or moved to the left if the number after the *E* is negative. For example, the E3 in the number 1.625E3 means to move the decimal place three places to the right, so that the number becomes 1625. The E-3 in the number 7.31E-3 means move the decimal point three places to the left, so that 7.31E-3 becomes .00731. Expressing a floating point number using exponential notation, using an *E* to denote the exponent, causes the number to be stored as a single-precision value. Using a *D* in place of the *E* forces the number to be stored as a double-precision value. In the absence of an explicit specification, the number is stored as a Variant type.

String Values

The third basic data value recognized by Visual Basic is a string value. Other names used for string values are messages, strings, string constants, and string literals. Strings were introduced in the previous chapter. To review, a string value consists of one or more characters enclosed within double quotes. Examples of valid strings are

```
"A"
"**&!##!!"
"$3,256.22"
"25.68"
"VELOCITY"
"HELLO THERE WORLD!"
```

The number of characters within a string is the length of the string. For example, the length of the string "$3,256.22" is nine and the length of the string constant "A" is one. Should it be required to include a double quote within a string constant, two double quotes are used. For example, the string "They said ""Hello"" to me" is a string of length 23 consisting of the characters

```
They(space)said(space)"Hello"(space)to(space)me
```

String constants are typically represented in a computer using the ANSI codes. ANSI, pronounced AN-SEE, is an acronym for American National Standards Institute. This code assigns individual characters to a specific pattern of 0s and 1s. Table 3-2 lists the correspondence between bit patterns and the uppercase letters of the alphabet used by the ANSI code.

Table 3-2 The ANSI Uppercase Letter Codes

Letter	ANSI Code	Letter	ANSI Code
A	01000001	N	01001110
B	01000010	O	01001111
C	01000011	P	01010000
D	01000100	Q	01010001
E	01000101	R	01010010
F	01000110	S	01010011
G	01000111	T	01010100
H	01001000	U	01010101
I	01001001	V	01010110
J	01001010	W	01010111
K	01001011	X	01011000
L	01001100	Y	01011001
M	01001101	Z	01011010

Using Table 3-2, we can determine how the string constant "SMITH", for example, is stored inside the computer. Using the ANSI code, this sequence of characters requires five bytes of storage (one byte for each letter) and would be stored as illustrated in Figure 3-1.

Figure 3-1
The Letters SMITH Stored Inside a Computer

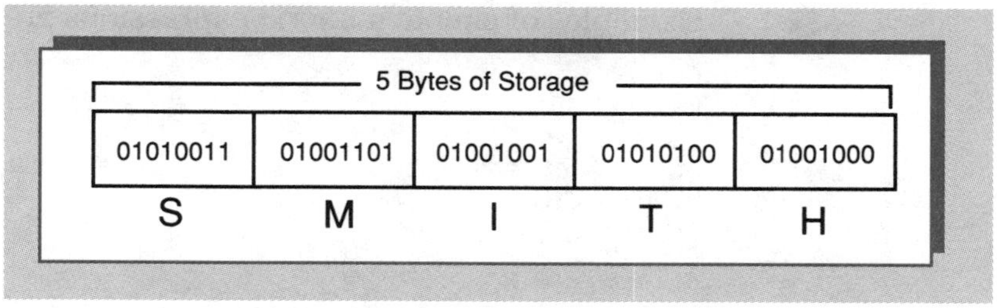

5 Bytes of Storage				
01010011	01001101	01001001	01010100	01001000
S	M	I	T	H

Boolean Values

There are only two boolean data values in Visual Basic. These values are the constants

True   False

The words **True** and **False** are restricted keywords in Visual Basic.

Boolean data is useful in programming because all programming languages have the ability to select a course of action based on the state of a programmer-specified condition. Any condition has one of two possible outcomes—either the condition is satisfied or it is not. In computer terms a condition that is satisfied is considered to be **True** and a condition that is not satisfied is considered to be **False**. The two boolean constants in Visual Basic correspond to these outcomes and are used extensively in programs that incorporate decision-making statements.

Numeric Operations

Integers and real numbers may be added, subtracted, multiplied, divided, and raised to a power. The symbols for performing these and other numeric operations in Visual Basic are listed in Table 3-3.

Table 3-3   Visual Basic's Numeric Operators

Operator	Operation
+	Addition
–	Subtraction
*	Multiplication
/	Division
\	Integer Division
^	Exponentiation (raising to a power)
Mod	Return a remainder

Each of these numeric operators is referred to as a *binary operator* because it requires two operands to operate on. A *simple numeric expression* consists of a numeric binary operator connecting two arithmetic operands and has the syntax

```
operand operator operand
```

Examples of simple numeric expressions are

```
6 + 2
17 - 5
12.75 + 9.3
0.06 * 14.8
26.7 / 3.0
3.1416 ^ 2
```

The spaces around the arithmetic operators in these examples are inserted strictly for clarity and may be omitted without affecting the value of the expression.

The value of any numeric expression can be displayed using either a **Print** or **MsgBox** statement. For example, the value of the expression 0.06 * 14.8 can be displayed on a form using the statement

```
Print 0.06 * 14.8
```

Here the expression, with no surrounding double quotes, is included directly in the **Print** statement. When this statement is executed, the indicated multiplication is performed and the output 0.888 is displayed on the form.

In addition to calculating and displaying the value of an expression, a **Print** statement can also include a message. For example, the **Print** statement

```
Print "The value of the expression 0.06 * 14.8 is"; 0.06 * 14.8
```

contains two items that will be printed directly on the form. The first item is a message, which is a string enclosed in double quotes, and the second item is an arithmetic expression. When an arithmetic expression is used, the **Print** method displays the numerical result of the expression. Positive numeric values are displayed with a single leading and trailing space, while negative values display a negative sign instead of the leading space. The semicolon between items causes Visual Basic to print one item immediately after another. Event Procedure 3-1 illustrates this statement within the context of a complete `Form_Click` event procedure.

Event Procedure 3-1

```
Private Sub Form_Click()
  Print "The value of the expression 0.06 * 14.8 is"; 0.06 * 14.8
End Sub
```

When this event procedure is executed the display produced on the screen is

```
The value of the expression .06 * 14.8 is 0.888
```

Notice that the space between items is produced by the leading space that Visual Basic always uses for positive numbers.

See if you can determine what output is produced by the Event Procedure 3-2:

Event Procedure 3-2

```
Private Sub Form_Click()
  Print "0.06 * 14.8"
  Print 0.06 * 14.8
  Print "0.06 * 14.8 is"; 0.06 * 14.8
End Sub
```

Figure 3-2
Program 3-1's Interface

The first **Print** statement in Event Procedure 3-2 contains a message, which is a string enclosed in double quotes. As the message consists of the characters 0.06 * 14.8, these characters will be displayed by the **Print** statement when it is executed. The second **Print** statement does not contain a message because no double quotes are used. Thus, the value of the expression 0.06 * 14.8, which is 0.888, is calculated and displayed when this statement is executed. Finally, the third **Print** statement contains both a message and an expression. When this statement is executed the message will be displayed first, and the value of the arithmetic expression will be calculated and displayed next. This produces the output:

```
0.06 * 14.8 is 0.888
```

Program 3-1 illustrates using **Print** statements to display the results of simple arithmetic expressions within the context of a complete program. The interface for this project is shown in Figure 3-2. As illustrated the form contains a Command button and a Picture box. The Picture box icon is in the top row in the second column of the Toolbox.

A Picture box is very similar to a Text box, with one important difference: unlike a Text box, which can be used for both input and output, a Picture box can only be used for output.

Table 3-4	The Properties Table for Program 3-1	
Object	**Property**	**Setting**
Form	Name	frmMain
	Caption	Program 3-1
Picture box	Name	picShow
	Height	1455
	Width	2175
	TabStop	False
Command button	Name	cmdOps
	Caption	&ShowOps

For this application the only procedure will be for the Command button's **Click** event. The required code is listed in Program 3-1's Event Code.

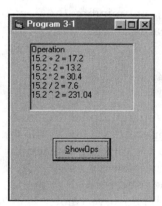

Figure 3-3
The Output Displayed by Program 3-1

Program 3-1's Event Code

```
Private Sub cmdOps_Click()
  picShow.Print "OPERATION"
  picShow.Print "15.2 + 2 ="; 15.2 + 2
  picShow.Print "15.2 - 2 ="; 15.2 - 2
  picShow.Print "15.2 * 2 ="; 15.2 * 2
  picShow.Print "15.2 / 2 ="; 15.2 / 2
  picShow.Print "15.2 ^ 2 ="; 15.2 ^ 2
End Sub
```

The output displayed in the Picture box by Program 3-1's Event procedure when the Command button is clicked is shown in Figure 3-3.

Expression Types

A numeric expression that contains only integer values is called an *integer expression*. The result of an integer expression can be either an integer or a floating point value. For example, 8 / 4 is the integer 2, while 15 / 2 is the floating point value 7.5. Similarly, an expression containing only floating point operands (single and double-precision) is called a *floating point expression*. The result of such an expression can also be either an integer or a floating point value. An expression containing both integer and floating point operands is called a *mixed-mode expression*.

Integer Division

A special numeric operation supplied in Visual Basic is integer division, which is designated by the slash operator, (\). This operator divides two numbers and provides the result as an integer. When the result of the division is not an integer, the result is truncated (that is, the fractional part is dropped). Thus, 15 \ 2 is 7. This is calculated by first performing the normal division, 15 / 2 = 7.5, and then truncating the result to 7.

When an operand used in integer division is a floating point number, the floating point number is automatically rounded to the nearest integer before the division is performed. Thus,

14.6 \ 2 is calculated as 15 / 2 = 7.5, which is then truncated to 7.
14 \ 2.8 is calculated as 14 / 3 = 4.667, which is then truncated to 4.
14.6 \ 2.8 is calculated as 15 / 3 = 5, which is left as the integer 5.

The Mod Operator

There are times when we would like to retain the remainder of an integer division. To do this Visual Basic provides an arithmetic operator that captures the remainder when two integers are divided. This operator, called the modulus operator, uses the symbol Mod. For example,

```
 9 Mod 4 is 1
17 Mod 3 is 2
14 Mod 2 is 0
```

Notice that in each case the result of the numeric expression is the remainder produced by the division of the second integer into the first. If any of the numbers used in the expression is a floating point number, the floating point number is automatically rounded to the nearest integer before calculating the remainder. Thus, 19 Mod 6.7 is 5, which is the same as 19 Mod 7, and 10.6 Mod 4.2 is 3, which is the same as 11 Mod 4.

A Unary Operator (Negation)

Besides the binary operators for addition, subtraction, multiplication, and division, Visual Basic also provides a few unary operators. One of these unary operators uses the same symbol that is used for binary subtraction (−). The minus sign used in front of a single numerical operand negates (reverses the sign of) the number. This operator can be used with all numeric types except the Byte type, because Bytes can only be positive values.

String Concatenation

String concatenation means the joining of two or more strings into a single string. Although string concatenation is not an arithmetic operation, it is the only operation that directly manipulates string data. Visual Basic provides two symbols, the ampersand (&) and the plus sign (+), for performing string concatenation. Both symbols produce the same effect when applied to string data. For example, the expression

```
"Hot" & " " & "Dog"
```

concatenates the three individual strings, `"Hot "`, `" "`, and `"Dog"` into the single string `"Hot Dog"`. The same result is obtained using the + symbol in place of the & symbol.

Operator Precedence and Associativity

Besides such simple numeric expressions as 5 + 12 and .08 * 26.2, we frequently need to create more complex expressions. Visual Basic, like most other programming languages, requires that certain rules be followed when writing expressions containing more than one operator. These rules are

1. Two binary operators must never be placed adjacent to one another. For example, 12 / Mod 6 is invalid because the two binary operators / and Mod are placed next to each other. The expression 12 / –6, however, is valid and does not violate this rule because the – here is recognized as a unary operator that simply makes the +6 a –6. Thus, the result of this expression is –2.

2. Parentheses may be used to form groupings, and all expressions enclosed within parentheses are evaluated first. For example, in the expression (6 + 4) / (2 + 3), the 6 + 4 and 2 + 3 are evaluated first to yield 10 / 5. The 10 / 5 is then evaluated to yield 2. Sets of parentheses may also be enclosed by other parentheses. For example, the expression (2 * (3 + 7)) / 5 is valid. When parentheses are used within parentheses, the expressions in the innermost parentheses are always evaluated first. The evaluation continues from innermost to outermost parentheses until the expressions of all parentheses have been evaluated. The number of right-facing parentheses, (, must always equal the number of left-facing parentheses,), so that there are no unpaired sets.

3. Parentheses cannot be used to indicate multiplication; the multiplication operator must be used. For example, the expression (3 + 4) (5 + 1) is invalid. The correct expression is (3 + 4) * (5 + 1).

As a general rule, parentheses should be used to specify logical groupings of operands and to indicate clearly to both the computer and any programmer reading the expression the intended order of arithmetic operations. In the absence of parentheses, expressions containing multiple operators are evaluated by the priority, or precedence, of each operator. Table 3-5 lists both the precedence and associativity of the operators considered in this section.

Table 3-5 Arithmetic Operator Precedence and Associativity

Operation	Operator	Associativity
Exponentiation	^	left to right
Negation (unary)	–	left to right
Multiplication and division	* /	left to right
Integer division	\	left to right
Modulo arithmetic	Mod	left to right
Addition and subtraction	+ –	left to right

The precedence of an operator establishes its priority relative to all other operators. Operators at the top of Table 3-5 have a higher priority than operators at the bottom of the table. In expressions with multiple operators, the operator with the higher precedence is used before an operator with a lower precedence. For example, in the expression 6 + 4 / 2 + 3, the division is done before the addition, yielding an intermediate result of 6 + 2 + 3. The additions are then performed to yield a final result of 11.

When the minus sign precedes an operand, as in the expression –A ^ B, the minus sign negates (reverses the sign of) the number with a higher priority level than all other operators except exponentiation. For example, the expression –6 ^ 2 is calculated as –(6^2), which equals –36.

Expressions containing operators with the same precedence are evaluated according to their associativity. This means that evaluation for addition and subtraction, as well as multiplication and division, is from left to right and successive exponents are evaluated from right to left as each operator is encountered. For example, in the expression 8 + 40 / 8 * 2 + 4, the multiplication and division operators are of higher precedence than the addition operator and are evaluated first. Both the multiplication and division operators, however, are of equal priority. Therefore, these operators are evaluated according to their left-to-right associativity, yielding

```
8 + 40 / 8 * 2 + 4 =
8 +      5 * 2 + 4 =
8 +         10 + 4 =
```

The addition operations are now performed, again from left to right, yielding

```
18 + 4 = 22
```

When two exponentiation operations occur sequentially the resulting expression is evaluated from left to right. Thus, the expression 2^2^4 is evaluated as 4^4, which equals 256.

Exercises 3.1

1. Determine data types appropriate for the following data:
   a. The average of four speeds
   b. The number of transistors in a radio
   c. The length of the Golden Gate Bridge
   d. The part numbers in a machine
   e. The distance from Brooklyn, NY to Newark, NJ
   f. The names of inventory items

2. Convert the following numbers into standard decimal form:

   6.34E5   1.95162E2   8.395E1   2.95E-3   4.623E-4

3. Write the following decimal numbers using exponential notation:

   126.   656.23   3426.95   4893.2   .321   .0123
   .006789

4. Show how the name KINGSLEY would be stored inside a computer using the ANSI code. That is, draw a figure similar to Figure 3-1 for the letters KINGSLEY.

5. Repeat Exercise 4 using the letters of your own last name.

6. Listed below are correct algebraic expressions and incorrect Visual Basic expressions corresponding to them. Find the errors and write corrected Visual Basic expressions.

	Algebra Expression	**Visual Basic**
a.	$(2)(3) + (4)(5)$	$(2)(3) + (4)(5)$
b.	$\dfrac{6 + 18}{2}$	$6 + 18 / 2$
c.	$\dfrac{4.5}{12.2 - 3.1}$	$4.5 / 12.2 - 3.1$
d.	$4.6(3.0 + 14.9)$	$4.6(3.0 + 14.9)$
e.	$(12.1 + 18.9)(15.3 - 3.8)$	$(12.1 + 18.9)(15.3 - 3.8)$

7 Determine the value of the following expressions:

a. `3 + 4 * 6`   e. `20 - 2 / 6 + 3`

b. `3 * 4 / 6 + 6`   f. `20 - 2 / (6 + 3)`

c. `2.0 * 3 / 12 * 8 / 4`   g. `(20 - 2) / 6 + 3`

d. `10 * (1 + 7.3 * 3)`   h. `(20 - 2) / (6 + 3)`

8 Assuming that `DISTANCE` has an integer value of 1, `V` has the integer value 50, `N` has the integer value 10, and `T` has the integer value 5, evaluate the following expressions:

a. `N / T + 3`   f. `-T * N`

b. `V / T + N - 10 * DISTANCE`   g. `-V / 20`

c. `V - 3 * N + 4 * DISTANCE`   h. `(V + N) / (T + DISTANCE)`

d. `DISTANCE / 5`   i. `V + N / T + DISTANCE`

e. `18 / T`

9 Enter and run Program 3-1 on your computer system.

10 Modify the **Click** event procedure used in Program 3-1 so that the Picture box is cleared immediately before any data is displayed in the box.

11 Rewrite Program 3-1 to remove the Picture box and display the results directly on the screen generated by the form. (**Hint**: Review Program 2-1 in Chapter 2).

12 Add a **Double-click** event to Program 3-1 that causes the contents of the Picture box to be cleared when the user double-clicks the box.

13 Since Visual Basic uses different representations for storing integer, real, and string values, discuss how a program might alert Visual Basic to the data types of the various values it will be using.

Note: For the following exercise the reader should have an understanding of basic computer storage concepts. Specifically, if you are unfamiliar with the concept of a byte, refer to Section 1.7 before doing the next exercise.

14 Although the total number of bytes varies from computer to computer, memory sizes of 65,536 to more than 1 million bytes are not uncommon. In computer language, the letter K is used to represent the number 1024, which is 2 raised to the 10th power and the letter m is used to represent the number 1,048,576, which is 2 raised to the 20th power. Thus, a memory size of 640K is really 640 times 1024, or 655,360 bytes, and a memory size of 4MB is really 4 times 1,048,576 or 4,194,304 bytes. Using this information, calculate the actual number of bytes in

a. A memory containing 512K bytes

b. A memory containing 2M bytes

c. A memory containing 8M bytes
d. A memory consisting 16M bytes
e. A memory consisting of 4M words, where each word consists of 2 bytes
f. A memory consisting of 4M words, where each word consists of 4 bytes
g. A floppy diskette that can store 1.44M bytes

3.2 ▶ Variables and Declaration Statements

All data used in an application is stored and retrieved from the computer's memory unit. Conceptually, individual memory locations in the memory unit are arranged like the rooms in a large hotel. Like hotel rooms, each memory location has a unique address ("room number"). Before high-level languages such as Visual Basic existed, memory locations were referenced by their addresses. For example, storing the integer values 45 and 12 in memory locations 1652 and 2548 (See Figure 3-4), respectively, required instructions equivalent to

> *put a 45 in location 1652*
> *put a 12 in location 2548*

Adding the two numbers just stored and saving the result in another memory location, for example at location 3000, required a statement comparable to

> *add the contents of location 1652*
> *to the contents of location 2548*
> *and store the result into location 3000*

Clearly this method of storage and retrieval is a cumbersome process. In high-level languages like Visual Basic, symbolic names are used in place of actual memory addresses. Symbolic names used in this manner are called variables. A *variable* is simply a name given by the programmer to a memory storage location. The term variable is used because the value stored in the variable can change, or vary. For each name the programmer uses, the computer keeps track of the corresponding actual memory address. In our hotel room analogy, this is equivalent to putting a name on the door of a room and referring to the room by this name, such as the BLUE room, rather than using the actual room number.

Figure 3-4
Enough Storage for Two Integers

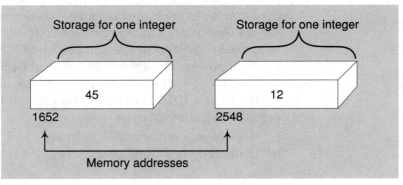

In Visual Basic the selection of variable names is left to the programmer, as long as the following rules are observed:

1. The name must begin with a letter;
2. The name cannot contain arithmetic operators or any of the following symbols: . % & ! # @ $;
3. The name cannot exceed 255 characters;
4. The name cannot be a Visual Basic keyword, such as **Print**.

A variable name should also be a mnemonic. A *mnemonic* (pronounced NI-MONIC) is a memory aid. It should convey information about what the name represents. For example, a mnemonic name for a variable used to store a total value would be sum or total. Similarly, the variable name width is a good choice, if the value stored in the variable represents a width. Variable names that give no indication of the value stored, such as r2d2, linda, bill, and dude should not be selected.

Now, assume the first memory location illustrated in Figure 3-4, assigned address 1652, is given the name num1. Also assume that memory location 2548 is given the variable name num2, and memory location 3000 is given the variable name total, as illustrated in Figure 3-5.

Using these variable names, storing 45 in location 1652, 12 in location 2548, and adding the contents of these two locations is accomplished by the Visual Basic statements

```
num1 = 45
num2 = 12
total = num1 + num2
```

These statements are called *assignment statements* because they tell the computer to assign (store) a value into a variable. Assignment statements always have an equal (=) sign and one variable name immediately to the left of the equal sign. The value on the right of the equal sign is determined first and this value is assigned to the variable on the left of the equal sign. The blank spaces in the assignment statements are inserted for readability. We will have much more to say about assignment statements in the next section, but for now we can use them to store values in variables.

A variable name is useful because it frees the programmer from concern over where data is physically stored inside the computer. We simply use the variable name and let the computer worry about where in memory the data is actually stored. Before storing a value into a variable, however, we must clearly define the type of data that is to be stored in it. This requires telling the computer, in advance, the names of the variables that will be used for

Figure 3-5
Naming Storage Locations

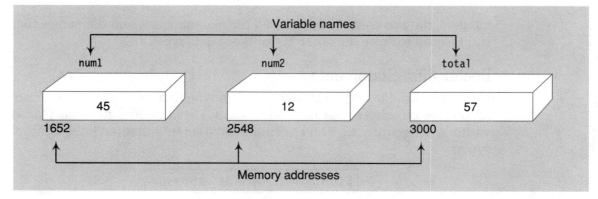

PROGRAMMERS NOTES

Hungarian Notation

In addition to being a mnemonic name that provides a clear understanding of a variable's usage (for example, the names BalanceNew and BalancePrev, when used to store new and previous balance amounts), an additional piece of information that can be provided with each name is the variable's data type. One of the original recommendations for providing this information was made by a Hungarian born Microsoft programmer, Charles Simonyi. His recommendations, which are collectively referred to as Hungarian notation, include a complete set of single letter prefixes and three letter tags; the *prefixes* indicate information as to whether the variable is an array, parameter, or flag, etc., while the *tag* indicates the data type. The most commonly used tags are shown below.

In each example notice that the tag is in lowercase letters and that the first letter of the variable's descriptive name, which is referred to as the *base*, is capitalized.

The original reason for introducing tags was that early computer languages such as Fortran, Basic, and C did not have strong data type checking mechanisms. For these languages, using Hungarian notation helped a programmer to minimize the possibility of misusing a variable or interpreting it incorrectly from its defined data type. Since Visual Basic's compiler catches all data type inconsistencies, using Hungarian notation for its original purpose makes little sense.

As part of a variable's name, however, tags still provide programmers with more complete information than its descriptive base name, and is a good learning tool. Its use, though, is very mixed among professional programmers and is a hotly debated issue. On the positive side the tags clearly enhance the ability to maintain and jointly develop code, while on the negative side, typing and carrying around three extra characters for each variable is not necessarily worth the effort. As you will encounter both adherents and non-adherents to this style, be prepared to adopt whatever standard is in use at your school or company.

(**Note:** A complete report on Hungarian notation can be obtained from the Help facility by entering the name Simonyi in the Search tab's Text box and pressing the List Topics Command button. An article entitled Naming Conventions for Microsoft Access, by S. Leszynsi and G. Reddick, is stored within the MSDN Technical Article and Background subsection of the MSDN Library.)

Tag	Meaning	Example
byt	Indicates a Byte data type	Dim bytChar As byte
bln	Indicates a Boolean data type	Dim blnYesNo As Boolean
cur	Indicates a Currency data type	Dim curInterest As Currency
dbl	Indicates a Double data type	Dim dblRate As Double
int	Indicates an Integer data type	Dim intCount As Integer
lng	Indicates a Long data type	Dim lngMaturity As Long
sng	Indicates a Single data type	Dim sngTotal As Single
str	Indicates a String data type	Dim strMessage As String
var	Indicates a Variant data type	Dim varInput As Variant

integers, the names that will be used for real numbers, and the names that will be used to store the other Visual Basic data types.

Declaration Statements

Naming a variable and specifying the data type that can be stored in it are accomplished using *declaration statements*. Declaration statements placed within a procedure are non-executable statements that have the general syntax

```
Dim variable-name As data-type
```

where *data-type* designates any of the Visual Basic data types listed in Table 3-1, such as Integer, Single, Boolean, and String, and *variable-name* is a user-selected variable name. For example, the declaration statement

```
Dim total As Integer
```

declares `total` as the name of a variable capable of storing an integer value. Variables used to hold single-precision values are declared using the keyword **Single**, variables that will be used to hold double-precision values are declared using the keyword **Double**, variables that will be used to hold boolean values are declared using the keyword **Boolean**, and variables used to hold strings are declared using the keyword **String**. For example, the statement

```
Dim firstnum As Single
```

declares `firstnum` as a variable that can be used to store a single-precision value (a number with a decimal point). Similarly, the statement

```
Dim secnum As Double
```

declares `secnum` as a variable that can be used to store a double-precision value, and the declaration statements

```
Dim logical As Boolean
Dim message As String
```

Figure 3-6
Program 3-2's Interface

declare `logical` as a boolean variable and `message` as a string variable.

Although declaration statements may be placed anywhere within a procedure, most declarations are typically grouped together and placed immediately after the procedure's header line. In all cases, however, a variable should be declared before it is used. If a variable is not declared, it is assigned the Variant type by default.

Program 3-2 illustrates using declaration statements within the context of a complete application. Except for the form and Command button captions, the application interface, shown in Figure 3-6, is essentially the same as we used in Program 3-1. As illustrated, the form contains a Command button and a Picture box.

For this application, the only procedure will be for the Command button's **Click** event. The required code is listed in Program 3-2's Event Code.

Program 3-2's Event Code

```
Private Sub cmdOps_Click()
  Dim grade1 As Single 'declare grade1 as a Single
  Dim grade2 As Single 'declare grade2 as a Single
  Dim total As Single 'declare total as a Single
  Dim average As Single 'declare average as a Single

  grade1 = 85.5
  grade2 = 97
  total = grade1 + grade2
  average = total / 2
  picShow.Print "grade1 is"; grade1
  picShow.Print "grade2 is"; grade2
  picShow.Print "The average grade is"; average
End Sub
```

Although the placement of the declaration statements in the event procedure is straightforward, notice the blank line after these statements. Placing

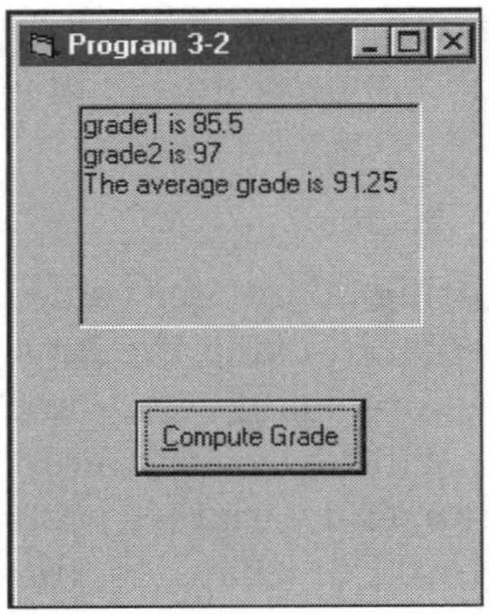

Figure 3-7
The Output Displayed by Program 3-2

Table 3-6   The Properties Table for Program 3-2

Object	Property	Setting
Form	Name	frmMain
	Caption	Program 3-2
Picture box	Name	picShow
	Height	1455
	Width	2175
	TabStop	False
Command button	Name	cmdOps
	Caption	&Compute Grade

a blank line after variable declarations is a common programming practice that improves both a procedure's appearance and readability: we will adopt this practice for all of our procedures. The output displayed by Program 3-2's event procedure when the Command button is clicked, is shown in Figure 3-7.

Single-Line Declarations

Visual Basic permits combining multiple declarations into one statement, using the syntax

```
Dim var-1 As data-type, var-2 As data-type,...,var-n As data-type
```

Using this syntax, the four individual declaration statements used in Program 3-2 can be combined into the single declaration statement.

```
Dim grade1 As Single, grade2 As Single, total As Single, average As Single
```

Notice that in a single-line declaration each variable must still be declared, individually, with its own data type and that commas are used to separate declarations. Unfortunately, there is no way to declare multiple instances of a single data type using only one **As** keyword. For example, the single-line declaration

```
Dim grade1, grade2, total, average As Single
```

does not declare all four variables as single-precision variables. Rather, when a specific data type is omitted, the variable is declared as the default

PROGRAMMERS NOTES

Atomic Data

The numeric and boolean variables we have declared have all been used to store atomic data values. An *atomic data value* is a value that is considered a complete entity by itself and not decomposable into a smaller data type supported by the language. For example, although an integer can be decomposed into individual digits, Visual Basic does not have a numerical digit data type. Rather, each integer is regarded

as a complete value by itself and, as such, is considered atomic data. Similarly, since the integer data type only supports atomic data values, it is said to be an atomic data type. As you might expect, boolean and all floating point data types are atomic data types also. The string data type is not considered an atomic data type because it is easily decomposable into individual characters and each string can be constructed by concatenation of individual characters.

Variant data type.[2] Thus, this declaration is actually a shortened form of the declaration

```
Dim grade1 As Variant, grade2 As Variant, total As Variant, average as Single
```

At the end of this section we will describe the characteristics of the Variant data type. In certain situations, for example, when a data type is not known beforehand, the Variant type becomes extremely useful. Unfortunately, however, it consumes four times as much memory space as a **Single** variable (16 as opposed to 4 bytes) and is less efficient in numeric expressions than pure numeric types. Thus, when the data type of a variable is known, it is more efficient to declare it with its actual data type.

In the case of a String declaration, an optional length specifier can be applied to individual variables. For example, the declaration

```
Dim S2 As String*20
```

declares S2 to always be a fixed-length string variable consisting of 20 characters. If you try to place more than 20 characters in this string, the string will be truncated. If you use less than 20 characters, the string will automatically be padded with trailing spaces to total 20 characters. In the absence of a length specification, a declared string defaults to a variable-length that expands or contracts, as data is assigned to it. For example, consider the following section of code:

```
Dim S As String, S4 As String*4

S = "Algorithm"
S4 = "Algorithm"
Print "S = "; S
Print "S4 = "; S4
```

The output produced on the screen by this code is

```
S = Algorithm
S4 = Algo
```

This output is produced because S has been declared as a variable-length string. As such, S expands to include all of the characters assigned to it. S4, however, has been declared as a fixed-length string that can only accommodate 4 characters. Thus, when the string "Algorithm" is assigned to S4, only the first four characters are actually stored.

Initialization

The first time a value is stored in a variable, the variable is said to be *initialized*. In Visual Basic all declared numeric variables are initialized, by default, to zero. Thus, if you print the value of a declared numeric variable before you explicitly assign it a value, the displayed value will be 0. Similarly, all declared variable length strings are initialized to zero length strings containing no characters at all. Fixed length strings are not initialized and retain whatever characters ("garbage" values) happen to be in the string's allocated memory space.

---

[2]There are two schools of thought on using single-line declarations. Some programmers insist that variables of the same data type should be declared, space permitting, on the same line; others insist, with equal vehemence, that each variable should be declared on an individual line with an optional comment as to its purpose. This second approach also tends to reduce errors that inadvertently create Variant variables. We prefer a middle ground where a single-line declaration can be used to save space if it is used. If a comment on an individual variable is advantageous, we will use separate declaration lines.

The Option Explicit Statement

Specifying the data type of a variable, using a declaration statement, is referred to as *explicit data typing*. Programming languages that require all variables to be declared by declaration statements before they can be used, are called *strongly typed* languages. In this regard, Visual Basic is considered a weakly typed language because it does not require a declaration statement for every variable. In the absence of a declaration, Visual Basic permits identifying the data type of a variable by appending one of the type-declaration characters listed in Table 3-7 to the end of the variable's name.[3] If no type-declaration character is used, the variable defaults to the Variant type.

Table 3-7   Type Declaration Characters

Data Type	Type-Declaration Character	Example
Integer	%	count%
Long	&	longcount&
Single	!	grade!
Double	#	yield#
Currency	@	dollar@
String	$	message$
Variant	(None)	invalue

For example, if the variables ALPHA%, BETA&, GAMMA!, DELTA#, and SIGMA$ are used in an event procedure without first being explicitly declared, the data types for the variables would be an integer, a long, a single, a double, and a string, respectively.

The use of implied data declarations is a carryover from very early versions of Basic. In Visual Basic this implied data typing can be changed using an **Option Explicit** statement, which provides a means of creating strongly typed programs. This is accomplished in the Code window by placing this statement in the **(Declarations)** section of the **(General)** object, as shown in Figure 3-8.

When an **Option Explicit** statement is placed in the declarations section of the **General** object, it is applied to all procedures contained within the form module (that is, every procedure entered in the form's Code window). This statement informs Visual Basic that no implied declarations are to be accepted in any procedure. The effect of this statement is that Visual

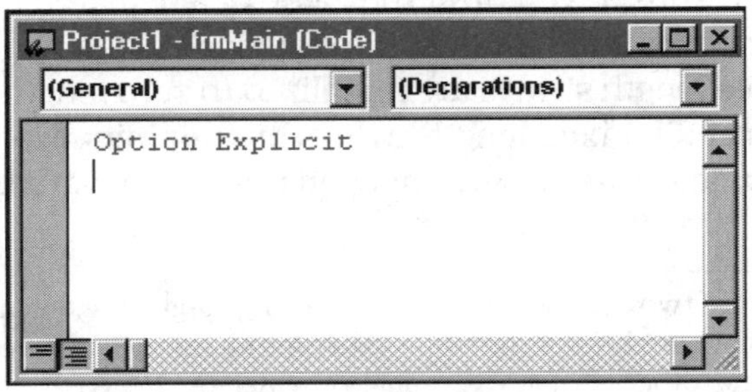

Figure 3-8

Entering the Option Explicit Statement

---

[3]There are no type-declaration characters for the other data types, such as Boolean and Date.

PROGRAMMERS NOTES

The Option Explicit Statement

The **Option Explicit** statement is a module level statement that can be placed in the (**Declarations**) section of the (**General**) form object. Placing the **Option Explicit** statement in the General declarations section activates it for every form module procedure,

which is any procedure entered in the form's Code window. To automatically have this statement inserted into the (**Declarations**) section of each form module:

1. From the Tools menu select Options.
2. Click on the Editor tab.
3. Click on the Require Variable Declaration box so that a check mark (✓) appears.

Basic will issue an error message for any undeclared variable, which eliminates an otherwise common and troublesome error caused by the misspelling of a variable's name within a program. For example, assume that a variable named `distance` is declared using the statement

```
Dim distance As Double
```

Now assume that this variable is assigned a value, but is later misspelled in the statement

```
mpg = distnce / gallons
```

Without the **Option Explicit** statement, Visual Basic would consider `distnce` as a new variable of type Variant. Variants are initialized with an empty value that is different from either a 0 or the zero-length string, `""`. When used in a numeric expression, the empty value is treated as a 0, and when used as a string, the empty value becomes a zero length string. Thus, in the previous numeric expression a value of zero would be assigned to `distnce`, resulting in a calculated result of zero for `mpg`. Finding this error, or even knowing that an error occurred, could be extremely troublesome. Such errors are impossible when the **Option Explicit** statement is used, because the interpreter will highlight `distnce` in the Code window when the program is run and display the error message `Variable not defined`. The interpreter cannot, of course, detect when one declared variable is typed in place of another variable.

All subsequent applications written in this text will include an **Option Explicit** statement within the (**General**) object's (**Declarations**) and explicitly declare all variable names in each procedure. The explicit declaration of variables is considered a good programming practice because it provides the programmer with an opportunity to carefully decide on variable names and their data types at the start of an application. It also provides a summary of all variables that have been used, which is extremely helpful if additional variables need to be named.

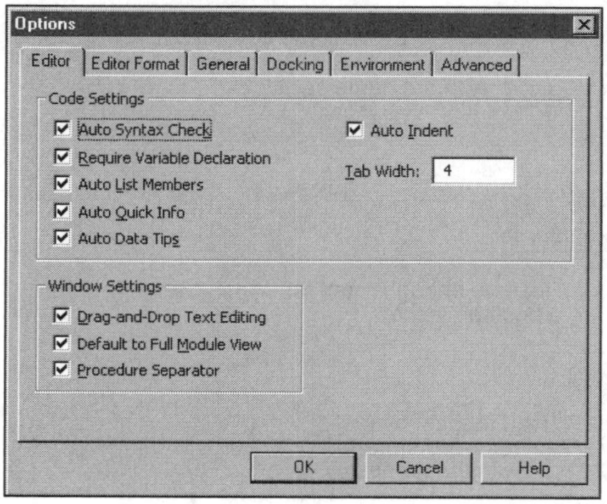

In order to have the **Option Explicit** statement automatically supplied by Visual Basic in every application that you create, without the need for you to type it in, do the following:

1. From the Tools menu select Options.
2. Select the Editor tab, which will produce the window shown in Figure 3-9.
3. Click on the Require Variable Declaration box so that a check mark (✓) appears.

Figure 3-9

Setting the Option Explicit Default

Specifying Storage Allocation

Declaration statements perform both a software and a hardware function. From a software perspective, declaration statements provide a convenient, up-front list of all variables and their data types. In addition to this software role, declaration statements also serve a distinct hardware task. Since each data type has its own storage requirements (see Table 3-1), the interpreter can only allocate sufficient storage for a variable after it knows the variable's data type. Because variable declarations provide this information, they also inform the interpreter of the physical memory storage that must be reserved for each variable. (In the hotel analogy introduced at the beginning of this section, this is equivalent to connecting adjoining rooms to form larger suites.)

Figure 3-10 illustrates the series of operations set in motion by declaration statements in performing their memory allocation function. As illustrated, declaration statements cause both sufficient memory to be allocated

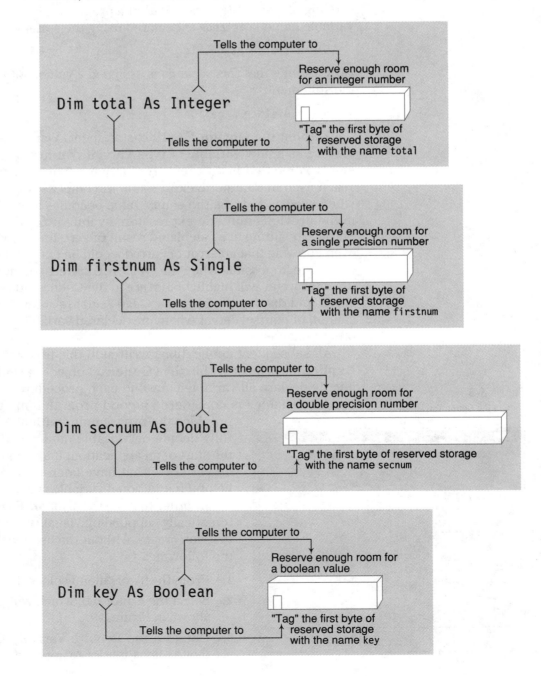

Figure 3-10a
Defining the Integer Variable Named `total`

Figure 3-10b
Defining the Single Variable Named `firstnum`

Figure 3-10c
Defining the Double Variable Named `secnum`

Figure 3-10d
Defining the Logical Variable Named `key`

for each data type and "tag" the reserved memory locations with a name. This name is, of course, the variable's name.

Within a program, the declared variable name is used by a programmer to reference the contents of the variable (that is, the variable's value). Where in memory this value is stored is generally of little concern to the programmer. Visual Basic, however, must be concerned with where each value is stored. In this task the interpreter uses the variable's name to locate the desired value. Knowing the variable's data type allows the interpreter to access the correct number of locations for each type of data.

The Variant Data Type[4]

The Variant data type in Visual Basic is capable of storing many kinds of data. Initially, a value stored in a Variant variable is stored as the data type requiring the least amount of storage. The stored value can then change, depending on the operation applied to it, or the stored value can remain the same but temporarily change data type within a computation. For example, consider the following code:

```
Dim thisval ' declare a Variant by default

thisval = "25" ' store the 2-character string "25"
Print "thisval - 5 ="; thisval - 5
Print "thisval & ""cents"" ="; thisval & "cents"
Print "thisval + ""cents"" ="; thisval + "cents
Print "thisval & ""5"" ="; thisval & "5"
Print "thisval + ""5"" ="; thisval + "5"
Print "thisval & 5 ="; thisval & 5
Print "thisval + 5 ="; thisval + 5
```

The display produced on the screen by this code is

```
thisval - 5 = 20
thisval & "cents" =25cents
thisval + "cents" =25cents
thisval & "5" =255
thisval + "5" =255
thisval & 5 =255
thisval + 5 = 30
```

In this particular example the value actually stored in thisval is always the string "25"; however, its usage changes from a string to a numeric within the various expressions. In the first **Print** statement the interpreter converts the string "25" into the number 25 and subtracts 5 from it, to produce a value of 20. In both the second and third **Print** statements

```
Print "thisval & ""cents"" ="; thisval & "cents"
Print "thisval + ""cents"" ="; thisval + "cents
```

the value in thisval is treated as a string in both expressions. Thus, both string concatenation operators (& and +) produce the same result, namely an output of 25cents. This same treatment of thisval as a string is retained when the string "5" is concatenated using the statements

```
Print "thisval & ""5"" = "; thisval & "5"
Print "thisval + ""5"" = "; thisval + "5"
```

---

[4] This topic may be omitted on first reading with no loss of subject continuity.

The string value produced by both of these statements is 255. Now notice what happens when we use the numeric value 5 in the last two **Print** statements. The concatenation operator (&) in the statement

```
Print "thisval & 5 ="; thisval & 5
```

clearly informs Visual Basic to perform a string concatenation, which again results in a string value of 255. But in the case of the expression `thisval + 5` used in the last **Print** statement

```
Print "thisval + 5 ="; thisval + 5
```

the interpreter assumes we mean arithmetic addition, and produces the value 30.

The importance of this example is to illustrate that Variant data can convert to various data types, depending on its usage. Many times this is an advantage, especially when data must be entered by a user. In such cases, it is very helpful to first store the entered data as a Variant, and then determine its exact type. We shall see how to do this in Section 7.2.

In almost all other cases when we know the type of value being stored, it is much more efficient to avoid a Variant declaration by specifying the variable as the appropriate data type directly. Doing so saves memory storage space and avoids the requirement of the interpreter first determining the proper data representation, before evaluating an expression.

Exercises 3.2

1. State whether the following variable names are valid or not. If they are invalid, state the reason.

prod_a	c1234	abcd	_c3	12345
newbal	Print	$total	new bal	a1b2c3d4
9ab6	sum.of	average	grade1	fin_grade

2. a. State whether the following variable names are valid or not. If they are invalid, state the reason.

salestax	a243	r2d2	first_num	cc_a1
harry	sue	c3p0	average	sum
maximum	okay	a	awesome	go forit
3sum	for	tot.a1	c$five	newpay

   b. List which of the valid variable names found in Exercise 2a should not be used because they clearly are not mnemonics.

3. a. Write a declaration statement to declare that the variable `count` will be used to store an integer.

   b. Write a declaration statement to declare that the variable `grade` will be used to store a single-precision number.

   c. Write a declaration statement to declare that the variable `yield` will be used to store a double-precision number.

4. For each of the following, write a single-line declaration statement:

   a. `num1`, `num2`, and `num3` used to store integer numbers

   b. `grade1`, `grade2`, `grade3`, and `grade4` used to store single-precision numbers

   c. `tempa`, `tempb`, and `tempc` used to store double-precision numbers

   d. `message1` and `message2` used to store strings

   e. `message1` and `message2` used to store fixed-length strings consisting of 15 characters each

⑤ For each of the following, write a single-line declaration statement:

   a. `firstnum` used to store an integer and `secnum` used to store a single-precision number

   b. `speed` used to store a single-precision number and `distance` used to store a double-precision number

   c. `years` to store an integer, `yield` to store a single-precision number, and `maturity` used to store a fixed-length string consisting of 8 characters

⑥ Rewrite each of these declaration statements as three individual declarations.

   a. `Dim month As Integer, day As Integer, year As Integer`
   b. `Dim hours As Single, rate As Single`
   c. `Dim price As Double, amount As Double, taxes As Double`
   d. `Dim inkey As String, choice As String * 5`

⑦ a. Enter and run Program 3-2 on your computer.

   b. Rewrite the event procedure in Program 3-2 so that it uses a single-line declaration statement.

⑧ a. Determine what event invokes the following procedure and the effect of each statement in the procedure.

```
Private Sub cmdButton1_Click()
  Dim num1 As Integer, num2 As Integer, total As Integer

  picShow.Cls
  num1 = 25
  num2 = 30
  total = num1 + num2
  picShow.Print num1; " +"; num2; " ="; total
End Sub
```

   b. What output will be printed when the event procedure listed in Exercise 8a. is run?

⑨ Write a Visual Basic program that stores the sum of the integer numbers 12 and 33 in a variable named `sum`. Have your program display the value stored in `sum`, along with an appropriate message telling the user what is being displayed. The display should appear in a Picture box when a Command button is pushed. There should also be a Command button to clear the Picture box display.

⑩ Write a Visual Basic program that stores the value 16 in the integer variable named `length` and the value 18 in the integer variable named `width`. Have your program calculate the value assigned to the variable perimeter, using the assignment statement

`perimeter = 2 * (length + width)`

and display the value stored in the variable perimeter. The display should appear in a Picture box when a Command button is clicked. There should also be a second Command button to clear the Picture box display. Make sure to declare all the variables as integers at the beginning of the event procedure.

⑪ Write a Visual Basic program that stores the integer value 16 in the variable `num1` and the integer value 18 in the variable `num2`. Have your program calculate the total of these numbers and their average. The total should be stored in an integer variable named `total` and the average in an integer variable named `average`. (Use the statement `average = total/2` to calculate the average.) The display of the total and average should appear in a Picture box when a Command button is pushed. There should also be a second Command button to clear the Picture box display. Make sure to declare all the variables as integers at the beginning of the event procedure.

12. Repeat Exercise 11, but store the number 15 in `num1` instead of 16. With a pencil, write down the average of `num1` and `num2`. What do you think your program will store in the integer variable that you used for the average of these two numbers? What change must you make in the event procedure to ensure that the correct answer will be printed for the average?

13. Write a Visual Basic program that stores the number 105.62 in the variable `firstnum`, 89.352 in the variable `secnum`, and 98.67 in the variable `thirdnum`. Have your program calculate the total of the three numbers and their average. The total should be stored in the variable `total` and the average in the variable `average`. (Use the statement `average = total/3` to calculate the average.) The display of the total and average should appear in a Picture box when a Command button is pushed. There should also be a second Command button to clear the Picture box display. Make sure to declare all the variables as either Single or Double at the beginning of the event procedure.

14. Every variable has at least two items associated with it. What are these two items?

Note: For Exercises 15 through 17: Use the storage allocations given in Table 3-1 and assume that variables are assigned storage in the order they are declared.

15. Using Figure 3-11, and assuming that the variable name `miles` is assigned to the byte at memory address 159, determine the addresses corresponding to each variable declared in the following statements:

```
Dim miles As Single
Dim count As Integer, num As Integer
Dim distance As Double, temp As Double
```

16. a. Using Figure 3-11, and assuming that the variable name `rate` is assigned to the byte having memory address 159, determine the addresses corresponding to each variable declared in the following statements. Also fill in the appropriate bytes with the data stored in each string variable (use letters for the characters, not the computer codes that would actually be stored).

```
Dim rate As Single
Dim message As String * 4
Dim taxes As Double
Dim num As Integer, count As Integer

message = "OKAY"
```

Figure 3-11
Memory Bytes for Exercises
15, 16, and 17

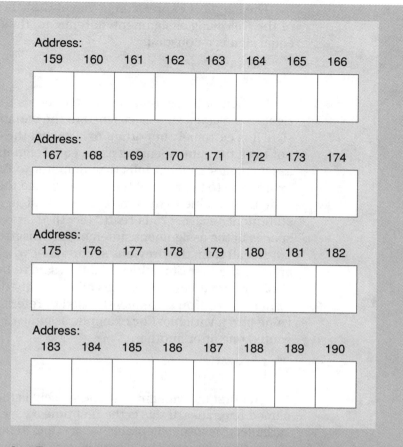

b. Repeat Exercise 16a, but substitute the actual byte patterns that a computer using the ANSI code would use to store the characters in the message variable. (**Hint:** Use Table 3-2.)

17. a. Using Figure 3-11, and assuming that the variable named `message` is assigned to the byte at memory address 159, determine the addresses corresponding to each variable declared in the following statements. Also, fill in the appropriate bytes with the data stored in the variables (use letters for the characters and not the computer codes that would actually be stored).

```
Dim message As String * 20
message = "HAVE A WONDERFUL DAY"
```

b. Repeat Exercise 17a but substitute the actual byte patterns that a computer using the ANSI code would use to store the characters in each of the declared variables. (**Hint:** Use Table 3-2.)

3.3 ▶ Assignment Statements

We have already used simple assignment statements in the previous section. An assignment statement provides the most basic way to both assign a value to a variable and to perform calculations. This statement has the syntax

```
variable = expression
```

The simplest expression in Visual Basic is a single constant, and in each of the following assignment statements, the expression to the right of the equal sign is a constant:

```
length = 25
width = 17.5
```

In each of these assignment statements the value of the constant to the right of the equal sign is assigned to the variable on the left side of the equal sign. It is extremely important to note that the equal sign in Visual Basic does not have the same meaning as an equal sign in algebra. The equal sign in an assignment statement tells the computer to first determine the value of the expression to the right of the equal sign and then to store (or assign) that value in the variable to the left of the equal sign. In this regard, the Visual Basic statement `length = 25` is read "`length is assigned the value 25`." The blank spaces in the assignment statement are inserted for readability only.

Recall from the previous section that when a value is assigned to a variable for the first time, the variable is said to be *initialized*. Although Visual Basic automatically initializes all explicitly declared variables to zero, the term initialization is frequently used to refer to the first time a user places a value into a variable. For example, assume the following statements are executed one after another:

```
temperature = 68.2
temperature = 70.6
```

The first assignment statement assigns the value of 68.2 to the variable named temperature. If this is the first time a user assigned value is stored in the variable, it is also acceptable to say that "temperature is initialized to 68.2." The next assignment statement causes the computer to assign a value of 70.6 to temperature. The 68.2 that was in temperature is overwritten with the new value of 70.6, because a variable can only store one value at a time. In this regard, it is sometimes useful to think of the variable to the left of the equal sign as a temporary parking spot in a huge parking lot. Just as an individual parking spot can only be used by one car at a time, each variable can only store one value at a time. The "parking" of a new value in a variable automatically causes the computer to remove any value previously parked there.

In its most common form, a Visual Basic expression is any combination of constants, variables, and operators that can be evaluated to yield a value[5]. Thus, the expression in an assignment statement can be used to perform calculations using the arithmetic operators introduced in Section 3.1 (see Table 3-3). Examples of assignment statements using expressions containing these operators are

```
sum = 3 + 7
difference = 15 - 6
taxes = 0.05 * 14.6
tally = count + 1
newtotal = 18.3 + total
price = 6.58 * quantity
totalweight = weight * factor
average = sum / items
newval = number ^ power
```

As always in an assignment statement, the equal sign directs the computer to first calculate the value of the expression to the right of the equal

---

[5]Expressions can also include functions, which are presented in the next section.

Figure 3-12
Values Stored in the Variables

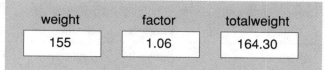

weight	factor	totalweight
155	1.06	164.30

sign and then store this value in the variable to the left of the equal sign. For example, in the assignment statement `totalweight = weight * factor`, the expression `weight * factor` is first evaluated to yield a value. This value, which is a number, is then stored in the variable `totalweight`.

In writing assignment statements, you must be aware of two important considerations. Since the expression to the right of the equal sign is evaluated first, all variables used in the expression must be assigned values, if the result is to make sense. For example, the assignment statement `totalweight = weight * factor` will only cause a valid number to be stored in `totalweight` if the programmer first takes care to put valid numbers in `weight` and `factor`. Thus, the sequence of statements

```
weight = 155.0
factor = 1.06
totalweight = weight * factor
```

ensures that we know the values being used to obtain the result that will be stored in the variable to the left of the equal sign. Figure 3-12 illustrates the values stored in the variables `weight`, `factor`, and `totalweight`.

The second consideration to keep in mind is that, since the value of an expression is stored in the variable to the left of the equal sign, there must only be one variable listed in this position. For example, the assignment statement

```
amount + extra = 1462 + 10 - 24
```

is invalid. The right-side expression evaluates to the integer 1448, which can only be stored in a variable. Since `amount + extra` is not the valid name of a memory location (it is not a valid variable name), the interpreter does not know where to store the value 1448.

Program 3-3 illustrates the use of assignment statements to calculate the volume of a cylinder. As illustrated in Figure 3-13, the volume of a cylinder is determined by the formula, Volume = $\pi r^2 h$, where r is the radius of the cylinder, h is the height, and π is the constant 3.1416 (accurate to four decimal places).

The interface for Program 3-3 is shown in Figure 3-14. For this application, the only procedure will be for the Command button's **Click** event. The required code is listed in Program 3-1's Event Code.

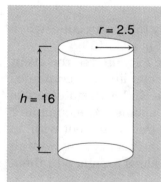

Figure 3-13
Determining the Volume of a Cylinder

Figure 3-14
Program 3-3's Interface

Table 3-8   The Properties Table for Program 3-3

Object	Property	Setting
Form	Name	frmMain
	Caption	Program 3-3
Picture Box	Name	picShow
	Height	615
	Width	2655
	TabStop	False
Command Button	Name	cmdVol
	Caption	&Volume

Program 3-3's Event Code

```
Private Sub cmdVol_Click()
  Dim radius As Single, height As Single, volume As Single

  picShow.Cls
  radius = 2.5
  height = 16.0 ' Note: this will get changed to 16#
  volume = 3.1416 * radius ^ 2 * height
  picShow.Print "The volume of the cylinder is"; volume;
End Sub
```

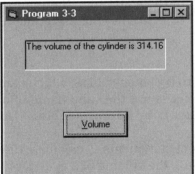

Figure 3-15
The Output Displayed by Program 3-3

The output displayed in the Picture box by this event code, when the Command button is clicked, is shown in Figure 3-15.

Notice the order in which statements are executed in the event procedure. The procedure begins with the header line and continues sequentially, statement by statement, until the **End Sub** statement is encountered. All procedures execute in this manner. The computer works on one statement at a time, executing that statement with no knowledge of what the next statement will be. This explains why all variables used in an expression must have values assigned to them before the expression is evaluated.

When the computer executes the statement volume = 3.1416 * radius ^ 2 * height, it uses whatever value is stored in the variables radius and height at the time the assignment statement is executed. If no values have been specifically assigned to these variables before they are used in the assignment statement, the procedure uses whatever values happen to occupy these variables when they are referenced (in Visual Basic all numeric variables are automatically initialized to zero). The procedure does not look ahead to see that you might assign values to these variables later in the program.

Assignment Variations

Although only one variable is allowed immediately to the left of the equal sign in an assignment expression, the variable on the left of the equal sign can also be used on the right of the equal sign. For example, the assignment statement total = total + 20 is valid. Clearly, in an algebraic equation total could never be equal to itself plus 20. But in Visual Basic, the statement total = total + 20 is not an equation; it is a statement evaluated in two distinct steps. The first step is to calculate the value of total + 20. The second step is to store the computed value in `total`. See if you can determine the output of Event Procedure 3-3, when the form **Click** event is triggered.

Event Procedure 3-3

```
Private Sub Form_Click()
  Dim total As Integer

  total = 15
  Print "The number stored in total is"; total
  total = total + 25
  Print "The number now stored in total is"; total
End Sub
```

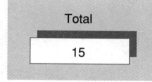

Figure 3-16
The Integer 15 Is Stored in `total`

The assignment statement `total = 15` assigns the value 15 to `total`, as shown in Figure 3-16. The first **Print** statement then causes both a message and the value stored in `total` to be displayed on the form. The output produced by this statement for the form **Click** event is

```
The number stored in total is 15
```

The second assignment statement in the procedure, `total = total + 25` causes the computer to retrieve the 15 stored in `total` and add 25 to this number, yielding the number 40. The number 40 is then stored in the variable on the left side of the equal sign, which is the variable `total`. The 15 that was in `total` is simply erased and replaced, that is, overwritten, with the new value of 40, as shown in Figure 3-17.

Accumulating

Assignment expressions like `total = total + 25` are very common in programming and are required in accumulating subtotals when data is entered one number at a time. For example, if we want to add the numbers 96, 70, 85, and 60 in calculator fashion, the following statements could be used.

Statement	Value in total
`total = 0`	0
`total = total + 96`	96
`total = total + 70`	166
`total = total + 85`	251
`total = total + 60`	311

The first statement initializes `total` to 0. This removes any number ("garbage" value) stored in the memory locations corresponding to `total` and ensures we start with 0 (this is equivalent to clearing a calculator before doing any computations). As each number is added, the value stored in `total` is increased accordingly. After completion of the last statement, `total` contains the total of all the added numbers.

Figure 3-17
`total = total + 25` Causes a New Value to Be Stored in `total`

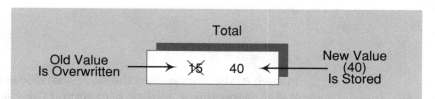

The form **Click** procedure listed in Event Procedure 3-4 illustrates the effect of these statements by displaying total's contents after each addition is made.

Event Procedure 3-4

```
Private Sub Form_Click()
  Dim total As Integer

  total = 0
  Print "The value of total is initially set to"; total
  total = total + 96
  Print " total is now"; total
  total = total + 70
  Print " total is now"; total
  total = total + 85
  Print " total is now"; total
  total = total + 60
  Print " The final value in total is"; total
End Sub
```

The output produced by the Form **Click** event in Event Procedure 3-4 is

```
The value of total is initially set to 0
 total is now 96
 total is now 166
 total is now 251
 The final value in total is 311
```

Although it is clearly easier to add the numbers by hand than to use the sequence of assignment statements listed, these statements do illustrate the subtotaling effect of repeated assignment statements having the form:

```
variable = variable + new value
```

We will find many important uses for this type of statement when we become more familiar with the repetition statements introduced in Chapter 6.

Counting

A variation of the accumulating assignment statement is the counting statement. Counting statements have the form:

```
variable = variable + fixed number
```

Examples of counting statements are

```
i = i + 1
totalStudents = totalStudents + 1
count = count + 1
j = j + 2
m = m + 2
kk = kk + 3
```

In each of these examples the same variable is used on both sides of the equal sign. After the statement is executed the value of the respective variable is increased by a fixed amount. In the first three examples the variables i, totalStudents, and count have all been increased by one. In the next two examples the respective variables have been increased by two, and in the final example the variable kk has been increased by three. Typically, integer variables with very simple names such as i, j, k, l, m, and n,[6] or more mnemonic names, such as count, are used for counter variables. The following sequence of statements illustrates the use of a counter.

Statement	Value in COUNT
count = 0	0
count = count + 1	1
count = count + 1	2
count = count + 1	3
count = count + 1	4

The Form_Click procedure listed in Event Procedure 3-5 illustrates the effect of these statements within the context of a complete procedure.

Event Procedure 3-5

```
Private Sub Form_Click()
  Dim count As Integer

  count = 0
  Print "The initial value of count is"; count
  count = count + 1
  Print " count is now"; count
  count = count + 1
  Print " count is now"; count
  count = count + 1
  Print " count is now"; count
  count = count + 1
  Print " count is now"; count
End Sub
```

The output produced by the Form **Click** event in Event Procedure 3-5 is

```
The initial value of count is 0
  count is now 1
  count is now 2
  count is now 3
  count is now 4
```

Type Conversions

It is important to understand that data type conversions take place across the assignment statement. That is, the value of the expression on the right side of the equal sign is converted to the data type of the variable to the left of the equal sign. For example, consider the evaluation of the expression

```
average = total / 2
```

where total is an integer variable having a stored value of 15 and average is also an integer variable. The result of the expression total / 2 will be 7.5, the correct average value. Since, however, the left side of the assignment operator is an integer variable, the value of the expression total / 2 is rounded to

---

[6]This is a carryover from the original version of the first high-level language, FORTRAN, in which any variable beginning in these letters was created as an integer variable.

an integer value and stored in the variable average. Thus, at the completion of this assignment statement, the value stored in average is 8.

Automatic type conversions due to assignment take place whenever possible. For example, consider the following section of code:

```
Dim s As String, number As Integer

s = "55"
number = s
```

Here, the value 55 is stored in number. If, however, the string "AB" is stored in s, the error Type mismatch will be displayed when the assignment statement number = s is executed.

To avoid unintentional conversions and type mismatch errors, the general rule is to always use the same data types on each side of the equal sign; that is, the integer types (byte, integer, and long) should be used with integer types, floating point types (single and double) with floating point types, strings with strings, and so on.

In addition to data type conversions made automatically across an equal sign, Visual Basic also provides for explicit user-specified type conversions. These conversion functions are presented in the next section.

Exercises 3.3

1. Write an assignment statement to calculate the circumference of a circle having a radius of 3.3 inches. The equation for determining the circumference, c, of a circle is $c = 2\pi r$, where r is the radius and π equals 3.1416.

2. Write an assignment statement to calculate the area of a circle. The equation for determining the area, a, of a circle is $a = \pi r^2$, where r is the radius and $\pi = 3.1416$.

3. Write an assignment statement to convert temperature in degrees Fahrenheit to degrees Celsius. The equation for this conversion is *Celsius = 5/9 (Fahrenheit – 32)*.

4. Write an assignment statement to calculate the round trip distance, d, in feet, of a trip that is s miles long, one way.

5. Write an assignment statement to calculate the length, in inches, of a line that is measured in centimeters. Use the fact that there are 2.54 centimeters in one inch.

6. Write an assignment statement to calculate the value, in dollars, of an amount of money in francs. Assume that five francs are worth one dollar.

7. Determine the output of the following procedure:

```
Private Sub Form_Click()  ' a procedure illustrating integer truncation
  Dim num1 As Integer, num2 As Integer

  Cls
  num1 = 9/2
  num2 = 17/4
  Print "The first integer displayed is"; num1
  Print "The second integer displayed is"; num2
End Sub
```

8 Determine the output produced by the following procedure:

```
Private Sub Form_Click()
   Dim average As Single

   Cls
   average = 26.27
   Print "The average is"; average
   average = 682.3
   Print "The average is"; average
   average = 1.968
   Print "The average is", average
End Sub
```

9 Determine the output produced by the following procedure:

```
Private Sub Form_Click()
   Dim sum As Single

   Cls
   sum = 0.0
   Print "The sum is"; sum
   sum = sum + 26.27
   Print "The sum is"; sum
   sum = sum + 1.968
   Print "The final sum is"; sum
End Sub
```

10 a. Determine what each statement causes to happen in the following procedure:

```
Private Sub Form_Click()
   Dim num1 As Integer, num2 As Integer
   Dim num3 As Integer, total As Integer

   Cls
   num1 = 25
   num2 = 30
   total = num1 + num2
   Print num1; " +"; num2; " ="; total
End Sub
```

b. What output will be produced when the event procedure listed in Exercise 10a. is triggered by clicking the mouse on the screen?

11 Determine and correct the errors in the following procedures:

a.
```
Private Sub Form_Click()
   width = 15
   area = length * width
   Print "The area is"; area
End Sub
```

b.
```
Private Sub Form_Click()
   Dim length As Integer, width As Integer, area As Integer

   area = length * width
   length = 20
   width = 15
   Print "The area is"; area
```

```
  c.  Private Sub Form_Click()
        Dim length As Integer, width As Integer, area As Integer

        length = 20
        width = 15
        length * width = area
        Print "The area is; area
      End Sub
```

12 Determine the output produced by the following event procedure:

```
Private Sub Form_Click()
  Dim sum As Integer

  sum = 0
  sum = sum + 96
  sum = sum + 70
  sum = sum + 85
  sum = sum + 60
  Print "The value of sum is initially set to"; sum
  Print " sum is now"; sum
  Print " sum is now"; sum
  Print " sum is now"; sum
  Print " The final sum is"; sum
End Sub
```

13 Using Program 3-3, determine the volume of cylinders having the following radii and heights.

Radius (in.)	Height (in.)
1.62	6.23
2.86	7.52
4.26	8.95
8.52	10.86
12.29	15.35

3.4 Using Intrinsic Functions

As we have seen, assignment statements can be used to perform numeric computations. For example, the assignment statement

```
tax = rate * income
```

multiplies the value in rate times the value in income and then assigns the resulting value to tax. Although the common numeric operations, such as addition, subtraction, and so on, are easily accomplished using Visual Basic's numeric operators, no such operators exist for finding the square root of a number, the absolute value of a number, and other useful mathematical values. To facilitate the calculation of such quantities as well as the conversion between data types and other useful operations, Visual Basic provides a set of preprogrammed routines, referred to as *intrinsic functions*, that can be included in a procedure.

Before using one of Visual Basic's intrinsic functions, you must know:

- The name of the desired intrinsic function,
- What the intrinsic function does,
- The type of data required by the intrinsic function, and
- The data type of the result returned by the intrinsic function.

In practice, all functions operate in a manner similar to procedures, with one major difference: *A function always directly returns a single value.* This is an extremely important difference because it allows functions to be included within expressions.

To illustrate the use of a Visual Basic intrinsic function, consider the intrinsic function named **Sqr**, which calculates the square root of a number. The square root of a number is computed using the expression

```
Sqr(number)
```

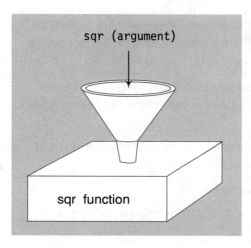

Figure 3-18

Passing Data to the Sqr Function

where the function's name, in this case **Sqr**, is followed by parentheses containing the number for which the square root is desired. The parentheses following the function name effectively provide a "funnel" through which data can be passed to the function (see Figure 3-18). The items passed to the function through the parentheses are called *arguments* of the function, and constitute its input data. For example, the following expressions are used to compute the square root of the arguments 4, 17, 25, 1043.29, and 6.4516:

```
Sqr(4)
Sqr(17)
Sqr(25)
Sqr(1043.29)
Sqr(6.4516)
```

The argument to the **Sqr** function can be any numeric expression that results in a positive value[7]. The **Sqr** function computes the square root of its argument and returns the result. The values returned by **Sqr** function for the previous expressions are

Expression	Value Returned
Sqr(4)	2
Sqr(17)	4.12310562561766
Sqr(25)	5
Sqr(1043.29)	32.3
Sqr(6.4516)	2.54

Although we have used the square root function to illustrate how intrinsic functions are used, the most useful functions for commercial purposes are those that deal with formatting numbers, converting between data types, and operating on string data. Table 3-9 lists the commonly used conversion functions. The Format function and string manipulation functions are presented in Sections 4.5 and 7.3, respectively.

---

[7]A negative argument value results in the error message Invalid procedure call when the function is called.

Table 3-9 Visual Basic's Conversion Functions

Function Name and Argument(s)	Returned Value
Asc(string)	The character code corresponding to the first letter in the string.
Chr$(string)	Same as Asc( ).
CBool(expression)	If expression is zero, **False** is returned; otherwise, **True** is returned.
Ccur(expression)	Convert the expression to a currency value.
CDbl(expression)	The expression as a double-precision number. If expression lies outside the acceptable range for the Double data type, an error occurs.
Int(expression)	The expression as an integer. If expression lies outside the acceptable range for the Integer data type, an error occurs. The expression is truncated.
CSng(expression)	The expression as a single-precision integer. If expression lies outside the acceptable range for the Single data type, an error occurs.
CStr(expression)	The expression as a string. The expression argument must be a valid numeric or string expression.
CVar(expression)	The expression as a variant data type.
Hex(n)	The hexadecimal value of n, returned as a string (n is rounded to the nearest integer).
Oct(n)	The octal value of n, returned as a string (n is rounded to the nearest integer).
Str(n)	Same as Cstr( ).
Val(string)	The first number in the string (the function stops reading the string at the first nonnumeric character, except for a period, which is recognized as a decimal point).
Var(variant)	Returns 2 if integer, 3 if long, 4 if single, 5 if double, 6 if currency, 7 if date, 8 if string.

Exercises 3.4

1. List the four items you must know before using a Visual Basic intrinsic function.
2. How many values does a call to a single Visual Basic function return?
3. Write function calls to determine:
   a. The square root of 6.37.
   b. The square root of $x - y$.
   c. The square root of $a^2 - b^2$.

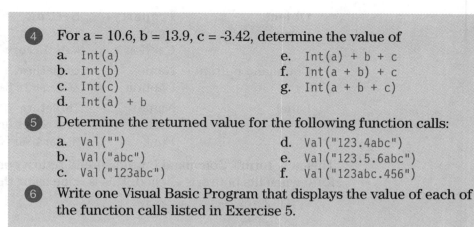

4. For a = 10.6, b = 13.9, c = -3.42, determine the value of

   a. `Int(a)`   e. `Int(a) + b + c`

   b. `Int(b)`   f. `Int(a + b) + c`

   c. `Int(c)`   g. `Int(a + b + c)`

   d. `Int(a) + b`

5. Determine the returned value for the following function calls:

   a. `Val("")`   d. `Val("123.4abc")`

   b. `Val("abc")`   e. `Val("123.5.6abc")`

   c. `Val("123abc")`   f. `Val("123abc.456")`

6. Write one Visual Basic Program that displays the value of each of the function calls listed in Exercise 5.

3.5 ▸ Focus on Program Design and Implementation:

Creating an Operational Form[8]

Currently, the Rotech Systems application consists of a Main Menu and Stub form, with sufficient event code to permit a user to cycle between forms. In this Focus section we make the Main Menu's Walk In button operational, so that it calls a new form that calculates and prints out invoices for walk in customers. This is done using the following three steps:

Step 1: Add a new Walk In stub form to the project.

   a. Provide the Walk In stub form with a single Command button that returns control to the Main Menu.

   b. Save the new form.

Step 2: Link the new stub form to the Main Menu.

   a. Modify the Main Menu Walk In Command button to display the new Walk In stub form rather than the Under Development stub form.

   b. Verify that a user can correctly cycle between the Main Menu and new stub form.

Step 3: Modify the Walk In stub form.

   a. Change the stub form to a fully functional operational form that performs its intended operational task.

   b. Verify that the new form performs correctly.

Figure 3-19

The New Stub Walk In Form

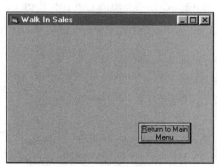

The first two steps are "cookbook" items, in that the same procedure is used whenever we modify an application to have the Main Menu call a new stub form rather than the generic Under Development stub form. Here is the procedure for performing these two steps, as they apply to our new Walk In form.

Step 1: Add a New Stub Form to the Project

Add a new form by either following the procedure used in the previous Focus section for the Under Development stub form or the summary procedure listed in this section's Programmers Notes box. Provide this new form with the following properties and make the form look like the one shown in Figure 3-19.

----

[8]Unless subsequent Focus sections are to be covered, the material in this section may be omitted with no loss of subject continuity.

Object	Property	Setting
Form	Name	frmWalkin
	Caption	Walk In Form
Command button	Name	cmdReturn
	Caption	&Return to Main Menu
Label	Name	lblReturn
	Text	Disk Sales Order Form
	Font	MS Sans Serif, Bold, Typeface = 10

This new form's Command button should return control to the Main Menu form when the button is clicked. This is done using the following event code:

```
Private Sub cmdReturn_Click()
  Unload Me
  frmMain.Show
End Sub
```

We have chosen to unload the form, rather than merely hide it, because this form will not be used extensively. Thus, when the form is not in use we might as well unload it altogether instead of keeping it in memory. The statement used to unload the form, Unload Me, can be replaced by the statement Unload frmWalkin. Once this is done, save the new form in the file named Walk using the Save As option from the File menu.

Step 2: Link the New Stub Form to the Main Menu

This is done by simply modifying one line in the Main Menu Walk In Command button's **Click** event code. Specifically, change the second line within the button's existing **Click** event procedure from frmStub.Show to frmWalk.Show. The completed event procedure should now be:

```
Private Sub cmdWalkins_Click()
  frmMain.Hide
  frmWalk.Show   ' this is the changed line
End Sub
```

Once this change is made, verify that the new Walk In form is displayed when the Main Menu Walk In Command button is clicked, and that the new form's Return button successfully redisplays the Main Menu form.

(**Note:** At this stage the project consists of three forms: a Main Menu form, an Under Development stub form and a Walk In stub form. The project, as it currently exists, can be found as the rotech3a.vbp project in the rotech3a folder on the Student Disk.)

The remaining task is to now modify the stub Walk In form illustrated in Figure 3-19 to that shown in Figure 3-20. As seen in this figure, the form has an input section for entering a customer's name, address, and the number of

---

PROGRAMMERS NOTES

Adding a New Form

To add a new form to an existing project, either:

1. Select the Add Form item from the Project menu, or

Press the Add Form button on the Standard Toolbar

2. Select the Form icon under the New tab.

This procedure displays a new Form and adds the new form to the Project Explorer Window. To switch between forms, simply click on the desired form in the Project Explorer Window.

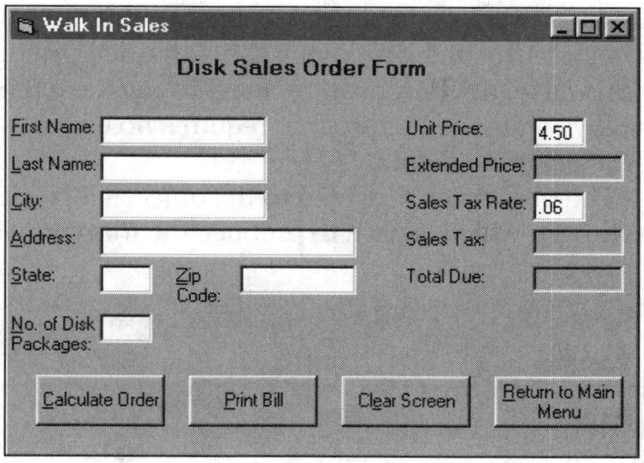

Figure 3-20
The Completed Walk In Form

diskette boxes purchased. Also included on the form are four Command buttons, whose function is indicated by their captions, and an output section for listing the total amount of the purchase. Recall from the original project specification given in Section 1.5 that the price of a box of diskettes is $4.50 and the sales tax rate is currently 6%.

The Walk In form's required tasks are listed in the TTL Table 3-10. Notice that the tasks have been organized as to function; that is input, output, and processing. The input tasks are all performed using Text boxes, while the

Table 3-10   The Walk In Form's TTL Table

| **Form:** Walk In (Order Entry) | **Trigger** | |
Task	**Object**	**Event**
Obtain customer data		
First name	txtFname	user entry
Last name	txtLname	user entry
Address	txtAddr	user entry
City	txtCity	user entry
State	txtState	user entry
Zip code	txtZip	user entry
Disk packs ordered	txtQuantity	user entry
Display output data		
Unit price	txtPrice	initial text with user over-write
Calculate and	cmdCalculate	Click
display extended price	picTotal	none
Sales tax rate	txtTrate	initial text with user over-write
Calculate and	cmdCalculate	Click
display tax due	pictax	none
Calculate and	cmdcalculate	Click
display total due	picFinal	none
Compute screen invoice	cmdCalculate	Click
Compute and print Invoice	cmdPrint	Click
Clear all screen inputs	cmdClear	Click
Return to Main Menu	cmdReturn	Click

output is produced using both Text and Picture boxes. In some cases, such as calculating and displaying the extended price, two objects are required; in this case, a **Click** event is used to perform the calculation and force the display, while the Picture box requires no event—it is just a passive recipient of the calculated data.

The properties provided to the object's listed in the TTL table are listed in Table 3-11, which is used to produce the form previously shown in Figure 3-20.

Table 3-11 The Walk In Form's Properties Table

Object	Property	Setting
Form	Name	frmWalk
	Caption	Walk In Sales
Label	Name	lblHeader
	Caption	Disk Sales Order Form
	Font	MS Sans Serif, Bold, Typeface = 10
Label	Name	lblFname
	Caption	&First Name:
	TabIndex	0
Text box	Name	txtFname
	Caption	(blank)
	TabIndex	1
Label	Name	lblLname
	Caption	&Last Name:
	TabIndex	2
Text box	Name	txtFname
	Caption	(blank)
	TabIndex	3
Label	Name	lblAddr
	Caption	&Address:
	TabIndex	4
Text box	Name	txtAddr
	Caption	(blank)
	TabIndex	6
Label	Name	lblCity
	Caption	&City:
	TabIndex	7
Text box	Name	txtCity
	Caption	(blank)
	TabIndex	8
Label	Name	lblState
	Caption	&State:
	TabIndex	9
Text box	Name	txtState
	Caption	(blank)
	TabIndex	10

continued on next page

Object	Property	Setting
Label	Name	lblZip
	Caption	&Zip:
	TabIndex	11
Text box	Name	txtZip
	Caption	(blank)
	TabIndex	12
Label	Name	lblQauntity
	Caption	&No. of Disk Packages:
	TabIndex	13
Text box	Name	txtQuantity
	Caption	(blank)
	TabIndex	14
Command button	Name	cmdcalculate
	Caption	&Calculate Order
	TabIndex	15
Command button	Name	cmdPrint
	Caption	&Print Bill
	TabIndex	16
Command button	Name	cmdClear
	Caption	Cl&ear Screen
	TabIndex	17
Command button	Name	cmdReturn
	Caption	&Return to Main Menu
	TabIndex	18
Label	Name	lblPrice
	Caption	Unit Price:
Text box	Name	txtPrice
	Caption	4.50
Label	Name	lblExtend
	Caption	Extended Price:
Picture box	Name	picTotal
Label	Name	lblTrate
	Caption	Sales Tax Rate:
Text box	Name	txtTrate
	Caption	.06
Label	Name	lblTax
	Caption	Sales Tax:
Picture box	Name	pictax
Label	Name	lblFinal
	Caption	Total Due:
Picture box	Name	picFinal

TIPS FROM THE PROS

Providing Text Boxes with Access Keys

Since Text boxes have no caption property, we cannot directly provide a box with an access key that will move focus to it. A useful and common "work-around" is to provide an access key within a label associated with the box. This can always be done since almost all Text boxes require an associated label. And if a label is not actually required, we provide one anyway.

The "trick" then is to manipulate the label's access key to move the focus to the Text box.

This is accomplished by providing the box with a **TabIndex** value that is one higher than its associated label. Since a label cannot receive focus, when the user activates the label's access key, focus will automatically shift to the object having the next highest **TabIndex** value, which, in this case is the Text box. From a user's viewpoint, it makes sense that the access key contained within the label forces the focus into the Text box, because it is the Text box, and not the label, that the user interfaces with. Thus, the operation of the label's access key will appear natural and correct to a user.

Except for the quantity of objects placed on the Walk In form, there is nothing significantly different here from the forms you have been using throughout the text. It is worth reviewing the **TabIndex** numbers in the Properties table, however, and the reason for their assignment. Notice that in each case a Text box's corresponding label is given a **TabIndex** number that is one less than the number assigned to the Text box. Also notice the Labels corresponding to Text boxes that will be used for input have been assigned an access key. Activating a Label's access key will attempt to move focus to the Label, but since Labels cannot receive focus, the focus automatically shifts to the object having the next highest **TabIndex** value. Thus, by giving the associated Text box the next **TabIndex** value in sequence, we have provided a means for users to tab into a text box using an access key.

Adding the Event Code

All that remains to do to complete our sales order form is to provide **Click** events so that each Command button performs the task assigned to it in the TTL table. Except for the Printing task, which is developed in the next Focus section, the required event code is rather simple and is listed as Rotech Event Code—Version 1.

Rotech Event Code—Version 1

```
Private Sub cmdCalculate_Click()
  Dim sTotal As Single, sTaxes As Single, sFinal As Single

  'Clear out the picture boxes
  picTotal.Cls
  picTax.Cls
  picFinal.Cls

  'Calculate and display new values
  sTotal = txtQuantity * txtPrice
  sTaxes = txtTrate * sTotal
  sFinal = sTotal + sTaxes
  picTotal.Print sTotal
  picTax.Print sTaxes
  picFinal.Print sFinal
End Sub
```

```
Private Sub cmdClear_Click()
  'Clear out the picture boxes
  picTotal.Cls
  picTax.Cls
  picFinal.Cls

  'Clear out the text boxes
  txtLname = ""
  txtFname = ""
  txtCity = ""
  txtState = ""
  txtZip = ""
  txtQuantity = ""
End Sub

Private Sub cmdReturn_Click()
  Unload Me
  frmMain.Show
End Sub
```

Each of these **Click** event codes should look familiar to you. Working from the bottom up, the Return button's code simply unloads the current form and shows the Main Menu form. The Clear button clears out the Text boxes by assigning blank strings to each box and calling the Cls method to clear the Picture boxes. Finally, the Calculate button's **Click** event declares three single-precision variables and uses these variables to store, and then display the calculated values of price, sales tax, and total amount due for the order.

Areas of Programmer Concern

The form that has been developed in this section contains a number of areas that would be of concern to a professional programmer. As these concerns are neither immediately apparent nor restricted to our order entry form, but represent more general problems encountered in all commercial applications, we will take a moment to consider them.

The first and most obviously noticeable concern when the form is activated is that displayed dollar values are not output in conventional currency format; that is, with a leading dollar sign and two digits following the decimal point. We address and rectify this problem in the next Focus section, after the material on output formatting is presented.

The second problem with the form is that pressing the ENTER key does not shift the focus from the current Text box to the next one. Users expect this type of operation; that is, when they press the ENTER key it signifies the end of the current input, at which point the focus should automatically shift to another object. Providing this feature requires correctly determining when the ENTER key is pressed, and then taking action. Detecting when a particular key is pressed is presented in Chapter 5, and we show how to use this detection to shift the input focus in that chapter's Focus section.

A third concern is that the form provides no user-input validation, which is a very serious flaw in the application. For example, if a user inadvertently enters the letters abc into the txtQuantity box, the application will crash. Since at some point in every system's lifetime incorrect types of data are entered, the application must provide some type of input validation to prevent a user from crashing the system simply by entering the wrong data type.

This concern is addressed in Chapter 6's Focus section, after Visual Basic's looping facilities are presented.

Our fourth item of concern is that we have not provided the Walk In form's Print button with any event code. As such, if a user clicks this button, nothing will happen. The obvious and correct solution to this problem is to have the button display a stub form. Since we will provide the code for this button's **Click** event as the next item in our application's development (done in the next Focus section), we can temporarily leave this button as is.

A more subtle problem with our sales order form is that the product is hard coded into the form. Thus, if an additional product is added to the promotion, the form itself must be modified, which requires action by a programmer. For many systems, such as the Rotech application, that are only used for the duration of a single promotion, this is not a problem. However, many systems need to provide a choice among many items, any of which can be purchased and any of which can change. For these situations asking the client to recall you each time an addition or modification needs to be made will only cause frustration, both for you and the client. A much better approach is to provide the application with a list of products, and give the user the means of adding items to the list, deleting items from the list, and modifying existing products already in the list. The means of doing this is presented in Chapter 8's Focus section.

In practice, each of these concerns is handled by a programmer as a normal course of constructing a commercial application, using standard techniques known by all professional programmers. By the time you finish this course you too should have a good understanding of how to address these concerns and how to correctly incorporate their use within your VB applications. Don't, however, be discouraged about how much still must be done. Successful programmers are aware of what they know as well as what they still don't know. This permits them to look further and get the answers to their questions. It is only the poor programmers who cannot conceive of any limitations in their work and never ask for help, either from their users or other programmers. So, although there is still much to learn before you complete a commercial project, you should also acknowledge how much you have learned and how far you have traveled. If you have completed the Rotech project to this point, you have built a solid foundation for your own programming work.

*(**Note:** The Rotech Systems project, at the stage of development begun in this section, can be found on the Student Disk in the* rotech3 *folder as project* rotech3.vbp. *The project, as it exists at the end of this section, can be found on the Student Disk in the* rotech3b *folder as project* rotech3.vbp.*)*

Exercises 3.5

1. Either construct the Rotech system as it has been developed in this section or locate and load the project from the Student Disk.

2. Modify the Rotech project so that pressing the Print Bill Command button displays a new form. This new form should have two Command buttons; one that returns control to the Walk In form and one that returns control directly to the Main Menu form.

3. Add a new form to the Rotech application to handle the Mail In orders. This form should look like Figure 3-21.

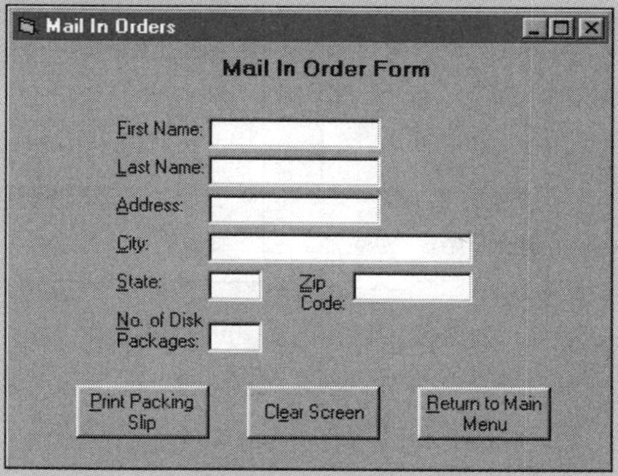

Figure 3-21
The Mail In Order Form

Figure 3-21
The Mail In Order Form

(**Hint:** Either start from scratch by adding a new form, setting the form's **Name** property to `frmMailin`, and adding the required controls, or make a copy of the existing `Walk In` form using the method described in the Programmers Notes box on this page, and then modify the copied form. Additionally, the project with a copied `Mail In` form that can be modified is found in the `rotech3b` folder, as project `rotech3b.vbp`, on the Student disk.)

4 (**Case study**) For your selected project (see project specifications at the end of Section 1.5) design an appropriate order entry form. To do this you can either make a preliminary pencil sketch or start designing it directly on a new form within Visual Basic's IDE. Be sure to construct a TTL table for the new form and save this table as part of your project's documentation.

PROGRAMMERS NOTES

Copying a Form

Many applications use similar forms. For example, in the Rotech project the `Walk In` and `Mail In` order entry forms are almost identical. As a programmer you can either develop each form anew, or you can copy an existing form and then make modifications to it. Copying a form, however, requires a good understanding of how Visual Basic actually stores each form, and the relationship between the form **Name** property and the file name under which the form is saved. Without this understanding, things can get very confusing. As a start in obtaining this understanding, review Sections 2.2's Programmers' Note on Visual Basic's File Structure.

To illustrate making a copy of a form, we will copy the `Walk In` form created for the Rotech project. Figure 3-22 shows the Project window for the project as it exists after the

`Walk In` form was created in Section 3.5. Notice that this form, which has the **Name** property `frmWalk` is saved in a file named `Walk.frm`. In this regard it is useful to consider the `Walk.frm` file as the package within which a form named `frmWalk` has been wrapped and stored. The Windows operating system knows the file as the name `Walk.frm`, and if you list the directory tree structure for the student disk, you will see a file named `Walk.frm` within the folder named

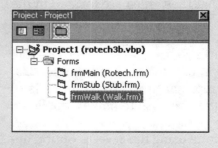

Figure 3-22a
The Initial Rotech Forms

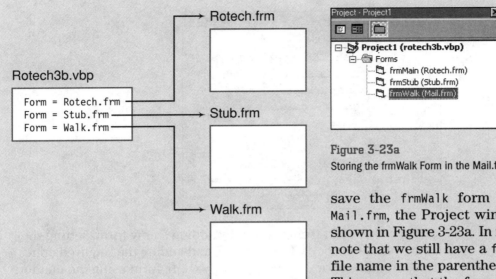

Figure 3-22b
The Initial Relationship between Rotech Project Files

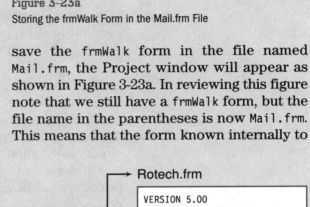

Figure 3-23a
Storing the frmWalk Form in the Mail.frm File

save the `frmWalk` form in the file named `Mail.frm`, the Project window will appear as shown in Figure 3-23a. In reviewing this figure note that we still have a `frmWalk` form, but the file name in the parentheses is now `Mail.frm`. This means that the form known internally to

`rotech3b`. Once this file is accessed by Visual Basic, the Visual Basic program opens it, takes out the form, and then deals with the form using it's **Name** property.

Figure 3-22b shows how each of the forms listed within the Project window shown in Figure 3-22a are packaged and stored as files within the operating system. It is important to understand that the project file, which is the file with the .vbp extension, is the controlling file that is always opened first. In Figure 3-22b this file is named rotech3b.vbp. Within the project file there are always one or more lines of code that begin with the word FORM. It is these lines of code that tell Visual Basic the names and locations of the files containing the forms needed to complete the application. The locations can be given either as full or relative path names, with the last item on the line being the file's name. Since only a file name is listed in each of the lines shown in the project file, it means that these files are located in the same folder as the project (.vbp) file. Compare Figures 3-22a and b and notice that the file names shown in Figure 3-22b are the same names shown in parentheses in Figure 3-22a.

The first step that needs to be taken is to save the form that we wish to make a duplicate of, in this case `frmWalk`, under a new file name. This is easily done using the `Save As` option under the `File` menu. If we use this option and

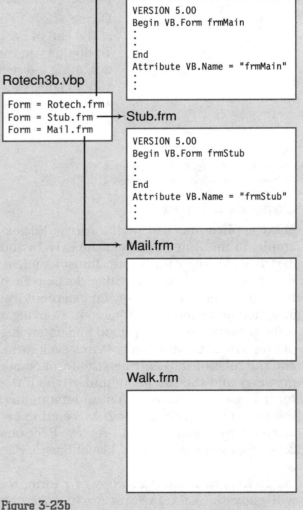

Figure 3-23b
The Files Structure Corresponding to Figure 3-23a

Visual Basic as the object with the **Name** property frmWalk is now stored externally in a file known to the operating system as Mail.frm.

What has happened, from a file standpoint is shown in Figure 3-23b. As seen in this figure we now have four form files, two of which contain a copy of the frmWalk form, but only one of which is actually linked to the application via the project (.vbp) file. It is important to understand that at this point the original Walk.frm file still exists as a distinct file stored on the disk, but that it is no longer a part of the current application, and that the frmWalk form is supplied to the application as the contents of the file Mail.frm. The contents of the Mail.frm file is, at this stage, an exact duplicate of the Walk.frm file (as such, this copy could also have been made outside of Visual Basic, either in a DOS window or by using Window's copy and renaming facilities). Within each of the .frm files shown in the figure, we have included the lines of code that identify the form by its Name property, and as it is known in Visual Basic. An interesting sidelight at the time this text was written is that the first line of code shown, Version 5.00, is produced even though the Rotech application was developed using Version 6.0 (and if you change this line to Version 6.0, it will be rejected by VB Version 6.0).

It is also important to note that no two forms within an application can have the same **Name** property. Thus, at this stage, we cannot link the Walk.frm file back into the application. First, we must change the name of the file stored in Mail.frm. This is easily done by displaying the currently active frmWalk form within Visual Basic, and changing its **Name** property. Renaming this form frmMail causes the Project window to change from that previously shown in Figure 3-23a to that shown in Figure 3-24a. The only change in these two figures is that the name and position of the highlighted form has changed. The form name is highlighted to indicate that it is the active form being worked on, and the position has changed because forms are listed alphabetically by **Name** property. So, at this stage, the frmMail form is stored in the Mail.frm file. Figure 3-24b illustrates how all of the files exist, as they are known by the operating system. Comparing Figure 3-24b to Figure 3-23b reveals that as far

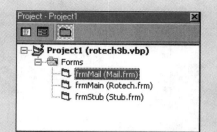

Figure 3-24a
Storing the frmMail Form in the Mail.frm File

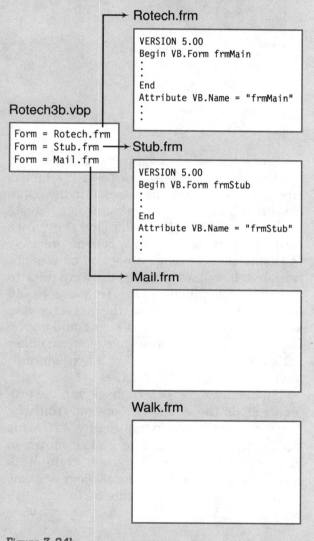

Figure 3-24b
The Files Structure Corresponding to Figure 3-24a

as the operating system is concerned, there is no difference as to the number and names of files being stored. It is only within the file named Mail.frm that the two lines of code containing the form's **Name** property have changed form Walk.frm to Mail.frm.

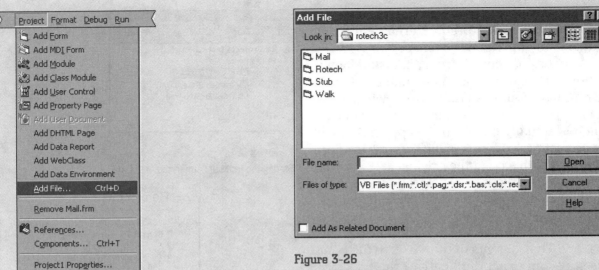

Figure 3-25
Adding a File into a Project

Figure 3-26
The Add File Dialog Box

Since the same form name is no longer used twice, we can now link `frmWalk`, which is stored in the `Walk.frm` file, back into the application. In fact, the process we used in saving the `Mail.frm` file before changing the form's **Name** property to `frmMail` was done precisely to ensure that the same object name was not repeated. If we had renamed the form prior to saving the file, the new `Mail.frm` name would have been saved in both the `Mail.frm` and `Walk.frm` files, and the next step could not be made (if you made this mistake, you can either start the process anew, or use a text editor to alter names within the `.frm` files).

To link the `frmWalk` form back into the project, select the <u>Add</u> <u>File</u> option from the <u>Project</u> menu, as shown in Figure 3-25. This will bring up the Add File dialog shown in Figure 3-26. Using this dialog, select the Walk form. Once this is done, the Project window will appear as shown in Figure 3-27a.

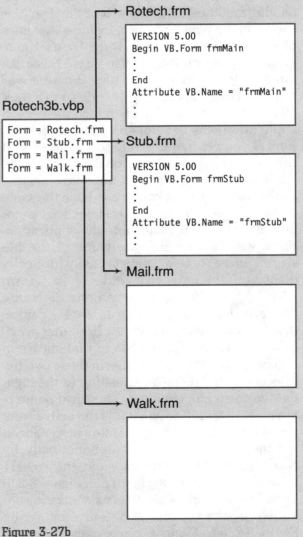

Figure 3-27b
The Files Structure Corresponding to Figure 3-27a

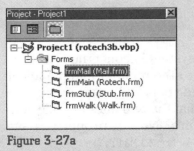

Figure 3-27a
The frmWalk Form Reattached

Notice in Figure 3-27a that the frmWalk form, contained within the Walk.frm file, is once again included within the project. Additionally, the project now has a frmMail, which is an exact duplicate of frmWalk. The added frmMail form can now be modified independently of, and with no effect on, frmWalk. Figure 3-27b shows how each of the five files associated with the application are stored with respect to the operating system, and linked from within the project definition (.vbp) file. As text files, all of the files shown in this figure can be opened, inspected, and modified using a text editor (one of the easiest to use is the full screen editor available in each DOS window by typing the command edit at the DOS prompt). However, you should not attempt to modify any of these files using a text editor unless you have made a copy of them using DOS or Windows techniques, and only if you understand what you are doing. One or two mistakes with the editor can easily trash your complete application.

3.6 ▶ Knowing About: The Basics of Form Design[9]

The purpose of a form, which is the interface between the application and the user, is to permit the user to interact with the application in a convenient way. To achieve this purpose, Visual Basic provides two categories of objects that can be placed on a form: data controls and graphic controls. Data controls include Text boxes, Option buttons, Check boxes, and any other control that is used to get and display data. The graphic controls include labels, lines, shapes, and images, which are generally used to add visual interest to the form. In this section we present basic guidelines for using data and graphic controls to create easy to use, attractive forms.

In designing a form it is useful to always remember that the form's main purpose is to control the flow of information to and from a user. It is also useful to understand that when a user views a screen, the user's eye will be attracted to a graphic first and then to text; with respect to text, a user will automatically start at the left top corner of the screen and move across and down the screen. Finally, users will judge an application based on how your screens look and how easy it is to use these screens and complete the tasks that the application is meant to accomplish. With this in mind, the following guidelines should always be observed, unless a special situation demands otherwise:

1. General Design Considerations

- Except for splash screens, which are meant to be advertisements (see Section 8.6), each form should have, at most, only a single small graphic that is placed toward the screen's upper-left corner. This makes the graphic unobtrusive and permits a user's eye to move in its natural pattern from the graphic into the screen's operational portion.
- Place frequently read information toward the top left or top center of a screen. Since this is where a user's eye normally focuses, it decreases eye movement and increases the screen's usability.
- Margins should be consistent around the screen, and should consist of a minimum of two dots from the screen's edge.
- Keep at least 40% of a screen's overall area blank.
- Make sure that all controls are surrounded by blank spaces.

---

[9]The material in this section may be omitted with no loss of subject continuity.

- Command buttons within a column or row should be the same size. They can all be touching or separated from each other by one or two dots. The most commonly used button should be placed either at the top of the left-most column of buttons or at the left side of a row of buttons.

- When placing Labels, Text boxes, or Picture boxes in a line across the screen, make sure that the line is filled no more than 75% with controls.

- Don't make a form larger than the screen's physical size. Although users can use scroll bars to access these areas, they are not used to doing so.

- Create additional forms as needed with Command buttons that allow the user to switch between forms.

- Design inconspicuous forms. Each form should be useful while going essentially unnoticed. User's should end up remembering and referring to each operational form by its function, such as the `Walk In` form, and not by its color or graphic.

2. Label and Text Considerations

- Use Labels to describe the purpose of a form and what information is being asked for or displayed.

- Provide every Text box with a Label. If the Text box is used for input, provide the Label with an access key and give it a TabIndex number that is one less than its associated Text box. This permits the user to force the focus into the Text box by activating the Label's access key.

- All labels should be positioned either above or to the left of their respective Text boxes. When placed above a Text box the label should align with the box's left side. When placed to the left of a text box, all labels in a column should be left-aligned.

- Use only one or two fonts that are easy to read, and use them for all text on the form. Generally, avoid script fonts (fonts that resemble handwriting) as they are harder to read than non-script fonts.

- Use a point size of 8 or more, as smaller point sizes are difficult to read. To distinguish important data or make titles clearly identifiable, use larger point sizes.

- For multi-word labels adopt a consistent style of either capitalizing all words in the label or only capitalizing the first word.

- Don't use exotic fonts that may not be available on one of your user's computers.

- Do not use underlining or italics, as they both make text hard to read.

3. Line and Shape Considerations

- Use lines and shapes to group related items on the form.

- Use lines and shapes to focus a user's eye on different sections of a form.

4. Color Considerations

- Use colors to create a soothing, rather than a dazzling, frenetic effect. User's quickly tire and become irritated when required to use a "glittery" or glaring form over an extended period of time. Blue colors tend to be soothing while "hot" colors, such as vivid pink or violet tent to be distracting.

- Use only two or, at most, three complimentary colors within a single form, in addition to the white, gray, or black colors used. Excessive colors tend to distract users.

- Use a darker color to emphasize headings or titles.

- Use different color combinations amongst multiple forms to create a coding scheme for your application. For example, a blue and white color scheme might be used for a Mail In order entry form and a red and gray scheme for a Walk In order entry form. These color schemes can be used on more than one form.

- Do not use red and green together. People who are color blind cannot distinguish between these colors.

3.7 Common Programming Errors and Problems

Part of learning any procedural programming language is making the elementary mistakes commonly encountered as you begin to use the language. These mistakes tend to be quite frustrating, since each language has its own set of common programming errors waiting for the unwary. Here is a list of the most common basic errors beginning Visual Basic programmers make:

1. Misspelling the name of a method; for example, typing `pint` instead of `Print`. A simple way to detect this is to type all entries in the Code window in lowercase. Keywords, such as **Print**, will then be automatically capitalized correctly and displayed in blue (or any other color selected under the <u>T</u>ools options). Any misspelled word will not be converted, making it easier to detect.

2. Forgetting to close messages to be displayed by the **Print** method within double quote symbols.

3. Incorrectly typing the letter O for the number zero (0), and vice versa.

4. Incorrectly typing the letter l ("el"), for the number 1 (one), and vice versa.

5. Forgetting to declare all the variables used in a program. This error is detected by Visual Basic, and an error message is generated for all undeclared variables, if the **Option Explicit** statement is used.

6. Forgetting to use the **As** `data-type` clause in a single-line declaration, which causes the variable to be declared as Variant by default. For example, the declaration `Dim quantity, amount As Single` *does not* declare both `quantity` and `amount` as singles. Rather, `amount` is declared as a Single and `quantity` as a Variant. In this case, the correct declaration is `Dim quantity As Single, amount As Single`.

7. Storing an inappropriate data type value in a declared variable. This results in the assigned value being converted to the data type of the declared variable.

8. Using a variable in an expression before an explicit value has been assigned to the variable. Here, whatever value happens to be in the variable will be used when the expression is evaluated, and the result is usually incorrect.

9. Using an intrinsic function without providing the correct number of arguments of the proper data type.

10. Being unwilling to test an event procedure in depth. After all, since you wrote the procedure you assume it is correct, or you would have

changed it before it was run. It can be very difficult to completely test your own software. As a programmer, you must constantly remind yourself that believing your program is correct does not make it so. Finding errors in your own program is a sobering experience, but one that will help you become a master programmer.

11. Saving an existing project using a new project name, without also saving all form modules using new form names so that both the original and new projects use the same form files. In this case, changing a form for the new project also changes the same form in the original project. Remember that the projects we have constructed are saved using two files—one for the project as a whole and one for the single form module it uses.

On a more fundamental level, it is worth repeating one of the errors mentioned in Chapter 1. A major programming error that almost all beginning programmers make is the rush to code and run a program before fully understanding what is required by each procedure. A symptom of this haste is the lack of either an outline of each proposed procedure or a written procedure itself. Many problems can be caught just by visually checking each procedure, either handwritten or listed from the computer, before it is ever run, and then testing it for a variety of inputs a user might enter.

3.8 ▶ Chapter Review

Key Terms

accumulating	expression	precedence
ANSI	floating point number	Print
assignment	Integer	Single
associativity	integer number	Single-precision number
counting	instrinsic function	String
declaration	long	type conversion
Double	mixed-mode	variable
double-precision number	mnemonic	

Summary

1. Five types of data were introduced in this chapter: integer, floating point, boolean, string, and variant.

2. Every variable in a Visual Basic program should be declared as to the type of value it can store. Declarations within a procedure may be placed anywhere after the header line, but are usually placed together at the top of a procedure. Single variable declarations use the syntax

```
Dim variable-name As data-type
```

An example of using this syntax is

```
Dim quantity As Double
```

Multiple variable declarations may also be made on the same line using the syntax

```
Dim var-1 As data-type, var-2 As data-type,...,var-n As data-type
```

An example using this syntax is

```
Dim amount As Single, price As Double, count As Integer
```

When the **As** data-type clause is omitted, the variable is declared as a Variant type by default.

3. Declaration statements always play a software role of defining a list of valid variable names. They also play a hardware role, because they cause memory storage locations to be set aside for each declared variable.

4. An *expression* is any combination of constants, variables, operators, and functions that can be evaluated to yield a value.

5. Expressions are evaluated according to the precedence and associativity of the operators used in them.

6. The **Print** method can be used to display both text and numerical results. Text should be enclosed in double quotes, and items to be printed should be separated by either a space or semicolon.

7. Assignment statements are used to store values into variables. The general syntax for an assignment statement is

```
variable = expression
```

8. Visual Basic provides intrinsic functions for calculating mathematical and string computations.

9. Data passed to a function are called *arguments* of the function. Arguments are passed to an intrinsic function by including each argument, separated by commas, within the parentheses following the function's name. Each function has its own requirements for the number and data types of the arguments that must be provided.

10. Every intrinsic function operates on its arguments to calculate a single value. To effectively use an intrinsic function you must know what the function does, the name of the function, the number and data types of the arguments expected by the function, and the data type of the returned value.

Test Yourself—Short Answer

1. Give an example of an expression.
2. Give an example of an assignment.
3. Name 3 Visual Basic keywords.
4. Define variable.
5. List the rules for naming a variable.
6. Declare a variable called PayAmt. It should be able to hold a decimal value.
7. Declare a variable called DeptName. It should hold alphabetic characters and have a fixed length of 14.
8. What is the code that will force you to declare all of your variables?

9. Write code that will declare a variable to hold the count of students riding a bus. Use the data type best suited to the number anticipated.

10. Write code that will store the sum of the numbers 78 and 2 into the variable **sum**.

Programming Projects

1. Construct a program that uses integer and string variables and the operations that can be performed on them. Follow the instructions below:

a. Integers

1. Open a new project called lab2.vbp and change the form's caption to "VB Data Types."

2. Create an Exit Command control on your form named cmdExit that can be used to end the program.

3. Create a Picture box and Command control on your form named `picDisplay1` and `cmdDisplay1`, respectively. Set the caption of the Command control to "Display results."

4. Add the following commands to the Command control's click event procedure, and run your program:

```
picDisplay1.Cls
picDisplay1.Print 1
picDisplay1.Print 3 + 4
picDisplay1.Print 3 + 4 - 5
picDisplay1.Print 3 + 4 * 5 - 10 / 2
picDisplay1.Print 3 / 4, 6 / 4, 8 / 4
picDisplay1.Print 6 ^ 2, 3 ^ 2 ^ 2
picDisplay1.Print 3;4;5;7-1
```

5. Now, add a Command button that causes the following code to be executed:

```
Dim a, b, c as Integer
picDisplay1.Cls
a = 5 : b = 2
picDisplay1.Print a + b, a - b
picDisplay1.Print a * b, a / b
picDisplay1.Print a ^ b; b ^ a;
picDisplay1.Print (a + b) / b * a - 13
picDisplay1.Print ((a - 3) * b) - 13 * 2
```

6. Now add a Command button to calculate and display the following:

- a * b where a = 10 and b = 7
- the average speed of a plane that traveled 600 miles in 2.5 hours
- the square root of 15

b. Strings

1. Create a new Picture box named `picDisplay2` and a Command button that activates the following code when it is clicked:

```
Dim today As String 'string variables
Dim fday As String
Dim tdate as String  'today's date, as a string
picDisplay2.Cls
picDisplay2.Print "Hello";
picDisplay2.Print "There!"
```

```
today = "01/24/98"
picDisplay2.Print today
fday = "Friday"
picDisplay2.Print "Today is ";
picDisplay2.Print fday + ", " + today
tdate = fday + ", " + today
picDisplay2.Print tdate
picDisplay2.Print "400 + 125 = "; 400 + 125
```

Adding two strings is called concatenation. The strings are simply "strung together." Adding two integers adds up the numbers.

2. Add a new Command button that executes the following code:

```
Dim irate As Single
Dim net As Single
Dim principal As Single
Dim phrase As String

irate = 0.065
principal = 1000
phrase = "The balance after a year is "
net = (1 + irate) * principal
picDisplay2.Print "Using an interest rate of ";
picDisplay2.Print irate * 100; "%",
picDisplay2.Print phrase; net
```

3. Create one last Picture box named `picDisplay3`, and a Command control to activate the following code:

```
Dim n1 As Integer, n2 As Integer, n3 As Integer
Dim f1 As Single, f2 As Single, f3 As Single
Dim s1 As String, s2 As String, s3 As String

n1 = 3 : n2 = 4 : n3 = 5
f1 = 3 : f2 = 4 : f3 = 5
s1 = "3" : s2 = "4" : s3 = "5"
picDisplay3.Cls
picDisplay3.Print n1 * n2 * n3, n1 * Val(s2) * n3
n2 = n3 / n1
f2 = f3 / f1
picDisplay3.Print n2, f2
picDisplay3.Print n1+n2+n3, s1+s2+s3
picDisplay3.Print s1, n2, f2
picDisplay3.Print
picDisplay3.Print Val(s1) + n2 + f2, Val(s1)+ n2+ Int(f2)
```

Extra Challenge Questions

1. Use the Help Facility to obtain information on the string functions **Left$**, **Right$**, **Mid$**, and **InStr**.
   a. What does the **Left$** function do?
   b. What does the **Right$** function do?
   c. What does the **Mid$** function do?
   d. What is the exact value of the expression Str(3.1415)?
   e. What does the **InStr** function return?

2. Create a Picture box and a Command control to activate the following code:

```
Dim S1 As String
Dim f1 As Single

s1 = "Hello There, World!"
```

continued

```
picDisplay4.Print Left$(s1, 5)
picDisplay4.Print Mid$ (s1,7,5)
picDisplay4.Print Right$(s1,6)
picDisplay4.Print Instr(s1,"W")
f1 = 3.1415927
picDisplay4.Print "/";Str$(f1);"/",Mid$(Str$(f1),4,4)
picDisplay4.Print (s1) + Str(f1)
```

3. Answer the following questions (Hint: Use the results of Exercise 1).

    a. What happens when you divide two integers together and store the result into an integer variable?

    b. What happens when you divide two integers together and store the result into a single-precision variable?

    c. What does the trailing semicolon do after a **Print** statement?

    d. What does the trailing comma do after a **Print** statement?

    e. What happens if a **Print** statement is called with nothing after it?

    f. How do you clear (erase) a Picture box?

    g. Is 3 ^ 2 ^ 2 equal to 81?

    h. What is the value of the expression 3 + 4 * 5?

    i. What is the value of the expression (3 + 4) * 5?

    j. What is the value of the expression "3 + 4 * 5"?

    k. What is the value of the expression "(3 + 4) * 5"?

    l. What happens when two strings are added together?

    m. What does an apostrophe do in Visual Basic?

    n. What does a colon do in Visual Basic?

    o. What does a comma do in a **Print** statement?

    p. What does a semicolon do in a **Print** statement?

    q. True or False: An assignment statement takes the right hand side of an equation and assigns it to the left hand side.

    r. Is the statement a + b = c + 5 a valid Visual Basic statement? Why or why not?

    s. What type of data does the **Val** function expect to operate on and what data type does it return?

    t. How do you ensure that each and every Visual Basic variable must be explicitly declared in a program?

4. Create a project that can be used by a business person on their laptop computer to determine exchange rates for China, Japan, England, and France. A form for this project is shown in Figure 3-28. For this project assume that there are 8.3 yuan per dollar, 120 yen per dollar, 0.6 pounds per dollar, and 5 francs per dollar.

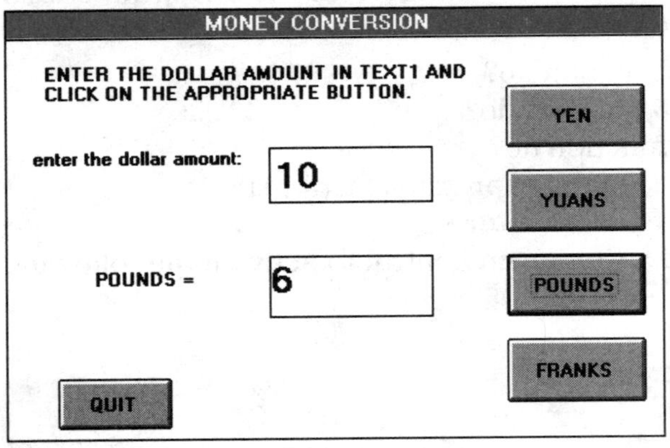

5. You're the owner of a clothing store. Business has been slow and you have too much of last season's merchandise so you decide to have a sale. Everything in the store will be 45% off. Write a program which will allow the clerk to enter the original price then hit a button and the discounted price, with the 6% sales tax added, appears. A suggested form for this project is shown in Figure 3-29.

    a. The following formulas are needed for the CAL-CULATE button.

DISCOUNTED PRICE = .55 * ORIGINAL PRICE
TAX = .06 * DISCOUNTED PRICE
FINAL PRICE = DISCOUNTED PRICE + TAX

Figure 3-28

Form for Exercise 4

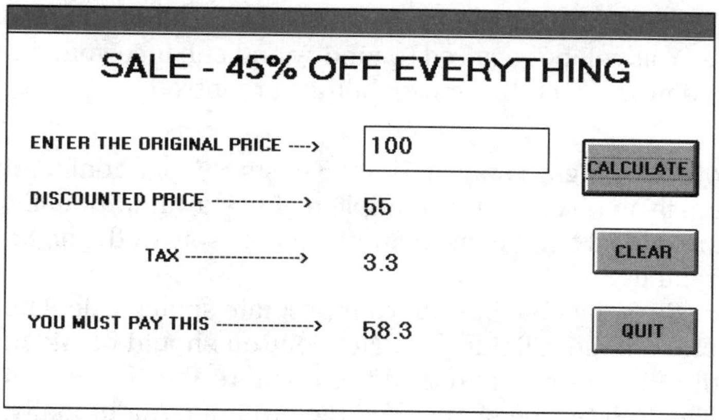

Figure 3-29
Suggested form for Exercise 5

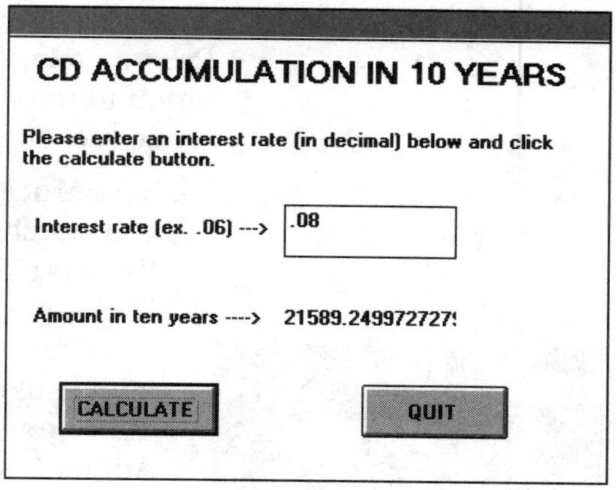

Figure 3-30
Form for Exercise 6

b. The CLEAR button clears the values in the Text box and the three labels used for the discounted price, tax, and final price.

6. In ten years you believe that you will need money to start a new business. At present you have about $10,000 which you can invest in a savings account or CD. Create a Visual Basic Project which will allow you to try out different interest rates and see how much money you will have in this savings account or CD in ten years. The formula needed for this Future Value program is: *Future value = Present value * (1 + interest rate) ^ years* where the Present value = $10,000, the interest rate is variable, and the years = 10. (This problem assumes that interest is compounded annually.)

You may prefer to use the FV (future value) function built in to Visual Basic rather than the above formula. Information on this function can be obtained using the Help facility. In calculating the future value, construct a form similar to that shown in Figure 3-30.

7. Create an application that permits a user to compare the cost of ordering equipment via mail order or buying the equipment locally. It is assumed that the local delivery entails no delivery charge but a sales tax of 6% is charged, while the mail order has no sales tax but requires a $100 shipping and handling charge. Using your application, fill out the following table:

Base Item Cost	Total Mail Order Cost	Total Local Order Cost
$ 500		
$1000		
$1500		
$2000		
$2500		
$3000		
$3500		
$4000		
$4500		
$5000		

Note: The following Motel 8 project is used in subsequent End-of-Chapter Programming Projects. You will be required to modify and enhance your solution to this project as new Visual Basic capabilities are introduce in subsequent chapter.

8. **The Motel 8 Project:** A night's stay at Motel 8 costs $30 per adult and $10 per child. There is no discount for multiple nights stay. Additionally, there is a 5% state and local tax that is computed on the sum of the nightly charges. Requirements:

When the user clicks the Calc button, your program should calculate and display the total charge. Clicking the New button should blank all Text boxes and the Picture box and give the focus to the Number of Adults Text box. The Exit button should end the program. Additionally:

a. Insure that the tab sequence is txtAdults, txtChildren, txtNights, cmdCalc, cmdNew, and cmdExit.
b. Use the VAL function to convert input in Text boxes to numeric values.
c. In the General Declaration section of your program, declare variables to hold values of Number of Adults, Number of Children, Number of Nights (all Integer variables) and Total Charge (a Currency variable).

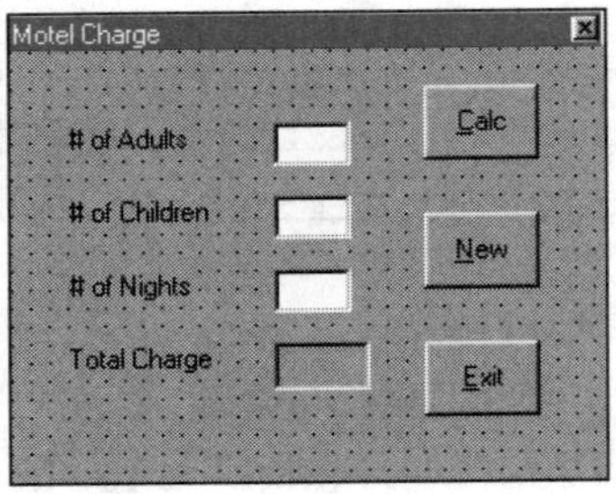

Figure 3-31
Form for Exercise 8

Note: The following Local Car Rental Company project is used in subsequent End-of-Chapter Programming Projects. You will be required to modify and enhance your solution to this project as new Visual Basic capabilities are introduced in subsequent chapters.

9. The Local Car Rental Company rents cars for $29.95 per day with unlimited mileage. There is a refueling fee of $12.95 regardless of the level of fuel when the car is returned. Write a program that will permit the user to input the customer's first and last name and the number of days that the car was rented. The program should compute the total charge for the car rental.

Requirements: When the user clicks the Calc button, your program should calculate and display the total charge. Clicking the New button should blank all Text boxes and Picture box and give the focus to the First Name Text box. The Exit button should end the program. Additionally:

a. Insure that the tab sequence is txtFirstName, txtLastName, txtDays,cmdCalc, cmdNew, and cmdExit.
b. Use the VAL function to convert input in Number of Days Text box to an integer numerical value.
c. Declare variables to hold values of Number of Days and Total Charge in the General Declaration section of the program.

Figure 3-32
Form for Exercise 9

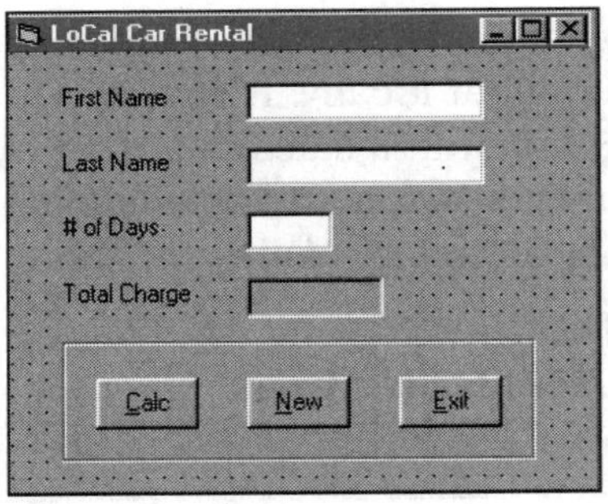

10. The LoCal Ice Cream Shoppe has asked you to write a program that will calculate the quantities of ice cream, nuts, and chocolate sauce they will probably need on the next day based on an estimate of the next day's sales. The Properties table is on page 180. The following is a list of the quantities used in their sundaes and shakes (their only two products).

Sundaes:

Ounces of ice cream per sundae	7
Ounces of nuts per sundae	1
Ounces of chocolate sauce per sundae	2

Shakes:

Ounces of ice cream per shake	12
Ounces of chocolate sauce per shake	1

Motel 8 Properties Table (Exercise 8)		
Object	**Property**	**Setting**
Form	Name	frmMotelCharge
	Caption	Room Charge
Label	Name	lblAdults
	Caption	# of Adults
Label	Name	lblChildren
	Caption	# of Children
Label	Name	lblNights
	Caption	# of Nights
Label	Name	lblCharges
	Caption	Total Charges
Label	Name	lblTotCharges
Text Box	Name	txtAdults
	Text	(Blank)
Text Box	Name	txtChildren
	Text	(Blank)
Text Box	Name	txtNights
	Text	(Blank)
Command Button	Name	cmdCalc
	Caption	&Calc
Command Button	Name	cmdNew
	Caption	&New
Command Button	Name	cmdExit
	Caption	&Exit

Local Car Rental Company Properties Table (Exercise 9)		
Object	**Property**	**Setting**
Form	Name	frmCarRental
	Caption	Local Car Rental Company
Label	Name	lblFirstName
	Caption	First Name
Label	Name	lblLastName
	Caption	Last Name
Label	Name	lblDays
	Caption	# of Days
Label	Name	lblTotCharge
	Caption	Total Charge
Text Box	Name	txtFirstName
	Text	(Blank)
Text Box	Name	txtLastName
	Text	(Blank)
Text Box	Name	txtDays
	Text	(Blank)
Label	Name	lblCharge
	Caption	(Blank)
Command Button	Name	cmdCalc
	Caption	&Calc
Command Button	Name	cmdNew
	Caption	&New
Command Button	Name	cmdExit
	Caption	&Exit

Figure 3-33
Form for Exercise 10

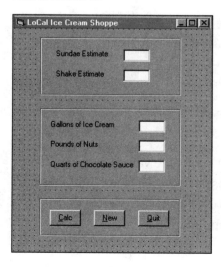

Your program should provide for input of the estimated amount of sundaes and shakes that will be sold the next day and display the quantities needed. The output list should display amount of ice cream in gallons, nuts in pound, and sauce in quarts.

11. Create an application that permits a user to determine how much an item depreciates over a five-year time span using straight line, declining balance, and sum of the years digits depreciation methods. The application should allow the user to

a. Input the item's original cost and its salvage value at the end of 5 years.

b. Enter the depreciation year of interest, which should be an integer from 1 to 5.

c. Exit the program.

LoCal ICe Cream Shoppe Properties Table (Exercise 10)

Object	Property	Setting
Form	Name	frmIceCream
	Caption	Local Ice Cream Shoppe
Frame	Name	fraInput
Label	Name	lblSundaes
	Caption	Sundae Estimate
Label	Name	lblShakes
	Caption	Shake Estimate
Text Box	Name	txtSundaes
	Text	(Blank)
Text Box	Name	txtShakes
	Text	(Blank)
Frame	Name	fraOutput
Label	Name	lblIcecream
	Caption	Gallons of Ice Cream
Label	Name	lblNuts
	Caption	Pounds of Nuts
Label	Name	lblChocolate
	Caption	Quarts of Chocolate Sauce
Label	Name	lblGalIceCream
	Caption	(Blank)
Label	Name	lblLbsNuts
	Caption	(Blank)
Label	Name	lblQtsChocolate
	Caption	(Blank)
Frame	Name	fraCommands
Command Button	Name	cmdCalc
	Caption	&Calc
Command Button	Name	cmdNew
	Caption	&New
Command Button	Name	cmdQuit
	Caption	&Quit

The required formulas are as follows:

Yearly straight line depreciation = (cost – salvage value)/5

Double declining depreciation = .4 * (cost – previous years depreciation)

Sum of the years digits depreciation = (6 – year)/15 * cost

Use a form of your own choosing for this application.

Controlling Input and Output

In the previous chapters we explored how data is stored and processed using variables and assignment statements. In this chapter we complete this exploration by presenting additional input, output, and processing capabilities. On the input side we show how both the **InputBox** function and Text box control can be used to obtain data from a user while an application is executing. On the output side we show how numerical data can be formatted using the **Format** function and displayed in either a Text or Picture box.

4.1 Interactive User Input

Data for applications that only need to be executed once may be included directly in the appropriate procedure. For example, if we wanted to multiply the numbers 30.5 and 0.06, we could use Event Procedure 4-1.

Event Procedure 4-1

```
Private Sub Form_Click()
  Dim num1 As Single, num2 As Single, product As Single

  num1 = 30.5
  num2 = 0.06
  product = num1 * num2
  Print num1; " times"; num2; "  is"; product
End Sub
```

The output displayed by this procedure is

```
30.5 times 0.06 is 1.83
```

Event Procedure 4-1 can be shortened to the even simpler Event Procedure 4-2. Both procedures, however, suffer from the same basic problem: they must be rewritten in order to multiply other numbers. Neither procedure allows the user to substitute different values into the multiplication operation.

Event Procedure 4-2

```
Private Sub Form_Click()
  Print 30.5; " times"; 0.06; "  is"; 30.5 * 0.06
End Sub
```

Except for the programming practice they provide, event procedures that perform a single, simple calculation are clearly not very useful. After all, it is easier to use a calculator to multiply two numbers than to enter and run either Event Procedure 4-1 or 4-2.

This section outlines two commonly used techniques for permitting a user to enter data into an executing Visual Basic application: the **InputBox** intrinsic function and the Text box control.

The InputBox Intrinsic Function

The **InputBox** intrinsic function provides a very simple way for users to enter a single input into a procedure while it is executing. A call to this function creates a dialog box that permits a user to enter a string at the terminal. The entered string, which frequently is converted to either an integer or a floating point number, is then stored directly in a variable. Figure 4-1 shows the relationship between an **InputBox** function used for entering string data, and a **MsgBox** statement used for displaying string data. (Recall from Section 2.3 that a dialog is any box requiring the user to supply additional information to complete a task.)

The most commonly used syntax for calling the **InputBox** function is

```
InputBox(prompt, title, default)
```

where *prompt* is a required string and both *title* and *default*, which are also strings, are optional. If a title string is used, it is displayed in the title bar of the dialog box; otherwise, the application's name is placed in the title bar. If a default string is provided, it is placed within the input area of the dialog box. A *prompt* is a message telling a user that input is required. The prompt, which is always required, is displayed as a string within the input dialog box. For example, the statement

```
s = InputBox("Enter a value", "Input Dialog")
```

calls the **InputBox** function with the arguments "Enter a value", which is the prompt, "Input Dialog", which is the title, and no default argument. When this statement is executed, the input dialog shown in Figure 4-2 is displayed.

Figure 4-1
An InputBox Dialog and MsgBox
Dialog

InputBox
MsgBox

Figure 4-2
A Sample InputBox Dialog

Figure 4-3
Program 4-1's Interface

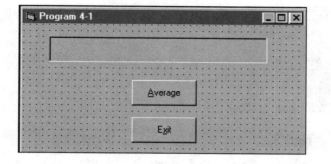

Further examples of the InputBox function are

```
s = InputBox("Enter a Value")
s = InputBox("Enter a Value", "Sample", "5")
s = InputBox("Enter a Value",, "10")
```

In all three examples, the prompt Enter a Value is displayed. In both the first and third examples the title bar is used to display the application's name, while in the second example, the title bar displays Sample. Finally, the last two examples provide default string values of 5 and 10 in the text input area. Notice that in the last example, where a default value is provided with no explicit title, the title argument is simply left blank but is separated from both the prompt and the default value by a comma.

Once an input dialog box is displayed, the keyboard is continuously scanned for data. As keys are pressed, the **InputBox** function displays them within the input area of the dialog. When either the (ENTER) key is pressed or one of the two command buttons in the box are clicked, input stops and the entered text is stored in the variable on the left side of the assignment statement. The procedure then continues execution with the next statement after the call to **InputBox**.

Program 4-1 illustrates using an **InputBox** function within the context of a complete application. The interface for this project is shown in Figure 4-3. As illustrated, the graphical user interface consists of two Command buttons and a Picture box.

For this application the only procedure is the Command button **Click** event, which is listed in Program 4-1's Event Code.

Program 4-1's Event Code

```
Private Sub cmdInput_Click()
  Dim num1 As Single, num2 As Single
  Dim average As Single

  picShow.Cls
  num1 = InputBox("Enter a number", "Input Dialog", "0")
  num2 = InputBox(("Great! Now enter another number", "Input Dialog", "0")
  average = (num1 + num2) / 2
  picShow.Print "The average of"; num1; " and"; num2; " is"; average
End Sub
```

The first input dialog displayed by Program 4-1's event procedure is shown in Figure 4-4. The 15 displayed in the input area of the dialog is the value that was entered from the keyboard. Before this value is entered the dialog displays a 0, which is the default provided in the **InputBox** function call.

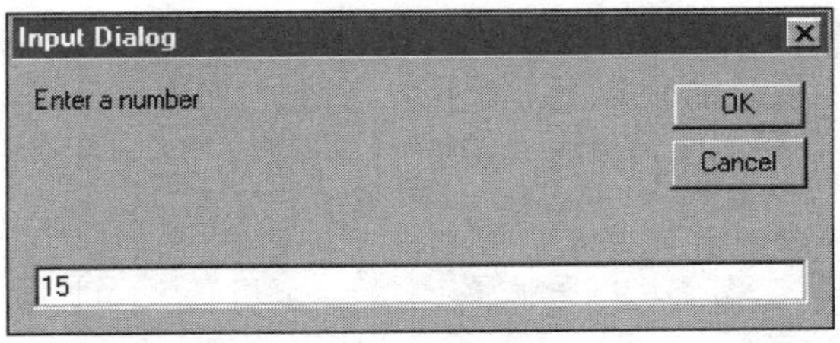

Figure 4-4
The First InputBox Dialog after Data is Entered

Table 4-1 The Properties Table for Program 4-1

Object	Property	Setting
Form	Name	frmMain
	Caption	Program 4-1
Picture box	Name	picShow
	Height	495
	Width	4095
	TabStop	False
Command button	Name	cmdInput
	Caption	&Average

Notice that the dialog prompt tells the user to enter a number. After this dialog is displayed, the **InputBox** function puts the application into a temporary paused state for as long as it takes the user to type in a value. The user signals the **InputBox** function that data entry is finished by clicking one of the Command buttons. If the user clicks the OK button (or presses the (ENTER) key when this button is in focus), the entered value is stored in the variable on the left side of the assignment statement, which in this case is num1, and the application is taken out of its pause. Program execution then proceeds with the next statement, which in Program 4-1's event procedure is another call to an **InputBox** function. The second **InputBox** dialog and the data entered in response to it, are shown in Figure 4-5.

While the second dialog is displayed, the application is again put into a temporary waiting state while the user types a second value. This second number is stored in the variable num2. Based on these input values, the output produced by Program 4-1 is shown in Figure 4-6.

Figure 4-5
The Second InputBox Dialog after Data Is Entered

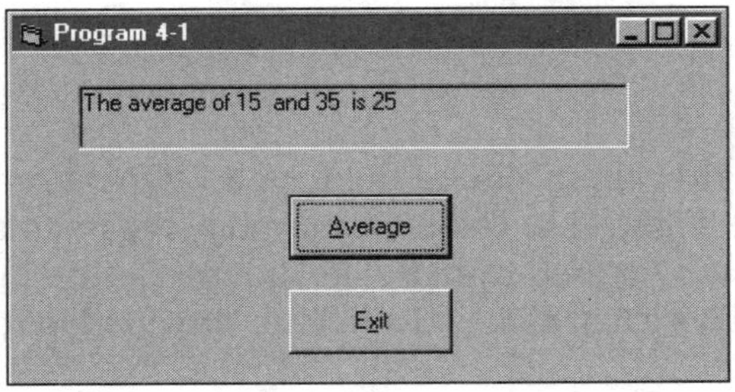

Figure 4-6
A Sample Output Produced by Program 4-1

We now explain why a default value of 0 was used for each **InputBox** dialog. The reason touches on a much broader issue of constant concern to all good programmers.

A default value will handle the case where a user presses the OK Command button accidentally, before any value is entered. Remember that the **InputBox** function actually accepts and returns a string, which allows a user to type in any text. Using a string as input provides a safety precaution because the programmer has no control over what a user might happen to enter. Accepting the input as a string ensures that whatever is typed will be accepted initially. After the data is entered, however, the programmer should validate the entered data. For example, if a number is required, the procedure should check that only digits, and possibly one decimal point, have been entered. Whenever invalid data is detected, an error message should be displayed and the user be given an opportunity to reenter valid data. Validating user input requires the selection statements presented in Chapter 5, so for now we can provide only minimal protection against invalid data entry. This is the reason for the default value.

If no default is provided and a user should accidentally click the OK button before any data is entered, the string returned from the dialog will contain no characters at all. This string is thus the zero-length empty string, "". Now notice that in Program 4-1's event procedure the first assignment statement stores the entered and returned value in the variable num1, which is declared as a **Single**. In executing this assignment, Visual Basic will automatically convert the returned string, if possible, into a single-precision number before storing it in num1. (If this is unfamiliar to you, refer to the type conversions presented in Section 3.3.) Thus, if the user enters only digits and possibly a single decimal point into the input dialog, the conversion can be made. If an entered string cannot be converted, the error message Type mismatch is displayed. Since an empty string has no valid numerical value, clicking on the OK button when no default or value has been entered would cause a Type mismatch error. Providing a zero default prevents this error from occurring.

Before leaving Program 4-1's event procedure, one last observation is worth making. Notice the parentheses in the statement

```
average = (num1 + num2) / 2
```

The parentheses here are required to produce a correct calculation. Without these parentheses, the only number that would be divided by two is the value in num2 (since division has a higher precedence than addition).

The Text Box Control Reconsidered

By far, the most versatile and commonly used object for interactive input is the Text box control. This control permits the user to enter a string at the terminal. The string is then stored as the value for the Text box's **Text** property. A Text box control for input is almost always used in conjunction with a Label control, where the Label acts as a prompt and the Text box provides the actual means for the user to input data. For example, consider the interface shown in Figure 4-8. Here the Label is Enter a Fahrenheit Temperature: and the Text box provides an input area. The Label and Text box icons, as they appear in the Toolbox, are illustrated on Figure 4-7.

The Text box provides the actual means for a user to enter data while a program is executing. All data entered in the Text box is assumed by Visual Basic to be string data. This means that if numbers are to be input, the

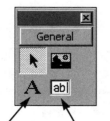

Label Control Icon   Text Box Control Icon

Figure 4-7
The Toolbox's Label and Text Box Icons

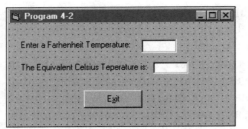

Figure 4-8
Program 4-2's User Interface

entered string must be converted to numerical data, either explicitly or implicitly. It also means that some data validation is typically required to ensure that a user does not enter data that will cause the application to crash.

For example, consider again the interface for Program 4-2 shown in Figure 4-8, where the user is prompted to enter a temperature in degrees Fahrenheit. Once a user enters a Fahrenheit temperature, the program will compute the corresponding temperature in degrees Celsius and display the calculated value in the picture box. The properties for Program 4-2 are listed in Table 4-2.

Table 4-2	Program 4-2's Property Table	
Object	**Property**	**Setting**
Form	Name	frmMain
	Caption	Program 4-2
Label	Name	lblFahr
	Caption	Enter a Fahrenheit Temperature:
	AutoSize	True
	WordWrap	False
Label	Name	lblCelsius
	Caption	The Equivalent Celsius Temperature is:
	AutoSize	True
	WordWrap	False
Text box	Name	txtFahr
	Text	(Blank)
Picture box	Name	picCelsius
	TabStop	False
Command button	Name	cmdExit
	Caption	E&xit

Now consider Program 4-2's event code, paying particular attention to the Text box **GotFocus** and **LostFocus** event procedures, as these are the two of the three procedures primarily used in processing Text box data.

Program 4-2's Event Code

```
Private Sub txtFahr_GotFocus()
  picCelsius.Cls
End Sub

Private Sub txtFahr_LostFocus()
  Dim celsius As Single

  celsius = 5 / 9 * (Val(txtFahr.text) - 32)
  picCelsius.Print celsius
End Sub

Private Sub cmdExit_Click()
  Beep
  End
End Sub
```

Figure 4-9

A Sample Run Using Program 4-2

The **GotFocus** event is triggered when an object receives focus and is used to perform any preprocessing associated with a user control. In Program 4-2 we use the Text box's **GotFocus** event to clear the Picture box of any data, prior to allowing a user to enter a new Fahrenheit temperature. This is done to ensure that a previously calculated Celsius temperature does not appear while the user is typing in new data.

The actual calculation and display of a Celsius temperature is performed by the Text box's **LostFocus** event. This event is triggered when the Text box loses focus, which occurs when the user signals completion of data entry either by pressing the TAB key or clicking on another control. The actual computation in the **LostFocus** event consists of the single calculation celsius = (5 / 9) * (Val(txtFahr.Text) - 32), which converts a Fahrenheit temperature to its Celsius equivalent. This is followed by a call to the Picture box's **Print** method to display the calculated result. Figure 4-9 illustrates a completed run using Program 4-2. Notice that the focus in this figure is on the E**x**it Command button.

Before leaving Program 4-2, take a closer look at the assignment statement used to calculate a Celsius value. Specifically, notice the term Val(txtFahr.Text). Here, the term txtFahr.Text accesses the data value entered in the Text box and stored in its **Text** property, which is a string value. Using this string as an argument to the **Val** function explicitly converts the string into a numerical value. Specifically, the **Val** function converts string data into numerical data for as many characters in the string as can be recognized as a number (see Table 3-9). Although the **Val** function will recognize a period as a decimal point, it stops the conversion at the first character that it cannot recognize as part of a number. For example, if the user entered the data 212abc, the **Val** function would return the number 212. The function also returns a numerical value of zero if the string does not begin in either a digit or a decimal point.

The purpose of using the **Val** function is that it prevents the program from crashing if the user types in a non-numeric input such as the characters abc. For example, without the **Val** function the assignment statement would appear as

```
celsius = (5 / 9) * (txtFahr.Text - 32)
```

This statement operates correctly when a user enters any string that can be considered as a number, such as 212, because the string is automatically converted to a numeric value within the expression (txtFahr.Text - 32). If a user inadvertently types in a string such as 212a, however, the program stops and produces the message Type mismatch error, because the entered string cannot be converted into a numerical value. Using the **Val** function ensures that this error will not occur, because the string is always converted to a numerical value prior to being processed as part of the calculation.

A First Look at User-Input Validation

Validating user input and ensuring that a program does not crash due to unexpected input is a sign of a well-constructed program. Programs that respond effectively to unexpected user input are referred to as "bullet-proof" programs, and one of your jobs as a programmer is to produce this type of program.

Program 4-2 only touches on the topic of validating user input by employing one of the more commonly used techniques associated with Text box input; this is to explicitly convert string data to numerical data, using the **Val** function when a numerical value is expected. This conversion is done in the **LostFocus** event code, immediately after the user has completed using the Text box. Clearly, this is an ideal place to verify and validate data. This is one of the primary uses of the **LostFocus** event—to verify and validate data before any computation is made.

Another very important type of validation occurs directly as the user is entering data. Typically, this type of validation is made using the **KeyPress** and **KeyDown** events. Each of these events returns the key just pressed and permits action to be taken before the key's value is accepted into the input string. The difference between these two events is the amount of information returned. The **KeyPress** procedure receives only the ANSI value of a character key as an argument, while the **KeyDown** event can detect and process the function, cursor, and shift keys in addition to the printable character keys. This type of validation, however, is based on selecting out desired characters and rejecting others from the entered string. The methods for performing such selections are described in the next chapter.

Using Scroll Controls for Input

Two additional controls for entering input numbers are the Horizontal and Vertical Scroll Bar controls. Except for their visual orientation (horizontal or vertical), both controls work the same way. In this section we present the Horizontal Scroll bar as an example for using either type of Scroll bar.

Figure 4-10 illustrates a form with a Horizontal Scroll bar. The Scroll bar is placed on a form in the same manner as all other toolbox controls; either by double-clicking the control or clicking and dragging the control to the desired form location.

In addition to a typical control's properties and events, Scroll bar controls have the following five unique properties that should be explicitly set at Design Time for each Scroll bar control placed on a form:

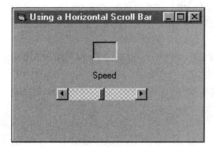

Figure 4-10
A Horizontal Scroll Bar Control

Property	Default Value
Max	32767
Min	0
Large Change	1
Small Change	1
Value	0

Each of these properties must be set to an integer value, because Scroll bars only work with integers. The first two of these properties, **Max** and **Min**, set the maximum and minimum values that can be set by the Scroll bar's thumb slide and scroll arrows. The maximum value is set when the scroll bar's thumb slide is moved to its furthest rightmost position, as shown in Figure 4-11a, while the minimum value is set when the thumb slide reaches

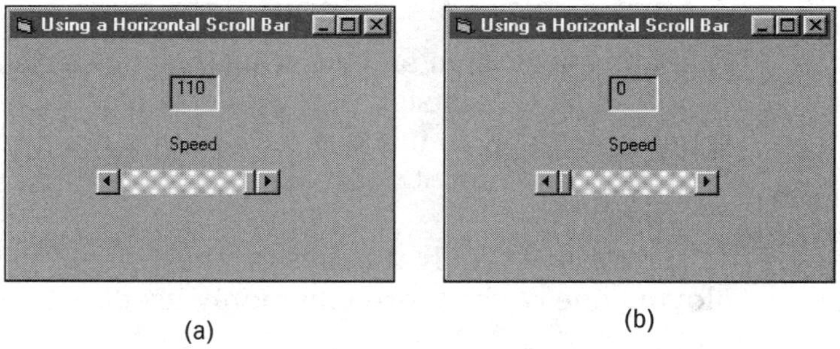

Figure 4-11
(a) Thumb Slide at Maximum Value; (b) Thumb Slide at Minimum Value

(a)

(b)

its furthest leftmost position, as shown in Figure 4-11b. For the Scroll bar shown in these figures the **Max** and **Min** values were set at Design Time to 110 and 0, respectively.

The **Value** property determines the thumb slide's initial position, and can be set to any integer value between **Min** and **Max**. When the **Value** setting is the same as the **Min** setting, the thumb slide is initially located at its left-most position, while if the **Value** setting is the same as the **Max** setting, the thumb slide will initially be at its rightmost position.[1] For the Scroll bar pre-viously shown in Figure 4-10 the **Value** setting is 55; since this is halfway be-tween the **Max** and **Min** values, the initial thumb slide position is in the middle of its scrollable area.

The **Small** change value determines the change in value whenever the Scroll bar's arrows are clicked or the thumb slide is moved. The **Large** change value determines how much the value is changed by clicking within the slide area on either side of the thumb slide.

For monitoring a Scroll bar's movement, either by clicking the arrows, moving the thumb slide, or clicking within the scroll area, the following two events are used:

Event	Description
Change	Occurs after the scroll arrows have been clicked and after the thumb slide has been moved to its final new position.
Scroll	Occurs while the thumb slide is being moved.

For the Scroll bar shown in Figure 4-11a and 4-11b, which is named hsbSpeed, Event Procedures 4-3 and 4-4 provide the code used to display the values shown in the associated Picture box, which is named picSpeed. The first event code causes the Picture box display to change as the thumb slide is being moved, while the second event code ensures the display also changes when the arrows are used.

Event Procedure 4-3

```
Private Sub hsbSpeed_Scroll()
  picSpeed.Cls
  picSpeed.Print hsbSpeed.Value
End Sub
```

Event Procedure 4-4

```
Private Sub hsbSpeed_Change()
  picSpeed.Cls
  picSpeed.Print hsbSpeed.Value
End Sub
```

Exercises  **4.1**

1. Write assignment statements that store the returned value from an **InputBox** dialog in a variable named test for the following Input dialog specifications:

   a. prompt = Enter a grade
   title = Input dialog
   default = 0

---

[1]The value of **Min** can be larger than the value of **Max**. In this case the Scroll bar will cause values to change from larger to smaller values.

b. prompt = Enter a temperature
title = Data Analysis
default = 98.6
c. prompt = Enter an interest rate
title = Yield Analysis
default = 0
d. prompt = Enter a name
title = Mail List Application
no default value
e. prompt = Enter a price
title = Pricing Application
default = 12.50

 2 Determine what value is placed in the variable num1 in Program 4-1's event procedure, if the Cancel button is clicked on the input dialog box.

3 **a.** Write, by hand, a Visual Basic event procedure named cmdTax_Click that can be used to display the following prompt in an Input dialog box:

Enter the amount of the bill:

After accepting a value for the amount of the bill, your procedure should calculate the sales tax, assuming a tax rate of 6 percent. The display of the sales tax, as a dollar amount, should appear in a Picture box named picShow when a Command button is clicked. A second Command button should be provided to terminate the application.

b. Include the event procedure written for Exercise 3a in a working program. For testing purposes, verify your program using an initial amount of $36.00. After manually checking that the result produced by your program is correct, use your program to complete the following table:

Amount (dollars)	Sales Tax (dollars)
36.00	
40.00	
52.60	
87.95	
125.00	
182.93	

4 **a.** Write a Visual Basic program that can be used to convert Celsius temperatures to their equivalent Fahrenheit values. Use a Label to display the following prompt:

Enter the temperature in degrees Celsius:

After accepting a value entered from the keyboard into a Text box, the program should convert the entered temperature to degrees Fahrenheit, using the equation *Fahrenheit = (9.0 / 5.0) * Celsius + 32.0*. The program should then display the temperature in degrees Fahrenheit, in a clearly labeled Picture box named picShow. A Command button should be provided to terminate the application.

b. Verify your program, by first calculating the Fahrenheit equivalent of the following test data by hand, and then using your program to see if it produces the correct results.

```
Test data set 1: 0 degrees Celsius
Test data set 2: 50 degrees Celsius
Test data set 3: 100 degrees Celsius
```

c. When you are sure your procedure is working correctly, use it to complete the following table:

Celsius	Fahrenheit
45	
50	
55	
60	
65	
70	

5 Write and execute a Visual Basic program that displays the following prompts, using two Label controls:

```
Enter the length of the office:
Enter the width of the office:
```

Have your program accept the user input in two Text boxes. When a Command button is clicked your program should calculate the area of the office and display the area in a Picture box. This display should be cleared whenever the input Text boxes receive the focus. A second Command button should be provided to terminate the application. Verify your procedure using the following test data:

```
Test data set 1: length = 12.5, width = 10
Test data set 2: length = 12.4, width = 0
Test data set 3: length = 0, width = 10
```

6 a. Write and execute a Visual Basic program that displays the following prompts and uses two Text boxes to receive the input data.

```
Enter the miles driven:
Enter the gallons of gas used:
```

The program should calculate and display the miles per gallon in a Picture box when a Command button is clicked. Use the equation *miles per gallon* = *miles / gallons used*. The display should be cleared whenever one of the Text boxes gets the focus. A second Command button should be provided to terminate the application. Verify your procedure using the following test data:

```
Test data set 1: Miles = 276, Gallons used = 10.
Test data set 2: Miles = 200, Gallons used = 15.5.
```

b. When you have completed your verification, use your procedure to complete the following table:

Miles Driven	Gallons Used	MPG
250	16.00	
275	18.00	
312	19.54	
296	17.39	

    c. For the procedure written for Exercise 6a, determine how many verification runs are required to ensure the procedure is working correctly, and give a reason supporting your answer.

7 Write a Visual Basic Program that displays the following prompts:

```
Enter the length of the swimming pool:
Enter the width of the swimming pool:
Enter the average depth of the swimming pool:
```

Have your program accept the user input in three Text boxes. When a Command button is clicked your program should calculate the volume of the swimming pool and display the volume in a Picture box. This display should be cleared whenever the input Text boxes receive the focus. A second Command button should be provided to terminate the application. In calculating the volume use the equation

$$volume = length * width * average\ depth$$

8 a. Write and execute a Visual Basic program that provides three Text boxes for the input of three user input numbers. There should be a single Label prompt that tells the user to enter three numbers in the boxes. When the user clicks a Command button the program should calculate the average of the entered numbers and then display the average in a clearly labeled Picture box. The displayed value should be cleared whenever one of the Text boxes receives the focus. A second Command button should be provided to terminate the application. Verify your procedure using the following test data:

```
Test data set 1: 100, 100, 100
Test data set 2: 100, 50, 0
```

When you have completed your verification, use your program to complete the following table:

Numbers	Average
92, 98, 79, 85	
86, 84, 75, 86	
63, 85, 74, 82	

9 Program 3-5's event procedure prompts the user to input two numbers, where the first value entered is stored in num1 and the second value is stored in num2. Using this procedure as a starting point, rewrite the procedure so that it swaps the values stored in the two variables.

10 Write a Visual Basic program that prompts the user to type in an integer number. Have your procedure accept the number as an integer and immediately display the integer. Run your procedure three times. The first time you run the procedure enter a valid integer number, the second time enter a floating point number, and the third time enter the string Help. Using the output display, see what numbers your procedure actually accepted from the data you entered.

11 Repeat Exercise 10, but have your procedure declare the variable used to store the number as a single-precision floating point variable. Run the procedure four times. The first time enter an integer, the second time enter a decimal number with less than fourteen decimal places, the third time enter a number having more than fourteen decimal places, and the fourth time enter the string Oops. Using the output display, keep track of what number your procedure actually accepted from the data you typed in. What happened, if anything, and why?

12 a. Why do you think that most successful applications procedures contain extensive data input validity checks? (**Hint**: Review Exercises 10 and 11.)

b. What do you think is the difference between a data type check and a data reasonableness check?

c. Assume that a procedure asks the user to enter the speed and acceleration of a car. What are some checks that could be made on the data entered?

4.2 Formatted Output

Although it is essential that an application display correct results, it is also important that it present these results attractively. Most applications are judged, in fact, on the ease of data entry and the style and presentation of their output. For example, displaying a monetary result as 1.897256 is not in keeping with accepted report conventions. The display should be either $1.90 or $1.89, depending on whether rounding or truncation is used.

The format of displayed numeric values can be controlled by the intrinsic **Format** function. The general syntax of this function is

```
Format(expression, format string)
```

The first argument supplied to the **Format** function is an expression to be formatted and the second argument is the desired format. The **Format** function formats the expression's value according to the given format string and returns the formatted expression as a string value. For numeric expressions the format string can be either one of the Visual Basic predefined format strings listed in Table 4-3,[1] or a user-defined format string. For example, the statement

```
Print Format(84675.03567, "Currency")
```

produces the printout

```
$84,675.04
```

---

[1] These formats can be found under Formats, Named, or Named Numeric Formats, using Visual Basic's Help facility.

Further examples illustrating the effect of the predefined formats listed in Table 4-3 are

Example	Returned String
`Format(1234.567, "Currency")`	$1,234.57
`Format(1234.567, "Fixed")`	1234.57
`Format(1234.567, "General Number")`	1234.567
`Format(0.1234567, "Percent")`	12.35%
`Format(1234.567, "Scientific")`	1.23E+03
`Format(1234.567, "Standard")`	1,234.57
`Format(1234.567, "Yes/No")`	Yes
`Format(1234.567, "True/False")`	True

Table 4-3   Predefined Numeric Format Strings

String	Description
Currency	Displays a number with a leading dollar sign, thousands separator, if required, and two digits (rounded) to the right of the decimal point.
Fixed	Displays a number with at least one digit to the left of the decimal point and two digits (rounded) to the right of the decimal point.
General Number	Displays the number as is.
Percent	Displays the number multiplied by 100, with at least one digit to the left of the decimal point and two digits to the right (rounded) of the decimal point and a percent sign.
Scientific	Uses standard scientific notation.
Standard	Same as Fixed, except uses thousands separator as required by the magnitude of the number.
Yes/No	Displays No if the number is 0; otherwise displays Yes.
True/False	Displays False if the number is 0; otherwise displays True.

User-defined formats are useful for creating specialized output. Table 4-4 lists the acceptable symbols that can be included in a user-defined format string. For example, the format string in the statement

```
Print Format(12345.678,"#,###.##")
```

Table 4-4   Symbols for User-Defined Format Strings

Symbol	Description
@	right-justified digit placeholder
#	left-justified digit placeholder
0	left-justified digit placeholder and automatic fill character
.	decimal placeholder
,	thousands separator

requires that the formatted number use a comma as a thousands separator and return two digits (rounded) to the right of the decimal place. In this case, the returned value is 12,345.68. Notice, however, that the statement

```
Print Format(345.60, "#,###.##")
```

produces the output 345.6. That is, if the # placeholder is used, and the number being formatted does not require all the places provided by the #s in the format string, on either side of the decimal point, the extra #s are ignored. If the integer part of the number exceeds the number of #s to the left of the decimal point, however, additional space is allocated to accommodate the number.

These same rules apply to the 0 placeholder, with one important difference: if the number does not fill the space designated by the 0s, a 0 will fill each unused space. For example,

```
Print Format(12345.678,"0,000.00")
```

produces the output

```
12,234.68
```

but the statement

```
Print Format(345.6, "0,000.00")
```

produces the output

```
0,345.60
```

Since leading zeros are typically not required for numeric output, the # format symbol is frequently used to specify the integer part of a number, while the 0 format symbol is used to force a fixed number of decimal digits for the fractional part. For example, the statement

```
Print Format(345.6, "#,###.00")
```

produces the output

```
345.60
```

In addition to numeric placeholders, other symbols can be placed directly within a user specified format and are included in the string returned by the **Format** function. For example, the statement

```
mystr = Format(18005551212,"#(###)###-####")
```

assigns the string value 1(800)555-1212 to the string variable named mystr.

Using a bar symbol (|) to clearly mark the beginning and end of the returned string, Table 4-5 on page 196 illustrates the effect of various user formats. Notice in Table 4-5 that the **Format** function ignores the specified integer format when the integer specification is too small, and always allocates enough space for the integer part of the number. The fractional part of a number is only displayed with the number of specified digits if the 0 placeholder is used. In this case, if the fractional part contains fewer digits than specified, the number is padded with trailing zeros. For both 0 and # placeholders, if the fractional part contains more digits than specified in the format, the number is rounded to the indicated number of decimal places.

Date and Time Formatting

In addition to formatting numbers, the **Format** function is also used to format date and time information. The current date and time are obtained using the Visual Basic **Now** function, which returns the date and time together as

Table 4-5 Examples of Numeric Formats

Format	Returned Number	String Value	Comments
"|##|"	3	|3|	Only one # position is used.
"|##|"	43	|43|	Both # positions are used.
"|##|"	143	|143|	# place holders ignored.
"|00|"	3	|03|	Leading 0 position is used.
"|00|"	43	|43|	Both 0 positions are used.
"|00|"	143	|143|	0 place holders ignored.
"|##.00|"	2.466	|2.47|	Fractional part rounded.
"|##.##|"	2.466	|2.47|	Fractional part rounded.
"|00.00|"	123.4	|123.40|	Leading place holders ignored. Fractional part forced to 2 decimal places.
"|00.##|"	123.4	|123.4|	Leading place holders ignored. Fractional part not forced to 2 decimal places.

a long integer. To format the date information contained within this long integer, the symbols d, m, and y are used as a format string within the **Format** function. Table 4-6 lists the effect of each of these symbols individually when applied to a date-time value.

Table 4-6 Date Formatting Symbols

Format String	Returned String Value	Example
"d"	Day as a one or two digit number	8
"dd"	Day as a two digit number	08
"ddd"	First three letters of the day	Tue
"dddd"	Complete day designation	Tuesday
"ddddd"	Date as dd/mm/yy	01/25/99
"dddddd"	Date as day, month day-number, year	Saturday, November 28, 1998
"m"	Month as a one or two digit number	3
"mm"	Month as a two digit number	03
"mmm"	First three letters of the month	Dec
"mmmm"	Complete month designation	December
"mmmmm"	Complete month and day date	December 25
"yy"	Year as a two digit number	02
"yyyy"	Year as a four digit number	2002

Following are example results that can be produced using various combinations of the formatting strings listed in Table 4-6.

Format	Result
Format(Now, "m/d/y")	5/18/99
Format(Now, "mm/dd/yy")	05/18/99
Format(Now, "ddddd")	5/18/99
Format(Now, "dddd, mmmm dd, yyyy"	Friday, December 25, 1999
Format(Now, "dddddd")	Friday, December 25, 1999
Format(Now, "d-mmm")	27-Nov
Format(Now,"mmmm-yyyy")	October-2000

To format the time portion of the date and time returned by **Now** you can use the symbols h, m, s, each delimited with a colon(:), an optional AM/PM symbol, or the format string "ttttt". Table 4-7 lists the effect of each of these formatting symbols individually when applied to a date-time value.

Table 4-7 Time Formatting Symbols

Format String	Returned String Value	Example
"h"	hour as a one or two digit number	5
"hh"	hour as a two digit number	05
"m"	minute as a one digit number	9
"mm"	minute as a two digit number	09
"s"	second as a one digit number	3
"ss"	second as a two digit number	03
"ttttt"	time as h:m:s AM/PM	6:19:44 PM

Following are example results that can be produced using various combinations of the formatting strings listed in Tables 4-6 and 4-7.

Format	Result
Format(Now, "hh:mm")	19:20
Format(Now, "hh:mm AM/PM")	07:20 PM
Format(Now, "h:mm:ss a/p")	8:22:05 a
Format(Now, "d-mmmm h:mm A/P")	5-February 7:15 A

In reviewing these examples notice that the date and time formats can be combined within the same format string. Also notice that the AM and PM within the AM/PM designation can be replaced by any combination of letters, such as a/p, A/P, am/pm, etc. Unless one of these designations is used, however, the displayed time will be based on a 24-hour clock. The "ddddd" and "ttttt" format strings return the date and time in displays appropriate to the settings supplied in the Windows Control Panel Regional Settings dialog

Table 4-8 International Formatting Examples

Format	Country	Result
Format(Now, "ddddd ttttt")	Canada	99-10-15 20:15:44
Format(Now, "ddddd ttttt")	Sweden	1999-10-15 20.15.44
Format(Now, "ddddd ttttt")	United Kingdom	15/10/99 20:15:44
Format(Now, "ddddd ttttt")	United States	10/15/99 8:15:44 PM

box. Table 4-8 on page 197 illustrates sample results using these two format strings for various regional settings.

Cursor Control Options

The real purpose of the semicolon in a **Print** statement is to control the cursor. When a semicolon is placed after an expression in a **Print** statement it causes the cursor to stop immediately after the last displayed character. For example, the sequence of statements

```
Print "Hello";
Print "There"
```

produces the output

```
HelloThere
```

This output occurs because the semicolon in the first statement forces the cursor to remain in position after displaying Hello. As we have seen, a semicolon performs in an identical manner when separating items in a single **Print** statement. For example, the same output is produced by the statement

```
Print "Hello"; "There"
```

Here, the **Print** statement first displays the string Hello, the semicolon causes the cursor to remain in the position it finds itself after the display, and then the string There is displayed. Within a single **Print** statement, a space performs the same function as the semicolon.

In addition to the simple cursor control provided by the semicolon, Visual Basic provides a number of other cursor control options. To see how these controls work, however, you first need to understand how characters are positioned within a line of text.

Each displayed line within an object, such as a Picture box or window, consists of a fixed number of columns starting with column 1. For display purposes, Visual Basic defines a print zone as 14 consecutive columns, with the first print zone beginning in column 1. Thus, as shown in Figure 4-12, print zone 1 occupies columns 1 through 14, print zone 2 occupies columns 15 through 28, and so on.

If a comma is encountered in a **Print** statement, the cursor automatically is moved to the first position in the next print zone. For example, assuming that the **Font** property is set to Courier, the statements

```
Print "12345678901234567890"
Print "Hello", "There"
```

produce the display

```
12345678901234567890
Hello          There
```

This display is produced because the comma in the second **Print** statement causes the cursor to move to the next print zone, which starts in column 15.

Print zones permit aligning data in fixed columns, assuming a fixed-size (or monospace) font, such as Courier, is used. In a Courier font each

Figure 4-12
Print Zones

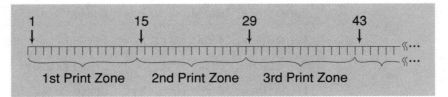

character moves the cursor by the same fixed amount, so that w and i, for example, both occupy the same amount of space on the display. This is not true for proportional fonts, such as Times Roman, where w occupies more space than i. Thus, if you are trying to align data on output, make sure to set the **Font** property to a fixed font, such as Courier. For proportional fonts, a print zone is defined as the width of 14 average character widths.

The Tab and Spc Functions

The tab function **Tab(n)** moves the cursor to the specified column number. For example, the statements

```
Print "12345678901234567890"
Print "Hello"; Tab(10); "There"
```

produce the display

```
12345678901234567890
Hello     There
```

Here the **Tab** function is used to tab over to column number 10. If the print position is beyond the column number in the **Tab** function call, the **Tab** function is ignored. A **Tab** by itself produces the same effect as a comma. Thus, the statement

```
Print "Hello"; Tab; "There"
```

produces the same output as the statement

```
Print "Hello", "There"
```

The space function, **Spc(n)**, moves the cursor over n spaces from its current position. As such, it effectively inserts n spaces into the output display. For example, the statements

```
Print "12345678901234567890"
Print "Hello"; Spc(5); "There"
```

produce the display

```
12345678901234567890
Hello     There
```

Centering Text

Every graphical object drawn on a form uses the coordinate system shown in Figure 4-13. The units of measurement for both the x and y axis are in *twips*, where there are 1,440 twips in an inch and 567 twips in a centimeter.

By default, the left and upper x and y positions of each object are defined as the coordinates (0,0) and printing always begins at these coordinates. To change the current starting coordinates, you can use the **CurrentX** and **CurrentY** properties. For example, the statements

```
CurrentX = 50
CurrentY = 100
```

set the form's current x and y coordinates to 50 and 100 twips, while the statements

```
picBox1.CurrentX = 30
picBox1.CurrentY = 40
```

Figure 4-13
A Form's Coordinate System

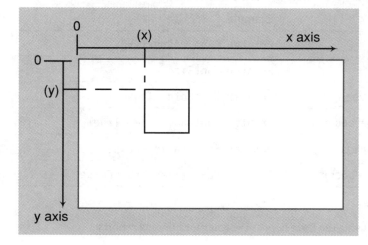

set the current x and y coordinates of the picBox1 object to 30 and 40 twips, respectively. Setting the **CurrentX** and **CurrentY** properties permits text to be easily centered within an object. For example, the statements

```
CurrentX = (Width - TextWidth("Hello World")) / 2
CurrentY = (Height - TextHeight("Hello World")) /2
Print "Hello World"
```

center the text Hello World within a form. The **TextWidth** and **TextHeight** methods return a string's width and height, respectively, taking into account the object's font size and style. In a similar manner, you can set the current print position to the beginning of line number n, using the statement syntax

```
CurrentX = 0
CurrentY = object-name.TextHeight(string) * (n - 1)
```

For example, the statements

```
CurrentX = 0
CurrentY = TextHeight("Hello World") * 9
```

set the cursor to the beginning of line 10 in the current form.

Printer Output

Output can be sent to the printer in the same manner as output displayed on a screen object. This is because Visual Basic defines the printer as an object named **Printer**. Thus, the statement

```
Printer.Print "Hello World"
```

causes the text Hello World to be output on the printer. To force output onto a new page, the page-eject command

```
Printer.Newpage
```

can be used. Similarly, to ensure that all data is sent to the printer and not stored in an internal buffer area, the statement

```
Printer.EndDoc
```

should be issued as the last command to the printer after all output has been sent.

Table 4-9 lists the most commonly used statements for controlling the display of printed text from within a Visual Basic event procedure.[2]

Table 4-9   Statements for Controlling Printed Text Display

Syntax	Example
Printer.Font = font	Printer.Font = "Courier"
Printer.FontSize = n	Printer.FontSize = 14
Printer.FontBold = boolean	Printer.FontBold = True
Printer.FontUnderline = boolean	Printer.FontUnderline = True
Printer.FontItalic = boolean	Printer.FontItalic = False
Printer.FontStrikethru = boolean	Printer.FontStrikethru = False

---

[2]Appendix H documents using the Data Report Designer for creating reports.

Exercises 4.2

1 Determine and write out the display produced by the following statements:

```
Format(155.986, "Currency")
Format(155.986, "Fixed")
Format(155.986, "General Number")
Format(0.155986, "Percent")
Format(155.986, "Scientific")
Format(155.986, "Standard")
Format(155.986, "Yes/No")
Format(155.986, "True/False")
```

2 Determine and write out the display produced by the following statements:

a. `Format(5, "##")`
b. `Format(5, "####")`
c. `Format(56829, "####")`
d. `Format(5.26, "###.##")`
e. `Format(5.267, "###.##")`
f. `Format(53.264, "###.##")`
g. `Format(534.264, "###.##")`
h. `Format(534., "###.##")`

3 Determine the errors in each of the following statements:

a. `Format("##", 5)`
b. `Format(56829, #####)`
c. `Format("526.768", "###")`
d. `Format("526.78", """.""")`

4 Write out the display produced by the following statements:

a. `Format(126.27, "###.##")`
    `Format(82.3, "###.##")`
    `Format(1.756, "###.##")`

b. `Format(26.27, "###.##")`
    `Format(682.3, "###.##")`
    `Format(1.968, "###.##")`
    `Print "------"`
    `Format(26.27 + 682.3 + 1.968", "###.##")`

c. `Format(26.27, "Currency")`
    `Format(682.3, "Currency")`
    `Format(1.968, "Currency")`
    `Print "------"`
    `Format(26.27 + 682.3 + 1.968, "Currency")`

d. `Format(34.164, "###.##")`
    `Format(10.003, "###.##")`
    `Print "------"`
    `Format(34.164 + 10.003, "###.##")`

4.3 Named Constants

Literal data is any data within a procedure that explicitly identifies itself. For example, the constants 2 and 3.1416 in the assignment statement

```
circumference = 2 * 3.1416 * radius
```

are also called literals because they are literally included directly in the statement. Additional examples of literals are contained in the following Visual Basic assignment statements. See if you can identify them.

```
perimeter = 2 * length * width
        y = (5 * p) / 7.2
salestax = 0.05 * purchase
```

The literals are the numbers 2, 5, and 7.2, and 0.05 in the first, second, and third statements, respectively.

Quite frequently, literal data used within a procedure have a more general meaning that is recognized outside the context of the procedure. Examples of these types of constants include the number 3.1416, which is the value of π accurate to four decimal places, 32.2 ft/sec^2, which is the gravitational constant, and the number 2.71828, which is Euler's number accurate to five decimal places.

The meaning of certain other constants appearing in a procedure are defined strictly within the context of the application being programmed. For example, in a procedure to determine bank interest charges, the value of the interest rate takes on a special meaning. Similarly, in determining the weight of various sized objects, the density of the material being used takes on a special significance. Constants such as these are sometimes referred to as both *manifest constants* and *magic numbers*. By themselves the constants are quite ordinary, but in the context of a particular application they have a special ("manifest" or "magical") meaning. Frequently, the same manifest constant appears repeatedly within the same procedure. This recurrence of the same constant throughout a procedure is a potential source of error, should the constant have to be changed. For example, if either the interest rate changes, or a new material is employed with a different density, the programmer has the cumbersome task of changing the value of the magic number everywhere it appears in the procedure. Multiple changes, however, are subject to error: if just one value is overlooked and not changed or if the same value used in different contexts is changed when only one of the values should have been, the result obtained when the procedure is run will be incorrect.

To avoid the problems of having such constants spread throughout a procedure, and to clearly permit identification of more universal constants, such as π, Visual Basic allows the programmer to give these constants their own symbolic names. Then, instead of using the constant throughout the procedure, the symbolic name is used instead. If the number ever has to be changed, the change need only be made once, at the point where the symbolic name is equated to the actual constant value. Equating numbers to symbolic names is accomplished using the **Const** statement. The syntax for this statement within a form's procedure is

```
Const name As data-type = expression
```

For example, the number 3.1416 can be equated to the symbolic name PI using the **Const** statement

```
Const PI As Single = 3.1416
```

Constants used in this fashion are called both *named constants* and *symbolic constants*, and we shall use both terms interchangeably. The constant's name must be selected using the same rules as those for choosing a variable's name. Once a constant has been named, the name can be used in any Visual Basic statement in place of the number itself. For example, the assignment statement

```
circumference = 2 * PI * radius
```

makes use of the symbolic constant PI. This statement must, of course, appear after the declaration of the named constant is made. Within a form module, all **Const** statements must be placed

- In the **(Declaration)** section of the **(General)** object, either before or after the **Option Explicit** statement; or
- Anywhere within a procedure, though for clarity they are usually placed immediately after the procedure's header line.

In the first case, the constant can be used by all procedures connected to the form and its objects. In the second case, the constant can only be used within the procedure from its point of declaration to the end of the procedure. In this case, the constant is said to be local to the procedure declaring it.

Although we have typed the named constant PI in uppercase letters, lowercase letters could have been used. It is common in Visual Basic, however, to use uppercase letters for symbolic constants, at least for the initial letter of the name. Then, whenever a programmer sees an initial uppercase letter in a procedure, he or she will know the name is a symbolic constant defined in a **Const** statement, not a variable name declared in a declaration statement.

Program 4-3 illustrates the use of the **Const** statement declared within an event procedure. The interface for this project is shown in Figure 4-14. As illustrated, the graphical user interface consists of two Command buttons and a Picture box, whose background color has been set to white.

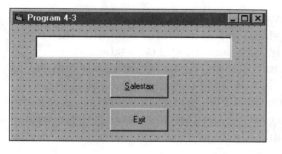

Figure 4-14
Program 4-3's Interface

For this application the only procedures will be for the Command button **Click** events. The required procedures are listed in Program 4-3's Event Code.

Program 4-3's Event Code

```
Private Sub cmdTax_Click()
  Const TAXRATE As Single = 0.05
  Dim amount As Single, taxes As Single, total As Single

  picShow.Cls
  amount = InputBox("Enter the amount purchased", "Input Box", "0")
  taxes = TAXRATE * amount
  total = amount + taxes
  picShow.Print "The sales tax is "; Format(taxes, "Currency")
  picShow.Print "The total bill is "; Format(total, "Currency")
End Sub
```

continued

```
Private Sub cmdExit_Click()
    Beep
    End
End Sub
```

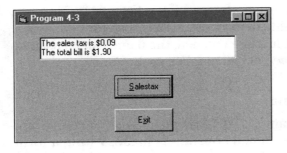

Figure 4-15

A Sample Output Displayed by Program 4-3

The output displayed in the Picture box, when the Command button is clicked and an input value of 1.81 is entered in the InputBox dialog, is shown Figure 4-15.

The advantage of using a symbolic constant such as PI is that it clearly identifies the value 3.1416 in terms recognizable to most people. The advantage of using the symbolic constant TAXRATE in Program 4-3 is that it permits a programmer to change the value of the sales tax, when required, without having to search through the procedure to see where it's used. A natural question arises, however, as to the actual difference between symbolic constants and variables.

The value of a variable can be altered anywhere within a program. By its nature, a symbolic constant is a constant value that must not be altered after it is defined. Naming a constant, rather than assigning its value to a variable, ensures that the value in the constant cannot be subsequently altered. Whenever a symbolic constant appears in an instruction, it has the same effect as the constant it represents. Thus, TAXRATE in Program 4-3 is simply another way of representing the number 0.05. Since TAXRATE and the number 0.05 are equivalent, the value of TAXRATE may not be subsequently changed within the program. Once TAXRATE has been defined as a constant, an assignment statement such as

```
TAXRATE = 0.06
```

is meaningless and will result in an error message, because TAXRATE is not a variable. Since TAXRATE is only a stand-in for the value 0.05, this last statement is equivalent to writing the invalid statement 0.05 = 0.06.

In addition to using the **Const** statement to name constants, as in Program 4-3, this statement can also be used to equate the value of a constant expression to a symbolic name. A constant expression is an expression consisting of operators and constants only (no variables or intrinsic functions are allowed). For example, the statement

```
Const CONVERT As Single = 3.1416/180
```

Table 4-10	The Properties Table for Program 4-3	
Object	**Property**	**Setting**
Form	Name	frmMain
	Caption	Program 4-3
Picture box	Name	picShow
	Backcolor	white window background (system tab)
	TabStop	False
Command button	Name	cmdTax
	Caption	&Salestax
Command button	Name	cmdExit
	Caption	E&xit

equates the value of the constant expression 3.1416/180 to the symbolic name CONVERT. The symbolic name, as always, can be used in any statement following its definition. For example, since the expression 3.1416/180 is required for converting degrees to radians, the symbolic name selected for this conversion factor can be conveniently used whenever such a conversion is required.

A previously defined, symbolic constant can also be used in a subsequent **Const** statement. For example, the following sequence of statements is valid:

```
Const PI As Single = 3.1416
Const CONVERT As Single = PI/180
```

Since the constant 3.1416 has been equated to the symbolic name PI, it can be used legitimately in any subsequent definition, even within another **Const** statement.

An interesting modification to the **Const** statement is that the **As** *data-type* clause may be omitted. When the data type is not explicitly declared, Visual Basic will select the data type that is most appropriate for the value. For example, if you use the statement

```
Const PI = 3.14159265358979
```

which has 14 digits of precision after the decimal point, Visual Basic will automatically make this a **Double** value.

Finally, you can place more than one constant declaration on a line, as long as each constant assignment is separated by a comma. For example, the following **Const** statement is valid:

```
Const PI = 3.1415, CONVERT = 360/PI
```

Exercises 4.3

1. Rewrite the following event procedure using a **Const** statement for the constant 3.1416.

```
Private Sub Form_Click()
  Dim radius As Single, area As Single
  Dim circumference as Single
  radius = InputBox("Enter a radius:", "Input Dialog", "0")
  circumference = 2 * 3.1416 * radius
  area = 3.1416 * radius ^ 2
  Print "The circumference of the circle is "; circumference
  Print "The area of the circle is "; area
End Sub
```

2. Rewrite the following event procedure so that the variable prime is changed to a symbolic constant.

```
Private Sub Form_Click()
  Dim prime As Single
  Dim amount As Single, interest As Single
  prime = 0.08      ' prime interest rate
  amount = InputBox("Enter the amount"; "Input Dialog", "0")
  interest = prime * amount
  Print "The interest earned is"; interest; " dollars"
End Sub
```

> **3** Rewrite the following procedure to use the symbolic constant
> FACTOR in place of the expression (5/9) used in the procedure.
>
> ```
> Private Sub Form_Click()
>   Dim fahren As Single, celsius As Single
>   fahren = InputBox("Enter a temperature in degrees Fahrenheit",,"0")
>   celsius = (5/9) * (fahren - 32)
>   Print "The equivalent Celsius temperature is "; celsius
> End Sub
> ```

4.4 ► Focus on Program Design and Implementation:

Formatting and Printer Output

Using this chapter's information on formatting and printer output, we can now address two problems associated with the Walk In form developed in the previous Focus section.[3] Figure 4-16 illustrates a sample, filled-in, order entry form for which the Calculate Order Command button was pressed. As shown, the calculated dollar amounts are not formatted in conventional currency notation. Also, at this stage in its development, the form's Print button has no associated code. Both of these problems are corrected in this Focus section.

All that is required to modify the Picture boxes' displayed dollar values is to use the **Format** function. When displaying the values in the variables sngtotal, sngtaxes, and sngfinal. This means replacing these variable names with the expressions Format(sngtotal, "Currency"), Format(sngtaxes, "Currency"), and Format(sngfinal, "Currency") in each Print statement. Making these replacements in the Calculate Order Command button's **Click** event procedure and using the **Val** and **CCur** conversion functions to convert all Text box data into numerical values, provides the event code shown at the top of the next page.

Figure 4-16
A Filled in Walk In Order Form

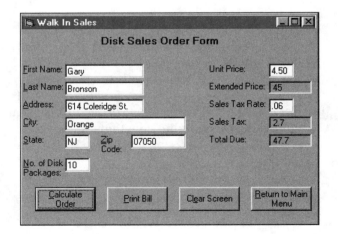

---

[3]The Rotech application, as it exists at the start of this Focus section can be found as the rotech3b.vbp project in the rotech3b folder on the Student Disk.

```
Private Sub cmdCalculate_Click()
    Dim sngtotal As Single, sngtaxes As Single, sngfinal As Single

    'Clear out the picture boxes
    picTotal.Cls
    picTax.Cls
    picFinal.Cls

    'Calculate and display new values
    sngtotal = Val(txtQuantity) * CCur(txtPrice)
    sngtaxes = Val(txtTrate) * sngtotal
    sngfinal = sngtotal + sngtaxes
    picTotal.Print Format(sngtotal, "currency")
    picTax.Print Format(sngtaxes, "currency")
    picFinal.Print Format(sngfinal, "currency")
End Sub
```

Figure 4-17
Formatting the Calculated Dollar
Amounts

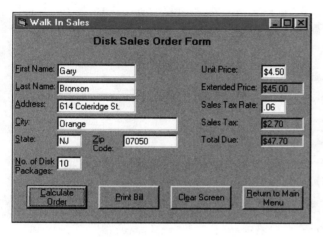

Figure 4-18
A Sample Printed Bill

Figure 4-17 illustrates a sample output produced using this modified **Click** event code. As shown, each calculated amount is now formatted in conventional currency notation. Notice that we have also modified the displayed unit price to show a dollar sign. Since a Text box displays string data, all that was required for this was to set the **Text** property, at Design Time, to the string $4.50. When this is done, however, the conversion of this string into an equivalent numerical value cannot be done using the **Val** function. The reason for this is that the **Val** function stops reading a string at the first non-numerical character, which includes both dollar signs and commas. Thus, the value of the expression Val($4.50) is 0, not 4.50. To avoid this problem we have used the **CCur** function instead (see Table 3-10 or Exercise 3), which correctly interprets dollar signs, commas, and periods.

All that remains now is to add code to the Print button's **Click** event, so that a bill is printed when this button is pressed. In practice, the bill would either be printed on a pre-printed form or a blank piece of paper would be used and the entire bill, including Rotech's name and address would be printed under control of the Print button's **Click** event. To illustrate the main points required for this event code, however, we will produce a simpler bill, a sample of which is shown in Figure 4-18.

As a practical matter, the Print button should also calculate the bill, because users would quickly tire of pressing the Calculate Order button each time before pressing the Print button.[4] Anticipating this, which makes the system easier to use, we will duplicate the Calculate Order button's calculate and display code and include it within the Print button's Click event code. Thus, if a customer only wants to know the final price, the user can press the

---

[4]Or, more likely, they would just press the Print button anyway, get a blank printed bill and complain that the system did not correctly compute the bill. At this point, after explaining the proper operation of the system, you would be asked to make the correction so that the Calculate button need not be pressed first. These are the types of situations that you should anticipate before the user brings them to your attention.

Calculate Order button. To produce a bill, however, the <u>P</u>rint button must be pressed. In pressing this latter button it will not matter whether the <u>C</u>alculate Order button was or was not pressed first. The required event code for the <u>P</u>rint button is:

```
Private Sub cmdPrint_Click()
    Dim sngtotal As Single, sngtaxes As Single, sngfinal As Single

    'Clear out the picture boxes
    picTotal.Cls
    picTax.Cls
    picFinal.Cls

    'Calculate and display new values
    sngtotal = Val(txtQuantity) * CCur(txtPrice)
    sngtaxes = Val(txtTrate) * sngtotal
    sngfinal = sngtotal + sngtaxes
    picTotal.Print Format(sngtotal, "currency")
    picTax.Print Format(sngtaxes, "currency")
    picFinal.Print Format(sngfinal, "currency")

    'Print a Bill
    Printer.Print
    Printer.Print
    Printer.Font = "Courier"
    Printer.FontSize = 12
    Printer.Print Spc(20); Format(Now, "mm/dd/yy")
    Printer.Print Spc(20); Format(Now, "h:m AM/PM")
    Printer.Print
    Printer.Print
    Printer.Print "Sold to: "; txtFname; " "; txtLname; ""
    Printer.Print Spc(9); txtAddr
    Printer.Print Spc(9); txtCity; " "; txtState; " "; txtZip
    Printer.Print
    Printer.Print
    Printer.Print "Quantity:"; Spc(1); txtQuantity
    Printer.Print "Unit Price:"; Spc(2); Format(txtPrice, "currency")
    Printer.Print "Total:"; Spc(6); Format(sngtotal, "currency")
    Printer.Print "Sales tax:"; Spc(3); Format(sngtaxes, "currency")
    Printer.Print "Amount Due:"; Spc(1); Format(sngfinal, "currency")
    Printer.EndDoc
End Sub
```

In reviewing this event code pay particular attention to the lines of code where the date and time are printed (because almost all printed forms require this type of information), where the printer font name is specified, where the font size is specified, and how spacing within a line is controlled by the **Spc** function. In practice, each of these items would be determined by your particular application, but the syntax required to set each item is always the same as that shown here. Also notice the next to last line, where the **EndDoc** method is used. This method, which can be replaced by a **NewPage** method, forces a page eject from the printer. If neither of these methods were used, the printer would not eject the printed page until either its buffer were full or the application was terminated.

Exercises **4.4**

(**Note:** The Rotech Systems project, at the stage of development begun in this section, can be found on the Student Disk in the `rotech3b` folder as project `rotech3b.vbp` . If you are developing the system yourself, following the procedures given in this section, we suggest that you first copy all of the files in the `rotech3b` folder into the `temp` folder, and then work out of this latter folder. When you have finished your changes you can compare your results to the files in the `rotech3b` folder.)

1. Either construct the Rotech system as it has been developed in this section or locate and load the project from the Student Disk in the rotech4 folder.

2. Modify the Rotech project so that pressing the <u>P</u>rint Packing Slip Command button on the Mail in form prints a packing slip on the printer. (Note: The Mail in form is contained within the current Rotech application stored on the Student Disk as project `rotech4.vbp` within the `rotech4` folder.

3. Using the Help facilities' Index tab, obtain information on the **CCur** conversion function used within both **Click** event procedures presented in this section.

4. Using the Help facilities' search tab, enter the string "Formatting Numbers, Dates, and Times" (include the double quotes) and search the MSDN's Technical articles to locate any information on these topics.

5. **CASE STUDY** For your selected project (see project specifications at the end of Section 1.5) complete the order entry form you developed in the previous chapter. Your order entry form should now be able to both calculate the total amount due on the entered order and print a bill for the order.

4.5 Knowing About: Version 6.0's Debugging Environment

Debugging refers to the process of finding errors, or "bugs," in program code and correcting them. Visual Basic provides a number of debugging tools that can help in this process by analyzing program execution and permitting a look inside application code as it is running. This is accomplished by setting *breakpoints* in your code, which stop a program when they are reached; running your code in *single-step mode,* which executes one instruction at a time; or setting *watch expressions,* which permit you to monitor the values of selected variables and expressions while a program is executing. To accomplish this, and other useful debugging tasks, Version 6.0 provides three distinct debugging windows, which are shown in Figure 4-19, and two dialog boxes. Each of these debugging elements is described in Table 4-11.

Figure 4-19
The Three Debug Windows

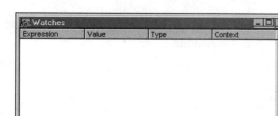

Table 4-11   The Debug Windows and Dialog Boxes

Name	Use
Immediate window	Displays information resulting from debugging statements in your code or from statements typed directly into this window. Useful for immediately determining the effect of a single-line statement (cannot accommodate multi-line statements). It is automatically opened in Break mode, but can also be used in Design mode. Code can be dragged, copied, and pasted between the Code and Immediate windows, but code cannot be saved in the Immediate window.
Watch window	Used in Break mode to display the values of all current watch expressions. This window will automatically appear when watch expressions are defined in a project and selected variables can be dragged into the Watch window from the Code window. Can be viewed in Design mode.
Locals window	Used in Break mode. This window automatically displays all of the declared variables in the current procedure and their values. The Locals window is automatically updated whenever there is a change from Run to Break mode or the Stack dialog box is accessed. Can be viewed in Design mode.
Quick Watch dialog	Only available in Break mode to display the current value of a single variable, property, or watch expression and the procedure in which it is currently being used.
Call Stack dialog	Only available in Break mode to list the procedure calls in an application that have started but are not yet completed.

Each of the three Debug windows can be activated in either Design or Break mode from within the View menu, as shown in Figure 4-20, while the dialog boxes can only be activated in Break mode. Additionally, the Debug windows and dialog boxes can be activated directly from the Debug toolbar, which is shown in Figure 4-21.

If the Debug toolbar is not visible, you can make it so using the Toolbars option from the View menu, as shown in Figure 4-22.

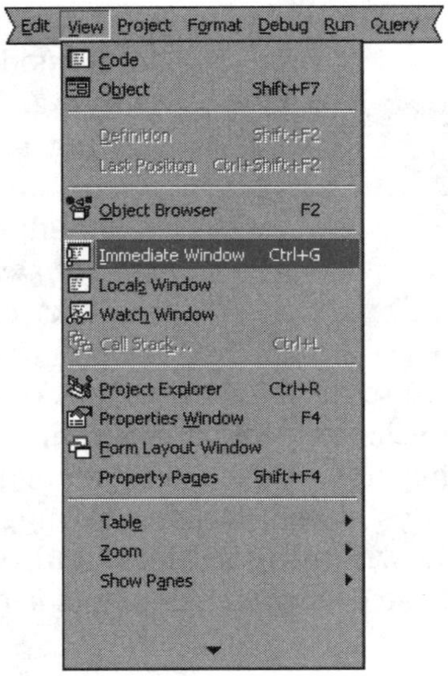

Figure 4-20

Activating the Debug Windows from the Menu Bar

Figure 4-21
The Debug Toolbar's Buttons

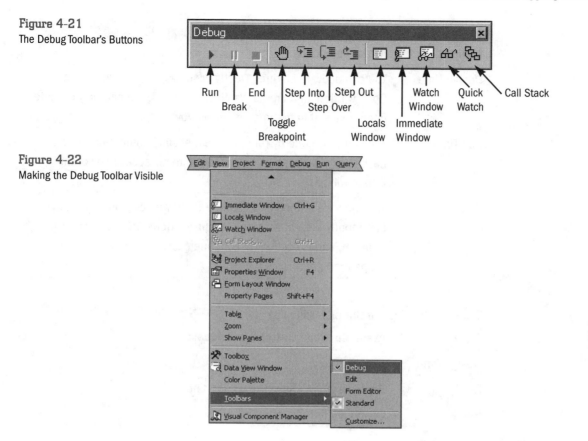

Figure 4-22
Making the Debug Toolbar Visible

The Watch and Locals windows are most effective when used in Break mode. In this mode, a program's execution is temporarily suspended and the various Debug windows are used to gain a "snapshot" view of the values of variables and expressions at the point in your code where execution has been temporarily suspended. Once in a Debug window, during Break mode, you can change the value of variables and properties to see how the changes affect the application.

Break mode can only be reached from Run Time mode. In Break mode program execution is suspended, which gives you an opportunity to both view and edit code. You can always determine the mode you are in by examining Visual Basic's title bar. Figure 4-23 shows how the title bar looks in each of the three modes: Design, Run, and Break.

The characteristics of each of Visual Basic's three operating modes, as they relate to Visual Basic's debugging facilities, are listed in Table 4-12.

Switching from one mode to another can be accomplished using Menu options, Function keys, or Toolbar buttons. For example, you already know how to switch from Design mode to Run mode by using either the Run menu option or pressing the F5 function key. Additionally, you can use one of the three Standard Toolbar buttons illustrated in Figure 4-24 to switch between modes. Table 4-13 lists the buttons that are active in each mode. Notice that when in Break mode, the Start button becomes a Continue button.

Figure 4-23
Identifying the Current Mode

Table 4-12   Debug Window Facilities by Mode

Mode	Available Facility
Design Time	You can activate all three Debug windows, set breakpoints in the Code window, and create Watch expressions. You can only execute code from within the Immediate window.
Run Time	You can view code by running in either single-step mode or by having set a breakpoint. You cannot directly access any of the Debug windows.
Break	You can view and edit code in the Code window. You can examine and modify data in all of the Debug windows. You can restart the program, end execution, or continue execution from the suspended point.

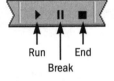

Figure 4-24
The Standard Toolbar's Run, Break, and End Buttons

Table 4-13   Toolbar Button Availability

Mode	Available Mode Buttons and Access Keys
Design TIme	Start ($\boxed{F5}$ key)
Run Time	Break ($\boxed{CTRL}$+$\boxed{BREAK}$ keys) and End
Break	Continue ($\boxed{F5}$ key) and End

With this as background, let's now write an application that uses the Immediate and Locals windows (in Section 7.8 we show how to use the Watch window). To do this, enter Event Procedure 4-5 in a new project.

Event Procedure 4-5

```
Private Sub Form_Click()
  Dim n As Single

  n = 5
  Cls
  Print n
  Debug.Print "Hello World!"
  Print
  Print n
End Sub
```

Once you have entered this event procedure, run the program but *do not* activate the form's **Click** event. Instead, press the Break toolbar button. At this point the Immediate window should appear (if it does not, activate it using the View menu options (see Figure 4-25). You can now use this window

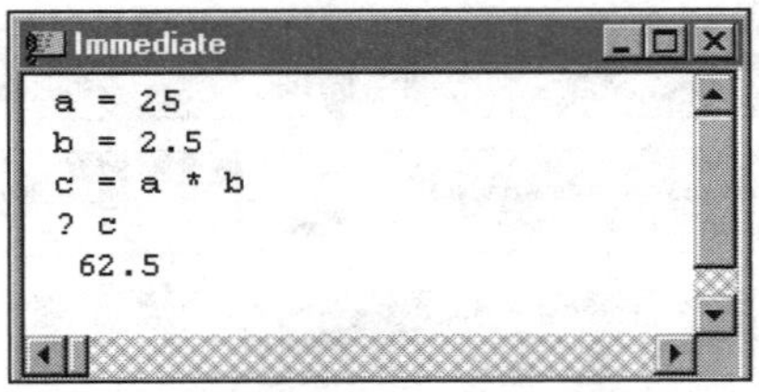

Figure 4-25
Using the Debug Immediate Window

```
Immediate
a = 25
b = 2.5
c = a * b
? c
 62.5
```

PROGRAMMERS NOTES

Activating Break Mode

You can only move to Break mode while a program is executing. To switch to Break mode from the Run Time mode, do one of the following:

1. Press the Break Toolbar button.
2. Start the program in single-step mode.
3. Press the (CTRL) and (BREAK) keys at the same time while the program is running.
4. Set a breakpoint in the program (see Section 7.8).

---

to examine the value of variables set in a program, change these values, or enter data to produce an immediate result. For example, type in the following lines in the Immediate window:[5]

```
a = 25
b = 2.5
c = a * b
? c
```

When you press the (ENTER) key, the Immediate window should appear as shown in Figure 4-25. Notice that the question mark, which is a shorthand way of asking, "What is the value of?" and is equivalent to the keyword **Print**, causes the value of c to be displayed.

Single-Step Mode

To illustrate how to use both the Locals and Immediate windows to view and change a variable's data, we will single step through Event Procedure 4-5. To begin this process make sure that the Code window illustrated in Figure 4-26 is showing on your design screen and then initiate single-step mode by using one of the following steps:

Figure 4-26

The Initial Code Window

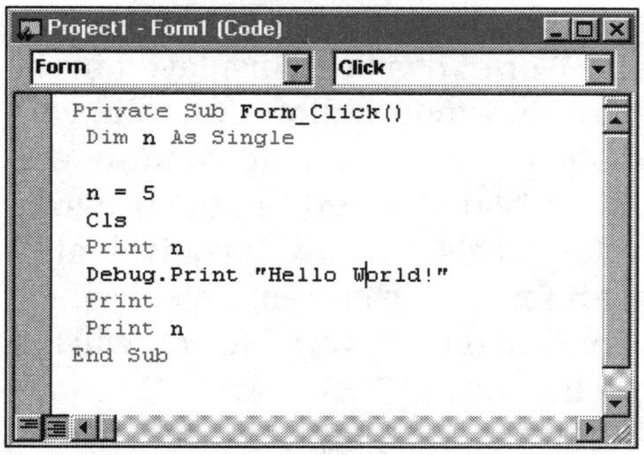

- Press the (F8) key, or
- Select the Step Into option from the Debug menu, as shown on Figure 4-27, or
- Press the Step Into tool button on the Debug Toolbar (see Figure 4-21).

Once the program is running, click the mouse. This will activate the form's **Click** event and will result in the screen shown in Figure 4-28. The highlighting of the procedure's

Figure 4-27

Activating Step Into Mode from the View Menu

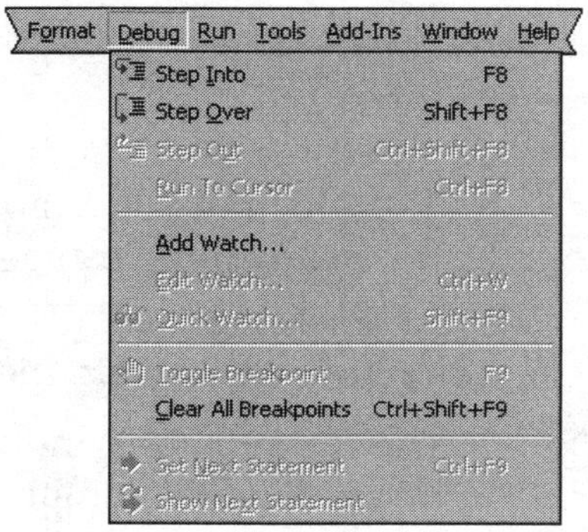

---

[5] The Immediate window can also be activated and viewed from the View menu in both Design or Run modes. It can only be used to evaluate immediate commands, however, in Break and Design modes.

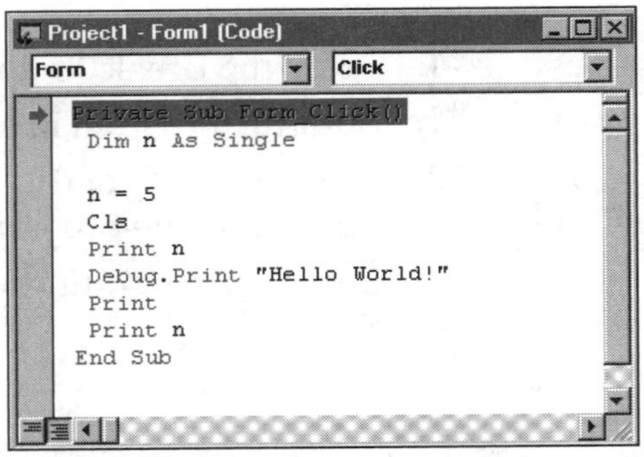

Figure 4-28
The Click Event Procedure in Single Step Mode

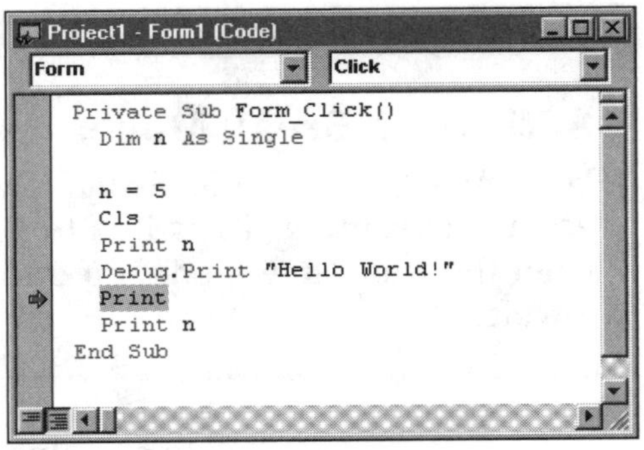

Figure 4-29
The Code Window after Five Single Steps

Figure 4-30
The Immediate Window after Five Single Steps

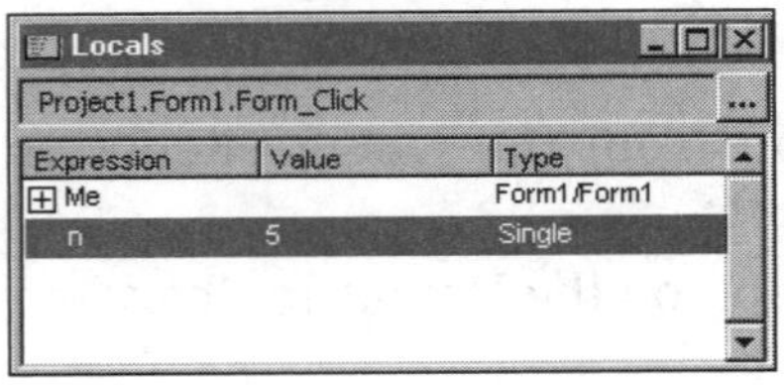

Figure 4-31
The Locals Window after Five Single Steps

header line and the arrow pointing to it indicate that this is the next statement to be executed. Continue pressing either the F8 key or the Step Into toolbar button until your screen appears as shown in Figure 4-29.

Notice in Figure 4-29 that the next statement to be executed is a **Print** statement, which will cause a blank line to be displayed on the form. At this point you are in Break mode. Activate both the Immediate and Locals windows using any of the following steps:

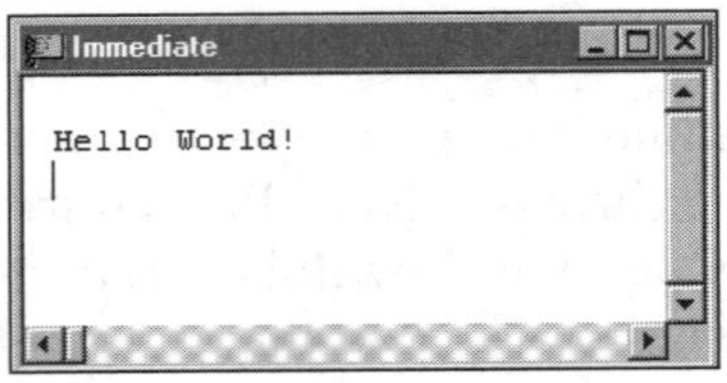

- Click on the partially hidden windows, or
- Select the windows from the View menu, or
- Select the windows from the Debug toolbar, or
- Press the CTRL+G keys (this is the access key sequence) to select the Immediate window.

At this point you should see the windows shown in Figures 4-30 and 4-31. Notice that the line Hello World! has been displayed in the Immediate window and that the Locals window shows that the variable n has a value of 5. The message in the Immediate window was printed by the statement Debug.Print "Hello World!" in the program code. The **Me** keyword listed in the Locals window is equivalent to an implicitly declared variable that refers to the current object, which in this case is the form object itself. If you click on this variable you will see the value of all properties associated with the form.

Once the Immediate and Locals windows are displayed we can use either of them to both examine and alter the current state of each of the program's variables.

PROGRAMMERS NOTES

Activating the Debug Windows

You can activate the various debug windows by doing one of the following:

1. Clicking on a partially hidden Debug window
2. Selecting the desired window from the View menu (see Figure 4-20)

3. Selecting the desired window from the Debug toolbar (see Figure 4-21)
4. Pressing the CTRL and G keys at the same time to activate the Immediate window

The Immediate window can be used in both Design and Break modes. Although, both the Locals and Watch windows can be viewed in Design mode, they are operationally only effective in Break mode.

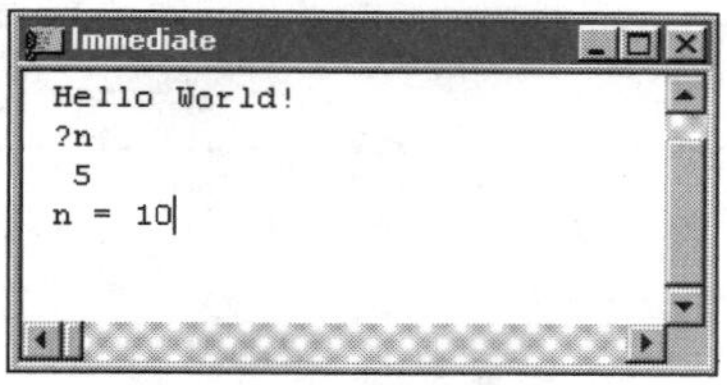

Figure 4-32

Examining and Altering n's Value
from the Immediate Window

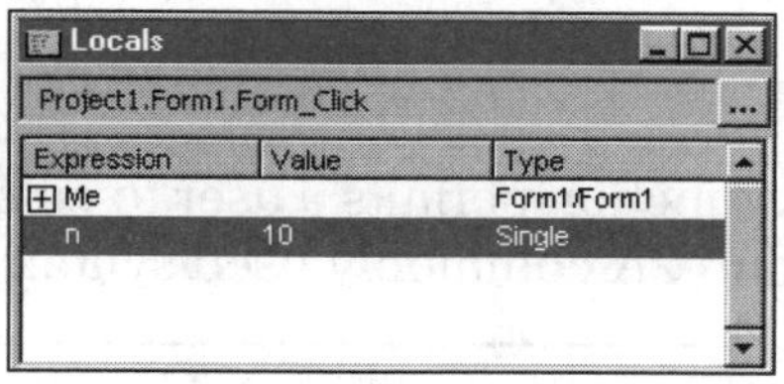

```
Immediate                        _ □ X
  Hello World!
  ?n
    5
  n = 10|
```

Figure 4-33

Examining n's Value in the Locals
Window

```
Locals                           _ □ X
Project1.Form1.Form_Click                 ...
Expression      Value        Type
⊞ Me                          Form1/Form1
  n             10            Single
```

For example, enter the following two lines directly in the Immediate
window:

```
? n
n = 10
```

The first line asks the value of the variable n, which was set to 5 by the
program. In response to this statement the value of 5 will be displayed in the
Immediate window. The second entered line changes the value of n to 10.
Once these lines have been entered, the Immediate and Locals windows will
appear as shown in Figure 4-32 and 4-33, respectively. Notice that once the
statement n = 10 is entered into the Immediate window and the (ENTER) key is
pressed, the value of n changed from 5 to 10 in the Locals window. The value
of this variable could just as easily have been changed directly in the Locals
window. In practice, the Locals window would be used, by itself, for examining and changing local variables, while the Immediate window is used for
entering a statement and immediately executing it to determine its effect.

Now press the Run toolbar button to continue program execution. This
will take the program out of single-step mode and complete the event code's
execution. In Section 7.8 we will complete our introduction to the debugging environment by showing you how to set breakpoints, create watch variables, and use the Watch window.

4.6 ▶ Common Programming Errors and Problems

The common programming errors and problems associated with the material presented in this chapter are:

1. Calling the **InputBox** function without assigning its return value to a
    variable. The **InputBox** function can only be used on the right-hand side
    of an assignment statement.

2. Forgetting to clear the **Text** property of a Text box control that will be
    used for input purposes, unless an initial value is to be inserted in the
    Text box.

3. Mixing up the argument order used in the **Format** function. The first ar-
    gument is the expression to be formatted, while the second argument is
    the desired format.

4. Forgetting to enclose the format argument in the **Format** function with-
    in double quotes.

4.7 Chapter Review

Key Terms

Format function   Label
InputBox   **MsgBox**

Summary

1. The **InputBox** function permits a user to enter a single value into an executing procedure. A commonly used syntax for calling this function is

   > InputBox(*prompt, title, default*)

   where *prompt* is a required string and both *title* and *default*, which are also strings, are optional. If a title string is used, it is displayed in the title bar of the dialog box; otherwise, the application's name is placed in the title bar. If a default string is provided, it is placed within the input area of the dialog box. A *prompt* is a message telling a user that input is required. The prompt, which is always required, is displayed as a string within the input dialog box. For example, the statement

   > S = InputBox("Enter a value", "Input Dialog", "0")

   calls the **InputBox** function with the arguments "Enter a value", which is the prompt, "Input Dialog", which is the title, and a default string value of 0. Here the returned value is assigned to the variable S.

2. Text boxes are the most commonly used method of providing interactive user input. The data entered into a text box becomes the value of the Text box's **Text** property, and is always stored as a string. In addition to being set at Run Time by the user, the **Text** property can also be set at Design Time and at Run Time under program control. The **Text** property value is accessed using the standard object dot notation, in which the property name is separated from the object name using a dot. For example, the identifier txtInput.Text refers to the **Text** property of a Text box named txtInput.

3. A Label control is commonly used as a prompt for a Text box.

4. A **Const** statement is used to equate a constant to a symbolic name. The syntax of this statement is

   > Const *name* As *data-type = constant expression*

   where a constant expression can only include constants and operators (no variables or intrinsic functions). For example, the number 3.1416 can be equated to the symbolic name PI using the **Const** statement

   Const PI As Single = 3.1416

   Once a symbolic name has been equated to a value, another value may not be assigned to the symbolic name.

Test Yourself—Short Answer

1. What is the difference between a **monospaced font** and a **proportional font**?

2. What is the difference between the "print zone" for a monospaced font and the "print zone" of a proportional font?

3. What will **Spc(5)** do in a print line?

4. What is the difference between the **InputBox** function and the **InputBox$** function?

5. The **Format** function is used to determine how values will be displayed on the screen or on paper. Some parameters for this function are pre-determined by Visual Basic. What is a user-defined Format?

6. What value will result when the following is executed?

```
Val(2345)
Val(218 Main Street)
Val(0)
Val(R456)
```

7. How is the text displayed by the statement `Print Text1.Text; Text2.Text; Text3.Text`?

8. Set the current x and current y coordinates in a Picture box called picShow to 100 and 200 respectively.

9. Write the code that will force printer output to go to a new page (the page eject command).

10. Write **Format** functions that will produce the following results from the given numbers:

Number	Result
22345	$22,345.00
5.26	005.2600
5.26	5.26E+00

Programming Projects

1. a. Implement a simple calculator like the one pictured in Figure 4-34. An executable example of the calculator can be found on the Student Disk as simpcalc.exe. Your calculator should have the following features:

   i. The buttons perform the indicated operation on the two text fields and display the answer in the Picture box to the right of the Answer label.

   ii. When the calculator starts up, the first Text box field, to the right of the label Num 1, has the focus.

   iii. The tab key switches between the two Text box fields.

   iv. The Clear button clears the Text boxes, the answer, and sets the focus to the first Text box.

   v. The End button ends the program.

   Hints:

   i. Create a form having the following controls: 2 Text boxes, 1 Picture box, 3 Labels, and 6 Command buttons.

   ii. Set the properties for all of the controls. Start with each control's name!

   iii. Deactivate the **TabStop** property for all but the two Text boxes, and set the **TabIndex** property of the Text boxes to 1 and 2, respectively.

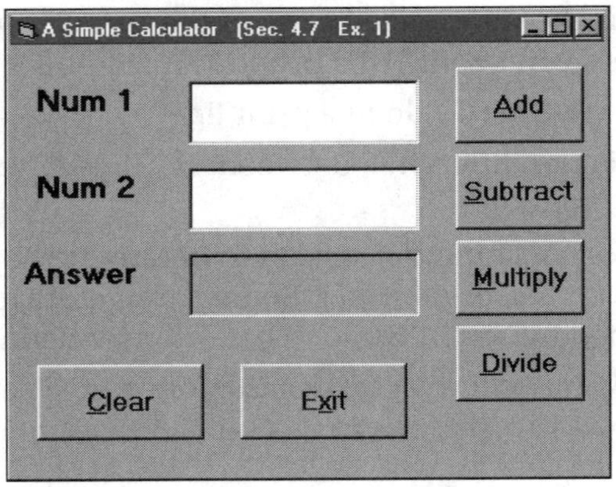

Figure 4-34

Form for Exercise 1

    iv. Write the code for each Command button's **Click** event procedure. The Clear button should call the **SetFocus** method for the first Text box.

  b. Extra challenges:

    i. Add a Square Root button that takes the square root of the answer.

    ii. Add a Negate button that negates (changes the sign of) the answer.

2. Create a project which will compare the income (after one year) from a tax exempt municipal bond to a similar risk taxable bond. It is assumed that the municipal bond has a 5% interest rate and $1000 will be invested in either type of bond. This project should allow the user to enter their income tax rate and the interest available on the taxable bond.

    The formula for calculating the income from the *taxable bond* is as follows:

Income = (1000 ∗ Bond interest rate) ∗ (1 – Tax rate)

    Obviously the tax exempt bond will earn $50 (1000 ∗ .05). This amount is entered in a label.

    A possible form for this project is shown in Figure 4-35.

3. Create an application that permits a user to determine how much an item depreciates over a five-year time span using straight line, declining balance, and sum of the years digits depreciation methods. The application should allow the user to:

  a. Input the item's original cost and its salvage value at the end of 5 years.

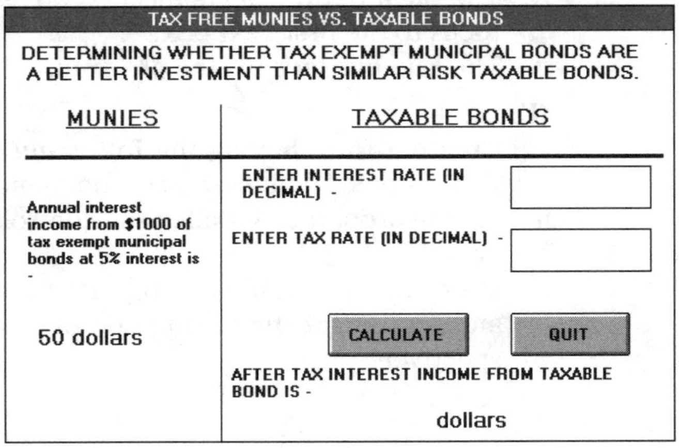

Figure 4-35

Form for Exercise 2

Figure 4-36

Form for Exercise 3

```
┌─────────────────────────────────────────────────────────┐
│                  DEPRECIATION OVER 5 YEARS                │
│      ENTER THE NAME, COST AND SALVAGE VALUE THEN SCROLL YEARS │
│                                                           │
│   NAME OF ITEM --->  [WIDGET]      STRAIGHT LINE     180  │
│                                    DEPRECIATION IS -      │
│   COST OF ITEM ---->  [1000]                             │
│                                    DECLINING BALANCE 144  │
│   SALVAGE VALUE -->   [100]        DEPRECIATION IS -      │
│                                                           │
│                                    "SUM OF THE YEARS      │
│           YEAR ----    3           DIGITS "              │
│                                    DEPRECIATION IS -  200 │
│        [◄]        [    ]       [►]                        │
│                                        [ QUIT ]          │
└─────────────────────────────────────────────────────────┘
```

b. Enter the depreciation year of interest, which should be an integer from 1 to 5.

c. Exit the program.

The required formulas are as follows:

Yearly straight line depreciation = (cost – salvage value)/5
Double declining depreciation = .4 * (cost – previous years depreciation)
Sum of the years digits depreciation = (6 – year)/15 * cost

Use the form shown in Figure 4-36.

4. a. Create a project that will permit users to determine the value of their current portfolio of stocks. A suggested form appears in Figure 4-37. The requirements for this project are:

   i. The stock names (Borland, IBM, Novell), the number of shares, and their purchase price are all entered at Design Time.

   ii. The amount invested is calculated when the form is loaded.

   iii. The current prices are entered with an **InputBox** when the UP-DATE Command button is clicked.

   iv. After the current prices are entered, the increase or decrease. totals, and current portfolio value are calculated.

   b. The user knows that he will need to remember the purchase date on each stock for income tax purposes. Change this form so that if a stock name is clicked, a message box appears reporting the purchase date for that stock. Similar click procedures should be written for the other stock name labels.

5. a. Develop an application that will calculate the Economic Order Quantity. The EOQ determines the most efficient order quantity for a

STOCK NAME	no. shares	purchase price	amt. invested	current price	INCREASE OR DECREASE
BORLAND	200	20	4000	18	-400
IBM	500	90	45000	100	5000
NOVELL	300	18	5400	20	600
TOTALS			54400		5200

PORTFOLIO EVALUATION

[UPDATE]   [QUIT]   CURRENT PORTFOLIO VALUE - 59600

Figure 4-37

Form for Exercise 4

Economic Order Quantity

14.14213562373l

ANNUAL DEMAND   1000
ORDERING COST   100
HOLDING COST   1000

[QUIT]   [ABOUT]

Figure 4-38

Form for Exercise 5a

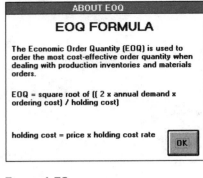

Figure 4-39
Form for Exercise 5b

part used in manufacturing. EOQ calculates the most cost effective order quantity when dealing with production inventories and materials orders. It uses the annual demand, holding cost, and ordering cost to determine this quantity. The equation for the EOQ is:

$$EOQ = \sqrt{2 \text{ (Annual demand) (Ordering cost)} / \text{Holding cost}}$$

i. The three quantities (Annual demand, Ordering cost, and Holding cost) should be entered by the user using either Scroll bars or Text boxes.

ii. The EOQ should appear on the form in a label.

iii. An Exit button should be included.

b. (Extra challenge) Add an <u>A</u>bout button that displays the About box shown in Figure 4-39. **Hint:** An About box is simply another form that must be loaded and unloaded in the same manner as all other forms. You can either create the form by adding controls to a new form, or change the default controls within the About Box provided when you select this form from the Add Form Dialog (see previous Figure 2-74 on page 105). Additionally, an About Box is further described in Section 8.6, when one is added to the Rotech project.

6. This assignment is a modification to the Motel 8 project (Section 3.8, Exercise 8).

a. Use constants (in your **General Declaration** section) to assign values for Cost per Adult (Integer value 30), Cost per Child (Integer value 10), and State-Local Tax (Currency value 0.05). Additionally, include an Option Explicit statement in the **General Declaration** section, and use a Currency format to display the total charges.

b. Add named constants to your project to hold values for the Daily Charge (Currency value 29.95) and Refueling Fee (Currency value 12.95).

7. You have been asked to write a program that will help new employees at the local Burger House return the correct change. The point of sale terminal displays the amount of change to be returned to the customer but does not tell the employee how to choose the coins. In an effort to train new employees to make change in the most efficient manner, your program will be used in that effort.

Program Requirements:

Your program will permit an integer value to be entered and will compute and display the number of quarters, dimes, nickels, and pennies for the value entered. Output is computed, starting with quarters and ending with pennies. For example, for change of 68 cents, your program should display 2 quarters, 1 dime, 1 nickel, and 3 pennies. All program variables should be declared as integers. (**Hint:** Use integer division and integer remainder operators (\ and MOD) in your calculations.) Create a form like the one shown in Figure 4-40.

Figure 4-40
Form for Exercise 7

Selection

A decision requires making a choice between two or more alternatives. As you might expect, given the dual nature of Visual Basic, decisions can be implemented by both graphical and procedural means.

The graphical features consist of Toolbox control objects specifically designed to provide a selection of input choices. These controls are listed in Table 5-1. The first two, the Check box and Option button controls are presented in Section 5.1. The remaining controls, except for the Scroll bars presented in Chapter 4, are described in Chapter 11 and Appendix D.

On the procedural side, *selection statements* are used to make decisions on what action or computation should be performed based upon either an expression or property value. Examples of such basic decisions include setting a type in bold only if a Check box has been selected, performing a division only if the divisor is not zero, printing different messages depending upon the value of a grade received, and so on. In this way, selection statements determine the flow of control of procedural code execution based on tested conditions being True or False.

The term *flow of control* refers to the order in which a program's procedural code statements are executed. Unless directed otherwise, the normal flow of control for procedural statements within an event procedure is sequential. This means that once a procedure is invoked, statements within that procedure are executed in sequence, one after the other.

Selection statements, presented in this chapter starting with Section 5.2, permit this sequential flow of control to be altered in precisely defined ways. Specifically, selection statements determine the procedural code to be executed next, based on a comparison operation. Repetition statements, which are used to repeat a set of procedural code, can also alter a procedure's flow of control. They are presented in the next chapter.

5.1 Selection Controls

Except for the Combo box control, which is a combination of a List box and a Text box control, all of the controls listed in Table 5-1 limit the user to selecting from a pre-defined set of choices. In this regard, both the Combo box and Text box controls are less restrictive. What this means in practice is that the procedural code used to decide what was entered in either a Text box or Combo box is generally more complex than that needed for the other controls listed in Table 5-1. We will see an example of this in Section 5-3, where the input from a Text box is processed to ensure that a user types in a legitimate value. The advantage of the controls listed in Table 5-1 (with the exception of the Combo box), is that they force a user to choose between programmer-defined choices. In this section we present the Check box and Option button input controls.

Table 5-1	Selection Controls
Control	**Use**
Check box	A Yes/No toggle selection.
Option button	Select only one option from a group.
List box	Select one or more options from a predefined list.
Combo box	Select from a predefined list or type in a selection.
Horizontal and Vertical Scroll bars	Select a number from a sequential range of numbers.

The Check Box Control

The Check box control provides a user with a simple Yes-or-No option. For example, in the interface shown in Figure 5-1 there are two Check boxes. The Properties table for this interface is listed in Table 5.2.

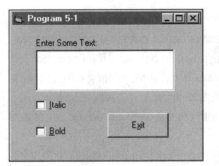

Figure 5-1
An Interface with Two Check Boxes

As illustrated in Figure 5-1, both Check boxes are unchecked initially. These settings were set at design time using the Check box's **Value** property and can be altered by the user at run time, either by clicking on the box, pressing the Space Bar key when the box is in focus, or pushing the access key defined for the box. They can also be changed at run time using program code, where settings of 0, 1, or 2 correspond to unchecked, checked, and grayed (which represents unavailable).

Each Check box in an application is independent of any other Check box. This means that the choice made in one box has no effect on, and does not depend on, the choice made in another box. As such, Check boxes are useful for providing a set of one or more options that can be in effect at the same time, provided that each option is individually of the Yes/No, On/Off, or True/False type. For example, in the interface shown in Figure 5-1 the Check box options consist of a set of two Check boxes that permit independent selection of how the text is to be displayed. Selecting or deselecting Bold has no effect on the choice for Italic or nonItalic.

Because of their On/Off nature, Check boxes are also known as toggle selections, where a user can effectively toggle (switch back and forth) between a check mark and no check mark. If no check mark appears in a box,

Table 5-2 The Properties Table for Figure 5-1

Object	Property	Setting
Form	Name	frmMain
	Caption	Program 5-1
Label	Name	lblPrompt
	Caption	Enter Some Text
Text box	Name	txtBox1
	Text	(Blank)
	Font	Ms Sans Serif
	FontBold	False
	FontItalic	False
	BackColor	White (Palette tab)
Check box 1	Name	chkItalic
	Caption	&Italic
	Value	0-Unchecked
Check box 2	Name	chkBold
	Caption	&Bold
	Value	0-Unchecked
Command button	Name	cmdExit
	Caption	E&xit

clicking on it changes its **Value** property to 1 and causes a check to appear; otherwise, if the box has a check, clicking on it changes its **Value** property to 0 and causes the check to be erased.

Although a Check box allows a user to make a selection easily, the programmer must still provide the code to activate that selection and then act appropriately on it. Doing so requires the **If-Else** selection statement described in the next section. In anticipation of this material, Program 5-1's event code is given below.

Program 5-1's Event Code

```
Private Sub chkItalic_Click()
  If chkItalic.Value = vbChecked Then
    txtBox1.FontItalic = True
  Else
    txtBox1.FontItalic = False
End Sub

Private Sub chkBold_Click()
  If chkBold.Value = vbChecked Then
    txtBox1.FontBold = True
  Else
    txtBox1.FontBold = False
End Sub

Private Sub cmdExit_Click()
  Beep
  End
End Sub
```

Notice in this event code that the **Click** events for both the Italic and Bold Check boxes use an **If** statement containing their respective **Value** properties. Based on the value, which will be either 1 or 0, the Text box **Font** property, **FontItalic** or **FontBold**, is set to either **True** or **False**. The term **vbChecked** is a system-defined named constant that has the value 1.

The Option Button Control

The Option button control provides a user with a set of one or more choices, only one of which can be selected. Selecting one Option button immediately deselects and clears all the other buttons in the group. Thus, the choices in an Option button group are mutually exclusive. Because Option buttons operate in the same manner as the channel selector buttons provided on radios, where selecting one channel automatically deselects all other channels, Option buttons are also referred to as "radio buttons."

As an example, consider a form that requires information on the marital status of an employee. As the employee can be either Single, Married, Divorced, or Widowed, selecting one category automatically means the other categories are not selected. This type of choice is ideal for an Option button group, as shown in Figure 5-2, where the group consists of four individual Option buttons.

Each Option button placed on a form is automatically part of a group. To create separate groups of Option buttons you can place these controls on a form directly or inside both Picture boxes and Frames. All Option buttons placed directly on a form constitute a single option group. To create separate groups within either a Picture box or Frame you must draw these controls on the GUI *before* placing an Option button within them. Placing an Option button outside of a Picture box or Frame and then dragging them into the control, or drawing a Picture box or Frame around existing Option buttons, will not produce the same result. In either of these cases, the Option buttons will remain part of their original group.

For example, in the interface shown in Figure 5-3, we have added an Option button group to the interface previously used in Program 5-1. This option group consists of three individual Option buttons with the captions Courier, SansSerif, and Serif, respectively. We will use these buttons to select the style of print displayed in the Text box. Since these styles are mutually exclusive, the use of Option buttons for this selection is appropriate. The Properties table for this interface is listed in Table 5-3.

Notice in Properties Table 5-3 that only one of the Option button's **Value** properties has been set to **True**. Setting the second Option button **Value** to **True** automatically sets the remaining Option button's **Value** property to **False**. The event code for these Option buttons is listed on the next page. The remaining event code for Program 5-2 is the same as listed for Program 5-1.

Figure 5-2
An Option Button Group

Figure 5-3
An Interface with an Option Button Group

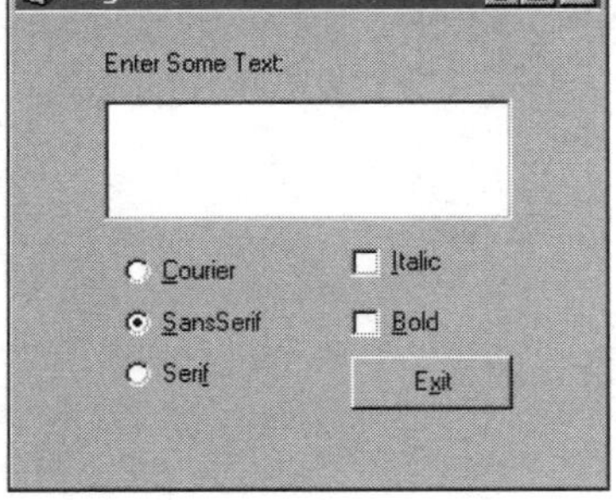

Table 5-3 Program 5-2's Properties Table

Object	Property	Setting
Form	Name	frmMain
	Caption	Program 5-1
Label	Name	lblPrompt
	Caption	Enter Some Text
Text box	Name	txtBox1
	Text	(Blank)
	Font	Ms Sans Serif
	FontBold	False
	FontItalic	False
	BackColor	White (Palette tab)
Check box 1	Name	chkItalic
	Caption	&Italic
	Value	0-Unchecked
Check box 2	Name	chkBold
	Caption	&Bold
	Value	0-Unchecked
Option button 1	Name	optCourier
	Caption	&Courier
	Value	False
Option button 2	Name	optSansSerif
	Caption	&SansSerif
	Value	True
Option button 3	Name	optSerif
	Caption	&Serif
	Value	False
Command button	Name	cmdExit
	Caption	E&xit

Program 5-2's Event Code

```
Private Sub optCourier_Click()
  txtBox1.Font = "Courier"
End Sub

Private Sub optSansSerif_Click()
  txtBox1.Font = "Ms Sans Serif"
End Sub

Private Sub optSerif_Click()
  txtBox1.Font = "Ms Serif"
End Sub
```

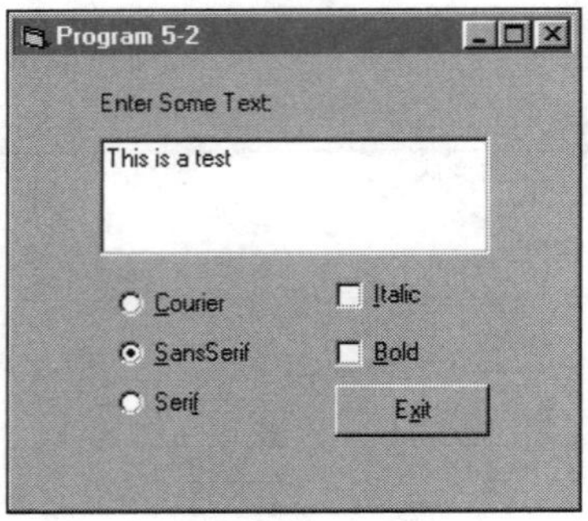

Figure 5-4

An Example of User-Entered Text

Notice that the event code for an Option button group does not require any selection statements. This is because only one Option button can be in effect at a time. Thus, the **Click** event for each button can unilaterally change the text box's **Font** property, without the need to first determine the values of the other Option buttons, using a selection statement like that used for the Check box event code in Program 5-1. As we will see in Chapter 7, however, there is an alternative method of processing an Option button group that does use a selection statement. This method makes each button's **Click** event code call the same general procedure. This single general procedure then uses a selection statement to first determine which button's **Value** property is **True**, before setting the Text box's **Font** property.

When Program 5-2 is executed, and before any Check box or Option button is checked, the typeface of user entered text is determined by the Text box's **Font**, **FontBold**, and **FontItalic** Property values set at design time (see Table 5-3). For these values the text This is a test would appear as shown in Figure 5-4.

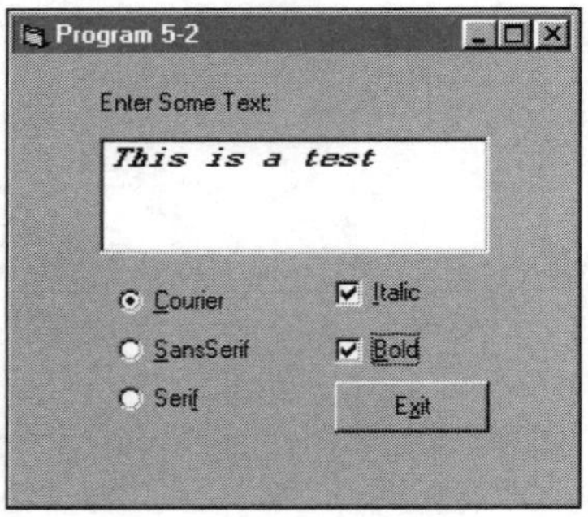

Figure 5-5

The Text in Courier Bold and Italic

The text illustrated in Figure 5-4 and any subsequently entered text can now be changed by the user using the Check boxes and Option buttons. An Option button is selected at run time in one of four ways:

- Clicking the mouse on the desired button;
- Tabbing to the Option button group and using the arrow keys;
- Using the access (hot) keys; or
- Assigning its **Value** property to **True** under program control, as for example, optSansSerif.Value = True.

For example, if the user checks the Bold and Italic Check boxes and the Courier Option button, the text will appear as shown in Figure 5-5.

The Frame Control

Frame controls, two of which are shown in Figure 5-6, are extremely useful for providing clearly defined visual areas and for grouping controls together. This is especially important when you need to have two or more groups of Option buttons on the same form. Since all Option buttons placed directly on a form, no matter where they are placed, constitute a single group of buttons, the only way to create additional groupings is to use either a Frame control or Picture box. All Option buttons placed within either of these two controls constitute a separate grouping of buttons.

A Frame control is placed on a form in the same manner as all other toolbox controls; either by clicking the control or clicking and dragging the control to the desired location. As with all controls, the Frame control can be resized using its resizing handles.

Figure 5-6

The Frame Control

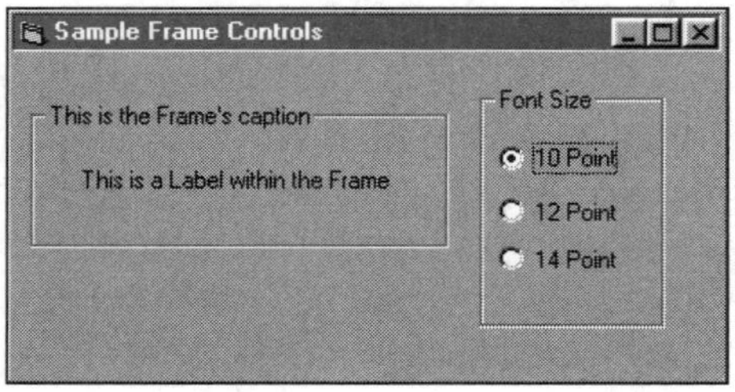

Besides setting the Frame control's size and position, the only other values that should be explicitly set at design time are its **Caption** property and the caption's font type, style, and size. These latter values are all set using the control's **Font** property.

A Frame control, which can be used to group a set of other controls, such as Option buttons, is referred to as a *container control*. The primary container control, of course, is a form, because all other controls are contained within it.

The relationship between a container control and all its internal controls is referred to as a *parent and child relationship*. In this relationship, the position of all child controls is relative to the upper Left and Top of its parent control. This means that if the parent control is moved, all of its internal child controls move, as a group, with it, and retain their relative positions within the parent control. Additionally, a child control cannot be moved outside of its parent.

When using a Frame control to group a set of controls, such as Option buttons or Check boxes, *you must always draw the Frame first, and then place the controls within the Frame*.[1] Doing this produces two important effects; first, it ensures that all of the controls within the Frame will automatically move when the Frame itself is relocated (controls drawn first and then moved onto a Frame will not move with the Frame), and secondly, it forces all internal controls to be grouped together, as an individual unit. This last effect is especially important when you need a separate grouping of Option buttons, because, unlike Check boxes, only one Option button can be active in a group. Therefore, if two or more Option buttons need to be active at the same time, you must construct additional container controls to hold them.

Additionally, when placing another control within a Frame control, double clicking the desired object's icon within the toolbox *will not* work; doing so only places the object on the form, over the existing Frame. To place an object within the Frame, click and drag the desired object to the proper position inside the Frame, and then release the mouse button.

Exercises 5.1

1. Determine whether the following choices should be presented on a GUI using either Check boxes or Option buttons:

   a. The choice of air conditioning or not on a new automobile order form.

   b. The choice of automatic or manual transmission on a new automobile order form.

   c. The choice of AM/FM, AM/FM Tape, or AM/FM CD radio on a new automobile order form.

   d. The choice of tape backup system or no tape backup system on a new computer order form.

   e. The choice of a 14-, 15-, or 17-inch color monitor on a new computer order form.

   f. The choice of CD-ROM drive or not on a new computer order form.

---

[1] If you have existing controls that need to be grouped together, you can select all of the controls and then cut and paste them into an existing Frame or Picture control.

g. The choice of a 4-, 6-, or 8-speed CD-ROM drive on a new computer order form.

h. The choice of a 100-, 120-, or 200-MHZ Pentium processor on a new computer order form.

② Enter and run Program 5-1 on your computer.

③ a. Modify Program 5-1 so that the choices presented by the Check boxes are replaced by Command buttons. (**Hint**: Each Check box can be replaced by two Command buttons.)

b. Based on your experience with Exercise 3a, determine what type of input choice is best presented using a Check box rather than Command buttons.

④ a. Modify Program 5-1 so that the choices presented by the Check boxes are replaced by Option buttons.

b. Based on your experience with Exercise 4a, determine what type of input choice is best presented using a Check box rather than an Option button.

⑤ Enter and run Program 5-2 on your computer.

⑥ Modify Program 5-2 so that the user can also specify the point size for the Text box. The default point size should be 10, with the user capable of choosing among 8, 10, and 12 points.

5.2 ▶ Relational Expressions

Besides providing computational capabilities (addition, subtraction, multiplication, division, etc.), all programming languages provide procedural operations for comparing quantities. Because many decision-making situations can be reduced to the level of choosing between two quantities, this comparison capability can be very useful.

The expressions used to compare quantities are called relational expressions. A *simple relational expression* consists of a relational operator that compares two operands as shown in Figure 5-7. While each operand in a relational expression can be any valid Visual Basic expression, the relational operators must be one of those listed in Table 5-4. These relational operators may be used with all of Visual Basic's data types, but must be typed exactly as given in Table 5-4. Thus, while the following examples are all valid:

```
age > 40      length <= 50    temp > 98.6
3 < 4         flag = done     id_num = 682
day <> 5      2.0 > 3.3       hours > 40
```

Figure 5-7
Structure of a Simple Relational Expression

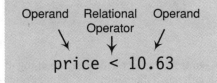

Table 5-4 Relational Operators

Operator	Meaning	Example
<	Less than	age < 30
>	Greater than	height > 6.2
<=	Less than or equal to	taxable <= 20000
>=	Greater than or equal to	temp >= 98.6
=	Equal to	grade = 100
<>	Not equal to	number <> 250

the following are invalid:

```
length =< 50     ' operator out of order
2.0 >> 3.3       ' invalid operator
```

Relational expressions are sometimes called *conditions*, and we will use both terms to refer to these expressions. Like all Visual Basic expressions, relational expressions are evaluated to yield a result. For relational expressions this result is one of the boolean values, **True** or **False**. For example, the expression 3 < 4 is always **True**, and the expression 2 > 3 is always **False**. Thus, the event code

```
Private Sub Form_Click()
  Print "The value of 3 < 4 is "; 3 < 4
  Print "The value of 2 > 3 is "; 2 > 3
End Sub
```

can be used to display the boolean value of the expressions 3 < 4 and 2 > 3, respectively, and produce the display

```
The value of 3 < 4 is True
The value of 2.0 > 3.0 is False
```

The value of a relational expression such as hours > 40 depends on the value stored in the variable hours. In Visual Basic, a condition such as this is typically used as part of a selection statement. In these statements, which are presented in the next section, the selection of which statement is to be executed next is based on the value of the condition (**True** or **False**).

In addition to numerical operands, character data can also be compared using relational operators. For example, in ANSI code the letter 'A' is stored using code with a lower numerical value than that storing the letter 'B', the code for a 'B' is lower in value than the code for a 'C', and so on. For character sets coded in this manner, the following conditions are evaluated as listed:

Expression	Value
'A' > 'C'	False
'D' <= 'Z'	True
'E' = 'F'	False
'G' >= 'M'	False
'B' <> 'C'	True

Comparing letters is essential in alphabetizing names or using characters to select a particular option.

Finally, two string expressions may be compared using relational operators. Each character in a string is stored in binary using ANSI code. In this code, a blank precedes (is less than) all letters and numbers; the letters of the alphabet are stored in order from A to Z; and the digits are stored in order from 0 to 9. It is important to note that in ANSI the digits come before, or are less than, the letters.

When two strings are compared, their individual characters are compared one character pair at a time (both first characters, then both second characters, and so on). If no differences are found, the strings are equal; if a difference is found, the string with the first lower character is considered the smaller string. If all characters are the same but the end of the first string is reached before the end of the second string, the first string is considered less than the second string. Thus,

> *"JONES" is less than "SMITH" because the first 'J' in JONES is less than the first 'S' in SMITH.*
>
> *"Hello" is less than "hello" because the first 'H' in Hello is less than the first 'h' in hello.*
>
> *"Hello" is less than "Hello " because the second string is longer.*
>
> *"Hello" is greater than "Good Bye" because the first 'H' in Hello is greater than the first 'G' in Good Bye.*
>
> *"Behop" is greater than "Beehive" because the third character, 'h', in Behop is greater than the third character, 'e', in Beehive.*
>
> *"123" is greater than "1227" because the third character, '3', in 123 is greater than the third character, '2', in 1227.*
>
> *"123" is less than "1237" because the first three characters are the same, but the first string is shorter.*

Logical Operators

In addition to using simple relational expressions as conditions, more complex conditions can be created using the logical operators **And**, **Or**, and **Not**.

When the **And** operator is used with two simple expressions, the condition is **True** only if both individual expressions are **True** by themselves. Thus, the compound condition

```
(age > 40) And (term < 10)
```

is **True** only if age is greater than 40 and term is less than 10.

The logical **Or** operator is also applied between two expressions. When using the **Or** operator, the condition is satisfied if either one or both of the two expressions is **True**. Thus, the compound condition

```
(age > 40) Or (term < 10)
```

is **True** if either age is greater than 40, term is less than 10, or both conditions are **True**.

For the declarations

```
Dim i As Integer, j As Integer
Dim a As Single, b As Single
Dim complete as Boolean
```

the following represent valid conditions:

```
a > b
(i = j) Or (a < b) Or complete
(a/b > 5) And (i <= 20)
```

Before these conditions can be evaluated, the values of a, b, i, j, and complete must be known. Assuming

```
a = 12.0, b = 2.0, i = 15, j = 30, and complete = False
```

the previous expressions yield the following results:

Expression	Value
a > b	True
(i = j) Or (a < b) Or complete	False
(a/b > 5) And (i <= 20)	True

The **Not** operator is used to change an expression to its opposite state; that is, if the expression is **True**, then **Not** expression is **False**. Similarly, if an expression is **False** to begin with, then **Not** expression is **True**. For example, assuming the number 26 is stored in the variable age, the expression age > 40 is **False** and the expression Not(age > 40) is **True**. Since the **Not** operator is used with only one expression, it is a unary operator.

Relational and logical operators have a hierarchy of execution similar to the arithmetic operators. Table 5-5 lists the precedence of these operators, in relation to the other operators we have used. Since relational operators have a higher precedence than logical operators, the parentheses in an expression such as

```
(age > 40) And (term < 10)
```

are not strictly needed. The evaluation of this expression is identical to the evaluation of the expression

```
age > 40 And term < 10
```

Table 5-5   Precedence of Operators

Operation	Operator	Associativity
Exponentiation	^	left to right
Negation	-	left to right
Multiplication and Division	* /	left to right
Integer Division	\	left to right
Modulo arithmetic	Mod	left to right
Addition and Subtraction	+ -	left to right
String Concatenation	&	left to right
Equality	=	left to right
Inequality	<>	left to right
Less than	<	left to right
Greater than	>	left to right
Less than or equal to	<=	left to right
Greater than or equal to	>=	left to right
Not	Not	left to right
And	And	left to right
Or	Or	left to right

The following example illustrates the use of an operator's precedence and associativity to evaluate relational expressions, assuming the stated declarations and assignments:

```
Dim i As Integer, j As Integer, k As Integer
Dim x As Single
Dim key As String*1
i = 5
j = 7
k = 12;
x = 22.5;
key = "m"
```

Expression	Equivalent Expression	Value
i + 2 = k - 1	(i + 2) = (k - 1)	False
3 * i - j < 22	(3 * i) - j < 22	True
i + 2 * j > k	(i + (2 * j)) > k	True
k + 3 <= -j + 3 * i	(k + 3) <= ((-j) + (3*i))	False
"a" <> "b"	"a" <> "b"	True
key < "p"	key < "p"	True
20.5 >= x + 10.2	25 >= (x + 10.2)	False

As with arithmetic expressions, parentheses can be used both to alter the assigned operator priority and to improve the readability of relational and logical expressions. Since expressions within parentheses are evaluated first, the following complex condition is evaluated as

```
(6 * 3 = 36 / 2) Or (13 < 3 * 3 + 4) And Not (6 - 2 < 5) =
     (18 = 18) Or (13 < 9 + 4) And Not (4 < 5) =
        (True) Or (13 < 13)  And Not (True) =
        (True) Or  (False)  And (False) =
        (True) Or (False) =
                  True
```

A Numerical Accuracy Problem

A problem that can occur with Visual Basic's relational expressions is a subtle numerical accuracy problem relating to floating point and double-precision numbers. Due to the way computers store these numbers, tests for equality of floating point and double-precision values and variables using the relational operator, =, should be avoided.

The reason for this is that many decimal numbers, such as 0.1, for example, cannot be represented exactly in binary using a finite number of bits. Thus, testing for exact equality for such numbers can fail. When equality of non-integer values is desired, it is better to require that the absolute value of the difference between operands be less than some extremely small value. Thus, for non-integer numerical operands, the general expression:

```
operand_1 = operand_2
```

should be replaced by the condition

```
Abs(operand_1 - operand_2) < 0.000001
```

where the value 0.000001 can be altered to any other acceptably small value. Thus, if the difference between the two operands is less than 0.000001 (or any other user selected amount), the two operands are considered essentially equal. For example, if x and y are single-precision variables, a condition such as

```
x/y = 0.35
```

should be programmed as

```
Abs(x/y - 0.35) < 0.000001
```

This latter condition ensures that slight inaccuracies in representing non-integer numbers in binary do not affect evaluation of the tested condition. Since all computers have an exact binary representation of zero, comparisons for exact equality to zero don't encounter this numerical accuracy problem.

Exercises 5.2

1. Determine whether the value of each of the following expressions is **True** or **False**. Assume a = 5, b = 2, c = 4, d = 6, and e = 3.

   a. `a > b`
   b. `a <> b`
   c. `d Mod b = c Mod b`
   d. `a * c <> d * b`
   e. `d * b = c * e`
   f. `Not(a = b)`
   g. `Not(a < b)`

2. Write relational expressions to express the following conditions (use variable names of your own choosing):

   a. A person's age is equal to 30.
   b. A person's temperature is greater than 98.6 degrees Fahrenheit.
   c. A person's height is less than 6 feet.
   d. The current month is 12 (December).
   e. The letter input is *m*.
   f. A person's age is equal to 30 and that person is taller than 6 feet.
   g. The current day is the fifteenth day of the first month.
   h. A person is older than 50 or has been employed at the company for at least 5 years.
   i. A person's identification number is less than 500 and that person is older than 55.
   j. A length is greater than 2 feet and less than 3 feet.

3. Determine the value of the following expressions, assuming a = 5, b = 2, c = 4, and d = 5.

   a. `a = 5`
   b. `b * d = c * c`
   c. `d Mod b * c > 5 Or c Mod b * d < 7`

4. Using parentheses, rewrite the following expressions to correctly indicate their order of evaluation. Then evaluate each expression, assuming all variables are integers and that a = 5, b = 2, and c = 4.

   a. `a / b <> c And c / b <> a`
   b. `a / b <> c Or c / b <> a`
   c. `b Mod c = 1 And a Mod c = 1`
   d. `b Mod c = 1 Or a Mod c = 1`

5. Write a Visual Basic program to determine the value of the condition (2 > 1) >= (2 < 1). What does your result tell you about how Visual Basic orders a **True** value relative to a **False** value?

5.3 The If-Then-Else Structure

The **If-Then-Else** structure directs a procedure to perform a series of one or more instructions, based on the result of a comparison. For example, the state of New Jersey has a two level state income tax structure. If a person's taxable income is less than $20,000, the applicable state tax rate is 2 percent. For incomes exceeding $20,000, a different rate is applied. The **If-Then-Else** structure can be used in this situation to determine the actual tax, based on whether the taxable income is less than or equal to $20,000. The general syntax of an **If-Then-Else** structure, which is referred to as a *block structure*, is

```
If condition Then
    statement(s)
Else
    statement(s)
End If
```

This block structure is constructed using three separate Visual Basic parts, each of which must reside on a line by itself: an **If** statement having the form **If** *condition* **Then**, an **Else** statement consisting of the keyword **Else**, and an **End If** statement consisting of the keywords **End** and **If**.

The condition in the **If** statement is evaluated first. If the condition is **True**, the first set of statements is executed. If the condition is **False**, the statements after the keyword **Else** are executed. Thus, one of the two sets of statements is always executed depending on the value of the condition. The flowchart for the **If-Then-Else** structure is shown in Figure 5-8.

As a specific example of an **If-Then-Else** statement, we will construct a Visual Basic application for determining New Jersey income taxes. As previously described, these taxes are assessed at 2 percent of taxable income for incomes less than or equal to $20,000. For taxable incomes greater than $20,000 state taxes are 2.5 percent of the income that exceeds $20,000 plus a fixed amount of $400. The expression to be tested is whether taxable income is less than or equal to $20,000. An appropriate **If-Then-Else** statement for this situation is

```
If taxable <= 20000.00 Then
    taxes = 0.02 * taxable
Else
    taxes = 0.025 * (taxable - 20000.00) + 400.00
End If
```

Recall that the relational operator <= represents the relation "less than or equal to." If the value of taxable is less than or equal to 20000.00, the condition is **True** and the statement taxes = 0.02 * taxable is executed. If the condition is **False**, the **Else** part of the statement is executed. Program 5-3 illustrates the use of this statement within the context of a complete application. The interface for this program is shown in Figure 5-9.

Figure 5-8

The If-Then-Else Flowchart

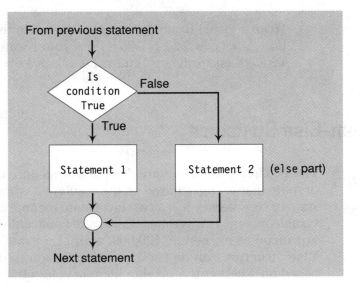

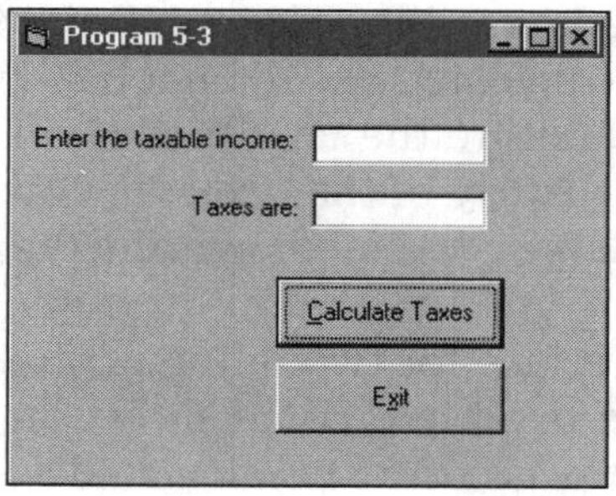

Figure 5-9
The Interface for Program 5-3

Table 5-6   Program 5-3's Properties Table

Object	Property	Setting
Form	Name	frmMain
	Caption	Program 5-3
Label	Name	lblIncome
	Caption	Enter the taxable income:
Label	Name	lblTaxes
	Caption	Taxes are:
Text box	Name	txtIncome
	Text	(Blank)
	BackColo	White (Palette tab)
Picture box	Name	chkItalic
	TabStop	False
	BackColor	White (Palette tab)
Command button	Name	cmdCalculate
	Caption	&Calculate Taxes
Command button	Name	cmdExit
	Caption	E&xit

The Properties table for Program 5-3 is given in Table 5-6. Notice that the **TabStop** property for the Picture box has been set to **False**. Thus, the user can only tab between the Text Box and the E<u>x</u>it Command button. Now look at Program 5-3's Event Code.

Program 5-3's Event Code

```
Private Sub txtIncome_GotFocus()
  pictaxes.Cls
End Sub

Private Sub cmdCalculate_Click()
  Const HIGHRATE As Single = 0.025
  Const LOWRATE As Single = 0.02
  Const FIXED As Single = 400.00
  Const CUTOFF As Single = 20000.00
  Dim taxable As Single, taxes As Single

  taxable = Val(txtIncome.Text)
  If taxable <= CUTOFF Then
    taxes = LOWRATE * taxable
  Else
    taxes = HIGHRATE * (taxable - CUTOFF) + FIXED
  End If

  pictaxes.Print Format(taxes, "Currency")
End Sub

Private Sub cmdExit_Click()
  Beep
  End
End Sub
```

Notice that the Text box's **GotFocus** event is used to trigger the Picture box's **Cls** method. This ensures that whenever a user moves into the Text

Figure 5-10
Entering a Taxable Income Less
Than $20,000

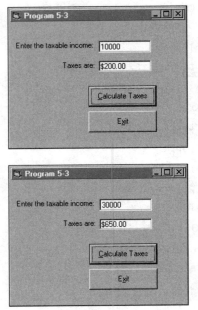

Figure 5-11
Entering a Taxable Income
Greater Than $20,000

box to enter an income value, the Picture box will be cleared. Doing this prevents the situation of a previously calculated tax amount being visible for a newly entered income level before the user moves off the Text box. The actual calculation and display of the taxes due on the entered amount uses an **If-Then-Else** statement within the cmdCalculate_Click event.

Figures 5-10 and 5-11 illustrate the interface for two different values of taxable income. Observe that the taxable income shown in Figure 5-10 was less than $20,000 and the tax is correctly calculated as 2 percent of the number entered. In Figure 5-11 the taxable income is more than $20,000 and the **Else** part of the **If-Then-Else** statement yields a correct tax computation of

$$0.025 * (\$30,000 - \$20,000) + \$400 = \$650$$

One-Way Selection and the Single-Line If-Then Statement

As we have seen, the **If-Then-Else** structure that we have been using consists of three separate Visual Basic parts: an **If-Then** part, an **Else** part, and an **End If** part. Any number of valid Visual Basic statements can be included with the **If** and **Else** parts of the structure. As a multi-line statement it must, however, always be terminated with an **End If** statement. Use of the **Else** part, however, is optional. When the **Else** statement is not used, the **If** statement takes the shortened and frequently useful form:

```
If condition Then
    statement(s)
End If
```

The statement or statements following the **If** condition are only executed if the condition is **True**. Figure 5-12 illustrates the flowchart for this combination of statements. This modified form of the **If** statement is called a *one-way If structure*. Program 5-4 uses this statement to selectively display a message in a Picture box for cars that have been driven more than 3000 miles. The program's interface is shown in Figure 5-13, and its Properties table is listed in Table 5-7.

Figure 5-12
Flowchart for One-Way If Structure

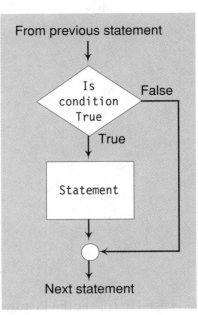

Table 5-7	Program 5-4's Properties Table	
Object	**Property**	**Setting**
Form	Name	frmMain
	Caption	Program 5-4
Label	Name	lblMiles
	Caption	Enter the Miles:
Text box	Name	txtMiles
	Text	(Blank)
	BackColor	White (Palette tab)
Picture box	Name	picError
	TabStop	False
	BackColor	White (Palette tab)
Command button	Name	cmdExit
	Caption	E&xit

PROGRAMMERS NOTES

What Is a Flag?

In current programming usage the term *flag* refers to an item, such as a variable or argument, that sets a condition usually considered as either active or nonactive. Flags are typically used in selecting actions based on the following pseudocode

> If the flag is set
>> do the statements here
> Else
>> do the statements here

where the flag being set means that the flag has a value that is **True**. Similarly, selection can also be based on the fact that the flag is not set, which corresponds to a **False** condition. Although the exact origin of the term *flag* in programming is not known, it probably originates from the use of real flags to signal a condition, such as the Stop, Go, Caution, and Winner flags commonly used at car races.

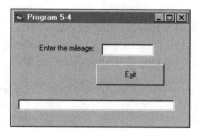

Figure 5-13
Program 5-4's Interface

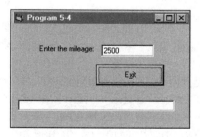

Figure 5-14

![Program 5-4 window showing mileage 2500]

Figure 5-15

Notice in the event code for Program 5-4 that the Text box **GotFocus** event is used to clear the Picture box of any text. The actual calculation is contained in the Text box **LostFocus** event, which uses a one-way **If** statement to check the value in the Text box and display the message

```
This car is over the mileage limit
```

only if `mileage` is greater than `LIMIT`.

Program 5-4's Event Code

```
Private Sub txtMiles_GotFocus()
  picError.Cls
End Sub

Private Sub txtMiles_LostFocus()
  Const LIMIT As Single = 3000.00
  Dim mileage As Single

  mileage = Val(txtMiles.Text)
  If mileage > LIMIT Then
    Beep
    picError.Print "This car is over the mileage limit"
  End If
End Sub

Private Sub cmdExit_Click()
  Beep
  End
End Sub
```

As an illustration of its one-way selection criteria in action, Program 5-4 was run twice, each time with different input data. Figure 5-14 illustrates the case where the input data causes the statements within the **If** to be executed, while in Figure 5-15 the input data is below the limit so that the message is not printed.

Input Data Validation

If statements can be used to select appropriate processing paths as in Programs 5-3 and 5-4. These statements can also validate input data and prevent undesirable data from being processed at all. For example, a date such as 5/33/98 contains an obviously invalid day. Similarly, division of any number by zero within a program, such as 14/0, should not be allowed. Each of these examples illustrates the need for *defensive programming*, in which code is used to check for improper input data before attempting to process it further. The defensive programming technique of checking user input data for erroneous or unreasonable data is called *input data validation*. We now have the tools to supply input data validation to Program 5-3.

Clearly, Program 5-3 expects that the user will enter a number and not a text string into the Text box. To ensure that only numerical data is entered, we can validate each typed character and reject any keystrokes that do not result in one of the characters 0–9. This can be done using the Text box's **KeyPress** event. The header line for this event is

```
Private Sub text-box-name_KeyPress(KeyAscii As Integer)
```

where the argument **KeyAscii** provides the ANSI value of the key that was pressed (Appendix C lists the ANSI values for each character.) Using a one-way **If** statement, this value can be compared to the ANSI values of the characters 0–9 using the following code:

```
If KeyAscii < Asc("0") Or KeyAscii > Asc("9") Then
  KeyAscii = 0
  Beep
End If
```

The **Asc** function in this code returns the ANSI value of its argument. For example, the value returned by ASC("0") is 48 and the value returned by ASC("9") is 57. Thus, the **If** statement checks whether the ANSI value of the typed character is outside the range 48 to 57, and is thus invalid. If the key is outside of this range the computer will beep and set the ANSI value to 0, which corresponds to the zero-length string (""). This effectively intercepts each key and replaces any non-numeric key with no key. The complete event code that can be used for this input validation is listed below.

```
Private Sub txtIncome_KeyPress(KeyAscii As Integer)
  If KeyAscii < Asc("0") Or KeyAscii > Asc("9") Then
    KeyAscii = 0
    Beep
  End If
End Sub
```

Before leaving this keychecking procedure, there is one additional verification we can make. Most users expect that pressing the ENTER key will terminate data input. Of course, this is not the case for Text boxes, where the user must either press the TAB key, click on another object, or use access ("hot") keys to move off the box. We can, however, check the value of the key just pressed, to determine if it was the ENTER key. Since the ANSI value of the ENTER key is 13, this check takes the form

```
Const ENTER As Integer = 13   ' the ANSI value of the Enter key
If KeyAscii = ENTER Then
  KeyAscii = 0
  cmdExit.SetFocus
End If
```

If the (ENTER) key has been pressed, the key is reset to no key and the focus is set to the cmdExit object using the **SetFocus** method. Including this code with the prior check for a digit key results in the following event procedure:

```
Private Sub txtMiles_KeyPress(KeyAscii As Integer)
  Const ENTER As Integer = 13 ' the ANSI value of the Enter key

  If KeyAscii = ENTER Then
    KeyAscii = 0
    cmdExit.SetFocus
  ElseIf KeyAscii < Asc("0") Or KeyAscii > Asc("9") Then
    KeyAscii = 0
    Beep
  End If
End Sub
```

Single-Line If-Then Statement

An alternative to the one-way **If-Then** statement can be used when only a single statement needs to be executed if the tested condition is **True**. For this case, the single-line **If** statement, having the simplified syntax

> **If** *condition* **Then** *statement*

will suffice. For example, the statements:

```
If speed > 22896.0 Then a = b
If number < 0 Then sum = sum + number
If balance < reorder And Time > 5 Then newbal = balance
```

are all examples of single-line **If-Then** statements. In each case, the single statement following the condition is executed only if the tested condition is **True** and no **End If** statement is required.

It is possible to have more than one statement following the **Then** part of a single-line **If-Then** statement, provided that all statements are on the same line and are separated by colons. For example, the following single-line **If-Then** statement is valid:

```
If number > 0 Then sum = sum + number: count = count + 1
```

The only other restriction on the single-line **If-Then** statement is that another **If-Then** statement or the **For/Next** statement described in the next chapter may not follow the **Then** part.

Exercises   5.3

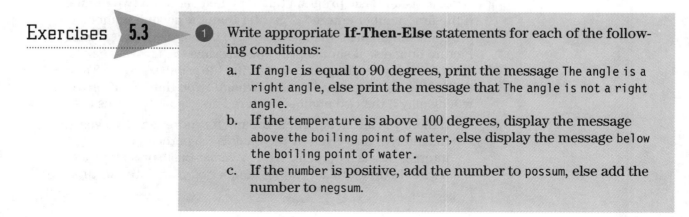

1. Write appropriate **If-Then-Else** statements for each of the following conditions:

    a. If angle is equal to 90 degrees, print the message The angle is a right angle, else print the message that The angle is not a right angle.

    b. If the temperature is above 100 degrees, display the message above the boiling point of water, else display the message below the boiling point of water.

    c. If the number is positive, add the number to possum, else add the number to negsum.

d.   If the `slope` is less than 0.5, set the variable `flag` to zero, else set `flag` to one.

e.   If the difference between `num1` and `num2` is less than 0.001, set the variable `approx` to zero, else calculate `approx` as the quantity (`num1 - num2`) `/ 2.0`.

f.   If the difference between `temp1` and `temp2` exceeds 2.3 degrees, calculate `error` as (`temp1 - temp2`) `* factor`.

g.   If `x` is greater than `y` and `z` is less than 20, read in a value for `p`.

h.   If `distance` is greater than 20 and it is less than 35, read in a value for `time`.

2 Write **If-Then-Else** statements corresponding to the conditions illustrated by each of the following flowcharts:

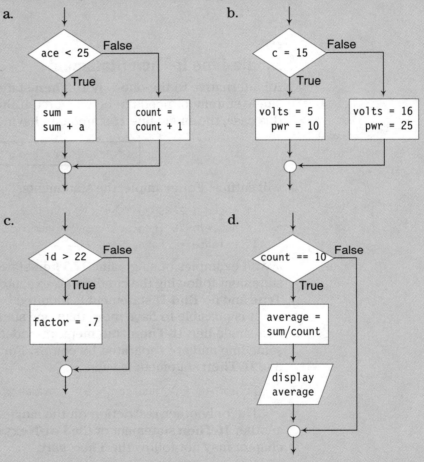

3 Write a Visual Basic program that lets the user input two numbers. If the first number entered is greater than the second number, the program should print the message `The first number is greater` in a Picture box, else it should print the message `The first number is smaller`. Test your program by entering the numbers 5 and 8 and then using the numbers 11 and 2. What do you think your program will display if the two numbers entered are equal? Test this case.

4 a.   If money is left in a particular bank for more than two years, the interest rate given by the bank is 5.5 percent, else the interest rate is 3 percent. Write a Visual Basic program that uses a Text box to accept the number of years into the variable

nyrs and display the appropriate interest rate in a Picture box, depending on the input value.

b. How many runs should you make for the program written in Exercise 4a. to verify that it is operating correctly? What data should you input in each of the program runs?

5 a. In a pass/fail course, a student passes if the grade is greater than or equal to 70 and fails if the grade is lower. Write a Visual Basic program that accepts a grade and prints the message A passing grade or A failing grade, as appropriate.

b. How many runs should you make for the program written in Exercise 5a. to verify that it is operating correctly? What data should you input in each of the program runs?

6 A student wrote the following code to both ensure that the input into a Text box was a number and to set the focus on the cmdExit button when the [ENTER] key was pressed. When testing the code, the student noticed that the focus did not shift when the [ENTER] key was pressed. Determine the error.

```
Private Sub txtMiles_KeyPress(KeyAscii As Integer)
  Const ENTER As Integer = 13 ' the ANSI value of the Enter key

  If KeyAscii < Asc("0") Or KeyAscii > Asc("9") Then
    KeyAscii = 0
    Beep
  ElseIf KeyAscii = ENTER Then
    KeyAscii = 0
    cmdExit.SetFocus
  End If
End Sub
```

5.4 The If-Then-ElseIf Structure

A modification to the **If-Then-Else** selection structure provided in Visual Basic uses an **ElseIf** part. When an **ElseIf** is included within an **If-Then-Else** statement, the complete syntax is

```
If condition-1 Then
    statement(s)
ElseIf condition-2 Then
    statement(s)
ElseIf condition-3 Then
    statement(s)
ElseIf condition-4 Then
        :
Else
    statement(s)
End If
```

Each condition is evaluated in the order it appears in this structure. For the first condition that is **True**, the corresponding statements between it and the next immediately following **ElseIf** or **Else** statement are executed; control is then transferred to the statement following the final **End If** statement. Thus, if condition-1 is **True**, only the first set of statements between condition-1 and conditon-2 are executed; otherwise, condition-2 is tested. If condition-2 is then **True**, only the second set of statements are executed; otherwise, condition-3 is tested. This process continues until a condition is satisfied or the **End If** statement is reached. The final **Else** statement, which is optional, is only executed if none of the previous conditions are satisfied. This serves as a default or "catch all" case that is frequently useful for detecting an error condition. Although only three **ElseIf** parts are illustrated, any number of **ElseIf**'s may be used in the structure, which must be terminated with an **End If** statement.

As a specific example, consider the following **If-Else-ElseIf** statement:

```
If Marcode = "M" Then
    picBox.Print "Individual is married."
ElseIf Marcode = "S" Then
    picBox.Print "Individual is single."
ElseIf Marcode = "D" Then
    picBox.Print "Individual is divorced."
ElseIf Marcode = "W" Then
    picBox.Print "Individual is widowed."
Else
    picBox.Print "An invalid code was entered."
End If
```

Execution through this **If** statement begins with the testing of the expression Marcode = M. If the value in Marcode is an M, the message Individual is married is displayed, no further expressions in the structure are evaluated, and execution resumes with the next statement immediately following the **End If** statement. If the value in Marcode was not an M, the expression Marcode = "S" is tested, and so on, until a **True** condition is found. If none of the conditions in the chain is **True**, the message An invalid code was entered is displayed. In all cases, execution resumes with whatever statement immediately follows the **End If**. Program 5-5 uses this **If-Then-Else** statement within a complete program. The interface and properties for Program 5-5 are illustrated in Figure 5-16 and Table 5-8, respectively.

Since the message in the Picture box depends on the Text box input, we will use our standard procedure of clearing the Picture box when the Text

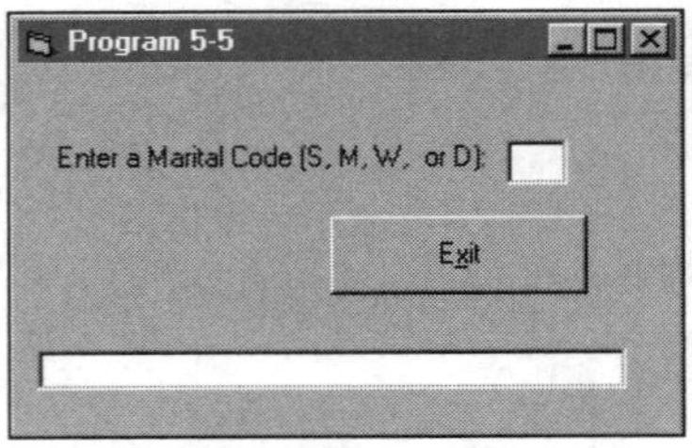

Figure 5-16
Program 5-5's Interface

Table 5-8	Program 5-5's Properties Table	
Object	**Property**	**Setting**
Form	Name	frmMain
	Caption	Program 5-5
Label	Name	lblMcode
	Caption	Enter a Marriage Code (S, M, D, or W):
Text box	Name	txtMcode
	Text	(Blank)
	BackColor	White (Palette tab)
Picture box	Name	picBox
	TabStop	False
	BackColor	White (Palette tab)
Command button	Name	cmdExit
	Caption	E&xit

box gets the focus, and calculate the message to be displayed based on the Text box's data when it loses the focus. This is accomplished by the Text box **GotFocus** and **LostFocus** event code. Within the **LostFocus** event code, the message that is displayed in the Picture box depends on the user input value for Marcode.

Program 5-5's Event Code

```
Private Sub txtMcode_GotFocus()
  picBox.Cls ' clear the picture box
End Sub

Private Sub txtMcode_LostFocus()
  Dim Marcode As String

  Marcode = txtMcode.Text

  If Marcode = "M" Then
    picBox.Print "Individual is married."
  ElseIf Marcode = "S" Then
    picBox.Print "Individual is single."
  ElseIf Marcode = "D" Then
    picBox.Print "Individual is divorced."
  ElseIf Marcode = "W" Then
    picBox.Print "Individual is widowed."
  Else
    picBox.Print "An invalid code was entered."
  End If
End Sub

Private Sub txtMcode_KeyPress(KeyAscii As Integer)
  Const ENTER As Integer = 13 ' the ANSI value of the Enter key

  If KeyAscii = ENTER Then
    KeyAscii = 0
    cmdExit.SetFocus
  End If
End Sub

Private Sub cmdExit_Click()
  Beep
  End
End Sub
```

As a final example illustrating the **If-Else** chain, let us calculate the monthly income of a computer salesperson using the following commission schedule:

Monthly Sales	Income
Greater than or equal to $50,000	$375 plus 16 percent of sales
Less than $50,000 but greater than or equal to $40,000	$350 plus 14 percent of sales
Less than $40,000 but greater than or equal to $30,000	$325 plus 12 percent of sales
Less than $30,000 but greater than or equal to $20,000	$300 plus 9 percent of sales
Less than $20,000 but greater than or equal to $10,000	$250 plus 5 percent of sales
Less than $10,000	$200 plus 3 percent of sales

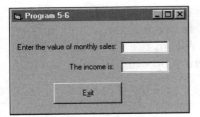

Figure 5-17
Program 5-6's Interface

Table 5-9 Program 5-6's Properties Table

Object	Property	Setting
Form	Name	frmMain
	Caption	Program 5-6
Label	Name	lblSales
	Caption	Enter the value of monthly sales:
Label	Name	lblIncome
	Caption	The income is:
Text box	Name	txtSales
	Text	(Blank)
	BackColor	White (Palette tab)
Picture box	Name	picBox
	TabStop	False
	BackColor	White (Palette tab)
Command button	Name	cmdExit
	Caption	E&xit

The following **If-Then-Else** structure can be used to determine the correct monthly income, where the variable MonthlySales is used to store the salesperson's current monthly sales:

```
If MonthlySales >= 50000.00 Then
   income = 375.00 + 0.16 * MonthlySales
ElseIf MonthlySales >= 40000.00 Then
   income = 350.00 + 0.14 * MonthlySales
ElseIf MonthlySales >= 30000.00 Then
   income = 325.00 + 0.12 * MonthlySales
ElseIf MonthlySales >= 20000.00 Then
   income = 300.00 + 0.09 * MonthlySales
ElseIf MonthlySales >= 10000.00 Then
   income = 250.00 + 0.05 * MonthlySales
Else
   income = 200.000 + 0.03 * MonthlySales
End If
```

Notice that this example makes use of the fact that the testing stops once a **True** condition is found. This is accomplished by checking for the highest monthly sales first. If the salesperson's monthly sales are less than $50,000, the **If-Then-ElseIf** chain continues checking for the next highest sales amount, until the correct category is obtained.

Program 5-6 uses this **If-Then-ElseIf** chain to calculate and display the income corresponding to the value of monthly sales input by the user in the Text box. The interface and properties for Program 5-6 are illustrated in Figure 5-17 and Table 5-9, respectively.

Program 5-6's Event Code

```
Private Sub txtSales_GotFocus()
  picBox.Cls
End Sub
```

```
Private Sub txtSales_LostFocus()
  Dim MonthlySales As Single
  Dim income As Single

  MonthlySales = Val(txtSales.Text)
  If MonthlySales >= 50000.00 Then
    income = 375.00 + 0.16 * MonthlySales
  ElseIf MonthlySales >= 40000.00 Then
    income = 350.00 + 0.14 * MonthlySales
  ElseIf MonthlySales >= 30000.00 Then
    income = 325.00 + 0.12 * MonthlySales
  ElseIf MonthlySales >= 20000.00 Then
    income = 300.00 + 0.09 * MonthlySales
  ElseIf MonthlySales >= 10000.00 Then
    income = 250.00 + 0.05 * MonthlySales
  Else
    income = 200.00 + 0.03 * MonthlySales
  End If

  picBox.Print Format(income, "Currency")
End Sub

Private Sub txtSales_KeyPress(KeyAscii As Integer)
  Const ENTER As Integer = 13 ' the ANSI value of the Enter key
  Const DECPOINT As Integer = 46 ' the ANSI value of the decimal point

  If KeyAscii = ENTER Then
    KeyAscii = 0
    cmdExit.SetFocus
  ElseIf (KeyAscii < Asc("0") Or KeyAscii > Asc("9")) And KeyAscii <> DECPOINT Then
    KeyAscii = 0
    Beep
  End If
End Sub

Private Sub cmdExit_Click()
  Beep
  End
End Sub
```

The selection code contained within the **LostFocus** event is simply the **If-Then-ElseIf** statement previously presented. A new feature of the event code, however, is contained within the **KeyPress** event procedure. Notice that we have included the ANSI code for the decimal point and have included the decimal point as one of the valid keys that may be pressed by a user when entering a number. Figure 5-18 illustrates a sample run using Program 5-6.

Figure 5-18
A Sample Run Using Program 5-6

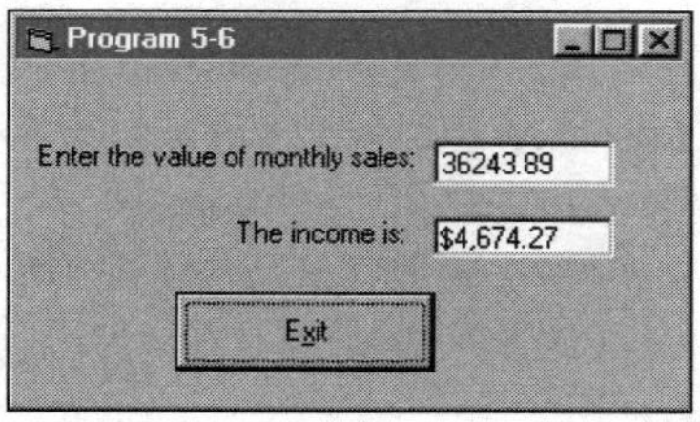

Exercises   **5.4**

1. Modify Program 5-5 to accept both lower- and uppercase letters as marriage codes. For example, if a user enters either an `m` or an `M`, the program should display the message `Individual is married`.

2. Write **If** statements corresponding to the compound conditions illustrated in each of the following flowcharts. (**Hint**: Use a logical operator.)

   a.   b.

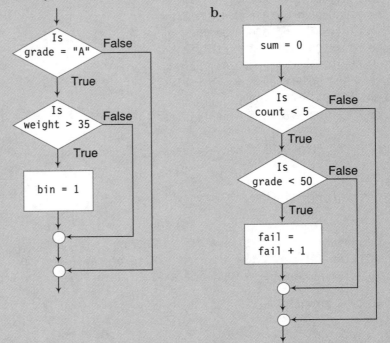

3. An angle is considered acute if it is less than 90 degrees, obtuse if it is greater than 90 degrees, and a right angle if it is equal to 90 degrees. Using this information, write a Visual Basic program that accepts an angle, in degrees, and displays the type of angle corresponding to the degrees entered.

4. The grade level of undergraduate college students is typically determined according to the following schedule:

Number of Credits Completed	Grade Level
Less than 32	Freshman
32 to 63	Sophomore
64 to 95	Junior
96 or more	Senior

   Using this information, write a Visual Basic program that accepts the number of credits a student has completed, determines the student's grade level, and displays the grade level.

5. A student's letter grade is calculated according to the following schedule:

Numerical grade	Letter grade
Greater than or equal to 90	A
Less than 90 but greater than or equal to 80	B
Less than 80 but greater than or equal to 70	C
Less than 70 but greater than or equal to 60	D
Less than 60	F

Using this information, write a Visual Basic program that accepts a student's numerical grade, converts the numerical grade to an equivalent letter grade, and displays the letter grade.

6　The interest rate used on funds deposited in a bank is determined by the amount of time the money is left on deposit. For a particular bank, the following schedule is used:

Time on deposit	Interest rate
Greater than or equal to 5 years	7.5 percent
Less than 5 years but greater than or equal to 4 years	7.0 percent
Less than 4 years but greater than or equal to 3 years	6.5 percent
Less than 3 years but greater than or equal to 2 years	5.5 percent
Less than 2 years but greater than or equal to 1 year	4.65 percent
Less than 1 year	3.58 percent

With this information, write a Visual Basic program that accepts the time funds are left on deposit and displays the interest rate corresponding to the time entered.

7　Using the commission schedule from Program 5-6, a student coded the Text box's **LostFocus** event procedure as follows:

```
Private Sub txtSales_LostFocus()
  Dim MonthlySales As Single
  Dim income As Single

  MonthlySales = Val(txtSales.Text)
  If MonthlySales >= 50000.00 Then
    income = 375.00 +.16 * MonthlySales
  End If
  If MonthlySales >= 40000.00 && MonthlySales < 50000.00 Then
    income = 350.00 +.14 * MonthlySales
  End If
  If MonthlySales >= 30000.00 && MonthlySales < 40000.00 Then
    income = 325.00 +.12 * MonthlySales
  End If
  If MonthlySales >= 20000.00 && MonthlySales < 30000.00 Then
    income = 300.00 +.09 * MonthlySales
  End If
  If MonthlySales >= 10000.00 && MonthlySales < 20000.00 Then
    income = 250.00 +.05 * MonthlySales
  End If
  If MonthlySales < 10000.00 Then
    income = 200.00 +.03 * MonthlySales
  End If
  picBox.Print Format(income, "Currency")
End Sub
```

a.　Will this code produce the same output as Program 5-6?
b.　Which program is better and why?

8 **a.** Will the following event code produce the same result as that used in Program 5-6?

```
Private Sub txtSales_LostFocus()
  Dim MonthlySales As Single
  Dim income As Single

  MonthlySales = Val(txtSales.Text)
  If MonthlySales < 10000.00
    income = 200.00 +.03 * MonthlySales
  ElseIf MonthlySales >= 10000.00 Then
    income = 250.00 +.05 * MonthlySales
  ElseIf MonthlySales >= 20000.00 Then
    income = 300.00 +.09 * MonthlySales
  ElseIf MonthlySales >= 30000.00 Then
    income = 325.00 +.12 * MonthlySales
  ElseIf MonthlySales >= 40000.00 Then
    income = 350.00 +.14 * MonthlySales
  ElseIf MonthlySales >= 50000.00 Then
    income = 375.00 +.16 * MonthlySales
  End If
  picBox.Print Format(income, "Currency")
End Sub
```

  b. What does the event procedure do?
  c. For what values of monthly sales does this procedure calculate the correct income?

9 **a.** Write a Visual Basic program that accepts two real numbers from a user, using individual Text boxes, and a Select code using an Option box group. If the entered Select code is 1, have the program add the two previously entered numbers and display the result; if the Select code is 2, the second number should be subtracted from the first number; if the Select code is 3, the numbers should be multiplied; and if the Select code is 4, the first number should be divided by the second number.

  b. Determine what the program written in Exercise 9. does when the entered numbers are 3 and 0, and the Select code is 3.

  c. Modify the program written in Exercise 9a so that division by 0 is not allowed and so that an appropriate message is displayed when such a division is attempted.

10 **a.** Write a program that displays the following two Labels:

```
Enter a month (use a 1 for Jan, etc.):
Enter a day of the month:
```

Have your program accept a user-input number in a Text box and store the number in a variable named month, in response to the first Label prompt. Similarly, accept and store a number entered in a second Text box in the variable day in response to the second Label prompt. If the month entered is not 1–12 (inclusive), print a message informing the user that an invalid month has been entered. If the day entered is not 1–31, print a message informing the user that an invalid day has been entered.

   b. What will your program do if the user types a number with a decimal point for the month? How can you ensure that your **If** statements check for an integer number?

   c. In a non-leap year, February has 28 days, the months January, March, May, July, August, October, and December have 31 days, and all other months have 30 days. Using this information, modify the program written in Exercise 10a. to display a message when an invalid day is entered for a user-entered month. For this program, ignore leap years.

11 All years that are evenly divisible by 400 or are evenly divisible by 4 and not evenly divisible by 100, are leap years. For example, since 1600 is evenly divisible by 400, the year 1600 was a leap year. Similarly, since 1988 is evenly divisible by 4 but not by 100, the year 1988 was also a leap year. Using this information, write a Visual Basic program that accepts the year as a user input, determines if the year is a leap year, and displays a message that tells the user if the entered year is or is not a leap year.

12 Based on an automobile's model year and weight, the state of New Jersey determines a car's weight class and registration fee using the following schedule:

Model Year	Weight	Weight Class	Registration Fee
1970 or earlier	Less than 2,700 lbs	1	$16.50
	2,700 to 3,800 lbs	2	$25.50
	More than 3,800 lbs	3	$46.50
1971 to 1979	Less than 2,700 lbs	4	$27.00
	2,700 to 3,800 lbs	5	$30.50
	More than 3,800 lbs	6	$52.50
1980 or later	Less than 3,500 lbs	7	$19.50
	3,500 or more lbs	8	$52.50

Using this information, write a Visual Basic program that accepts the year and weight of an automobile and determines and displays the weight class and registration fee for the car.

5.5 The Select Case Structure

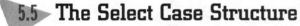

An alternative to the **If-Then-ElseIf** structure presented in the previous section is the **Select Case** structure. The syntax of the **Select Case** construct is

```
Select Case expression
   Case value-1
      statement(s)
   Case value-2
      statement(s)
         .
         .
   Case value-n
      statement(s)
   Case Else
      statement(s)
End Select         ' End of Select Structure
```

The **Select Case** structure uses three new Visual Basic statements, a single **Select Case** statement, one or more **Case** statements, and a required **End Select** statement. Let us see how these statements are used. The **Select Case** statement, which has the general form

> `Select Case` *expression*

identifies the start of the **Select Case** structure. The expression in this statement is evaluated and the result of the expression is compared to various alternative values contained within each **Case** statement.

Internal to the **Select Case** construct, the **Case** statement, which has the general syntax

> `Case` *list of values*

is used to identify individual values that are compared to the value of the **Select Case** expression. The expression's value is compared to each of these **Case** values, in the order that these values are listed, until a match is found. Execution then begins with the statement immediately following the matching **Case** and ends when either the next **Case** or **End Select** statement is encountered. The **Select Case** structure is then exited and program execution continues with the statement following the **End Select** statement. Thus, as illustrated in Figure 5-19, the value of the expression determines where in the **Case** construct execution actually begins.

Any number of **Case** labels may be contained within a **Select Case** structure, in any order; the only requirement is that the values in each **Case** statement must be of the same type as the expression in the **Select Case** statement. If the value of the expression does not match any of the case values, however, no statement within the structure is executed unless a **Case Else** statement is encountered. The keyword **Else** is optional in a **Select Case** structure and produces the same effect as the last **Else** in an **If-ElseIf**

Figure 5-19
The Expression Determines an Entry Point

```
                                      switch case expression
Start here if  ───────────►  case value-1
expression equals value-1       .
                                .
                                .
Start here if  ───────────►  case value-2
expression equals value-2       .
                                .
                                .
Start here if  ───────────►  case value-3
expression equals value-3       .
                                .
                                .
Start here if  ───────────►  case value-n
expression equals value-n       .
                                .
                                .
Start here if  ───────────►  Case Else
no previous match               .
                                .
                                .
```

structure. If the value of the **Select Case** expression does not match any of the **Case** values, and the **Case Else** statement is present, execution begins with the statement following the word **Else**.

Once an entry point has been located by the **Select Case** structure, all further **Case** evaluations are ignored and execution continues until either a **Case** or **End Select** statement is encountered.

When writing a **Select Case** structure, you can use multiple case values to refer to the same set of statements; the **Case Else** is optional. For example, consider the following:

```
Select Case number
  Case 1
    Print "Have a Good Morning"
  Case 2
    Print "Have a Happy Day"
  Case 3, 4, 5
    Print "Have a Nice Evening"
End Select
```

If the value stored in the variable number is 1, the message Have a Good Morning is displayed. Similarly, if the value of number is 2, the second message is displayed. Finally, if the value of number is 3 or 4 or 5, the last message is displayed. Since the statement to be executed for these last three cases is the same, the cases for these values can be "stacked together," as shown in the example. Also, since there is no **Case Else**, no message is printed if the value of number is not one of the listed case values. Although it is good programming practice to list case values in increasing order, this is not required by the **Select Case** statement. A **Select Case** statement may have any number of case values, in any order; only the values being tested for need be listed.

A **Select Case** structure can also be used to test the value of a string expression. For example, assuming that letter is a string variable, the following **Select Case** statement is valid:

```
Select Case letter
  Case "a", "e", "i", "o", "u", "A", "E", "I", "O", "U"
    Print "The character is a vowel"
  Case Else
    Print "The character is not a vowel"
End Select
```

Exercises 5.5

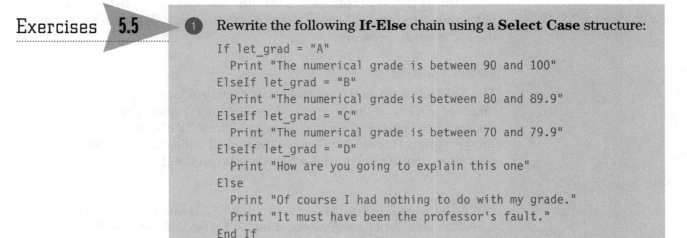

1. Rewrite the following **If-Else** chain using a **Select Case** structure:

```
If let_grad = "A"
  Print "The numerical grade is between 90 and 100"
ElseIf let_grad = "B"
  Print "The numerical grade is between 80 and 89.9"
ElseIf let_grad = "C"
  Print "The numerical grade is between 70 and 79.9"
ElseIf let_grad = "D"
  Print "How are you going to explain this one"
Else
  Print "Of course I had nothing to do with my grade."
  Print "It must have been the professor's fault."
End If
```

2 Rewrite the following **If-Else** chain using a **Select Case** structure:

```
If res_typ = 1
   a = b + c
ElseIf res_typ = 2
   a = b * c
ElseIf res_typ = 3
   a = b / c
ElseIf res_typ = 4
   a = 4
ElseIf res_typ = 5
   a = c/b
ElseIf res_typ = 6
   a = b + c/d
```

3 Each disk drive in a shipment of these devices is stamped with a code 1–4, which indicates a drive from among the following types:

Code	Disk	Drive Type
1	360 Kilobyte Drive	(5 1/2-inch)
2	1.2 Megabyte Drive	(5 1/2-inch)
3	722 Kilobyte Drive	(3 1/4-inch)
4	1.4 Megabyte Drive	(3 1/4-inch)

Write a Visual Basic program that accepts the code number as an input and, based on the value entered, displays the correct disk drive type.

5.6 ▶ Focus on Program Design and Implementation:

Focus Control and On-the-Fly Data Validation

Figure 5-20 illustrates the Rotech project's current Walk In order-entry form.[2] With the information provided in this chapter we can now provide this form with two additional features required of all commercial applications: focus control features that automatically move the focus to the next input control when the ENTER key is pressed, and input data validation, so that a user cannot enter data that will cause the program to crash. We start by providing the focus control feature.

Focus Control

The **TabIndex** property controls how focus shifts when a user presses either the TAB key or the SHIFT-TAB keys together; pressing the tab key moves the focus to the control with the next highest **TabIndex** value, while the SHIFT-TAB keys moves the focus in the opposite direction. In addition to this operation, users expect that when they press the ENTER key, input to the

---

[2]The Rotech project, as it should exist at the start of this section (which includes all of the capabilities built into it through the end of Section 4.4) can be found on the Student Disk as the rotech4.vbp project within the rotech4 folder.

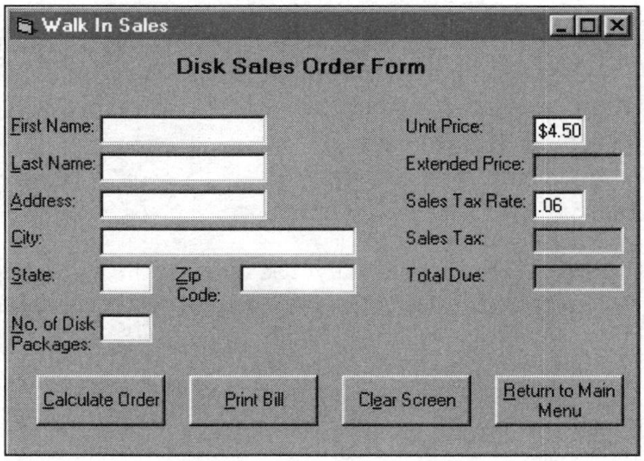

Figure 5-20
The Current Walk in Order Entry
Form

current control will stop, and focus will shift to the next input control. Unfortunately, this operation is not built into Visual Basic. To force this type of focus shift we can use each control's **KeyPress** event to detect when the ⌧ENTER⌧ key has been pressed, and then use the **SetFocus** method to explicitly shift the focus to another control when the detection is made. Event Procedure 5-1 illustrates the code that can be used for the First Name Text box shown in Figure 5-20 (named txtFname) to shift focus to the Last Name Text box (named txtLname) when the ⌧ENTER⌧ key is pressed. If this code is unfamiliar to you, review Section 5.3's Input Data Validation section, where the code is described in detail.

Event Procedure 5-1

```
Private Sub txtFname_KeyPress(KeyAscii As Integer)
  Const ENTER As Integer = 13 ' the ANSI value of the Enter key

  If KeyAscii = ENTER Then
    KeyAscii = 0
    txtLname.SetFocus
  End If
End Sub
```

One drawback to Event Procedure 5-1's code is that the control's name to which the focus is shifted must be included with the **SetFocus** method. That is, there is no Visual Basic statement that uses the **TabIndex** property to focus on the next **TabIndex** value. Event Procedures 5-2 illustrate the complete set of procedures, including Event Procedure 5-1, that can be used to control the shifting of focus, using the ⌧ENTER⌧ key, for Rotech's Walk In order entry form.

Event Procedures 5-2

```
Private Sub txtFname_KeyPress(KeyAscii As Integer)
  Const ENTER As Integer = 13 ' the ANSI value of the Enter key

  If KeyAscii = ENTER Then
    KeyAscii = 0
    txtLname.SetFocus
  End If
End Sub
```

continued

```
Private Sub txtLname_KeyPress(KeyAscii As Integer)
  Const ENTER As Integer = 13 ' the ANSI value of the Enter key
  If KeyAscii = ENTER Then
    KeyAscii = 0
    txtAddr.SetFocus
  End If
End Sub

Private Sub txtAddr_KeyPress(KeyAscii As Integer)
  Const ENTER As Integer = 13 ' the ANSI value of the Enter key
  If KeyAscii = ENTER Then
    KeyAscii = 0
    txtCity.SetFocus
  End If
End Sub

Private Sub txtCity_KeyPress(KeyAscii As Integer)
  Const ENTER As Integer = 13 ' the ANSI value of the Enter key
  If KeyAscii = ENTER Then
    KeyAscii = 0
    txtState.SetFocus
  End If
End Sub

Private Sub txtState_KeyPress(KeyAscii As Integer)
  Const ENTER As Integer = 13 ' the ANSI value of the Enter key
  If KeyAscii = ENTER Then
    KeyAscii = 0
    txtZip.SetFocus
  End If
End Sub

Private Sub txtZip_KeyPress(KeyAscii As Integer)
  Const ENTER As Integer = 13 ' the ANSI value of the Enter key
  If KeyAscii = ENTER Then
    KeyAscii = 0
    txtQuantity.SetFocus
  End If
End Sub

Private Sub txtQuantity_KeyPress(KeyAscii As Integer)
  Const ENTER As Integer = 13 ' the ANSI value of the Enter key
  If KeyAscii = ENTER Then
    KeyAscii = 0
    cmdCalculate.SetFocus
  End If
End Sub
```

In reviewing the procedures contained within Event Procedures 5-2, notice that all procedures are essentially copies of Event Procedure 5-1, with the only difference being the object named for the **SetFocus** method. Thus, once you have coded one of these procedures, you can use standard copy and paste techniques to include the code within each subsequent event procedure, and then change the object named to receive focus.

Also, notice that the last event procedure listed shifts the focus to the Calculate, rather than the Print Command button. Although most of the time a user will want to print a bill from the order entry form, shifting focus to the Calculate button prevents a user from inadvertently printing a bill by unconsciously pressing the [ENTER] key one too many times. Pressing the [ENTER] key while the focus is on the Calculate button will simply fill in the order form with the calculated data, and still force the user to make a conscious choice of either tabbing over to the Print button or using this button's access key when a bill is needed.

On-the-Fly Input Data Validation

The user input to the Walk In form that can easily cause the system to crash is the quantity of disks ordered. If the data entered here is either not numeric or cannot be converted to numeric data, the system will crash when it uses this quantity to calculate a total amount. The most powerful way to ensure correct data is to verify each keystroke made by the user as data is being entered. This type of input data validation, where each keystroke is checked immediately after being pressed, is referred to as on-the-fly validation. For our particular case, the entered data must be an integer, which means each key pressed should either be the [ENTER] key or correspond to a digit between 0 and 9. This type of validation was presented in Section 5.3, and the relevant code is repeated below for convenience:

```
If KeyAscii < Asc("0") Or KeyAscii > Asc("9") Then
  KeyAscii = 0
  Beep
End If
```

This code can easily be incorporated into the existing If statement within the txtQuantity Text box **KeyPress** event code listed in Event Procedures 5-2. Doing so, provides the code listed in Event Procedure 5-3. Notice that in this code we have also added a Message box to inform the user that an incorrect character was entered.

Event Procedure 5-3

```
Private Sub txtQuantity_KeyPress(KeyAscii As Integer)
  Const ENTER As Integer = 13 ' the ANSI value of the Enter key

  If KeyAscii = ENTER Then
    KeyAscii = 0
    cmdCalculate.SetFocus
  ElseIf KeyAscii < Asc("0") Or KeyAscii > Asc("9") Then
    KeyAscii = 0
    Beep
    MsgBox "You can only enter a number here.", vbCritical, "Data Entry Error"
  End If
End Sub
```

Exercises ▶ 5.6

(**Note:** The Rotech Systems project, at the stage of development begun in this section, can be found on the Student Disk in the rotech4 folder as project rotech4.vbp. The project, as it exists at the end of this section, can be found on the Student Disk in the rotech5 folder as project rotech5.vbp. If you are developing the system yourself, following the procedures given in this section, we suggest that you first copy all of the files in the rotech4 folder into the temp folder, and then work out of this latter folder. When you have finished your changes you can compare your results to the files in the rotech5 folder.)

1. a. Either add the data validation and (ENTER) key focus shifting code described in this section to the Rotech system or locate and load the project from the Student Disk.
   b. Test that the (ENTER) key correctly shifts control focus as expected, and that the data validation procedure correctly works when a quantity is entered into the Walk In Order Entry form.

2. Add the same type of focus shifting and input data validation to Rotech system's Mail In form as was made to the Walk In form.

3. Using the Help facilities' Index tab, obtain information on the **SetFocus** method used within all of the **Click** event procedures presented in this section.

4. a. Modify the Walk in form's <u>P</u>rint button's event code to provide the following two features:
      i. If both the first and last name Text boxes are blank, the name printed on the bill and displayed in the txtFname Text box should be "Cash."
      ii. If no quantity is entered in the quantity Text box, a Message box should be displayed indicating that a bill will not be printed unless an amount is entered.
   b. Would you classify the data validation code written for Exercise 4a as on-the-fly validation? Why or why not?

5. **CASE STUDY**
   For your selected project (see project specifications at the end of Section 1.5) complete the order entry form you developed in the previous chapter by adding appropriate input data validation and (ENTER) key activated focus shifting.

5.7 Knowing About: Errors, Testing, and Debugging

The ideal in programming is to efficiently produce readable, error-free programs that work correctly and can be modified or changed with a minimum of testing required for reverification. In this regard, it is useful to know the different types of errors that can occur, when they are detected, and how to correct them.

Design-Time and Run-Time Errors

A program error can be detected at a variety of times:

1. During design time,
2. During run time,
3. After the program has been executed and the output is being examined, or
4. Not at all.

Errors detected by the compiler are formally referred to as *design-time* errors and errors that occur while the program is being run are formally referred to as *run-time* errors.

Methods are available for detecting errors both before and after a program has been executed. The method for detecting errors after a program has been executed is called *program verification and testing*. The method for detecting errors before a program is run is called *desk checking* because the programmer sits at a desk or table and checks the program, by hand, for syntax and logic errors.

Syntax and Logic Errors

There are two primary types of errors, referred to as syntax and logic errors, respectively. A *syntax* error is an error in the structure or spelling of a statement. For example, the statements

```
If a < b
   Print "There are four syntax errors here
   Pint " can you find tem"
End
```

contain four syntax errors. These errors are

1. The keyword **Then** is missing in the first line.

2. A closing double quote is missing in line two.

3. The keyword **Print** is misspelled in line three.

4. The **End** keyword in line four should be **End If**.

All of these errors will be detected by Visual Basic when the program is translated for execution. This is true of all syntax errors since they violate the basic rules of the language.[3] In some cases the error message is clear and the error is obvious; in other cases it takes a little detective work to understand the error message. Note that the misspelling of the word tem in the second **Print** statement is not a syntax error. Although this spelling error will result in an undesirable output line being displayed, it is not a violation of Visual Basic's syntactical rules. It is a simple case of a typographical error, commonly referred to as a "typo."

Logic errors result directly from some flaw in the program's logic. These errors, which are never caught during translation, may be detected by desk checking, by program testing, by accident when a user obtains an obviously erroneous output, while the program is executing, or not at all. If the error is detected while the program is executing, a run-time error occurs that results in an error message being generated and/or abnormal and premature program termination.

Since logic errors may not be detected during translation, they are always more difficult to detect than syntax errors. If not detected by desk checking, a logic error will reveal itself in several predominant ways.

1. **No output**
    This is caused either by an omission of an output statement or by a sequence of statements that inadvertently bypasses an output statement.

2. **Unappealing or misaligned output**
    This is caused by an error in an output statement.

3. **Incorrect numerical results**
    This is caused either by incorrect values assigned to the variables used in an expression, the use of an incorrect arithmetic expression, an

---

[3]They may not, however, all be detected at the same time. Frequently, one syntax error masks another error and the second error is only detected after the first error is corrected.

omission of a statement, a roundoff error, or the use of an improper sequence of statements.

Sometimes faulty or incomplete program logic will cause a run-time error. Examples of this type of logic error are attempts to divide by zero or to take the square root of a negative number.

Testing and Debugging

In theory, a comprehensive set of test runs would reveal all possible program errors and ensure that a program will work correctly for any and all combinations of input and computed data. In practice this requires checking all possible combinations of event activation and statement execution. Due to the time and effort required, this is an impossible goal except for extremely simple programs. Let us see why this is so. Consider the following event code that is activated on a Command button **Click** event:

```
Private Sub cmdTest_Click()
  Dim num As Integer

  num = val(txtBox.text)
  If num = 5 Then
    Print "Bingo!"
  Else
    Print "Bongo!"
  End If
End Sub
```

This event code has two paths that can be traversed when the event code is activated. The first path, which is executed when the input number is 5, consists of the statement:

```
Print "Bingo!"
```

The second path, which is executed whenever any number except 5 is input, consists of the statement

```
Print "Bongo!"
```

To test each possible path through this event code requires two activations of the **Click** event, with a judicious selection of test input data to ensure that both paths of the **If** statement are exercised. The addition of one more **If-Else** statement in the program increases the number of possible execution paths by a factor of two and requires four (2^2) runs of the program for complete testing. Similarly, two additional **If-Else** statements increase the number of paths by a factor of four and requires eight (2^3) runs for complete testing, and three additional **If-Else** statements would produce a program that required sixteen (2^4) test runs.

Now consider a modestly sized application consisting of only ten event procedures, with each procedure containing five **If-Else** statements. Assuming the procedures are always activated in the same sequence, there are 32 possible paths through each module (2 raised to the fifth power) and more than 1,000,000,000,000,000 (2 raised to the fiftieth power) possible paths through the complete application (all modules executed in sequence). The time needed to create individual test data to exercise each path and the actual computer run time required to check each path make the complete testing of such a program impossible to achieve.

The inability to fully test all combinations of statement execution sequences has led to the claim that there is no error-free program. It has also led to the realization that any testing should be well thought out to maximize the possibility of locating errors. At a minimum, test data should include appropriate values for input values, illegal input values that the program should reject, and limiting values that are checked by selection statements within the program.

Another important realization is that, although a single test can reveal the presence of an error, it cannot guarantee the absence of one. The fact that one error is revealed by a particular verification run does not indicate that another error is not lurking somewhere else in the program, and the fact that one test revealed no errors does not indicate that there are no errors.

Although there are no hard-and-fast rules for isolating the cause of an error, some useful techniques can be applied. The first of these is preventive. Many errors are simply introduced by the programmer in the rush to code and run a program, before fully understanding what is required and how the result is to be achieved. A symptom of this haste to get a program entered into the computer is the lack of an outline of the proposed program (pseudocode or flowcharts) or a handwritten program itself. Many errors can be eliminated simply by desk checking a copy of each procedure before it is ever entered or translated.

A second useful technique is to mimic the computer and execute each statement, by hand, as the computer would. This means writing down each variable as it is encountered in the program and listing the value that should be stored in the variable, as each input and assignment statement is encountered. Doing this also sharpens your programming skills, because it requires that you fully understand what each statement in your program causes to happen. Such a check is called *program tracing*.

A third debugging technique is to use one or more diagnostic **Print** statements to display the values of selected variables. In this same manner, another use of **Print** statements in debugging is to immediately display the values of all input data. This technique is referred to as *echo printing*, and is useful in establishing that the computer is correctly receiving and interpreting the input data.

The fourth and most powerful debugging technique is to use the debugger that comes with Visual Basic. The debugger was introduced in Chapter 4 and is discussed further in Chapter 7.

Finally, no discussion of program verification is complete without mentioning the primary ingredient needed for successful isolation and correction of errors. This is the attitude and spirit you bring to the task. Since you wrote the program, your natural assumption is that it is correct, or you would have changed it before it was executed. It is extremely difficult to back away and honestly test and find errors in your own software. As a programmer, you must constantly remind yourself that just because you *think* your program is correct does not make it so. Finding errors in your own programs is a sobering experience, but one that will help you become a master programmer. It can also be exciting and fun, if approached as a detection problem with you as the master detective.

5.8 ▶ Common Programming Errors and Problems

The common programming errors related to Visual Basic's selection statements include the following:

1. Omitting the keyword **Then** from an **If-Else** statement.

2. Writing the keyword **ElseIf** as the two words, **Else** and **If**.

3. Trying to use a logical operator without a relational expression or logical variable immediately following it. For example, the expression

```
age >= 35 And < 40
```

is invalid. The expression

```
age >= 35 And age < 40
```

which uses the **And** operator to connect the two relational expressions is valid.

4. This error presents a typical debugging problem. Here an **If** statement appears to select an incorrect choice and the programmer mistakenly concentrates on the tested condition as the source of the problem. For example, assume that the following **If-Else** statement is part of your program:

```
If key = "F" Then
  temp = (5.0 / 9.0) * (temp - 32.0)
  txtBox.text = "Conversion to Celsius completed"
Else
  temp = (9.0 / 5.0) * temp + 32.0
  txtBox.text = "Conversion to Fahrenheit completed"
End If
```

This statement will always display `Conversion to Celsius completed` when the variable `key` contains an `F`. Therefore, if this message is displayed when you believe `key` does not contain F, investigation of `key`'s value is called for. As a general rule, whenever a selection statement does not act as you think it should, make sure to test your assumptions about the values assigned to the tested variables, by displaying these values. If an unanticipated value is displayed, you have at least isolated the source of the problem to the variables themselves, rather than the structure of the **If-Then** statement. From there you will have to determine where and how the incorrect value was obtained.

5.9 ▶ Chapter Review

Key Terms

Check box
condition
flag
If-Then-Else structure
input data validation
logical operators

nested **If**
one-way selection
Option button
Select Case structure
simple relational expression

Summary

1. Relational expressions, which are also called *simple conditions*, are used to compare operands. The value of a relational expression is either **True** or **False**. Relational expressions are created using the following relational operators:

Relational Operator	Meaning	Example
<	Less than	age < 30
>	Greater than	height > 6.2
<=	Less than or equal to	taxable <= 20000
>=	Greater than or equal to	temp >= 98.6
=	Equal to	grade = 100
<>	Not equal to	number <> 250

2. More complex conditions can be constructed from relational expressions using Visual Basic's **And**, **Or**, and **Not** logical operators.

3. An **If** statement is used to select one or more statements for execution based on the value of a condition. The **If** statement has the syntax

```
If condition Then
```

and must always be used with an **End If** statement. Additionally, one **Else** statement and any number of **ElseIf** statements may be used with an **If** statement to provide multiple selection criteria. The common selection structures that can be created using an **If** statement include the following forms:

Form 1—Simple **If**:

```
If condition Then
   statement(s)
End If
```

Here, the statements between the **If** and **End If** statements are only executed if the condition being tested is **True**. The **If** and **End If** statements must be written on separate lines.

Form 2—Simple **If-Else**:

```
If condition Then
   statement(s)
Else
   statement(s)
End If
```

This is a two-way selection structure. Here the **Else** statement is used with the **If** to select between two alternative sets of statements based on the value of a condition. If the condition is **True**, the first set of statements is executed; otherwise, the set of statements following the keyword **Else** are executed. The **If**, **Else**, and **End If** statements must be written on separate lines.

Form 3—Simple **If-ElseIf-Else**:

```
If condition-1 Then
   statement(s)
ElseIf condition-2 Then
   statement(s)
Else
   statement(s)
End If
```

This is a three-way selection structure. Once a condition is satisfied, only the statements between that condition and the next **ElseIf** or **Else** are executed, and no further conditions are tested. The **Else** statement is optional, and the statements corresponding to the **Else** statement are only executed if neither condition-1 nor condition-2 is **True**. The **If**, **ElseIf**, **Else**, and **End If** statements must be written on separate lines.

Form 4—Multiple **Else-Ifs**:

```
If condition-1 Then
   statement(s)
ElseIf condition-2 Then
   statement(s)
       .
       .
       .
ElseIf condition-n Then
   statement(s)
Else
   statement(s)
End If
```

This is a multi-way selection structure. Once a condition is satisfied, only the statements between that condition and the next **ElseIf** or **Else** are executed and no further conditions are tested. The **Else** statement is optional, and the statements corresponding to the **Else** statement are only executed if none of the conditions tested are **True**. The **If**, **Else**, and **End If** statements must be written on individual lines.

4. The **Then** keyword can be omitted if a one-way **If** statement fits on a single line:

```
If condition statement
```

Test Yourself—Short Answer

1. The **Select Case** statement always ends with the statement _____.

2. If you click a "grayed" Check box, what will happen?

3. The method for detecting errors before a program is run is called _____ because the programmer sits at a desk or table and checks the program by hand, for syntax and logic errors.

4. If your form has a single group of 5 Check boxes and a single group of 5 Option buttons, how many of the Check boxes can be true at the same time? How many of the option buttons can be true at the same time?

5. Write a **Select Case** statement that will check the value of a variable myNum and process as following:

myNum Value	Required Processing
1 or 7 or 15	Add 100 to myNum
2 or 9 or 21	Add 150 to myNum
3 or 6 or 13	Add 200 to myNum
none of the above	print "Can't find it"

Programming Projects

1. Implement a calculator similar to the one pictured in Figure 5-21. An executable example of this calculator can be found on the Student Disk as calc.exe. Although you are free to design your calculator interface and functionality however you like, the button operation must be consistent with a typical calculator.

   Requirements:

   i. There can only be one number display (like a calculator).
   ii. Your calculator must have support for: addition, subtraction, multiplication, and division.
   iii. Your calculator needs to have (at least) the following features:
      A square root function
      An additive inverse function (+/- key to negate the display)
      A multiplicative inverse function (1/x to get the reciprocal of the display)
      A clear key.
   iv. The Divide button needs to check for divide by zero using an **If-Then** statement.

   Although you can start with the simple calculator completed for Programming Project 1 in the previous chapter, significant redesign will need to be done.

2. Create the interface shown in Figure 5-22. Using the interface to select a desired display, clicking the update button should update the text in the Text box. Also, make sure that each group of Option and Check boxes are enclosed within their own Frame control. An executable example of this program can be found on the Student Disk as font.exe.

   To do this Project:

   i. Create the interface (the form and its controls).
   ii. Add Visual Basic code to the "Update" button's **Click** event procedure. This code will consist of a series of **If-Then** type statements to set the properties of the Text box.
   iii. Set the **FontName** property before the size and style properties, or inconsistent results can occur!

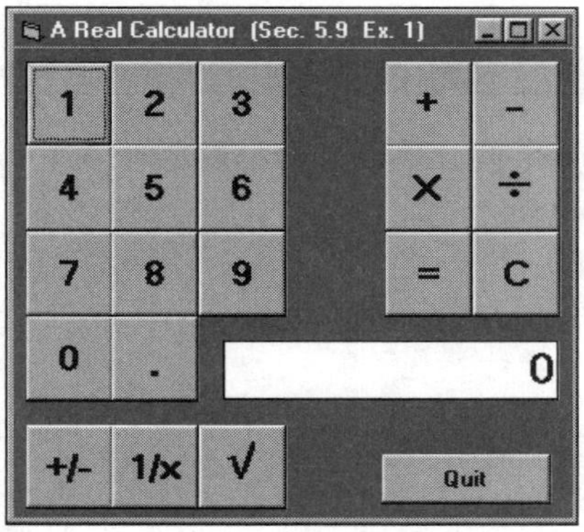

Figure 5-21
Form for Programming Project 1

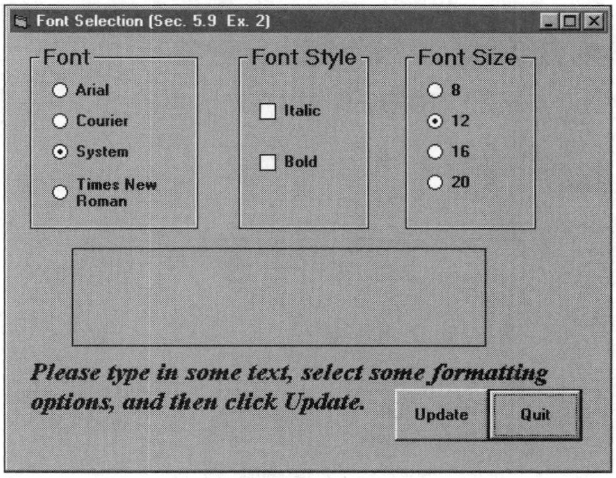

Figure 5-22
Form for Programming Project 2

iv. Make sure to put the Frame control on the interface first, and then place the desired set of Option boxes or Check boxes within the Frame control.

3. a. Change the RETIREMENT PARTY form created in Program 1 from Chapter 2 to include the following features:

    i. Increase the size of the form to accommodate the following additions.

    ii. A line at the bottom of the invitation area named linBase. This line will be used to determine the area to be printed.

    iii.. Two Check boxes that will be used to select bold and italic fonts for the invitation's title.

    iv. Three Option buttons in a frame that will be used to color the invitations title.

Your form should look like that shown in Figure 5-23.

b. **Extra Challenge.** Use the Help facility for information on the **PrintForm** method, and use this method to print the form (party invitation), up to the linBase line, on the printer.

4. Create a program that will calculate the cost of the purchase of donuts. Below is a list of the types of donuts offered and their price at Dopey's Donut Shop. Dopey needs a program which will calculate the cost of a donut purchase (price per donut * quantity of that donut) with the tax added in (6% sales tax).

Donut Type	Cost
chocolate frosted cake	50¢
cherry vanilla cake	60¢
plain glazed yeast	40¢
German chocolate cake	55¢
plain cake	35¢

A suggested form for this programming project is shown in Figure 5-24.

5. Create a project that calculates the user's actual tax rate by including social security and medicare contributions in the tax rate. The user is asked to indicate his tax rate (choices are presented in Radio buttons and a Frame), enter his monthly income, amount of this monthly income

Figure 5-23
Form for Programming Project 3

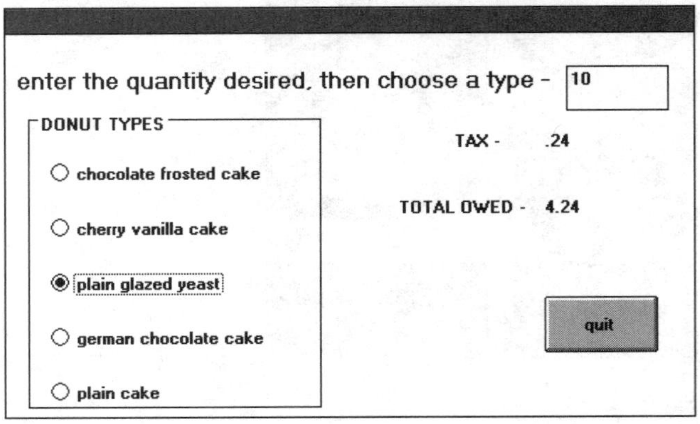

Figure 5-24
Suggested Form for Programming
Project 4

devoted to social security, and the amount devoted to medicare. The user then clicks on a calculate button which uses the following formulas:

Percent used for SS = ($ amount to SS/ monthly income * 100)

Percent used for medicare = ($ amount to medicare/
                                          monthly income * 100

The Option button choice can be saved in an invisible label and then used as follows:

User's actual tax rate = percent used for SS
                                    + percent used for medicare
                                    + income tax rate (saved in label) * 100

(**Note:** A person's tax rate is actually a bit lower than the 15% to 39.6% used for exemptions.)

A suggested form for this project is shown as Figure 5-25.

6. Develop a program for Rambling Wreck Auto Rentals to determine the daily rental rate on its vehicles. The daily rate is calculated as follows:

    i.   Base rate for sedans is $30 (convertible) and $25 (hardtop), for mini-vans is $32, and for trucks is $35.
    ii. All convertibles are sedans.
    iii. If the vehicle is large, the day rate increases by 10%.
    iv. After the above has been calculated, if the vehicle is rented on the weekend, the day rate is cut by 50%.
    v.   If the renter requires insurance, $5 is added to the day rate.
    vi. The day rate is calculated by a Calculate button and displayed in currency format.

    A suggested form is shown in Figure 5-26.

7. This assignment is a modification to the Motel 8 Project (Section 3.8, Exercise 8)

Figure 5-25
Suggested Form for Programming Project 5

Figure 5-26
Form for Exercise 6

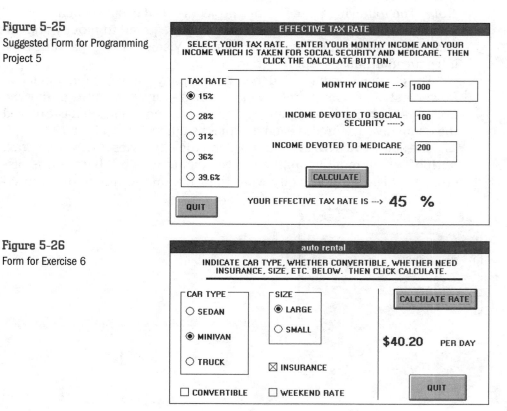

Additional Program Requirements: Motel 8 requires at least one adult registered in each room. Therefore, if the Number of Adults Text box is left empty, display a Message box indicating the need for at least one adult in the room. Use the vbCritical type and reposition the focus to the Number of Adults Text box. (**Hint:** take a look at both the **LostFocus** and **GotFocus** event procedures.)

Additionally, the entry in the number of nights Text box should be a positive value integer. If the value in the Number of Nights Text box is not a positive value, display a Message box indicating the need for a positive value for Number of Nights. Use the vbCritical type and reposition the focus to the Number of Nights Text box.

The customer will be given a 15% discount (before state-local taxes are computed) when the Number of Nights is greater than four. Use a named constant to represent the discount value.

8. This assignment is a modification to Local Car Rental Company Project (Section 3.8, Exercise 9).

Additional Program Requirements: For all miles in excess of 200 per day, there is a $.10 per mile charge; i.e., the first 200 miles per day are free. Use named constants to represent the number of miles per day (200) over which mileage will be charged and the per mile charge (0.10).

There is no refueling fee charge if the car is returned with a full tank; otherwise, the customer is charged the $12.95 refueling fee regardless of the amount of fuel in the tank (not full). Use a Check box (chkTankFull) to indicate that the car was returned with a full tank.

All input fields (txtFirstName, txtLastName, txtDays) must be non-empty. Use a Message box to alert the user of any empty Text box and reset the focus to the appropriate empty field. A suggested form is shown in Figure 5-27.

9. **THE STATE UTILITIES COMMISSION PROJECT**

Note: The following State Utilities project is used in subsequent End-of-Chapter Programming Projects. You will be required to modify and enhance your solution to this project as new Visual Basic capabilities are introduced in subsequent chapters.

The commission has ruled that the company you work for, Municipal Power and Light, has overcharged customers for two months during the previous year. To compensate customers, the commission has ordered the company to decrease each customer's bill next month by 12%.

The state levies a 3.5% utility tax and the city levies a 1.5% utility tax, both of which must be applied to the customer's bill before it is discounted. (The state and city want their tax on the full, undiscounted

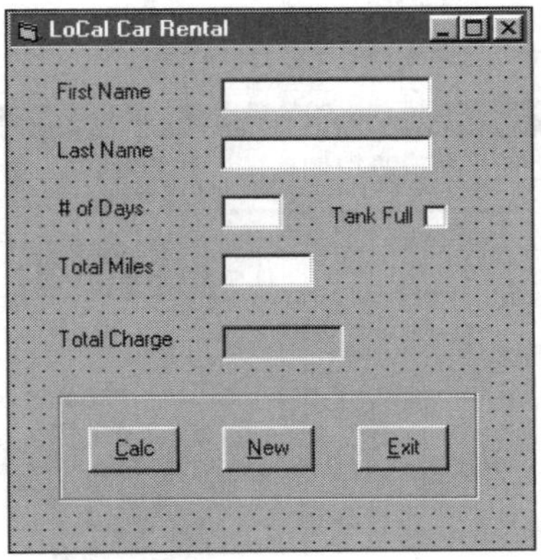

Figure 5-27

Form for Exercise 8

amount, and the 12% discount does not apply to the utility taxes.) Municipal Power and Light charges are as follows:

KWH Used	Cost Scale
less than 1000	$0.052 per KWH used
at least 1000 but less than 1300	$0.052 per KWH for first 1000 KWH used $0.041 per KWH for KWH used over 1000
at least 1300 but less than 2000	$0.052 per KWH for first 1000 KWH used $0.041 per KWH for next 300 KWH used $0.035 per KWH for KWH used over 1300
at least 2000	$0.052 per KWH for first 1000 KWH used $0.041 per KWH for next 300 KWH used $0.035 per KWH for next 700 KWH used $0.03 per KWH for KWH used over 2000

Input for your program should include the customer name and number of KWH's used during the current month. Output should include:

> base, undiscounted, untaxed bill amount
> discount amount
> state utility tax amount
> city utility tax amount
> total amount due

Remember that the state and city taxes are computed on the first amount in the above list. Your solution should use a form like that shown in Figure 5-28.

Object	Property	Setting
Form	Name	frmPowerBill
	Caption	Municipal Power & Light
Frame	Name	fraInput
Label	Name	lblCustomer
	Caption	Customer Name
Text box	Name	txtCustomer
	Text	<blank>

continued

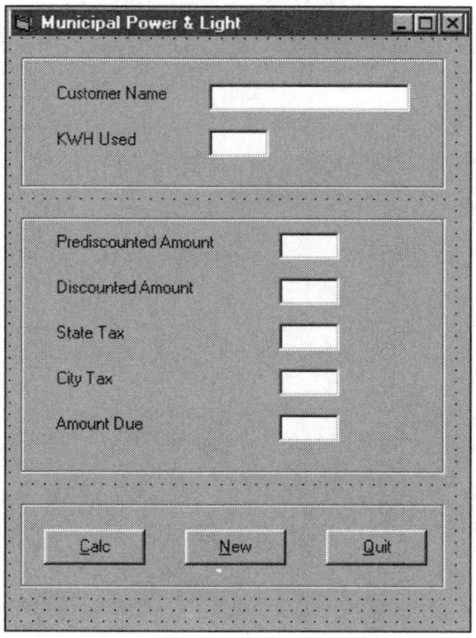

Figure 5-28
Form for Exercise 9

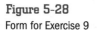

Municipal Power & Light

Customer Name

KWH Used

Prediscounted Amount

Discounted Amount

State Tax

City Tax

Amount Due

Calc   New   Quit

Object	Property	Setting
Label	Name	lblKWHUsed
	Caption	KWH Used
Text box	Name	txtKWHUsed
	Text	<blank>
Frame	Name	fraOutput
Label	Name	lblPreDiscountAmt
	Caption	Prediscounted Amount
Text box	Name	txtPreAmt
	Text	<blank>
Label	Name	lblDiscountAmt
	Caption	Discounted Amount
Text box	Name	txtDiscountAmt
	Text	<blank>
Label	Name	lblStateTax
	Caption	State Tax
Text box	Name	txtStateTax
	Text	<blank>
Label	Name	lblCityTax
	Caption	City Tax
Text box	Name	txtCityTax
	Text	<blank>
Label	Name	lblAmtDue
	Caption	Amount Due
Text box	Name	txtAmtDue
	Text	<blank>
Frame	Name	fraCommands
Command button	Name	cmdCalc
	Caption	&Calc
Command button	Name	cmdNew
	Caption	&New
Command button	Name	cmdQuit
	Caption	&Quit

Repetition Structures

The applications examined so far have illustrated the programming concepts involved in input, output, assignment, and selection capabilities. By this time you should have gained enough experience to be comfortable with these concepts and the mechanics of implementing them using Visual Basic. Many problems, however, require a repetition capability, in which the same calculation or sequence of instructions is repeated, over and over, using different sets of data. Examples of such repetition include continual checking of user data entries until an acceptable entry, such as a valid password, is entered; counting and accumulating running totals; and recurring acceptance of input data and recalculation of output values that only stops upon entry of a designated value.

This chapter explores the different methods that programmers use to construct repeating sections of code and how they can be implemented in Visual Basic. A repeated procedural section of code is commonly called a *loop* because, after the last statement in the code is executed, the program branches or loops back to the first statement and starts another repetition. Each repetition is also referred to as an *iteration* or *pass* through the loop.

6.1 Introduction

The real power of most computer programs resides in their ability to repeat the same calculation or sequence of instructions many times over, each time using different data, without the necessity of rerunning the program for each new set of data values. This ability is realized through repetitive sections of code. Such repetitive sections are written only once, but include a means of defining how many times the code should be executed.

Figure 6-1
A Pretest Loop

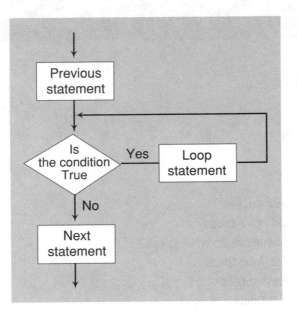

Constructing repetitive sections of code requires four elements:

1. A *repetition statement* that both defines the boundaries containing the repeating section of code and controls whether or not that code will be executed. There are three different forms of repetition structures, all of which are provided in Visual Basic: **Do While** structures, **For** structures, and **Do / Loop Until** structures.

2. A *condition* that needs to be evaluated. Valid conditions are identical to those used in selection statements. If the condition is **True**, the code is executed; if it is **False**, the code is not executed.

Figure 6-2
A Posttest Loop

3. A *statement* that initially *sets the condition*. This statement must always be placed before the condition is first evaluated to ensure correct loop execution the first time.

4. A *statement* within the repeating section of code that *allows the condition to become **False***. This is necessary to ensure that, at some point, the repetitions stop.

Pretest and Posttest Loops

The condition being tested can be evaluated at either the beginning or the end of the repeating section of code. Figure 6-1 illustrates the case where the test occurs at the beginning of the loop. This type of loop is referred to as a *pretest loop*, because the condition is tested before any statements within the loop are executed. If the condition is **True**, the executable statements within the loop are executed. If the initial value of the condition is **False**, the executable statements within the loop are never executed at all, and control transfers to the first statement after the loop. To avoid infinite repetitions, the condition must be updated within the loop. Pretest loops are also referred to as *entrance-controlled loops*. Both the **Do While** and **For** loop structures are examples of such loops.

A loop that evaluates a condition at the end of the repeating section of code, as illustrated in Figure 6-2, is referred to as *posttest* or *exit-controlled loop*. Such loops always execute the loop

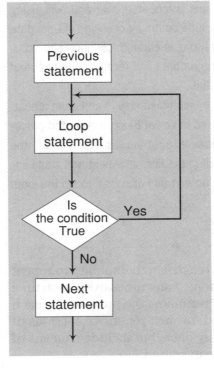

statements at least once before the condition is tested. Since the executable statements within the loop are continually executed until the condition becomes **False**, there always must be a statement within the loop that updates the condition and permits it to become **False**. The **Do / Loop Until** structure is an example of a posttest loop.

Fixed Count Versus Variable-Condition Loops

In addition to where the condition is tested (pretest or posttest), repeating sections of code are also classified as to the type of condition being tested. In a *fixed-count loop*, the condition is used to keep track of how many repetitions have occurred. For example, we might want to produce a very simple fixed design such as

```
*************************
*************************
*************************
*************************
```

In each of these cases, a fixed number of calculations is performed or a fixed number of lines is printed, at which point the repeating section of code is exited. All of Visual Basic's repetition statements can be used to produce fixed-count loops.

In many situations, the exact number of repetitions is not known in advance or the items are too numerous to count beforehand. For example, if we are working with a large amount of market research data, we might not want to take the time to count the number of actual data items that must be entered and so we would use a variable-condition loop. In a *variable-condition loop*, the tested condition does not depend on a count being achieved, but rather on a variable that can change interactively with each pass through the loop. When a specified value is encountered, regardless of how many iterations have occurred, repetitions stop. All of Visual Basic's repetition statements can also be used to create variable-condition loops. In this chapter we will encounter examples of both fixed-count and variable-condition loops.

6.2 ▷ Do While Loops

In Visual Basic, a **Do While** loop is constructed using the following syntax:

```
Do While expression
    statement(s)
Loop
```

The expression contained after the keywords **Do While** is the condition tested to determine if the statements provided before the **Loop** statement are executed. The expression is evaluated in exactly the same manner as that contained in an **If-Else** statement; the difference is in how the expression is used. As we have seen, when the expression is **True** in an **If-Else** statement, the statement or statements following the expression are executed once. In a **Do While** loop the statement or statements following the expression are executed repeatedly, as long as the expression remains **True**.

Considering the expression and the statements following it, the process used by the computer in evaluating a **Do While** loops is

1. Test the expression, and
2. If the expression is **True**:
   a. Execute all statements following the expression up to the **Loop** statement, and
   b. Go back to Step 1.

   Else

   Exit the **Do While** statement and execute the next executable statement following the **Loop** statement.

Notice that Step 2b. forces program control to be transferred back to Step 1. This transfer of control back to the start of a **Do While** statement, in order to reevaluate the expression, is what forms the program loop. The **Do While** statement literally loops back on itself to recheck the expression until it becomes **False**. This naturally means that somewhere in the loop it must be possible to alter the value of the tested expression so that the loop ultimately terminates its execution.

The looping process produced by a **Do While** statement is illustrated in Figure 6-3. A diamond shape is used to show the entry and exit points required in the decision part of the **Do While** statement.

To make this a little more tangible, consider the relational expression `count <= 10` and the statement `Print count`. Using these, we can write the following valid **Do While** loop:

```
Do While count <= 10
   Print count;
Loop
```

Although the above loop structure is valid, the alert reader will realize that we have created a situation in which the **Print** statement either is called

Figure 6-3

Anatomy of a Do While Loop

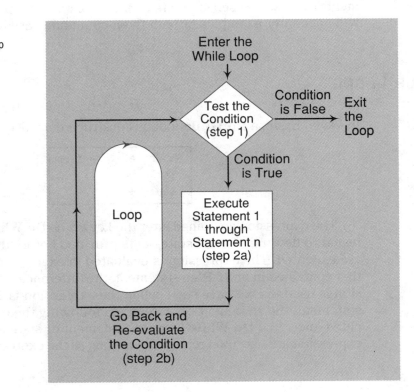

forever (or until we stop the program) or it is not called at all. Let us see why this happens.

If count has a value less than or equal to 10 when the expression is first evaluated, the **Print** statement is executed. When the **Loop** statement is encountered, the structure automatically loops back on itself and retests the expression. Since we have not changed the value stored in count, the expression is still **True** and another call to the **Print** method is made. This process continues forever, or until the program containing this statement is prematurely stopped by the user. However, if count starts with a value greater than 10, the expression is **False** to begin with and the **Print** method is never used.

How do we set an initial value in count to control what the **Do While** statement does the first time the expression is evaluated? The answer, of course, is to assign values to each variable in the tested expression before the **Do While** statement is encountered. For example, the following sequence of instructions is valid:

```
count = 1
Do While count <= 10
  Print count;
Loop
```

Using this sequence of instructions, we ensure that count starts with a value of 1. We could assign any value to count in the assignment statement—the important thing is to assign some value. In practice, the assigned value depends on the application.

We must still change the value of count so that we can finally exit the **Do While** loop. To do this requires an expression such as count = count + 1 to increment the value of count each time the **Do While** statement is executed. All that we have to do is add a statement within the **Loop** structure that modifies count's value so that the loop ultimately terminates. For example, consider the following expanded loop:

```
count = 1  ' initialize count
Do While count <= 10
  Print count;
  count = count + 1 ' increment count
Loop
```

Note that the **Do While** structure begins with the keywords **Do While** and ends with the keyword **Loop**. For this particular loop, we have included two statements within the Loop structure:

```
Print count;
count = count + 1 ' increment count
```

Let us now analyze the complete section of loop code to understand how it operates. The first assignment statement sets count equal to 1. The **Do While** structure is then entered and the expression is evaluated for the first time. Since the value of count is less than or equal to 10, the expression is **True** and the two statements internal to the **Loop** structure are executed. The first statement within the loop is a **Print** statement that displays the value of count. The next statement adds 1 to the value currently stored in count, making this value equal to 2. The **Do While** statement now loops back to retest the expression. Since count is still less than or equal to 10, the loop statements are executed once again. This process continues until the value of count reaches 11. Event Procedure 6-1 illustrates these statements within the context of a complete **Form_Click** event procedure.

Event Procedure 6-1

```
Private Sub Form_Click
  Dim count As Integer

  count = 1  ' initialize count
  Do While count <= 10
    Print count;
    count = count + 1 ' increment count
  Loop
End Sub
```

The following output will appear on the screen when Event Procedure 6-1 is activated:

```
1 2 3 4 5 6 7 8 9 10
```

There is nothing special about the name count used in Event Procedure 6-1. Any valid integer variable could have been used.

Before we consider other examples of the **Do While** statement, two comments concerning Event Procedure 6-1 are in order. First, the statement count + 1 can be replaced with any statement that changes the value of count. The statement count = count + 2, for example, would cause every second integer to be displayed. Second, it is the programmer's responsibility to ensure that count is changed in a way that ultimately leads to a normal exit from the **Do While**. For example, if we replace the expression count + 1 with the expression count - 1, the value of count will never exceed 10 and an infinite loop will be created. An *infinite loop* is a loop that never ends. The computer will not reach out, touch you, and say, "Excuse me, you have created an infinite loop." It just keeps displaying numbers, until you realize that the program is not working as you expected.

Now that you have some familiarity with the **Do While** structure, see if you can read and determine the output of Event Procedure 6-2.

Event Procedure 6-2

```
Private Sub Form_Click
  Dim I as integer

  I = 10  ' initialize I
  Do While I >= 1
    Print I;
    I = I - 1    ' subtract 1 from i
  Loop
End Sub
```

The assignment statement in Event Procedure 6-2 initially sets the integer variable I to 10. The **Do While** statement then checks to see if the value of I is greater than or equal to 1. While the expression is **True**, the value of I is displayed by the **Print** method and the value of I is decremented by 1. When I finally reaches zero, the expression is **False** and the program exits the **Do While** statement. Thus, the following display is obtained when Event Procedure 6-2 is activated:

```
10 9 8 7 6 5 4 3 2 1
```

To illustrate the power of **Do While** loops, consider the task of printing a table of numbers from 1 to 10 with their squares and cubes. This can be done with a simple **Do While** loops structure, as illustrated by Event Procedure 6-3.

Event Procedure 6-3

```
Private Sub Form_Click()
  Dim num As Integer

  Cls ' clear the form
  Font = "Courier"
  Print "NUMBER", "SQUARE", "CUBE"
  Print "------", "------", "----"

  num = 1
  Do While num < 11
    Print num, num ^ 2, num ^ 3
    num = num + 1  ' increment num
  Loop
End Sub
```

When Event Procedure 6-3 is activated, the following display is produced on the form:

NUMBER	SQUARE	CUBE
------	------	----
1	1	1
2	4	8
3	9	27
4	16	64
5	25	125
6	36	216
7	49	343
8	64	512
9	81	729
10	100	1000

Note that the expression used in Event Procedure 6-3 is num < 11. For the integer variable num this expression is exactly equivalent to the expression num <= 10. The choice of which to use is entirely up to you.

If we want to use Event Procedure 6-3 to produce a table of 1000 numbers, all that needs to be done is to change the expression in the **Do While** statement from num < 11 to num < 1001. Changing the 11 to 1001 produces a table of 1000 lines—not bad for a simple five-line **Do While** structure.

All the program examples illustrating the **Do While** statement are examples of fixed-count loops, because the tested condition is a counter that checks for a fixed number of repetitions. A variation on the fixed-count loop can be made, where the counter is not incremented by one each time through the loop, but by some other value. For example, consider the task of producing a Celsius to Fahrenheit temperature conversion table. Assume that Fahrenheit temperatures corresponding to Celsius temperatures ranging from 5 to 50 degrees are to be displayed in increments of five degrees. The desired display can be obtained with the following series of statements:

```
celsius = 5   ' starting Celsius value
Do While celsius <= 50
  fahren = 9.0/5.0 * celsius + 32.0
  Print celsius, fahren
  celsius = celsius + 5
Loop
```

As before, the **Do While** loop consists of everything from the words **Do While** through the **Loop** statement. Prior to entering the **Do While** loop, we have made sure to assign a value to the counter being evaluated, and there is a statement to alter the value of celsius within the loop (in increments of 5), to ensure an exit from the **Do While** loop. Event Procedure 6-4 illustrates the use of this code within the context of a complete Form_Click event.

Event Procedure 6-4

```
Rem - a procedure to convert Celsius to Fahrenheit
Private Sub Form_Click()
  Const MAX_CELSIUS As Integer = 50
  Const START_VAL As Integer = 5
  Const STEP_SIZE As Integer = 5
  Dim celsius As Integer
  Dim fahren As Single

  Cls ' clear the form
  Font = "Courier"

  Print "Degrees", " Degrees"
  Print "Celsius", "Fahrenheit"
  Print "-------", "----------"

  celsius = START_VAL
  Do While celsius <= MAX_CELSIUS
    fahren = (9.0/5.0) * celsius + 32.0
    Print celsius, fahren
    celsius = celsius + STEP_SIZE
  Loop
```

The following display is obtained on a form when Event Procedure 6-4 is activated:

```
Degrees           Degrees
Celsius           Fahrenheit

-------           ----------
  5                 41
 10                 50
 15                 59
 20                 68
 25                 77
 30                 86
 35                 95
 40                104
 45                113
 50                122
```

Exercises 6.2

1. Rewrite Event Procedure 6-1 to print the numbers 2 to 10 in increments of two. The output of your program should be

    ```
    2 4 6 8 10
    ```

2. Rewrite Event Procedure 6-4 to produce a table that starts at a Celsius value of –10 and ends with a Celsius value of 60, in increments of ten degrees.

3. a. For the following code, determine the total number of items displayed. Also determine the first and last numbers printed.

```
Dim num as integer
num = 0
Do While num <= 20
    num = num + 1
    Print num;
Loop
```

   b. Enter and run code from Exercise 3a. as a `Form_Click` event procedure to verify your answers to the exercise.

   c. How would the output be affected if the two statements within the loop were reversed, that is, if the **Print** statement were made before the `Num = Num + 1` statement ?

4. Write a Visual Basic program that converts gallons to liters. The program should display gallons from 10 to 20 in one-gallon increments and the corresponding liter equivalents. Use the relationship that there are 3.785 liters to a gallon.

5. Write a Visual Basic program to produce the following display on a form.

```
0
 1
  2
   3
    4
     5
      6
       7
        8
         9
```

6. Write a Visual Basic program to produce the following displays on a form.

   a.
```
****
  ****
    ****
      ****
```

   b.
```
    ****
  ****
 ****
****
```

7. Write a Visual Basic program that converts feet to meters. The program should display feet from 3 to 30 in three-foot increments and the corresponding meter equivalents. Use the relationship that there are 3.28 feet to a meter.

8. A machine purchased for $28,000 is depreciated at a rate of $4,000 a year for seven years. Write and run a Visual Basic program that computes and displays a depreciation table for seven years. The table should have the form shown at the top of the next page.

Year	Depreciation	End-of-year value	Accumulated depreciation
1	4000	24000	4000
2	4000	20000	8000
3	4000	16000	12000
4	4000	12000	16000
5	4000	8000	20000
6	4000	4000	24000
7	4000	0	28000

9. An automobile travels at an average speed of 55 miles per hour for four hours. Write a Visual Basic program that displays the distance driven, in miles, that the car has traveled after 0.5, 1.0, 1.5, . . . hours, until the end of the trip.

10. An approximate conversion formula for converting Fahrenheit to Celsius temperatures is

$$\text{Celsius} = \text{Fahrenheit} - 30 / 2$$

a. Using this formula, and starting with a Fahrenheit temperature of zero degrees, write a Visual Basic program that determines when the approximate equivalent Celsius temperature differs from the exact equivalent value by more than four degrees. (**Hint:** use a **Do While** loop that terminates when the difference between approximate and exact Celsius equivalents exceeds four degrees.)

b. Using the approximate Celsius conversion formula given in Exercise 10a, write a Visual Basic program that produces a table of Fahrenheit temperatures, exact Celsius equivalent temperatures, approximate Celsius equivalent temperatures, and the difference between the correct and approximate equivalent Celsius values. The table should begin at zero degrees Fahrenheit, use two-degree Fahrenheit increments, and terminate when the difference between exact and approximate values differs by more than four degrees.

6.3 ▶ Interactive Do While Loops

Combining interactive data entry with the repetition capabilities of the **Do While** loop produces very adaptable and powerful programs. To understand the concept involved, consider Program 6-1, where a **Do While** statement is used to accept and then display four user-entered numbers, one at a time. Although it is simple, the program highlights the flow of control concepts needed to produce more useful programs.

For this application, the only procedure code is the Command button's **Click** event, which is listed in Program 6-1's event code.

Figure 6-5 illustrates a sample run of Program 6-1 after four numbers have been input. The **InputBox** control that is displayed by the program for the data entry is shown in Figure 6-6.

Figure 6-4
Program 6-1's Interface

Table 6-1 The Properties Table for Program 6-1

Object	Property	Setting
Form	Name	frmMain
	Caption	Program 6-1
Command button	Name	cmdRun
	Caption	&Run Program
Command button	Name	cmdExit
	Caption	E&xit

Program 6-1's Event Code

```
Private Sub cmdRun_Click()
  Const MAXNUMS As Integer = 4
  Dim count As Integer
  Dim num As Single

  Cls
  Print "This Program will ask you to enter"; MAXNUMS; "numbers"

  count = 1
  Do While count <= MAXNUMS
    num = Val(InputBox("Enter a number", "Input Dialog", 0))
    Print "The number entered is"; num
    count = count + 1
  Loop
End Sub

Private Sub cmdExit_Click()
  Beep
  End
End Sub
```

Let us review the program so we clearly understand how the output illustrated in Figure 6-5 was produced. The first message displayed is caused by execution of the first **Print** statement. This statement is outside and before the **Do While** loop, so it is executed once before any statement within the loop.

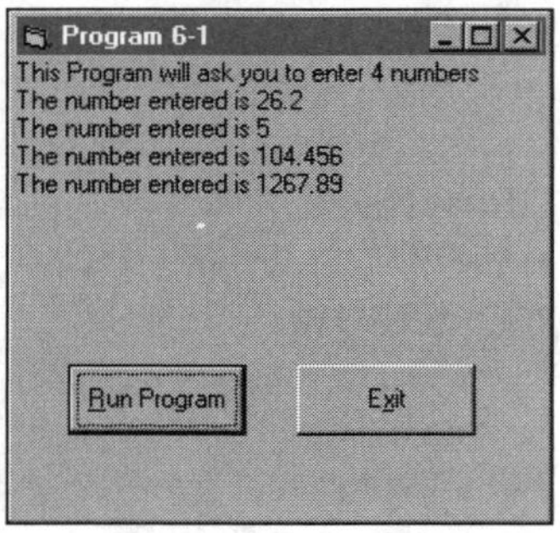

Figure 6-6
The InputBox Displayed by
Program 6-1

Figure 6-5
A Sample Run of Program 6-1

Once the **Do While** loop is entered, the statements within the loop are executed while the tested condition is **True**. The first time through the loop, the statement

```
num = InputBox("Enter a number", "Input Dialog", "0")
```

is executed. The call to the **InputBox** function displays the **InputBox** dialog shown in Figure 6-6, which forces the computer to wait for a number to be entered at the keyboard. Once a number is typed and the [Return] or [Enter] key is pressed, the **Print** statement within the loop displays that number. The variable count is then incremented by one. This process continues until four passes through the loop have been made and the value of count is 5. Each pass causes the **InputBox** and the message The number entered is to be displayed. Figure 6-7 illustrates this flow of control.

Program 6-1 can be modified to use the entered data rather than simply displaying it. For example, let us add the numbers entered and display their

Figure 6-7
Flow of Control Diagram for the cmdRun Click Event Procedure

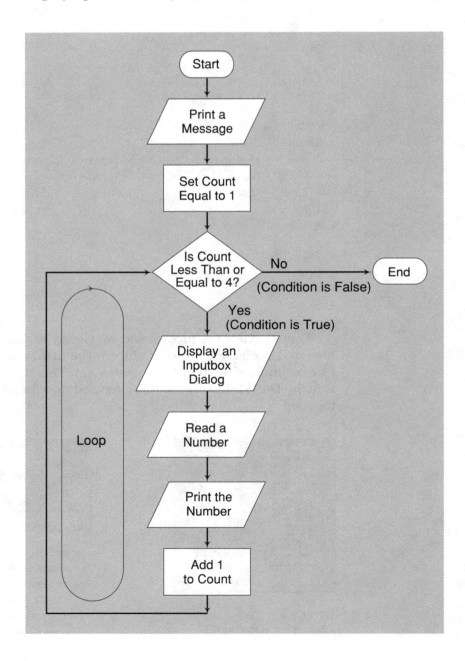

total. To do this we must be very careful about how we add the numbers since the same variable, num, is used for each number. Because of this, the entry of a new number in Program 6-1 automatically causes the previous number stored in num to be lost. Thus, each number entered must be added to the total, before another number is entered. The required sequence is

Enter a number

Add the number to the total

How do we add a single number to a total? A statement such as total = total + num does the job perfectly. This is the accumulating statement introduced in Section 3.3. After each number is entered, the accumulating statement adds the number into the total, as illustrated in Figure 6-8. The complete flow of control required for adding the numbers is illustrated in Figure 6-9.

Observe that in Figure 6-9 we have made a provision for initially setting the total to zero before the **Do While** loop is entered. If we cleared the total inside the **Do While** loop, it would be set to zero each time the loop was executed and any value previously stored would be erased. As indicated in the flow diagram shown in Figure 6-9, the statement total = total + num is placed immediately after the call to the **InputBox** function. Putting the accumulating statement at this point in the program ensures that the entered number is immediately added to the total.

Program 6-2 incorporates the necessary modifications to Program 6-1 to total the numbers entered. The significant difference between Program 6-1 and 6-2 is the Run Program Command button's event code.

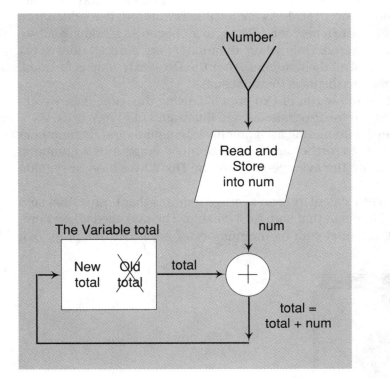

Figure 6-8
Accepting and Adding a Number to a Total

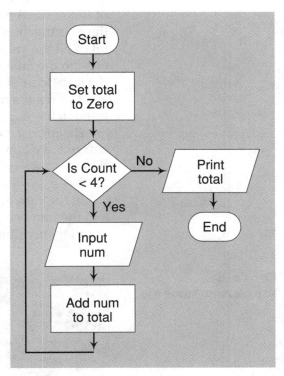

Figure 6-9
Accumulation Flow of Control

Program 6-2's Event Code

```
Private Sub cmdRun_Click()
  Const MAXNUMS As Integer = 4
  Dim count As Integer
  Dim num As Single
  Dim total As Single

  Cls
  Print "This Program will ask you to enter"; MAXNUMS; "numbers"

  count = 1
  total = 0
  Do While count <= MAXNUMS
    num = InputBox("Enter a number", "Input Dialog", "0")
    total = total + num
    Print "The number entered is"; num
    Print "The total is now"; total
    count = count + 1
  Loop
  Print "The final total is"; total
End Sub
```

Let us review this event code. The variable `total` was created to store the total of the numbers entered. Prior to entering the **Do While** statement, the value of `total` is set to zero. This ensures that any previous value present in the storage locations assigned to the variable `total` is erased. Within the **Do While** loop, the statement `total = total + num` is used to add the value of the entered number into `total`. As each value is entered, it is added into the existing total to create a new total. Thus, `total` becomes a running subtotal of all the values entered. Only when all numbers are entered does `total` contain the final sum of all the numbers. After the **Do While** loop is finished, the last **Print** statement displays the final sum.

The results of a sample run of Program 6-2, using the same data we entered in the sample run for Program 6-1, are illustrated in Figure 6-10.

Having used an accumulating assignment statement to add the numbers entered, we can now go further and calculate the average of the numbers. Where do we calculate the average—within the **Do While** loop or outside of it?

In the case at hand, calculating an average requires that both a final sum and the number of items in that sum be available. The average is then computed by dividing the final sum by the number of items. At this point, we

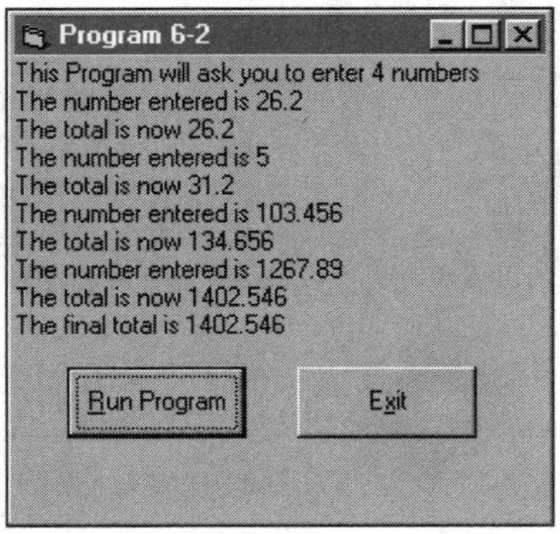

Figure 6-10
A Sample Run of Program 6-2

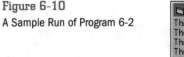

```
Program 6-2
This Program will ask you to enter 4 numbers
The number entered is 26.2
The total is now 26.2
The number entered is 5
The total is now 31.2
The number entered is 103.456
The total is now 134.656
The number entered is 1267.89
The total is now 1402.546
The final total is 1402.546
```

[Run Program] [Exit]

must ask, "At what point in the program is the correct sum available, and at what point is the number of items available?" In reviewing Program 6-2's event code, we see that the correct sum needed for calculating the average is available after the **Do While** loop is finished. In fact, the whole purpose of the **Do While** loop is to ensure that the numbers are entered and added correctly to produce a correct sum. With this as background, see if you can read and understand the event code used in Program 6-3.

Program 6-3's Event Code

```
Private Sub cmdRun_Click()
  Const MAXNUMS As Integer = 4
  Dim count As Integer
  Dim num As Single
  Dim total As Single
  Dim average As Single

  Cls
  Print "This Program will ask you to enter"; MAXNUMS; "numbers"

  count = 1
  total = 0
  Do While count <= MAXNUMS
    num = InputBox("Enter a number", "Input Dialog", "0")
    total = total + num
    Print "The number entered is"; num
    count = count + 1
  Loop
  average = total / MAXNUMS
  Print "The average of these numbers is"; average
End Sub
```

Program 6-3 is almost identical to Program 6-2, except for the calculation of the average. We have also removed the constant display of the total within and after the **Do While** loop. The loop in Program 6-3 is used to enter and add four numbers. Immediately after the loop is exited, the average is computed and displayed.

A sample run of Program 6-3 is illustrated in Figure 6-11.

The Do Until Loop Structure

In a **Do While** loop structure, the statements within the loop are executed as long as the condition is **True** (has a non-zero value). A variation of **Do While** loop is the **Do Until** loop, which executes the statements within the

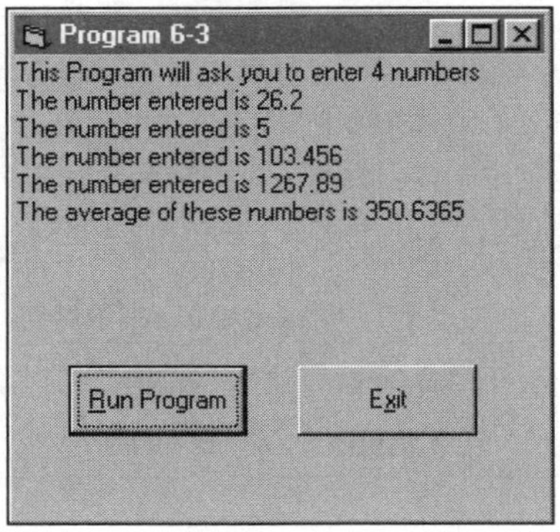

Figure 6-11
A Sample Run of Program 6-3

```
Program 6-3
This Program will ask you to enter 4 numbers
The number entered is 26.2
The number entered is 5
The number entered is 103.456
The number entered is 1267.89
The average of these numbers is 350.6365



  Run Program        Exit
```

loop, as long as the condition is **False** (has a zero value). The syntax of a **Do Until** loop is

```
Do Until condition
    statement(s)
Loop
```

The **Do Until** loop, like its **Do While** counterpart, is an entrance-controlled loop. Unlike the **Do While** loop, which executes until the tested condition becomes **False**, a **Do Until** loop executes until the condition becomes **True**. If the condition tested in a **Do Until** loop is **True** to begin with, the statements within the loop will not execute at all. Generally, **Do Until** loops are not used extensively, for two reasons. First, most practical programming problems require performing a repetitive set of tasks while a condition is **True**. Next, if an entrance-controlled loop is required until a condition becomes **True**, it can always be restated as a loop that needs to be executed while the same condition remains **False**, using the syntax

```
Do While Not condition
    statement(s)
Loop
```

Sentinels

All of the loops we have created thus far have been examples of fixed-count loops, where a counter controls the number of loop iterations. By means of a **Do While** statement variable-condition loops may also be constructed. For example, when entering grades we may not want to count the number of grades that will be entered, but would prefer to enter the grades one after another and, at the end, type in a special data value to signal the end of data input.

In computer programming, data values used to signal either the start or end of a data series are called *sentinels*. The sentinel values must, of course, be selected so as not to conflict with legitimate data values. For example, if we were constructing a program to process a student's grades, and assuming that no extra credit is given that could produce a grade higher than 100, we could use any grade higher than 100 as a sentinel value. Program 6-4 illustrates this concept. In Program 6-4's event procedure, the grades are serially requested and accepted until a number larger than 100 is entered. Entry of a number higher than 100 alerts the program to exit the **Do While** loop and display the sum of the grades entered.

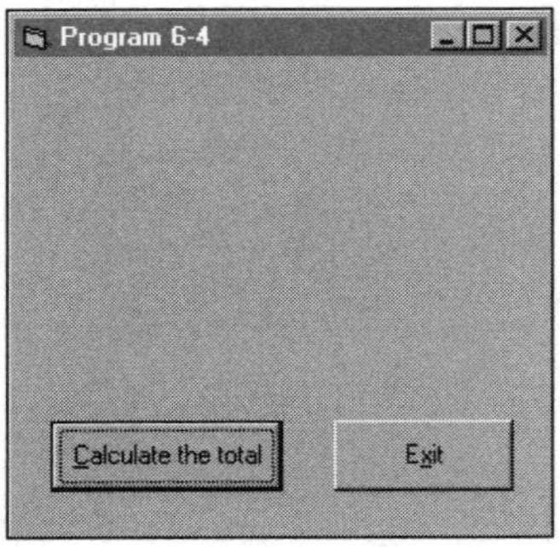

Object	Property	Setting
Table 6-2 The Properties Table for Program 6-4		
Form	Name	frmMain
	Caption	Program 6-2
Command button	Name	cmdTotal
	Caption	&Calculate the total
Command button	Name	cmdExit
	Caption	E&xit

Figure 6-12
Program 6-4's Interface

Program 6-4's Event Code

```
Private Sub cmdTotal_Click()
  Const HIGHGRADE As Integer = 100
  Dim grade As Single, total As Single

  grade = 0
  total = 0
  Print "To stop entering grades, type in"
  Print "any number greater than 100."

  Do While grade <= HIGHGRADE
    grade = InputBox("Enter a grade", "Input Dialog", "0")
    Print "The grade just entered is"; grade
    total = total + grade
  Loop
  Print "The total of the valid grades is "; total - grade
End Sub

Private Sub cmdExit_Click()
  Beep
  End
End Sub
```

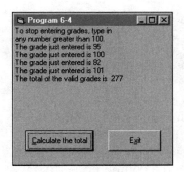

Figure 6-13
A Sample Run Using
Program 6-4

A sample run using Program 6-4 is illustrated in Figure 6-13. As long as grades less than or equal to 100 are entered, the program continues to request and accept additional data. When a number less than or equal to 100 is entered, the program adds this number to the total. When a number greater than 100 is entered, the program exits the loop and displays the sum of the grades.

Notice that the event procedure used in Program 6-4 differs from previous examples, in that termination of the loop is controlled by an externally supplied value, rather than a fixed-count condition. The loop in Program 6-4 will continue indefinitely until the sentinel value is encountered.

Breaking Out of a Loop

It is sometimes necessary to prematurely break out of a loop when an unusual error condition is detected. The means of doing this is provided by an **Exit Do** statement. For example, execution of the following **Do While** loop is immediately terminated if a number greater than 76 is entered.

```
Count = 1
Do While count <= 10
num = InputBox("Enter a number", "Input Dialog", "0")
If num > 76 Then
  Print "You lose!"
  Exit Do        ' break out of the loop
End If
Print "Keep on trucking!\n"
count = count + 1
Loop
  ' break jumps to here
```

The **Exit Do** statement violates pure structured programming principles because it provides a second, nonstandard exit from a loop. Nevertheless, this statement is extremely useful and valuable for breaking out of a **Do** loop.

Exercises 6.3

1. Write a **Do While** loop to do the following:
   a. Display the multiples of 3 backward from 33 to 3, inclusive.
   b. Display the capital letters of the alphabet backward from Z to A.

2. Rewrite Program 6-2 to compute the average of eight numbers.

3. Rewrite Program 6-2 to display the following prompt in an InputBox:

   `Please type in the total number of data values to be added`

   In response to this prompt, the program should accept a user-entered number from the InputBox and then use this number to control the number of times the **Do While** loop is executed. Thus, if the user enters 5 in the InputBox, the program should request the input of five numbers, and display the total after five numbers have been entered.

4. a. Write a Visual Basic program to convert Celsius degrees to Fahrenheit. The program should request the starting Celsius value, the number of conversions to be made, and the increment between Celsius values. The display should have appropriate headings and list the Celsius value and the corresponding Fahrenheit value. Use the relationship Fahrenheit = 9.0 / 5.0 * Celsius + 32.0.
   b. Run the program written in Exercise 4a on a computer. Verify that your program starts at the correct Celsius value and contains the exact number of conversions specified in your input data.

5. a. Modify the program written in Exercise 4 to request the starting Celsius value, the ending Celsius value, and the increment. Thus, instead of the condition checking for a fixed count, the condition will check for the ending Celsius value.
   b. Run the program written in Exercise 5a on a computer. Verify that your output starts and ends on the correct values.

6. Rewrite Program 6-3 to compute the average of ten numbers.

7. Rewrite Program 6-3 to display the following prompt in an InputBox:

   `Please type in the total number of data values to be averaged`

   In response to this prompt, the program should accept a user-entered number from the InputBox, and then use this number to control the number of times the **Do While** loop is executed. Thus, if the user enters 6, the program should request the input of six numbers and display the average of the next six numbers entered.

8. By mistake, a programmer put the statement `average = total / count` within the **Do While** loop immediately after the statement `total = total + num` in Program 6-3. Thus, the **Do While** loop becomes

```
count = 1
total = 0
Do While count <= MAXNUMS
  num = InputBox("Enter a number", "Input Dialog", "0")
  total = total + num
  Print "The number just entered is"; num
```

```
    average = total / count
    count = count + 1
Loop
Print "The average of these numbers is"; average
```

Will the program yield the correct result with this **Do While** loop?

From a programming perspective, which **Do While** loop is better to use, and why?

9. a. The following data was collected on a recent automobile trip:

	Mileage	**Gallons**
Start of trip:	22495	Full tank
	22841	12.2
	23185	11.3
	23400	10.5
	23772	11.0
	24055	12.2
	24434	14.7
	24804	14.3
	25276	15.2

Write a Visual Basic program that accepts a mileage and gallons value and calculates the miles per gallon (mpg) achieved for that segment of the trip. The mpg is obtained as the difference in mileage between fill-ups divided by the number of gallons of gasoline used in the fill-up.

b. Modify the program written for Exercise 9a to compute and display the cumulative mpg achieved after each fill-up. The cumulative mpg is calculated as the difference between each fill-up mileage and the mileage at the start of the trip divided by the sum of the gallons used to that point in the trip.

10. a. A bookstore summarizes its monthly transactions by keeping the following information for each book in stock:

- International Standard Book Number (ISBN),
- Inventory balance at the beginning of the month,
- Number of copies received during the month, and
- Number of copies sold during the month.

Write a Visual Basic program that accepts this data for each book, and then displays the ISBN and an updated book inventory balance using the following relationship:

New balance = Inventory balance at the beginning of the month
+ Number of copies received during the month
– Number of copies sold during the month

Your program should use a **Do While** loop with a fixed-count condition, so that information on only three books is requested.

b. Run the program written in Exercise 10a on a computer. Review the display produced by your program and verify that the output produced is correct.

11. Modify the program you wrote for Exercise 10a to keep requesting and displaying results until a sentinel identification value of 999 is entered. Run the program on a computer.

6.4 For/Next Loops

As we have seen, the condition used to control a **Do While** loop can either test the value of a counter or test for a sentinel value. Loops controlled by a counter are referred to as fixed-count loops, because the loop is executed a fixed number of times. The creation of fixed-count loops always requires initializing a counter variable, testing the counter variable, and modifying the counter variable. The general form we have used for these steps is

```
Initialize counter
Do While counter <= final value
    statement(s)
    counter = counter + increment
Loop
```

The need to initialize, test, and alter a counter to create a fixed-count loop is so common that Visual Basic provides a special structure, called the **For/Next** loop, that groups all of these operations together on a single line. The general syntax of a **For/Next** loop is

```
For variable = start To end Step increment
    statement(s)
Next variable
```

Although the **For/Next** loop looks a little complicated, it is really quite simple, if we consider each of its parts separately. A **For/Next** loop begins with a **For** statement. This statement, which begins with the keyword **For**, provides four items that control the loop: a variable name, a starting value for the variable, an ending value, and an increment value. Except for the increment, each of these items must be present in a **For** statement, including the equal sign and the keyword **To**, used to separate the starting and ending values. If an increment is included, the keyword **Step** must also be used, to separate the increment value from the ending value.

The variable name in the **For** statement can be any valid Visual Basic name and is referred to as the *loop counter* (typically the counter is chosen as an integer variable); *start* is the starting (initializing) value assigned to the counter; *end* is the maximum or minimum value the counter can have and determines when the loop is finished; and *increment* is the value that is added to or subtracted from the counter each time the loop is executed. If the increment is omitted, it is assumed to be one. Examples of valid **For** statements include:

```
For count = 1 To 7 Step 1
For I = 5 To 15 Step 2
For kk = 1 To 20
```

In the first **For** statement, the counter variable is named count, the initial value assigned to count is 1, the loop will be terminated when the value in count exceeds 7, and the increment value is 1. In the next **For** statement, the counter variable is named I, the initial value of I is 5, the loop will be terminated when the value in I exceeds 15, and the increment is 2. In the last **For** statement, the counter variable is named kk, the initial value of kk is equal to 1, the loop will be terminated when the value of kk exceeds 20, and a default value of one (1) is used for the increment.

For each **For** statement there must be a matching **Next** statement. The **Next** statement both defines where the loop ends and is used to increment the counter variable by the increment amount defined in the **For** statement. If no increment has been explicitly listed in the **For** statement, the counter is incremented by one.

The **Next** statement formally marks the end of the loop and causes the counter to be incremented. It then causes a transfer back to the beginning of the loop. When the loop is completed, program execution continues with the first statement after the **Next** statement.

Consider the loop contained within Event Procedure 6-5, as a specific example of a **For/Next** loop.

Event Procedure 6-5

```
Private Sub Form_Click()
  Dim count As Integer

  Cls
  Font = "Courier"
  Print "NUMBER", "SQUARE ROOT"
  Print "------", "-----------"
  For count = 1 To 5
    Print count, Format(Sqr(count), ".000000")
  Next count
End Sub
```

When Event Procedure 6-5 is executed, the following display is produced:

```
NUMBER      SQUARE ROOT
------      -----------
  1         1.000000
  2         1.414214
  3         1.732051
  4         2.000000
  5         2.236068
```

The first two lines displayed by the program are produced by the two **Print** statements placed before the **For** statement. The remaining output is produced by the statements within the **For/Next** loop. This loop begins with the **For** statement and ends with the **Next** statement.

The initial value assigned to the counter variable count is 1. Since the value in count does not exceed the final value of 5, the statements in the loop, including the **Next** statement, are executed. The execution of the **Print** statement within the loop produces the display:

```
  1     1.0000000
```

The **Next** statement is then encountered, which increments the value in count to 2, and control is transferred back to the **For** statement. The **For** statement then tests if count is greater than 5, and repeats the loop, producing the display:

```
  2     1.414214
```

This process continues until the value in count exceeds the final value of 5, producing the complete output table. For comparison purposes, an equivalent **Do While** loop to the **For/Next** loop contained in Event Procedure 6-5 is shown at the top of page 290.

```
count = 1
Do While count <= 5
  Print count, Format(Sqr(count), ".000000")
  count = count + 1
Loop
```

As seen in this example, the difference between the **For/Next** and **Do While** loops is the placement of the initialization, condition test, and incrementing items. The grouping together of these items in a **For** statement is very convenient when fixed-count loops must be constructed. See if you can determine the output produced by Event Procedure 6-6.

Event Procedure 6-6

```
Private Sub Form_Click()
  Dim count As Integer

  Cls
  Font = "Courier"
  For count = 12 To 20 Step 2
    Print count
  Next count
End Sub
```

Did you figure it out? The loop starts with count initialized to 12, stops when count exceeds 20, and increments count in steps of two. The actual statements executed include all statements following the **For** statement, up to and including the **Next** statement. The output produced by Event Procedure 6-6 is

```
12
14
16
18
20
```

For/Next Loop Rules

Now that we have seen a few simple examples of **For/Next** loop structures, it is useful to summarize the rules that all **For/Next** loops must adhere to.

1. The first statement in a **For/Next** loop must be a **For** statement, and the last statement in a **For/Next** loop must be a **Next** statement.

2. The **For/Next** loop counter variable may be either a real or integer variable.

3. The initial, final, and increment values may all be replaced by variables or expressions, as long as each variable has a value previously assigned to it, and the expressions can be evaluated to yield a number. For example, the **For** statement

```
For count = begin To begin + 10 Step augment
```

is valid and can be used as long as values have been assigned to the variables begin and augment before this **For** statement is encountered in a program.

4. The initial, final, and increment values may be positive or negative, but the loop will not be not executed at all, if either of the following is true:

a. The initial value is greater than the final value and the increment is positive, or

b. The initial value is less than the final value and the increment is negative.

5. An infinite loop is created if the increment is zero.

6. An **Exit For** statement may be embedded within a **For/Next** loop, to cause a transfer out of the loop.

Once a **For/Next** loop is correctly structured, it is executed as follows:[1]

Step 1. The initial value is assigned to the counter variable.

Step 2. The value in the counter is compared to the final value.

For positive increments, if the value is less than or equal to the final value:

- All **Loop** statements are executed; and
- The counter is incremented and Step 2 is repeated.

For negative increments if the value is greater than or equal to the final value:

- All **Loop** statements are executed; and
- The counter is decremented and Step 2 is repeated.

Else

- The loop is terminated.

It is extremely important to realize that no statement within the loop should ever alter the value in the counter because the increment or decrement of the loop counter is automatically done by the **Next** statement. The value in the counter may itself be displayed, as in Event Procedures 6-5 and 6-6, or used in an expression to calculate some other variable. It must, however, never be used either on the left-hand side of an assignment statement or altered within the loop. Also notice that when a **For/Next** loop is completed, the counter contains the last value that exceeds the final tested value.

Figure 6-14 (on page 292) illustrates the internal workings of the **For/Next** loop for positive increments. To avoid the necessity of always illustrating these steps, a simplified flowchart symbol has been created. Using the following flowchart symbol to represent a **For/Next** statement

complete **For/Next** loops can be illustrated as shown in Figure 6-15 on page 292.

To understand the enormous power of **For/Next** loops, consider the task of printing a table of numbers from 1 to 10, including their squares and cubes, using a **For/Next** statement. Such a table was previously produced, using a **Do While** loop in Event Procedure 6-3. You may wish to review Event Procedure 6-3 and compare it to Event Procedure 6-7 to get a further sense of the equivalence between **For/Next** and **Do While** loops. Both Event Procedures 6-3 and 6-7 produce the same output.

---

[1]The number of times that a **For/Next** loop is executed is determined by the expression:

Int((final value – initial value + increment) / increment)

If this expression results in a negative value, the loop is not executed.

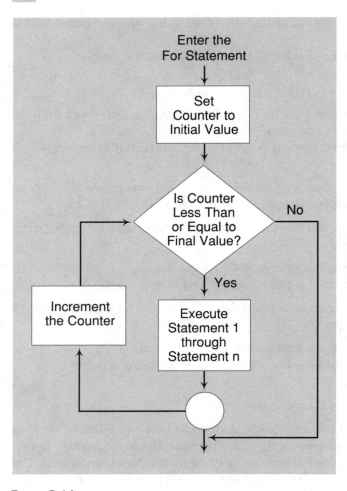

Figure 6-14
For/Next Loop Flowchart for
Positive Increments

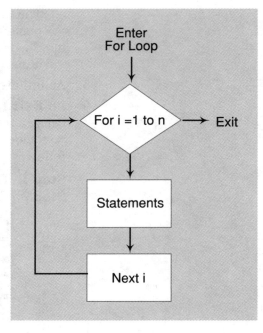

Figure 6-15
Simplified For/Next Loop
Flowchart

Event Procedure 6-7

```
Private Sub Form_Click()
  Dim num As Integer

  Cls ' clear the form
  Font = "Courier"
  Print "NUMBER", "SQUARE", "CUBE"
  Print "------", "------", "----"

  For num = 1 To 10
    Print num, num ^ 2, num ^ 3
  Next num
End Sub
```

PROGRAMMERS NOTES

Which Loop Should You Use?

Beginning programmers often ask which structure they should use—a **For** or **Do While** loop?

In Visual Basic, the answer is relatively straightforward, because the **For** statement can only be used to construct fixed-count loops. Thus, in Visual Basic, although both **For** and **Do While** loops create pretest loops, you should generally use a **For/Next** loop when constructing fixed-count loops and **Do While** loops when constructing variable-condition loops.

When Event Procedure 6-7 is activated, the following display is produced on the form:

```
NUMBER  SQUARE   CUBE
------  ------   ----
  1       1       1
  2       4       8
  3       9       27
  4      16       64
  5      25       125
  6      36       216
  7      49       343
  8      64       512
  9      81       729
 10     100       1000
```

In the **For/Next** statement of Procedure 6-7, simply changing the number 10 to 1000 creates a loop that is executed 1000 times and produces a table of numbers from 1 to 1000. As with the **Do While** loop, this small change produces an immense increase in the processing and output provided by the program.

Exercises 6.4

1. Write individual **For** statements for the following cases:

   a. Use a counter named I that has an initial value of 1, a final value of 20, and an increment of 1.

   b. Use a counter named count that has an initial value of 1, a final value of 20, and an increment of 2.

   c. Use a counter named J that has an initial value of 1, a final value of 100, and an increment of 5.

   d. Use a counter named count that has an initial value of 20, a final value of 1, and an increment of –1.

   e. Use a counter named count that has an initial value of 20, a final value of 1, and an increment of –2.

   f. Use a counter named count that has an initial value of 1.0, a final value of 16.2, and an increment of 0.2.

   g. Use a counter named xcnt that has an initial value of 20.0, a final value of 10.0, and an increment of –0.5.

2. Determine the number of times that each **For/Next** loop is executed for the statements written in Exercise 1.

3. Determine the value in total, after each of the following loops is executed.

   a.
   ```
   total = 0
   For I = 1 To 10
      total = total + I
   Next I
   ```

   b.
   ```
   total = 1
   For count = 1 To 10
      total = total * 2
   Next count
   ```

   c.
   ```
   total = 0
   For I = 10 To 15
      total = total + I
   Next I
   ```

   d.
   ```
   total = 50
   For I = 1 To 10
      total = total - I
   Next I
   ```

   e.
   ```
   total = 1
   For icnt = 1 To 8
      total = total * icnt
   Next icnt
   ```

   f.
   ```
   total = 1.0
   For J = 1 To 5
      total = total / 2.0
   Next J
   ```

4 Determine the errors in the following **For/Next** statements:

   a. For I = 1,10
   b. For count 5,10
   c. For JJ = 1 To 10 Increment 2
   d. For kk = 1, 10, –1
   e. For kk = –1, –20

5 Determine the output of the following **For** loop:

```
Dim I as Integer
For I = 20 To 0 Step -4
  Print I
Next I
```

6 Modify Event Procedure 6-7 to produce a table of the numbers 0 through 20 in increments of 2, with their squares and cubes.

7 Modify Event Procedure 6-7 to produce a table of numbers from 10 to 1, instead of 1 to 10 as it currently does.

8 Write a Visual Basic program that uses a **For/Next** loop to accumulate the sum $1 + 2 + 3 + \ldots + N$, where N is a user-entered integer. Then evaluate the expression $N * (N + 1) / 2$ to verify that this expression yields the same result as the loop.

9 a. An old Arabian legend has it that a fabulously wealthy but unthinking king agreed to give a beggar one cent the first day and double the previous day's amount for 64 days. Using this information write, run, and test a Visual Basic program that displays how much the king must pay the beggar on each day. The output of your program should appear as follows:

```
Day      Amount Owed
---      -----------
 1         0.01
 2         0.02
 3         0.04
 .          .
 .          .
 .          .
64          .
```

   b. Modify the program you wrote for Exercise 9a to determine on which day the king will have paid a total of one million dollars to the beggar.

10 Write and run a program that calculates and displays the amount of money available in a bank account that initially has $1000 deposited in it and that earns 8 percent interest a year. Your program should display the amount available at the end of each year for a period of ten years. Use the relationship that the money available at the end of each year equals the amount of money in the account at the start of the year plus 0.08 times the amount available at the start of the year.

11 A machine purchased for $28,000 is depreciated at a rate of $4000 a year for seven years. Write and run a Visual Basic program that uses a **For/Next** loop to compute and display a seven-year depreciation table. The table should have the form:

```
Depreciation Schedule
------------ --------

Year          Depreciation   End-of-year     Accumulated
                             value           depreciation

----          ------------   -----------     ------------
1             4000           24000           4000
2             4000           20000           8000
3             4000           16000           12000
4             4000           12000           16000
5             4000           8000            20000
6             4000           4000            24000
7             4000           0               28000
```

12 A well-regarded manufacturer of widgets has been losing 4 percent of its sales each year. The annual profit for the firm is 10 percent of sales. This year, the firm has had $10 million in sales and a profit of $1 million. Determine the expected sales and profit for the next 10 years. Your program should complete and produce a display similar to the following:

```
              Sales and Profit Projection
              -----------------------------
Year          Expected  sales   Projected  profit

----          ---------------   ------------------
1             $10000000         $1000000
2             $ 9600000         $ 960000
3                  .   .
   .               .   .
   .               .   .
   .               .   .
10                 .   .
              ---------------------------------------------
Totals:       $ .               $ .
```

13 According to legend, the island of Manhattan was purchased from the Native American population in 1626 for $24. Assuming that this money was invested in a Dutch bank paying 5 percent simple interest per year, construct a table showing how much money this would grow to at the end of each twenty-year period, starting in 1626 and ending in 2006.

6.5 ► Nested Loops

There are many situations in which it is very convenient to have a loop contained within another loop. Such loops are called *nested loops*. A simple example of a nested loop is

```
For I = 1 To 4     ' Start of Outer Loop
  Print "I is now"; I
  For J = 1 To 3  ' Start of Inner Loop
    Print " J = "; J
  Next J    ' End of Inner Loop
Next I      ' End of Outer Loop
```

Figure 6-16

For Each I, J Makes a Complete Loop

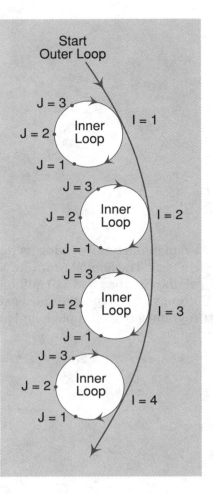

The first loop, controlled by the value of I, is called the *outer loop*. The second loop, controlled by the value of J, is called the *inner loop*. Notice that all statements in the inner loop are contained within the boundaries of the outer loop, and that we have used a different variable to control each loop. For each single trip through the outer loop, the inner loop runs through its entire sequence. Thus, each time the I counter increases by one, the inner **For/Next** loop executes completely. This situation is illustrated in Figure 6-16.

To understand the concept involved, consider Program 6-5, which uses a nested **For/Next** loop.

For this application, the procedure code for the Command button **Click** events is listed in Program 6-5's event code.

Figure 6-17

Program 6-5's Interface

Table 6-3	The Properties Table for Program 6-5	
Object	**Property**	**Setting**
Form	Name	frmMain
	Caption	Program 6-5
Command button	Name	cmdRun
	Caption	&Show Nested Loop
Command button	Name	cmdExit
	Caption	E&xit

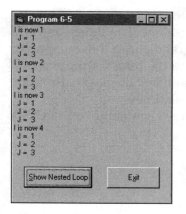

Figure 6-18
The Display Produced by
Program 6-5

Program 6-5's Event Code

```
Private Sub cmdRun_Click()
  Dim I As Integer, J As Integer

  Cls
  For I = 1 To 4  ' <----------- Start of Outer Loop
    Print "I is now"; I
    For J = 1 To 3 ' <------ Start of Inner Loop
      Print " J = "; J
    Next J    ' <------------ End of Inner Loop
  Next I      ' <------------- End of Outer Loop
End Sub

Private Sub cmdExit_Click()
  Beep
  End
End Sub
```

Figure 6-18 illustrates the display produced when Program 6-5 is executed. In creating nested loops, using any of Visual Basic's loop structures (and the various structures can be nested within one another), the only requirements are

1. An inner loop must be fully contained within an outer loop,
2. The inner loop and outer loop control variables cannot be the same, and
3. An outer loop control variable must not be altered within an inner loop.

Let us use a nested loop to compute the average grade for each student in a class of 20 students. Assume that each student has taken four exams during the course of the semester. The final grade for each student is calculated as the average of the four examination grades. The pseudocode for this example is

Do 20 times
    Set student total to zero
    Do 4 times
        Read in a grade
        Add the grade to the student total
    End inner Do
  Calculate student's average grade
  Print student's average grade
End outer Do

Figure 6-19
Program 6-6's Interface

Table 6-4 The Properties Table for Program 6-6

Object	Property	Setting
Form	Name	frmMain
	Caption	Program 6-6
Command button	Name	cmdRun
	Caption	&Calculate Average
Command button	Name	cmdExit
	Caption	E&xit

As described in the pseudocode, an outer loop consisting of 20 passes will be used to calculate the average for each student. The inner loop will consist of four passes, with one examination grade entered in each inner loop pass. As each grade is entered, it is added to the total for the student, and at the end of the loop, the average is calculated and displayed. Program 6-6 uses a nested loop to make the required calculations.

For this application, the procedure code for the Command button **Click** event is listed in Program 6-6's event code.

Program 6-6's Event Code

```
Private Sub cmdRun_Click()
Rem: This program calculates the average grade for MAXSTUDENTS no. of students
    Const MAXSTUDENTS As Integer = 20
    Const NUMGRADES As Integer = 4

    Dim i As Integer, j As Integer
    Dim grade As Single, total As Single, average As Single

    Rem: This is the start of the outer loop
    For i = 1 To MAXSTUDENTS
      total = 0
      Rem: This is the start of the inner loop
      For j = 1 To NUMGRADES
          grade = InputBox("Enter an exam grade for this student", "Input Dialog", "0")
          total = total + grade
      Next j  ' End of inner loop
      average = total / NUMGRADES
      Print "The average for student"; i; "is ", average
    Next i  ' End of outer loop
End Sub

Private Sub cmdExit_Click()
    Beep
    End
End Sub
```

In reviewing Program 6-6, pay particular attention to the initialization of `total` within the outer loop before the inner loop is entered. `total` is initialized 20 times, once for each student. Also notice that the average is calculated and displayed immediately after the inner loop is finished. Since the statements that compute and print the average are also contained within the outer loop, 20 averages are calculated and displayed. The entry and addition of each grade within the inner loop use summation techniques we have seen before, which should now be familiar to you.

Exercises 6.5

1. Four experiments are performed, each consisting of six test results. The results for each experiment are given below. Write a program using a nested loop to compute and display the average of the test results for each experiment.

First experiment results:	23.2	31.5	16.9	27.5	25.4	28.6
Second experiment results:	34.8	45.2	27.9	36.8	33.4	39.4
Third experiment results:	19.4	16.8	10.2	20.8	18.9	13.4
Fourth experiment results:	36.9	39.5	49.2	45.1	42.7	50.6

② Modify the program written for Exercise 1, so that the number of test results for each experiment is entered by the user. Write your program so that a different number of test results can be entered for each experiment.

③ a. A bowling team consists of five players. Each player bowls three games. Write a Visual Basic program that uses a nested loop to enter each player's individual scores and then computes and displays the average score for each bowler. Assume that each bowler has the following scores:

First bowler:	286	252	265
Second bowler:	212	186	215
Third bowler:	252	232	216
Fourth bowler:	192	201	235
Fifth bowler:	186	236	272

b. Modify the program written for Exercise 3a., to calculate and display the average team score. (**Hint:** Use a second variable to store the total of all the players' scores.)

④ Rewrite the program written for Exercise 3a., to eliminate the inner loop. To do this, you will have to input three scores for each bowler rather than one at a time.

⑤ Write a program that calculates and displays values for Y when

$$Y = X * Z / (X - Z)$$

Your program should calculate Y for values of X ranging between 1 and 5, and values of Z ranging between 2 and 10. X should control the outer loop and be incremented in steps of one, and Z should be incremented in steps of one. Your program should also display the message `Value Undefined` when the X and Z values are equal.

⑥ Write a program that calculates and displays the yearly amount available if $1000 is invested in a bank account for 10 years. Your program should display the amounts available for interest rates from 6 percent to 12 percent inclusively, in 1 percent increments. Use a nested loop, with the outer loop controlling the interest rate and the inner loop controlling the years. Use the relationship that the money available at the end of each year equals the amount of money in the account at the start of the year, plus the interest rate times the amount available at the start of the year.

⑦ In the Duchy of Penchuck, the fundamental unit of currency is the Penchuck Dollar, PD. Income tax deductions are based on Salary in units of 10,000 PD and on the number of dependents the employee has. The formula, designed to favor low-income families, is

Deduction PD = Dependents * 500 + 0.05 * (50,000 – Salary)

Beyond five dependents and beyond 50,000 PD, the deduction does not change. There is no tax, hence no deduction, on incomes of less than 10,000 PD. Based on this information, create a table of Penchuck income tax deductions, with dependents 0 to 5 as the column headings and salaries of 10000, 20000, 30000, 40000, and 50000 as the rows.

6.6 ▶ Exit-Controlled Loops

The **Do While** and **For/Next** loops are both entrance-controlled loops, which means that they evaluate a condition at the start of the loop. A consequence of testing a condition at the top of the loop is that the statements within the loop may not be executed at all.

There are cases, however, where we always require a loop to execute at least once. For such cases, Visual Basic provides two exit-controlled loops, the **Do/Loop While** and **Do/Loop Until** structures. Each of these loop structures tests a condition at the bottom of a loop, which ensures that the statements within the loop are executed at least one time. The syntax for the most commonly used exit-controlled loop is

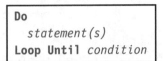

```
Do
    statement(s)
Loop Until condition
```

The important concept to notice in the **Do/Loop Until** structure is that all statements within the loop are executed at least once before the condition is tested, and the loop is repeated until the condition becomes **True** (another way of viewing this is that the loop executes while the condition is **False**). A flowchart illustrating the operation of the **Do/Loop Until** structure is shown in Figure 6-20.

As illustrated in Figure 6-20, all statements within the **Do/Loop Until** loop are executed once before the condition is evaluated. Then, if the condition is **False**, the statements within the loop are executed again. This process continues until the condition becomes **True**.

As an example of a **Do/Loop Until** structure consider the following loop:

```
i = 0
Do
   Print i;
   i = i + 5
Loop Until i > 20
```

Figure 6-20

The Do/Loop Until Structure's Flowchart

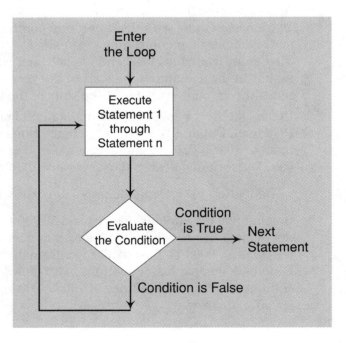

The output produced by this code is

0   5   10   15   20

The important point to notice here is that the condition is tested after the statements within the **Loop** structure have been executed, rather than before. This ensures that the loop statements are always executed at least once. Also notice that exit-controlled loops require that you correctly initialize all variables used in the tested expression before the loop is entered, in a manner similar to that used in entrance-controlled loops. Similarly, within the loop itself, these same variables must be altered to ensure that the loop eventually terminates.

The Do/Loop While Structure

In a **Do/Loop Until** structure, the statements within the loop are executed as long as the condition is **False** (has a zero value). A variation of **Do/Loop Until** structure is the **Do/Loop While** structure, which executes the statements within the loop as long as the condition is **True** (has a non-zero value). The syntax of a **Do/Loop While** loop is

```
Do
    statement(s)
Loop While condition
```

The **Do/Loop While** structure, like its **Do/Loop Until** counterpart, is an exit-controlled loop. Unlike the **Do/Loop Until** loop, which executes until the condition becomes **True**, a **Do/Loop While** structure executes until the condition becomes **False**. If the condition tested in a **Do/Loop While** loop is **False** to begin with, the statements within the loop will only execute once.

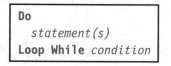

Figure 6-21
Program 6-7's Interface

Validity Checks

Exit-controlled loops are particularly useful for filtering user-entered input and validating that the correct type of data has been entered. For example, assume that a program is being written to provide the square root of any user input number. For this application, we want to ensure that a valid number has been entered. Any invalid data, such as a negative number or a non-numeric input, should be rejected and a new request for input made, until the user actually enters a valid number. Program 6-7 illustrates how this request can easily be accomplished using a **Do/Loop Until** structure.

Program 6-7's Event Code

```
Private Sub cmdRun_Click()
  Dim num As String

  Do
    picsquare.Cls
    num = InputBox("Enter a number", "Input Request", "0")
    If IsNumeric(num) And num >= 0 Then
      picsquare.Print Sqr(num)
    Else
      MsgBox "Invalid data was entered", vbInformation, "Error Message"
    End If
  Loop Until IsNumeric(num) And num >= 0

End Sub
```

continued

```
Private Sub cmdExit_Click()
   Beep
   End
End Sub
```

Notice that, in the Run button's **Click** code, a request for a number is repeated until a valid number is entered. This code is constructed so that a user cannot "crash" the program by entering either a non-numeric string or a negative number. This type of user-input validation is essential for programs that will be used extensively by people other than the programmer and is a mark of professionally written programs.

Exercises 6.6

1. a. Using a **Do/Loop Until** structure, write a program to accept a grade. The program should continue to request a grade until a valid grade is entered. A valid grade is any grade greater than or equal to 0 and less than or equal to 100. After a valid grade has been entered, your program should display the value of that grade.

   b. Modify the program written for Exercise 1a. so that it allows the user to exit the program by entering the number 999.

   c. Modify the program written for Exercise 1b. so that it automatically terminates after five invalid grades are entered.

2. a. Modify the program written for Exercise 1a as follows: if the grade is less than 0 or greater than 100, your program should print an appropriate message informing the user that an invalid grade has been entered; otherwise, the grade should be added to a total. When a grade of 999 is entered, the program should exit the repetition loop and compute and display the average of the valid grades entered.

   b. Run the program written in Exercise 2a on a computer and verify the program, using appropriate test data.

3. a. Write a program to reverse the digits of a positive integer number. For example, if the number 8735 is entered, the number displayed should be 5378. (**Hint:** Use an exit-controlled loop, and continuously strip off and display the units digit of the number.) If the variable num initially contains the number entered, the units digit is obtained as num Mod 10. After a units digit is displayed, dividing the number by 10 sets up the number for the next iteration. Thus, 8735 Mod 10 is 5 and 8735 / 10 is 873. The loop should repeat as long as the remaining number is not zero.

   b. Run the program written in Exercise 3a on a computer and verify the program, using appropriate test data.

4. a. The outstanding balance on Rhona Karp's car loan is $8000. Each month, Rhona is required to make a payment of $300, which includes both interest and principal repayment of the car loan. The monthly interest is calculated as 0.10/12 of the outstanding balance. After the interest is deducted, the remaining part of the payment is used to pay off the loan. Using this information, write a Visual Basic program that produces a table indicating the beginning monthly balance, the interest payment,

the principal payment, and the remaining loan balance after each payment is made. Your output should resemble and complete the entries in the following table until the outstanding loan balance is zero.

Beginning Balance	Interest Payment	Principal Payment	Ending Loan Balance
----------	--------	----------	-----------
8000.00	66.67	233.33	7766.67
7766.67	64.73	235.28	7531.39
75531.39	.	.	.
.	.	.	.
.	.	.	.
.	.	.	0.00

b. Modify the program written in Exercise 4a to display the total of the interest and principal paid at the end of the table produced by your program.

5 Write, run, and test a Visual Basic program that prompts the user for the amount of a loan, the annual percentage rate, and the number of years of the loan, using InputBox functions that display the following prompts:

```
What is the amount of the loan?
What is the annual percentage rate?
How many years will you take to pay back the loan?
```

From the input data, produce a loan amortization table similar to the one shown below:

	Amount 1500	Annual % 14	Interest	Years 1	Monthly Payment 134.68	
Payment Number	Interest Paid	Principal Paid	Cumulative Interest	Total Paid to Date	New Balance Due
1	17.50	117.18	17.50	134.68	1382.82
2	16.13	118.55	33.63	269.36	1264.27
3	14.75	119.93	48.38	404.04	1144.34
4	13.35	121.33	61.73	538.72	1023.01
5	11.94	122.75	73.67	673.40	900.27
6	10.50	124.18	84.17	808.08	776.09
7	9.05	125.63	93.23	942.76	650.46
8	7.59	127.09	100.81	1077.45	523.37
9	6.11	128.57	106.92	1212.13	394.79
10	4.61	130.07	111.53	1346.81	264.72
11	3.09	131.59	114.61	1481.49	133.13
12	1.55	133.13	116.17	1616.17	0

In constructing the loop necessary to produce the body of the table, the following initializations must be made:

```
New balance due = Original loan amount
Cumulative interest = 0.0
Paid to date = 0.0
Payment number = 0
Monthly Interest Rate = Annual Percentage Rate / 1200
```

$$\text{Monthly Payment} = \frac{(\text{Loan Amount}) * (\text{Monthly Interest Rate})}{1 - (1 + \text{Monthly Interest Rate})^{-(\text{Number of Months})}}$$

Within the loop, the following calculations and accumulations should be used:

Payment number = Payment number + 1
Interest paid = New balance due * Monthly interest rate
Principal paid = Monthly payment - Interest paid
Cumulative interest = Cumulative interest + Interest paid
Paid to date = Paid to date + Monthly payment
New balance due = New balance due - Principal paid

 6 Modify the program written for Exercise 5 to prevent the user from entering an illegal value for the interest rate. That is, write a loop that asks the user repeatedly for the annual interest rate, until a value between 1.0 and 25.0 is entered.

6.7 ▶ Focus on Program Design and Implementation:[2]

After-the-Fact Data Validation and Creating Function Hot Keys

In the last chapter's Focus section, key stroke input validation was applied to the Rotech[3] Walk in order entry form's quantity Text box. This type of validation consists of checking each entered character, and only permitting selected keys to be entered as valid input data. In addition to this key stroke-by-key stroke data validation, overall validation of a completed input entry is also used to ensure that (1) a required field has not been skipped over, and (2) that data contained within a field is reasonable. This second type of data validation is referred to as after-the-fact validation.

As a practical example of this type of data validation, consider Rotech's Mail in form, a copy of which is shown in Figure 6-22.

In an extreme situation, a user could enter no data at all into any of the input Text boxes shown in Figure 6-22, and still attempt to print out a packing slip. Even using key stroke validation for the quantity Text box won't help, because a user can simply jump over this box without entering any

Figure 6-22
The Rotech Mail In Form

```
┌─ Mail In Orders ──────────── _ □ X ┐
│                                      │
│           Mail In Order Form         │
│                                      │
│   First Name: [            ]         │
│                                      │
│   Last Name: [            ]          │
│                                      │
│   Address: [            ]            │
│                                      │
│   City: [                ]           │
│                                      │
│   State: [  ]    Zip    [      ]     │
│                  Code:               │
│   No. of Disk [  ]                   │
│   Packages:                          │
│                                      │
│  [Print Packing]  [Clear Screen]  [Return to Main] │
│  [    Slip    ]                 [    Menu    ]      │
└──────────────────────────────────────┘
```

---

[2]This section can be omitted with no loss of subject continuity, unless the Rotech project is being followed.

[3]The Rotech project, as it should exist at the start of this section (which includes all of the capabilities built into it through the end of Section 5.6) can be found on the Student Disk as the `rotech6.vbp` project within the `rotech6` folder.

quantity into it all. After-the-fact validation can be used to correct this type of situation. Specifically, for the Mail in form we will apply after-the-fact validation to ensure the following requirements are met:

A packing slip will not be prepared if any name or address fields are empty or if there is not a positive number in the quantity Text box. We will also assume that each customer is limited to a maximum of 5 free disk packages, so the quantity cannot exceed this value.

Additionally, we will add after-the-fact data validation to ensure that the Walk in form adheres to the following requirements:

A bill will only be printed if the quantity field contains a positive number. Since the customer is purchasing disk packs, there will be no limit check on the maximum number that can be entered for this quantity. Additionally, if both the first and last name fields have been left blank, the bill will be made out to Cash.[4]

There are two predominant techniques for informing a user that a particular data entry item has either been incorrectly filled in or is missing completely. In the first method, each individual field is examined and a message displayed, one-at-a-time, for each incorrectly completed item. For more than two fields this method tends to annoy users and should be avoided. For example, assume that you inform the user that the Address item has not been filled in. Then, after the user corrects this field, you provide another message that the City item is missing. After this item is entered, yet another message appears indicating that the State has not been entered. From a user's standpoint this is extremely annoying, and a much better scheme is to provide a single message that gives a complete list of all missing items.

Figure 6-23 shows how such a message would look for our Mail in form, assuming that all of the Mail in form's name and address fields were left empty when the Print Packing Slip Command button was pressed. Notice that the Message box lists all of the missing address items. The quantity input, which is not part of the address data, will be given its own set of error messages. Figures 6-24 and 6-25 show the two possible error messages that a user could receive for this input. Thus, in total, a user will receive at most two separate error messages (one for the address data and one for the quantity input), which is within most user's tolerance zone. Clearly, these error messages can and will recur if the user does not correct the problem, but this recurrence will not be blamed on the system, but rather on the user's inattention to detail.

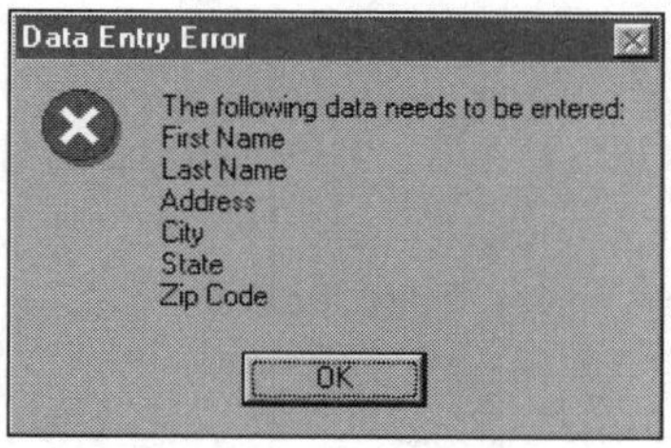

Figure 6-23
A Sample Address Information
Error Message

Figure 6-24
The Error Message for a Missing
Quantity

Figure 6-25
The Error Message for Too Large a
Quantity

---

[4]This is a common custom in business. For customers who do not wish to give their names or addresses, the transaction is simply posted as a cash transaction.

Creating a Carriage Return and Line Feed

The terms *carriage return* and *line feed* are holdovers from the early days of computing, when a typewriter-like printer was used for creating all hardcopy output. The printing mechanism in these printers was a movable device, called a *carriage*, that traveled across the paper from left to right. When a return code was sent to the printer, the carriage would return to the left side of the paper and the paper would move up by one line. This movement of the printer was described as a carriage return followed by a line feed. These same terms are still used to describe cursor movement on a screen. Here, however, the term carriage return means moving the cursor to the left side of the current text area, and line feed means moving down one row.

The need to construct a new line on the screen occurs frequently, but is complicated by the fact that there are no printable characters for forcing the correct cursor motion. The programming trick to creating a new line within a string of text is to convert the non-printing ANSI codes for a carriage return and line feed, which are the decimal values 13 and 10, respectively, into printable characters using Visual Basic's Chr$ function. For example, the code:

```
Dim CRLF as String
CRLF = Chr$(13) + Chr$(10)
```

provides a string variable named CRLF that can be used to explicitly force a new screen line. Using this variable, for example, the single statement Print "One" + CRLF + "Two" + CRLF + "Three" will cause three lines to be displayed on the screen. Clearly, the same output can be produced using five **Print** statements, but the single statement version is much cleaner. (Note that a single Print statement, by itself, creates a new line by internally issuing the same carriage return and line feed codes.)

Event Procedure 6-8 illustrates the code used in the Rotech application to validate the Mail in form's input before a packing slip is printed. The first item to notice is that from a user's viewpoint, the procedure is meant to print a packing slip—but that from a programming viewpoint the majority of the procedure is concerned with validating data. This is true for most real-world code; the code itself should validate all data and ensure that any data required for processing cannot inadvertently cause the system to crash or produce clearly silly results. For example, it is the program's responsibility not to print a packing slip with a blank address or an unreasonable quantity of product. Clearly, all the validation in the world cannot stop a user from entering a misspelled name or a non-existent address, but that is an error that cannot be fixed by the application.

Event Procedure 6-8

```
Private Sub cmdPrint_Click()
   Dim CRLF As String   ' this will be a carriage return and line feed
   Dim strErrorPrompt As String
   Dim strErrorMsg As String
   Dim strListEmptyBoxes As String ' the list of empty Text boxes
   Dim strErrorMin As String
   Dim strErrorMax As String

   Const MAXALLOWED As Integer = 5

   'Set the standard strings that will be printed
   CRLF = Chr$(13) & Chr$(10)
   strErrorPrompt = "Data Entry Error"
```

```
strErrorMsg = "The following data needs to be entered: " + CRLF
strListEmptyBoxes = ""
strErrorMin ="You must enter the No. of disk packages ordered."
strErrorMax = "The quantity ordered cannot exceed " + Str(MAXALLOWED)

'Locate all empty name and address text boxes
If Len(txtFname) = 0 Then
   strListEmptyBoxes = strListEmptyBoxes + "First Name " + CRLF
End If
If Len(txtLname) = 0 Then
   strListEmptyBoxes = strListEmptyBoxes + "Last Name " + CRLF
End If
If Len(txtAddr) = 0 Then
   strListEmptyBoxes = strListEmptyBoxes + "Address " + CRLF
End If
If Len(txtCity) = 0 Then
   strListEmptyBoxes = strListEmptyBoxes + "City " + CRLF
End If
If Len(txtState) = 0 Then
   strListEmptyBoxes = strListEmptyBoxes + "State " + CRLF
End If
If Len(txtZip) = 0 Then
   strListEmptyBoxes = strListEmptyBoxes + "Zip Code "
End If


' Inform the user of all empty text boxes
If Len(strListEmptyBoxes) > 0 Then
    MsgBox strErrorMsg + strListEmptyBoxes, vbCritical, strErrorPrompt
ElseIf Val(txtQuantity) < 1 Then
   MsgBox strErrorMin, vbCritical, strErrorPrompt
ElseIf Val(txtQuantity) > MAXALLOWED Then
   MsgBox strErrorMax, vbCritical, strErrorPrompt
Else ' Print the packing slip
  Print a; Packing; slip
  Printer.Print
  Printer.Print
  Printer.Font = "Courier"
  Printer.FontSize = 12
  Printer.Print Spc(20); Format(Now, "mm-dd-yy-hh:mm:ss")
  Printer.Print
  Printer.Print
  Printer.Print Spc(5); "To: "; txtFname; " "; txtLname; ""
  Printer.Print Spc(9); txtAddr
  Printer.Print Spc(9); txtCity; " "; txtState; " "; txtZip
  Printer.Print
  Printer.Print
  Printer.Print Spc(5); "Quantity Shipped:"; Spc(1); txtQuantity
  Printer.EndDoc
  End If
End Sub
```

Now look at the first section of code printed in black in Event Procedure 6-8. Notice that the maximum allowable disk order quantity and all of the standard messages used as prompts in Figures 6-23 through 6-25 have been assigned at the top of this section, near the beginning of the procedure. The advantage of this is that if any change must be made to any of these values, the value can be easily located and modified.

Now notice that the name and address validation code at the end of this first black section consists of a series of six individual **If** statements. Within each statement an individual Text box string is checked using Visual Basic's **Len** function. Although this function is explained more fully in the next chapter, its usage here is easily understood. The **Len** function returns a string's length, which consists of the total number of characters in the string. A length of zero means that the string has no characters, which indicates that no data has been entered for it. For each Text box that has no data, the name of the equivalent data field and a carriage return/line feed combination are appended to the string variable named strListEmptyBoxes. Thus, after the last **If** statement is executed, this string variable will contain a list of all empty name and address items. (See the "Tips from the Pros" box on page 306 for a description of how the carriage return/line feed variable CRLF is constructed.)

Finally, look at second section of code printed in black, which contains the validation code for the quantity of disk packages ordered. Here there are two possibilities; either the quantity has been left blank, or the number of ordered packages exceeds the value in the MAXALLOWED named constant (we don't have to check for either a negative or fractional value being entered, because the key stroke validation will prevent a minus sign or period from being entered). The two **ElseIf** statements within this second shaded region check for each of these conditions.

The Walk in form's after-the-fact validation is listed as Event Procedure 6-9. As the majority of the code listed in this procedure was previously described in Section 4.4, we will only comment on the code specifically added for data validation. The first black section provides the prompts that we will use for an error Message box, which is the same as that previously illustrated in Figure 6-24 for the Mail in form. The second black section contains two individual **If** statements. The first **If** statement checks that both a first name and last name have been entered; if not, the string "Cash" is substituted for

---

TIPS FROM THE PROS

Checking for Completed Inputs

The method used in Event Procedure 6-8 individually tests and identifies each Text box that contains an empty string. When this individual identification is not necessary, a much quicker validation can be obtained by multiplying the length of all the input strings together. Then, if one or more of the strings is empty, the result of the computation will be zero.

As a specific example, assume that you need to check that three Text boxes, named txtPrice, txtQuantity, and txtDescription, have all been filled in. The code below does the trick:

Notice that this code does not identify which, or how many of the input items is blank. However, if one or more of the items is blank, at least one of the operands in the multiplication will be zero, and the result of the computation is zero. And this is the only way we can get a zero, because if all of the inputs are filled in, the result of the multiplication will be a positive number. Thus, a zero result ensures that at least one of the inputs has not been filled in.

This programming trick is very prevalent in real-world applications, and you are sure to see many applications of it in your programming work.

```
If (Len(txtPrice) * Len(txtQuantity) * Len(txtDescription)) = 0
   MsgBox "One or more of the fields has not been filled in!"
Endif
```

the first name (see the "Tips from the Pros" box on page 308 for an alternative way of making this check). The second **If** statement validates that the number of disks ordered is greater than zero.

Event Procedure 6-9

```
Private Sub cmdPrint_Click()
  Dim sngtotal As Single, sngtaxes As Single, sngfinal As Single
  Dim strErrorPrompt As String
  Dim strErrorMin As String

  'Set the standard strings that will be printed
  strErrorPrompt = "Data Entry Error"
  strErrorMin ="You must enter the No. of disk packages ordered."

  'Clear out the picture boxes
  picTotal.Cls
  picTax.Cls
  picFinal.Cls

  'Calculate and display new values
  sngtotal = Val(txtQuantity) * CCur(txtPrice)
  sngtaxes = Val(txtTrate) * sngtotal
  sngfinal = sngtotal + sngtaxes
  picTotal.Print Format(sngtotal, "currency")
  picTax.Print Format(sngtaxes, "currency")
  picFinal.Print Format(sngfinal, "currency")

  ' Validate the Name and Quantity
  If Len(txtFname) = 0 AND Len(txtLname) = 0 Then
    txtFname = "Cash"
  End If
  If Val(txtQuantity) < 1 Then
    MsgBox strErrorMin, vbCritical, strErrorPrompt
  Else ' Print a Bill
    Printer.Print
    Printer.Print
    Printer.Font = "Courier"
    Printer.FontSize = 12
    Printer.Print Spc(20); Format(Now, "mm/dd/yy")
    Printer.Print Spc(20); Format(Now, "h:m AM/PM")
    Printer.Print
    Printer.Print
    Printer.Print "Sold to: "; txtFname; " "; txtLname; ""
    Printer.Print Spc(9); txtAddr
    Printer.Print Spc(9); txtCity; " "; txtState; " "; txtZip
    Printer.Print
    Printer.Print
    Printer.Print "Quantity:"; Spc(1); txtQuantity
    Printer.Print "Unit Price:"; Spc(2); Format(txtPrice, "currency")
    Printer.Print "Total:"; Spc(6); Format(sngtotal, "currency")
    Printer.Print "Sales tax:"; Spc(3); Format(sngtaxes, "currency")
    Printer.Print "Amount Due:"; Spc(1); Format(sngfinal, "currency")
    Printer.EndDoc
  End If
End Sub
```

Using Function Keys as Hot Keys

Many applications reserve the function keys (F1, F2, etc.) for use as "Hot" keys. A Hot key is a single key, or combination of keys, that performs a distinct task, no matter when or where in the application that it is pressed.

For example, a common practice is to allocate the F1 key as the Hot key for calling up a Help screen, so that whenever this key is pressed, a Help screen appears. Another use is to allocate a function key as a "Return to Main Menu" Hot key. Using the designated key, no matter where it is pressed in an application, guarantees unloading or hiding of the currently displayed form and display of the Main Menu form. For applications with long chains of forms, where one form is used to call another, a specific function key can also be used as a "Return to Previous Form" Hot key. Here, by pressing the designated key, the user recalls the prior form. This permits a user to back-up as many forms as necessary, even to the point of recalling the first screen displayed by the application.

The first requirement for capturing a pressed function key, independent of which specific control has the focus when the key is pressed, is to set a form's KeyPreview property to True. Doing this ensures that no matter which control has focus, the keyboard events KeyDown, KeyUp, and KeyPress will be invoked as **Form** events before they are invoked for any control placed on a form. Because the form's keyboard events supercede all other control keyboard events, the desired function key is detected as a **Form** event first and is recognized as such no matter where on the form or within a control that the key is pressed.

As a specific example, assume that we want to make the F10 key a "Return to Main Menu" Hot key. The following event code does the trick:

```
Private Sub Form_KeyDown(KeyCode As Integer, Shift As Integer)
  If KeyCode = vbKeyF10 Then  ' check for F10 key
    KeyCode = 0
    Me.Hide
    frmMain.Show
  End If
End Sub
```

In this event code we check for the constant vbKeyF10, which is the named constant for the KeyCode returned by the F10 key (the value of this constant is 0x79, which is the decimal number 121—thus, the more ambiguous expression If KeyCode = 121 also works). When the F10 function key is pressed, the **If** statement first resets the KeyCode to 0 to ensures that the key is not passed on to the specific control currently having the focus, the current form is hidden, and the frmMain form is displayed. Assuming this is the name of the Main Menu form, the user now sees this form displayed.

All that remains is to explicitly set each form's KeyPreview property to True, which is necessary to ensure that the form level keyboard event is triggered. This is easily done within the code that displays each form for which we want the function keys to be active at the form level. For example, the following event code, which is used to display the Walk in form from Rotech's Main Menu screen, illustrates how this form's KeyPreview property is set just before the form is displayed.

```
Private Sub cmdWalkins_Click()
  frmWalk.KeyPreview = True
  Me.Hide
  frmWalk.Show
End Sub
```

Although the example presented here applies to the [F10] key, it is easily extended to any key for which you know the KeyCode. Exercise 4 at the end of this section shows how to obtain these codes using the Help facility.

Finally, as a technical note, a KeyCode is recognized within all keyboard event procedures, while the KeyAscii codes used in the last chapter's Focus section are only recognized within KeyPress events.

Exercises 6.7

(**Note:** The Rotech Systems project, at the stage of development begun in this section, can be found on the Student Disk in the rotech5 folder as project rotech5.vbp. The project, as it exists at the end of this section, can be found on the Student Disk in the rotech6 folder as project rotech6.vbp. If you are developing the system yourself, following the procedures given in this section, we suggest that you first copy all of the files in the rotech5 folder into the temp folder, and then work out of this latter folder. When you have finished your changes you can compare your results to the files in the rotech6 folder.)

1. a. Either add the data validation code described in this section to the Rotech Mail In and Walk In forms or locate and load the rotech6.vbp project from the Student Disk.
   b. Test that the data validation procedures correctly work for each form.

2. a. Make the [F10] function key a Hot key for both the Mail In and Walk In forms, as described in this section.
   b. Test that the Hot key created in Exercise 2a works correctly for both the Mail In and Walk In form.

3. Using the Help facility's Index tab, obtain information on the KeyPreview method used to create the Hot key described in this section.

4. Using the Help facility, obtain information on the KeyCode constant names and values used for all of the function keys. **Hint:** Enter the words Keycode Constants in the Index tab's Text box.

5. The key stroke validation used for the quantity Text box in both the Mail In and Walk In forms is actually a bit too restrictive, in that it does not permit entry of the [BACKSPACE] key to delete an entered digit (a user can still use the arrow keys and the [DELETE] key to edit the Text box's data). Using the fact that the named constant for the backspace key is vbKeyBack, which you can verify by completing Exercise 4, modify the key stroke validation for the txtQuantity Text box to permit entry of the [BACKSPACE] key.

6. Event Procedure 6-8 uses the following series of six individual **If** statements to check each name and address Text box:

```
If Len(txtFname) = 0 Then
   strListEmptyBoxes = strListEmptyBoxes + "First Name " + CRLF
End If
If Len(txtLname) = 0 Then
   strListEmptyBoxes = strListEmptyBoxes + "Last Name " + CRLF
End If
If Len(txtAddr) = 0 Then
   strListEmptyBoxes = strListEmptyBoxes + "Address " + CRLF
End If
```

continued

```
If Len(txtCity) = 0 Then
   strListEmptyBoxes = strListEmptyBoxes + "City " + CRLF
End If
If Len(txtState) = 0 Then
   strListEmptyBoxes = strListEmptyBoxes + "State " + CRLF
End If
If Len(txtZip) = 0 Then
   strListEmptyBoxes = strListEmptyBoxes + "Zip Code "
End If
```

Determine the effect of replacing this set of statements by the following single **If-Then-ElseIf** structure:

```
If Len(txtFname) = 0 Then
   strListEmptyBoxes = strListEmptyBoxes + "First Name " + CRLF
ElseIf Len(txtLname) = 0 Then
   strListEmptyBoxes = strListEmptyBoxes + "Last Name " + CRLF
ElseIf Len(txtAddr) = 0 Then
   strListEmptyBoxes = strListEmptyBoxes + "Address " + CRLF
ElseIf Len(txtCity) = 0 Then
   strListEmptyBoxes = strListEmptyBoxes + "City " + CRLF
ElseIf Len(txtState) = 0 Then
   strListEmptyBoxes = strListEmptyBoxes + "State " + CRLF
ElseIf Len(txtZip) = 0 Then
   strListEmptyBoxes = strListEmptyBoxes + "Zip Code "
End If
```

7 Event Procedure 6-9 uses the following **If** statement to check that neither a first nor last name has been entered in their respective Text boxes:

```
If Len(txtFname) = 0 AND Len(txtLname) = 0 Then
   txtFname = "Cash"
End If
```

Determine the effect of replacing this statement with the following code. (**Hint:** see the "Tips from the Pros" on page 308.)

```
If (Len(txtFname) * Len(txtLname)) = 0 Then
   txtFname = "Cash"
End If
```

8 **CASE STUDY:** For your selected project (see project specifications at the end of Section 1.5) complete all order entry forms by adding appropriate after-the-fact data validation code into the appropriate event procedures.

6.8 Knowing About: Programming Costs

Any project that requires a computer incurs both hardware and software costs. The costs associated with hardware relate to the physical components of the system. These components include the computer itself, peripherals, and any other items, such as air conditioning, cabling, and associated equipment required by the project. The software costs include all costs associated with initial program development and subsequent program maintenance.

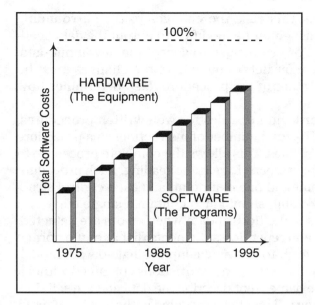

Figure 6-26
Software Is the Major Cost of Most Engineering Projects

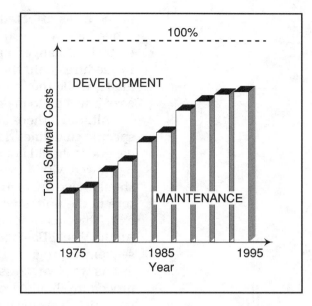

Figure 6-27
Maintenance Is the Predominant Software Cost

As illustrated in Figure 6-26, software costs represent the greatest share of most computer projects.

The reason that software costs contribute so heavily to total project costs is that these costs are labor intensive; that is, they are closely related to human productivity, while hardware costs are more directly related to manufacturing technologies. For example, microchips that cost over $500 per chip 10 years ago can now be purchased for under $1 per chip.

It is far easier, however, to dramatically increase manufacturing productivity by a thousand, with the consequent decrease in hardware costs, than it is for people to double either the quantity or the quality of their thought output. So, as hardware costs have plummeted, the ratio of software costs to total system costs (hardware plus software) has increased dramatically. As was previously noted in Section 1.2, (see Figure 1-11, repeated as Figure 6-27, for convenience) maintenance of existing programs accounts for the majority of software costs.

How easily a program can be maintained (debugged, modified, or enhanced) is related to the ease with which the program can be read and understood, which is directly related to the modularity with which the program was constructed. Modular programs are constructed using procedures, each of which performs a clearly defined and specific task. If each procedure is clearly structured internally and the relationship between procedures clearly specified, each procedure can be tested and modified with a minimum of disturbance or undesirable interaction with the other procedures in the program.

Just as hardware designers frequently locate the cause of a hardware problem by using test methods designed to isolate the offending hardware subsystem, modular software permits the software engineer to similarly isolate program errors to specific software units.

Once a bug has been isolated, or a potential new feature identified, the required changes can be confined to appropriate procedures, without radically affecting other procedures. Only if the procedure in question requires different input data or produces different outputs are its surrounding procedures affected. Even in this case the changes to the surrounding procedures are clear: they must either be modified to output the data needed by the changed procedure or be changed to accept the new input data. Procedures help the programmer determine where the changes must be made, while the internal structure of the procedure itself determines how easy it will be to make the change.

Although there are no hard-and-fast rules for well-written procedures, specific guidelines do exist. The total number of instructions in a procedure generally should not exceed 50 lines. This allows the complete procedure to be viewed within two scrollable screens for ease of reading. Each procedure should have one entrance point and one exit point, and each control structure in the unit, such as a **Do** loop, should also contain a single entry and exit. This makes it easy to trace the flow of data when errors are detected. All the Visual Basic selection and repetition statements that alter the normal sequential program flow, conform to this single-input–single-output model.

As we have stressed throughout the text, instructions contained within a procedure should use variable names that describe the data and are self-documenting. This means that they tell what is happening without a lot of extra comments. For example, the statement

```
x = (a - b) / (c - d)
```

does not contain intelligent variable names. A more useful set of instructions, assuming that a slope is being calculated, is

```
slope = (y2 - y1) / (x2 - x1)
```

Here, the statement itself "tells" what the data represents, what is being calculated, and how the calculation is being performed. Always keep in mind that the goal is to produce programs that make sense to any programmer reading them, at any time. The use of mnemonic data names makes excessive comments unnecessary. The program should contain a sufficient number of comments explaining what a procedure does and any information that would be helpful to other programmers; excessive comments, however, are usually a sign of insufficient program design or poorly constructed coding.

Another sign of a good program is the use of indentation to alert a reader to nested statements and indicate where one statement ends and another begins. Consider the following pseudocode listing the algorithm for determining "What to Wear":

> *If it is below 60 degrees*
> *If it is snowing*
> *wear your lined raincoat*
> *Else*
> *wear a topcoat*
> *If it is below 40 degrees*
> *wear a sweater also*
> *If it is below 30 degrees*
> *wear a jacket also*
> *ElseIf it is raining*
> *wear an unlined raincoat*

Because the **If** and **Else** statement matchings are not clearly indicated, the instructions are difficult to read and interpret. For example, consider what you would wear if the temperature is 35 degrees and it is raining. Now consider the following version of "What to Wear":

If it is below 60 degrees
  If it is snowing
    wear your lined raincoat
  Else
    wear a topcoat
  If it is below 40 degrees
    wear a sweater also
  If it is below 30 degrees
    wear a jacket also
ElseIf it is raining
  wear an unlined raincoat

The second version is indented, making it clear that we are dealing with one main **If-ElseIf** statement. If it is below 60 degrees, the set of instructions indented underneath the first **If** will be executed; otherwise the **ElseIf** condition will be checked. Although a Visual Basic program essentially ignores indention and will always pair an **ElseIf** with the closest matching **If**, indention is extremely useful in making code understandable to the programmer.

6.9 Common Programming Errors and Problems

Three errors are commonly made by beginning Visual Basic programmers when using repetition statements.

1. Testing for equality in repetition loops when comparing floating-point or double-precision operands. For example, the condition num = 0.01 should be replaced by a test requiring that the absolute value of num - 0.01 be less than an acceptable amount. The reason for this is that all numbers are stored in binary form. Using a finite number of bits, decimal numbers such as .01 have no exact binary equivalent, so that tests requiring equality with such numbers can fail.

2. Failure to have a statement within a **Do** loop that alters the tested condition in a manner that terminates the loop.

3. Modifying a **For** loop's counter variable within the loop.

6.10 Chapter Review

Key Terms

counter loop
Do/Loop Until loop
Do/Loop While loop
Do Until loop
Do While loop

Exit Do
fixed-count loop
For/Next loop
infinite loop
nested loop

posttest loop
pretest loop
sentinel values
variable-condition loop

Summary

1. A section of repeating code is referred to as a *loop*. The loop is controlled by a repetition statement that tests a condition to determine whether the code will be executed. Each pass through the loop is referred to as a *repetition* or *iteration*. The tested condition must always be explicitly set, prior to its first evaluation by the repetition statement. Within the loop there must always be a statement that permits altering the condition so that the loop, once entered, can be exited.

2. There are three basic type of loops:
   a. **Do While**,
   b. **For/Next**, and
   c. **Do/Loop Until**.

   The **Do While** and **For/Next** loops are pretest or entrance-controlled loops. In this type of loop, the tested condition is evaluated at the beginning of the loop, which requires that the tested condition be explicitly set prior to loop entry. If the condition is **True**, loop repetitions begin; otherwise the loop is not entered. Iterations continue as long as the condition remains **True**.

   The **Do/Loop Until** loop is a posttest or exit-controlled loop, where the tested condition is evaluated at the end of the loop. This type of loop is always executed at least once. **Do/Loop Until** loops continue to execute as long as the tested condition is **False**, and terminate when the condition becomes **True**.

3. Loops are also classified as to the type of tested condition. In a *fixed-count loop*, the condition is used to keep track of how many repetitions have occurred. In a *variable-condition loop* the tested condition is based on a variable that can change interactively with each pass through the loop.

4. In Visual Basic, the **Do While** loop has the syntax

```
Do While condition
    statement(s)
Loop
```

The condition is tested to determine if the statement or statements within the loop are executed. The condition is evaluated in exactly the same manner as a condition contained in an **If-Else** statement; the difference is how the condition is used. In a **Do While** statement, the statement(s) following the condition is (are) executed repeatedly, as long as the expression is **True**. An example of a **Do While** loop is

```
count = 1              ' initialize count
Do While count <= 10
   Print count;
  count = count + 1  ' increment count
Loop
```

The first assignment statement sets count equal to 1. The **Do While** loop is then entered and the condition is evaluated for the first time. Since the value of count is less than or equal to 10, the condition is **True** and the statements within the loop are executed. The first statement displays the value of count. The next statement adds 1 to the value currently stored in count, making this value equal to 2. The **Do While** structure now loops back to retest the condition. Since count is still less than or equal to 10, the two statements within the loop are again executed. This process continues until the value of count reaches 11.

The **Do While** loop always checks a condition at the top of the loop. This requires that any variables in the tested expression must have values assigned before the **Do While** is encountered. Within the **Do While** loop there must be a statement that alters the tested condition's value.

5. Sentinels are prearranged values used to signal either the start or end of a series of data items. Typically, sentinels are used to create **Do While** loop conditions that terminate the loop when the sentinel value is encountered.

6. The **For/Next** structure is extremely useful in creating loops that must be executed a fixed number of times. The initializing value, final value, and increment used by the loop are all included within the **For** statement. The general syntax of a **For/Next** loop is

```
For counter = start value To end value Step increment value
   statement(s)
Next counter
```

7. Both **Do While** and **For/Next** loops evaluate a condition at the start of the loop. The **Do/Loop Until** structure is used to create an exit-controlled loop, because it checks its expression at the end of the loop. This ensures that the body of the loop is executed at least once. The syntax for this loop structure is

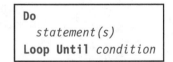

```
Do
   statement(s)
Loop Until condition
```

The important concept to notice in the **Do/Loop Until** structure is that all statements within the loop are executed at least once before the condition is tested, and the loop is repeated until the condition becomes **True** (another way of viewing this is that the loop executes while the condition is **False**). Within the loop, there must be at least one statement that alters the tested expression's value.

Test Yourself–Short Answer

1. A section of repeating code is referred to as a _____.
2. A prearranged value used to signal either the start or end of a series of data items is called a _____.
3. In the **For Next** loop statement, For X = 1 to 100 Step 5 , what is the purpose of the Step clause?
4. List the 4 elements required in the construction of repetitive sections of code.
5. Explain the difference between a pretest loop and a posttest loop.

Problems

1. Determine the output of the following program segment, assuming that all variables have been declared As Single.

```
sngNum = 1734527
sngComputedValue = 0
sngCounter = 0
Do While sngComputedValue < 20
   sngSmallNum = sngNum / 10
   sngLargeNum = Int(sngSmallNum)
   sngDigit = sngNum - sngLargeNum * 10
   sngComputedValue = sngComputedValue + sngDigit
   sngNum = sngLargeNum
   picOutput.Print "sngCounter = "; sngCounter
   picOutput.Print " sngComputedValue  = "; sngComputedValue
   sngCounter = sngCounter + 1
Loop
```

2. Write a loop that displays the numbers 1 to 10 on two lines in a Picture box.

3. Write a loop that displays the even numbers from 2 to 20 on two lines in a Picture box.

4. Write a loop that displays the first 50 numbers in the following sequence: 1, 2, 4, 7, 11, 16, 33, . . .

5. Write a loop that displays all integer less than 1000 whose square roots are integers (i.e., 1, 4, 16, 25, . . .).

6. Write a loop that displays the following table:

```
1 2 3 4
2 3 4 5
3 4 5 6
4 5 6 7
5 6 7 8
6 7 8 9
7 8 9 10
```

7. Write a loop that displays the following table:

```
1 2 3 4 5
2 3 4 5 6
3 4 5 6 7
4 5 6 7 8
5 6 7 8 9
6 7 8 9 10
```

8. Write a loop that displays the following table:

```
1
2 4
3 6 9
4 8 12 16
5 10 15 20 25
```

9. Write a loop that displays the following:

```
*
**
***
****
*****
******
```

10. Write a loop that displays the following:

```
******
*****
****
***
**
*
```

Programming Projects

1. a. The purpose of this project is to create a moving car. An executable example of the required program can be found on the Student Disk enclosed with the text as carrace.exe. You don't have to reproduce the program exactly, but your program should work in a somewhat similar manner. To create your program you will need a loop for moving the car. You will also need to locate and use two icons that are provided on the VB6.0 CDRom named Trffc16.ico and Cloud.ico, which must be placed into either Picture or Image boxes at design time.

Hint: The basic idea for moving the car is to subtract a set increment form the top coordinate of the Image box using an algorithm such as:

Do until "Car is off the screen"
  imgCar.top = imgCar.top – increment
Loop

b. Extra Challenge: Make the clouds of smoke move as the car moves. To do this, first create a control array of five Picture boxes, each containing a small cloud icon, all of whose **Visible** property is set to **False**. (See Section 8.3 for information on Control arrays.) Then, using a **For** loop, set each cloud image's **Visible** property to **True** when the bottom of the car image passes the top of the cloud image.

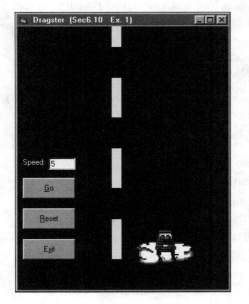

Figure 6-28
Form for Exercise 1

2. a. Create an application that determines the most efficient change to be given from a one-dollar bill. The change should be given in terms of quarters, dimes, nickels, and pennies. For example, a purchase of 44 cents would require change of 2 quarters, a nickel, and a penny (2 quarters and 6 pennies would not be correct). Your program should:

  i. Accept the amount of purchase in terms of the number of cents (integer, no decimals).

  ii. Calculate the change required.

  iii. Determine the number of quarters, dimes, nickels, and pennies necessary for the *most efficient* change.

  iv. Add a <u>C</u>lear button to clear all the quarters, dimes, nickels, and pennies and set the focus to the input Text box.

A suggested form is shown in Figure 6-29 on page 320.

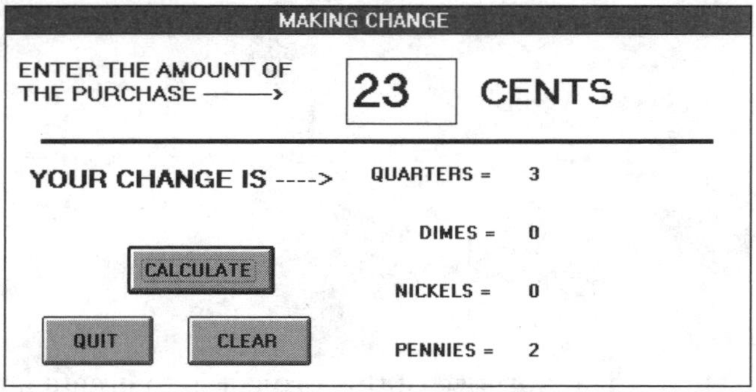

Figure 6-29
Form for Exercise 2

b. Change your code so that if the amount of purchase is over $1 or less than 0, an error message is given and the input Text box receives the focus.

3. Credit scoring is a common practice for businesses that offer credit to their customers. Some of the factors generally used in credit scoring include whether the customer owns a home, has a telephone in their own name, has a savings or checking account, the years employed at their present job, etc. In this project you are to construct a program that determines a credit score. The credit scoring algorithm used by the company requesting the program is

   i. Add 5 points for each of the following: phone (in customer's name), owns home, has a savings or checking account.

   ii. If the customer has been at the same job for less than two years, add no points; if he/she has been at the same job for two years but less than four years, add 3 points, and if he/she has been at the same job for four or more years, add 5 points. For example, for three years at the same job, add 3 points.

   iii. If the customer has been at the same residence for less than two years, add no points; if he/she has been at the same residence for two years but less than four years, add 3 points, and if he/she has been at the same residence for four or more years, add 5 points. For example, three years at the same residence, add 3 points.

   iv. If the customer has other debt, the percent of this debt relative to total income is evaluated as follows:

   no dept, add 10 points
   up to 5% of income, add 5 points
   5% to less than 25% of income, no points
   25% or more of income, subtract10 points

   v. If the credit score is over 25, credit is granted.

   Your program should permit a user to enter all the above information. It should then display the credit score (number of points) based on the entered data. A form for this application is shown in Figure 6-30.

4. Wind chill is calculated by subtracting wind speed times 1.5 from the current temperature. For example, if the current temperature is 40 degrees and the wind speed is 10 miles per hours, then Wind Chill = 40 − 1.5 * 10 = 40 − 15 = 25 degrees. For this project the input for your program should include current temperature and a minimum value for wind speed (value should be at least 0). Your program should display a list or table of 10 values for wind speed and corresponding wind chill, starting with the input value for wind speed. For each pair of values, increment

Figure 6-30

Form for Exercise 3

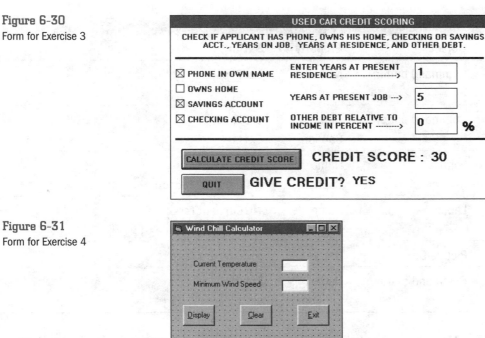

Figure 6-31

Form for Exercise 4

wind speed by 2. Use a **Do While** loop structure to handle the repetition. Output the pairs of values to a second form. Express wind chill as an integer value. Figure 6-31 illustrates the form you should construct for this project.

For the form shown, the <u>D</u>isplay Command button should display a second form with the table values. The <u>C</u>lear button should clear all input entries on the input form, and the E<u>x</u>it button should end the program. The second from should have a <u>R</u>eturn that hides the form and redisplays the input form. For this project, use the following properties table.

Table 6-5 Properties Table for Exercise 4

Object	Property	Setting
Form	Name	frmWindSpeed
	Caption	Wind Chill Calculator
Label	Name	lblCurrentTemp
	Caption	Current Temperature
Label	Name	lblMinWindSpeed
	Caption	Minimum Wind Speed
Text box	Name	txtCurrentTemp
	Text	<blank>
Text box	Name	txtMinWindSpeed
	Text	<blank>
Command button	Name	cmdDisplay
	Caption	<u>D</u>isplay

(continued)

Properties Table for Exercise 4 (*continued*)

Object	Property	Setting
Command button	Name	cmdClear
	Caption	Clear
Command button	Name	cmdExit
	Caption	Exit
Form	Name	frmWindChill
	Caption	Wind Chill Factor
Label	Name	lblCurrentTemp
	Caption	For a temperature of:
Picture Box	Name	picCurrentTemp
Command button	Name	Return
	Caption	OK

5. Modify your solution to Exercise 4 to have your program display a two-way table of wind chill factors for pairs of wind speed and temperature. Input for the program should include a minimum value for temperature and a minimum value for wind speed. Output should be displayed on a separate form. All numeric values should be integers. Column headings should represent incremented values of temperature and row headings should represent incremented values of wind speed. Increment wind speed by 2 and temperature by 5.

6. A loan officer at a local bank has asked you to write a program that displays a range of monthly payments for a sequence of interest rates. Your program should provide for input of loan amount, length of loan (in years), and a lower bound on the yearly loan interest rate. Calculate 12 monthly loan payments and increment the interest rate by .25% for each successive calculation. Display the interest rates and corresponding payments in a table format. (**Hint:** you might use a List box.) Use the PMT function to compute monthly payment. Figure 6-32 illustrates the form you should construct for this project.

Figure 6-32
Form for Exercise 6

Table 6-6   Property Table for Exercise 6

Object	Property	Setting
Form	Name	frmLoanPmt
	Caption	Loan Payment
Label	Name	lblName
	Caption	Name
Text box	Name	txtName
	Text	<blank>
Label	Name	lblLoanAmt
	Caption	Loan Amount
Text box	Name	txtLoanAmt
	Text	<blank>
Label	Name	lblYears
	Caption	Years
Text box	Name	txtYears
	Text	<blank>
Label	Name	lblIntRate
	Caption	Interest Rate
Text box	Name	txtIntRate
	Text	<blank>
List box	Name	lstMoPmt
Command button	Name	cmdCalc
	Caption	Calculate
Command button	Name	cmdClear
	Caption	Clear
Command button	Name	cmdPrint
	Caption	Print
Command button	Name	cmdExit
	Caption	Exit

Sub Procedures and Functions

7

As we have seen, the central element of a Visual Basic program is the form, which is stored in a form module. The basic processing units on a form consist of event-driven procedures, which are attached to the objects placed on the form. In addition to event procedures, Visual Basic programs may also contain any number of additional subprogram, function, and property procedures. To distinguish these procedure types from event procedures, these three new types of procedures are collectively referred to as *general* procedures. By definition then, general procedures are not associated with specific events. Each Visual Basic general procedure is identified using one of three keywords: *Sub, Function,* or *Property*. In this chapter we learn how to write *Sub* and *Function* general procedures, how to pass data to these procedures, how to have the procedures process the passed data, and how they can be used to return a result.

Professional programs are designed, coded, and tested very much like hardware, as a set of modules integrated to perform a completed whole. A good analogy of this is an automobile, where one major module is the engine, another is the transmission, a third the braking system, a fourth the body, and so on. Each of these modules is linked together and ultimately placed under the control of the driver, which can be compared to a supervisor or main program module. The whole now operates as a complete unit, able to do useful work, such as driving to the store. During the assembly process, each module is individually constructed, tested, and freed of defects (bugs) before it is installed in the final product.

Now think of what you might do if you wanted to improve your car's performance. You might have the existing engine altered or removed altogether and replaced with a new engine. Similarly, you might change the transmission or tires or shock absorbers, making each modification individually, as your budget allows.

PROGRAMMERS NOTES

What Is a Subprogram?

User-defined, non-event procedures are generically referred to as subprograms. In Visual Basic, subprograms are constructed as both **Sub** and **Function** procedures. In Pascal, they are referred to as procedures and functions. Modula-2 names them PROCEDURES (even though some of them are actually functions). In C and C++, they are referred to as functions, while in JAVA they are called methods. COBOL refers to them as paragraphs, while FORTRAN refers to them as subroutines and functions.

In this analogy, each of the major components of a car can be compared to a procedure designed to perform a specific task. For example, the driver calls on the engine when the gas pedal is pressed. The engine accepts inputs of fuel, air, and electricity to turn the driver's request into a useful product, power, and then sends this output to the transmission for further processing. The transmission receives the output of the engine and converts it to a form that can be used by the drive axle. An additional input to the transmission is the driver's selection of gears (reverse, neutral, first, second, etc.).

In each case, the engine, transmission, and other modules only "know" the universe bounded by their inputs and outputs. The driver need know nothing of the internal operation of the engine, transmission, drive axle, and other modules that are being controlled. The driver simply "calls" on a module, such as the engine, brakes, air conditioning, or steering, when that module's output is required. Communication between modules is restricted to passing needed inputs to each module as it is called upon to perform its task, and each module operates internally in a relatively independent manner. This same modular approach is used by programmers to create and maintain reliable Visual Basic applications, using general procedures in addition to event-specific procedures.

7.1 ▶ Sub Procedures

Each event procedure we have created is an example of a **Sub** procedure. The only restriction on these event procedures is that they are called into action by a specific event, such as clicking a button control. A second type of **Sub** procedure, which is referred to as a *general procedure*, has the same form as an event procedure but is called into action by the application code, rather than by a specific event. As their name indicates, such general procedures are meant to handle tasks broader in scope than a specific event. For example, as illustrated in Figure 7-1, an application might have three Text boxes, each of which is meant to receive numeric input from a user. For each

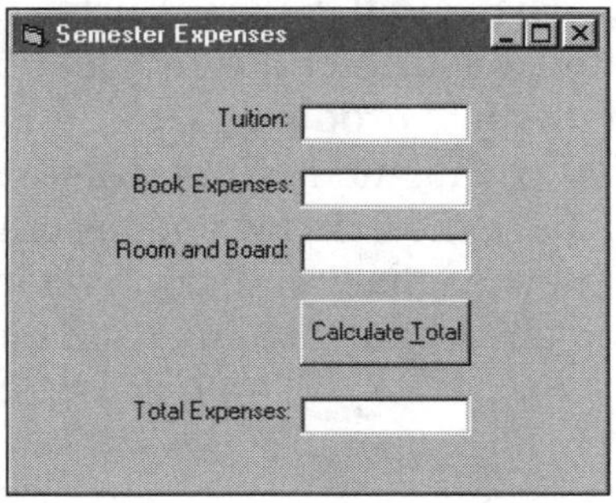

Figure 7-1

An Application that Requires the Input of Three Numbers

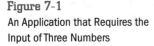

Figure 7-2
Using a Single General Procedure
to Validate Numeric Input

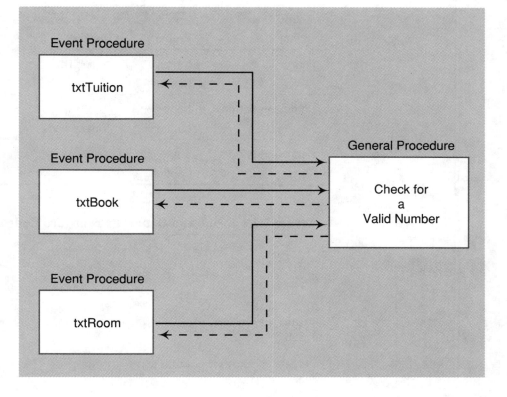

Text box's **Lost_Focus** event, we could include a check that a valid number was entered. Instead of repeating the same code, however, a more efficient strategy would be to create a general procedure that accepts a string and determines if the entered string represents a numeric value. Assuming such a general procedure was written, each Text box's **Lost_Focus** event could then activate this same general procedure. Figure 7-2 illustrates the connection between the general procedure and its three invoking event procedures. It is important to notice that when the called procedure has completed execution, control is returned to the calling procedure.

As illustrated in Figure 7-2, a **Sub** procedure is distinct in its own right, very similar to an event procedure. Its purpose is to receive data, operate on that data, and return as few or as many values as required. Although Figure 7-2 shows the **Sub** procedure being invoked by an event procedure, this is not a requirement. General procedures can be invoked by either event or other **Sub** procedures. They can also be written either as general procedures in a specific form, or in standard modules saved with a .bas extension.

A general procedure is called into action (invoked) using a **Call** statement.[1] For example, the statement

```
Call Message
```

initiates the execution of a general procedure named Message. This statement is used in Program 7-1 to call a general procedure that displays the message Hello World.

---

[1]Although the keyword **Call** is optional, we will always include it to explicitly indicate that a call to a general procedure is being made.

Table 7-1 Program 7-1's Properties Table

Object	Property	Setting
Form	Name	frmMain
	Caption	Program 7-1
Command button	Name	cmdDisplay
	Caption	&Display
Command button	Name	cmdExit
	Caption	E&xit

Figure 7-3
Program 7-1's Interface

Figure 7-4
The Output Created by Pressing
Program 7-1's Display Button

Program 7-1's Event and General Procedure Code

```
Private Sub cmdDisplay_Click()
  Call Message
End Sub

Public Sub Message()
  Print "Hello World"
End Sub

Private Sub cmdExit_Click()
  Beep
  End
End Sub
```

In reviewing Program 7-1's code, notice that the **Click** event for the cmdDisplay command button makes a call to the Message procedure. The Message procedure, which is a general procedure, simply displays the message Hello World on the form, as illustrated on Figure 7-4. Notice that the Message procedure has been declared as **Public**. This designation permits the procedure to be called from any procedure and function residing on any form or module attached to the application. A **Private** declaration restricts it to be called from procedures residing on the module containing the procedure. Also notice that since the general procedure code resides in the (**General**) section of the form's Code window, the **Print** method refers to the current form, by default. If this general procedure was coded on a standard (.bas) form, the reference to this method would have to be explicitly written as

```
Public Sub Message()
  frmMain.Print "Hello World"
End Sub
```

As written, Program 7-1 makes no provision for passing data into the general procedure nor for transmitting data back from it. The program does, however, clearly illustrate the connection between one procedure making a call to another procedure. Before seeing how data can be exchanged between two procedures, let's see how to create the general procedure used in Program 7-1.

Creating a General Procedure

The steps necessary for creating a general procedure on a form module are as follows:

1. Make sure that the Code window is activated by

- Double-clicking on a form object, or
- Pressing the F7 function key, or
- Selecting the <u>C</u>ode option from the <u>V</u>iew menu.

Once the Code window is active, type a procedure header line directly into the Code window. This line should have the form

> `Public Sub` *procedure-name()*

Visual Basic will complete the template for the new procedure when you have entered the header line (if you omit the **Public** keyword, the procedure will become **Public** by default). After Visual Basic has created the procedure's template, type in the required code in the same manner as you would for event procedures. Once you have created a general procedure you can always view or edit it by clicking on the (**General**) object and selecting the desired procedure in the Code window.

Exchanging Data with a General Procedure

In exchanging data with a general procedure, we must be concerned with both the sending and receiving sides of the data exchange. Let us look at the sending of data into a general procedure first.

In its most general syntax, a general procedure is called into action using a **Call** statement having the form

> `Call` *procedure-name(argument list)*

Except for the addition of the parentheses and the argument list, this is identical to the **Call** statement used in Program 7-1. As always, the keyword **Call** tells the program to transfer control into a general procedure. The general procedure name, as illustrated in Figure 7-5 on page 330, identifies which procedure is to be executed; the argument list is used to exchange data with the called general procedure.[2]

PROGRAMMERS NOTES

Where to Place General Procedures

General procedures can be placed in either form (.frm), standard (.bas), or class (.cls) modules. In all of these cases the general procedures are coded directly in the Code window in the (General) object list section.

For simple applications using a single form, you would place all of the general procedures in the existing form module.

In the case where your procedure has more generality and can be used by a number of applications, you would open a standard module by selecting the <u>A</u>dd Module option from the <u>P</u>roject menu and code the procedure in the Code window. Standard modules, by definition, contain only Visual Basic code and are typically used to construct Program Libraries. In its simplest configuration a Program Library consists of one or more a standard modules containing well-tested and efficient procedures guaranteed to perform without error if the arguments supplied to the procedure are correct.

Finally, if you are constructing general procedures applicable to classes, you would include the procedures in a class module. Class modules are presented in Chapter 12.

---

[2] Again, the keyword **Call** is optional. If this keyword is not used, the arguments must not be enclosed in parentheses. Thus, for example, the calls `Call Display(2.78, 8)` and `Display 2.67, 8` are equivalent.

Figure 7-5
Calling a General Procedure

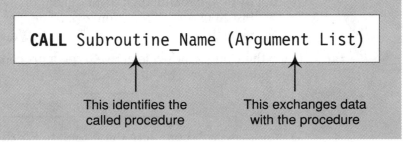

```
CALL Subroutine_Name (Argument List)
```

This identifies the   This exchanges data
called procedure   with the procedure

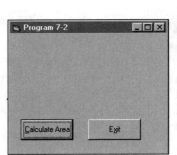

Figure 7-6
Program 7-2's Interface

Table 7-2   Program 7-2's Properties Table

Object	Property	Setting
Form	Name	frmMain
	Caption	Program 7-2
Command button	Name	cmdRun
	Caption	&Calculate Area
Command button	Name	cmdExit
	Caption	E&xit

The arguments in a **Call** statement consist of constants, variables, or expressions that can be evaluated to yield a value at the time of the call. For example, the statement

```
Call Circumference(3.5)
```

both calls a general procedure named `Circumference` and makes the number 3.5 available to it. Here the argument list consists of a single argument, the constant 3.5. Similarly, the statement

```
Call Display(2.67, 8)
```

calls a general procedure named `Display` and makes two arguments, the real constant 2.67 and the integer constant 8, available to the called general procedure. In the following **Call** statement

```
Call Area(radius)
```

the general procedure `Area` is called using a variable named `radius` as an argument. To illustrate the use of this **Call** statement from within an event procedure, consider Program 7-2. Included within it is a general procedure named `Area` appropriate to receive the transmitted data.

In reviewing Program 7-2's code, notice that the **Call** statement in the `cmdCalculate_Click()` procedure both calls the `Area` general procedure into action and makes one argument available to it. Let's now see how the general procedure `Area` has been constructed to correctly receive this argument.

Program 7-2's Event and General Procedure Code

```
Private Sub cmdCalculate_Click()
  Dim radius As Single

  radius = InputBox("Enter the radius", "Input Request", "0")
  Call Area(radius)
End Sub

Public Sub Area(r As Single)
  Const PI As Single = 3.1416
```

```
        Cls
        Print "For a circle with radius"; r
        Print "The area is "; Format(PI * r ^ 2, ".0000")
      End Sub

      Private Sub cmdExit_Click()
        Beep
        End
      End Sub
```

Like all procedures, a general procedure begins with a header line and ends with an **End Sub** line, as illustrated in Figure 7-7. In addition to naming the general procedure, the procedure header is used to exchange data between the general procedure and its calling procedure. The purpose of the statements after the header line is to process the passed data and produce any values to be returned to the calling procedure.

The general **Sub** procedure header line must include the keyword **Sub**, the name of the general procedure, and the names of any parameters that will be used by it. Here we have retained the convention that a *parameter* refers to the procedure's declaration of what data it will accept, while an *argument* refers to the data sent by the calling function (another name for a parameter is a *formal argument*, while the data sent by the calling procedure is sometimes referred to as *actual arguments*). For example, the header line of the general procedure in Program 7-2

```
      Public Sub Area(r as Single)
```

Figure 7-7

The Structure of a General Sub Procedure

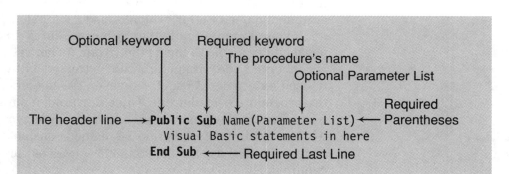

```
Optional keyword      Required keyword
                           The procedure's name
                                Optional Parameter List

                                                   Required
The header line ──▶ Public Sub Name(Parameter List) ◀── Parentheses
                    Visual Basic statements in here
              End Sub ◀────── Required Last Line
```

PROGRAMMERS NOTES

Creating and Using Standard (.bas) Modules

To create the first General Procedure on a new standard (.bas) module:

1. Select the <u>A</u>dd Module option from the <u>P</u>roject menu. You will then be presented with a choice of activating a Code window in either a new or existing standard module with a (**General**) object.

2. Type a procedure header line into the Code window.

This line should have the syntax

```
Public Sub procedure-name()
```

Once a header line is entered, Visual Basic will complete the template for the new procedure. If the **Public** keyword is omitted, the procedure will still be **Public** by default. This permits the procedure to be called from within any form or module attached to the application.

3. Enter the desired code for the new General Procedure.

PROGRAMMERS NOTES

Viewing and Editing a General Procedure

To view and edit an existing general procedure on a form:

1. Make sure that the Code window is activated by

- Double-clicking on a form object, or
- Pressing the F7 function key, or
- Selecting the Code option from the View menu.

2. Select (**General**) from the Code window's object selection box.

3. Select the procedure's name from the Code window's procedure selection box.

contains a single parameter named r. The names of parameters are selected by the programmer according to the same rules used to select variable names. It should be noted that the names selected for parameters may, but need not be, the same as the argument names used in the **Call** statement.

The purpose of the parameters in a general procedure header is to provide names by which the general procedure can access values transmitted through the **Call** statement. Thus, the argument name r is used within the general procedure to refer to the value transmitted by the **Call** statement. In this regard, it is extremely useful to visualize arguments and parameters as containers or pipelines through which values can be transmitted between called and calling program units. As illustrated in Figure 7-8, the parameter named r effectively opens one side of the container through which values will be passed between the cmdCalculate_Click and Area procedures. Within the cmdCalculate_Click event procedure, the same container is known as the argument named radius, which is also a variable of this event procedure.

It is important to note that **Sub** procedures do not know where the values made available to them come from. As far as the Area general procedure is concerned, the parameter r can be treated as a variable that has been initialized externally. As such, however, parameters must still be declared in the procedure's header line. Once declared, a parameter can be used anywhere within the general procedure the same way a variable can be used. Also, as illustrated in Program 7-2, named constants used by the general procedure (in this case the constant PI) as well as variables internal to the procedure must also be declared.

In addition, the individual data types of each argument and its corresponding parameter must be the same. Thus, if a general procedure's first

Figure 7-8

Exchanging Data with a Sub Procedure

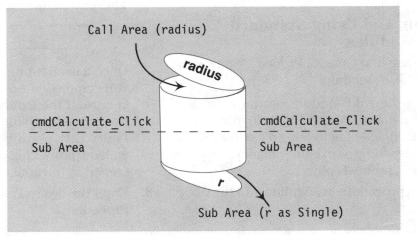

parameter is declared as an integer, then an integer variable, integer constant, or integer expression must be used as an argument when the procedure is called. If the general procedure's second parameter has been declared as **Single**, then the second argument in the **Call** statement must also be a **Single**.

Argument and parameter mismatches will result in an `argument type mismatch` error message when the program is run.

CAUTION: Since an argument and its corresponding parameter both reference the same memory locations (see Figure 7-8), the rule concerning the correspondence between numbers and data types of arguments and parameters is simple: they must MATCH! If there are two arguments in a general procedure call, there must be two parameters in the general procedure's parameter list. The first argument becomes the first parameter and the second argument becomes the second parameter.

A Practical Application Illustrating Input Data Validation

The examples presented so far have been useful in illustrating how to construct and call **Sub** procedures. Clearly, however, the **Sub** procedure calls were not necessary because the code in these general procedures could have been included directly in the event procedures making the calls. We now present an application that uses **Sub** procedures in a more useful and practical way.

Consider Figure 7-9, which illustrates the interface for a loan payment program. The program calculates the monthly payment due on a loan after the user enters the amount of the loan, the time in years, and the annual interest rate for the loan. The program uses the standard convention that payments must be made monthly and that the interest is calculated as a monthly compounded rate.

In addition to the three Text boxes shown in Figure 7-9 that will be used for data entry, the form contains two Picture boxes. The first Picture box, which is named `picPay`, will be used to display the calculated monthly payment for the loan. The second Picture box, at the bottom of the form, is named `picError`, and is used to display error messages. Table 7-3 on page 334 lists the properties table for this interface.

As a practical matter, only positive numbers should be accepted for the user-entered data. Rather than including individual input validation code for each of the three Text boxes, a single data entry validation **Sub** procedure, named `CheckVal`, will be constructed. This procedure is called from each

Figure 7-9
Program 7-3's Interface

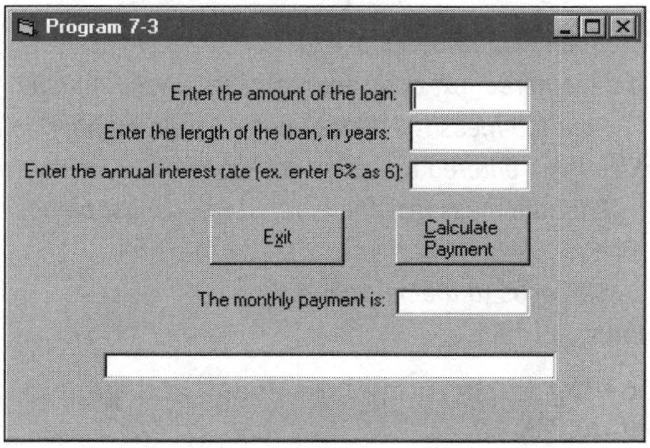

Table 7-3 Program 7-3's Properties Table

Object	Property	Setting
Form	Name	frmMain
	Caption	Program 7-3
Label	Name	lblAmt
	Caption	Enter the amount of the loan:
Label	Name	lblTime
	Caption	Enter the length of the loan, in years:
Label	Name	lblRate
	Caption	Enter the annual interest rate (ex. Enter 6% as 6):
Text box	Name	txtAmt
	Text	(Blank)
	BackColor	White (Palette tab)
Text box	Name	txtTime
	Text	(Blank)
	BackColor	White (Palette tab)
Text box	Name	txtRate
	Text	(Blank)
	BackColor	White (Palette tab)
Picture box	Name	picPay
	TabStop	False
	BackColor	White (Palette tab)
Picture box	Name	picError
	TabStop	False
	BackColor	White (Palette tab)
Command button	Name	cmdPay
	Caption	&Calculate Payment
Command button	Name	cmdExit
	Caption	E&xit

Text box when the user signals completion of data entry in the box. This is done using the Text box's **KeyPress** event. For each Text box we "capture" the key press and determine when the ENTER key was pressed (see Section 4.3 for a review of this). Once this key has been detected, the CheckVal data validation procedure is called. The algorithm used in CheckVal is

> *Clear all Picture boxes of text*
> *If the entered text does not represent a valid number*
> > *Print the message "Please enter a valid number" in the Error Picture box*
> *Else if the entered text does not represent a positive number*
> > *Print the message "The entered value must be positive" in the Error Picture box*
> *Else*
> > *Set focus to the next control*
> *Endif*

Following is the complete event and general procedure code used in Program 7-3.

Program 7-3's Event and General Procedure Code

```
Rem: These named constants are entered in
Rem: the (General) object declarations section
Rem: As such, they can be used by any procedure on the form
Const ENTER As Integer = 13 ' the ANSI value of the Enter key
Const FromAmt As Integer = 1
Const FromTime As Integer = 2
Const FromRate As Integer = 3

Rem: These three event procedures clear the Picture boxes
Rem: whenever the Text boxes receive focus
Private Sub txtAmt_GotFocus()
  Call Clear
End Sub

Private Sub txtRate_GotFocus()
  Call Clear
End Sub

Private Sub txtTime_GotFocus()
  Call Clear
End Sub

Rem: These three event procedures accept data from
Rem: the Text boxes
Private Sub txtAmt_KeyPress(KeyAscii As Integer)
  If KeyAscii = ENTER Then
    Call CheckVal(txtAmt.Text, FromAmt)
  End If
End Sub

Private Sub txtTime_KeyPress(KeyAscii As Integer)
  If KeyAscii = ENTER Then
    Call CheckVal(txtTime.Text, FromTime)
  End If
End Sub

Private Sub txtRate_KeyPress(KeyAscii As Integer)
  If KeyAscii = ENTER Then
    Call CheckVal(txtRate.Text, FromRate)
  End If
End Sub

Rem: This is the event procedure that calculates the payment
Private Sub cmdPay_Click()
  Dim amt As Single, time As Single, rate As Single
  Dim payment As Single

  amt = Val(txtAmt.Text)
  time = Val(txtTime.Text) * 12 ' convert years to months
  rate = Val(txtRate.Text) / 1200 ' convert to monthly rate
  If amt * time * rate <> 0 Then
    payment = (amt * rate) / (1 - (1 + rate) ^ -time)
    picPay.Print Format(payment, "Currency")
  Else
    picError.Print "Please check all of the input data"
  End If
End Sub

Rem: This is the input data validation general Sub procedure
Private Sub CheckVal(s1 As String, fromwhere As Integer)
  Call Clear
```

continued

```
    If Not (IsNumeric(s1)) Then
      picError.Print "Please enter a valid number"
    ElseIf Val(s1) <= 0 Then
      picError.Print "The entered value must be positive"
    Else ' a valid data was entered, so we shift the focus
      Select Case fromwhere
        Case FromAmt
          txtTime.SetFocus
        Case FromTime
          txtRate.SetFocus
        Case FromRate
          cmdPay.SetFocus
      End Select
    End If
End Sub

Rem: This is a general Sub procedure used to clear all Picture boxes
Private Sub Clear()
  picPay.Cls
  picError.Cls
End Sub

Private Sub cmdExit_Click()
  Beep
  End
End Sub
```

In reviewing Program 7-3's code, first notice that the **GotFocus** event procedures for each Text box call the Clear **Sub** procedure. This procedure simply clears both Picture boxes of text. The reason for this is that the Text boxes are used in this application for data entry. The rationale is that, once an input area receives the focus, all output messages and any calculations from prior data should be cleared.

Now concentrate on the three **KeyPress** event procedures and notice that each of these procedures calls the CheckVal **Sub** procedure when the (ENTER) key has been pressed. The value for the (ENTER) key has been set as a named constant in the declarations section of the (**General**) object; as such, this named constant can be used by any procedure on the form.

The CheckVal **Sub** procedure uses two parameters, a string and an integer. The string represents the text value from either the Amount, Time, or Rate Text boxes, while the integer is used to communicate which Text box event made the call. In addition, we have used three named constants for the integer arguments used in the **Call** statement. The named constants were entered in the (**General**) object of the Code window under the **Declarations** section. Like the ENTER named constant, each of these constants apply to the form module as a whole, and can be used by any procedure on the form.

The first task accomplished by the CheckVal procedure is to call the procedure Clear, which clears any prior text in the Picture boxes. Then, the procedure either produces an error message and keeps the focus in the current Text box, or moves the focus to the next control in the Tab sequence.

Finally, take a look at the cmdPay_Click procedure. This event procedure uses a common programming "trick" to determine when to make its calculation. If any of the Text box values are zero, a valid payment cannot be calculated. Rather than checking each Text box for a zero value, however, we can check all boxes at once by checking the expression Val(txtAmt.Text) * Val(txtTime.Text) * Val(txtRate.Text). If any of the individual values are zero, the product of all three values will also be zero. Thus, we only make

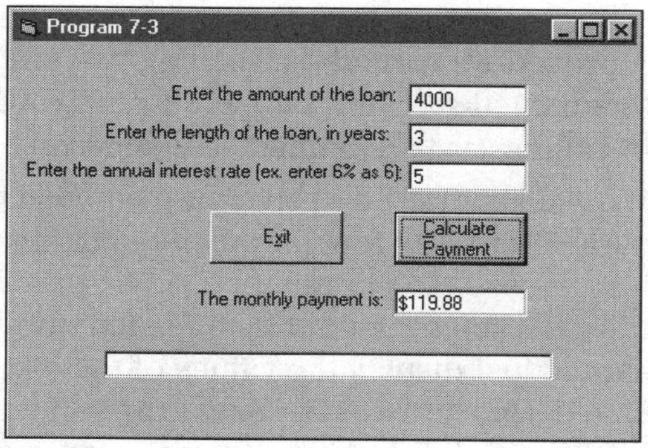

Figure 7-10
A Sample Run Using Program 7-3

```
Program 7-3                                    _□X

        Enter the amount of the loan:  4000

      Enter the length of the loan, in years:  3

Enter the annual interest rate (ex. enter 6% as 6):  5


              Exit          Calculate
                            Payment

        The monthly payment is:  $119.88


```

the payment calculation if all three boxes have a nonzero value. The calculation of the payment is made using the formula

$$\text{Monthly Payment} = \frac{(\text{Loan Amount}) * (\text{Time of Loan in Months})}{1 - (1 + \text{Monthly Interest Rate})^{-\text{Time of Loan in Months}}}$$

Since the input of interest rate is an annual percentage rate, and the time is in years, the entered rate is first divided by 1200 to convert it to a monthly decimal rate, and the number of years is multiplied by 12 to convert it to a time in months. Figure 7-10 illustrates a sample run using Program 7-3, once valid input data has been entered.

Exercises 7.1

1. For the following general **Sub** procedure headers, determine the number, type, and order (sequence) of the arguments that must be passed to the procedure:

   a. `Public Sub Factorial(n As Integer)`
   b. `Public Sub Price(type As Integer, yield As Single, maturity As Single)`
   c. `Public Sub Yield(type As Integer, price As Double, maturity As Double)`
   d. `Public Sub Interest(flag As Boolean, price As Double, time As Double)`
   e. `Public Sub Total(amount As Single, rate As Single)`
   f. `Public Sub Roi(a As Integer, b As Integer, c As String, d As String, e As Single)`
   g. `Public Sub Get_val(item As Integer, iter As Integer, decflag As Boolean, delim As Boolean)`

2. Write **Sub** procedure header lines and **Call** statements for the following:

   a. A procedure named `Test` having a single-precision parameter named `exper`. The corresponding argument used in calling `Test` is named `value`.
   b. A procedure named `Minute` having an integer parameter named `time`. The corresponding argument used in calling `Minute` is named `second`.
   c. A procedure named `Key` having a boolean parameter named `codeflag`. The corresponding argument used in calling `Key` is also named `codeflag`.
   d. A procedure named `Yield` having a single-precision parameter named `rate` and an integer parameter named `n`. The arguments used in calling `Yield` are named `coupon` and `years`.

e. A procedure named `Rand` having two single-precision parameters named `seed` and `randno`, respectively. The arguments used in calling `Rand` are named `Seed` and `Rval`.

3 a. Write a general **Sub** procedure named `Check`, which has three parameters. The first parameter should accept an integer number, the second parameter a single-precision number, and the third parameter a double-precision number. The procedure should just display the values of the data passed to it when it is called. (**Note:** When tracing errors in general **Sub** procedures, it is very helpful to have the procedure display the values it has been passed. Quite frequently, the error is not in what the procedure does with the data, but in the data received and stored.)

   b. Include the general **Sub** procedure written in Exercise 3a in a working program. Test the procedure by passing various data to it. For example, when the procedure is invoked by the statement `Call Check(5, 6.27, -18.98765432)` it should display the values 5, 6.27, and -18.98765432.

4 a. Write a general **Sub** procedure named `Find_abs` that accepts a double-precision number passed to it, computes its absolute value, and displays the absolute value. The absolute value of a number is the number itself, if the number is positive, and the negative of the number, if the number is negative.

   b. Include the general **Sub** procedure written in Exercise 4a in a working program. Test the procedure by passing various data to it.

5 a. Write a general **Sub** procedure named `Mult` that accepts two single-precision numbers as parameters, multiplies these two numbers, and displays the result.

   b. Include the general **Sub** procedure written in Exercise 5a in a working program. Test the procedure by passing various data to it.

6 a. Write a general **Sub** procedure named `SquareIt` that computes the square of the value passed to it and displays the result. The procedure should be capable of squaring numbers with decimal points.

   b. Include the general **Sub** procedure written in Exercise 6a in a working program. Test the procedure by passing various data to it.

7 a. Write a general **Sub** procedure named `RectangleArea` that accepts two parameters named `width` and `length` as **Single** data. The procedure should calculate the area of a rectangle by multiplying the passed data, and then display the calculated area.

   b. Include the `Area` general procedure written for Exercise 7a in a working program. The calling procedure should correctly call and pass the values 4.4 and 2.0 to `Area`. Make sure to do a hand calculation to verify the result displayed by your program.

7.2 Returning Values

In addition to receiving inputs when it is called, every **Sub** procedure has the capability of returning one or more values to its calling routine. The mechanism for doing this relies on the correspondence between arguments used in the **Call** statement and the parameters used in the general procedure header.

To illustrate how this correspondence can be used to return values from a general procedure, consider Procedure Code 7-1.

Procedure Code 7-1

```
Rem: Here is the calling procedure
Private Sub Form_Click()
  Dim firnum As Single, secnum As Single

  firnum = Val(InputBox("Enter a number", "Input Request", "0"))
  secnum = Val(InputBox("Enter a number", "Input Request", "0"))
  Print "The value entered for firnum was:"; firnum
  Print "The value entered for secnum was:"; secnum

  Call Newval(firnum, secnum)

 Print
 Print "After the call to Newval:"
 Print "The value in firnum is now"; firnum
 Print "The value in secnum is now"; secnum
End Sub

Rem: Here is the called procedure
Public Sub Newval(xnum As Single, ynum As Single)
  xnum = 86.5
  ynum = 96.5
End Sub
```

In the Newval **Sub** procedure within Procedure Code 7-1, it is extremely important to understand the connection between the arguments used in the **Call** statement and the parameters used in the general procedure header. *Both reference the same data items*. The significance of this is that the value in a calling argument can be altered by the general procedure, using the corresponding parameter name, and provides the basis for returning values from a general procedure. Thus, the parameters xnum and ynum do not store copies of the values in firnum and secnum, but directly access the locations in memory set aside for these two arguments. This type of general procedure call, where a general procedure's parameters reference the same memory locations as the arguments of the calling unit, is formally referred to as a *pass by reference*, which in Visual Basic is named as a **ByRef** call. The equivalence between argument and parameter names used in Procedure Code 7-1 is illustrated in Figure 7-11. As before, it is useful to consider both argument and parameter names as different names referring to the same value. The calling procedure refers to the value, using an argument name, while the general procedure refers to the same value, using its parameter name.

Figure 7-11

The Equivalence of Arguments and Parameters in Procedure Code 7-1

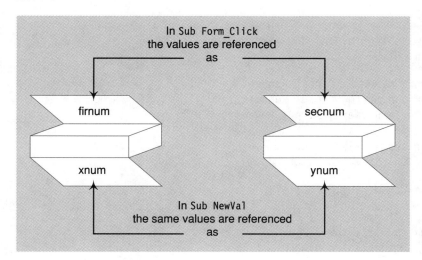

A sample output produced by Procedure Code 7-1 is

```
The value entered for firnum was: 10
The value entered for secnum was: 20
```

After the call to `Newval`:

```
The value in firnum is now 86.5
The value in secnum is now 96.5
```

In reviewing this output, notice that the values displayed for the variables `firnum` and `secnum` have been changed immediately after the call to the `Newval` general procedure. This is because these two variables were used as arguments in the **Call** statement, which gives `Newval` access to them. Within `Newval`, these arguments are known as the parameters `xnum` and `ynum`, respectively. As illustrated by the final displayed values, the assignment of values to `xnum` and `ynum` within `Newval` is reflected in the calling procedure as the altering of `firnum`'s and `secnum`'s values.

The equivalence between calling arguments and a **Sub** procedure's parameters, illustrated in Procedure Code 7-1, provides the basis for returning any number of values from a **Sub** procedure. For example, assume that a **Sub** procedure is required to accept three values, compute these values' sum and product, and return these computed results to the calling routine. Naming the **Sub** procedure `Calc` and providing five parameters (three for the input data and two for the returned values), the following general procedure can be used:

```
Public Sub Calc(x as Single, y as Single, z as Single, total as Single, product as Single)
   total = x + y + z
   product = x * y * z
End Sub
```

This general procedure has five parameters, named `x`, `y`, `z`, `total`, and `product`, all declared as Single arguments. Within the general procedure, only the last two arguments are altered. The value of the fourth argument, `total`, is calculated as the sum of the first three arguments, and the last argument, `product`, is computed as the product of the arguments `x`, `y`, and `z`. Procedure Code 7-2 shows how this **Sub** procedure could be called from an event procedure.

Procedure Code 7-2

```
Rem: Here is the calling procedure
Private Sub Form_Click()
   Dim firnum As Single, secnum As Single, thirdnum as Single
   Dim sum As Single, prod As Single

   firnum = Val(InputBox("Enter a number", "Input Request", "0"))
   secnum = Val(InputBox("Enter a number", "Input Request", "0"))
   thirdnum = Val(InputBox("Enter a number", "Input Request", "0"))
   Print "The value entered for firnum was:"; firnum
   Print "The value entered for secnum was:"; secnum
   Print "The value entered for thirdnum was:"; thirdnum

   Call Calc(firnum, secnum, thirdnum, sum, prod)

   Print
   Print "The sum of these numbers is:"; sum
   Print "The product of these numbers is:"; prod
End Sub
Rem: Here is the called procedure
Public Sub Calc(x as Single, y as Single, z as Single, total as Single, product as Single)
   total = x + y + z
   product = x * y * z
End Sub
```

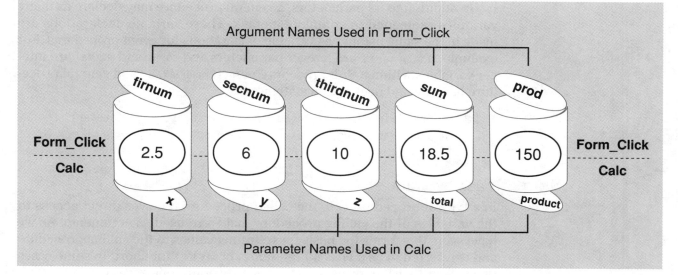

Argument Names Used in Form_Click

Parameter Names Used in Calc

Figure 7-12

Relationship Between Arguments and Parameters for Procedure Code 7-2

Within the calling event procedure, the `Calc` general procedure is called, using the five arguments `firnum`, `secnum`, `thirdnum`, `sum`, and `prod`. As required, these arguments agree in number and data type with the parameters declared by general procedure `Calc`. Of the five arguments passed, only `firnum`, `secnum`, and `thirdnum` are assigned values when the call to `Calc` is made. The remaining two arguments are not explicitly initialized and will be used to receive values back from `Calc` (these arguments will initially contain zero values). Figure 7-12 illustrates the relationship between argument and parameter names and the values they contain after the return from `Calc` for the following sample run using this procedure code:

```
The value entered for firnum was: 2.5
The value entered for secnum was: 6
The value entered for thirdnum was: 10


The sum of these numbers is: 18.5
The product of these numbers is: 150
```

Once `Calc` is called, it uses its first three parameters x, y, and z to calculate values for `total` and `product` and then returns control to the calling program. Because of the order of its calling arguments, the calling procedure knows the values calculated by `Calc` as `sum` and `prod`, which are then displayed.

Although all of the examples we have used have illustrated calling a general procedure from a event procedure, this is not required in Visual Basic. A general procedure can be called by any procedure, including another general procedure, including itself (as described in Section 7.5).

In general, the arguments used in calling a general procedure can be variables, as illustrated in Procedure Code 7-2, single constants, or more complex expressions yielding the correct argument data type. For example, one valid call to `Calc` is

```
Call Calc(2.0,3.0,6.2,sum,product)
```

When an argument is a constant value the corresponding parameter in the called general procedure must never be used on the left-hand side of an assignment statement. To do so would be an attempt to change the value of a constant within the called procedure.

In addition to its parameters, a general procedure may declare as many variables as needed to complete its task. These variable declarations are made in the same manner as variable declarations for event procedures. For example, if i, j, and k are integer parameters and count and maxval are integer variables within a **Sub** procedure named Findmax, a valid general procedure heading and declaration statement is

```
Public Sub Findmax(i as Integer, j as Integer, k as Integer)
    Dim count as Integer, maxval as Integer
```

Pass by Value

In a typical procedure call, the called procedure receives direct access to the variables of the calling procedure that were used as arguments. As we have seen, this forms the basis for returning values to the calling procedure and is referred to as a *pass by reference*, or **ByRef** for short. In some cases you may not wish to provide the called procedure this access.

To prevent a called procedure from having access to the calling procedure's arguments, a *pass by value* call can be made. In a pass by value, the called procedure is provided numeric values that cannot be altered. We have already seen one method of doing this. For example, the statement

```
Call Calc (10, 20, 30, sum, prod)
```

calls the Calc procedure with three arguments that are values. Regardless of what the receiving parameter names are, changing these parameters' values will not alter the constants 10, 20, and 30 in the calling statement. In a similar manner, *the values of variables used as arguments can also be transmitted to a called procedure by enclosing the variable names within parentheses.* For example, the statement Call Calc((firnum), (secnum), (thirdnum), sum, prod) passes the first three arguments by value and the last two by reference. This is because the parentheses around each of the first three arguments causes Visual Basic to evaluate the expressions within the parentheses. The evaluation of an expression, even one consisting of a single variable, is a value. That value is then transmitted to the called procedure.

Finally, in writing a general procedure, you can ensure that only a value is received. This is accomplished by placing the keyword **ByVal** in front of the parameter's name when the parameter is declared. For example, the header line

```
Public Sub Calc(ByVal x As Single, ByVal y As Single, ByVal Z As Single, total As Single, product As Single)
```

ensures that the parameters x, y, and z are effectively named constants for the values being transmitted. As such, the values in x, y, and z cannot be altered from within Calc.

Exercises 7.2

1. a. Write a general **Sub** procedure, named Find_abs, that accepts a double-precision number passed to it, computes its absolute value, and returns the absolute value to the calling function. The absolute value of a number is the number itself if the number is positive, and the negative of the number if the number is negative.

b. Include the function written in Exercise 1a. in a working program. Have the calling procedure display the returned value. Test the function by passing various data to it.

2 a. Write a general **Sub** procedure, named `Mult`, that accepts two double-precision numbers as parameters, multiplies these two numbers, and returns the result to the calling function.

b. Include the function written in Exercise 2a. in a working program. Have the calling procedure display the returned value. Test the function by passing various data to it.

3 a. Write a general procedure, named `Findmax`, that accepts two parameters named `firnum` and `secnum` as single-precision values and returns the largest of these parameters in a third parameter named `max`.

b. Include the `Findmax` general procedure written for Exercise 3a. in a working program.

4 a. Write a general procedure, named `RightTriangle`, that accepts the lengths of two sides of a right triangle and one of the angles as the parameters `a`, `b`, and `angle`, respectively. All of these parameters should be declared as Singles. The general procedure should determine and return the both the hypotenuse and the remaining angle of the triangle. (**Hint:** use the Pythagorean Theorem that $c^2 = a^2 + b^2$.)

b. Include the `RightTriangle` procedure written for Exercise 4a. in a working program.

5 a. The time in hours, minutes, and seconds is to be passed to a general procedure named `Totsec`. Write `Totsec` to accept the input data, determine the total number of seconds in the passed data, and display the calculated value.

b. Include the `Totsec` procedure written for Exercise 5a. in a working program. Use the following test data to verify your program's operation: hours = 10, minutes = 36, and seconds = 54. Make sure to do a hand calculation to verify the result displayed by your program.

6 a. Write a general procedure named `Time` that accepts an integer number of seconds in the parameter named `totsec` and returns the number of hours, minutes, and seconds corresponding to the total seconds in the three parameters named `hours`, `mins`, and `secs`.

b. Include the `Time` procedure written for Exercise 6a. in a working program.

7 Write a general procedure named `Daycount` that accepts a month, day, and year as integer parameters, and estimates the total number of days from the turn of the century corresponding to the passed date, and returns the estimate, as a long integer, to the calling procedure. For this problem assume that each year has 365 days and each month has 30 days. Test your general procedure by verifying that the date 1/1/00 returns a day count of one.

8 Write a general **Sub** procedure named `Liquid` that is to be called using the statement Call Liquid(cups, gallons, quarts, pints). The procedure should determine the number of gallons, quarts, pints,

and cups in the passed value named cups, and directly alter the respective arguments in the calling procedure. Use the relationships of two cups to a pint, four cups to a quart, and 16 cups to a gallon.

9. **a.** A clever and simple method of preparing to sort dates into either ascending (increasing) or descending (decreasing) order is to first convert a date having the form month/day/yr into a long integer number using the formula date = year * 10000 + month * 100 + day. For example, using this formula the date 12/6/1988 converts to the long integer 19881206 and the date 2/28/1990 converts to the long integer 19900228. Sorting the resulting integer numbers automatically puts the dates into the correct order. Using this formula, write a general **Sub** procedure named Convert that accepts a month, day, and year; converts the passed data into a single integer; and returns the integer to the calling procedure.

b. Include the Convert procedure written for Exercise 9a. in a working program. The main procedure should correctly call Convert and display the integer returned by the general procedure.

10. **a.** Write a general procedure named Date that accepts a long integer of the form described in Exercise 9a., determines the corresponding month, day, and year, and returns these three values to the calling procedure. For example, if Date is called using the statement

```
Call Date(19901116, month, day, year)
```

the number 11 should be returned in month, the number 16 in day, and the number 1990 in year.

b. Include the Date procedure written for Exercise 10a. in a working program.

7.3 Function Procedures

Visual Basic provides two types of functions: intrinsic and subprogram. We are already familiar with intrinsic functions, such as **Abs**, **Sqr**, **Exp**, and so on (see Section 3.4), which are part of the Visual Basic language. Subprogram functions perform in a manner identical to intrinsic functions, except that they are user-written. A subprogram function, like a **Sub** procedure, is a distinct procedure containing multiple statements. The difference between **Sub** procedures and function procedures, however, is that a function is intended to directly return a single value to its calling procedure (see Figure 7-13).

Figure 7-14 illustrates the general form of a function. As with **Sub** procedures, the purpose of the function header is to provide the function with a name and to specify the number and order of parameters expected by the function. In addition, the header identifies the data type of the value returned by the function. The statements after the header line are used to operate on the passed parameters and return a single value back to the calling function.

Figure 7-13
A Function Directly Returns a
Single Value

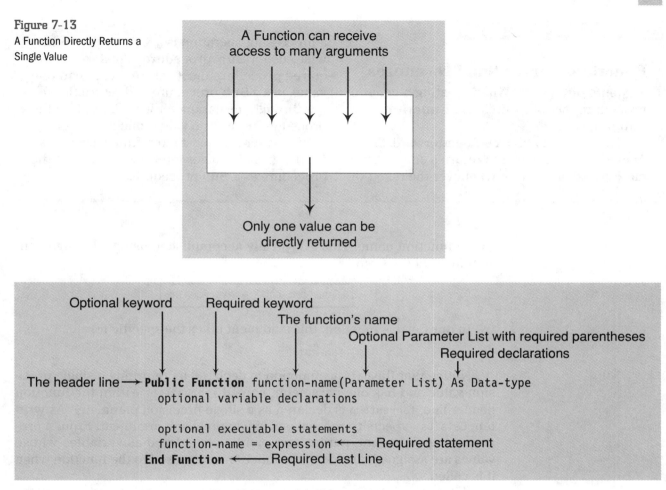

Figure 7-14
The Structure of a Function
Procedure

Notice that a function's header line includes a declaration of the data type of the value that will be returned by the function. This can be any of Visual Basic's data types. The parameters in the header line are intended for passing data into the function. For example, the following function header line can be used for a subprogram function named Fmax that receives two values and returns a single-precision value:

```
Public Function Fmax(x as Single, y as Single) As Single
```

The names of the parameters in the function header line, in this case x and y, are chosen by the programmer. Since the header declaration for Fmax includes two parameters, this function expects to receive two data items when it is called. Instead of the parameter names x and y, any two valid variable names could have been used to refer to the data passed to the function. Even if the function does not have any parameters, which is an extremely rare occurrence, the parentheses following the function name must always be included. As a specific application, consider the function Celsius that converts a Fahrenheit temperature into its equivalent Celsius value:

```
Public Function Celsius(fahrentemp As Single) As Single
  Celsius = 5 / 9 * (fahrentemp - 32)
End Function
```

The Celsius function illustrates a new feature found in function procedures; this is that the function must contain a statement that assigns a value

PROGRAMMERS NOTES

Functions versus Sub Procedures

Students often ask, "When creating a general procedure, should I create a **Function** or a **Sub** procedure?"

The answer is rather straightforward. Since functions are designed to return a single value directly, use a function whenever the result of a processing operation is a single value; otherwise, use a **Sub** procedure. Thus, if the required procedure must return more than one value, use a **Sub** procedure and return the values through the parameter list. Similarly, if the procedure returns no values and is used either to display data, request input from a user, or alter the graphical user interface, construct the procedure as a **Sub** procedure.

to the function name. This is typically accomplished using an assignment statement of the form

```
function-name = expression
```

In our Celsius function, this statement takes the specific form

```
Celsius = 5 / 9 * (fahrentemp - 32)
```

Notice that the Celsius function is declared as returning a single-precision value and has one parameter, named fahrentemp. Within the function header line, fahrentemp is declared as a single-precision parameter. As written, Celsius expects to receive one single-precision argument. From a programming viewpoint, parameters can be considered as variables whose values are assigned outside of the function and passed to the function when it is called.

Within the Celsius function, the assignment statement both calculates an equivalent Celsius value and assigns the calculated value to Celsius, which is the name of the function. The function is then completed with the **End Function** statement.

Calling a Function Procedure

Having written a function named Celsius, we now turn our attention to how this function can be called by other procedures. User-written functions are called the same way intrinsic functions are called—by giving the function's name and passing any data to it in the parentheses following the function name (see Figure 7-15). At the same time the function is called, attention must be given to using its calculated value corectly.

Figure 7-15

Calling and Passing Data to a Function

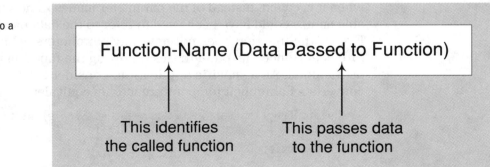

Figure 7-16
Program 7-4's Interface

Table 7-4 Program 7-4's Properties Table

Object	Property	Setting
Form	Name	`frmMain`
	Caption	`Program 7-4`
Label	Name	`lblFahr`
	Caption	`Enter a Fahrenheit Temperature:`
Label	Name	`lblCelsius`
	Caption	`The Equivalent Celsius Temperature is:`
Text box	Name	`txtFahr`
	Text	`(Blank)`
	BackColor	`White (Palette tab)`
Picture box	Name	`picCelsius`
	TabStop	`False`
	BackColor	`White (Palette tab)`
Command button	Name	`cmdConvert`
	Caption	`&Convert to Celsius`
Command button	Name	`cmdExit`
	Caption	`E&xit`

To clarify the process of sending data to a function and using its returned value, consider Program 7-4, which calls the function `Celsius`.

As illustrated in Program 7-4, calling a function is rather trivial. It requires only that the name of the function be used and that any data passed to the function be enclosed within the parentheses following the function name. The items enclosed within the parentheses are called *arguments* of the called function. As illustrated in Figure 7-17, the parameter `fahrentemp` within `Celsius` references the argument `fahrenheit` in the `cmdConvert_Click` event procedure.[3] The function itself does not know which procedure made the function call. The calling procedure must, however, provide arguments that match in number, order, and data type to the parameters declared by the function. As with general procedures, no data type conversions are made between arguments and parameters.

Figure 7-17
Assigning Arguments to
Parameters

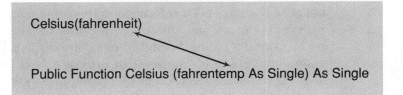

```
Celsius(fahrenheit)


Public Function Celsius (fahrentemp As Single) As Single
```

---

[3] The argument named `fahrenheit` was used here to illustrate the equivalence between arguments and parameters. Thus, the `cmdConvert_Click()` event could just have easily been written using the single statement

```
picCelsius.Print Celsius(Val(txtFarh.text))
```

Program 7-4's Event and General Procedure Code

```
Rem: This event procedure clears the picture box
Rem: whenever the text box gets focus
Private Sub txtFahr_GotFocus()
  picCelsius.Cls
End Sub

Rem: This event procedure calls the Function
Private Sub cmdConvert_Click()
  Dim fahrenheit as Single

  fahrenheit = Val(txtFahr.Text)
  picCelsius.Print Celsius(fahrenheit)
End Sub

Rem: This Function converts a Fahrenheit temperature to Celsius
Public Function Celsius(fahrentemp As Single) As Single
  Celsius = 5 / 9 * (fahrentemp - 32)
End Function

Rem: This is the Exit event procedure
Private Sub cmdExit_Click()
  Beep
  End
End Sub
```

At the time a function is called, the program must also have a way to use the value provided by the function. We must either provide a variable to store the value or use the value directly in an expression, as was done in Program 7-4. Storing the returned value in a variable is accomplished using a standard assignment statement. For example, the assignment statement

```
thistemp = Celsius(fahrenheit)
```

assigns Celsius' returned value in the variable named thistemp. This assignment statement does two things: the right-hand side calls Celsius and the result returned by the Celsius function is stored in the variable thistemp. Since the value returned by Celsius is single-precision, the variable thistemp must also be declared as a **Single** data-typed variable within the calling procedure's variable declarations.

CAUTION: It is important to know that when a variable is used as an argument to a function, the function receives direct access to the variable. This is because the pass is by reference in the same manner as data is passed to a **Sub** procedure. Thus, the function can alter a calling procedure's variable by returning a value through the parameter list. For example, the calling statement Celsius(fahrenheit) in Program 7-4 gives Celsius access to variable fahrenheit, even though this variable is "known" as fahrentemp within Celsius. Thus, if the assignment statement fahrentemp = 22.5 is contained in the function, both the value in fahrentemp and the value in fahrenheit, are changed from within the called procedure. The reason for this, as illustrated in Figure 7-18, is that both fahrenheit and fahrentemp *refer to the same storage location and are simply different names for the same variable.* Because of this equivalence, it is important that functions never assign values to their parameters.

Figure 7-18
The Relationship between
Arguments and Parameters

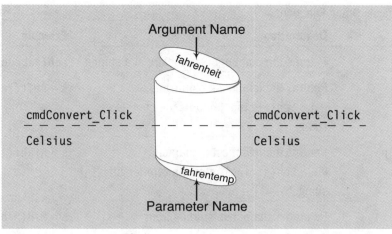

As with **Sub** procedures, you can pass data to functions by value, either by placing parentheses around the arguments or by placing the keyword **ByVal** in front of the parameter's name when the parameter is declared. For example, the header line

```
Public Function Celsius(ByVal fahrentemp As Single)
```

ensures that the `fahrentemp` parameter is effectively a named constant for the values being transmitted. As such, the value in `fahrentemp` cannot be altered from within `Celsius`.

If a function must use a parameter in a way that will alter its value, the parameter should first be assigned to a new variable declared within the function. This variable name should then be used in subsequent expressions in place of the parameter name. Then, any change to the variable inside the function, even if the variable has the same name as a variable in another procedure, has no effect outside of the function.

String Functions

User-written functions that return a string value are written the same way as any other function procedures, except that the return data type must be declared as a string. For example, the header line

```
Public Function Addchar(s1 As String) As String
```

declares that the `Addchar` function accepts a string parameter named `s1` and returns a string. A commonly used default provided by Visual Basic is that the return **String** data declaration can be omitted if a dollar sign is appended to the end of the function's name. Thus, the declaration for `Addchar` can be written

```
Public Function Addchar$(s1 As String)
```

Here, the name of the function is `Addchar$`, and this complete name must be used whenever the function is being referred to. In general, functions that return strings are not often needed, because Visual Basic provides an extremely extensive set of intrinsic string functions. The more commonly used of these are listed in Table 7-5.

In addition to the string functions listed in Table 7-5, strings can be compared using Visual Basic's relational operators. Each character in a string is stored in binary, using the ANSI code. In the ANSI code, a blank precedes (is less than) all letters and numbers; the letters of the alphabet are stored in order from A to Z; and the digits are stored in order from 0 to 9. It is also

Table 7-5 Intrinsic String Functions

Name	Description	Example
Len(string)	Returns the number of characters in a string.	`Len("abcde") returns a 5`
Left(string, n)	Returns the leftmost n characters. If n > `Len(string)`, returns the complete string.	`s = Left("abcd",2) sets s = "ab"`
Right(string, n)	Returns the rightmost n characters. If n > `Len(string)` returns a zero-length string.	`s = Right("abc",2) sets s = "bc"`
Mid(string, m, n)	Returns n characters starting from position m. If m > `Len(string)` returns a zero-length string.	`s = Mid("abc",2,1) sets s = "b"`
InStr(n, string, str)	Returns the position of the first occurrence of str within string starting from position n.	`InStr(1,"abcd","b") returns a 2`
LTrim(string)	Trims leading blanks.	`s = LTrim("    abcd") sets s = "abcd"`
RTrim(string)	Trims trailing blanks.	`s = RTrim("abcd    ") sets s = "abcd"`
Trim(string)	Trims leading and trailing blanks.	`s = Trim("  abcd  ") sets s = "abcd"`
StrConv(string, const)	Returns an uppercase string if `const = vbUppercase` or a lowercase string if `const = vbLowercase`.	`s = ("ab",vbUppercase) sets s = "AB"`
IsNumeric(string)	Returns a boolean value indicating whether the string can be evaluated as a number.	`s = IsNumeric("12.4") sets s to True`

important to note that, in ANSI, the digits come before, or are less than, the letters, and that uppercase letters come before lowercase letters.

Typically, Visual Basic's intrinsic string functions are used to create useful string manipulation **Sub** procedures. For example, consider Program 7-5, which processes a string to determine the number of vowels it contains.

Program 7-5's Event and General Procedure Code

```
Rem: This event procedure clears the picture box
Rem: whenever the text box gets focus
Private Sub txtVowels_GotFocus()
  picVowels.Cls
End Sub

Rem: This event procedure calls the Procedure
Private Sub cmdShow_Click()
  Call ShowVowels(txtVowels.Text)
End Sub

Rem: This Procedure displays the vowels
Public Sub ShowVowels(s1 As String)
  Dim n As Integer
  Dim i As Integer
```

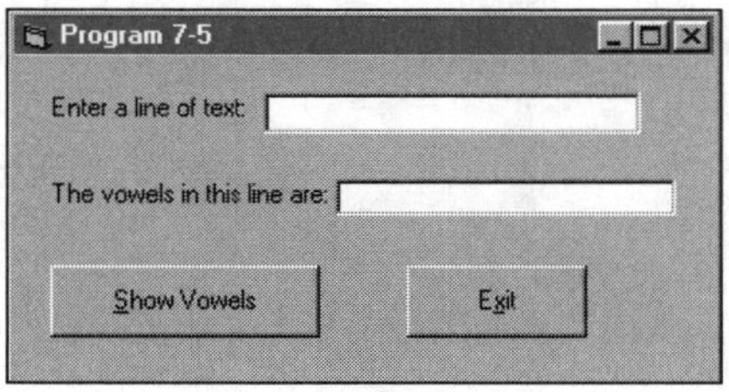

Figure 7-19
Program 7-5's Interface

Table 7-6 Program 7-4's Properties Table

Object	Property	Setting
Form	Name	frmMain
	Caption	Program 7-5
Label	Name	lblInput
	Caption	Enter a line of text:
Label	Name	lblVowels
	Caption	The vowels in this line are:
Text box	Name	txtVowels
	Text	(Blank)
	BackColor	White (Palette tab)
Picture box	Name	picVowels
	TabStop	False
	BackColor	White (Palette tab)
Command button	Name	cmdShow
	Caption	&Show Vowels
Command button	Name	cmdExit
	Caption	E&xit

```
Dim c As String * 1, clower As String * 1
Dim out As String

out = ""
n = Len(s1) ' find the string's length
For i = 1 To n
  c = Mid(s1, i, 1) ' extract next character
  clower = StrConv(c, vbLowerCase)
  Select Case clower
    Case "a", "e", "i", "o", "u"
      out = out & c
  End Select
Next i
  picVowels.Print out
End Sub

Rem: This is the Exit event procedure
Private Sub cmdExit_Click()
  Beep
  End
End Sub
```

In reviewing the Showvowels **Sub** procedure, notice that the length of the string is used to determine the terminating value of the **For** loop. In this loop, each character is "stripped off" using the **Mid** function and converted to its lowercase form. This is done so that both uppercase and lowercase vowels can be recognized by comparing all letters to the lowercase forms of the vowels. The converted character is then compared to the lowercase characters a, e, i, o, and u. If there is a match to one of these characters, the original character is appended to the output string. After each character in

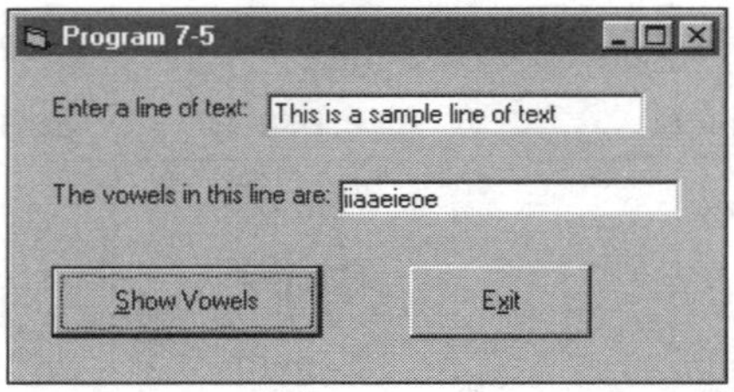

Figure 7-20
A Sample Output Produced by
Program 7-5

the string has been examined, the output string is displayed in the Picture box. Figure 7-20 illustrates a sample output produced by Program 7-5.

Exercises 7.3

1 For the following function header lines determine the number, type, and order (sequence) of the values that must be passed to the function and the type of value returned by the function:

   a. `Public Function IntToSingle(n As Integer) As Single`
   b. `Public Function Volts(res As Single, amp As Single) As Single`
   c. `Public Function Power(type As Boolean, cap As Single) As Double`
   d. `Public Function Flag(type As Boolean, time As Double)`
      `As Boolean`
   e. `Public Function Energy(pow As Double, time As Double) As Double`
   f. `Public Function Roi(a As Single, b As Single, c As Single,`
      `d As Integer) As Single`
   g. `Public Function Getval(item As Integer, delim As String)`
      `As Double`
   h. `Function Locase(c As String) As String`

2 a. Write a function named `Check` that has three parameters. The first parameter should accept an integer, the second parameter a single-precision number, and the third parameter a string. The function should display the values of the data passed to the function when it is called, and return a value of 1. (**Note:** When tracing errors in functions, it is very helpful to have the function display the values it has been passed. Quite frequently, the error is not in what the function does with the data, but in the data it receives and stores.)

   b. Include the function written in Exercise 2a in a working program.

3 Write a function named `CelToFahr` that converts a Celsius temperature to a Fahrenheit temperature according to the formula *Fahrenheit = 9/5(Celsius) + 32*.

4 Write a function named `Hyptns` that accepts the lengths of two sides of a right triangle and determines the triangle's hypotenuse. (The hypotenuse of a right triangle is equal to the square root of the sum of the squares of the other two sides.) Include `Hyptns` in a working program and verify that it works properly by passing various values to it, displaying the returned value, and checking that the displayed value is correct.

5 Write a function with the header line

   `Public Function Absdif(x As Single, y As Single)`

   that returns the absolute value of the difference between two real numbers. For example, the function calls `Absdif(2,10)`, `Absdif(-1,`

-10), and `Absdif(-2,10)` should return the values, 8, 9, and 12, respectively. Include the function `Absdif` in a Visual Basic program and test the function, by passing various numbers to it, displaying the returned value, and checking that the displayed value is correct.

6. Write and execute a Visual Basic function that accepts an integer parameter and determines whether the passed integer is even or odd. (**Hint:** Use the **Mod** operator.)

   a. Write a function named `Round` that rounds any single-precision value to two decimal places. Rounding to two decimal places is obtained using the following steps:

   Step 1: Multiply the passed number by 100.
   Step 2: Add 0.5 to the number obtained in Step 1.
   Step 3: Take the integer part of the number obtained in Step 2.
   Step 4: Divide the result of Step 3 by 100.

   b. Include the function written in Exercise 7a in a working program. Test the function by passing various data to it and verifying the displayed values.

7. a. Modify the function written for Exercise 7a to accept two values. The second passed value is the number of decimal places to which the first passed value should be rounded. For example, `Round(27.6485, 2)` should return the value 27.65 and `Round(27.6485, 3)` should return the value 27.649.

   b. Include the function written in Exercise 8a. in a working program. Test the function by passing various data to it and verifying the displayed values.

8. Modify the `Vowels` procedure in Program 7-5 to count and display the total number of vowels contained in the string passed to it.

9. Modify the `Vowels` procedure in Program 7-5 to count and display the numbers of each individual vowel contained in the string. That is, the function should display the total number of *a*s, *e*s, and so forth.

10. a. Write a Visual Basic function to count the total number of non-blank characters contained in a string. For example, the number of non-blank characters in the string " abc def " is six.

    b. Include the function written for Exercise 11a in a complete working program.

11. Write and test a procedure that reverses the characters in a string.

7.4 ▶ Variable Scope

By their very nature, Visual Basic procedures are constructed to be independent modules. This implies that variables declared in one procedure, be it an event or general procedure, cannot be accessed by another procedure, unless specific provisions are made to allow such access. As we have seen, one such access is provided through a procedure's parameter list. Given this fact, both event and general procedures may be compared to a closed box, with slots at the top through which values may be exchanged with the calling procedure.

The metaphor of a closed box is useful because it emphasizes the fact that what goes on inside the procedure, except for the altering of a parameter's value, is hidden from all other procedures. This includes any variables declared within the procedure. These internally declared variables, available only to the procedure itself, are said to be "local to the procedure," and are called *procedure-level* or *local variables*. This term refers to the *scope* of a variable, where scope is defined as the section of the program where the variable is valid, visible, or "known." A variable can have either a local, form-level, or global scope. A variable with a local scope is simply one that has had storage locations set aside for it by a declaration statement made within a procedure. Local variables are only meaningful when used in expressions or statements inside the procedure that declared them. This means that the same variable name can be declared and used in more than one procedure. For each procedure that declares the variable, a separate and distinct variable is created.

By definition, all Visual Basic variables that are declared within a procedure using the **Dim** keyword are local variables. Visual Basic does, however, provide two different means of extending the scope of a variable from one procedure into another. One way is to use a variable as an argument in a **Call** statement, which gives the called procedure access to the variable. The second method is to use module-level variables. *Module-level variables*, which are said to have *module-level scope*, are declared in the declarations section of the (**General**) object in a Code window. Such variables must be declared as either **Private** or **Public** (declaring a module-level variable with the **Dim** keyword is the same as making it **Private**). Module level variables that have been declared **Private** are accessible only to procedures in the module, and are referred to as *form-level* variables. **Public** module-level variables are available and shared between all modules in a project and their procedures, and are referred to as *global* and *project-level* variables. Table 7-7 lists the scope of variables in Visual Basic. It should be noted that procedures share

Figure 7-21
A Procedure Can Be Considered a Closed Box

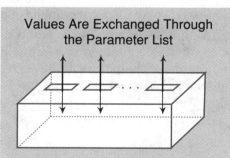

Values Are Exchanged Through the Parameter List

Table 7-7 Variable Scope		
Scope	**Private or Dim**	**Public**
Procedure-Level (Local Variables)	Variables are private to the procedure in which they are declared.	Not applicable. Local variables cannot be declared as Public.
Module-Level (Form-Level and Global Variables)	Variables are private within the module in which they are declared, and are referred to as form-level variables. They are shared and can be accessed by every procedure in the module.	Variables are available to all modules, and are referred to as global variables. They are shared and can be accessed by any procedure in the project, no matter where that procedure is located.

the same scope rules as module-level variables. That is, a **Public** procedure can be called from any module in an application, while a **Private** procedure can only be called by other procedures residing on the same module.

To illustrate the scope of both local and module-level variables, consider Procedure Code 7-3.

Procedure Code 7-3

```
Private firstnum As Integer ' create a module-level variable named firstnum

Private Sub Form_Click()
  Call First
End Sub

Public Sub First()
  Dim secnum As Integer  'creates a local variable named secnum

  firstnum = 10 ' store a value into the module-level variable
  secnum = 20   ' store a value into the local variable
  Cls
  Print "From First: firstnum = "; firstnum
  Print "From First: secnum = "; secnum

 Call Second
  Print

  Print "From First again: firstnum = "; firstnum
  Print "From main again: secnum = "; secnum
End Sub

Private Sub Second()
  Dim secnum As Integer ' create a second local variable named secnum

 secnum = 30 ' this only affects this local variable's value

  Print
  Print "From Second: firstnum = "; firstnum
  Print "From Second: secnum = "; secnum

 firstnum = 40  ' this changes firstnum for both procedures
End Sub
```

The variable `firstnum` in Procedure Code 7-3 is a module-level variable because its storage is created by a declaration statement located outside a procedure. Specifically, the declaration for this variable was entered in the declarations section of the (**General**) object in the Code window. Since both procedures, `First` and `Second`, are located on the form module in which `firstnum` is declared, both of these procedures can use this form-level variable with no further declaration needed. Procedure Code 7-3 also contains two separate local variables, both named `secnum`. Storage for the `secnum` variable named in `First` is created by the declaration statement located in `First`. A different storage area for the `secnum` variable in `Second` is created by the declaration statement located in the `Second` procedure. Figure 7-22 illustrates the three distinct storage areas reserved by the three declaration statements used in Procedure Code 7-3.

Each of the variables named `secnum` are local to the procedure in which their storage is created, and each of these variables can only be used from

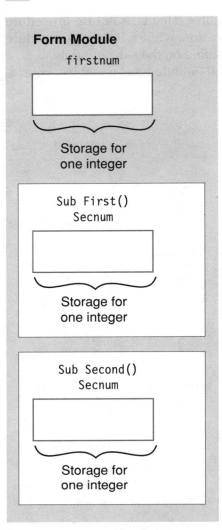

Form Module

firstnum

Storage for
one integer

Sub First()
Secnum

Storage for
one integer

Sub Second()
Secnum

Storage for
one integer

Figure 7-22

The Three Storage Areas Created
by Procedure Code 7-3

within the appropriate procedure. Thus, when secnum is used in First, the storage area reserved by First for its secnum variable is accessed, and when secnum is used in Second, the storage area reserved by Second for its secnum variable is accessed. The following output is produced when the Form_Click event in Procedure Code 7-3 is activated:

```
From First: firstnum = 10
From First: secnum = 20

From Second: firstnum = 10
From Second: secnum = 30

From First again: firstnum = 40
From First again: secnum = 20
```

Let us analyze the output produced by Procedure Code 7-3. Since firstnum is a form-level variable, both the First and Second procedures can use and change its value. Initially, both procedures print the value of 10 that First stored in firstnum. Before returning, Second changes the value of firstnum to 40, which is the value displayed when the variable firstnum is next displayed from within First.

Since each procedure only "knows" its own local variables, First can only display the value of its secnum and Second can only display the value of its secnum variable. Thus, whenever secnum is printed from First, the value of 20 is displayed, and whenever secnum is printed from Second, the value 30 is displayed.

Visual Basic does not confuse these two secnum, variables because only one procedure can execute at a given moment. While a procedure is executing, only those variables that are "in scope" for that procedure (module-level and local) can be accessed.

The scope of a variable in no way influences or restricts the data type of the variable. Local variables can be a character, integer, single, double, or any of the other data types (long, boolean, etc.) we have introduced, as can module-level variables. The scope of a variable is determined by a placement of the declaration statement that reserves storage for it. Finally, if both a module-level and local variable have the same name, the local variable will be accessed by the procedure in which that local variable is declared.

Using Module-Level Variables

Module-level variables are useful if a variable must be shared between many procedures. Rather than passing the same variable to each procedure, it is easier to define it once as module-level. Doing so also alerts anyone reading the program that many procedures use the variable. Most large programs make use of a few module-level variables and the majority of these variables should be named constants. Such named constants can then be shared by all procedures as "read-only" variables, which restricts any one procedure from altering the constant's value. Smaller programs containing a few procedures, however, should rarely contain module-level variables, though they may contain module-level named constants. The reason for this is that module-level variables allow the programmer to "jump around' the normal safeguards provided by procedures. By indiscriminately making variables module-level you destroy the safeguards Visual Basic provides to make procedures independent and insulated from each other, including the necessity of carefully designating the type of parameters needed by a procedure, the variables used in the procedure, and the values returned.

By their very nature module-level variables provide all procedures with the ability to access and change their values. Since no single procedure has exclusive use of such a variable, it is often difficult to determine which procedure actually accessed and changed a given variable's value. This makes debugging and maintaining code much more difficult.

Static Variables

The scope of a variable defines the location within a program where that variable can be used. Given any program, you could take a pencil and draw a box around the section of the program where each variable is valid. The space inside the box would represent the scope of each variable. From this viewpoint, the scope of a variable can be thought of as the space within the program where a variable is valid.

In addition to the space dimension represented by its scope, variables also have a time dimension. The time dimension refers to the length of time that storage locations are reserved for a variable. This time dimension is sometimes called the variable's "lifetime." For example, all local variable storage locations are released back to the computer when a procedure is finished running. Consider Procedure Code 7-4, where the **Sub** procedure Test is called four times when the Form_Click event is activated.

Procedure Code 7-4

```
Private Sub Form_Click()
  Dim count As Integer

  Cls
  count = 1
  For count = 1 To 4
    Call Test
  Next count
End Sub
Private Sub Test()
  Dim num As Integer

  Print "The value of num is "; num
  num = num + 1
End Sub
```

When the Form_Click procedure in this code is executed, the display produced is

```
The value of num is 0
The value of num is 0
The value of num is 0
The value of num is 0
```

This output is produced because each time Test is called, the local variable num is created and initialized to zero. When the **Sub** procedure returns control to the event procedure Form_Click, the variable num is destroyed along with any value stored in it. Thus, the effect of incrementing num in Test is lost.

The initialization used in Test is called a run-time initialization because it occurs each time the **Sub** procedure containing the variable is called. There are cases, however, where we would like a subroutine to preserve the value of its local variables between calls. This can be accomplished by declaring a variable inside a procedure using the **Static** keyword, rather than **Dim** keyword. For example, consider Procedure Code 7-5, which is identical to Procedure Code 7-4, except that local variable num in the **Sub** procedure Test has been declared as **Static**.

Procedure Code 7-5

```
Private Sub Form_Click()
  Dim count As Integer
  Cls

  count = 1
  For count = 1 To 4
    Call Test
  Next count
End Sub
Private Sub Test()
  Static num As Integer

  Print "The value of num is "; num
  num = num + 1
  End Sub
```

The output produced by the activation of this code is

```
The value of num is 0
The value of num is 1
The value of num is 2
The value of num is 3
```

As illustrated by this output, the variable num is set to zero only once. The **Sub** procedure Test then increments this variable, just before relinquishing control back to its calling procedure. The value that num has when Test is finished executing is retained and displayed when Test is next called. The reason for this is that local **Static** variables are not created and destroyed each time the procedure declaring the static variable is called. Once created, they remain in existence for the life of the program.

Since local **Static** variables retain their values, they are not initialized in the same way as variables declared as **Dim**. Their initialization is done only once, when the program is translated into executable form. At translation time all **Static** numeric variables are created and initialized to zero.[4] Thereafter, the value in each variable is retained each time the function is called. To make all of the variables **Static** in a procedure, the procedure itself can be declared **Static**. This is done by placing the keyword **Static** immediately before the procedure's designation as either a **Sub** or **Function** procedure. For example, the heading

```
Private Static Sub Test()
```

makes all of Test's variables Static. By definition, since all module level variables retain their values until an application is finished executing, the **Static** designation makes no sense for such variables.

---

[4]**String** variables are initialized to zero-length strings.

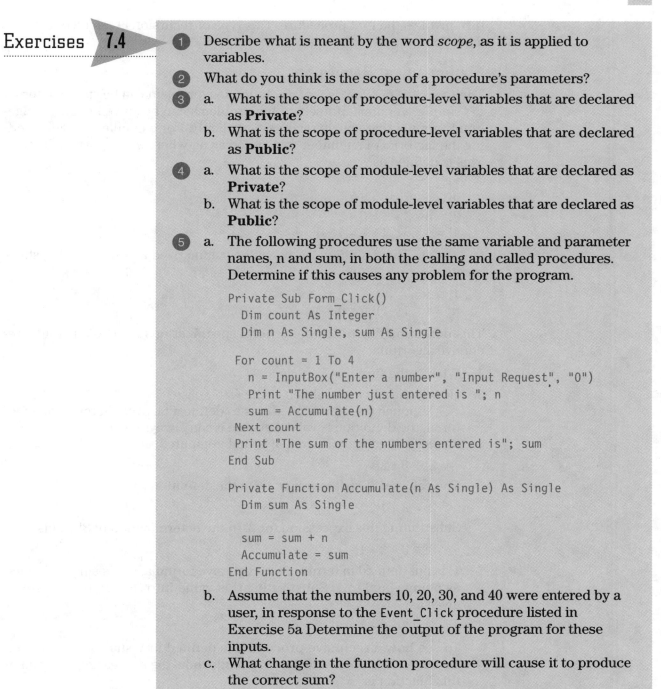

Exercises 7.4

1. Describe what is meant by the word *scope*, as it is applied to variables.

2. What do you think is the scope of a procedure's parameters?

3. a. What is the scope of procedure-level variables that are declared as **Private**?
   b. What is the scope of procedure-level variables that are declared as **Public**?

4. a. What is the scope of module-level variables that are declared as **Private**?
   b. What is the scope of module-level variables that are declared as **Public**?

5. a. The following procedures use the same variable and parameter names, n and sum, in both the calling and called procedures. Determine if this causes any problem for the program.

```
Private Sub Form_Click()
  Dim count As Integer
  Dim n As Single, sum As Single

  For count = 1 To 4
    n = InputBox("Enter a number", "Input Request", "0")
    Print "The number just entered is "; n
    sum = Accumulate(n)
  Next count
  Print "The sum of the numbers entered is"; sum
End Sub

Private Function Accumulate(n As Single) As Single
  Dim sum As Single

  sum = sum + n
  Accumulate = sum
End Function
```

   b. Assume that the numbers 10, 20, 30, and 40 were entered by a user, in response to the Event_Click procedure listed in Exercise 5a Determine the output of the program for these inputs.
   c. What change in the function procedure will cause it to produce the correct sum?

7.5 Recursion[5]

Because Visual Basic allocates new memory locations for parameters and local variables each time a procedure is called, it is possible for all general procedures to call themselves. Procedures that do so, which can be both **Sub** and **Function** procedures, are referred to as *self-referential* or *recursive* procedures. When a procedure invokes itself, the process is called *direct recursion*. Similarly, a procedure can invoke a second procedure, which in

---

[5]This topic may be omitted on first reading with no loss of subject continuity.

turn invokes the first procedure. This type of recursion is referred to as *indirect* or *mutual recursion*.

Mathematical Recursion

The recursive concept is that a solution to a problem can be stated in terms of "simple" versions of itself. Some problems can be solved using an algebraic formula that shows recursion explicitly. For example, consider finding the factorial of a number n, denoted as n!, where n is a positive integer. This is defined as

$$1! = 1$$
$$2! = 2 * 1 = 2 * 1!$$
$$3! = 3 * 2 * 1 = 3 * 2!$$
$$4! = 4 * 3 * 2 * 1 = 4 * 3!$$

and, so on. The definition for n! can be summarized by the following statements:

$$1! = 1$$
$$n! = n * (n\text{-}1)! \text{ for } n > 1$$

This definition illustrates the general specifications in constructong a recursive algorithm;

1. What is the first case?

2. How is the nth case related to the *(n-1)* case?

    Although the definition seems to define a factorial in terms of a factorial, the definition is valid, because it can always be computed. For example, using the definition, 3! is first computed as

$$3! = 3 * 2!$$

The value of 3! is determined from the definition as

$$2! = 2 * 1!$$

Substituting this expression for 2! in the determination of 3! yields

$$3! = 3 * 2 * 1!$$

1! is not defined in terms of the recursive formula, but is simply defined as being equal to 1. Substituting this value into the expression for 3! gives us

$$3! = 3 * 2 * 1 = 6$$

To see how a recursive procedure is defined in Visual Basic, we construct the function `Factorial`. In pseudocode, the processing required of this function is

> *If n = 1*
> > *Factorial = n*
> *Else*
> > *Factorial = n * Factorial(n - 1)*

Notice that this algorithm is simply a restatement of the recursive definition previously given. In Visual Basic, this can be written as

```
Public Function Factorial(n As Long) As Long
   If n = 1 Then
     Factorial = 1
   Else
     Factorial = n * Factorial(n - 1)
   End If
End Function
```

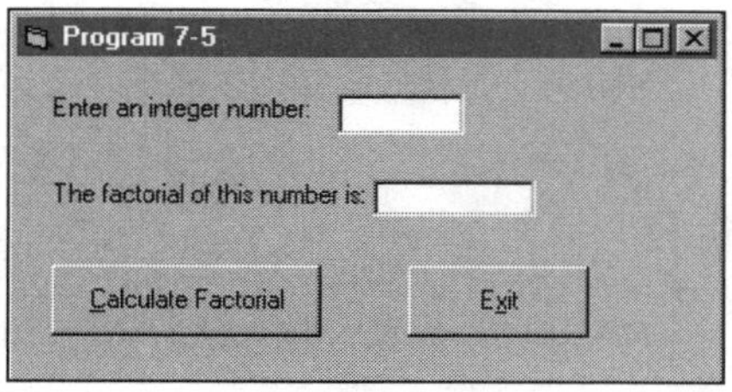

Figure 7-23
Program 7-5's Interface

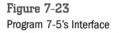

Table 7-8 The Properties Table for Program 7-5

Object	Property	Setting
Form	Name	frmMain
	Caption	Program 7-5
Label	Name	lblInput
	Caption	Enter an integer number:
Label	Name	lblFactorial
	Caption	The factorial of this number is:
Text box	Name	txtInput
	Text	(Blank)
	BackColor	White (Palette tab)
Picture box	Name	picFactorial
	TabStop	False
	BackColor	White (Palette tab)
Command button	Name	cmdFactorial
	Caption	&Calculate Factorial
Command button	Name	cmdExit
	Caption	E&xit

Notice that n has been declared as a long integer. The reason for this is that the factorial can easily exceed the bounds of an integer, which has a valid range from –32,768 to +32,767. (For example, the factorial of 8 is 40,320.) Program 7-5 illustrates the Factorial function within the context of a complete program.

Program 7-5's Event and General Procedure Code

```
Rem: This event procedure clears the picture box
Rem: whenever the txtInput box gets focus
Private Sub txtInput_GotFocus()
 picFactorial.Cls
End Sub

Rem: This event procedure calls the Factorial Function
Private Sub cmdFactorial_Click()
 Dim n As Long
 Dim fact As Long

 n = Int(Val(txtInput.Text))
 fact = Factorial(n)
 picFactorial.Print fact
End Sub
```

continued

```
Rem: This function calculates the factorial recursively
Public Function Factorial(n As Long) As Long
 If n = 1 Then
 Factorial = 1
 Else
 Factorial = n * Factorial(n - 1)
 End If
End Function

Rem: This is the Exit event procedure
Private Sub cmdExit_Click()
 Beep
 End
End Sub
```

Figure 7-24 illustrates a sample run of Program 7-5.

How the Computation Is Performed

The sample run of Program 7-5 initially invoked Factorial with a value of 3, using the call

```
fact = Factorial(n)
```

Let's see how the computer actually performs the computation. The mechanism that makes it possible for a Visual Basic procedure to call itself is that Visual Basic allocates new memory locations for all procedure parameters as each procedure is called. This allocation is made dynamically, as a program is executed, in a memory area referred to as the stack.

A *stack* is simply an area of memory used for rapidly storing and retrieving data. It is conceptually similar to a stack of trays in a cafeteria, where the last tray placed on top of the stack is the first tray removed. This last-in/first-out mechanism provides the means for storing information in order of occurrence. Each procedure call simply reserves memory locations on the stack for its parameters, its local variables, a return value, and the address where execution is to resume in the calling procedure when the called procedure has completed execution. Thus, when the procedure call Factorial(n) is made, the stack is initially used to store the address of the instruction being executed (fact = Factorial(n)); the parameter value for n, which is 3; and a space for the value to be returned by the Factorial procedure. At this stage, the stack can be envisioned as shown in Figure 7-25. From a program execution standpoint, the procedure that made the call to Factorial, in this case the cmdFactorial **Click** event, is suspended and the compiled code for the Factorial procedure starts executing.

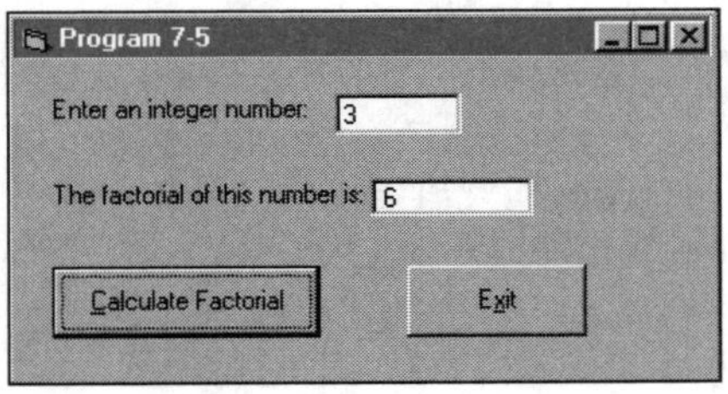

Figure 7-24

A Sample Output of Program 7-5

Within the `Factorial` procedure itself, another procedure call is made. That this call is to `Factorial`, is irrelevant as far as Visual Basic is concerned. The call is simply another request for stack space. In this case, the stack stores the address of the instruction being executed in `Factorial`, the number 2, and a space for the value to be returned by the procedure. The stack can now be envisioned as shown in Figure 7-26. At this point, a second version of the compiled code for `Factorial` begins execution, while the first version is temporarily suspended.

Once again, the currently executing code, which is the second invocation of `Factorial`, makes a procedure call. That this call is to itself, is irrelevant in Visual Basic. The call is once again handled in the same manner as any procedure invocation and begins with allocation of the stack's memory space. Here the stack stores the address of the instruction being executed in the calling procedure, which happens to be `Factorial`, the number 1, and a space for the value to be returned by the function. The stack can now be envisioned as shown in Figure 7-27. At this point the third and final version of the compiled code for `Factorial` begins execution, while the second version is temporarily suspended.

This third call to `Factorial` results in a returned value of 1 being placed on the stack. This completes the set of recursive calls and permits the suspended calling procedures to resume execution and be completed in reverse order. The value of 1 is used by the second invocation of `Factorial` to complete its operation and place a return value of 2 on the stack. This value is then used by the first invocation of `Factorial` to complete its operation and place a return value of 6 on the stack, with execution now returning to the `cmdFactorial_Click` event procedure. The original calling statement within this procedure stores the return value of its invocation of `Factorial` into the variable `fact`.

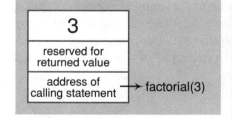

Figure 7-25
The Stack for the First Call to Factorial

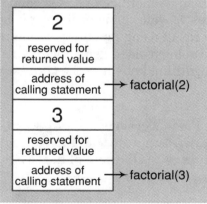

Figure 7-26
The Stack for the Second Call to Factorial

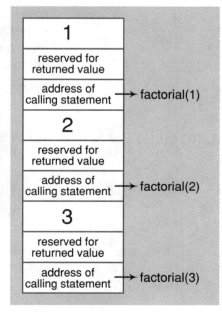

Figure 7-27
The Stack for the Third Call to Factorial

Recursion Versus Iteration

The recursive method can be applied to any problem in which the solution is represented in terms of solutions to simpler versions of the same problem. The most difficult tasks in implementing a recursive solution, however, are deciding how to create the process and visualizing what happens at each successive invocation.

Any recursive procedure can always be written in a nonrecursive manner using an iterative solution. For example, the factorial procedure can be written using an iteration algorithm as

```
Public Function Factorial(n As Long) As Long
   Dim fact As Long

   fact = 1
   Do
     fact = fact * n
     n = n - 1
   Loop While n > 0
   Factorial = fact
End Function
```

Since recursion is usually a difficult concept for beginning programmers, under what conditions would you use it in preference to a repetitive solution? The answer is rather simple.

If a problem solution can be expressed repetitively or recursively with equal ease, the repetitive solution is preferable because it executes faster (there are no additional procedure calls, which consume processing time) and uses less memory (the stack is not used for the multiple procedure calls needed in recursion). There are times, however, when recursive solutions are preferable.

First, some problems are simply easier to visualize using a recursive algorithm than a repetitive one. A second reason for using recursion is that it sometimes provides a much simpler solution. In these situations, obtaining the same result using repetition would require extremely complicated coding that can be avoided using recursion. An example of this is an advanced sorting algorithm known as the *Quicksort*.

Exercises 7.5

1. The Fibonacci sequence is 0, 1, 1, 2, 3, 5, 8, 13, . . . such that the first two terms are 0 and 1, and each term thereafter is defined recursively as the sum of the two preceding terms; that is,

   Fib(n) = Fib(n − 1) + Fib(n − 2)

   Write a recursive procedure that returns the *n*th number in a Fibonacci sequence, when *n* is passed to the procedure as a parameter. For example, when *n* = 8, the procedure should return the eighth number in the sequence, which is 13.

2. The sum of a series of consecutive numbers from 1 to *n* can be defined recursively as

   sum(1) = 1;
   sum(n) = n + sum(n − 1)

   Write a recursive Visual Basic procedure that accepts *n* as a parameter and calculates the sum of the numbers from 1 to *n*.

3. a. The value of x^n can be defined recursively as

$$x^0 = 1$$
$$x^n = x * x^{n-1}$$

Write a recursive procedure that computes and returns the value of x^n.

b. Rewrite the procedure written for Exercise 3a so that it uses a repetitive algorithm for calculating the value of x^n.

4. a. Write a procedure that recursively determines the value of the nth term in a geometric sequence defined by the terms

$$a, ar, ar^2, ar^3, \ldots ar^{n-1}$$

The parameters of the procedure should be the first term, a, the common ratio, r, and the value of n.

b. Modify the procedure written for Exercise 4a so that the sum of the first n terms in the sequence is returned.

5. a. Write a procedure that recursively determines the value of the nth term of an arithmetic sequence defined by the terms

$$a, a+d, a+2d, a+3d, \ldots a+(n-1)d$$

The parameters of the procedure should be the first term, a, the common difference, d, and the value of n.

b. Modify the procedure written for Exercise 5a so that the sum of the first n terms of the sequence is returned. (**Hint:** This is a more general form of Exercise 2.)

7.6 ▶ Focus on Program Design and Implementation:[6]

A General Procedure Main Menu System

Figure 7-28 illustrates Rotech's Main Menu form as it was developed in Section 2.6 and has been used throughout subsequent Focus sections. As shown, this form has five Command buttons.

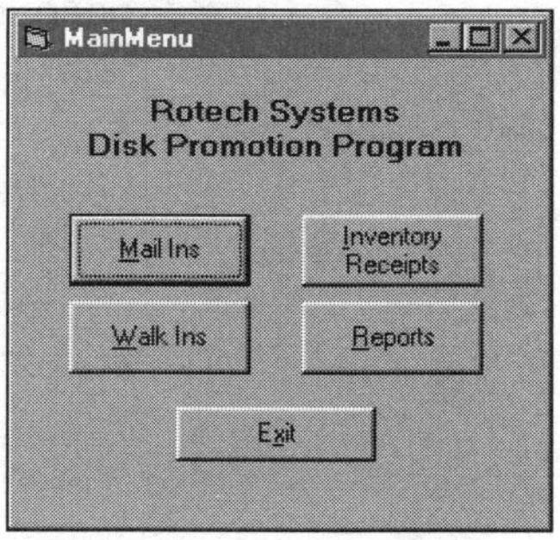

Figure 7-28
Rotech's Main Menu Form

---

[6]The Rotech project, as it should exist at the start of this section (which includes all of the capabilities built into it through the end of Section 6.7.) can be found on the Student Disk as the `rotech6.vbp` project within the `rotech6` folder.

As currently implemented, each Command button shown in Figure 7-28, except for the Exit button, uses its individual **Click** event to unload the Main Menu form and display an appropriate second form. Figure 7-29 illustrates the underlying structure of this relationship. Except for the form's name, each button repeats the same three lines of code. As a specific example of this code, Procedure Code 7-6 lists the code triggered by clicking the Walk Ins Command button.

Procedure Code 7-6

```
Private Sub cmdWalkins_Click()
    frmWalk.KeyPreview = True
    Me.Hide
    frmWalk.Show
End Sub
```

The structure shown in Figure 7-29 is an example of one type of programming style, called *disbursed programming*, where each event code sets its own preconditions, such as unloading the current form and setting the **KeyPreview** property, and is responsible for determining the next displayed form. A second programming style, called *centralized programming*, gathers similar tasks together into a single general procedure, and requires that the appropriate event codes simply make a call to this single procedure. The structure of this approach, as it applies to a Main Menu, is illustrated in Figure 7-30. Although this second approach requires the addition of a new general procedure, it does have the advantage of centralizing the code for what is essentially the single task of hiding the current form and displaying a second one. The new general procedure is usually placed on the same form as the Command buttons.

Procedure Code 7-7 illustrates how the call to the general procedure would be made within each Command button's **Click** event, for Rotech's Main Menu. Notice that each call uses a single named constant argument to identify which button was pressed. These named constants are always defined in the General Declarations section.

Figure 7-29
Disbursed Display Controls

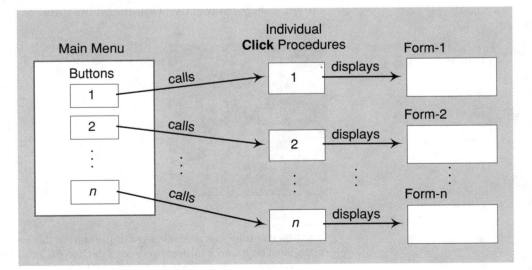

Figure 7-30
Centralized Display Control

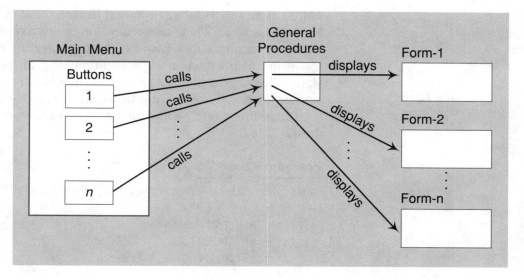

Procedure Code 7-7

```
Rem:(General) Declarations Section Code
Option Explicit

Rem: These constants are used to identify which button was pressed
Const intMAILBUTTON As Integer = 1
Const intWALKBUTTON As Integer = 2
Const intEXITBUTTON As Integer = 5
Const intSTUB As Integer = 99

Rem: Here are the Command buttons' Click Event Code

Private Sub cmdMailins_Click()
 Call mainmenu(intMAILBUTTON)
End Sub

Private Sub cmdWalkins_Click()
  Call mainmenu(intWALKBUTTON)
End Sub

Private Sub cmdInvRec_Click()
  Call mainmenu(intSTUB)
End Sub

Private Sub cmdReports_Click()
  Call mainmenu(intSTUB)
End Sub

Private Sub cmdExit_Click()
  Call mainmenu(intEXITBUTTON)
End Sub
```

Notice that each **Click** event in Event Procedure 7-7 is a call to the same general procedure, which we have named mainmenu, with a single argument that clearly identifies the clicked button. Since, at this stage there are five Command buttons, we have assigned the last, or Exit button, the number 5. We have also assigned the intSTUB constant the number 99, which is much higher than the number of actual buttons that will ever be placed on the Main Menu form. Then, as we develop the two remaining forms and use the existing button's **Click** Event code to trigger the forms' display in place of the Stub form, we will assign the numbers 3 and 4 to two new named constants. If we add a new button to the Main Menu (as we do in the next Focus section), we will use the number 6, and so on, for each added button.

Procedure Code 7-8 shows the code for the new `mainmenu` general procedure.

Procedure Code 7-8

```
Public Sub mainmenu(intFromButton As Integer)
  Me.Hide
  Select Case intFromButton
    Case intMAILBUTTON
      frmMail.KeyPreview = True
      frmMail.Show
      frmMail.Refresh
    Case intWALKBUTTON
      frmWalk.KeyPreview = True
      frmWalk.Show
      frmWalk.Refresh
    Case intSTUB
      frmStub.Show
      frmStub.Refresh
    Case intEXITBUTTON
      Beep
      End
  End Select
End Sub
```

In reviewing this `mainmenu` procedure, notice that the first statement in the procedure hides the current Main Menu form.[7] This statement is only made once, as opposed to being included within each **Click** event's code. A **Select Case** statement is then used to determine the action to take depending on the value of the passed parameter. In each case, except when the E**x**it button is pressed, a second form is displayed. The reason for using both a **Show** and **Refresh** method in the `mainmenu` procedure is that, although the **Show** method automatically performs a load of the designated window, if the form's **AutoRefresh** property is set to **False**, all graphical elements on the form may not be displayed. Calling the **Refresh** method forces a redraw of all graphical elements on the form, which ensures a correct display (this is described more fully in Chapter 11). Now, as a new form is added to replace the Stub form, we only need to add a new named constant, replace the `intSTUB` constant in the appropriate event procedure's **Call** structure, and add an appropriate **Case** statement within the **Select Case** statement. We will do this in Section 8.6, when we add an About Box to our program.

Although the centralized approach may initially appear more complicated than the disbursed approach, in practice it is very convenient to have the names of all displayed forms and all of the display code located together in

---

[7]An alternative is to use the statement `frmMain.Hide`, which explicitly names the Main Menu form.

a single place. In either case, you will encounter both approaches in your programming work, and which one you adopt is a matter of both programming style and required policy.

Exercises 7.6

(**Note:** The Rotech Systems project, at the stage of development begun in this section, can be found on the Student Disk in the otech6 folder as project rotech6.vbp. The project, as it exists at the end of this section, can be found on the Student Disk in the rotech7 folder as project rotech7.vbp.)

1 a. Make the changes to the Main Menu form described in this section or locate and load the project from the Student Disk.

b. Test that all Command buttons on the Main Menu form work correctly after you have made the changes for Exercise 1a.

2 Add a new Command button named cmdAbout to the Main Menu form. The button's caption should be set to <u>A</u>bout. When this new button is clicked the Stub form should be displayed.

3 **CASE STUDY**

Redo the Main Menu form for your selected project (see project specifications at the end of Section 1.5) to conform to the centralized programming style described in this section.

7.7 Knowing About:

Breakpoints, Watch Variables, and Step-Over Execution

In Section 4.5 we introduced the three Debug windows (Immediate, Watch, and Local) and the single-step method of running a program. Single-step execution is extremely useful for analyzing both small programs and small sections of code contained within a larger program. For debugging larger programs a combination of breakpoints, single-step execution, step-over execution, and watch variables are typically used. In this section we introduce these new techniques and show how they can be used together for debugging larger sections of code.

Breakpoints

A breakpoint statement, called a *breakpoint*, for short, is simply a designated statement at which program execution automatically stops and the mode switches from Run to Break. Once in Break mode the Immediate or Local Debug window can be activated and either window used to both examine and alter one or more variable's value. The program can then be continued in either single-step, step-over, or run mode.

Breakpoint statements are designated in either Design or Break mode in the Code window. This is accomplished by first placing the cursor on the designated line and

1. Pressing the [F9] key, or
2. Selecting the <u>T</u>oggle Breakpoint option from the <u>D</u>ebug menu, or
3. Pressing the Toggle Breakpoint (the hand) button on the Debug toolbar.

Figure 7-31
Event Code with Two Breakpoint
Statements

```
Project1 - frmMain (Code)                          _ □ ×
Form                    ▼    Click                  ▼
        Dim i As Long, j As Long '
        Dim total As Long

●       Print "Starting Loop Execution"
        For i = 1 To 1000
           Rem: A do nothing loop to kill time
           For j = 1 To 100000
           Next j
           Call AddToSum(i, total)
        Next i
●       Print "Total = "; total
        End Sub
```

Once a statement has been designated as a breakpoint statement, it will be both highlighted in the Code window and bulleted in the Code window's left-side margin. As an example of setting breakpoints, consider the event code illustrated in the Code window shown in Figure 7-31.

Notice in Figure 7-31 that two statements are highlighted and each of these statements has a bullet mark in the Code window's left-side margin. The highlighting and bulleting indicate that these two statements are breakpoint statements. This means that execution during run-time will stop just prior to each statement being executed. When this occurs an appropriate Debug window can be activated for examining and modifying all program variables. Run-time mode can then be restarted by pressing either the Run toolbar button (or the F5 key), the Step Into toolbar button (or the F8 key) for single-step execution, or the Step Over toolbar button (or the SHIFT and F8 keys together) if execution was suspended at a line that called either a **Sub** or **Function** procedure (the Debug toolbar is shown in Figure 7-32).

To explicitly clear breakpoints you must also be in either Design or Break mode. For specific breakpoints simply place the cursor on the desired statement in the Code window and repeat one of the steps used to set the breakpoint. For example, if the breakpoint is on, the F9 key will toggle it off. To explicitly clear all breakpoints in a program:

1. Press the CTRL + SHIFT + F9 keys at the same time, or
2. Select the Clear All Breakpoints option from the Debug menu.

In any case, all breakpoints are implicitly cleared in a saved project. That is, breakpoints *are not* saved when the file containing the code is saved.

To illustrate how breakpoints work, create and execute the program containing the code previously shown in Figure 7-31. Notice that when the Form_Click event is activated the program suspends execution at the first breakpoint statement and opens up a Code window. For now, simply press the Continue toolbar button to restart program execution at the breakpoint statement. Notice that the code contains a nested **For** loop that uses the

Figure 7-32
The Debug Toolbar

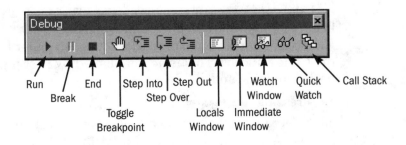

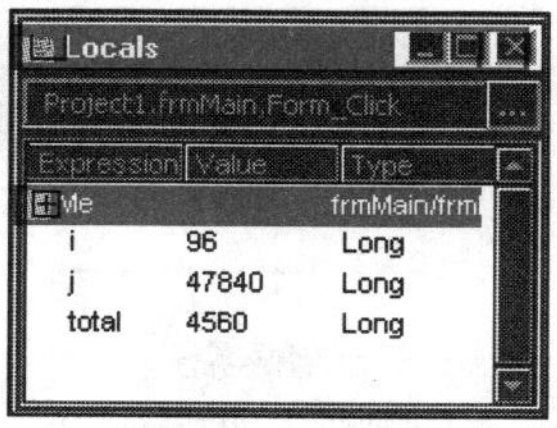

Figure 7-33a
The Locals Window

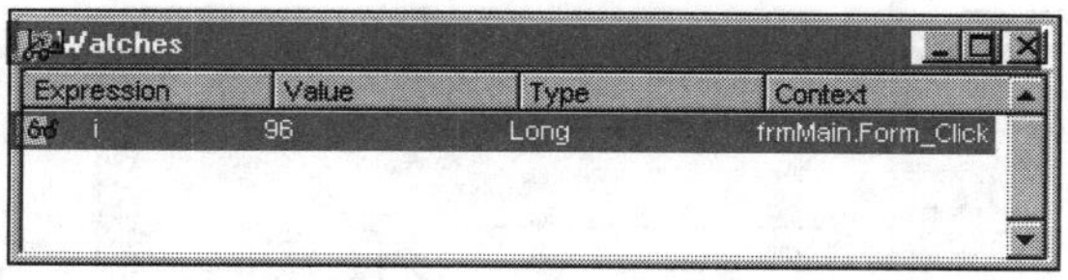

Figure 7-33b
The Immediate Window

inner loop simply to waste time. This gives you sufficient time to experiment moving into Break mode by

1. Pressing the Break toolbar button or
2. Pressing the CTRL and BREAK keys at the same time.

Try one or both of these methods to switch back to Break mode once the program has been restarted. Once in Break mode you activate the desired Debug window by

1. Clicking on the window, if it is visible,
2. Selecting the window from the View menu,
3. Selecting the window using a Debug toolbar icon, or
4. Pressing the CTRL and G keys at the same time to activate the Immediate window.

Figure 7-33 illustrates how the Locals and Immediate windows appeared for one such switch into Break mode. Clearly, the Locals window is easier to use because you don't have to enter either a question mark or a **Print** statement to display a variable's value, as is required with the Immediate window. After you restart the program notice that the program automatically switches back to Break mode once again just prior to executing the **Print** statement located after the nested loop. This is because this statement is a breakpoint statement.

Watch Variables and Expressions

Frequently, while debugging a section of code, you will be interested in a selected group of variables or a selected expression. Instead of displaying all

---

PROGRAMMERS NOTES

Creating and Clearing Breakpoint Statements

Breakpoint statements are created and cleared using the same steps. In both cases you must either be in Design or Break mode. When you are on the desired line of code:

1. Press the F9 key, or
2. Select the Toggle Breakpoint option from the Debug menu, or
3. Press the Toggle Breakpoint (the hand) button on the Debug toolbar.

Each of these steps is a toggle that both selects and deselects a statement as a breakpoint. To clear all breakpoints in either Design or Break mode do one of the following:

1. Press the CTRL+SHIFT+F9 keys at the same time, or
2. Select the Clear All Breakpoints option from the Debug menu.

Breakpoints are not saved when the code containing them is saved.

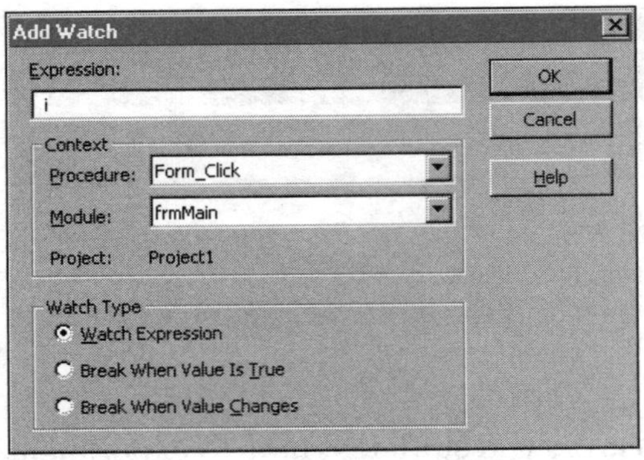

Figure 7-34
Adding the Variable i to the
Watched Variables List

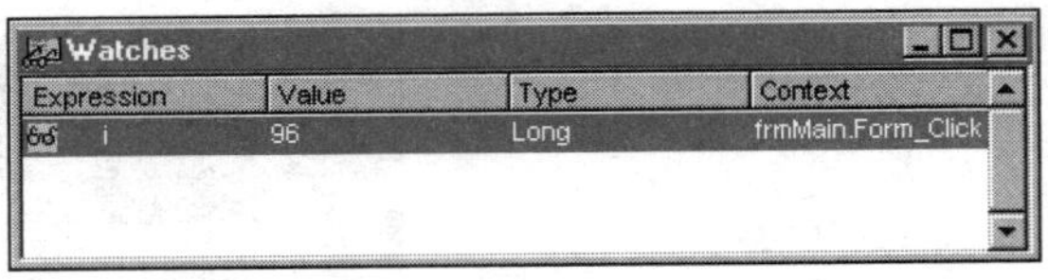

Figure 7-35
A Watch Window

local variables in the Locals window, or printing out the value of the expression in the Immediate window, you can have selected variables and expressions automatically displayed in the Watch window. This is accomplished by designating one or more variables and expressions as *watched*. This allows you to observe their value in the Watch window, because such variables and expressions are automatically updated and displayed in that window whenever Break mode is entered. To designate a variable or expression as watched, first highlight the selected variable or expression in the Code window and then select the Add Watch option from the Debug menu. This will bring up the Add Watch dialog box shown in Figure 7-34.

Pressing the OK Command button on the Add Watch dialog box causes the selected variable to be added to a list of watched variables. Or, if you need to watch an expression that is not in your code, but consists of variables whose values can be watched, simply type in the expression directly in the Add Watch dialog box. Now, whenever you enter Break mode and display the Watch window the watched expression and its value will automatically be displayed in the Watch window, as illustrated in Figure 7-35.

If you simply need to determine the value of a variable or expression quickly, you can highlight the variable or expression and activate the Quick Watch toolbar button. This will both display the value of the variable or expression and also provide you with the opportunity of making the highlighted item a watched expression.

Step-Over Execution

A very useful debugging procedure in conjunction with single-stepping through a section of code is to use the Step Over toolbar button whenever a call to a **Sub** procedure or function is encountered. The Step Over button causes the complete called procedure to execute but puts the program back into Break mode when the called procedure has completed execution. Thus, when you encounter a call to a general procedure and are interested in single-stepping through it use the Step Into toolbar button; otherwise use the Step Over toolbar button to complete the called procedure's execution and move to the next executable statement in the calling procedure's code.

7.8 Common Programming Errors

The common errors associated with general procedures are

1. Forgetting to use the word **Sub** or **Function** on the header line before the general procedure's name.

2. Using an argument list that does not match with the general procedure's parameter list. These errors fall into the following categories:

    a. The number of arguments is not the same as the number of parameters.

    b. The order of arguments and corresponding parameters do not match.

    c. The data types of arguments and corresponding parameters do not match.

3. Attempting to alter the value of a passed constant, expression, or function result. For example, assume that a general procedure named `Area` has the header line

   ```
   Public Sub Area(radius As Single)
   ```

   and is called using the statement

   ```
   Call Area(Rad)
   ```

   Here, the value in `Rad` is referenced within the general procedure as the parameter `radius`. If the general procedure subsequently alters the value of `radius`, the value of `Rad` is also changed. This is a consequence of the fact that both `Rad` and `radius` reference the exact same storage location area. Now assume that the general procedure is called using the following statement

   ```
   Call Area(3.62)
   ```

   Here the value in `radius` cannot be changed within `Area`. An attempt to do so is effectively an attempt to redefine the value of the constant 3.62, which usually causes a run-time error.

4. Inadvertently changing the value of a parameter inside a general procedure when the calling unit did not expect the change. This is an unwanted side effect that can be avoided by passing argument values by value, rather than by reference.

7.9 Chapter Review

Key Terms

actual argument	form-level variables	recursive procedures
arguments	formal argument	scope
ByRef	general procedure	stack
ByVal	global variables	**Static**
call by reference	local scope	static variables
call by value	local variables	subprograms
called procedure	module-level variable	
calling procedure	parameters	

Summary

1. The most commonly used syntax for a general **Sub** procedure is

   ```
   Public Sub Name(Parameter List)
      Visual Basic statements in here
   End Sub
   ```

Even if the **Sub** procedure has no parameter list, the parentheses must be present.

2. A general **Sub** procedure is called using a **Call** statement having the form

> **Call** procedure-name(argument list)

The arguments in the **Call** statement may be constants, variables, or expressions using combinations of constants and variables. The data type, number, and order of the arguments used in the **Call** statement must agree with the data type, number, and order of the corresponding parameters in the general procedure's parameter list. In addition, the parentheses surrounding the argument list can be omitted. If there are no arguments, the parentheses must be omitted.

3. Except for constants, arguments are passed by reference. This means that the called procedure can change the argument's value. To pass an argument by value, either enclose the argument in parentheses or declare the corresponding parameter using the **ByVal** keyword. For example, the declaration

```
Public Sub Test(ByVal radius As Single)
```

declares that the radius parameter references a value. Similarly, the **Call** statement

```
Call Message((Rad), (Angle))
```

passes values to the Message **Sub** procedure.

4. All functions (intrinsic and user-written) calculate and directly return a single value. The most commonly used syntax for a user-written function is

> **Public Function** *function-name(Parameter List) As Data-type*
>   optional variable declarations
>
>   optional executable statements
>   function-name = expression
> **End Function**

5. Functions that return a string can be declared as such by appending a dollar sign to the function's name. For example, the declarations

```
Public Function Test(s As String, n As Integer) As String
```

and

```
Public Function Test$( s As String, n As Integer)
```

are equivalent.

6. A function is called by using its name and passing any data to it in the parentheses following the name.

7. The arguments passed to a function must agree in type, order, and number with the function's parameters.

8. Every variable used in a procedure has a *scope*, which determines where in the program the variable can be used. The scope of a variable is either *local* or *module-level* and is determined by where the variable's definition statement is placed. A local variable is defined within a procedure and can only be used within its defining procedure. A module-level variable

is defined outside a procedure. If the module-level variable is declared as **Private**, it can be used by any procedure located on the same module in which it is declared. If it is declared as **Public**, it can be used by every procedure on any module in a project.

9. Global variables are in scope for the life of the application. Local variables are effectively destroyed when they go out of scope. To keep a local variable's value from being destroyed, the variable can be declared as **Static**. Additionally, placing the **Static** keyword immediately in front of the keywords **Sub** and **Function** in a general procedure's header line makes all of the procedure's variables **Static**.

10. Procedures also have scope. **Private** procedures can only be called from procedures residing on the same module as the **Private** procedure, while **Public** procedures can be called by every procedure in the application, regardless of the module containing the calling procedure.

11. A recursive solution is one in which the solution can be expressed in terms of a "simpler" version of itself. A recursive algorithm must always specify:

 a. The first case or cases, and

 b. How the *n*th case is related to the *(n–1)* case.

12. If a problem solution can be expressed repetitively or recursively with equal ease, the repetitive solution is preferable because it executes faster and uses less memory. In many advanced applications recursion is simpler to visualize and is the only practical means of implementing a solution.

Test Yourself—Short Answer

1. General Procedures can be placed in any of three different places:

 a. _____,

 b. _____, and

 c. _____ modules.

2. Explain the difference between a **Sub** procedure designated as **Public** and one designated as **Private**.

3. Data can be exchanged between the calling procedure and the procedure being called through the use of the _____.

4. Consider the statement `Call XYZ(x, (y), z)` and the procedure header line

 `Public Sub XYZ(x as integer, ByVal y as integer, z as integer)`

 Will the procedure XYZ be able to make changes to any of the values of x or y or z? Why or why not?

5. Explain the difference between passing arguments `by value` or passing the arguments `by reference`.

6. Determine what characters get assigned to `strMessage` for the statement

 `strMessage = Right("The Cat in the Hat", 3)`

7. Determine what characters get assigned to `strMessage` for the statement

 `strMessage = InStr("The Cat in the Hat", "t")`

8. Determine what characters get assigned to `strMessage` for the statement

 `strMessage = InStr(8,"The Cat in the Hat", "t")`

9. Write a Call statement that could be used to call the **Sub** procedure having the header line

```
Public Sub Message(x as string, y as integer)
```

10. Write a **Sub** procedure header line and a `Call` statement for a procedure called `Mine` having a single-precision parameter named `price`. The corresponding argument used in calling `Mine` is named `dollar`.

Programming Projects

1. Qualification for a loan from a local bank is based upon criteria with respect to employment, home ownership, major credit cards, and assets. Points are awarded or taken away based upon responses to questions about the above categories.

Loan Criteria:
With respect to employment, if the applicant has full-time employment, award one point and display a Text box to input number of years at present employer. If the applicant has been employed at least three years, award an additional point; at least six years, award an additonal two points; more than 10 years, award an additional three points. (Thus, an applicant can receive 1, 2, 3, or 4 points for full-time employment.)

With respect to home ownership, award two points if applicant owns a home, zero points otherwise.

With respect to major credit cards, these conditions apply for EACH credit card (MasterCard, VISA, AMEX): award one point with credit balance less than $500; deduct one point for credit balance at least $500; deduct two points for credit balance at least $3000; deduct three points for credit balance at least $5000. Thus, an applicant gets either +1, –1, –2, or –3 points depending upon the credit balance of the credit card. Display a Text box to input credit balance for each check box that is selected.

With respect to financial assets, these conditions apply for EACH instance: award one point if asset is at least 20% of loan amount; award two points if asset is at least 50% of loan amount; award three points if asset is at least 100% of loan amount. Display a Text box to input asset amount for each check box that is selected. Thus, an applicant gets either 0, 1, 2, or 3 points depending upon the size of the asset with respect to the amount of the loan.

The applicant will qualify for a loan if the number of points awarded totals at least eight. Use a Message box to display an appropriate message that the applicant has either qualified or not qualified for a loan.

Program Requirements:
The user should be able to check/uncheck choices in any order so that if a change is made, the appropriate category points are recalculated. (Hint: this can be done in the Check box and Option button **Click** event procedures.)

Use **Sub** functions to calculate points for credit card and asset balances. The same **Sub** function should be called to calculate the appropriate number of points for each credit card account that is listed on the application form. For each asset listed by the applicant, the same **Sub** function should be called to calculate the appropriate number of points. These **Sub** functions should be placed in a standard module (.bas file).

Figure for Programming
Project 1

2. The Texas Fence Company has asked you to write a program that will calculate the amount of materials needed for a fence given its length and width.

Requirements:
All fences are rectangular and the gate (only one) is always placed on the longer side. The gate occupies four linear feet. Every fence contains four corner fence posts, two gateposts, and a gate.

Fence posts that are neither corner posts nor gate posts are called intermediate posts. The fence may contain intermediate fence posts depending upon the length of fencing required. The maximum distance between any two fence posts (corner, intermediate, and gate) is 10 feet. Therefore, if the length of a side is 10 feet or less, no intermediate fence post is required for that side.

Three connectors are required at each intermediate fence post, three connectors are required at each gate post, and six connectors are required at each corner fence post.

Your output should display the number of connectors, corner posts, intermediate posts, gate posts, gates (only one for this problem) and fencing. You may assume that the length and width are sufficient to include a four-foot gate. In the General Declaration section of your program, declare variables to hold values of length, width, number of connectors, number of corner posts, number of intermediate posts, number of gate posts, and amount of fencing.

Because specifications for constructing a fence may change in the future, use named constants to represent the number of connectors needed for each type of fence post. Perform all calculations in a **Sub** procedure. Store the **Sub** procedure in a standard module (.bas file).

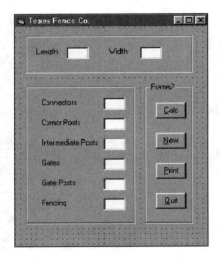

Figure for Programming Project 2

Project Property Table		
Object	**Property**	**Setting**
Form	Name	frmFence
	Caption	Texas Fence Co.
Frame	Name	fraInput
Label	Name	lblLength
	Caption	Length
Text Box	Name	txtLength
	Text	<blank>
Label	Name	lblWidth
	Caption	Width
Text Box	Name	txWidth
	Text	<blank>
Frame	Name	fraOutput
Label	Name	lblConnectors
	Caption	Connectors
Text box	Name	txtConnectors
	Text	<blank>
Label	Name	lblCornerPosts
	Caption	Corner Posts
Text box	Name	txtCornerPosts
	Text	<blank>
Label	Name	lblIntermediatePosts
	Caption	Intermediate Posts
Text box	Name	txtGates
	Text	<blank>
Text box	Name	txtGatePosts
	Text	<blank>
Label	Name	lblFencing
	Caption	Fencing
Text box	Name	txtFencing
	Text	<blank>
Frame	Name	fraCommands
Command button	Name	cmdCalc
	Caption	&Calc
Command button	Name	cmdNew
	Caption	&New
Command button	Name	cmdPrint
	Caption	&Print
Command button	Name	cmdQuit
	Caption	&Quit

Figure for Programming
Project 3

3. This assignment is a modification to project 2. In addition to computing the number of fence components needed for a given job, your program should also compute the corresponding cost for each component. Use the following unit costs in your program.

Material Cost per Unit:

Connector	$.75
Corner post	$6.50
Intermediate post	$5.00
Gate post	$7.50
Gate	$35.00
Fencing	$1.00 per linear foot

Your program should permit at most two gates; if two gates are required, they should not be placed between the same pair of corner posts. Since cost of materials will certainly change in the future, you should use named constants to represent the unit costs for fence materials, and perform all calculations in a **Sub** procedure.

Part Two

Data Structures and Storage

Structured Data

The variables we have used so far have shared a common characteristic: each could store only one value at a time. For example, although the variables key, count, and grade declared in the statements

```
Dim key As String*1
Dim count As Integer
Dim grade As Single
```

are of different data types, each variable can store only one value of the declared data type. These types of variables are called *atomic variables*. An atomic variable, which is also referred to as a scalar variable, has a value that cannot be further subdivided or separated into a legitimate data type.

Another method of storing and retrieving data is to use a data structure. A data structure is a data type whose values can be decomposed into individual data elements, each of which is either atomic or another data structure and provides an access scheme for locating individual data elements within the structure. One of the simplest and most widely used *data structures*, which is referred to as an *array*, consists of a set of logically related individual items, all of which have the same data type. For example, Table 8-1 illustrates three groups of items. The first group is a list of five single-precision temperatures, the second group is a list of four character codes, and the last group is a list of six integer grades.

In this chapter we describe how arrays are declared, initialized, stored inside a computer, and used. We also introduce record structures. A *record structure* is a user-defined data type whose elements need not all be of the same data type. Both arrays and record structures require Visual Basic's built-in procedural operations for individual element access and manipu-

Table 8-1	Three Individual Lists	
Temperatures	**Codes**	**Grades**
95.75	Z	98
83.0	C	87
97.625	K	92
72.5	L	79
86.25		85
		72

lation. In Chapter 12 we present an advanced data structure, referred to as a **Class**, that requires the programmer to define both the type of data and the operations that can be used on individual elements in the data structure.

8.1 One-Dimensional Arrays

A *one-dimensional* array, which is also referred to as either a *single-dimensional* array or a *vector*, is a list of related values, with the same data type, stored using a single group name.[1] In Visual Basic, as in other computer languages, the group name is referred to as the array name. For example, consider the list of grades illustrated in Table 8-2.

All the grades in this list are integer numbers and must be declared as such. However, the individual items in the list do not have to be declared separately. The items in the list can be declared as a single unit and stored under a common variable name called the array name. For convenience, we will choose grades as the name for the list shown in Table 8-2. The general syntax for declaring a one-dimensional array is

```
Dim arrayname(Lower-Index-Value To Upper-Index-Value) As data-type
```

For example, the declaration

```
Dim grades(1 To 6) As Single
```

specifies that grades is to store six individual integer values. Notice that this declaration statement gives the array (or list) name, the data type of items in the array, and the beginning and ending designations for items in the array. Figure 8-1 illustrates the grades array in memory with the correct designation for each array element.

Each item in an array is called an *element* or *component* of that array. The individual elements stored in the array illustrated in Figure 8-1 are stored sequentially, with the first array element stored in the first reserved location, the second element stored in the second reserved location, and so on, until the last element is stored in the last reserved location. This sequential storage allocation for the list is a key feature of arrays because it provides a simple mechanism for easily locating any single element in the list.

Table 8-2 A List of Grades
Grades
98
87
92
79
85
72

Figure 8-1
The grades Array in Memory

---

[1]Note that lists can be implemented in a variety of ways. An array is simply one implementation of a list in which all the list elements are of the same type and each element is stored consecutively in a set of contiguous memory locations.

PROGRAMMERS NOTES

Structured Data Types

In contrast to atomic types, such as integer and single-precision data, there are structured types. A structured type, which is sometimes referred to as a data structure, is any type whose values can be decomposed and are related by some defined structure. Additionally, operations must be available for retrieving and updating individual values in the data structure.

Single-dimensional arrays are examples of a structured type. In a single-dimensional array, such as an array of integers, the array is composed of individual integer values, where integers are related by their position in the list. Indexed variables provide the means of accessing and modifying values in the array.

Since elements in the array are stored sequentially, any individual element can be accessed by giving the name of the array and the element's position. This position is called the element's *index* or *subscript* value (the two terms are synonymous). As declared, the first element of the `grades` array has an index of 1, the second element has an index of 2, and so on, up to the number specified last in parentheses in the **Dim** statement used to declare the array. In Visual Basic, the array name and index of the desired element are combined by listing the index in parentheses after the array name. For example, given the declaration

```
Dim grades(1 To 6) As Integer:
```

- `grades(1)` refers to the first grade stored in the `grades` array,
- `grades(2)` refers to the second grade stored in the `grades` array,
- `grades(3)` refers to the third grade stored in the `grades` array,
- `grades(4)` refers to the fourth grade stored in the `grades` array,
- `grades(5)` refers to the fifth grade stored in the `grades` array, and
- `grades(6)` refers to the sixth grade stored in the `grades` array.

The indexed variable, `grades(1)`, is read as "grades sub one." This is a shortened way of saying "the grades array subscripted (that is, indexed) by one," and distinguishes the first element in an array from an atomic variable that could be declared as `grades1`. Similarly, `grades(2)` is read as "grades sub two," `grades(3)` as "grades sub three," and so on.

The Starting Index Number

In declaring an array, we have listed both the starting and ending index numbers. For example, in the following declarations

```
Dim temp(1 To 7) As Integer
Dim sample(3 To 6) As Single
Dim foo(0 To 5) As Double
```

the `temp` array has been declared with a starting index value of 1, the `sample` array with a starting index of 3, and the `foo` array with a starting index of 0.[2] Thus, the `temp` array consists of the seven elements from `temp(1)` to `temp(7)`, `sample` consists of the four elements from `sample(3)` to `sample(6)`, and `foo` consists of the six elements from `foo(0)` to `foo(5)`. A very useful option is to eliminate the starting index altogether, which forces the array to start with an index value of either 0 or 1, depending upon the default starting base value

---

[2] Negative starting and ending index values are valid. The only restriction is that the ending value must be larger than the starting value.

that is set using the **Option Base** statement. For example, the statement `Option Base 1` sets the default starting index value to 1, while the statement `Option Base 0` sets the default starting index value to 0. These are the only two forms of this statement, and if an explicit **Option Base** statement has not been set, the starting value will be 0 by default. For example, the declaration statement

```
Dim temp(5) As integer
```

creates an array of six integers consisting of elements `temp(0)` to `temp(5)`, except if the statement

```
Option Base 1
```

has been used. The **Option Base** statement is declared only once in the **Declarations** section of the (**General**) Code window. Once this statement is used, all subsequently declared arrays, no matter where in the module they are declared, will begin at 1, not 0. For example, if you include this statement in the **Declarations** section and subsequently declare a `temp` array as `Dim temp(5) As Integer`, an array of exactly five locations will be created, with the first available location being `temp(1)` and the last available location being `temp(5)`. For all subsequent programs, we will use this form of the **Option Base** statement so that all of our arrays begin with the element having an index value of 1.[3]

Where to Declare Arrays

Arrays may be declared at either the procedure, module, or project level. An array declared within a procedure is local to the procedure and can only be accessed from within the procedure, unless it is passed as an argument to another procedure. An array declared in the **Declarations** section of a module's (**General**) code object will have either module or project scope, depending on the keyword used to declare the array. If the **Dim** keyword is used, the array will have module scope (that is, it can be accessed from any procedure in the module); otherwise, if the **Public** keyword is used, the array will have *project scope* (that is, it can be accessed from *any* procedure in any module attached to the project). Additionally, to create a local static array (one that will retain its elements' values between procedure calls) the array can be declared as **Static** within a procedure. Table 8-3 summarizes this information.

Table 8-3	Declaring Arrays	
Placement	**Declaration Keyword**	**Scope**
Within a Procedure	Dim	Procedure Level
Within a Procedure	Static	Procedure Level but retains values between procedure calls
Declaration section of the General code object	Dim	Module Level
Declaration section of the General code object	Public	Project Level

---

[3]Another option is to simply ignore the fact that a zeroth element is available by not using it.

All of our programs will declare arrays at either the procedure or module level. Additionally, we will always use the `Option Base 1` statement to ensure that our arrays use a starting index value of 1. With this convention, good programming practice requires defining the upper index value (equivalent to the number of array items) as a named constant before declaring the array. Thus, our array declarations will always use two statements such as

```
Const NUMGRADES As Integer = 6
Dim grades(NUMGRADES) As Integer
```

Further examples of this type of array declaration include:

```
Const NUMELS As Integer = 5
Dim temperature(NUMELS) As Integer

Const ARRAYSIZE As Integer = 4
Dim code(1 To ARRAYSIZE) As String*1

Const SIZE As Integer = 100
Dim amount(1 To SIZE) As Single
```

In these declaration statements, each array is allocated sufficient memory to hold the declared number of data items. Thus, the array named `temperature` has storage reserved for five integer numbers, the array named `code` has storage reserved for four characters, and the array named `amount` has storage reserved for 100 single-precision numbers. The constant identifiers, `NUMELS`, `ARRAYSIZE`, and `SIZE` are programmer-selected names.

Using Indexed Variables

Indexed variables can be used anywhere that scalar variables are valid. Examples using the elements of the `grades` array are

```
grades(1) = 98
grades(2) = grades(1) - 11
grades(3) = grades(2)/2
grades(4) = 79
grades(4) = (grades(1) + grades(2) + grades(3)) / 2.2
sum = grades(1) + grades(2) + grades(3) + grades(4)
```

The index contained within parentheses need not be an integer constant; any expression that evaluates to an integer may be used as an index. In each case, of course, the value of the expression must be within the valid index range defined when the array is declared. For example, assuming that i and j are integer variables, the following indexed variables are valid:

```
grades(i)
grades(2*i)
grades(j-i)
```

One extremely important advantage of using integer expressions as indices is that it allows sequencing through an array by using a loop. This makes statements like

```
sum = grades(1) + grades(2) + grades(3) + grades(4)
```

unnecessary. The index values in this statement can be replaced by a **For** loop counter to access each element in the array sequentially. For example, the code

```
sum = 0        ' initialize the sum to zero
For i = 1 To 5
  sum = sum + grades(i)  ' add in a grade value
Next i
```

sequentially retrieves each array element and adds the element to sum. Here the variable i is used both as the counter in the **For** loop and as an index. As i increases by one each time through the loop, the next element in the array is referenced. The procedure for adding the array elements within the **For** loop is similar to the accumulation procedure we have used many times before.

The advantage of using a **For** loop to sequence through an array becomes apparent when working with larger arrays. For example, if the grades array contained 100 values rather than just five, simply changing the number 5 to 100 in the **For** statement is sufficient to sequence through the 100 elements and add each grades value to the sum.

As another example of using a **For** loop to sequence through an array, assume that we want to locate the maximum value in an array of 1000 elements named grades. The procedure we will use initially assumes that the first element in the array is the largest number. As we sequence through the array, the maximum is compared to each new element. When an element with a higher value is located, that element becomes the new maximum. The following code does the job.

```
Const NUMELS As Integer = 1000  ' This is declared in the General code
                                ' Declaration section

maximum = grades(1)             ' set the maximum to element one
For  i = 2 To NUMELS            ' cycle through the rest of the array
  If grades(i) > maximum  Then  ' compare each element to the maximum
    maximum = grades(i)         ' capture the new high value
  End If
Next i
```

In this code, the **For** statement consists of one **If** statement. The search for a new maximum value starts with the second element of the array and continues through the last element. Each element is compared to the current maximum, and when a higher value is encountered, it becomes the new maximum.

Input and Output of Array Values

Individual array values can be assigned values and have their values displayed in the same manner used for scalar variables. Examples of individual data assignment statements include:

```
grades(1) = InputBox("Enter a value for grade 1", "Input request", "0")
grades(2) =  96.5
grades(3) = grade(2) * 1.2
```

In the first statement a single value will be read and stored in the indexed variable named grades(1). The second statement causes the value 96.5 to be in the indexed variable grades(2), while the last statement multiples grades(1) by 1.2 and assigns the value of this computation to grades(3).

Typically, for interactive data input, a loop is used to cycle through the array and each pass through the loop is used to assign a value to an array element. For example, the code

```
Const NUMELS As Integer = 5

message = "Enter a grade"
For i = 1 To NUMELS
   grades(i) = InputBox(message, "Input Dialog", "0")
Next i
```

prompts the user for five grades. The first value entered is stored in grades(1), the second value entered in grades(2), and so on until five grades have been input.

During output, individual array elements can be displayed using the **Print** method and complete sections of the array can be displayed by including a **Print** method within a loop. Examples of this include:

```
Print grades(2)
```

and

```
Print "The value of element "; i ;"  is"; grades(i)
```

and

```
Const NUMELS As Integer = 20

For  k = 5 To NUMELS
  Print k; amount(k)
Next k
```

The first statement displays the value of the indexed variable grades(2). The second statement displays the value of the index i and the value of grades(i). Before this statement can be executed, i would have to have an assigned value. Finally, the last example includes a **Print** method within a **For** loop. Both the value of the index and the value of the elements from 5 to 20 are displayed.

Program 8-1 illustrates these input and output techniques, using an array named grades that is defined to store six integer numbers. Included in the program are two **For** loops. The first **For** loop is used to cycle through each array element and allows the user to input individual array values. After six values have been entered, the second **For** loop is used to display the stored values.

Figure 8-2
Program 8-1's Interface

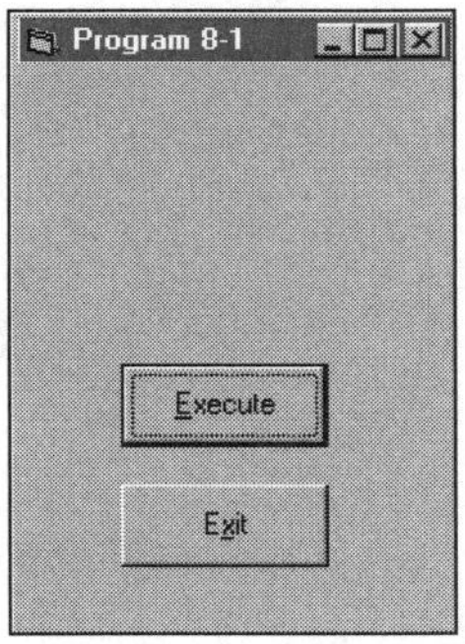

Table 8-4	Program 8-1's Properties Table	
Object	**Property**	**Setting**
Form	Name	frmMain
	Caption	Program 8-1
Command button	Name	cmdExecute
	Caption	&Execute
Command button	Name	cmdExit
	Caption	E&xit

Program 8-1's Event and General Object Code

```
Rem: General Object Declarations
Option Explicit
Option Base 1
Const MAXGRADES As Integer = 6
Dim grades(MAXGRADES)  ' create an array with 5 elements

Private Sub cmdShow_Click()
  Rem: preconditions - MAXGRADES and grades() set at the module level
  Dim i As Integer
  For i = 1 To MAXGRADES  ' Enter the grades
  grades(i) = InputBox("Enter a grade", "Input Dialog", "0")
  Next i
```

continued

```
      For i = 1 To MAXGRADES       ' Print the grades
        Print "grades("; i; ") is "; grades(i)
      Next i
    End Sub

    Private Sub cmdExit_Click()
      Beep
      End
    End Sub
```

A sample run of Program 8-1 produced the output illustrated in Figure 8-3.

In reviewing the output produced by Program 8-1, pay particular attention to the difference between the index value displayed and the numerical value stored in the corresponding array element. The index value refers to the location of the element in the array, while the indexed variable refers to the value stored in the designated location.

In addition to simply displaying the values stored in each array element, the elements can also be processed by appropriately referencing the desired element. For example, assume that the cmdShow_Click event procedure in Program 8-1 is modified to Procedure Code 8-1.

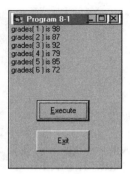

Figure 8-3
A Sample Output Using Program 8-1

Procedure Code 8-1

```
Private Sub cmdShow_Click()
    Rem: preconditions - MAXGRADES and grades() set at the module level
    Dim i As Integer
    Dim total As Integer
    Dim basestring As String
    Dim message As String

    basestring = "Enter grade "
    For i = 1 To MAXGRADES   ' Enter the grades
      message = basestring + Str(i)
      grades(i) = InputBox(message, "Input Dialog", "0")
    Next i

    Cls
    Print "The total of the grades"
    For i = 1 To MAXGRADES      ' Print the grades
      Print grades(i)
      total = total + grades(i)
    Next i
    Print "is"; total
End Sub
```

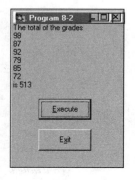

Figure 8-4
A Sample Output Using Program 8-2

In this modified code the value of each element is accumulated in a total, which is displayed after the display of each array element. Also notice in this event code that we have included an "individualized" message within the **InputBox** function by concatenating the string version of the index i to the output message. Thus, the message displayed in first input box will be Enter grade 1, the message displayed in the second input request will be Enter grade 2, and so on. This event code is used in Program 8-2, which is identical in all respects to Program 8-1, except for the form's caption and the new cmdShow_Click event procedure. A sample output produced by executing this event code is shown in Figure 8-4.

Notice that in the output displayed in Figure 8-4, unlike that shown in Figure 8-3, only the values stored in each array element are displayed.

Although the second **For** loop was used to accumulate the total of each element, the accumulation could also have been accomplished in the first loop by placing the statement `total = total + grades(i)` after the **InputBox** function was used to enter a value. Also notice that the **Print** used to display the total is made outside of the second **For** loop, so that the total is displayed only once, after all values have been added to the total. If this **Print** statement were placed inside of the **For** loop, six totals would be displayed, with only the last displayed total containing the sum of all of the array values.

The LBound and UBound Functions

Two useful Visual Basic functions that provide the smallest and largest available subscript value of an array, respectively, are the **LBound** and **UBound** functions. These function names are derived from the terms *Lower Bound* and *Upper Bound*. For example, if the array `test` is declared using the declaration statement

```
Dim test(10) As Integer
```

then `UBound(test)` will return a value of 10, and `LBound(test)` will return either a 0 or 1, depending on the setting or the **Option Base**. Similarly, for the declaration

```
Dim test(-5 to 7) As Integer
```

`UBound(test)` will return 7, and `LBound(test)` will return –5. These two functions are useful in processing array elements within **For** loops using the syntax

```
For i = LBound(array-name) To UBound(array-name)
    statement(s)
Next i
```

Exercises 8.1

1. Using the **Dim** keyword, write array declarations for the following:
   a. a list of 100 single-precision grades
   b. a list of 50 single-precision temperatures
   c. a list of 30 characters, each representing a code
   d. a list of 100 integer years
   e. a list of 32 single-precision velocities
   f. a list of 1000 single-precision distances
   g. a list of 6 integer code numbers

2. Write appropriate notation for the first, third, and seventh elements of the following arrays, assuming that the `Option Base 1` statement has been used.
   a. `Dim grade(20) As Integer`   d. `Dim distance(15) As Integer`
   b. `Dim grade(10) As Single`   e. `Dim velocity(25) As Single`
   c. `Dim amps(16) As Single`   f. `Dim time(100) As Single`

3. a. Write individual **InputBox** function calls that can be used to enter values into the first, third, and seventh elements of each of the arrays declared in Exercises 2a through 2f.
   b. Write a **For** loop that can be used to enter values for the complete array declared in Exercise 2a.

④ a. Write individual **Print** statements that can be used to print the values from the first, third, and seventh elements of each of the arrays declared in Exercises 2a through 2f.

b. Write a **For** loop that can be used to display values for the complete array declared in Exercise 2a.

⑤ List the elements that will be displayed by the following sections of code:

a.
```
For m = 1 To 5
   Print a(m)
Next m
```

b.
```
For  k = 1 To 5 Step 2
   Print  a(k)
Next k
```

c.
```
For j = 3 To 10 Step 1
   Print b(j)
Next j
```

d.
```
For  k = 3 To 12  Step 3
   Print b(k)
Next k
```

e.
```
For  i = 2 To  11 Step 2
   Print c(i )
Next i
```

⑥ a. Write a program to input the following values into an array named prices: 10.95, 16.32, 12.15, 8.22, 15.98, 26.22, 13.54, 6.45, 17.59. After the data has been entered, have your program output the values.

b. Repeat Exercise 6a, but after the data has been entered, have your program display it in the following form:

```
10.95   16.32   12.15
 8.22   15.98   26.22
13.54    6.45   17.59
```

⑦ Write a program to input eight integer numbers into an array named temp. As each number is input, add the numbers into a total. After all numbers are input, display the numbers and their average.

⑧ a. Write a program to input 10 integer numbers into an array named fmax and determine the maximum value entered. Your program should contain only one loop and the maximum should be determined as array element values are being input. (**Hint:** Set the maximum equal to the first array element, which should be input before the loop used to input the remaining array values.)

b. Repeat Exercise 8a, keeping track of both the maximum element in the array and the index number for the maximum. After displaying the numbers, print these two messages

```
The maximum value is: ___
This is element number ___ in the list of numbers
```

Have your program display the correct values in place of the underlines in the messages.

c. Repeat Exercise 8b, but have your program locate the minimum of the data entered.

⑨ a. Write a program to input the following integer numbers into an array named grades: 89, 95, 72, 83, 99. As each number is input, add the numbers to a total. After all numbers are input and the total is obtained, calculate the average of the numbers and use the average to determine the deviation of each value from the average. Store each deviation in an array named `deviation`. Each deviation is obtained as the element value less the average of all the data. Have your program display each deviation alongside its corresponding element from the `grades` array.

b. Calculate the variance of the data used in Exercise 9a. The variance is obtained by squaring each individual deviation and dividing the sum of the squared deviations by the number of deviations.

10 Write a program that stores the following prices in an array named `prices`: 9.92, 6.32, 12.63, 5.95, 10.29. Your program should also create two arrays named `units` and `amounts`, each capable of storing five double-precision numbers. Using a **For** loop and an **InputBox** function call, have your program accept five user-input numbers into the `units` array when the program is run. Your program should store the product of the corresponding values in the `prices` and `units` arrays in the `amounts` array (for example, `amounts(1) = prices(1) * units(1)`) and display the following output (fill in the table appropriately).

```
Price   Units   Amount
-----   -----   ------
 9.92     .       .
 6.32     .       .
12.63     .       .
 5.95     .       .
10.29     .       .
                ------
Total:            .
```

11 Write a program that specifies three one-dimensional arrays named `prices`, `quantity`, and `amount`. Each array should be capable of holding 10 elements. Using a **For** loop, input values for the `prices` and `quantity` arrays. The entries in the `amount` array should be the product of the corresponding values in the `prices` and `quantity` arrays (thus, `amount(i) = price(i) * quantity(i)`). After all the data has been entered, display the following output:

```
Price   Quantity    Amount
-----   --------    ------
```

Under each column heading, display the appropriate value.

12 a. Write a program that inputs 10 float numbers into an array named `raw`. After 10 user-input numbers are entered into the array, your program should cycle through `raw` 10 times. During each pass through the array, your program should select the lowest value in `raw` and place the selected value in the next available slot in an array named `sorted`. Thus, when your program is complete, the `sorted` array should contain the numbers in `raw` in sorted order from lowest to highest. (**Hint:** Make sure to reset the lowest value selected during each pass to a very high number so that it is not selected again. You will need a second **For** loop within the first **For** loop to locate the minimum value for each pass.)

> b. The method used in Exercise 12a to sort the values in the array is very inefficient. Can you determine why? What might be a better method of sorting the numbers in an array?

8.2 Additional Array Capabilities

The sizes of all the arrays we have considered have been declared at design time. There are times, however, when you might want to set the array size during run time based on user input, rather than at design time. How this is done is described in this section. Also described is the method for passing local arrays into procedures as arguments. Finally, additional array processing techniques are presented, including the declaration and processing of multi-dimensional arrays.

Dynamic Arrays

There are times when you, as a designer, will not know how large an array must be. Fortunately, Visual Basic provides a means of changing an array's size at run time. Such arrays are referred to as *dynamic arrays*. A dynamic array can be resized at any time during program execution. For example, you might need a very large array for a short period of time. Rather than allocate a fixed array size that will remain in effect throughout the program's execution, you can create a dynamic array. Then, when you no longer need the array, you can redimension it to a smaller size.

The method for creating a dynamic array is rather simple. First, in the **Declarations** section of the (**General**) code object, declare the array using either the **Public** or **Dim** keyword, to give the array either a project or module level scope, respectively. Alternatively, if you want the array to be local to a particular procedure, declare it using either the **Dim** or **Static** keyword within a procedure. The key, however, is to give the array an empty dimension value. For example, the declaration

```
Dim Dynar() As Integer
```

creates an integer dynamic array named Dynar. To actually set the size of the array you must use the **ReDim** statement, which can only appear within a procedure. The **ReDim** statement is an executable statement that redimensions the size of the array at run time. For example, the statements:

```
n = InputBox("Enter the number of grades", "Input Dialog", "0")
ReDim Dynar(n)
```

will cause the Dynar array to have the number of elements entered by the user in response to the Input dialog request. Similarly, the statement:

```
ReDim Dynar(10)
```

causes the Dynar array to be redimensioned to accommodate 10 integers.

Unless specific steps are taken to preserve the values in a dynamic array, these values will be lost when the array is redimensioned. If you want to resize an array without losing the existing element values, use the **Preserve** keyword. Thus, the statement

```
ReDim Preserve Dynar(UBound(Dynar) + 15)
```

enlarges the Dynar array by 15 elements, without losing the existing element values.

Arrays as Arguments

An individual array element can be passed to a general procedure (**Sub** and **Function**) in the same manner as any scalar variable. For a single array element this is done by including the element as an indexed variable in a **Call** statement's argument list. For example, the procedure call

```
Call Fmax(temp(2),temp(5))
```

makes the individual array elements temp(2) and temp(5) available to the Fmax procedure.

Passing a complete array to a procedure is, in many respects, an easier operation than passing individual elements. For example, if temp is an array, the statement Call Fmax(temp) makes the complete temp array available to the Fmax procedure.

On the receiving side, the called procedure must be alerted that an array is being made available. For example, assuming temp was declared as Dim temp(5) As Integer, a suitable procedure heading and parameter declaration for the Fmax procedure is

```
Public Sub Fmax(vals() As Integer)
```

In this procedure heading, the parameter name vals is local to the procedure. However, vals refers to the original array created outside the procedure. This is made clear in Procedure Code 8-2, where the temp array that is declared local to the Form_Click event procedure is passed to the Fmax procedure.

Procedure Code 8-2

```
Private Sub Form_Click()
  Dim temp(5) As Integer

  temp(1) = 2
  temp(2) = 18
  temp(3) = 1
  temp(4) = 27
  temp(5) = 6
  Call Fmax(temp)
End Sub

Public Sub Fmax(vals() As Integer)
  Dim i As Integer, max As Integer

  max = vals(1)
  For i = 2 To 5
    If max < vals(i) Then max = vals(i)
  Next i
  Print "The maximum value is"; maximum
End Sub
```

Only one array is created in Procedure Code 8-2. In the Form_Click procedure this array is known as temp, and in Fmax, the array is known as vals. As illustrated in Figure 8-5, both names refer to the same array. Thus, in Figure 8-5 vals(3) is the same element as temp(3).

Figure 8-5
Only One Array Is Created

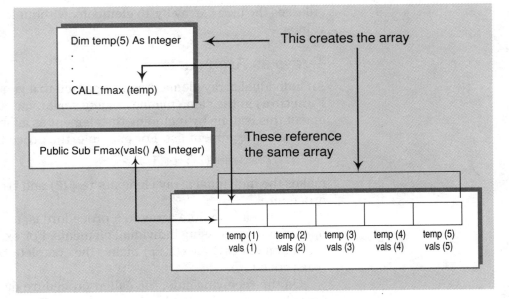

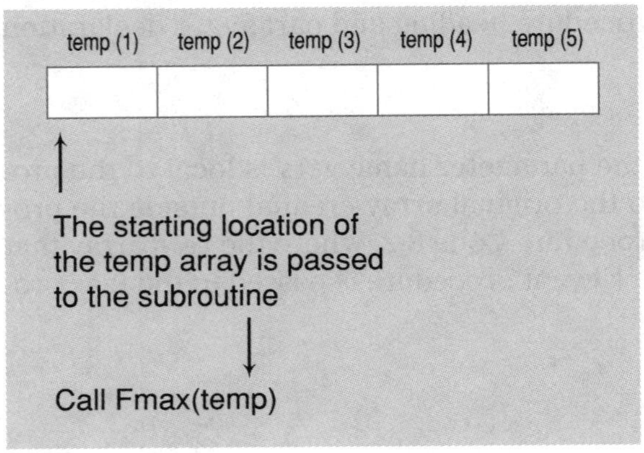

Figure 8-6
The Starting Location of the Array
Is Passed

Notice that the parameter declaration for vals in Fmax does not contain the number of elements in the array. This makes sense when you realize that only one item is actually passed to Fmax when the procedure is called. As you might have suspected, the item passed is the starting location of the temp array. This is illustrated in Figure 8-6.

Now let us generalize Fmax to find and return the maximum value of an integer array of arbitrary size. Consider Procedure Code 8-3.

Procedure Code 8-3

```
Private Sub Form_Click()
  Const NUMELS As Integer = 5
  Dim temp(NUMELS) As Integer
  Dim maximum As Integer

  temp(1) = 2
  temp(2) = 18
  temp(3) = 1
  temp(4) = 27
  temp(5) = 6
  Call Fmax(temp, NUMELS, maximum)
  Print "The maximum value is"; maximum
End Sub

Public Sub Fmax(vals() As Integer, final As Integer, max As Integer)
  Dim i As Integer, max As Integer

  max = vals(1)
  For i = 2 To final
    If max < vals(i) Then max = vals(i)
  Next i
End Sub
```

The more general form of Fmax listed in Procedure Code 8-3 returns the maximum value in any single-dimensioned integer array passed to it. The procedure expects that an integer array and the number of elements in the array will be passed into it as arguments. Then, using the number of elements as the boundary for its search, the procedure's **For** loop causes each array element to be examined in sequential order to locate the maximum value. This value is passed back to the calling routine through the third argument in the function call. The output displayed when the code is executed is

```
The maximum value is 27
```

Multi-Dimensional Arrays

In addition to one-dimensional arrays, Visual Basic provides the capability of defining and using larger array sizes. A *two-dimensional* array consists of both rows and columns of elements. For example, the array of numbers

8	16	9	52
3	15	27	6
14	25	2	10

is called a two-dimensional array of integers. This array consists of three rows and four columns. To reserve storage for this array, both the number of rows and the number of columns must be included in the array's declaration. For example, the declaration

```
Dim vals(3, 4) As Integer
```

specifies that vals is a two-dimensional array having 3 rows and 4 columns.[4] Similarly, the declarations

```
Dim volts(10,5) As Single
Dim code (6,26) As String *4
```

specify that the array volts consists of 10 rows and 5 columns of single-precision numbers and that the array code consists of 6 rows and 26 columns, with each element capable of holding 4 characters.

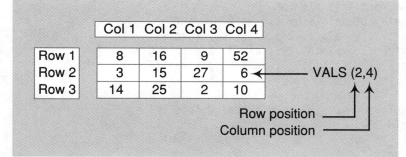

Figure 8-7

Each Array Element Is Identified by Its Row and Column Position

To make it possible to locate an element in a two-dimensional array, each element is identified by its position in the array. As illustrated in Figure 8-7, the term vals(2,4) uniquely identifies the element in row 2, column 4. As with one-dimensional array variables, two-dimensional array variables can be used anywhere that scalar variables are valid. Examples using elements of the vals array are

```
watts = vals(2,3)
vals(1,1) = 62
newnum = 4 * (vals(2,1) - 5)
sumrow1 = vals(1,1) + vals(1,2) + vals(1,3) + vals(1,4)
```

The last statement causes the values of the four elements in row 1 to be added and the sum to be stored in the scalar variable sumrow1.

As with one-dimensional arrays, two-dimensional arrays can be declared either at the project, module, or procedure level. Additionally, as with one-

---

[4]This assumes **Option Base** has been set to 1. The more general declaration syntax is **Dim** array-name(n1 To n2, m1 To m2), where n1 and m1 represent the lower bounds, and n2 and m2 represent the upper bounds on the first and second index values, respectively.

dimensional arrays, two-dimensional array elements are processed and displayed using individual element notation, as illustrated in Procedure Code 8-4.

Procedure Code 8-4

```
Rem: This code is in the [General] object's [declaration section]
Option Explicit
Option Base 1
Const ROWS As Integer = 3
Const COLS As Integer = 4
Dim vals(ROWS, COLS) As Integer

Rem: This is a [General] procedure used to initialize the array
Private Sub setvals()
    vals(1, 1) = 10
    vals(1, 2) = 20
    vals(1, 3) = 30
    vals(1, 4) = 40
    vals(2, 1) = 15
    vals(2, 2) = 25
    vals(2, 3) = 35
    vals(2, 4) = 54
    vals(3, 1) = 50
    vals(3, 2) = 60
    vals(3, 3) = 70
    vals(3, 4) = 80
End Sub

Private Sub Form_Click()
    Dim i As Integer, j As Integer
    Call setvals
    Cls
    Rem: display by explicit element
        Print "Display of vals() by explicit element"
        Print vals(1, 1); vals(1, 2); vals(1, 3); vals(1, 4)
        Print vals(2, 1); vals(2, 2); vals(2, 3); vals(2, 4)
        Print vals(3, 1); vals(3, 2); vals(3, 3); vals(3, 4)
    Rem: Display using a nested loop
        Print
        Print "Display of vals() using a nested loop"
        For i = 1 To ROWS
          For j = 1 To COLS
            Print vals(i, j);
          Next j
        Print
        Next i
End Sub
```

Following is the display produced when Procedure Code 8-4 is executed:

```
Display of vals() by explicit element
10   20   30   40
15   25   35   45
50   60   70   89
Display of vals() using a nested loop
10   20   30   40
15   25   35   45
50   60   70   89
```

The first display of the vals array produced by Procedure Code 8-4 is constructed by explicitly designating each array element. The second display of array element values, which is identical to the first, is produced using a nested **For** loop. Nested loops are especially useful when dealing with two-dimensional arrays, because they allow the programmer to easily designate and cycle through each element. In Procedure Code 8-4, the variable i controls the outer loop and the variable j controls the inner loop. Each pass through the outer loop corresponds to a single row, with the inner loop supplying the appropriate column elements. After a complete column is printed, a new line is started for the next row. The effect is a display of the array in a row-by-row fashion.

Once two-dimensional array elements have been assigned to an array, processing can begin. Typically, **For** loops are used to process two-dimensional arrays because, as was previously noted, they allow the programmer to easily designate and cycle through each array element. For example, the nested **For** loop in the following code is used to multiply each element in the vals array by the scalar number 10.

```
For i = 1 To ROWS
  For j = 1 To COLS
    vals(i,j) = 10 * vals(i,j)
  Next j
Next i
```

Although arrays with more than two dimensions are not commonly used, Visual Basic does allow larger arrays to be declared. This can be done by listing the maximum size of all indices for the array. For example, the declaration response(4, 10, 6) specifies a three-dimensional array. Assuming the **Option Base** has been set to 1, the first element in the array is designated as response(1,1,1) and the last element as response(4,10,6).[5]

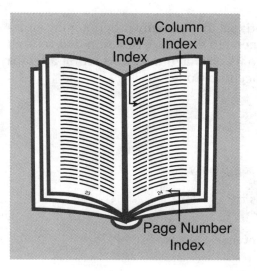

Conceptually, as illustrated in Figure 8-8, a three-dimensional array can be viewed as a book of data tables. Using this visualization, the first index can be thought of as the location of the desired row in a table, the second index value as the desired column, and the third index value as the page number of the selected table.

Similarly, arrays having at most sixty dimensions can be declared. Conceptually, a four-dimensional array can be represented as a shelf of books, where the fourth dimension is used to specify a desired book on the shelf, and a five-dimensional array can be viewed as a bookcase filled with books where the fifth dimension refers to a selected shelf in the bookcase. Using the same analogy, a six-dimensional array can be considered as a single row of bookcases where the sixth dimension references the desired bookcase in the row. Finally, a seven-dimensional array can be considered as multiple rows of bookcases where the seventh dimension references the desired row. Alternatively, three-, four-, five-, six-, and seven-dimensional arrays can be viewed as mathematical *n*-tuples of order three, four, five, six, and seven, respectively.

Figure 8-8
Representation of a Three-Dimensional Array

Passing Multi-Dimensional Arrays

Multi-dimensional arrays can be passed as arguments in a process identical to passing one-dimensional arrays. The called procedure receives access to the entire array. For example, consider Procedure Code 8-5.

---

[5]Again, as with single- and double-dimensioned arrays, both the lower and upper bounds of each index can be specified in the declaration statement for larger dimensioned arrays.

Procedure Code 8-5

```
Private Sub Form_Click()
  Dim vals(2, 2) As Integer
  vals(1, 1) = 10
  vals(1, 2) = 20
  vals(2, 1) = 30
  vals(2, 2) = 40
  Call average(vals)
End Sub

Private Sub show(nums() As Integer)
  Dim i As Integer, j As Integer
  Print nums(1, 1)
  Print nums(1, 2)
  Print nums(2, 1)
  Print nums(2, 2)
End Sub
```

Only one array is created in Procedure Code 8-5. This array is known as vals in the calling procedure and as nums in the show procedure. Thus, vals(1,2) refers to the same element as nums(1,2). The following display is produced when this procedure code is executed:

```
10
20
30
40
```

Arrays and Strings

Arrays and strings are frequently used together in many programming situations. For example, assume that we need to develop a function that returns the day of the week corresponding to its ordinal number. As a first attempt at solving this problem, consider Procedure Code 8-6.

Procedure Code 8-6

```
Private Sub Form_Click()
  Dim thisday As String
  Dim d As Integer
  d = InputBox("Enter a day (ex. 1 for Sunday)")
  thisday = Dayname(d)
  Print "This corresponds to "; thisday
End Sub

Public Function Dayname(dayint As Integer) As String
  Dim days(7) As String * 3

  days(1) = "Sun"
  days(2) = "Mon"
  days(3) = "Tue"
  days(4) = "Wed"
  days(5) = "Thu"
  days(6) = "Fri"
  days(7) = "Sat"
  Dayname = days(dayint)
End Function
```

The function Dayname listed in Procedure Code 8-6 uses an array of strings to store the seven day names, and selects the correct day, using each day's ordinal value as an index into the days array. While this solution works, we can actually do much better by considering the string data as a single array of characters. Using this conceptualization, the day name data is incorporated into a single days string as follows:

```
days ="SunMonTueWedThuFriSat"
```

In this string each group of three characters constitutes a day's name and the complete string is simply a convenient way of holding seven individual pieces of data. To extract any single name requires knowing the starting index position of the beginning letter and then extracting three characters from this position. For example, the expression Mid(days,4,3) extracts the characters Mon, starting from position 4 in the days string. Procedure Code 8-7 illustrates how this expression can be used within the Dayname function to locate and return the correct day.

Procedure Code 8-7

```
Private Sub Form_Click()
  Dim thisday As String
  Dim d As Integer

  d = InputBox("Enter a day (ex. 1 for Sunday)")
  thisday = Dayname(d)
  Print "This corresponds to "; thisday
End Sub

Public Function Dayname(dayint As Integer) As String
  Const DAYLENGTH As Integer = 3
  Dim days As String

  days = "SunMonTueWedThuFriSat"
  Dayname = Mid(days, DAYLENGTH * (dayint - 1) + 1, DAYLENGTH)
End Function
```

Notice that the starting index value into the string is determined by the expression DAYLENGTH * (dayint - 1) + 1, where DAYLENGTH is a named constant having a value of 3 and is the length of each day's name. Once the starting position is located, the next three characters are extracted. In using strings in this manner, the "trick" is always determining an expression that correctly locates the effective starting index value.

Arrays and Variants

Array elements can be of any type, including **Variants**, which we will consider shortly. First, however, we will create a **Variant** that contains an array. Although this is conceptually different from an array whose elements are of type **Variant**, the way that elements are accessed is the same. For example, consider the following code:

```
Dim A As Variant, B As Integer
A = Array(10, 20, 30, 40)
B = A(3)
A(4) = 50
```

Notice that A is a scalar variable of type **Variant**. The **Array** function is an intrinsic Visual Basic function that returns a **Variant** *containing* an array. Thus, the statement A = Array(10, 20, 30, 40) assigns an array of 4 integers to the variable A. At this point, A can be processed as a typical array. Thus, in the third statement we access an element from the Variant array and assign its value to the scalar variable B, while the last statement uses standard array notation to alter an element's value.

A very useful structure in connection with **Variant** variables is the **For Each** loop having the syntax

```
For Each element In variant-variable
    statement(s)
Next element
```

As an example using this repetition statement, consider Procedure Code 8-8.

Procedure Code 8-8

```
Private Sub Form_Click()
  Dim item As Variant
  Dim A As Variant
  Dim total As Single

  A = Array(10, 20, 30, 40)
  For Each item In A
    total = total + item
  Next item
  Print "The total is"; total
End Sub
```

The output produced by Procedure Code 8-8 is

```
The total is 100
```

The advantage of using a **For Each**, rather than a **For/Next** loop, is that the exact number of elements in the array need not be known. The disadvantage is that it requires an additional variable that must be a **Variant** data type. The loop itself, however, is not restricted to **Variant** arrays. For example, in Procedure Code 8-9 a **For Each** loop is used to cycle through an array of integers.

Having constructed a single **Variant** variable as an array using the **Array** function, as in Procedure Code 8-8, we can extend this concept by making each array element an array. For example, consider Procedure Code 8-10.

Procedure Code 8-9

```
Private Sub Form_Click()
  Const NUMELS As Integer = 4
  Dim item As Variant
  Dim a(NUMELS) As Integer
  Dim total As Single

  a(1) = 10
  a(2) = 20
  a(3) = 30
  a(4) = 40
  For Each item In a
    total = total + item
  Next item
  Print "The total is"; total
End Sub
```

Procedure Code 8-10

```
Private Sub Form_Click()
  Const NUMELS As Integer = 3
  Dim unit As Variant
  Dim bowler(NUMELS) As Variant
  Dim total As Single
  Dim i As Integer, j As Integer

  Cls
  bowler(1) = Array("Abrams, B.", 180, 219, 210)
  bowler(2) = Array("Bohm, P.", 155, 250, 207)
  bowler(3) = Array("Ernst, T.", 195, 245, 235)

  For i = 1 To 3
    total = 0
    Print "Bowler: "; bowler(i)(1)
    For j = 2 To 4
      total = total + bowler(i)(j)
    Next j
    Print "  Average Score:"; total / 3
  Next i
End Sub
```

In this code we have constructed an array of three **Variants**, each of which contains an array. The outer loop accesses each **Variant** element, while the inner loop accesses individual elements within each **Variant**. Notice, however, the unusual notation. For example, `bowler(1)` refers to the first **Variant** array. Within this array, the notation `bowler(1)(1)` refers to the first element, which is the name `Abrams, B`. Effectively, we have produced a one-dimensional array of one-dimensional arrays.

The **For** loop in Procedure Code 8-10 can be replaced by the following, which uses an **If** statement to determine the type of element being processed:

```
For i = 1 To 3
  total = 0
  For Each unit In bowler(i)
    If IsNumeric(unit) Then
      total = total + Val(unit)
    Else
      Print "Bowler: "; unit
    End If
  Next unit
  Print "  Average Score:"; total / 3
Next i
```

In using **Variant** variables, you should be aware of the following considerations:

1. A **Variant** variable has an **Empty** value before it is assigned a value. This is a special value, different from either the number 0 or the zero-length string " ".

2. A **Variant** with an **Empty** value can still be used in an expression. Depending on the context, it will be treated either as a 0 or zero-length string.

3. The **Empty** value disappears as soon as a value is assigned to the **Variant**.

4. A **Variant** variable can be set back to an **Empty** value by assigning the keyword **Empty** to the variable.

5. A **Variant** variable can also be assigned the named constant **Null**.

6. The **IsNull** function can be used to test if a **Variant** variable contains the **Null** value.

7. The **VarType** function can be used to test the type of value in a **Variant** or any variable, except for a user-defined type. This function is typically used within an **If** statement

```
If VarType(variable) = constant Then
  statement(s)
End If
```

where **constant** is one of the named constants listed in Table 8-5.

The named constants listed in Table 8-5 are specified by Visual Basic and can be used in any procedure code.

Table 8-5 VarType Function Return Values

Constant	Value	Variable Argument's Data Type
vbEmpty	0	Empty (uninitialized)
vbNull	1	Null (no valid data)
vbInteger	2	Integer
vbLong	3	Long integer
vbSingle	4	Single-precision floating-point number
vbDouble	5	Double-precision floating-point number
vbCurrency	6	Currency
vbDate	7	Date
vbString	8	String
vbObject	9	Ole object
vbError	10	Error
vbBoolean	11	Boolean
vbVariant	12	Variant (used only with arrays of Variants)
vbDataObject	13	Non-OLE object
vbByte	17	Byte
vbArray	8192	Array

Exercises ▶ 8.2

1. Modify the Fmax procedure in Procedure Code 8-3 to locate and return the minimum value of the passed array.

2. Write a program that stores the following numbers into a local array named grades: 65.3, 72.5, 75.0, 83.2, 86.5, 94.0, 96.0, 98.8, 100. There should be a procedure call to show that accepts the grades array as a parameter named grades and then displays the numbers in the array.

3. Write a program that declares three one-dimensional arrays named price, quantity, and amount. Each array should be capable of holding 5 single-precision numbers. The numbers that should be stored in price are 10.62, 14.89, 13.21, 16.55, 18.62. The numbers that should be stored in quantity are 4, 8.5, 6, 7.35, 9. Your program should pass these three arrays to a procedure called extend, which should calculate the elements in the amount array as the product of the equivalent elements in the price and quantity arrays (for example, amount(1) = price(1) * quantity(1)). After extend has put values into the amount array, the values in the array should be displayed from within the procedure that called extend.

4. Write a program that includes two functions named average and variance. The average function should calculate and return the average of the values stored in an array named testvals. The testvals array should be declared as a local array and include the

values 89, 95, 72, 83, 99, 86. The `variance` function should calculate and return the variance of the data. The variance is obtained by subtracting the average from each value in `testvals`, squaring the values obtained, adding them, and dividing by the number of elements in `testvals`. The values returned from `average` and `variance` should be displayed from within the procedure that called these functions.

5. Write appropriate declaration statements for
   a. an array of integers with 6 rows and 10 columns named `nums`
   b. an array of integers with 2 rows and 5 columns named `nums`
   c. an array of single characters with 7 rows and 12 columns named `codes`
   d. an array of single characters with 15 rows and 7 columns named `codes`
   e. an array of single-precision numbers with 10 rows and 25 columns named `vals`
   f. an array of single-precision numbers with 16 rows and 8 columns named `vals`

6. Write a Visual Basic function that can be used to add the values of all elements in the `nums` array used in Exercise 5a and returns the total.

7. Write a Visual Basic program that adds equivalent elements of the two-dimensional arrays named `first` and `second`. Both arrays should have two rows and three columns. For example, element (1,2) of the resulting array should be the sum of `first(1,2)` and `second(1,2)`. The `first` and `second` arrays should be initialized as follows:

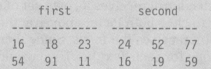

```
    first           second
 -------------   -------------
 16   18   23    24   52   77
 54   91   11    16   19   59
```

8. a. Write a Visual Basic program that finds and displays the maximum value in a two-dimensional array of integers. The array should be declared as a two-by-three array of integers and initialized with the following numbers: 16, 22, 99, 4, 18, –258.
   b. Modify the program written in Exercise 8a so that it also displays the maximum value's row and column index values.

9. Write a procedure that multiplies each element of a three-row-by-four-column array by a scalar number. Both the array name and the number by which each element is to be multiplied are to be passed into the procedure as parameters.

10. Modify Procedure Code 8-7 so that the complete name of each day is returned. **Hint:** You will have to make `DAYLENGTH` equal to the length of the longest day name.

11. Write a function named `Moname` that returns a month's name corresponding to the integer that represents the month. Use the string `months = "JanFebMarAprMayJunJulAugSepOctNovDec"` in your function.

12. a. Write a function named `Seasons` that returns a season's name corresponding to the integer representing the season. Use the

relationship that the numbers 1, 2, 3, and 4 correspond to the seasons Winter, Spring, Summer, and Autumn, respectively.

b. Modify the function written for Exercise 12a so that it returns the season corresponding to each month. Use the following assignments:

Months	**Season**
Dec, Jan, Feb	Winter
Mar, Apr, May	Spring
Jun, Jul, Aug	Summer
Sep, Oct, Nov	Autumn

Hint: Convert the month to an equivalent season using the expression (m Mod 12) / 3 + 1.

8.3 ▶ Control Arrays

Just as variables of the same data type can be grouped in an array, a set of controls having the same type can also be grouped as an array of controls.

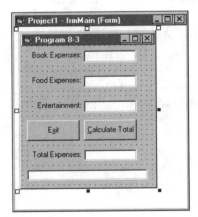

Figure 8-9
Program 8-3's Design-Time
Interface

When this is done, a group of controls is referred to as a *control array*. Each control in the array shares the common group name, and individual controls are distinguished by an index number. Using control arrays can save coding because all the controls in the array share the same event procedures as well as the same group name. To see how this works in practice, consider the design-time interface shown in Figure 8-9 (Properties Table on page 408).

If each Text box in Program 8-3's interface is given a unique name, then each control receives its own set of event codes. Let's assume that we want to clear both Picture boxes at the bottom of the form whenever a Text box receives the focus. Since there are three sets of **GotFocus** events (one for each Text box), we would have to code each event separately. Assuming the Picture boxes are named `picTotal` and `picError`, respectively, we would either have to include the two statements

```
picTotal.Cls
picError.Cls
```

in each Text box's **GotFocus** event procedure, or include these statements in a general procedure and place a call to this procedure in each Text box's **GotFocus** event procedure. Another solution is to give all three Text boxes the same name. When this is done the **Index** property of the first box gets automatically set to 0, the second box gets an **Index** value of 1, and the third an **Index** value of 2 (by default, each of these boxes has an initial **Index** property that is blank). Once a control has an **Index** value, it is accessed by giving both its **Name** and **Index** value (with the **Index** enclosed in parentheses). For example, assuming that the Text boxes in Figure 8-9 are all named `txtExpense`, then

```
txtExpense(0) refers to the Text box with Index value 0
txtExpense(1) refers to the Text box with Index value 1
txtExpense(2) refers to the Text box with Index value 2
```

All of these Text boxes now share the same name but have a unique **Index** property value used to distinguish one element of the control array from another. Each time one of the controls in the group activates an event,

Visual Basic calls a common event procedure and passes the **Index** value as an argument. It is this **Index** value that identifies which control triggered the event. For example, the header line for the `txtExpense_GotFocus` event procedure is

```
Private Sub txtExpense_GotFocus(Index As Integer)
```

Thus, if the first Text box gets the focus, Visual Basic passes 0 to the **Index** parameter, if the second Text box gets the focus, a 1 is passed to the **Index** parameter, and so on. This **Index** parameter can then be used or not, as required, within the event procedure. In our application, for example, we will want to clear both Picture boxes, no matter which Text box receives the focus. So for this application the **GotFocus** event procedure will not need to distinguish between Text boxes. The code that we will use for this event is

```
Private Sub txtExpense_GotFocus(Index As Integer)
  picError.Cls
  picTotal.Cls
End Sub
```

The advantage here is that we have written one event code that is shared by three controls. In a similar manner, we will want to call an input validation procedure whenever the (ENTER) key is pressed. Again, one event procedure will suffice for all three Text boxes in the control array. The code that we will use is

```
Private Sub txtExpense_KeyPress(Index As Integer, KeyAscii As Integer)
  If KeyAscii = ENTER Then
    Call CheckVal(txtExpense(Index).Text, Index)
  End If
End Sub
```

The header line for this event code is supplied by Visual Basic, and since we are using Text boxes that have the same name, the **Index** value of the Text box from which the **KeyPress** was activated is passed into the event procedure. In this case we first use the **Index** parameter within the event procedure to locate the correct Text value using the expression `txtExpense(Index).Text`. This **Text** value and the **Index** value are then used as arguments in the call to `CheckVal`. Thus, if the **KeyPress** event was activated from the first Text box, the arguments sent to `CheckVal` are `txtExpense(0).Text` and 0. Similarly, when the **KeyPress** event is triggered from the second Text box, the arguments `txtExpense(1).Text` and 1 are sent to `CheckVal`. Finally, when the **KeyPress** event is triggered from the third Text box, the arguments `txtExpense(2).Text` and 2 are sent to `CheckVal`. This event code is incorporated into Program 8-3. Table 8-6 provides the program's Properties table.

Program 8-3's Event and General Object Code

```
Rem: These are (General) declarations
Option Explicit
Const ENTER As Integer = 13 ' ANSI value of the ENTER key

Private Sub txtExpense_GotFocus(Index As Integer)
  picError.Cls
  picTotal.Cls
End Sub

Private Sub txtExpense_KeyPress(Index As Integer, KeyAscii As Integer)
  If KeyAscii = ENTER Then
```

continued

```
            Call CheckVal(txtExpense(Index).Text, Index)
        End If
End Sub

Private Sub cmdTotal_Click()
  Dim i As Integer
  Dim total As Single

  For i = 0 To 2
    total = total + Val(txtExpense(i).Text)
  Next i
  picTotal.Print Format(total, "Currency")
End Sub

Private Sub CheckVal(s1 As String, fromwhere As Integer)
  If Not (IsNumeric(s1)) Then
    picError.Print "Please enter a valid number"
  Else  ' a valid data was entered, so we shift the focus
    Select Case fromwhere
      Case 0, 1
        txtExpense(fromwhere + 1).SetFocus
      Case 2
        cmdTotal.SetFocus
    End Select
  End If
End Sub
```

Table 8-6   Program 8-3's Properties Table

Object	Property	Setting
Form	Name	frmMain
	Caption	Program 8-3
Text box	Name	txtExpense()
	Index	0 to 3
	Text	(blank)
	BackColor	White (Palette tab)
Command button	Name	cmdTotal
	Caption	&Calculate Total
Command button	Name	cmdExit
	Caption	E&xit
Picture box	Name	picError
	TabStop	False
	BackColor	White (Palette tab)
Picture box	Name	picTotal
	TabStop	False
	BackColor	White (Palette tab)
Label	Name	lblBooks
Label	Name	lblFood
Label	Name	lblEnt
Label	Name	lblTotal

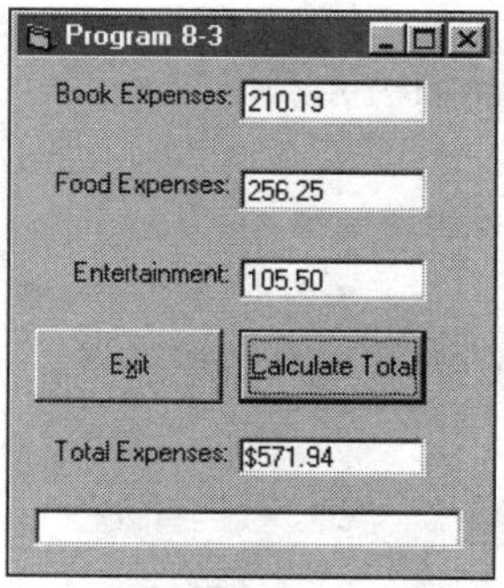

Figure 8-10

A Sample Output Using Program 8-3

The two event codes listed for Program 8-3 are the common procedures relating to the Text box control array that have already been discussed. Notice in the `cmdTotal_Click` event procedure that the total of the values in the Text boxes are obtained by cycling through each Text box's **Text** property, using a **For** loop and indexed Text box names. Finally, in the `CheckVal` general procedure notice, that the `fromwhere` parameter is used within the `Select Case` statement as an index value in the statement `txtExpense(fromwhere + 1).SetFocus`. The index expression `fromwhere + 1` identifies the next Text box in the control array from the Text box that activated the `CheckVal` procedure. Thus, if the parameter `fromwhere` is either 0 or 1, which identifies the current Text box that activated the general procedure, the focus will be set on the next Text box in the control array at either **Index** value 1 or 2, respectively. Figure 8-10 illustrates a sample run using Program 8-3.

Constructing Control Arrays

Any set of the same type of control can be made into a control array. Thus, you can make control arrays from Option buttons, Check boxes, Text boxes, Picture boxes, Labels, etc. In addition, control arrays can be constructed at either design- or run time. At design time a control array can be created by

1. Assigning the same name to more than one control, or
2. Setting the **Index** property of a control to an integer value, or
3. Copying an existing control and then pasting in back onto a form.

The easiest method is the third one, which can be performed using the following steps:

1. Create one control of the desired type on the form.
2. Set the **Name** property and any other property value that you want reproduced for all controls in the array.
3. Press CTRL+C to copy the control to the Clipboard.
4. Press CTRL+V to copy the control back onto the form—when the system displays a message box asking if you want to create a control array, answer Yes.
5. Repeat Step 4 to produce the desired number of control copies.

Using these steps, the first control will be assigned an **Index** property value of 0, and each new copy will have an **Index** property value that is incremented by 1.

Control arrays can also be added and removed at run time. To do so, however, you must have created at least one control at design time with its **Index** property set, usually to 0. New controls are added to the array, using the **Load** statement, which has the syntax

Load *objectname(index number)*

where *objectname* is the name of the control object and *index number* is the value that you want to assign to its **Index** property. To make the newly added control visible, you must subsequently set its **Visible** property to **True**. You will also have to set its **Left** and **Top** properties to correctly position the box on the form.

An existing control within a control array can be deleted at run time using the **UnLoad** statement, which has the syntax

UnLoad *objectname(index number)*

Exercises 8.3

1. Create a user interface that has three Command buttons—all members of the same control array.

2. Create a user interface that has four Labels—all members of the same control array.

3. Modify Program 8-3 so that the four Label and two Picture controls are members of their respective control arrays.

4. a. Create the user interface shown in Figure 8-11 so that the labels are in one control array, the four Text boxes in a second control array, and the Command buttons in a third control array.

   b. Write procedure code for the interface constructed in Exercise 4a, so that the program calculates a correct result based on the selected Command button.

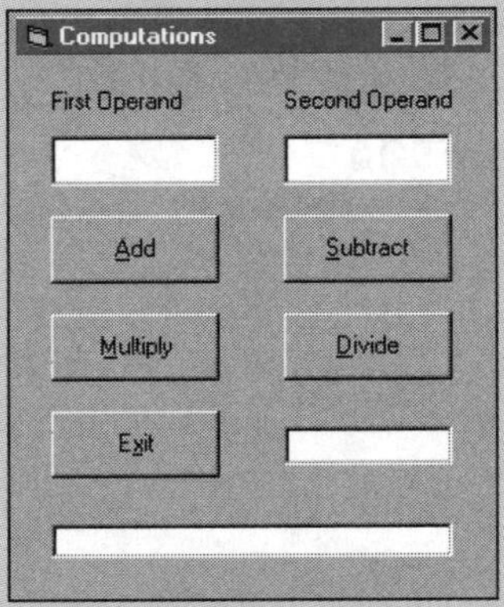

Figure 8-11

5. a. Create the user interface shown in Figure 8-12 so that the Option buttons are in one control array and the three Text boxes are in a second control array.

   b. Write procedure code for the interface constructed in Exercise 4a so that the program calculates the correct result based on the selected Option button.

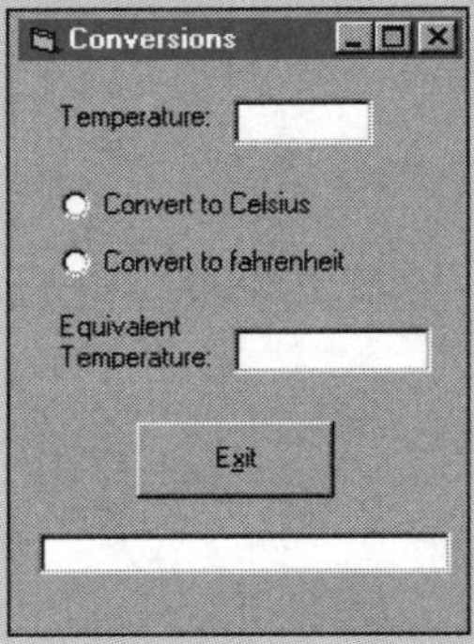

Figure 8-12

8.4 Structures

Name:
Type:
Location in Dungeon:
Strength Factor:
Intelligence Factor:
Type of Armor:

Figure 8-13
Typical Components of a Video Game Character

An array allows access to a list or table of data of the same data type, using a single variable name. At times, however, we may want to store information of varying types—such as a string name, an integer part number, and a real price—together in one structure. A data structure that stores different types of data under a single variable name is called a *record*.[6]

To make the discussion more tangible, consider data items that might be stored for a video game character, as illustrated in Figure 8-13.

Each of the individual data items listed in Figure 8-13 is an entity by itself, referred to as a *data field*. Taken together, all the data fields form a single unit, referred to as a *record*. In Visual Basic, a record is referred to as a *structure*.

---

[6]It should be noted that a single record can also be created using a **Variant** and the **Array** function, as described in Section 7.3. Similarly, an array of records can be created as an array of **Variants**.

Homogeneous and Heterogeneous Data Structures

Both arrays and records are structured data types. The difference between these two data structures is the types of elements they contain. An array is a homogeneous data structure, which means that each of its components must be of the same type. A record is a heterogeneous data structure, which means that each of its components can be of different data types. Thus, an array of records would be a homogeneous data structure whose elements are of the same heterogeneous type.

Name: Golgar
Type: Monster
Location in Dungeon: G7
Strength Factor: 78
Intelligence Factor: 15
Type of Armor: Chain Mail

Figure 8-14

The Form and Contents of a Record

Although there could be hundreds of characters in a video game, the form of each character's record is identical. In dealing with records, it is important to distinguish between a record's form and its contents.

A *record's form* consists of the symbolic names, data types, and arrangement of individual data fields in the record. The *record's contents* consists of the actual data stored in the symbolic names. Figure 8-14 shows acceptable contents for the record form illustrated in Figure 8-13.

Using a structure requires that the record must be created and variables declared to be of the new structure type. Then specific values can be assigned to individual variable elements. Creating a structure requires listing the data types, data names, and arrangement of data items. For example, the declaration

```
Type Birthdate
    month As Integer
    day As Integer
    year As Integer
End Type
```

creates a structure named `Birthdate` that consists of three data items or fields, called *members* of the structure.

The term `Birthdate` is a structure type name: It creates a new data type that is a data structure of the declared form. By convention the first letter of a user-selected data type name is uppercase, as in the name `Birthdate`, which helps to identify it as a data type when it is used in subsequent declaration statements. Here, the declaration for the `Birthdate` structure creates a new data type and describes how individual data items are arranged within the structure. To use a structure, you must declare variables of that type. For example, the declaration statement

```
Dim mybirthday As Birthdate
```

declares the variable `mybirthday` to be of type `Birthdate`. Assigning actual data values to the data items of a structure is called *populating* the structure, and is a relatively straightforward procedure. Each member of a structure is accessed by giving both the variable's name and individual data item name, separated by a period. Thus, `mybirthday.month` refers to the first member of the `mybirthday` structure, `mybirthday.day` refers to the second member of the structure, and `mybirthday.year` refers to the third member. Table 8-7 lists where structures may be created and the scoping rules for their declaring variables of a structure type.

The individual members of a structure are not restricted to integer data types, as illustrated by the `Birthdate` structure. Any valid Visual Basic data type can be used.

Table 8-7   Structure Creation and Declaration Scope

Procedure/Module	Creation of a Structure	Variable Declarations
Procedure	Not Permitted	Local only
Form Module	Private only	Private only
Standard Module	Private or Public	Private or Public
Class Module	Private only	Private only

For example, consider an employee record consisting of the following data items:

Name:
Identification Number:
Regular Pay Rate:
Overtime Pay Rate:

A suitable structure for these data items is

```
Type Payrec
  name As String *20
  idnum As Long
  regrte As Single
  otrate(3) As Single    ' this is an array of three elements
End Type
```

Before leaving single structures, it is worth noting that the individual members of a structure can be any valid Visual Basic data type, including both arrays and structures. For example, the otrate member of Payrec consists of an array. Accessing an element of a member array requires giving the structure's variable name, followed by a period, followed by the array designation. For example, if employee is of type Payrec, then employee.otrate(2) refers to the second value in the employee.otrate array.

Declaring an array of structures is the same as declaring an array of any other variable type. For example, an array of ten Payrec structures can be declared using the statement:

```
Dim employee(10) As Payrec
```

This declaration statement constructs an array named employee consisting of 10 elements (assuming **Option Base** is 1), each of which is a structure of the data type Payrec. Notice that the creation of an array of 10 structures has the same form as the creation of any other array. For example, creating an array of 10 integers named employee requires the declaration

```
Dim employee(10) As Integer
```

In this declaration the data type is Integer, while in the former declaration for employee the data type is Payrec. Once an array of structures is declared, a particular data item is referenced by giving the position of the desired structure in the array followed by a period and the appropriate structure member. For example, the variable employee(2).idnum references the idnum member of the second employee structure in the employee array.

Exercises 8.4

1. Declare a structure data type named `Stemp` for each of the following records:

   a. a student record consisting of a student identification number, number of credits completed, and cumulative grade point average

   b. a student record consisting of a student's name, birth date of type `Birthdate`, number of credits completed, and cumulative grade point average

   c. a mailing list consisting of a first name, last name, street address, city, state, and zip code

   d. a stock record consisting of the stock's name, the price of the stock, and the date of purchase

   e. an inventory record consisting of an integer part number, part description, number of parts in inventory, and an integer reorder number

2. For the individual data types declared in Exercise 1, define a suitable structure variable name, and initialize each structure with the appropriate following data:

   a. Identification Number: 4672
      Number of Credits Completed: 68
      Grade Point Average: 3.01

   b. Name: Rhona Karp
      Birth date: 8/4/60
      Number of Credits Completed: 96
      Grade Point Average: 3.89

   c. Name: Kay Kingsley
      Street Address: 614 Freeman Street
      City: Indianapolis
      State: IN
      Zip Code: 07030

   d. Stock: IBM
      Price Purchased: 134.5
      Date Purchased: 10/1/86

   e. Part Number: 16879
      Description: Battery
      Number in Stock: 10
      Reorder Number: 3

3. a. Write a Visual Basic program that prompts a user to input the current month, day, and year. Store the data entered in a suitably defined record and display the date in an appropriate manner.

   b. Modify the program written in Exercise 3a to use a record that accepts the current time in hours, minutes, and seconds.

4. Write a Visual Basic program that uses a structure for storing the name of a stock, its estimated earnings per share, and its estimated price-to-earnings ratio. Have the program prompt the user to enter these items for five different stocks, each time using the same structure to store the entered data. When the data has been entered for a particular stock, have the program compute and display the anticipated stock price based on the entered earnings and

price-per-earnings values. For example, if a user entered the data XYZ 1.56 12, the anticipated price for a share of XYZ stock is (1.56)*(12) = $18.72.

(5) Write a Visual Basic program that accepts a user-entered time in hours and minutes. Have the program calculate and display the time one minute later.

(6) a. Write a Visual Basic program that accepts a user-entered date. Have the program calculate and display the date of the next day. For purposes of this exercise, assume that all months consist of 30 days.

  b. Modify the program written in Exercise 6a to account for the actual number of days in each month.

(7) Define arrays of 100 structures for each of the data types described in Exercise 1 of this section.

8.5 Searching and Sorting

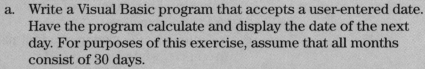

Most programmers encounter both the need to sort and search a list of data items at some time in their programming careers. For example, numerical data might have to be arranged in either increasing (ascending) or decreasing (descending) order for statistical analysis, lists of names may have to be sorted in alphabetical order, or a list of dates may have to be rearranged in ascending date order. Similarly, a list of names may have to be searched to find a particular name in the list, or a list of dates may have to be searched to locate a particular date. In this section we introduce the fundamentals of both sorting and searching lists. Although it is not necessary to sort a list before searching it, as we shall see, much faster searches are possible if the list is in sorted order.

Search Algorithms

A common requirement of many programs is to search a list for a given element. For example, in a list of names and telephone numbers, we might search for a specific name so that the corresponding telephone number can be printed, or we might wish to search the list simply to determine if a name is there. The two most common methods of performing such searches are the linear and binary search algorithms.

Linear Search

In a *linear search*, also known as a *sequential search*, each item in the list is examined in the order in which it occurs in the list until the desired item is found or the end of the list is reached. This is analogous to looking at every name in the phone directory, beginning with Aardvark, Aaron, until you find the one you want or until you reach Zzxgy, Zora. Obviously, this is not the most efficient way to search a long alphabetized list. However, a linear search has two advantages:

1. The algorithm is simple, and
2. The list need not be in any particular order.

In a linear search, the search begins at the first item in the list and continues sequentially, item by item, through the list. The pseudocode for a function performing a linear search is

> Set the location to a –1
> For all the items in the list
>   Compare the item with the desired item
>   If the item was found
>   Set the location to the index value of the current item
>   Exit the For loop
>   Endif
> EndFor
> Return the location

Notice that the return value indicates whether the item was found or not. If the return value is –1, the item was not in the list, otherwise, the return value within the **For** loop provides the index of where the item is located within the list. The function `linearSearch`, which is included in Program 8-4's procedure code, implements this linear search algorithm as a Visual Basic function. For testing purposes we have constructed the list as a **Variant** array (see Section 8.3).

Program 8-4's Event and General Object Code

```
Rem: This is the code contained in the [General] object section
Option Explicit
Option Base 1

Rem:  this function returns the location of key in the list
Rem: a -1 is returned if the value is not found
Public Function linearSearch(list As Variant, size As Integer, key As Integer) As Integer
    Dim i As Integer
    Dim location As Integer

  location = -1
  For i = 1 To size
    If list(i) = key Then
      location = i
        Exit For
    End If
  Next i
linearSearch = location
End Function

Private Sub cmdSearch_Click()
  Const NUMEL As Integer = 10
  Dim nums As Variant
  Dim item As Integer
  Dim location As Integer

  nums = Array(5, 10, 22, 32, 45, 67, 73, 98, 99, 101)

  item = Val(txtSearch.Text)
  location = linearSearch(nums, NUMEL, item)
  If location > -1 Then
    picSearch.Print "The item was found at index location "; location
```

continued

```
    Else
      picSearch.Print "The item was not found in the list"
    End If

Private Sub txtSearch_GotFocus()
    picSearch.Cls
End Sub

Private Sub cmdExit_Click()
    Beep
    End
End Sub
```

Figure 8-15

The Desired Item Is Found

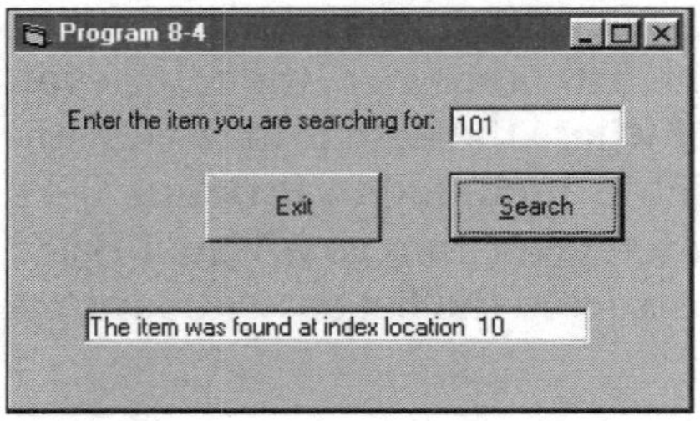

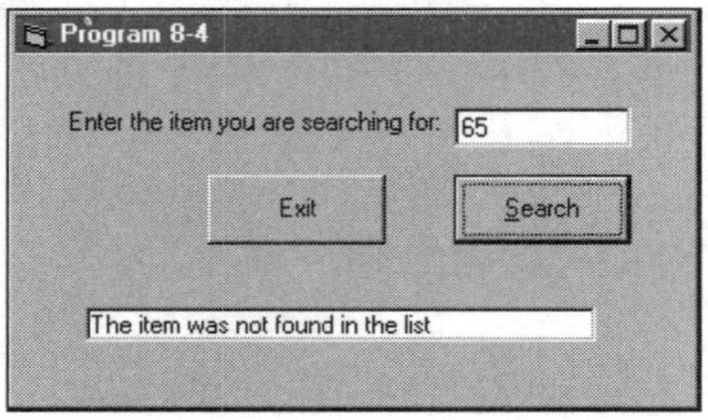

Figure 8-16

The Desired Item Is Not
in the List

In reviewing the `linearSearch` function, notice that the **For** loop is simply used to access each element in the list, from first element to last, until a match is found with the desired item. If the desired item is located, the index value of the current item is returned, which causes the loop to terminate; otherwise, the search continues until the end of the list is encountered. Two sample runs of Program 8-4 are illustrated in Figures 8-15 and 8-16, respectively.

As has already been pointed out, an advantage of linear searches is that the list does not have to be in sorted order to perform the search. Another advantage is that if the desired item is toward the front of the list, only a small number of comparisons will be done. The worst case, of course, occurs when the desired item is at the end of the list. On average, however, and assuming that the desired item is equally likely to be anywhere within the list, the number of required comparisons will be N/2, where N is the list's size. Thus, for a 10-element list, the average number of comparisons needed for a linear search is 5, and for a 10,000-element list, the average number of comparisons needed is 5000. As we show next, this number can be significantly reduced using a binary search algorithm.

Binary Search

In a *binary search*, the list must be in sorted order. Starting with an ordered list, the desired item is first compared to the element in the middle of the list. (For lists with an even number of elements, either of the two middle elements can be used.) Three possibilities present themselves once the comparison is made: the desired item may be equal to the middle element, it may be greater than the middle element, or it may be less than the middle element.

In the first case, the search has been successful, and no further searches are required. In the second case, since the desired item is greater than the middle element, if it is found at all, it must be in the bottom part of the list. This means that the upper part of the list, consisting of all elements from the first to the midpoint element, can be discarded from any further search. In the third case, since the desired item is less than the middle element, if it is found at all, it must be found in the upper part of the list. For this case, the bottom part of the list, containing all elements from the midpoint element to the last element, can be discarded from any further search.

The algorithm for implementing this search strategy is illustrated in Figure 8-15 and defined by the following pseudocode:

Set the lower index to 1
Set the upper index to the size of the list
Begin with the first item in the list

Do While the lower index is less than or equal to the upper index
Set the midpoint index to the integer average of the lower and upper index values
Compare the desired item to the midpoint element
If the desired element equals the midpoint element
Return the index value of the current item
Else If the desired element is greater than the midpoint element
Set the lower index value to the midpoint value plus 1
Else if the desired element is less than the midpoint element
Set the upper index value to the midpoint value less 1
Endif
End Do
Return –1 because the item was not found

As illustrated by both the pseudocode and the flowchart of Figure 8-17, a **Do While** loop is used to control the search. The initial list is defined by

Figure 8-17
The Binary Search Algorithm

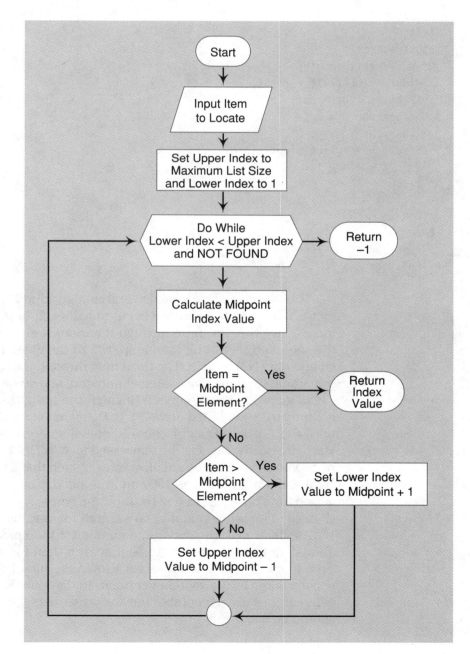

setting the lower Index value to 1 and the upper Index value to the number of elements in the list. The midpoint element is then taken as the integerized average of the lower and upper values. Once the comparison to the midpoint element is made, the search is subsequently restricted by moving either the lower Index to one integer value above the midpoint, or by moving the upper Index one integer value below the midpoint. This process is continued until the desired element is found or the lower and upper Index values become equal. The function binarySearch presents the Visual Basic version of this algorithm.

```
Rem: this function returns the location of key in the list
Rem: a -1 is returned if the value is not found
Public Function binarySearch(list As Variant, size As Integer, key As Integer) As Integer
   Dim left As Integer, right As Integer, midpt As Integer
   Dim location As Integer

   location = -1
   left = 1
   right = size
   Do While left <= right
     midpt = Int((left + right) / 2)
     If key = list(midpt) Then
       location = midpt
       Exit Do
     ElseIf key > list(midpt) Then
       left = midpt + 1
     Else
       right = midpt - 1
     End If
   Loop
     binarySearch = location
End Function
```

The value of using a binary search algorithm is that the number of elements that must be searched is cut in half each time through the **Do While** loop. Thus, the first time through the loop, N elements must be searched, the second time through the loop, N/2 of the elements have been eliminated and only N/2 remain. The third time through the loop, another half of the remaining elements have been eliminated, and so on.

In general, after p passes through the loop, the number of values remaining to be searched is $N/(2^p)$. In the worst case, the search can continue until there is less than or equal to one element remaining to be searched. Mathematically, this can be expressed as $N/(2^p) \leq 1$. Alternatively, this may be rephrased as p is the smallest integer such that $2^p \geq N$. For example, for a 1000-element array, N is 1000 and the maximum number of passes, p, required for a binary search is 10. Table 8-8 compares the number of loop passes needed for a linear and binary search for various list sizes.

As illustrated, the maximum number of loop passes for a 50-item list is almost 10 times more for a linear search than for a binary search, and is even more spectacular for larger lists. As a rule of thumb, 50 elements are usually taken as the switchover point: for lists smaller than 50 elements, linear searches are acceptable but for larger lists, a binary search algorithm should be used.

Table 8-8 A Comparison of Do While Loop Passes for Linear and Binary Searches

Array Size	10	50	500	5,000	50,000	500,000	5,000,000
Average Linear Search Passes	5	25	250	2,500	25,000	250,000	2,500,000
Maximum Linear Search Passes	10	50	500	5,000	50,000	500,000	5,000,000
Maximum Binary Search Passes	4	6	9	13	16	19	23

Big O Notation

On average, over a large number of linear searches with N items in a list, we would expect to examine half (N/2) of the items before locating the desired item. In a binary search the maximum number of passes, p, occurs when $N/2^p = 1$. This relationship can be algebraically manipulated to $2^p = N$, which yields $p = \log_2 N$, which approximately equals $3.33 \log_{10} N$.

For example, finding a particular name in an alphabetical directory with N = 1000 names would require an average of 500 (=N/2) comparisons using a linear search. With a binary search, only about 10 (= $3.33 * \log_{10} 1000$) comparisons would be required.

A common way to express the number of comparisons required in any search algorithm using a list of *N* items is to give the order of magnitude of the number of comparisons required, on average, to locate a desired item. Thus, the linear search is said to be of order N and the binary search of order $\log_2 N$. Notationally, this is expressed as O(N) and O($\log_2 N$), where the O is read as "the order of."

Sort Algorithms

For sorting data, two major categories of sorting techniques exist, called internal and external sorts, respectively. *Internal sorts* are used when the data list is not too large and the complete list can be stored within the computer's memory, usually in an array. *External sorts* are used for much larger data sets that cannot be accommodated within the computer's memory, as a complete unit.

Here we present two internal sort algorithms that are commonly used when sorting lists with less than approximately 50 elements. For larger lists, more sophisticated sorting algorithms are typically employed.

Selection Sort

One of the simplest sorting techniques is the selection sort. In a *selection sort*, the smallest value is initially selected from the complete list of data and exchanged with the first element in the list. After this first selection and exchange, the next smallest element in the revised list is selected and exchanged with the second element in the list. Since the smallest element is already in the first position in the list, this second pass need only consider the second through last elements. For a list consisting of *N* elements, this process is repeated *N-1* times, with each pass through the list requiring one less comparison than the previous pass.

For example, consider the list of numbers illustrated in Figure 8-18. The first pass through the initial list results in the number 32 being selected and exchanged with the first element in the list. The second pass, made on the reordered list, results in the number 155 being selected from the second through fifth elements. This value is then exchanged with the second

Figure 8-18
Sample Selection Sort

Initial List	Pass 1	Pass 2	Pass 3	Pass 4
690	32	32	32	32
307	307	155	155	155
32	690	690	307	307
155	155	307	690	426
426	426	426	426	690

element in the list. The third pass selects the number 307 from the third through fifth elements in the list and exchanges this value with the third element. Finally, the fourth and last pass through the list selects the remaining minimum value and exchanges it with the fourth list element. Although each pass in this example resulted in an exchange, no exchange would have been made in a pass if the smallest value were already in the correct location.

In pseudocode, the selection sort is described as

Set interchange count to zero (not required, but done just to keep track of the interchanges)
For each element in the list from first to next-to-last
   Find the smallest element from the current element being referenced to the last element by:
   Setting the minimum value equal to the current element
   Saving (storing) the index of the current element
   For each element in the list from the current element + 1 to the last element in the list
   If element(inner loop index) < minimum value
      Set the minimum value = element(inner loop index)
      Save the index the new found minimum value
   Endif
   EndFor
   Swap the current value with the new minimum value
   Increment the interchange count
EndFor
Return the interchange count

The function `selectionSort` incorporates this algorithm into a Visual Basic function.

```
Public Function selectionSort(num As Variant, NUMEL As Integer) As Integer
  Dim i As Integer, j As Integer
  Dim min As Integer, minidx As Integer
  Dim temp As Integer, moves As Integer

  moves = 0
  For i = 1 To (NUMEL - 1)
    min = num(i)       ' assume minimum is the first array element
    minidx = i         ' index of minimum element
    For j = i + 1 To numel
      If num(j) < min Then   ' if we've located a lower value
        min = num(j)         ' capture it
        minidx = j
      End If
```

```
        Next j
        If min < num(i) Then        ' check if we have a new minimum
          temp = num(i)             ' and if we do, swap values
          num(i) = min
          num(minidx) = temp
          moves = moves + 1
        End If
      Next i
      selectionSort = moves  ' return the number of moves
    End Function
```

The selectionSort function expects two arguments, the list to be sorted and the number of elements in the list. As specified by the pseudocode, a nested set of **For** loops performs the sort. The outer **For** loop causes one pass through the list. For each pass, the variable min is initially assigned the value num(i), where i is the outer **For** loop's counter variable. Since i begins at 1 and ends at NUMEL-1, each element in the list except the last is successively designated as the current element.

The inner loop is used as the function cycles through the elements below the current element to select the next smallest value. Thus, this loop begins at the index value i+1 and continues through the end of the list. When a new minimum is found, its value and position in the list are stored in the variables named min and minidx, respectively. Upon completion of the inner loop, an exchange is made only if a value less than that in the current position was found.

Program 8-5 was constructed to test selectionSort. This program implements a selection sort for the same list of 10 numbers previously used to test our search algorithms. For later comparison to the other sorting algorithms, the number of actual moves made by the program to get the data into sorted order is counted and displayed. For convenience, only the event code contained within Program 8-5 that calls the selection sort function is listed.

Program 8-5's Event Procedure Code

```
Private Sub Form_Click()
  Const numel As Integer = 10
  Dim nums As Variant
  Dim i As Integer, moves As Integer

  nums = Array(22, 5, 67, 98, 45, 32, 101, 99, 73, 10)
  moves = selectionSort(nums, numel)
  Cls
  Print "The sorted list, in ascending order, is:"
  For i = 1 To numel
    Print "  "; nums(i);
  Next i
  Print
  Print moves; " moves were made to sort this list"
End Sub
```

Figure 8-19
The Output Produced by Program 8-5

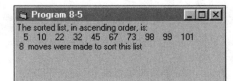

The output produced by Program 8-5 is shown in Figure 8-19.

Clearly, the number of moves displayed depends on the initial order of the values in the list. An advantage of the selection sort is that the maximum number of moves that must be made is N–1, where N is the number of items in the list. Further, each move is a final move that results in an element residing in its final location in the sorted list.

A disadvantage of the selection sort is that N(N–1)/2 comparisons are always required, regardless of the initial arrangement of the data. This number of comparisons is obtained as follows: the last pass always requires one comparison, the next-to-last pass requires two comparisons, and so on, to the first pass, which requires N–1 comparisons. Thus, the total number of comparisons is

$$1 + 2 + 3 + \ldots + N{-}1 = N(N{-}1)/2 = N^2/2 - N/2.$$

For large values of N, the N^2 dominates, and the order of the selection sort is $O(N^2)$.

Exchange ("Bubble") Sort

In an *exchange sort*, elements of the list are exchanged with one another in such a manner that the list becomes sorted. One example of such a sequence of exchanges is provided by the bubble sort, where successive values in the list are compared, beginning with the first two elements. If the list is to be sorted in ascending (from smallest to largest) order, the smaller value of the two being compared is always placed before the larger value. For lists sorted in descending (from largest to smallest) order, the smaller of the two values being compared is always placed after the larger value.

For example, assuming that a list of values is to be sorted in ascending order, if the first element in the list is larger than the second, the two elements are interchanged. Then the second and third elements are compared. Again, if the second element is larger than the third, these two elements are interchanged. This process continues until the last two elements have been compared and exchanged, if necessary. If no exchanges were made during this initial pass through the data, the data is in the correct order and the process is finished; otherwise, a second pass is made through the data, starting from the first element and stopping at the next-to-last element. The reason for stopping at the next-to-last element on the second pass is that the first pass always results in the most positive value "sinking" to the bottom of the list.

As a specific example of this process, consider the list of numbers illustrated in Figure 8-20. The first comparison results in the interchange of the first two element values, 690 and 307. The next comparison, between elements two and three in the revised list, results in the interchange of values between the second and third elements, 690 and 32. This comparison and possible switching of adjacent values is continued until the last two elements have been compared and possibly switched. This process completes the first pass through the data and results in the largest number moving to the bottom of the list. As the largest value sinks to its resting place at the bottom of the list, the smaller elements slowly rise, or "bubble," to the top of the list. This bubbling effect of the smaller elements is what gave rise to the name "bubble" sort for this sorting algorithm.

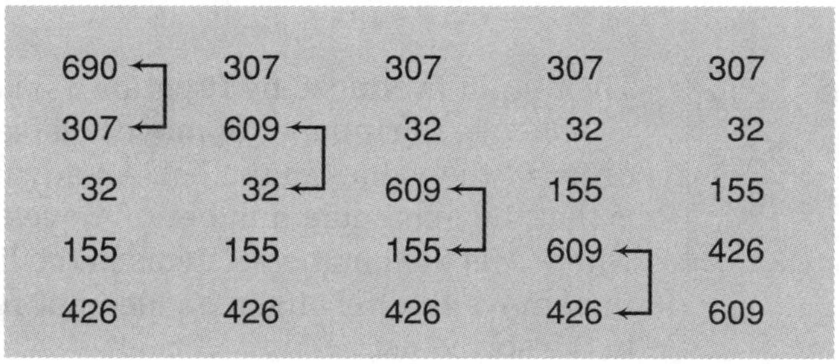

Figure 8-20

The First Pass of an Exchange Sort

690	307	307	307	307
307	609	32	32	32
32	32	609	155	155
155	155	155	609	426
426	426	426	426	609

Because the first pass through the list ensures that the largest value always moves to the bottom of the list, the second pass stops at the next-to-last element. This process continues, with each pass stopping at one higher element than the previous pass, until either N–1 passes through the list have been completed or no exchanges are necessary in any single pass. In both cases the resulting list is in sorted order. The pseudocode describing this sort is

> *Set interchange count to zero (not required, but done just to keep track of the*
> > *interchanges)*
> *For the first element in the list to one less than the last element (i index)*
> > *For the second element in the list to the last element (j index)*
> > > *If num(j) < num(j − 1)*
> > > > *Swap num(j) with num(j − 1)*
> > > > *Increment interchange count*
> > > *End If*
> > *End For*
> *End For*
> *Return interchange count*

This sort algorithm is coded in Visual Basic as the function bubbleSort, which is included within Program 8-6 for testing purposes. This program tests bubbleSort with the same list of 10 numbers used in Program 8-5. For comparison to the earlier selection sort, the number of adjacent moves (exchanges) made by bubbleSort is also counted and displayed.

Program 8-6's General and Event Object Code

```
Rem: This is the code contained in the [General] object section
Option Explicit
Option Base 1

Public Function bubbleSort(num As Variant, numel As Integer) As Integer
  Dim i As Integer, j As Integer
  Dim temp As Integer, moves As Integer

  moves = 0
  For i = 1 To (numel - 1)
    For j = 2 To numel
      If num(j) < num(j - 1) Then
        temp = num(j)
        num(j) = num(j - 1)
        num(j - 1) = temp
        moves = moves + 1
      End If
    Next j
  Next i
  bubbleSort = moves
End Function

Private Sub Form_Click()
  Const numel As Integer = 10
  Dim nums As Variant
  Dim i As Integer, moves As Integer

  nums = Array(22, 5, 67, 98, 45, 32, 101, 99, 73, 10)
  moves = bubbleSort(nums, numel)
```

continued

```
        Cls
        Print "The sorted list, in ascending order, is:"
        For i = 1 To numel
            Print "  "; nums(i);
        Next i
        Print
        Print moves; " moves were made to sort this list"
End Sub
```

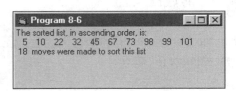

Figure 8-21
The Output Produced by
Program 8-6

Figure 8-21 illustrates the output produced by Program 8-6.

As with the selection sort, the number of comparisons using a bubble sort is $O(N^2)$ and the number of required moves depends on the initial order of the values in the list. In the worst case, when the data is in reverse sorted order, the selection sort performs better than the bubble sort. Here both sorts require $N(N–1)/2$ comparisons, but the selection sort needs only $N–1$ moves, while the bubble sort needs $N(N–1)/2$ moves. The additional moves required by the bubble sort result from the intermediate exchanges between adjacent elements to "settle" each element into its final position. In this regard, the selection sort is superior, because no intermediate moves are necessary. For random data, such as that used in Programs 8-5 and 8-6, the selection sort generally performs equal to or better than the bubble sort. A modification to the bubble sort, which causes the sort to terminate when the list is in order, regardless of the number of passes made, can make the bubble sort operate as an $O(N)$ sort in specialized cases.

Exercises **8.5**

1. a. Modify Program 8-5 to use a list of 100 randomly generated numbers and determine the number of moves required to put the list in order using a selection sort. Display both the initial list and the reordered list.

   b. Redo Exercise 1a using a bubble sort.

2. For the functions `selectionSort` and `bubbleSort`, a simple modification can allow the sorting to be done in decreasing order. In each case, identify the required changes and then rewrite each function to accept a parameter indicating whether the sort should be in increasing or decreasing order. Modify each function to correctly receive and use this parameter.

3. The selection and bubble sort both use the same technique for swapping list elements. Replace the code in these two functions that performs the swap, by a call to a procedure named `swap`.

4. a. Modify Program 8-6 to use a larger test list consisting of 20 numbers.

   b. Modify Program 8-6 to use a list of 100 randomly selected numbers.

5. A company currently maintains two lists of part numbers, where each part number is an integer. Write a Visual Basic program that compares these lists of numbers and displays the numbers, if any, that are common to both. (**Hint:** Sort each list prior to making the comparison.)

6. Redo Exercise 5, but display a list of part numbers that are only on one list, but not both.

7. Rewrite the binary search algorithm to use recursion rather than iteration.

8.6 Focus on Program Design and Implementation:

About Dialog Boxes and Splash Screens

In addition to operational forms, such as Rotech's order entry form, most applications include informational About boxes and a Splash screen. Both of these forms are added into a project using the same techniques, but are usually displayed in very different ways. In this Focus section we describe these forms, how they are created, and how their display is triggered within an application.

Adding an About Dialog Box

Figure 8-22

A Sample About Box

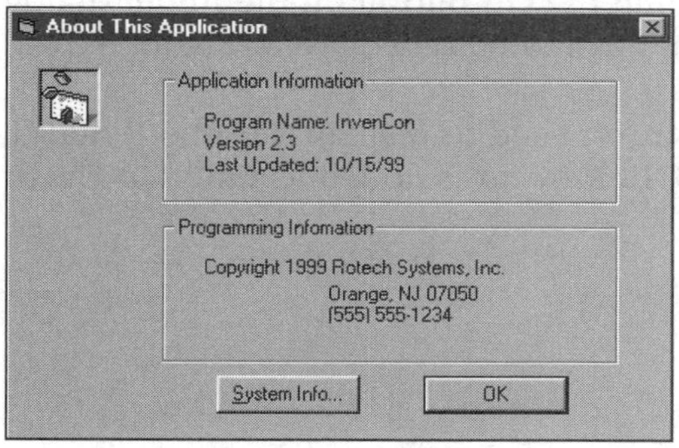

An About dialog box is an informational screen that typically provides general information about an application, such as its name, version number, programming company, and/or programmer. In addition, About dialogs can also be used to provide help information. From a design viewpoint an About dialog box, which is also referred to as an About box, is just another form that is added into a project. As such, an application can have as many About boxes as needed, with the first one usually providing general information about the program, such as that shown in Figure 8-22, and with additional ones acting as help screens.

About boxes can be constructed either by using the Application Wizard presented in the next section or manually by adding a new form into an existing project, as described next.

Manually adding an About box to an application is accomplished either by using the Project menu's Add Form option, as shown in Figure 8-23, or by clicking the Standard Toolbar's Add Form icon, which is shown in Figure 8-24. Either of these procedures displays the Add Form dialog shown in Figure 8-25. As shown in this figure, you now have the opportunity to select a variety of form types, such as an About dialog, Splash screen, or simply a second generic form. For our particular purpose we will select the About dialog icon.[7] This will add the About box form shown in Figure 8-26, which contains only images, labels, and lines, and two Command buttons, one of which is used to return control to the form from which the box is called. This default About box, which is referred to as the **About box template form**, is automatically named frmAbout and is added directly into your project. As such, it becomes part of your application and can be modified to your own specifications.

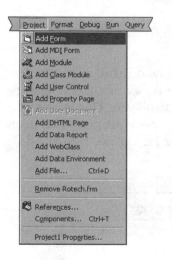

Figure 8-23

Adding a Form to a Project

---

[7]Alternatively, you can select the Form icon and create your own About box using any of the Toolbox controls in the same manner as you have created all of your Visual Basic frmMain forms.

Figure 8-24
The Standard Toolbar's Add Form
Icon

Add Form Icon

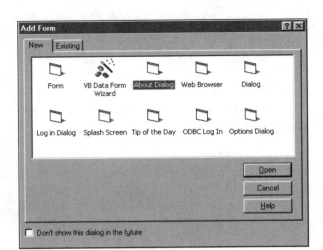

Figure 8-25
Selecting an About Box Form

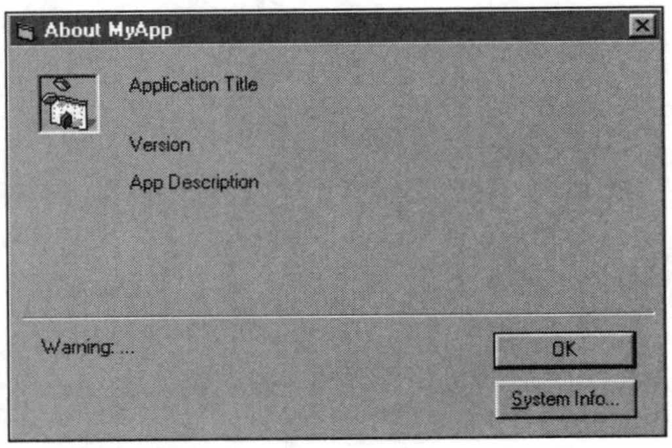

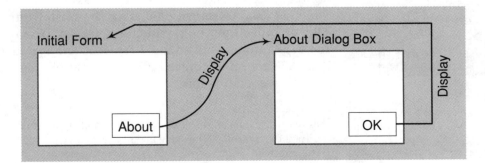

Figure 8-26
The Default About Box

Once an About dialog has been added into a project it must be linked in operationally, so that it can be displayed under user control. This is usually done using two Command buttons; one on your application's first form that triggers the About dialog's display, and the OK button on the About dialog that causes your application's initial form to be redisplayed. Figure 8-27 illustrates this relationship.

Assuming that the Command button used to display the About dialog box has been named cmdAbout, its **Click** event is coded as listed in Event Procedure 8-1.

Event Procedure 8-1

```
Private Sub cmdAbout_Click()
  Me.Hide
  frmAbout.Show
  frmAbout.Refresh
End Sub
```

This procedure first hides the currently displayed form, and then displays the About dialog box. It is followed by a **Refresh** method to ensure that all of the About box's graphical elements are displayed. This is simply a safety to cover the case where this form's **AutoRefresh** property has been set to **False**, and is explained more fully in Chapter 11. Figures 8-28 and 8-29

Figure 8-27
Displaying an About Box and
Returning

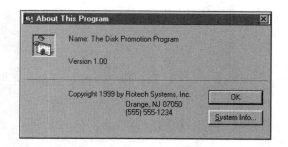

Figure 8-28
Including an <u>A</u>bout Button on the
Rotech Main Menu

Figure 8-29
The Rotech Application About Box

show the Rotech Main Menu form with an added <u>A</u>bout Command button
and the About dialog box that is displayed when this button is pressed.

On the return side, the About box's OK button would use the code listed
in Event Procedure 8-2 to redisplay the frmMain form. The body of this event
code is a copy of Event Procedure 8-1, with a name change for the form to
be displayed.

Event Procedure 8-2

```
Private Sub cmdOK_Click()
   Me.Hide
   frmMain.Show
   frmMain.Refresh
End Sub
```

Adding a Splash Screen

A Splash screen is an initial informational form that is displayed for a few
seconds before the main application form is presented. Typically a Splash
screen is used to present a company's name and the name or purpose of the

---

TIPS FROM THE PROS

Elusive About Dialog Box Settings

When you first change the default About dialog's form **Caption** property, as well as some of the label captions, you may find that they appear differently at run time than when set at design-time. The reason for this is that the default About dialog box uses its **Form_Load** event to set these properties when the box is displayed. Since the **Show** method used to display the dialog first loads an unloaded form before displaying it, the **Form_Load** event code is executed and the run-time assignments within the code will overwrite your design-time settings. The actual event code provided for the default About box is listed at the bottom of this Tips box.

Therefore, if you change the default property settings at design time, make sure to delete the three lines of code in the **Form_Load** event code listed below. Alternatively, you can leave the default design-time settings alone and make the changes directly within the **Form_Load** event code. Doing this sets the respective caption values at run time rather than at design time.

```
Private Sub Form_Load()
   Me.Caption = "About " & App.Title
   lblVersion.Caption = "Version " & App.Major & "." & App.Minor & "." & App.Revision
   lblTitle.Caption = App.Title
End Sub
```

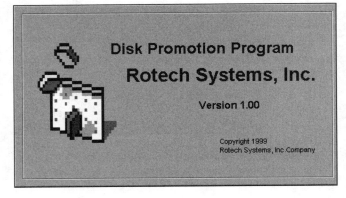

Figure 8-30
A Sample Splash Screen

executing application, as for example, the screen illustrated in Figure 8-30. Splash screens are created in the same manner as About dialog boxes.

To manually add a splash screen into an application either use the Project menu's Add Form option, as previously shown in Figure 8-23, or click the Standard Toolbar's Add Form icon, which was shown in Figure 8-24. Either of these two operations causes the Add Form dialog shown in Figure 8-31 to be displayed.[8] At this point select the Splash Screen icon. This will add the form shown in Figure 8-32, which contains only images, labels, and lines. This form, which is automatically added to your project, can be modified to your own specifications.[9]

The trick now is to display this splash screen for a few seconds as the initial screen when an application is first executed, immediately followed by the frmMain screen, which becomes the application's second screen.

By default, a project's first form is designated as the **startup form**. When an application is run, this startup form is automatically displayed, and the first code to execute is the form's **Initialize** event procedure. There are times, however, when you might want a different form than frmMain to be initially loaded and displayed, as is the case with a splash screen. There are two solutions to this problem: either designate the splash screen as the first form to be loaded, and have the splash screen display the frmMain screen, or designate a separate procedure to begin processing before any form is loaded, and have this procedure load the appropriate forms in sequence. Although the second solution is the preferred one, for reasons which will become apparent, we consider each of these solutions in turn, as they both yield insight into moving from one form to another within a single application.

To explicitly designate the frmSplash screen as the initial form to be loaded, select the last option from the Project menu (see Figure 8-33). When

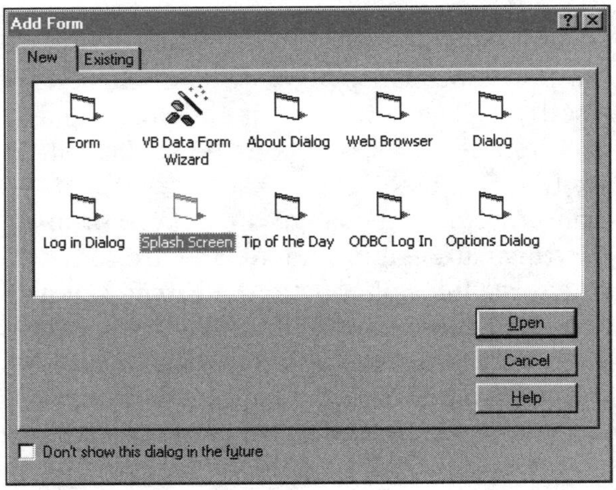

Figure 8-32
The Default Splash Screen

Figure 8-31
Selecting a Splash Screen Form

---

[8]Alternatively, and as with the About box, a splash screen can also be created using the Application Wizard presented in the next section.

[9]You can also select the Form icon and create your own Splash screen, as you would any other form.

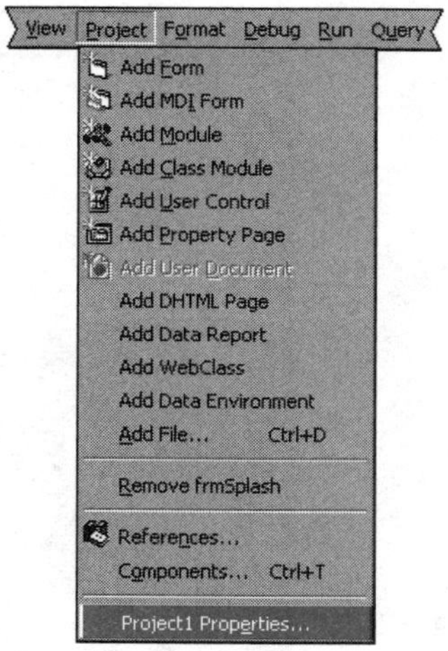

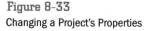

Figure 8-33
Changing a Project's Properties

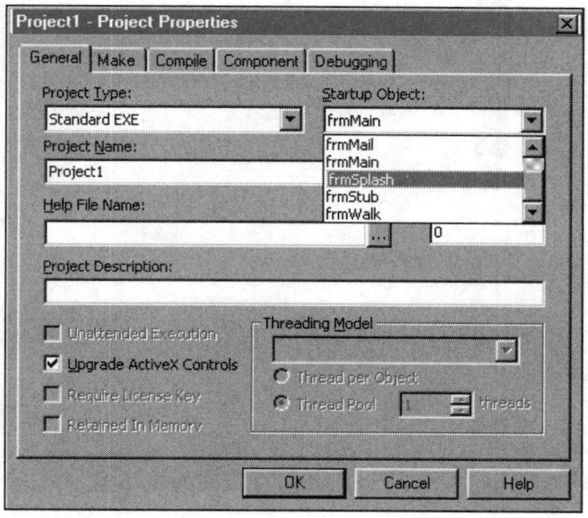

Figure 8-34
Selecting an Alternative Startup Form

this option is selected , a dialog box similar to the one shown in Figure 8-34 is displayed. As illustrated, we have selected the frmSplash form from the drop-down list as the Startup Object, rather than frmMain form. Pressing the OK button causes this selection to take effect and to become the startup form. Although this will cause the splash screen to be displayed, we are still left with the problem of unloading this screen and loading the frmMain form when we want the "working" part of the program to begin.

One method of switching from the splash screen to the Main Menu form is to use a Command button on the splash screen, and have its **Click** event trigger the display of the Main Menu form. Assuming we have named this control cmdContinue, its click event would be coded as listed in Event Procedure 8-3.

Event Procedure 8-3

```
Private Sub cmdContinue_Click()
  Me.Hide
  frmMain.Show
  frmMain.Refresh
End Sub
```

This procedure has been our standard one for unloading the current form and displaying a new one. The use of the **Refresh** method is to ensure that all graphical elements are displayed. This is a safety procedure to cover the case where the form's AutoRefresh property has been set to False.

Although the code listed in Event Procedure 8-3 is code that is familiar to us (it is similar to Event Procedure 8-2, which has been used extensively within the Rotech project), the more conventional method for displaying a Splash screen is to start the application with a procedure containing a timing loop. To do this the startup procedure must be named Sub Main and must be contained within a standard code (.bas) module.

The addition of this standard code module is accomplished by first selecting the Project menu's Add Module option, as shown in Figure 8-35. You will then be presented with the Add Module Dialog shown in Figure 8-36.

When the Add Module Dialog is displayed, make sure the New tab is active and press the Open Command button to create a new module. At this point the Code window shown in Figure 8-37 will appear.

Figure 8-35
Adding a Module to a Project

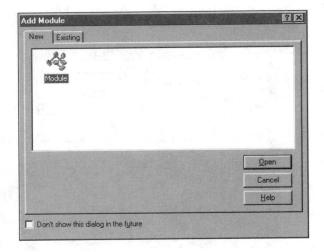

Figure 8-36
The Add Module Dialog

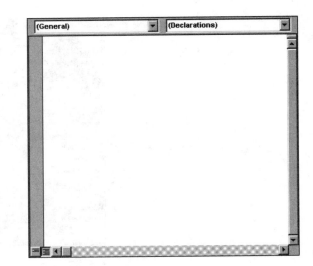

Figure 8-37
The New Module's Code Window

Once the Code window shown in Figure 8-37 is displayed, enter the code listed below as Procedure Code 8-11. Notice that when you enter the Sub procedure's name, the name displayed at the top right of the Code window changes from (Declarations) to Main (compare Figure 8-37 to Figure 8-38).

Procedure Code 8-11

```
Public Sub Main()
    Const sngDISPTIME As Single = 2
    Dim sngStart As Single

    frmSplash.Show
    frmSplash.Refresh
    sngStart = Timer   ' set start time using the Timer function
    Do While Timer < sngStart + sngDISPTIME
    Loop
    frmSplash.Hide
    frmMain.Show
    frmMain.Refresh
End Sub
```

Figure 8-38
The Completed Sub Main
Procedure

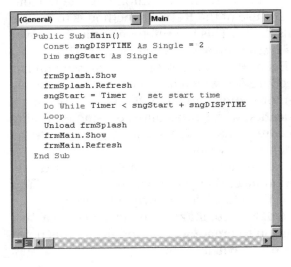

When you are finished typing, the Code window should look like that shown in Figure 8-38.

Let's take a moment to review what the Sub Main procedure code shown in Figure 8-38, and listed as Procedure Code 8-11 accomplishes.

First, the named constant in this code, sngDISPTIME, sets the number of seconds that the splash screen is displayed, while the sngStart variable is used to keep track of the elapsed time within a timing loop. The procedure then shows the frmSplash form and immediately invokes the form's **Refresh** method. This is done to ensure that all graphical elements are displayed in the event that the form's **AutoRefresh** property has been set to **False** (see Chapter 11). A timing loop is then used to wait for two seconds, at which point the frmSplash screen is unloaded

TIPS FROM THE PROS

Two Elusive Splash Settings

Two of the label captions provided by the default splash screen are set at run time by the form's **Form_Load** event code. Since the **Show** method used to display the splash screen first loads an unloaded form before displaying it, this **Form_Load** event code is executed and the run-time assignments take effect, regardless of the settings you have made at design time. The actual event code provided by the default splash screen is shown at the bottom of this Tips box.

Therefore, if you change the default caption values of the two labels listed in this code at design time, make sure to delete the two lines of code in the **Form_Load** event code listed below. Alternatively, you can leave the default design time settings alone and make the changes directly within the **Form_Load** event code. Doing this sets the respective caption values at run time rather than at design time.

```
Private Sub Form_Load()
    lblVersion.Caption = "Version " & App.Major & "." & App.Minor & "." & App.Revision
    lblProductName.Caption = App.Title
End Sub
```

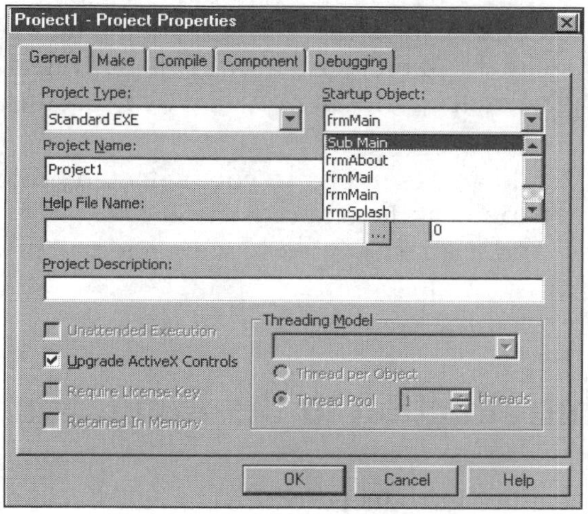

Figure 8-39

Selecting a Startup Procedure

and the `frmMain` screen is displayed. Here, use is made of the Timer function which returns the number of elapsed seconds from midnight (see Exercise 3).

All that remains is to ensure that our `Sub Main` procedure is initially executed when the application is run. This is accomplished using settings within the Project menu. When the last option in this menu item is selected (see Figure 8-33), a dialog box similar to the one shown in Figure 8-39 will be displayed. As illustrated, the current Startup Object is `frmMain`. To change this, select the `Sub Main` procedure in the drop-down list and press the `OK` button. Doing this explicitly selects the `Sub Main` procedure as the initial code executed when the application is run.

Exercises 8.6

(**Note:** The Rotech Systems project, at the stage of development begun in this section, can be found on the Student Disk in the `rotech7` folder as project `rotech7.vbp`. The project, as it exists at the end of this section, which includes an About dialog box and a Splash screen, can be found on the Student Disk in the `rotech8` folder as project `rotech8.vbp`.)

1 a. Add the About box shown in Figure 8-29 to the Rotech project. Add a Command button named cmdAbout to the project's Main Menu and use Event Procedure 8-1 to display the box. Event Procedure 8-2 should be used with the About box's OK button to redisplay the Main Menu form.

   b. Test the About box constructed in Exercise 1a to ensure that it can be displayed from the Main Menu and that it, in turn, can be used to redisplay the Main Menu.

2 a. Add the splash screen shown in Figure 8-30 to the Rotech project. Use Procedure Code 8-11 to display this screen.

   b. Test that the project initially displays the splash screen and then displays the Main Menu form when the application is executed.

3 Enter the words Timer function in the Help facility's Index tab to obtain documentation on the Timer function used in Procedure Code 8-11. Make sure to click on the Examples link in the documentation to see a complete example that uses this function.

4 Add a Command button to the splash screen constructed in Exercise 2a. The button should have the caption OK, and if it is pressed the splash screen should unload itself immediately and display the Main Menu form. This button should be in addition to the normal operation provided by Procedure Code 8-11.

5 a. **CASE STUDY**
      Add an About box to your selected project (see project specifications at the end of Section 1.5).

   b. Add a splash screen to your selected project.

8.7 ▸ Knowing About: Introduction to the Application Wizard

A new feature introduced with Version 5.0 and modified slightly in Version 6.0 is the Application Wizard, or App Wizard, for short. The App Wizard can be used to create the foundation for an application, which can then be edited to fit your particular needs. In this section we will show you how to use the Application Wizard to create a remarkably functional application that includes a menu bar, toolbar, and status bar. Each of these bars will be created as dockable objects that can be detached and dragged across the screen. Additionally, we will let the App Wizard create a splash screen like the ones discussed in Section 8.6. We will then explore how this screen is called, so you can create your own splash screens independent of the App Wizard.

To create an application using the App Wizard, select the App Wizard icon when you start a new project, as shown in Figure 8-40. This selection will cause the App Wizard to display a series of dialog boxes, each of which elicits information about the basic structure of the application. Table 8-9 lists the information you specify in each dialog box and the sequence of dialog box presentation.

After selecting the Application Wizard from the New Project dialog box, the introductory screen shown in Figure 8-41 is displayed. Clicking the Next button on this dialog brings up the Interface Dialog shown in Figure 8-42.

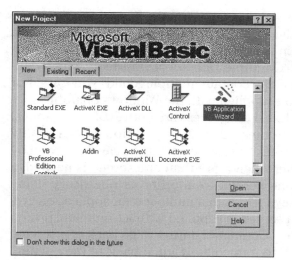

Figure 8-40
Specifying the Application Wizard

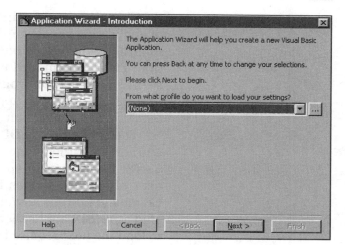

Figure 8-41
The App Wizard's Introduction Dialog (Screen 1)

Figure 8-42
The Interface Dialog (Screen 2)

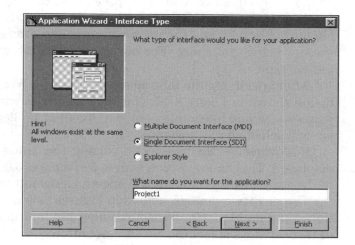

Table 8-9	Application Wizard Dialog Requests		
Seq No.	**Example**	**Name**	**Purpose**
1	Fig. 8-41	Introduction	Instructional
2	Fig. 8-42	Interface Type	Specify the type of application—SDI, MDI, Tools, Window, Explorer and its Name
3	Fig. 8-43	Menus	Specify the menu options—File, Edit, View, and Help
4	Fig. 8-44	Toolbar	Customize the Standard Toolbar
5	Fig. 8-45	Resources	Specify if a Resource file is required
6	Fig. 8-46	Internet Connectivity	Specify if you want the application to access the Internet
7	Fig. 8-47	Standard Forms	Specify if you want a Login Dialog, Splash Screen, About Box, or Options Dialog
8	Fig. 8-48	Data Access Forms	Specify if you want to connect to a Database (see Section 9.8)
9	Fig. 8-49	Finished!	Name the application, generate a summary report, and set Wizard defaults
10	Fig. 8-50	Application Created	Informational—indicates a successful completion of the Wizard's process

The purpose of the Interface dialog is to inform the Wizard as to the type of application you desire. Here the acronym SDI refers to a Single Document Interface, where only one screen at a time can be displayed by an application. The acronym MDI refers to Multiple Document Interface, which consists of a single main window that can contain multiple "child" windows. For example, the Notepad application supplied with the Windows operating system is an SDI application, while Excel and Access are both MDI applications.

The selection of SDI does not mean that an application can have only one screen; rather, it means that only one screen at a time can be viewed by a user. In this type of application, when more than one screen is needed, a user effectively moves from one screen to another as necessary using Command buttons and/or hot keys. Thus, in a multi-screen application created as an SDI application, each screen is supplied with a Command button to load the next required screen, a Command button to go back one screen, and possibly a Command button to immediately jump back to the opening screen. This is, in fact, the exact type of operation that the Application Wizard uses to move from one screen to the next as it requests information from you. Frequently, in an SDI application, hot keys may also be provided for these tasks. In an MDI application all screens are contained within a single master screen and the user can jump and drag-and-drop data between screens using the mouse. For our application, we will select SDI as the interface type.

After specifying the interface type, the App Wizard presents the Menus dialog shown in Figure 8-43. This dialog permits you to specify what menu items you would like implemented in the final application. For our purposes we will select all of the menus.

Following the Menus selection dialog, the dialog shown in Figure 8-44 is displayed. This dialog, which is new for Version 6.0, permits customization of the Standard Toolbar. We will accept its default selections.

The next two dialogs, shown in Figures 8-45 and 8-46, request information about multi-platform resource files and Internet connectivity. For both of these dialogs select the No Option button.

The seventh dialog box requests information about the additional forms that you want created for the application. For our purposes we will only select a Splash screen, as indicated in Figure 8-47.

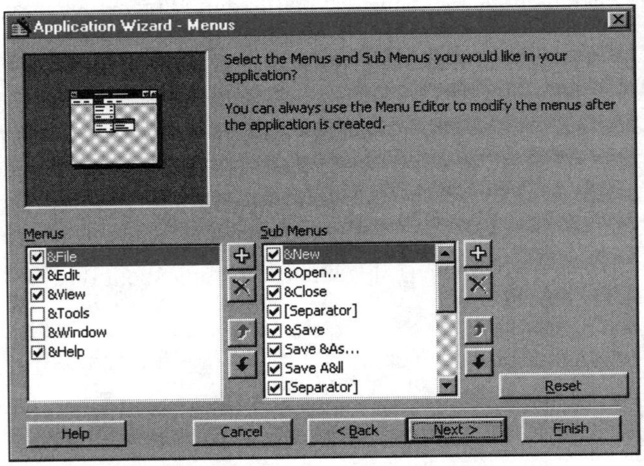

Figure 8-43
The Menus Dialog (Screen 3)

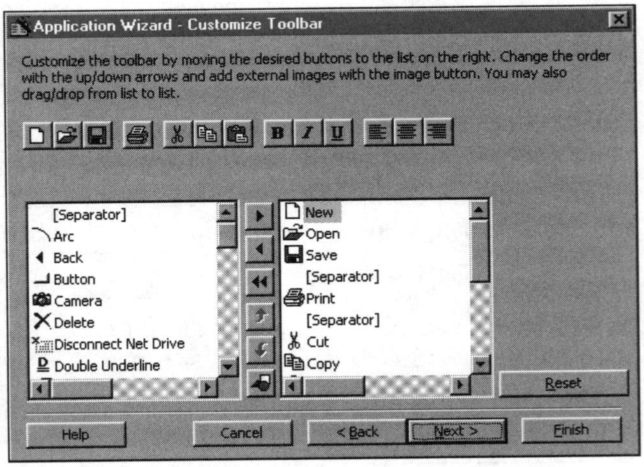

Figure 8-44
The Toolbar Dialog (Screen 4)

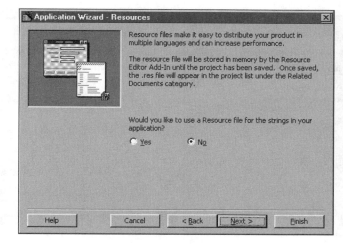

Figure 8-45
The Resources Dialog (Screen 5)

Figure 8-46
The Internet Connectivity Dialog (Screen 6)

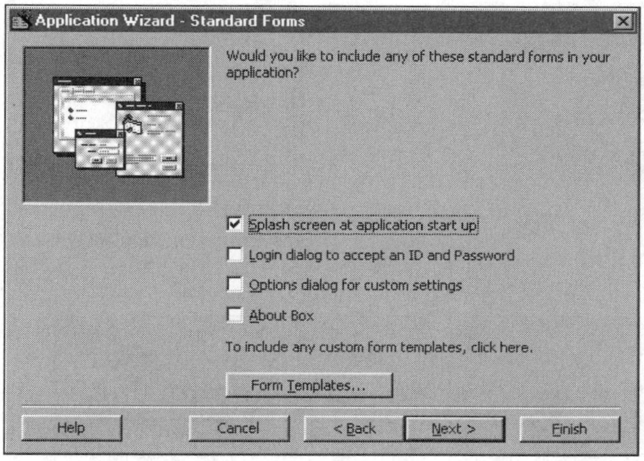

Figure 8-47
The Standard Forms Dialog (Screen 7)

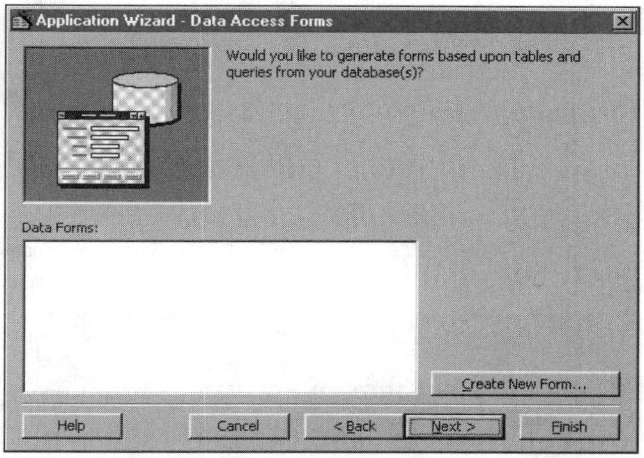

Figure 8-48
The Data Access Forms Dialog (Screen 8)

After you complete the Standard Forms dialog, the Data Access Forms dialog, illustrated in Figure 8-48, is displayed. For now we will leave the Data Forms section blank, which means our current application will not access a database. (In section 9.7 we will show how this dialog is used to create a Visual Basic database application.)

Pressing the <u>N</u>ext button on the Data Access Forms dialog brings up the Finished! dialog, which is shown in Figure 8-49. Press the <u>F</u>inish button to have the Wizard create an application that meets the specifications entered in prior dialogs. When the application is completed, the Wizard will display the screen shown in Figure 8-50.

The application created by the Wizard is a skeleton one that contains the essential elements you can use to "flesh out" your particular specifications. Nevertheless, the completed application has quite a bit of functionality built into it. Figure 8-51 shows the Project window for the created application, which contains two forms and a code module.

The frmSplash form contains the splash screen, which is shown in Figure 8-52a. This screen is easily modified to produce a custom splash screen by simply changing the labels the Wizard placed on the form. Figure 8-52b

Figure 8-49
The Finished! Dialog (Screen 9)

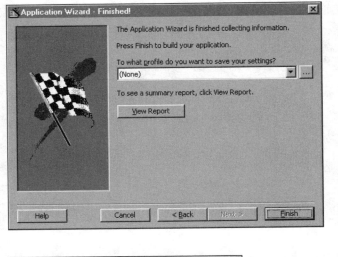

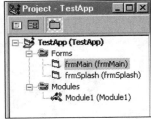

Figure 8-50
The Application Created Notification

Figure 8-51
The Application's Project Window

Figure 8-52a
The Initial Splash Screen

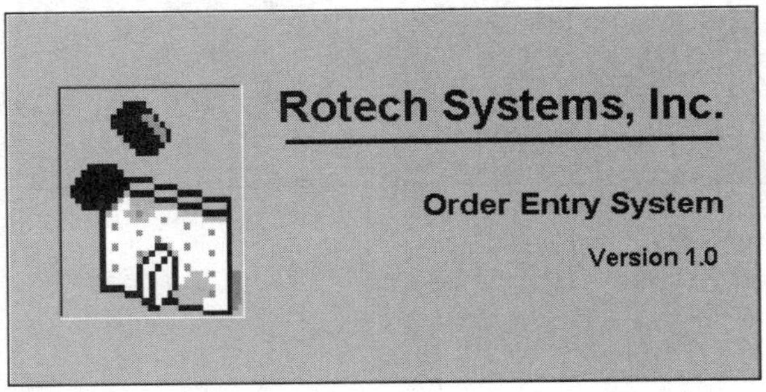

Figure 8-52b
A Modified Splash Screen

Figure 8-53
The frmMain Screen

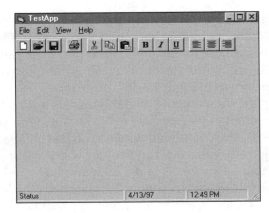

illustrates one such modified screen. Finally, Figure 8-53 shows the application's `frmMain` form with a Standard Toolbar, and a menu consisting of File, Edit, View, and Help options.

The code module shown in the application's Project window (see Figure 8-51) contains a `Sub Main` general procedure that is used to display the `frmSplash` screen, followed by the `frmMain` screen. Unfortunately, the splash screen is displayed so quickly that it is almost not visible. To control the amount of time that the splash screen is displayed, you should modify the code within this default `Sub Main` procedure to that listed as Procedure Code 8-11 in the previous section.

8.8 Common Programming Errors

Four common errors are associated with using arrays:

1. Forgetting to declare the array. This error results in a compiler error message equivalent to "Type mismatch" each time an indexed variable attempting to access the array is encountered.

2. Using a subscript that references a nonexistent array element. For example, declaring the array to be of size 20 and using a subscript value of 25. This error results in a run-time error and message that the "Subscript is out of range."

3. Not using a large enough conditional value in a **For** loop counter to cycle through all the array elements. This error usually occurs when an array is initially specified to be of size n and there is a **For** loop within the program of the form `For i = 1 To n`. The array size is then expanded but the programmer forgets to change the terminating value in the **For** loop. Declaring an array's size using a named constant and consistently using the named constant throughout the procedure eliminates this problem.

4. Forgetting to initialize the array. Although Visual Basic automatically sets all elements of numerical arrays to zero, all elements of string arrays to zero-length, and all elements of **Variants** to the **Empty** value, it is up to the programmer to ensure that each array is correctly initialized before processing of array elements begins.

8.9 Chapter Review

Key Terms

big O notation	indexed variable	single-dimensional array
binary search	linear (sequential) search	subscript
bubble sort	one-dimensional array	subscripted variable
Index	selection sort	two-dimensional array

Summary

1. A single-dimensional array is a data structure that can store a list of values of the same data type. Such arrays must be declared by giving the data type of the values stored in the array and the array size. For example, the declaration

```
Dim num(100) As Integer
```

creates an array of 100 integers. It is preferable to first use a named constant to set the array size, and then use this constant in defining the array. For example:

```
Const int MAXSIZE As Integer = 100
```

and

```
Dim num(MAXSIZE) As Integer
```

2. Array elements are stored in contiguous locations in memory and referenced using the array name and a subscript, for example, `num(22)`. Any integer valued expression can be used as an Index.

3. A two-dimensional array is declared by listing both a row and a column size with the data type and name of the array. For example, the statements

```
Const ROWS As Integer = 5
Const COLS As Integer = 7
Dim vals(ROWS, COLS) As Integer
```

creates a two-dimensional array consisting of five rows and seven columns of integer values.

4. Visual Basic permits the declaration of arrays with a maximum of sixty dimensions.

5. Arrays are passed to procedures by using the name of the array as an argument. Within the procedure, a parameter must be specified for the passed array name.

6. The linear search is an *O(N)* search. It examines each item in a list until the searched item is found or until it is determined that the item is not in the list.

7. The binary search is an $O(\log_2 N)$ search. It requires that a list be in sorted order before it can be applied.

8. The selection and exchange sort algorithms require an order of magnitude of N^2 comparisons for sorting a list of N items.

Test Yourself—Short Answer

1. A one-dimensional array requires one _____ to identify which element is being referred to in a statement.

2. The _____ function will return an array's lower limit.

3. What is the purpose of the **Option Base** statement? Where will it be found?

4. What is the difference between a fixed array and a dynamic array?

5. Visual Basic assigns a unique number, called a(n) _____ to each of the controls in a control array.

6. What will be the results of the execution of the statement `Dim MyArray(5 to 10) as Integer`

7. Write a declaration statement for an array named `aintQuantities` to hold 10 integer numbers.

8. Write a declaration statement for an array named `afltPrices` to hold 10 floating point numbers.

9. Declare an array named `astrMessages` that will hold 10 strings, with each string having a maximum of 15 characters each.

10. Declare a two-dimensional array named `aintPartNums` capable of holding 4 rows and 5 columns of integers.

Programming Projects

1. In this project you will create three integer arrays. The elements in the third array will be obtained by multiplying corresponding elements in the first two arrays. Finally, the sum and average of each array's elements will be computed and displayed.

   Specifically, you are to write a Visual Basic program that stores the odd numbers from 1 to 20 in one array and the even numbers from 1 to 20 in another array. The program should then multiply the first element of the first array by the first element in the second array and store the product into a third array. The cross multiplication of corresponding elements in the first two arrays should continue until the product of the 10th element in each of the first two arrays is stored in the 10th element of the third array. Your program must then calculate and display the sum and average of the numbers in each of the three arrays.

First Array	Second Array	Third Array
1	2	2
3	4	12
5	6	30
.	.	.
.	.	.
19	20	3800

   Notes: An array is like a super variable. Instead of storing a single value, it stores a set of values under the same name. The array index distinguishes one element from another. For example, where the declaration statement:

   ```
   Dim a As Integer
   ```

   creates a single integer variable that is capable of storing a single integer value, a statement such as:

   ```
   Dim a (10) As Integer
   ```

   creates an array that is capable of storing 11 integer values in the variables named a(0), a(1), a(2), . . ., a(10). If the statement `Option Base 1` has been executed, the array will only store 10 integer values in the variables a(1) through a(10).

2. Write a Visual Basic program that accepts two numbers from the user (in Text boxes) representing the rows and columns of a table. Using this input, display a multiplication table with the number of input rows and columns in a Picture box, such as that shown in the accompanying figure. The maximum number of rows is 15 and the maximum number of columns is 10. An executable example of this calculator can be found on the Student Disk as `mult.exe`.

   In constructing your program, be sure to:

   1. Comment your program.
   2. Use proper formatting, indenting, etc.
   3. Use Visual Basic constants (Const) where appropriate.

Figure 8-54
Form for Programming Project 2

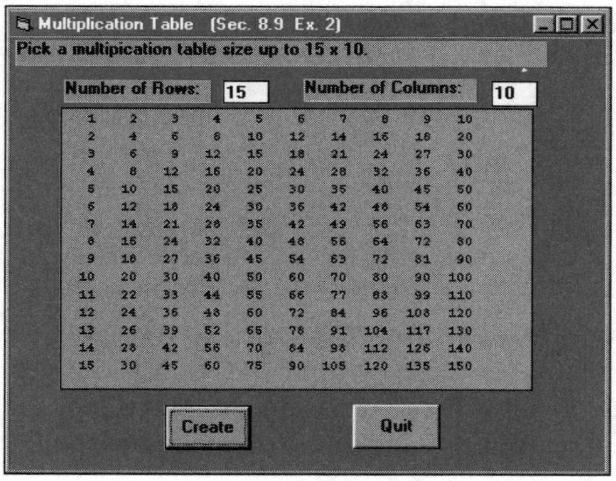

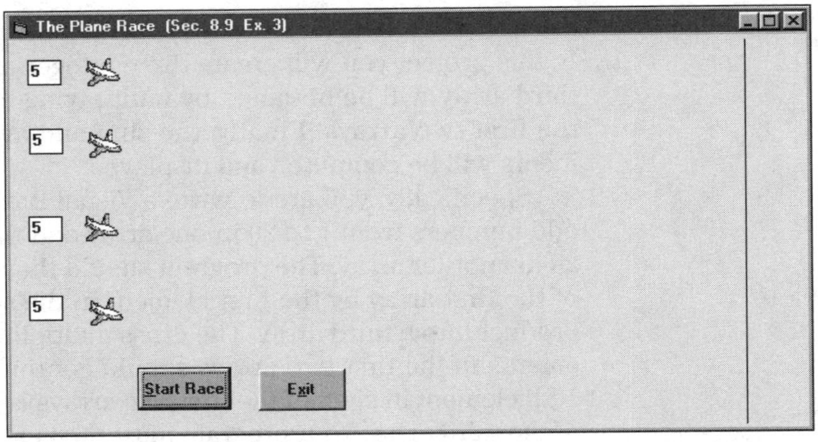

Figure 8-55

Form for Programming Project 3

3. Write a Visual Basic program that implements four racing planes. The planes should move across the screen and the first one across a finish line is the winner. The planes' speed is to be interactively controlled by a single Text box in which a user can enter a maximum speed for all of the planes. An executable example of this program can be found on the Student Disk as `planes.exe`. The plane image is name `Plane.ico` on the VB6.0 CDROM.

   For this project you are required to have a Command button with the caption `Start Race`. When the race is over, the caption on this button should change to `Reset`, and the button should act as a reset button that positions each plane at its starting point. You will also need a Command button with the caption `Exit`, that can be used to terminate the program. At a high level, here's the algorithm that you will need to conduct the race:

   When the Start Race button is clicked:

      Using a For-Next loop move each plane

        Until one of them crosses the finish line (use a Do-Until loop)

   For each movement the planes should move from 1 to maxspeed units where maxspeed is the number entered in the Text box.

   Hint: To generate a number between 1 and maxspeed, use the code:

   ```
   speed = Rnd * Val(txtSpeed.Text)
   ```

   Rnd is an intrinsic Visual Basic function that generates a random number between 0 and 1.

4. This assignment is a modification to the Motel 8 project (Section 5.9, Exercise 7). The untaxed cost for a night's stay at Motel 8 equals the adult charge plus the child charge, each based upon the number of adults and children respectively in the room. The following table enumerates the charges:

Adults	Charge	Children	Charge
1	$30	0	$0
2	$50	1	$15
3	$60	2	$25
4	$65	3	$30

   There is no discount for multiple nights stay. Additionally, there is a 5% state and local tax that is computed on the sum of the nightly charges. Using this information, write a Visual Basic program that calculates the final bill for a stay at the motel. Your application should use a form like the one shown in Figure 8-56.

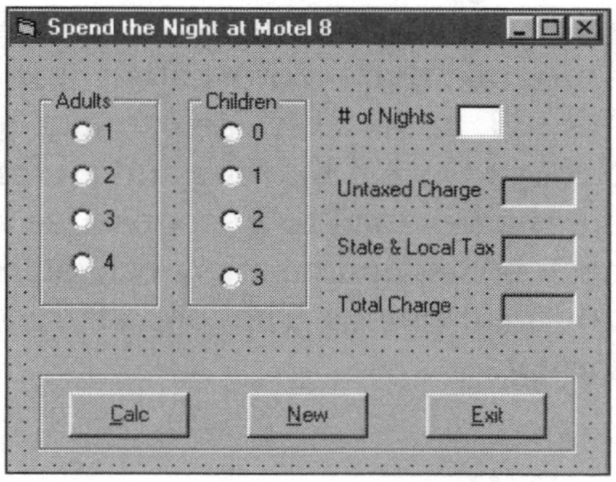

Figure 8-56
Form For Exercise 4

For this project, use one control array to group the set of "Number of Adults" option buttons and a second control array for the set of "Number of Children" option buttons. The corresponding charges for 1 to 4 adults and the charges for 0 to 3 children should be stored in two integer arrays, respectively.

Input the number of nights stay in a Text box and use the Val function to convert the entered data to a numeric value. In the General Declaration section of your program, declare variables to hold values of the number of nights stay, as an integer variable, and currency variables for untaxed charge, state and local tax, and total charge.

5. The LoCal Ice Cream Shoppe sells ice cream to its customers in either a cup or a cone. The charges for number of scoops and topping is as follows:

Scoops	Charge	Toppings	Charge
1	$1.25	0	$0.00
2	$1.85	1	$0.40
3	$2.35	2	$0.80
		3	$1.10

For a cone, the customer is charged an additional $0.25. Using this information, write a Visual Basic program to calculate the total charge for each order..

Use one control array for a set of Number of Scoops Option buttons and a second for the Number of Toppings Option buttons. Additionally, supply the application with a Check box for the choice of a cone or cup of ice cream. Your project should also use an array of type Single to store the charge for 1 to 3 scoops, as well as a second Single array for the 0 to 3 toppings charge. The total charge for each order should be displayed, in currency format, in a Picture box.

6. After performing a cost study on the price of toppings, the LoCal Ice Cream Shoppe plans to change the way in which they charge for toppings. Their new price structure will reflect the type of topping. The charge for number of scoops and an additional charge for cones will stay the same (as defined in Exercise 5).

Toppings	Charge
Chocolate sprinkles	$0.45
Chocolate sauce	$0.45
Shredded coconut	$0.40
Cherries	$0.35
Chopped nuts	$0.50
Butterscotch sauce	$0.40

Either modify the program written for Exercise 5 or write a new Visual Basic program that incorporates these additional prices in the final customer's bill. As in Exercise 5, use a control array for the set of Number of Scoops Option buttons and an array of Singles to store the corresponding charges for 1 to 3 scoops. Use a control array to name the Toppings Check boxes and an array of Singles to store the corresponding charges for the toppings. The total charge should be displayed using a currency format.

Accessing Databases

A growing area of importance for Visual Basic is the construction of database applications, which includes both the maintenance of existing data and the rapid retrieval and display of information stored in the database. In Section 9.1 we introduce the terminology and fundamental structures used in database design. The remaining sections then present the controls, methods, and events that permit construction of Visual Basic database applications.

9.1 Introduction to Databases

A *database* is defined as any collection of related data used by an organization. In this context *organization* is a generic term that refers to any self-contained social unit, such as a company, university, hospital, or family. Such organizations may wish to use:

- Student data,
- Patient data,
- Employee data,
- Customer data,
- Expense data,
- Product data, or
- Sales data.

The data in a database always consists of two types:

1. *Entities* about which the organization needs to store information, such as employees, customers, suppliers, and products; and

2. *Relationships* that link the entities together and express the associations between them.

As a specific example illustrating these concepts, consider that Rotech Systems, Inc. is a small corporation operating from two office locations. Assume that the company currently employs 20 people, each assigned to one of the two offices. In addition, the company employs ten salespeople working out of their homes and reporting to one of the two offices. The relevant data for these employees is listed in Tables 9-1 through 9-3.

Before examining the relationships among Tables 9-1 through 9-3, let's take a moment to concentrate on the tables themselves.

First, notice that the data stored in each table is relevant to a specific entity; for our example there are three tables corresponding to three entities: internal employee phone numbers, external sales force addresses, and office locations. Individually, each table is constructed to be a logical grouping of related information arranged in rows and columns. Mathematically, such a two-dimensional table is referred to as a *relation* if the following conditions hold:

1. Each location in the table can contain a single value;
2. Each column in the table has a unique identifying name;

Table 9-1	Internal Employee Telephone Directory[*]		
ID	**Name**	**Ext**	**Office**
1	Bronson, Bill	321	HM
2	Engle, Alan	234	HM
3	Dieter, Frank	289	F1
4	Dreskin, James	367	HM
5	Farrell, Mike	564	F1
7	Ford, Sue	641	F1
9	Gent, Hillary	325	HM
10	Grill, John	495	F1
11	Jones, Kay	464	F1
12	Jones, Mary	790	HM
14	Macleod, Jim	761	HM
15	Miller, Harriet	379	HM
21	O'Neil, Pat	856	F1
22	Schet, David	485	F1
23	Smith, Bill	251	F1
24	Smith, Dave	893	HM
26	Swan, Kurt	168	HM
27	Ward, Ann	726	F1
28	Williams, John	673	HM
30	Bass, Harriet	893	HM

[*](Table name is PhoneBook, the primary index is the ID field, and the table is also indexed on the Name field)

3. All values in a column have the same data type;

4. The data in each row is distinct (that is, no two rows have the same data);

5. No information is lost by reordering columns; and

6. No information is lost by reordering rows.

A *relational database* is defined as a collection of relations. As a practical matter, then, a relational database is simply any database that stores all of its data in table form. Since Visual Basic and most of the currently popular database programs, such as Access, Paradox, and dBase, deal with relational databases, this is the only type of database we will consider.

Each column in a table is designated by a heading, which is referred to as both a *field name* and an *attribute name* (the two terms are synonymous). For example, the four columns in Table 9-1 have the field names ID, Name, Ext, and Office, respectively. In a similar manner, each row in a table is referred to as a *record*. Thus, Table 9-1 has 20 records, Table 9-2 has 10 records, and Table 9-3 has two records.

In addition to storing information about each entity, a database must also provide information as to how the entities are related. Relationships between entities are typically signified by phrases such as "is related to," "is associated with," "consists of," "is employed by," "works for," and so forth. Such relationships between entities is conveniently expressed using an entity-relationship diagram (ERD), in which a straight line connects two or more entities. The exact relationship between entities is then marked on the line using the symbols illustrated in Figure 9-1.

Table 9-2 Sales Representatives Mailing Addresses*

ID	Office	FName	MI	LName	Addr1	Addr2	City	State	Zip
1	HM	Mary	A	Gerardo	614 Tremont Ave.		Hoboken	NJ	07030
2	HM	Bill	J	Bottlecheck	892 Freeman St.		Orange	NJ	07050
3	HM	Jayne		Scott	Apt. 12	56 Lyons Ave.	Bloomfield	NJ	07060
4	HM	Melissa	V	Smyth	78 Barnstable Rd.		Summit	NJ	07045
5	HM	Brian		Russell	93 Fairmont Ter.		Mountainside	NJ	07036
6	HM	Sara		Blitnick	832 Addison Drive		Maplewood	NJ	07085
7	F1	Blake		DiLorenzo	642 Schuller Dr.		Cherry Hill	NJ	07961
8	F1	Helen		Thomas	745 SkyLine Dr.		Camden	NJ	07920
9	F1	Mark		Somers	Apt. 3B	17 Turney St.	Trenton	NJ	07936
10	F1	Scott		Edwards	Apt. 46	932 Coleridge Rd.	Atlantic City	NJ	07018

*(Table name is SalesForce, the primary index is the ID field, and the table is also indexed on the LName field)

Table 9-3 Office Location List*

ID	Office	Address	City	State	Zip
1	HM	33 Freeman St.	Orange	NJ	07050
2	F1	614 Tremont Ave.	Trenton	NJ	07936

*(Table name is Offices and the primary index is the ID field)

Figure 9-1
ERD Symbols

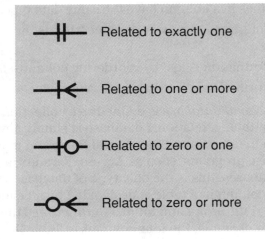

For example, Figure 9-2 illustrates the relationship between an employee and a company. ERD diagrams are always meant to be read from left-to-right and then from right-to-left. When reading from one entity to another, the ERD symbol attached to the starting entry is ignored. Thus, reading Figure 9-2 from left to right, and ignoring the symbol closest to the company entity, we see that a company employs zero or more employees. Reading from the right entity to the left entity, and again ignoring the symbol closest to the starting entity, we see that an employee is "employed by" exactly one company. The designation "zero or more," or "exactly one" is termed the *cardinality* of the relationship and refers to the number of one entity that is related to another entity.

Figure 9-3 is the ERD diagram for our Rotech Company database. As illustrated in this diagram, the database consists of three entities. Reading from the Office entity to the Employees entity, we see that an office consists of one or more employees, and reading from the Office entity to the Sales Reps entity, we see that an office consists of one or more sales representatives. Similarly, reading the ERD diagram from right-to-left, we see that an employee is related to exactly one office, as are the sales representatives.

The relationships illustrated in Figure 9-3 are both examples of *one-to-many* relationships. That is, one office may consist of many internal employees but each internal employee can only be associated with one office. This same one-to-many relationship exists for the sales force.

Figure 9-2
A Relationship between Entities

Figure 9-3
The Rotech Company ERD
Diagram

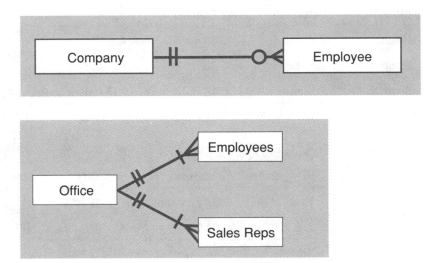

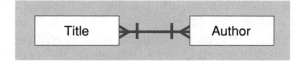

Figure 9-4
A Many-to-Many Relationship

In addition to a one-to-many relationship there is a many-to-many relationship. Such a relationship is illustrated in Figure 9-4, which relates authors to the books they write. As seen in this figure, an individual author can be associated with one or more titles, while an individual title can have more than one author.

Stored and Index Ordering

As each record is added to a table it is typically appended to the end of an existing set of records. This ordering of records is referred to as the table's original, or *stored*, order. For example, notice the ordering of the telephone records illustrated in Table 9-1. These records are in stored order, the order in which records were added to the table.

Frequently, it is convenient to have a table's records ordered either alphabetically, numerically, or chronologically. Rather than resorting all of the records, which can be time consuming for large databases, indexes are used. An *index* is a separate table of record positions, called *pointers*, which list the positions of the table's records in the desired order. For example, if we frequently wanted to access Table 9-1 in alphabetical name order, we would create an index based on the Name field. The first entry in the Name index table would be record number 30, followed by record number 1, followed by record numbers 3 and 4, and so. Reading the telephone table in Name index order would then provide us with an alphabetical list of names and their respective extensions.

Each index created for a table relies on one or more fields. The field on which a table's records are ordered is referred to as a *key field*. Thus, if the records in Table 9-1 are ordered by the Name field, the key field for this ordering is the Name field. A *compound key* is one in which two or more fields are used to create the index. For example, you might wish a table of employees to be listed in departmental order and then in alphabetical last name order. Creating a compound key consisting of department name followed by last name, and then indexing the table based on this key, would produce the desired result.

In constructing a database table, it is advisable that each record have at least one key field that can be used to uniquely identify each record in a table. When a key field is used in this manner it is referred to as a primary key field, or *primary key*, for short. Typically, in the absence of any other key field, the record number is taken to be the primary key. The record number is assigned sequentially, starting from 1, to each new record added to a table. If a record is deleted from the table, the record number is also deleted and not used again. In all of our tables we will assume that the record number is the primary key. Thus, displaying a table in record number order is the same as displaying it in what we previously referred to as its stored order.

Structured Queries

In addition to ordering a table's records in either stored or index order, you will encounter situations that require either listing a single table's records in a manner that is different from an existing index order, combining records from one or more tables, or asking and answering specific question about the data. For example, you might need to determine how many customers have a balance outstanding over sixty days, or how many customers have exceeded their credit limit. In almost all of these situations you could construct a new index, based on outstanding days or outstanding amounts, for example, use the data in the new indexed order, and then delete the index when you have completed the task at hand. An alternative, however, is to use a structured query. A *structured query* is a statement, written according to the rules of a language called Structured Query Language (SQL—pronounced as both sequel or the letters S-Q-L), that uniquely identifies a set of records from one or more tables.[1] For example, a requirement such as

> *Select all of the internal employee names from the PhoneBook table (Table 9-1) who are assigned to the Office designated as HM*

should result in all of the names being listed for those employees in Table 9-1 who are assigned to the home office. When this statement is written as an SQL structured statement, it becomes

```
Select Names From PhoneBook Where Office = "HM"
```

In Section 9.6 we present structured queries in detail, show how to construct such statements, and incorporate them within Visual Basic to create subsets of records from one or more tables.

The Jet Engine and RecordSets

A database management system (DBMS) is defined as a package of one or more computer programs designed to establish, maintain, and use a database. The underlying DBMS provided with Visual Basic is Microsoft's *Jet* database engine, which is referred to as the Jet engine, for short.[2] The Jet engine is responsible for opening a database, locating records from among the tables, providing access to these records, maintaining the security of the records as defined for the database, and other such capabilities requisite to a DBMS.

When accessed by Visual Basic the Jet engine creates a workspace into which the engine writes a set of records that may be manipulated by Visual Basic controls and code. This set of records, referred to as a *RecordSet*, consists of one of the following:

1. All of the records in a single table, in stored order, or
2. All of the records in a single table, in an indexed order, or
3. A select group of records, from one or more tables, constructed using a structured query.

To accommodate the different type of records that the Jet engine can create in a workspace, three different types of RecordSets can be constructed. Table 9-4 lists the three available types and their usage.

Table 9-4	RecordSet Types	
Type	**Name**	**Usage**
0	Table-Type	Construct a set of records that uses an index and can be updated, given the proper permissions.
1	Dynaset-Type	Construct a set of records that is either in stored order or is determined by a structured query, and can be updated, given the proper permissions.
2	Snapshot-Type	Construct a set of records that is either in stored order or is determined by a structured query, and that can only be examined but not updated.

---

[1] The set of records can be empty; i.e., no records meet the selected criteria.

[2] The Jet engine is also the DBMS that underlies Microsoft's Access Database system.

In the following sections we will explore how to use Visual Basic to create and use each of the RecordSet types listed in Table 9-4. This can be accomplished using code, using a Data control, or by a combination of these two techniques. Although both of these techniques, code and control, are presented in this chapter, we begin our exploration using the control technique.

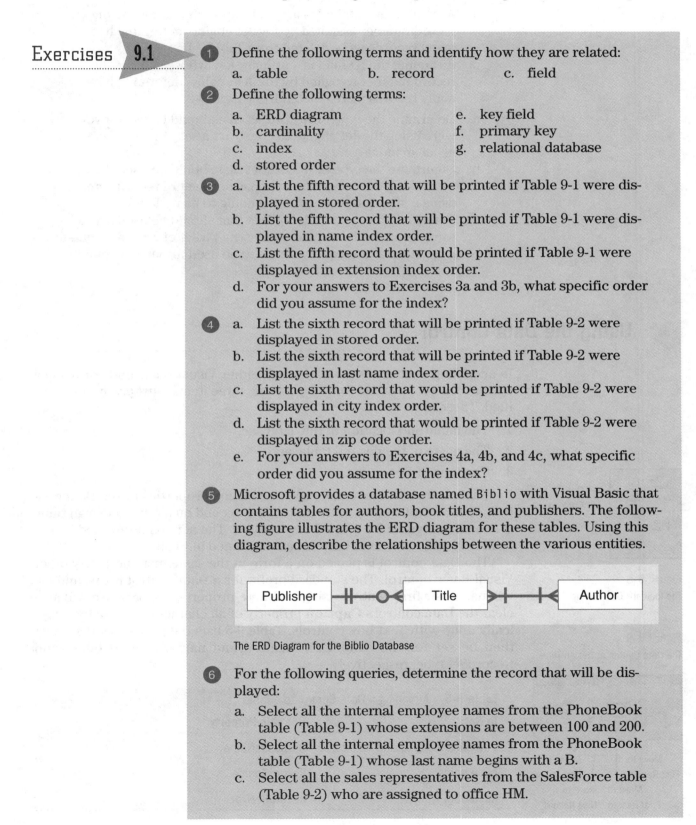

Exercises 9.1

1. Define the following terms and identify how they are related:
   a. table   b. record   c. field

2. Define the following terms:
   a. ERD diagram   e. key field
   b. cardinality   f. primary key
   c. index   g. relational database
   d. stored order

3. a. List the fifth record that will be printed if Table 9-1 were displayed in stored order.
   b. List the fifth record that will be printed if Table 9-1 were displayed in name index order.
   c. List the fifth record that would be printed if Table 9-1 were displayed in extension index order.
   d. For your answers to Exercises 3a and 3b, what specific order did you assume for the index?

4. a. List the sixth record that will be printed if Table 9-2 were displayed in stored order.
   b. List the sixth record that will be printed if Table 9-2 were displayed in last name index order.
   c. List the sixth record that would be printed if Table 9-2 were displayed in city index order.
   d. List the sixth record that would be printed if Table 9-2 were displayed in zip code order.
   e. For your answers to Exercises 4a, 4b, and 4c, what specific order did you assume for the index?

5. Microsoft provides a database named `Biblio` with Visual Basic that contains tables for authors, book titles, and publishers. The following figure illustrates the ERD diagram for these tables. Using this diagram, describe the relationships between the various entities.

The ERD Diagram for the Biblio Database

6. For the following queries, determine the record that will be displayed:
   a. Select all the internal employee names from the PhoneBook table (Table 9-1) whose extensions are between 100 and 200.
   b. Select all the internal employee names from the PhoneBook table (Table 9-1) whose last name begins with a B.
   c. Select all the sales representatives from the SalesForce table (Table 9-2) who are assigned to office HM.

d. Select all the sales representatives from the SalesForce table (Table 9-2) who live in Orange, New Jersey.

e. Select all the sales representatives from the SalesForce table (Table 9-2) who have a middle initial.

7. a. Assuming the ID field is a primary key whose value is the record number assigned by the Jet engine, determine how many records were deleted from Table 9-1.

b. Assuming the ID field is a primary key whose value is the record number assigned by the Jet engine, determine how many records were deleted from Table 9-2.

8. a. Determine the type of RecordSet that should be used if you were using the Jet engine to construct a set of records created using an index.

b. Determine the type of RecordSet that should be used if you were using the Jet engine to construct a set of records created using a structured query and needing to be updated.

c. Determine the type of RecordSet that should be used if you were using the Jet engine to construct a set of records created using a structured query that is to be used for viewing only.

9.2 Using the Data Control

In accessing a database table, through either Visual Basic code or using a special control provided for this purpose, three items must always be specified. These are

1. The name and location of the database,
2. The name of the desired table, and
3. The type of RecordSet.

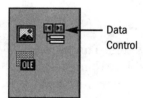

Data Control

Figure 9-5
The Toolbar's Data Control Icon

Figure 9-6
The Data Control at Design-Time

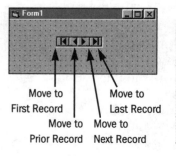

Move to First Record
Move to Last Record
Move to Prior Record
Move to Next Record

Each of these items can be specified using properties of the Data control. This control, as it appears in the Toolbox and on a form at design time, is shown in Figures 9-5 and 9-6 respectively. The actions performed by the Data control's movement buttons are also listed in Figure 9-6.

The Data control is placed on a form in the same manner as any other Visual Basic control. The standard prefix for a Data control is dat, and we will name our first control, using its **Name** property, datPhone. We will also clear the Data control's **Caption** property of all characters, as we have typically done with Text box controls. Table 9-5 lists the properties that must then be set for the database's location and name, desired table, and RecordSet type, respectively.

Table 9-5   Attaching a Data Control to a Table

To Set:	Use this Property:
Database location and name	DatabaseName
Table name	RecordSource
RecordSet Type	RecordSetType

PROGRAMMERS NOTES

Using a Data Control

For each set of records you wish to access, you can either set up a Data control or use Visual Basic code. If you use a control, the rule is one Data control per RecordSet. To set up and use a Data control, you must, at a minimum, set the following three properties:

1. DatabaseName, which names the desired database and defines where it is located,

2. RecordSource, which names the table or structured query from which a RecordSet is created,

and

3. RecordSetType, which defines the type of RecordSet that the Jet engine will create.

The third property, RecordSetType, does not have to be explicitly set, because it uses a default Dynaset type. The Dynaset is fine for stored-order or structured-query defined record sets that can be updated. If you are going to use an index, however, you must explicitly select a Table-type RecordSet.

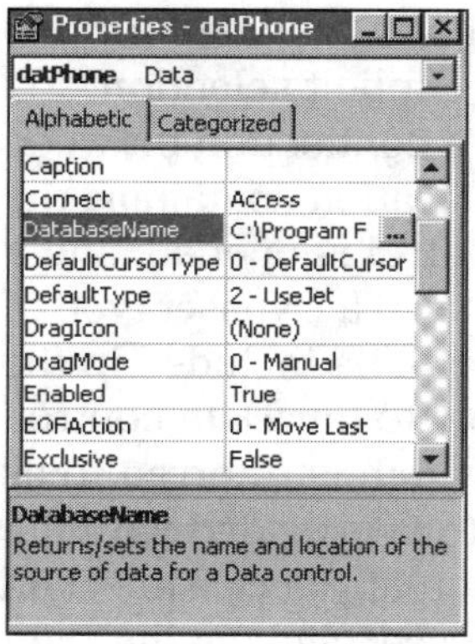

Figure 9-7

Setting the DatabaseName Property

Each of the properties listed in Table 9-5, must be set for the Data control to be correctly attached to a specific table and to permit the Jet engine to produce a set of records that can be manipulated in Visual Basic. The general rule for Data controls is one control per table. At run time the Data control calls upon the Jet engine to create a single workspace into which a single RecordSet is automatically written. Since our fist application will only use the PhoneBook table (Table 9-1), we will need only one Data control.

Figure 9-7 shows how the database's location and name appear in the **DatabaseName** property setting box. The complete Company database, which includes Tables 9-1 through 9-3, is provided on the Student Disk that comes with this text book. On our computer, this database resides in the directory named \Program Files\Microsoft Visual Basic. Thus, the complete path name for the file, placed in the **DatabaseName** property, is C:\Program Files\Microsoft Visual Basic\Company.mdb.[3] If you don't want to type this path name into the DatabaseName setting box, you can click on the ellipses (. . .) to the right of the setting box. This will bring up the standard Database dialog, illustrated in Figure 9-8, and you can designate the database's location from within this dialog.

In reviewing Figure 9-8, notice the Biblio database. This database is provided by Microsoft with Visual Basic and is one that we will use both in the section exercises and later in this chapter. Also, notice by their icons and

Figure 9-8

Using the DatabaseName Dialog Box

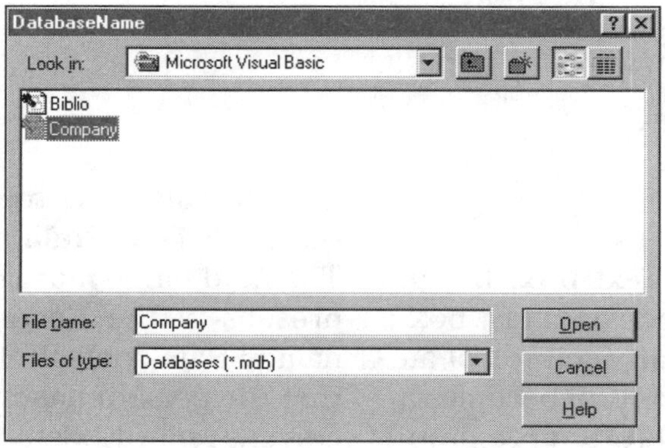

---

[3] Change this to A:Company.mdb to use the database on the Student Disk in the A drive.

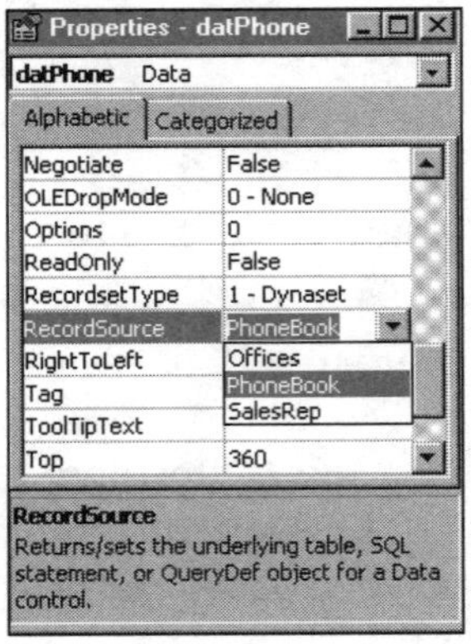

Figure 9-9

Setting the RecordSource Property

Figure 9-9

Setting the RecordSource Property

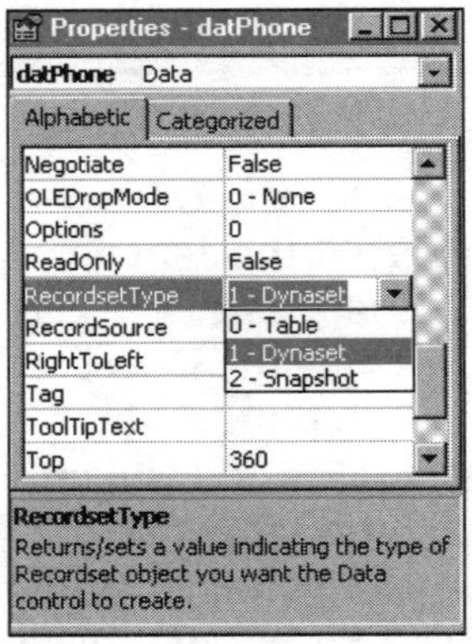

Figure 9-10

Setting the RecordSet Type
Property

extensions (.mdb) that both the Company and Biblio databases are Access data-bases. This database type is the default used in Visual Basic. If you are work-ing with a database created in another application, such as dBase or Paradox, you must change the database application name set for the **Connect** property.

Having set the location and database name using the **DatabaseName** property, we now continue to link the Data control to a specific database table. This is done, as indicated in Table 9-5, using the **RecordSource** prop-erty. As shown in Figure 9-9, once the **DatabaseName** has been set, Visual Basic will provide a drop-down list of available tables in the database, when the **RecordSource** property is accessed. In this case, we will select the PhoneBook table (Table 9-1).

The last property that must be set is the **RecordSetType**. Table 9-4, pre-sented at the end of the previous section, provides the basis for the **RecordSetType** selection. As indicated in this table, if an index is to be used, the **RecordSetType** must be a Table-type; otherwise, either a Dynaset- or Snapshot-type can be used depending upon whether or not the records are to be updated.

For our first application we will simply use the Data control to display and update the PhoneBook's records in stored order. From Table 9-4 we see that the proper RecordSet for this usage is a Dynaset. Since this is the de-fault value used for the **RecordSetType** property, no explicit setting need be made. Figure 9-10, however, shows the drop-down box provided for this property, and the three RecordSet types available for explicit selection.

The sole purpose of the Data control is to provide a connection between an application and an external database—when the application containing the control is executed, the table assigned to the Data control is opened, and a RecordSet created. In our specific case, since we have used a Dynaset type of RecordSet, all of the records in the PhoneBook table will be included in the RecordSet created by the Jet engine and made available to our Data control.

To move through the records in the RecordSet, which is referred to as *browsing* or *navigating* the table, we can use the buttons provided with the Data control. At any point in time, only one record is actually accessible, and this record is referred to as the *current record*. In our case, clicking the Data control's left-most button (see Figure 9-6) makes the PhoneBook's first record the current record, while clicking the right-most button makes the Phone-Book's last record the current record. Similarly, clicking the Previous Button and Next Button moves the record position forward and backward through the records contained in the RecordSet. There remains one significant prob-lem, however, and this is that we have made no provision for actually seeing the data in the current record. This is accomplished using bound controls.

PROGRAMMERS NOTES

Creating a Bound and Data-Aware Control

A Bound control can be a Text box, Label, Picture Box, Image box, Check box, List box, Combo box, a custom third-party control, or an OLE Container control. The control becomes a Bound control by setting its **DataSource** prop-erty to the name of a Data control.

The control is then made data-aware by setting its **DataField** property to a field name. The field name must represent a field that is present in the RecordSet accessed by the named Data control. Being *data-aware* means that the control has immediate access to the current record's data field value as identified by the control's **DataField** property setting.

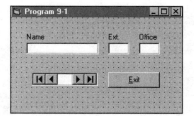

Figure 9-11
Program 9-1's Interface

Figure 9-12
Binding a Control to the datPhone
Data Control

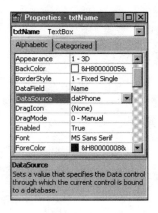

Figure 9-13
Setting the DataField Property

Bound Controls

Figure 9-11 illustrates Program 9-1's interface. As shown, three Text boxes are used to display the data in a current record's Name, Ext, and Office fields. To do this we will bind each of the three Text box controls to the Data control. Then, as we move through the RecordSet using the Data control's buttons, the field values from the current record will automatically be picked up and displayed in the designated Text boxes.

Binding an individual control, such as a Text box, to a Data control creates what is called a *data-aware* control. This means that the control has access to, or becomes aware of, the data field value in the current record identified by a Data control. Such controls, which can be a Text box, Label, Picture Box, Image box, Check box, List box, Combo box, custom third-party controls, or OLE container controls, are then referred to as *bound controls*.

Binding a control, such as a Text box, to a Data control requires setting the control's **DataSource** and **DataField** properties. Setting the **DataSource** property binds the control to a specific Data control, while setting the **DataField** property makes the bound control aware of (that is, attached to) a specific field. For example, look at Figure 9-12, which shows the setting for the Text box that will be used to display the PhoneBook's **Name** field. Since all of the Text boxes used in Program 9-1 will be used for PhoneBook data, each of these controls will be bound to the datPhone Data control using the setting shown in Figure 9-12.

Once a control is bound to a Data control, it is made data-aware by setting its **DataField** property. As illustrated in Figure 9-13, Visual Basic provides a drop-down list of all of the fields that can be assigned to the control. These fields are, of course, the fields for the RecordSet identified by the Data control. In our specific example, these include all of the PhoneBook table's fields.

Table 9-6 on page 454 lists the relevant property settings for Program 9-1's controls (see Figure 9-11). As listed in this table, all of the Text boxes are bound to the datPhone Data control. The significant difference between each box is the field in the PhoneBook table that each box is made aware of. Label controls are provided as a means of clearly identifying the displayed fields.

If Program 9-1 is now run, without adding any code, the Text boxes will display the values of the current record determined by the Data control's push buttons. As we will see in Section 9-5, any changes made in the Text boxes will automatically be made to the underlying PhoneBook data, if appropriate access privileges are set.

Typically, applications that use a Data control do provide some code for the control. At a minimum, this code sets and maintains the Data control's **Caption** property to identify the currently displayed record. Doing this requires a single line of code, but first we must consider the Data control's event procedures to determine where this line of code should be placed.

Data Control Event Procedures

A number of event procedures and methods are particularly useful for applications that use a Data control. Some of these, like the **Form_Load** event, have much broader uses. Others, such as the **Refresh** method, have more limited use, but still have applicability beyond their connection to the Data control. Still others, such as the **Reposition** event, only have applicability to a Data control. We will examine each of these events and methods as they relate to the Data control.

Table 9-6 Program 9-1's Properties Table

Object	Property	Setting
Form	Name	frmMain
	Caption	Program 9-1
Label	Name	lblName
	Caption	Name
Label	Name	lblExt
	Caption	Ext.
Label	Name	lblOffice
	Caption	Office
Text box	Name	txtName
	Text	(Blank)
	DataSource	datPhone
	DataField	Name
Text box	Name	txtExt
	Text	(Blank)
	DataSource	datPhone
	DataField	Ext
Text box	Name	txtOffice
	Text	(Blank)
	DataSource	datPhone
	DataField	Office
Data control	Name	datPhone
	Caption	(Blank)
	DatabaseName[4]	C:\Program Files\Microsoft Visual Basic\Company.mdb
	RecordSource	PhoneBook
	RecordSetType	Dynaset
Command button	Name	cmdExit
	Caption	E&xit

The first method that we will examine is the **Refresh** method. As it relates to a Data control, this method is used to either open a database and build a new RecordSet, reopen a database and recreate a RecordSet with updated data, or reopen a database and rebuild a new RecordSet when one of the Data control properties listed in Table 9-7 has been changed at run time.

For our immediate purposes we will invoke the **Refresh** method from within a **Form_Load** event to explicitly open a Data-control specified database. Although the database would eventually be opened implicitly, by explicitly using the **Refresh** method at form-load time we ensure that a RecordSet is immediately available and can be directly manipulated using code as the need arises. This is a typical use for the **Form_Load** event—to include initialization code for a form, to specify initial control settings at run time rather than at design time, and to explicitly open all files used by an ap-

---

[4]Change the stting to A:Company.mdb to use the database on the Student Disk on the A drive.

Table 9-7 Effect of Using the Refresh Method

If this property is changed:	This is the effect of a Refresh operation:
DatabaseName	Database is reopened and the RecordSet rebuilt.
RecordSource	RecordSet is rebuilt.
Options	RecordSet is rebuilt.
Connect	Database is reopened and the RecordSet rebuilt.
Exclusive	Database is reopened and the RecordSet rebuilt.
ReadOnly	Database is reopened and the RecordSet rebuilt.

plication. Thus, for our datPhone Data control the **Form_Load** event will initially appear as

```
Private Sub Form_Load()
  datPhone.Refresh
End Sub
```

In reviewing this code, pay particular attention to the dot notation used. Here, the **Refresh** method is applied to the Data control table named datPhone, and will cause the Jet engine to open and build a RecordSet when the form is loaded. Before leaving the **Form_Load** event, there is one other item that should be addressed—what to provide for the Data control's initial **Caption**. The three generally used options are

1. Provide the initial record's position in the RecordSet;
2. Provide a unique identification associated with the initial record, such as its key value; and
3. Leave the **Caption** blank.

The first option is the one most commonly used and the one that we will use. This is accomplished by expanding the **Form_Load** event procedure to the following:

```
Private Sub Form_Load()
  datPhone.Refresh
  datPhone.Caption = 1
End Sub
```

Figure 9-14

The Opening Screen Presented by Program 9-1

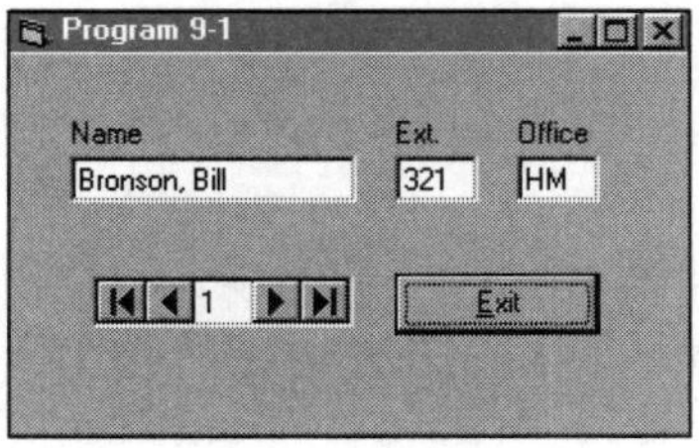

Figure 9-14 shows the effect of setting the **Caption** property to 1 in the **Form_Load** event by illustrating how the application looks when it is first executed.

Identifying the first record in a RecordSet with a caption of 1 is reasonable, because users generally expect to see the first record presented as record number 1, the second record as record number 2, and so on.

However, this approach does have a drawback because a record's position in the RecordSet can vary, depending on what is done to the records. For example, a record's position can change whenever a record is deleted or whenever a RecordSet is rebuilt. Thus, the record initially identified with a caption value of 2 may later become the first record in the set and be identified with a caption value of 1. Although this is usually not a problem, occasionally a user may either wonder about or complain that the same record appears to have two different record numbers.

The alternatives to assigning a possibly transient record position to the Data control's **Caption** value are either to provide no caption at all or to use a non-changing value, stored as a field value, that uniquely identifies each record. For the PhoneBook records, such a value is provided by the ID field. The following statement shows how this field's value is accessed and can be used to set the Data control's **Caption** property:

```
datPhone.Caption = datPhone.Recordset("ID")
```

Notice a specific field is identified by enclosing the quoted field name within parentheses. The drawback to using a specific field's value, however, is that as a user sequentially moves through the RecordSet using the Data control's push buttons, the displayed caption value can appear to "jump." For example, if a user moves through the records from the first to the last in the RecordSet created by Program 9-1, the **Caption** value will change from 15 to 21 when the user moves from the twelfth record, corresponding to Harriet Miller, to the thirteenth record, corresponding to Pat O'Neil (see Table 9-1). For most users this type of jump is very disconcerting. A way around this problem is to attach a textual identification with the caption, as in the following statement:

```
datPhone.Caption = "ID No = " & datPhone.Recordset("ID")
```

Regardless of which approach you select, it is always important to try and anticipate how your decisions will affect a user. For small decisions, such as how a caption or label will appear, the program designer should make the decision, explain how it works, and be prepared to make modifications based on user feedback. For more important decisions, users should always be consulted beforehand. Be aware, however, that asking users for decisions on minor design criteria and especially on *how* an operation is performed, is typically construed as bothersome and an indication that the programmer is inexperienced. Similarly, not asking users for input on matters that directly affect them, such as *what* data they require as output from an application, is typically construed as an indication that the programmer is insensitive to their needs. Obtaining the proper balance is what distinguishes both very successful programmers from the not-so-successful, and very successful applications from annoying ones.

Having now selected the initial value displayed for the Data control's **Caption** (we will use the record number approach), it only remains to keep the caption current as the user moves through the RecordSet. To do this, we will use the Data control's **Reposition** event. This event is triggered *after* one of the control's push buttons has been activated and the current record has been changed. The required event procedure is

```
Private Sub datPhone_Reposition()
  datPhone.Caption = datPhone.Recordset.AbsolutePosition + 1
End Sub
```

The **AbsolutePosition** method, which is only applicable to Dynaset- and Snapshot-type RecordSets, returns the relative record position of the RecordSet's current record, with the first record identified as position 0. Adding 1 to the returned value alters the record position to begin with the number 1. The complete code provided for Program 9-1 is listed below.

Program 9-1's Event Code

```
Private Sub Form_Load()
  datPhone.Refresh
  datPhone.Caption = 1
End Sub
```

```
Private Sub datPhone_Reposition()
  datPhone.Caption = datPhone.Recordset.AbsolutePosition + 1
End Sub

Private Sub cmdExit_Click()
  Beep
  End
End Sub
```

The only change you might want to make in Program 9-1's event code is to replace the setting of the Data control's **Caption** to 1 in the **Form_Load** event with the setting method used in the **Reposition** event code. Both approaches to initializing the caption are equally valid.

Before leaving this event code, we make note of the fact that the **Form_Load** event procedure can also be used to set a Data control's **DatabaseName** and **RecordSource** properties at run time. For example, the statements

```
datPhone.DatabaseName = App.Path & "\Company.mdb"
datPhone.RecordSource = "PhoneBook"
```

can be included in the **Form_Load** event procedure to set the respectively named property values. These statements would appear before the **Refresh** method is invoked. In setting the **DatabaseName** property, the keyword **App** is the name of a globally defined object that provides information about an application's title, path, and executable file name. When the **Path** method is applied to this object it specifies the path of the *project* file when the application is executed from the development environment, or the path of the *executable* file when the application is run as an executable file. Assuming that the Company database is located in the same directory, the expression App.Path & "\Company.mdb" correctly identifies the location and name of the desired database. An alternative is to provide the complete path name for the database, which is necessary if the database is located in a different directory than the application's form.

Index Ordering

When Program 9-1 is executed, the records built for the RecordSet will be in stored order. Typically, however, a user will expect the names to be accessed alphabetically, from A to Z. There are two approaches to creating this anticipated ordering. The first approach, which uses the **Name** index created for the PhoneBook table, is described next. The second approach, and a more powerful programming technique that uses structured queries, is presented in the next section.

To present the names provided by Program 9-1 in alphabetical order using an index requires minor changes to the program. The first modification, which is indicated by the information previously provided in Table 9-4, requires that the RecordSet type be a Table-type to accommodate a RecordSet built using an index. The final set of modifications is concerned with the code, which must set the active index to **Name** and update the Data control's **Caption** property correctly. To understand these changes, review Program 9-2's event code.

Program 9-2's Event Code

```
Private Sub Form_Load()
  datPhone.Refresh
  datPhone.Recordset.Index = "Name"
  datPhone.Caption = "ID = " & datPhone.Recordset("ID")
End Sub

Private Sub datPhone_Reposition()
  datPhone.Caption = "ID = " & datPhone.Recordset("ID")
End Sub

Private Sub cmdExit_Click()
  Beep
  End
End Sub
```

The first change to notice in the event code is the modification to the **Form_Load** event. Here we have used the **Index** method to explicitly set the index to **Name**. If this explicit setting was omitted, the RecordSet would be built using the table's primary index.

Figure 9-15

The Opening Screen Presented by Program 9-2

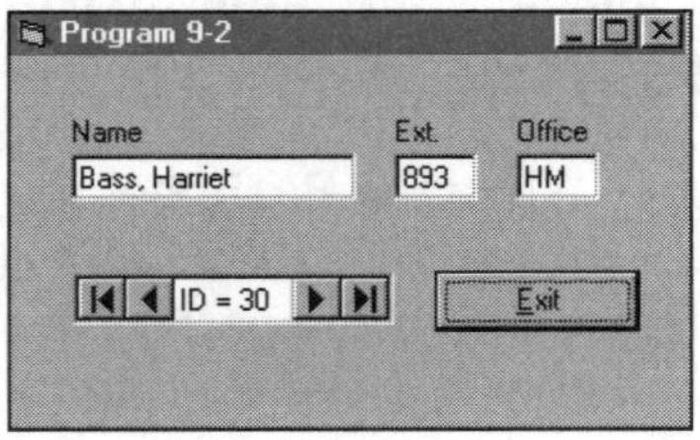

Next, notice that the Data control's **Caption** property is set and maintained using each record's ID value. Since the **AbsoluteProperty** method cannot be used with Table-type RecordSets, we must either keep track of record numbers by determining which push button was activated, or use the **Caption** property to display some other information, such as an ID value. We have chosen the latter approach both because of its simplicity and to reinforce use of the syntax required in directly accessing a record's field value.

Figure 9-15 shows how Program 9-2 appears when it is first executed. Notice that the first record displayed is, alphabetically, the first record in the PhoneBook table that was previously listed as Table 9-1. Also notice that the Data control **Caption** correctly identifies this as the record whose ID value is 30.

Exercises 9.2

1. List the three Data control properties that must be set to correctly build a RecordSet.

2. a. Under what circumstances would you use a Table for a Data control's RecordSet property?
   b. Under what circumstances would you use a Dynaset for a Data control's RecordSet property?
   c. Under what circumstances would you use a Snapshot for a Data control's RecordSet property?

3. a. What is a bound control?
   b. List the controls that can be used as bound controls.
   c. List the properties that must be set to create a bound control.

4. Using the Code window, determine and list all event procedures associated with a Data control.

5. Using the Help facility, obtain documentation on the following terms:
   a. AbsolutePosition Property
   b. Dynaset-type RecordSet
   c. Snapshot-type RecordSet
   d. Table-type RecordSet
   e. Path Property
   f. Refresh Method
   g. Validate Event

(6) Enter and execute Program 9-1 on your computer.

(7) a. Modify Program 9-1 so that the Data control's **Caption** displays the current record's ID field value.

b. Modify Program 9-1 so that the Data control's **Caption** is always blank.

(8) Enter and execute Program 9-2 on your computer.

(9) Modify Program 9-2 so that the displayed names are presented in Extension value order. (**Hint:** The PhoneBook table has an index named Ext.)

(10) a. Write a Visual Basic Program that uses a Data control to display the records in the Company database's SalesRep table (see Table 11-2.) The records should be displayed as they are stored in the table.

b. Modify the program written for Exercise 10a to display the records in last-name indexed order. (**Hint:** The SalesRep table has an index named LName.)

(11) Write a Visual Basic Program that uses a Data control to display the records in the Company database's Office table (see Table 9-3.) The records should be displayed as they are stored in the table.

9.3 Creating RecordSets Using SQL

Using a table's name as a Data control's **RecordSource** property restricts us to viewing a single table's records in either stored or indexed order. There will be times, however, when you will need to either view records in an order for which no index exists, create a set of records that is constructed from more than one table, or view a subset of records that meets one or more criteria. For example, you might need to create a list of people whose outstanding balance is over sixty days old, or create a list of people who owe more than $500, or possibly cross check two tables to determine names that appear in both. For situations such as these, structured queries can be used as a **RecordSource** property value in place of a table's name.

For example, in Program 9-1, the **RecordSource** property was set to PhoneBook at design time, which caused the Jet engine to create a RecordSet consisting of all this table's records in stored order. Instead of setting the **RecordSource** property to a table's name, a structured query can be used. For example, the same RecordSet created by Program 9-1 can be created by entering the following structured query into the **Record-Source** property:

```
Select * From PhoneBook
```

This statement is rather easy to read, once you understand that the * is a shortcut that means all fields are to be listed, in the order they appear in the table. Thus, this statement is read "select *all fields* from the PhoneBook table." Since no further constraints are placed on the table, the default is to select all of the table's records.

A structured query **Select** statement is quite different from Visual Basic's **Select Case** statement. As previously defined in Section 9.1, a *structured query* is a statement written according to the rules of a language called Structured Query Language (SQL—pronounced as both sequel or the letters S-Q-L), that uniquely identifies a set of records from one or more tables. Although obtaining all of the record's in a table is accomplished easier by using a table's name as the **RecordSource** property value, structured queries provide much more flexibility to create and order individualized sets of records. Structured queries can be entered as a **RecordSource** value either at design time or set at run time, and we show how to do both in this section. First, however, we must become familiar with the SQL **Select** statement.

SQL was developed by IBM in the 1970s, and became the foundation of its DB2 data management system. In 1986, an American National Standards Institute (ANSI) standard was approved for this language, and since that time many commercial DBMS products, including Microsoft's Jet engine, support it as an extremely powerful technique for extracting data from database tables.

The basic syntax of an SQL **Select** command, which is referred to as a structured query, is

```
Select field-name(s) From table(s) Where condition(s) Order By field-name(s)
```

Formally, this statement consists of four clauses; a **Select** clause, a **From** clause, a **Where** clause, and an **Order By** clause. The words **Select, From, Where**, and **Order By**, are all SQL keywords.

At a minimum, a structured query must contain both a **Select** and **From** clause; the **Select** clause specifies the field values that will be returned by the query, while the **From** clause specifies the table or tables whose records will be searched. Additionally, if any restrictions are placed on the data to be selected, or if the selected information is to be presented in a specified order, the **Where** or **Order** clauses must be included, respectively. For example, in the statement

```
Select * From PhoneBook Order By Ext
```

the **Select** * clause specifies that all fields are to be obtained, the **From** clause specifies that the fields are to come from the PhoneBook table, and the **Order** clause specifies that the RecordSet is to be constructed in increasing (that is, ascending) order based on the values in the Ext field. If descending order is desired (that is, from highest to lowest extension values) the SQL keyword **Desc** must be placed after the field name in the **Order** clause. Thus, the SQL statement

```
Select * From PhoneBook Order By Ext Desc
```

performs the same function as the previous SQL statement, but returns the data in descending extension number order. If an index exists for the field name upon which the data is being ordered, the Jet engine will automatically use this index to sort the data; if no index exists, the Jet engine sorts the data in the specified order before creating the returned RecordSet. Because structured queries are so versatile and can be used to construct RecordSets that contain records constructed from more than one table, they are used extensively as the **RecordSource** property for many Visual Basic database applications. This, of course, implies that either a Dynaset- or Snapshot-type value is used for the **RecordsetType** property, because only these two types of RecordSets can be constructed using a structured query (see Table 9-4).

To illustrate the usefulness of creating RecordSets using structured queries, we present a number of examples using the SQL **Select** statement. In the first two examples we use the Company database, whose tables were previously listed as Tables 9-1 through 9-3. We then construct RecordSets with records derived from two tables. For these latter examples we will use the `Biblio` database provided by Microsoft with Visual Basic.

Example 1:
Using the PhoneBook table, create a RecordSet consisting of all fields for employees in the home office.

The structured query for this example is

```
Select * From PhoneBook Where Office = 'HM'
```

Here we have used a **Where** clause, which creates a set of records where each record must meet the specified condition to be included in the final RecordSet. The resulting set of records is frequently referred to as a *filtered set*, and the **Where** clause itself is commonly referred to as a *filter*. In reviewing this clause, notice that the value being searched for (HM) is enclosed in single quotes. This is required in SQL when the field type of the desired item is a string type. If the field type were numeric, the value in the SQL **Where** clause would not be enclosed in single quotes. As always, the asterisk (*) in the query results in all fields in the selected records being included in the RecordSet, in the order that they exist in the underlying table. If you want to change this order, you can individually list the fields in the desired order. For example, the structured query

```
Select Office, Name, Ext, ID From PhoneBook Where Office = 'HM'
```

extracts the same data as the prior query, but creates a RecordSet in which each record has the field order listed in the **Select** statement. This ordering makes no difference to an application using a Data control, as long as the fields required by the data-aware controls are included in the query. Each data-aware control will subsequently extract its required field from the resulting RecordSet, no matter where the field is physically located within a record. If, however, a field is missing from the record required by a data-aware control, the error message `Item not found in this collection` is displayed.

Finally, notice that when explicit fields are listed within a **Select** clause, the individual field names are separated by commas. To cause this query to be the actual source of a RecordSet at design time, it must be entered as a Data control's **RecordSource** property value.

Example 2:
Using the SalesForce table, create a RecordSet consisting of all fields for employees living in Orange.

The structured query for this example is

```
Select * From SalesForce Where City = 'Orange'
```

In reviewing this query, notice that once again, since the `City` is a string field, we have enclosed the value being searched for within single quotes. As always, the query defines both the fields to be included in the RecordSet and the table from which these fields are to be taken. Additionally, the **Where** clause creates a filtered record set, where each selected record meets the stated requirement.

Although both of the preceding two examples have used a simple relational expression in the **Where** clause, compound expressions using the **And** and **Or** keywords are valid. For example, the structured query

```
Select Name From PhoneBook Where Ext < 300 And Ext > 900
```

Table 9-8 Publishers

PubID	Name	Company Name	Address
1	ACM	Association for Computing Machinery	11 W. 42nd St., 3rd flr.
2	Addison-Wesley	Addison-Wesley Publishing Co Inc.	Rte 128
3	Bantam Books	Bantam Books Div of: Bantam Doubleday Dell	666 Fifth Ave.
4	Benjamin/Cummings	Benjamin-Cummings Publishing Company Subs.	390 Bridge Pkwy.
5	Brady Pub.	Brady Books Div. of Prentice Hall Pr.	15 Columbus Cir.
6	Computer Science Press	Computer Science Press Inc Imprint	41 Madison Ave.
7	ETN Corporation	ETN Corp.	RD 4, Box 659
8	Gale	Gale Research, Incorporated	835 Penobscot Bldg.
9	IEEE	IEEE Computer Society Press	10662 Los Vaqueros
10	Intertext	Intertext Publications/Multiscience	2633 E. 17th Ave.

produces a set of records consisting of the Name field only for those individuals having an extension number either less than 300 or greater than 900. Notice that since the Ext field is defined as a numeric field, the values within the relational expression have not been enclosed in single quotes.

Relationships Reconsidered

The Company database we have used consists of three tables that, in practice, would be used almost independently of each other. That is, we could easily construct three forms, each of which uses its own Data control to assess and display data from each of the three tables individually.

It is not unusual to encounter databases with tables that are related in a more significant manner. As an example of such a database, we will use the Biblio database provided by Microsoft with Visual Basic. This database consists of tables containing information about publishers, titles, and authors of current computer science text books. Tables 9-8 through 9-11 list the names and the first ten records of each of the four tables that comprise the Biblio database. The relationship between the Publishers, Titles, and Authors tables is shown by the ERD diagram illustrated in Figure 9-16.

As shown in Figure 9-16, and reading from left to right, a publisher can be associated with zero or more titles, and a title can have one or more authors. Similarly, reading from right to left, an author can be associated with one or more titles, while a title can only be associated with a single publisher. Using Tables 9-8 through 9-10 we can easily establish RecordSets for any of the one-to-many relationships shown in Figure 9-16. This is accomplished by matching a desired field value in the appropriate table. For example, if we needed to locate all titles associated with the publisher ETN, the following structured query could be entered as a **RecordSource** property value:

```
Select * From Titles Where PubID = 7
```

Figure 9-16
The ERD Diagram for the Biblio.mdb Database

City	State	Zip	Telephone	Fax	Comments
New York	NY	10036	212-869-7440		
Reading	MA	01867	617-944-3700	617-964-9460	
New York	NY	10103	800-223-6834	212-765-3869	GENERAL TRA
Redwood City	CA	94065	800-950-2665	415-594-4409	
New York	NY	10023	212-373-8093	212-373-8292	
New York	NY	10010	212-576-9400	212-689-2383	Introductory
Montoursville	PA	17754-9433	717-435-2202	717-435-2802	Technical book
Detroit	MI	48226-4094	313-961-2242	313-961-6083	
Los Alamitos	CA	90720	800-272-6657	714-821-4010	PROFESSION
Anchorage	AK	99508			

Table 9-9 Titles

Title	Year Published	ISBN	PubID	Description/Notes	Subject
Database management; developing application	1989	0-0131985-2-1	17	xx, 441 p. : il	
Select-- SQL ; the relational database language	1992	0-0238669-4-2	12	xv, 446 p.	
dBase IV programming	1994	0-0280042-4-8	73		
Step-by-step dBase IV	1995	0-0280095-2-5	52		
Guide to ORACLE	1990	0-0702063-1-7	13	xii, 354 p. : ill/Includes I	ORACLE
The database experts' guide to SQL	1988	0-0703900-6-1 00703	10		
Oracle/SQL; a professional programmer's guide	1992	0-0704077-5-4	13	xx, 543 p. : il	
SQL 400: A Professional Programmer's Guide	1994	0-0704079-9-1	52		
Database system concepts	1986	0-0704475-2-7	13		
Microsoft FoxPro 2.5 applications programming	1993	0-0705015-3-X	61	xiii, 412 p. : i	

This type of query, which is a straightforward lookup in a single table, is typical of that used for a one-to-many relationship. The standard practice here is simply to locate all records in the table on the many sides of the relationship that have a matching field value for the single entity on the one side of the relationship. Unfortunately, no such simple lookup generally exists for locating matching entries corresponding to a many-to-many relationship.

Table 9-10	Authors	
Au_ID	**Author**	**Year Born**
1	Adams, Pat	
2	Adrian, Merv	
3	Ageloff, Roy	1943
4	Andersen, Virginia	
5	Antonovich Michael P.	
6	Arnott, Steven E.	
7	Arntson, L. Joyce	
8	Ault, Michael R.	
9	Avison, D. E.	
10	Bard, Dick	1941

Table 9-11	TitleAuthor
ISBN	**Au_ID**
0-0131985-2-1	13
0-0238669-4-2	113
0-0280042-4-8	11
0-0280042-4-8	120
0-0280095-2-5	171
0-0702063-1-7	26
0-0702063-1-7	65
0-0702063-1-7	104
0-0703900-6-1	96
0-0704077-5-4	59

For example, assume that we need to locate all authors associated with a single title. Since the titles-to-authors relationship is a many-to-many relationship, each title can have one or more associated authors and each author can be associated with one or more titles. To handle such relationships, tables referred to as both *cross-reference, correlation,* and *intersection* tables (all three terms are synonymous) are used. An example of a correlation table is illustrated by Table 9-11. Here, all authors associated with a particular ISBN number can be identified by locating all occurrences of the same ISBN number in the first column. Similarly, all books written by a single author can be identified by locating all occurrences of the author's ID number in the second column. Thus, if we needed to locate all the authors associated with the book entitled *Guide to ORACLE,* which has an ISBN number 0-0702063-1-7 (see the fifth record in Table 9-9), we could use the following structured query:

```
Select * From TitleAuthor Where ISBN = '0-0702063-1-1'
```

Similarly, if we needed to identify all books associated with the author named Virginia Andersen (the fourth author listed in Table 9-10), who has the author identification number 4, we could use the following structured query:

```
Select * From TitleAuthor Where Au_ID = 4
```

Notice that in the first query the "looked for" value has been enclosed in single quotes, while in the second query no quotes are used. This is because the ISBN field is defined as a string field, while the Au_ID field is defined as a numeric field in the TitleAuthor table.

Creating Multi-Table RecordSets

In addition to using structured queries to either filter or order data from a single table, they can be used to create sets of records derived from two or more tables. To illustrate this use of structured queries, we will again use the Biblio database (see Tables 9-8 through 9-11).

As a specific example, assume that we want to create a set of records that consist of a book's title and its publisher. Additionally, we want the final list of records to be in alphabetical order by publisher. To create this record set we would use the Titles table to locate all of the titles, and the Publishers table to locate all of the publishers. To connect a title with its publisher we use a **Where** clause with the condition that the PubID fields between the two tables match. Specifically, the following structured query locates the desired records and places them in the desired order:

```
Select Titles.Title, Publishers.Name
  From Titles, Publishers
  Where Titles.PubID = Publishers.PubID
  Order By Publishers.Name
```

For clarity we have written the query across four lines to easily identify each of the individual clauses. In practice, this single statement can be written as a single line in a Data control's **RecordSource** value.

In reviewing this query you should notice two items. The first is that the **From** clause identifies two tables. As with the **Select** clause where multiple fields can be identified, the **From** clause can include multiple table names. When this is done, individual table names must be separated by commas. The second item to note is the manner in which the field names have been identified throughout the query. Since we are dealing with two tables, both of which use the same field names, we must clearly establish which field is being referenced. This is accomplished using standard dot notation by listing the table name before the field name, and separating the two with a period. Thus the name `Titles.PubID` refers to the `PubID` field in the Titles table, and `Publishers.PubID` refers to the `PubID` in the Publishers table. This notation can be used wherever a field name is required, but if there is no ambiguity about which table is being used, the table name can always be omitted. Thus, the field name `Titles.Title` in the **Select** clause can be written simply as `Title`, because this field only exists in one of the tables referenced in the **From** clause.

Run-Time Structured Queries

As we have already seen, a structured query can be entered as a Data control's **RecordSource** property value at design time. For large queries, however, this can become error prone and provide queries that are cumbersome to debug. For example a query such as

```
Select Titles.Title, Publishers.Name
  From Titles, Publishers
  Where Titles.PubID = Publishers.PubID
  Order By Publishers.Name
```

is really too long to be conveniently entered as a **RecordSource** value. An alternative to entering such queries as design-time values is to set them at run time. For example, consider Event Procedure 9-1, which uses the **Form_Load** event to set and refresh the RecordSet of a Data control named `datSQL`.

Event Procedure 9-1

```
Private Sub Form_Load()
  Dim Sel As String, Frm As String
  Dim Whr As String, Ord As String
  Dim SQ As String
```

continued

```
            Sel = "Select Titles.Title, Publishers.Name"
            Frm = " From Titles, Publishers"
            Whr = " Where Titles.PubID = Publishers.PubID"
            Ord = " Order By Publishers.Name"
            SQ = Sel & Frm & Whr & Ord

            datSQL.RecordSource = SQ
            datSQL.Refresh
            datSQL.Caption = 1
        End Sub
```

The last two statements in this event procedure are the same as were previously used in Program 9-1. The new feature illustrated by this event procedure is the construction of a string named SQ and the assignment of this string to datSQL.RecordSource. Although we have constructed the SQ string from four strings, each of which highlights an individual SQL clause, this was done for the convenience of making each line a manageable size. The final setting of the **RecordSource** property could also have been made using the single statement

```
datSQL.RecordSource = "Select Titles.Title, Publishers.Name From Titles, Publishers Where
              Titles.PubID = Publishers.PubID Order By Publishers.Name"
```

Table 9-12　Program 9-3's Properties Table

Object	Property	Setting
Form	Name	frmMain
	Caption	Program 9-3
Data control	Name	datSQL
	Caption	(Blank)
	DatabaseName	C:\Program Files\Microsoft Visual Basic\Biblio.mdb
	RecordSource	(Blank)
	RecordSetType	Dynaset
Label	Name	lblTitle
	Caption	Title
Label	Name	lblPub
	Caption	Publisher
Text box	Name	txtTitle
	Text	(Blank)
	DataSource	datSQL
	DataField	Title
Text box	Name	txtPub
	Text	(Blank)
	DataSource	datSQL
	DataField	Name
Command button	Name	cmdExit
	Caption	E&xit

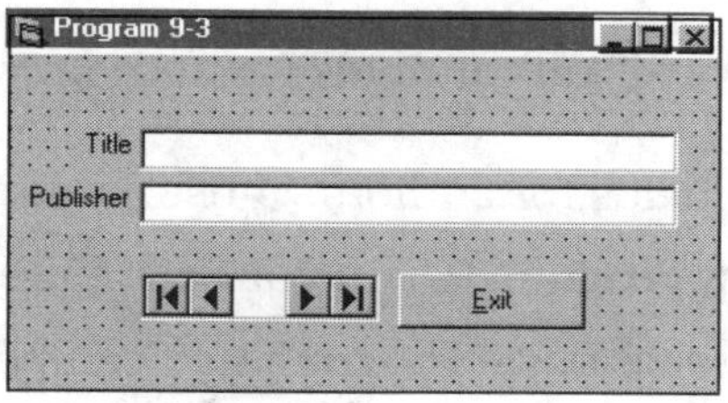

Figure 9-17
Program 9-3's Interface

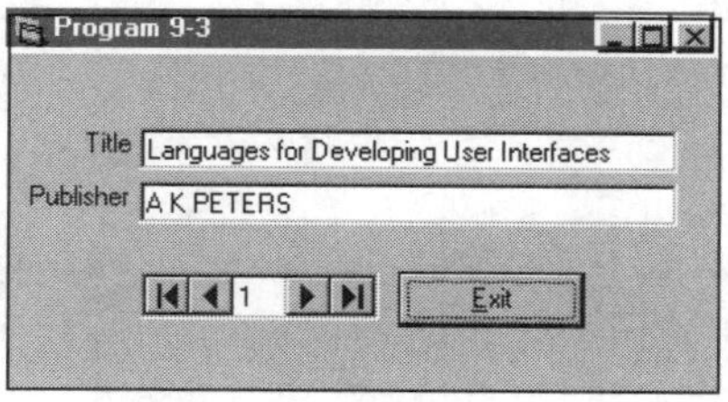

Figure 9-18
The Opening Screen Presented by Program 9-3

Notice that the final **RecordSource** setting is identical to that which could have been entered as the RecordSource at design time. Event Procedure 9-1 is used in Program 9-3, whose interface is shown in Figure 9-17.

Except for Event Procedure 9-1, the only other code used by Program 9-3 is the Exit procedure and Data control **Reposition** procedure previously used in Programs 9-1 and 9-2.

When Program 9-3 is executed the **Form_Load** event causes the Jet engine to create a RecordSet consisting of records constructed from both the Titles and Publishers tables. Each record in the set will consist of two fields, a Titles field, whose values come from the Titles table, and a Name field, whose values come from the Publishers table. Additionally, the records in the set will be in alphabetical order, by publisher's name. The screen that appears when this program is first run is shown in Figure 9-18.

Exercises 9.3

1. a. List the four clauses that can be present in a structured query.
   b. What are the two clauses that must be present in a structured query.

2. Using the Company database (Tables 9-1 through 9-3) write a structured query to create a RecordSet consisting of all fields for the following criteria:
   a. All records from the SalesRep table (Table 9-2) whose representatives are assigned to office HM.
   b. All records from the SalesRep table (Table 9-2) whose representatives live in Orange, New Jersey.
   c. All records from the SalesRep table (Table 9-2) whose representatives have a middle initial.
   d. All records from the PhoneBook table (Table 9-1) of employees whose last name begins with a B.
   e. All records from the PhoneBook table (Table 9-1) of employees who have an extension number between 100 and 200.

3. Using the Publishers Table (Table 9-8), write a structured query to create a RecordSet consisting of all fields for the following criteria:
   a. All records with a New York City field value.
   b. All records with a New York State field value.
   c. All records with both a New York City and State field value.
   d. All records with a Name field value beginning in the letter A.
   e. All records with a Zip code between 07000 and 07999.

4. Using the Authors Table (Table 9-10), write a structured query to create a RecordSet consisting of the indicated fields for the following criteria:
   a. All Author names for authors born before 1943.

b. All Au_ID and Author fields for authors whose birth date field is blank.

c. All Au_ID fields for authors whose name begins with the letter *C*.

5 Enter and run Program 9-3 on your computer.

6 a. Write a Visual Basic Program that can be used to display all Titles, ISBN numbers and Year Published from the Titles table (Table 9-9) in Year Published order.

b. If you have access to the `Biblio` database, run the program you wrote for Exercise 6a.

7 a. Modify the program written for Exercise 6a so that only texts published between 1989 and 1992 are accessed by your program.

b. If you have access to the `Biblio` database, run the program that you wrote for Exercise 7a.

8 a. Write a Visual Basic Program that can be used to display all fields of the Author table (Table 9-10) for records that do not have any data in their Year Born field.

b. If you have access to the `Biblio` database, run the program you wrote for Exercise 8a, and enter data into a Text box bound to the Year Born field. Describe what happens when you enter data, move to another record and then move back to the record in which you entered a date. Did the date remain with the record or was it erased?

9.4 Locating and Moving Through Records

The only means we currently have to locate a specific record is to move sequentially through a RecordSet using a Data control's push buttons. In this section we present alternative methods for directly locating a specific record and then moving through a RecordSet. We first introduce the **Find** methods, which can only be used with Dynaset- or Snapshot-type RecordSets, and then present the **Move** methods. Combining the **Move** methods with the **Find** methods permits us to construct a user interface that quickly locates a specific record and then cycles through any other records that match the search criteria. The last topic presented is the **Seek** method, which can only be used with indexes and Table-type RecordSets.

The Find Methods

The **Find** methods, which are listed in Table 9-13, can only be used with Dynaset- or Snapshot-type RecordSets. The syntax for each of the **Find** methods is

```
table.Recordset.Findmethod criteria
```

where

- *table* is the name of an existing Dynaset or Snapshot RecordSet;
- *Findmethod* is one of the **Find** methods listed in Table 9-13; and
- *criteria* is a string expression used to locate the desired record. It is constructed in the same manner as a structured query, but without the **Where** keyword.

Table 9-13 The Find Methods

Method Name	Search Begins At	Search Direction
FindFirst	Beginning of RecordSet	End of RecordSet
FindLast	End of RecordSet	Beginning of RecordSet
FindNext	Current Record Position	End of RecordSet
FindPrevious	Current Record Position	Beginning of RecordSet

For example, if we wanted to locate the first occurrence of extension number 464 in the PhoneBook table, the following statement can be used:

```
datPhone.Recordset.FindFirst "Ext = 464"
```

In a similar manner, to locate the first occurrence of the name John Grill, the following statement is valid:

```
datPhone.Recordset.FindFirst "Name = 'Grill, John' "
```

In reviewing these statements notice that the same convention is used for the **Find** criteria as that required in SQL: if the field value being searched for is a string, the value must be enclosed in single quotes. Also notice that the criteria itself, if it is a string literal, must be enclosed within double quotes.

When Visual Basic encounters a **Find** method, it searches through the RecordSet in the manner indicated in Table 9-13. If a record is found that matches the criteria, this record becomes the current record displayed by the Data control; otherwise the current record remains unchanged.

To indicate whether or not a search was successful, Visual Basic provides a **NoMatch** property. The value of this property is set either to **True** or **False** depending on whether the **Find** method was or was not successful in locating a record matching the given criteria. Typically, the **NoMatch** property is used in code such as the following:

```
datPhone.Recordset.FindFirst "Name = 'Grill, John' "
If datPhone.Recordset.NoMatch Then
  MsgBox "No match found"
Else
  Rem: include any desired processing of the located record in here
End If
```

Although all of the examples we have considered have tested for exact equality, this is not a requirement for the relational expression used within a search criteria. Any of Visual Basic's relational and logical operators can be used to construct a search criteria. For example, the statement

```
datPhone.Recordset.FindFirst "Ext >= 464"
```

can be used to find the first record whose extension field value is greater than or equal to 464. If a record exists that has this exact value, it becomes the current record; if not, the first record with an extension greater that 464 becomes the current record. If two or more records have the same value, the first record with this value becomes the current record.

In practice, a greater than or equal criteria, such as "Name >= 'S' " is used more often than a criteria that demands exact equality, such as "Name = 'S' ". The reason for this is that the searched for value is typically entered by a user, and the user may not know the exact name or value being searched for, may misspell an entered name, or transpose an entered number. Under these

Figure 9-19

Program 9-4's Interface

conditions a search for exact equality may fail, while a search using the >= relationship will move the current record close to the desired record. As a specific example of this, consider Program 9-4, which lets a user search the PhoneBook table for a desired name. The program's interface is presented in Figure 9-19. Except for the addition of the controls needed for finding a specific record, which include a Label, Text box, and the <u>F</u>ind Command button, this interface is identical to that used in Programs 9-1 and 9-2. For this reason, Table 9-14 only lists the controls whose properties differ from these earlier programs.

Table 9-14	Changed and Added Properties From Programs 9-1 and 9-2	
Object	**Property**	**Setting**
Form	Name	frmMain
	Caption	Program 9-4 Single Locate Using The Find Method
Data control	Name	datPhone
	Caption	(Blank)
	DatabaseName	C:\Program Files\Microsoft Visual Basic\Company.mdb
	RecordSource	Select * From datPhone Order By Name
	RecordSetType	Dynaset
Label	Name	lblFind
	Caption	Enter a Last Name:
Text box	Name	txtFind
	Text	(Blank)
	DataSource	(Blank)
	DataField	(Blank)
Command button	Name	cmdFind
	Caption	&Find

In reviewing Table 9-14 notice that the txtFind box is not bound to a data control. The box's sole purpose is to provide a data entry area for a user to enter either a full or partial name. It is this entered string value that will be searched for when the <u>F</u>ind control is pushed.

Next, pay attention to the fact that the Data control's **RecordSource** property is an SQL statement that orders the RecordSet in Name order. *Ordering records by the eventual search field or fields is essential if the Find methods are to operate in a manner expected by most users.* For example, if the PhoneBook RecordSet was constructed in its original order (see Table 9-1) and a search for a record having a name greater than or equal to 'D' was undertaken, the located record would end up being for the name *Engle*. This occurs because, in unsorted order, the name *Engle* appears before any name beginning in the letter D. Thus, a search for a name greater than or equal to 'D,' starting from the beginning of the table, will stop at the name beginning in E, because 'E' is greater than or equal to 'D.'

Now consider Program 9-4's event code, which is identical to that used in Program 9-1 except for the addition of the **cmdFind_Click( )** procedure. The first feature to notice is the construction of the search criteria as the string named target. This string is constructed in a manner that encloses the value entered in the txtFind Text box within single quotes; it is used as the search criteria by the **FindFirst** method contained in the very next statement. Finally, notice the use of the **NoMatch** property to alert the user when the **Find** method fails to find a record that matches the designated criteria.

Program 9-4's Event Code

```
Private Sub Form_Load()
  datPhone.Refresh
  datPhone.Caption = 1
End Sub

Private Sub datPhone_Reposition()
  datPhone.Caption = datPhone.Recordset.AbsolutePosition + 1
End Sub

Private Sub cmdExit_Click()
  Beep
  End
End Sub

Private Sub cmdFind_Click()
  Dim target As String

  target = "Name >=" & "'" & txtFind.Text & "'"

  datPhone.Recordset.FindFirst target
  If datPhone.Recordset.NoMatch Then
    MsgBox "No match found"
  Else
    datPhone.Caption = datPhone.Recordset.AbsolutePosition + 1
  End If
End Sub
```

Although Program 9-4 illustrates using the **FindFirst** method, it does have one drawback. As constructed, all the F̲ind Command button can be used for is to locate the first record that matches a user entered name. In many cases, however, more than one record will satisfy a given criteria. For example, there are two *Smiths* in the PhoneBook table and four names that begin in the letter *S*. As written, Program 9-4 will correctly locate only the first occurrence of each of these criteria. Operationally, the F̲ind button effectively "sticks" to the first matching record, no matter how many additional matching records exist. To examine any remaining matches, or even to know that another matching record exists, the user must move the focus from the F̲ind button and click the Data control's **MoveNext** button.

A more user-considerate and professional approach is to have the **Find** button not only locate the first matching record in a set, but then have it cycle through all of the remaining matching records as it is continuously pushed. This type of operation is easily accomplished using a **Move** method, which is described next. Besides their value for our immediate purposes, these **Move** methods have greater applicability in cycling through and processing groups of records, independent of a Data control. Some of these additional uses are also presented.

The Move Methods

The current record , as we have seen, is the record in a RecordSet currently accessible and displayed by any controls bound to a Data control. Only one record can be the current record at any given time. This record can be changed by a Data control's push buttons or by using a **Find** or **Move** method in code. Moving around or changing the current record, as we have already noted, is referred to as *navigating* or *browsing* through a RecordSet.

Table 9-15 lists the **Move** methods that can be applied to a RecordSet to alter the current record. Each of these methods permits navigating through a RecordSet using code. For example, the statement:

```
datPhone.Recordset.MoveFirst
```

makes the first record in the RecordSet the current record. Similarly, the statement

```
datPhone.Recordset.MoveLast
```

makes the last record in the RecordSet the current record.

Table 9-15 The Move Methods

Name	Action	Example
MoveFirst	Make the first record in the RecordSet the current record.	`datPhone.RecordSet.MoveFirst`
MoveNext	Make the next record in the RecordSet the current record.	`datPhone.RecordSet.MoveNext`
MoveLast	Make the last record in the RecordSet the current record.	`datPhone.RecordSet.MoveLast`
MovePrevious	Make the prior record in the RecordSet the current record.	`datPhone.RecordSet.MovePrevious`

Each of the Data control push buttons performs one of the equivalent **Move** methods listed in Table 9-15, except that the Data control is programmed so that it will not move past either the first or last record in a RecordSet. When explicitly using a **Move** method, these same checks can be incorporated in your code using the RecordSet properties named **EOF** and **BOF**, which stand *for End of File* and *Beginning of File*, respectively.

The End of File (**EOF**) property is set to **True** only when the current record is positioned after the last record in a RecordSet. Similarly, the Beginning of File (**BOF**) is set to **True** only when the current record is positioned in front of the first record in a RecordSet. When either of these two property values is **True**, it means that the current record being pointed to is not valid. Table 9-16 lists the conditions indicated by various combinations of **EOF** and **BOF** property settings.

By checking either the **EOF** or **BOF** values, you can safely code loops that traverse a RecordSet from any direction. For example, the following code can be used as the basis for starting at the beginning of the PhoneBook table and correctly processing and cycling through each subsequent record.

```
datPhone.Recordset.MoveFirst
Do While datPhone.Recordset.EOF = False
   ' process the current record as needed
  datPhone.Recordset.MoveNext
Loop
```

Now that we have the **Move** methods to work with, we can modify the **cmdFind_Click( )** event code used in Program 9-4, to not only locate the first occurrence of a name, but to correctly cycle through each subsequent

Table 9-16   EOF/BOF Property Settings

Property Value	Meaning
EOF = True	The current record is positioned after the last record. Thus, the current record being pointed to is invalid.
BOF = True	The current record is positioned before the first record. Thus, the current record being pointed to is invalid.
EOF and BOF both True	There are no records in the RecordSet, and the current record being pointed to is invalid.
EOF and BOF both False	The current record is valid unless it has been deleted and no movement has occurred in the RecordSet.

name in the RecordSet that matches the entered criteria. When the last matching record is reached, we want the code to cycle back to the first match. Thus, for example, if a user enters the letter S, Program 9-5's <u>F</u>ind button (see Figure 9-20) should locate the first name beginning in *S*, and then cycle through the remaining names beginning in *S* as the <u>F</u>ind button is repeatedly pressed. When the last *S* name is located, the code should then relocate the current record to the first *S* name and begin the cycle again. This should work no matter how many letters the user enters. So, for example, if the user enters the letters Sm, the search should only locate names beginning in *Sm*, and so on. The required code algorithm is as follows:

> *Set the variable n equal to the length of the entered search string*
> *If the first n characters of the current record do not match the entered search string*
> > *Find and display the first record matching the search string*
>
> *Else*
> > *Move to the next record*
> > *If the current record's position is past the last record*
> > > *Find and display the first record matching the search string*
> >
> > *Else if the first n characters of the current record do not match the search string*
> > > *Find and display the first record matching the search string*
> >
> > *End If*
>
> *End If*
> *If there is no match*
> > *Display a message indicating that there is no match*
>
> *Else*
> > *Display the current record's position*
>
> *End If*

The first **If** statement in the algorithm checks whether the current record matches the entered criteria. If there is no match, the algorithm locates and displays the first matching record; otherwise, the current record matches the search criteria and we move to the next record. At that point, one of three things has happened: we have either moved to another match, moved past the last record, or moved to a record that does not match the criteria. In the latter two cases we have positioned the current record beyond the last record that matches the search criteria, and we then relocate back to the first matching occurrence; however, we must test for the first

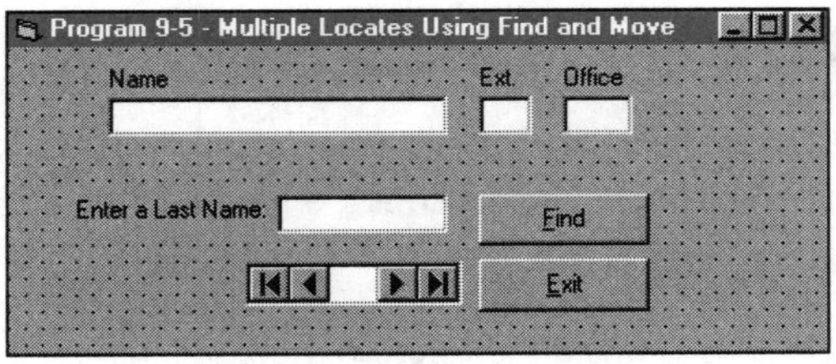

Figure 9-20
Program 9-5's Interface

possibility by itself, for if we have positioned ourselves beyond the last record, any string test will result in an error since no valid current record exists. Finally, the last **If** statement informs the user if no record matches the given criteria.

The procedural code for this algorithm, which uses both **Find** and **Move** methods, is listed as Program 9-5's cmdFind_Click() event code. The interface for Program 9-5 is shown in Figure 9-20. Except for the form's caption and the revised cmdFind_Click() event code, Program 9-5 is identical to Program 9-4.

Program 9-5's cmdFind_Click() Event Code

```
Private Sub cmdFind_Click()
  Dim target As String
  Dim n As Integer

  n = Len(txtFind.Text)
  target = "Name >=" & "'" & txtFind.Text & "'"

  If Mid(datPhone.Recordset("Name"), 1, n) <> txtFind.Text Then
        datPhone.Recordset.FindFirst target
  Else ' current record matches the search criteria
    datPhone.Recordset.MoveNext
    If datPhone.Recordset.EOF = True Then
       datPhone.Recordset.FindFirst target
    ElseIf Mid(datPhone.Recordset("Name"), 1, n) <> txtFind.Text Then
      datPhone.Recordset.FindFirst target
    End If
  End If
  If datPhone.Recordset.NoMatch Then
    MsgBox "No match found"
  Else
    datPhone.Caption = datPhone.Recordset.AbsolutePosition + 1
  End If
End Sub
```

The Seek Method

Just as the **Find** methods can only be used with Dynaset- or Snapshot-type RecordSets, the **Seek** method is used to locate records in an indexed Table-type RecordSet. Specifically, the **Seek** method locates the first record in an indexed set that meets the specified criteria and makes that record the current record. The general syntax for the **Seek** method is

```
table.Recordset.Seek comparison, value-1, value-2, . . . value-n
```

where

- *table* is the name of an existing Table-type RecordSet object;
- *comparison* is one of the string expressions "<", "<=", "=", ">=", or ">"; and
- *value-1, value-2, ...* are one or more values corresponding to the underlying table's index setting.

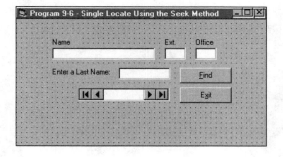

Figure 9-21
Program 9-6's Interface

For example, the statement

```
datPhone.Recordset.Seek ">=", txtFind.Text
```

sets the current record to the first record that matches the string in the txtFind Text box and then sets the **NoMatch** property to **False**. If no record matches the criteria, the **NoMatch** property is set to **True**, and the current record is undefined. To use the **Seek** method a current index must be set. If the key value being searched for is not unique, the **Seek** method will locate the first record that matches the criteria.

Program 9-6, whose interface is shown in Figure 9-21, uses the **Seek** method to locate a user entered string value. The properties for this program are identical to those of Program 9-4 and 9-5, except for the form's caption and that the datPhone data control's **Recordset- Type** has been set to Table. The **Seek** method is used in the **cmdFind_Click()** event code listed within Program 9-6's event code.

Program 9-6's Event Code

```
Private Sub Form_Load()
  datPhone.Refresh
  datPhone.Recordset.Index = "Name"
  datPhone.Caption = "ID = " & datPhone.Recordset("ID")
End Sub

Private Sub datPhone_Reposition()
  datPhone.Caption = "ID = " & datPhone.Recordset("ID")
End Sub

Private Sub cmdExit_Click()
  Beep
  End
End Sub

Private Sub cmdFind_Click()
  Dim target As String
  datPhone.Recordset.Seek ">=", txtFind.Text
  If datPhone.Recordset.NoMatch Then
    MsgBox "No match found"
  Else
    datPhone.Caption = "ID = " & datPhone.Recordset("ID")
  End If
End Sub
```

In reviewing Program 9-6's event code pay particular attention to the fact that the index for the table has been set in the **Form_Load()** event. Finally, notice the **Seek** method call in the **cmdFind_Click()** event. Here the method uses the value entered in the txtFind Text box as its search criteria. The comparison used (">=") means that the user does not have to enter an exact name for a match to occur. For example, if the user enters the letter S in the Text box, the search will locate the first record with a name beginning in the letter *S*. Finally, notice that a comma is used as a delimiter between the comparison expression and the value being searched for.

Exercises **9.4**

1. Use Visual Basic's Help facility to obtain documentation on the following:
   a. The **Find** methods
   b. The **Move** methods
   c. The **Seek** method
   d. **EOF** and **BOF**
   e. Positioning the Current Record Pointer (**Hint:** First search for "positioning current record.")

2. List and describe the functions of the four **Find** methods.

3. Assuming that the PhoneBook table (see Table 9-1) is the **RecordSource** for a Data control named datPhone, write **Find** method calls to locate records matching the following criteria:
   a. The first occurrence of the office value F1.
   b. The next occurrence of the office value F1.
   c. The last occurrence of the office value F1.
   d. The previous occurrence of the office value F1.

4. Assuming that the TitleAuthor table (see Table 9-11) is the **RecordSource** for a Data control named datTAuth, write **Find** method calls to locate records matching the following criteria:
   a. The first occurrence of an Au_ID equal to 59.
   b. The next occurrence of an Au_ID equal to 59.
   c. The last occurrence of an Au_ID equal to 96.
   d. The previous occurrence of an Au_ID equal to 96.

5. a. Define the term *current record*?
   b. How many current records can exist at one time?

6. List and describe the functions of the four **Move** methods.

7. Assuming that the Publishers table (see Table 9-8) is the **RecordSource** for a Data control named datPub, write **Move** method calls to
   a. Make the current record the first record in the RecordSet.
   b. Make the current record the next record in the RecordSet.
   c. Make the current record the last record in the RecordSet.
   d. Make the current record the previous record in the RecordSet.

8. Enter and run Program 9-4 on your computer.

9. Enter and run Program 9-5 on your computer.

10. Enter and run Program 9-6 on your computer.

11. Just as Program 9-5 modifies the **cmdFind_Click( )** event to sequentially search for additional records that satisfy the search criteria, Program 9-6 can also be modified to do the same. Modify Program 9-6 in such a manner that repeated clicking of the cmdFind button causes the program to locate the next record that satisfies the entered criteria value. When the last match has been found, clicking the cmdFind button should revert to locating the first matching record.

12. If you have access to the Biblio database provided by Microsoft with Visual Basic, write a Visual Basic program that allows users to examine records in the Titles table (see Table 9-9). The specific

fields that should be displayed are the title, year published, and ISBN number.

13 Modify the Program written for Exercise 12 so that records can be located by entering a title. The locate should work even if a partial title name is entered.

14 If you have access to the `Biblio` database provided by Microsoft with Visual Basic, write a Visual Basic program that allows users to examine records in the Publishers table (see Table 9-8). The specific fields that should be displayed are the company name, address, city, state, and zip code.

15 Modify the Program written for Exercise 14 so that records can be located by entering a company's name. The locate command should work even if a partial company name is entered.

9.5 ▸ Programming the Data Control

Programming a Data control means writing code to alter the control's current record. Effectively, we have already programmed a Data control by using the **Find**, **Move**, and **Seek** methods, since each of these methods typically does change a Data control's current record. In this section we complete this programming process by providing an interface that allows a user to update records using procedural code. In this context, the term *update* refers to either adding, deleting, or editing records in a RecordSet and its underlying database table. In addition, we will also show how edits and additions can be also be accomplished using a Data control without additional programming. The update methods provided by Visual Basic for programming a Data control are listed in Table 9-17.

Table 9-17   Database Methods

Method Name	Description
AddNew	Creates a new record for both a Dynaset and Table-type RecordSet. This method sets all fields to Nulls, or any predefined default values. After the new record has been created and the fields edited, either an Update method or movement to another record (using either a movement method or the Data control's push buttons) must be used to make the changes permanent.
Delete	Deletes the current record in both an open Dynaset and Table-type RecordSet, and in the underlying database table.
Edit	Copies the current record from both a Dynaset and Table-type RecordSet to a copy buffer for subsequent editing.
Update	Saves the contents of the copy buffer to the specified Dynaset or Table RecordSet and the underlying database table.

To illustrate how the methods listed in Table 9-17 are used in practice, we will incorporate them into Program 9-7, whose interface is shown in Figure 9-22. Specifically, we will incorporate the **AddNew** and **Update**

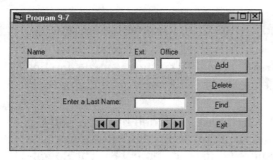

Figure 9-22
Program 9-7's Interface

methods within the <u>A</u>dd Command button's **Click** event and the **Delete** method within the <u>D</u>elete Command button's **Click** event. We will then show how to edit and save all editing changes using the E<u>x</u>it Command button's **Click** event. Table 9-18 lists the relevant properties for these Command buttons, which have the captions <u>A</u>dd, <u>D</u>elete, and E<u>x</u>it, respectively. Except for the form's caption, the remaining form objects and their associated code are identical to that of Program 9-4.

Table 9-18 Program 9-7's Update Command Control Properties

Object	Property	Setting
Command button	Name	cmdAdd
	Caption	&Add
Command button	Name	cmdDel
	Caption	&Delete
Command button	Name	cmdExit
	Caption	E&xit

Before you update (add, delete, or edit) a record, two items should be understood. The first is that the Jet database engine uses a special reserved location, called the *copy buffer*, to hold the contents of the record currently being updated. When the **AddNew** method is invoked, this copy buffer is cleared of its contents and any default values specified for the new record are set, while the **Edit** method causes the current record's contents to be copied into the buffer. Finally, the **Update** method causes all data in the copy buffer to be transferred and saved into both the RecordSet and the underlying database table.

The second item concerns the permissions that must be set for updating to take place. Although the correct permissions are created by default, and we assume that the correct permissions have been set, the required permissions are explicitly presented at the end of this section.

Adding a Record

Records can be added to a RecordSet either by using the **AddNew** method in code, by setting a Data control's **EOFAction** property, or by using a combination of both techniques. We examine each of these techniques, in turn.

For example, to add a new PhoneBook record using the code in Program 9-7, the following statement is required:

```
datPhone.Recordset.AddNew
```

What this statement does is to clear the copy buffer and set any required default field values. Event Code 9-1 illustrates how this statement is used for Program 9-7's cmdAdd Command button's **Click** event.

When the cmdAdd Command button is clicked, the first statement in Event Code 9-1 causes the Jet engine to clear the copy buffer. The procedure then requests that a name, extension, and office location be entered. Upon completion of these requests, the **Update** method is invoked, which causes the entered data to be appended both to the PhoneBook table and the Record-Set. To correctly order the RecordSet in Name order, the **Refresh** method is invoked, which rebuilds the RecordSet according to the structured query defined for the Data control's **RecordSource** property. Since this query orders the records by Name (see Table 9-14), the added name will subsequently appear to the user in its correct alphabetical position.

Event Code 9-1

```
Private Sub cmdAdd_Click()
   datPhone.Recordset.AddNew   ' clear the copy buffer
   datPhone.Recordset("Name") = InputBox("Enter the Name")
   datPhone.Recordset("Ext") = InputBox("Enter an Extension")
   datPhone.Recordset("Office") = InputBox("Enter an Office code (HM or F1)")
   datPhone.Recordset.Update   ' write the copy buffer to the Recordset & database
   datPhone.Refresh
End Sub
```

The Data control's **EOFAction** property can also be used to add new records. The default setting for this property is 0, which corresponds to a system constant named **vbEOFActionMoveLast**. This default setting disables the Data control's MoveNext button when the current record is the last record in a RecordSet. By changing the **EOFAction** property to the named constant **vbEOFActionAddNew**, which has a numerical value of 2, the MoveNext button *is not* disabled at the last record; rather, the current record is positioned to a new record in the copy buffer. From an operational viewpoint, all bound controls will either be cleared, or set to the default values contained in the copy buffer. The user can then change any and all values in the new record using the bound controls (formally, the user is actually *editing* the new record at this point). By moving to a new record, using the **Move**, **Find**, or **Seek** methods, or by using any of the Data control's Command buttons, the new record is automatically saved. Similarly, invoking the **Update** method also causes the new record to be saved.

Deleting a Record

To delete a record from a Data control's RecordSet and its underlying table, program code must be used. For example, to delete the current record displayed by Program 9-7's bound controls, the following statement is required:

```
datPhone.Recordset.Delete
```

In using this statement, however, we must provide for two contingencies. First, since all information in a deleted record is lost, we should build in a safety mechanism to protect against a user inadvertently activating the Delete button. The next item that we must take care of is to determine which record is to become the current record after a deletion has occurred. In relation to this second item, we will position the Data control according to the following algorithm:

> *If the last record in a RecordSet has been deleted*
> > *Position the Data control on the last record in the remaining set of records*
> *Else if the first record in the RecordSet has been deleted*
> > *Position the Data control on the first record in the remaining set of records*
> *Else*
> > *Position the Data control on the record immediately after the deleted record*

Making use of the **EOF** and **BOF** properties, the procedural code for this algorithm becomes that shown at the top of the following page.

```
datPhone.Recordset.Delete
If datPhone.Recordset.EOF = True Then
  datPhone.Recordset.MoveLast
ElseIf datPhone.Recordset.BOF = True Then
  datPhone.Recordset.MoveFirst
Else
  datPhone.Recordset.MoveNext
End If
```

Figure 9-23
The Delete Warning Message Box

Prior to invoking this code, however, we first want to ensure that the user really wants to proceed with the deletion. This "safety check" can be handled with a Message box similar to the one shown in Figure 9-23. As illustrated, the Message box consists of a critical icon and two Command buttons, with the default being the second, or Cancel button. Thus, if a user accidentally presses the ENTER key, the deletion will not take place, and only a positive action on the part of the user will cause the deletion to occur. Using the Message box constants listed in Appendix E, the appropriate Message box can be created using the following code:

```
Dim MboxType As Integer

MboxType = vbCritical + vbOKCancel + vbDefaultButton2
goahead = MsgBox("Press OK to Delete", MboxType)
```

The combination of the "safety check" code and the positioning of the Data control after a deletion forms the basis for Program 9-7's cmdDel control's **Click** event, which is listed as Event Code 9-2.

Event Code 9-2

```
Private Sub cmdDel_Click()
 Dim MboxType As Integer
 Dim goahead As Integer

 MboxType = vbCritical + vbOKCancel + vbDefaultButton2
 goahead = MsgBox("Press OK to Delete", MboxType)
 If goahead = vbOK Then
 datPhone.Recordset.Delete
 If datPhone.Recordset.EOF = True Then
 datPhone.Recordset.MoveLast
 ElseIf datPhone.Recordset.BOF = True Then
 datPhone.Recordset.MoveFirst
 Else
 datPhone.Recordset.MoveNext
 End If
 End If
 datPhone.Caption = datPhone.Recordset.AbsolutePosition
End Sub
```

Notice that when a record is deleted using Event Code 9-2, the position of the remaining records in the RecordSet can change. For example, if the first record in the set is deleted, all subsequent records move up one position in the RecordSet. Thus, the record that was previously identified with a Data control **Caption** of 2 will now have a **Caption** of 1. This generally is no problem for most users, but you may either have to explain this operation or choose not to use the **Caption** property for displaying record positions. Also notice that since a record's position in a RecordSet can change, either due to deletions or a rebuild caused by a **Refresh**, the **AbsolutePosition** property should not be used to locate records. The recommended way of retaining and returning to a given position in a RecordSet is to use **Bookmarks**.

Finally, the **Delete** method can be used to delete a complete set of records using a loop. For example, the following code deletes every record in the PhoneBook table whose Office field is equal to 'F1'.

```
datphone.DatabaseName = "Company.mdb"
datPhone.RecordSource = "Select * From PhoneBook Where [Office] = 'F1' "
datPhone.Refresh
Do While datPhone.RecordSDet.EOF = False
  Print "Deleting "; datPhone.Recordset("Name")
  datPhone.Recordset.Delete
  datPhone.Recordset.MoveNext
Loop
```

In this code a **MoveNext** method is used after each deletion. This is necessary because a deleted record contains invalid data and if subsequently accessed as the current record, will cause an error. Using the **MoveNext** method ensures that the Data control correctly points to a valid current record.

Editing a Record

An existing record's fields can be edited by modifying the desired field in the current record and then saved by using either the Data control's movement buttons or in code using either an **Update**, **Find**, **Move**, or **Seek** method. To edit a record without programming the Data control, do the following:

1. Make the desired record the current record (this can be done either by locating a record using one of the techniques described in the previous section or by using the Data control's movement buttons).
2. Assign new values to the desired fields.
3. Click one of the Data control's movement buttons, which causes the changes to be saved.

This procedure is generally the easiest for making changes to an existing record. The only pitfall occurs when a user makes a final editing change and immediately presses the Exit button. Since no movement button was pressed, this last change will not be saved. The solution is to either provide a Save command control, program the Exit command control to detect if a change was made to the current record and save this last change (possibly with user confirmation), or use both techniques. Generally, providing a Save button is not a good idea, because it tends to confuse most users: either they forget whether they pressed the button for one of their changes and become unsure whether a change was actually saved, or think that they can revert to the original record's contents by not pressing the Save button. Thus, it is typically easier simply to explain that any change is automatically made once the user moves to another record and not provide a separate Save button. To ensure that the last change is saved, however, it is a good idea to program the Exit button explicitly to save changes made to the last record. This can be accomplished using the algorithm at the top of page 482.

> *If the Exit button is pressed and the last record in a RecordSet has been modified*
>> *Request confirmation to save the changes*
>> *If confirmation is received*
>>> *Save the changes*
>> *End If*
> *End If*
> *End the application*

Notice that this algorithm asks for user confirmation to save any changes made to the last record. A case can be made that, since the user does not explicitly confirm changes made to any other records, the changes to the last record should also be automatically saved without explicit confirmation. Both approaches are used in practice. We continue with the approach that asks for confirmation to illustrate how to detect that a change has actually occurred.

To determine whether a bound control's value has been changed we use its **DataChanged** property. This property, which is only available at run time, returns a boolean value of **True** only if the data in the bound control has been changed by a process other than that of retrieving data from the current record. Thus, to determine if any changes have been made to the current record, the following code segment can be used:

```
Dim DataChanged As Boolean

' Determine if any changes were made to the last record
DataChanged = txtName.DataChanged Or txtExt.DataChanged Or
txtOffice.DataChanged
If DataChanged = True Then
    ' Statements to execute if the DataChanged is True
End If
```

Notice that the condition tested within the **If** statement is the value of the expression `DataChanged = True`. This tested expression can be replaced by a shorter expression that only uses the boolean variable's name. Thus, the statement

```
If DataChanged = True Then
```

can be replaced by the shorter statement

```
If DataChanged Then
```

Although this may appear confusing at first, the second statement is certainly more compact than the longer version. Here, if the value of the variable `DataChanged` is **True**, the expression itself is **True**. Since boolean variables are frequently tested by advanced Visual Basic programmers using just their name, as in the latter **If** statement, it is worthwhile being familiar with this convention. Event Code 9-3 incorporates this code segment, with the shorter **If** statement, within the final code used for Program 9-7's `cmdExit` control's **Click** event.

Event Code 9-3

```
Private Sub cmdExit_Click()
  Dim MboxType As Integer
  Dim MboxMessage As String
  Dim goahead As Integer
  Dim DataChanged As Boolean

  MboxType = vbCritical + vbYesNo
  MboxMessage = "Do you want to save the changes made to the last record?"
```

```
' Determine if any changes were made to the last record
DataChanged = txtName.DataChanged Or txtExt.DataChanged Or txtOffice.DataChanged
If DataChanged Then
  goahead = MsgBox(MboxMessage, MboxType)
  If goahead = vbYes Then
    datPhone.Recordset.Edit
    datPhone.Recordset.Update
  End If
End If
Beep
End
End Sub
```

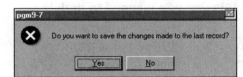

Figure 9-24
Program 9-7's Save Message Box

The only section of Event Code 9-3 that we have not discussed is the coding of the Message box. As coded, this box consists of a critical icon consisting of Yes and No Command buttons (see Appendix E for a description of these constants) and produces the Message box shown in Figure 9-24. As is seen in this figure, the default Command button is the first, or Yes button. Thus, if the user inadvertently presses the ENTER key, any changes to the last record are saved.

Finally, as with the other update methods, editing can be accomplished in code without using a bound control, as illustrated by the following code segment:

```
datphone.DatabaseName = "Company.mdb"
datPhone.RecordSouce = "PhoneBook"
datPhone.Refresh
datPhone.Recordset.Edit
datPhone.Recordset("Ext") = "711"
datPhone.Recordset.Update
```

This code sets the value of the Ext field to 711 for the current record, which in this case is the first record in the RecordSet.

Permissions

For changes to be made to a table's records using either code or the Data control directly, the following conditions must always be met:

1. The database itself must have permissions set that allow it to be updated, which is typically the default.

2. The desired field being edited must have been created to be updatable, which is typically the default.

3. The Data control's **ReadOnly** property has been set to **False**, which is the default value.

4. The RecordSet's **Updatable** property has been set to **True**, which is the default for Dynaset- and Table-types. Snapshot-type RecordSets are not updatable.

Each of these conditions can be checked using code. For example, assuming that the **RecordSource** for a Data control named datPhone has been set to PhoneBook, the following code can be used to check that the PhoneBook table can be updated (that is, either edited, added to, or deleted from):

```
If datPhone.Database.Updatable = False Or datPhone.ReadOnly = True _
Or datPhone.Recordset.Updatable = False Then
  MsgBox "This data cannot be altered"
End If
```

In a similar manner, the ability of a specific field to be updated can be tested by examining its **Attributes** property and its **dbUpdatableField** bit. For example, the following code can be used to determine if the PhoneBook table's Name field can be altered:

```
If datPhone.Recordset.Fields("Name").Attributes = True And
dbUpdatableField = 0 Then
  MsgBox "This field cannot be altered"
End If
```

Exercises 9.5

1. a. Describe what the phrase *Programming a Data Control* means.
   b. List and describe the four methods that can be used to update a Data control's records.

2. What update task cannot be accomplished without using program code.

3. List the ways in which changes to the current record become saved.

4. List and describe the four conditions that must be set for a record's fields to be updatable.

5. a. Enter and run Program 9-7.
   b. Modify Program 9-7 so that any change made to a record is automatically saved when the Exit button is pressed, whether or not it was updated using the Data control's movement buttons.

6. An interesting feature of Data controls is that they have an **Invisible** property. In this exercise you will be asked to set this property to **True**, which makes the control invisible at run time. You will then be asked to replace the move functions provided by the Data control's movement buttons with programmed Command controls. To accomplish this, modify Program 9-7 as follows:

   ● Set the Data control's **Invisible** property to **True**.
   ● Add four Command buttons having the captions First, Next, Previous, and Last, respectively.

   Once you have made these changes, code each of the new Command controls, using appropriate **Move** methods, to move to the location in the RecordSet indicated by each control's caption.

9.6 Focus on Program Design and Implementation:

Connecting to a Database

In this Focus section we connect the existing Mail In and Walk In forms to a database for storage of all transactions entered using these two order-entry screens. We then add an operational form for entering and storing disk package receipts into inventory. All three of these forms will require a Data control to provide access to the required data table; we will not, however, make any of the existing form controls data-aware by binding them to the Data controls. In this manner the forms are strictly used for input only, and not

TIPS FROM THE PROS

The Text Data Type

Beginning programmers frequently make the mistake of assuming that a data value that appears to be a number should be stored as a numerical data type. Doing this can cause real problems, which you can see in the following example. Consider the zip code values 92034, 47390, 07078, and 91843, as well as the phone extensions 7604, 5419, 2834, and 0365. If these zip codes are stored as numbers, the leading zero in the 07078 zip code will not displayed when it is printed. The same is true for the phone extension 0365, if the extension numbers are stored in number fields. The reason for this is that the default in all database programs is to suppress all leading zeros for any printed number value.

The correct rule to follow when assigning data types is the following: *Unless the normal mathematical operations of addition, subtraction, averaging, etc. make sense for values that appear as numbers, store the values as text.* Doing so ensures that when the values are printed, all leading zeros will be displayed.[5]

for viewing or changing existing records. The actual writing of the entered data items into the data table is accomplished by programming the Data control.

Before connecting the application to a data table, however, we must clearly understand the record structure that we will be interfacing with. So this item is considered first.

The Data Table

The data table we will use to store all inventory receipts and disbursements, which is named RecDis, can be found in the Disktrans.mdb database located on the Student Disk. This database was constructed using Microsoft's Access database program. The table's record structure, which consists of its field names and specifications, is listed in Table 9-19 (page 486). Currently, the RecDis table contains 20 records, of which the relevant fields for our immediate purpose are listed in Table 9-20 (page 486).

Notice that the last field listed in Table 9-20 provides the date of each transaction. It is extremely important to always add a date (and possibly time) stamp to each stored transaction. The reason for this is that, inevitably, in addition to asking you *if* a transaction took place, you will be asked to provide information about *when* it took place. For example, imagine that in six months a mail-in customer sends a letter to the manufacturer asking about the free disk package they requested but never received. You subsequently get a call from the disk manufacturer requesting information about this. You then confidently look up the person's name and address, and report to the manufacturer that this request was fulfilled. The next question, of course, is "When did you fulfill it?" If you cannot answer this question, your credibility as a programmer can come into question. This is typical of the type of inquiries you must anticipate if you are to successfully program commercial applications. So, as a general rule, always mark each transaction with the date that it occurred.

---

[5]The author was once called in to determine the problem with an existing program that had printed a number of mailing labels for New Jersey, in which all of the zip codes appeared as 4-digit rather than 5-digit numbers. Except for the expense and time in printing the original labels, the problem was easily fixed by changing the zip code field type from number to text, which ensured that the leading 0 in the New Jersey zip codes were printed. An alternative fix would have been to use the Format function to explicitly force the display of all leading zeros.

Table 9-19 The RecDis Field Specifications

Field Name	Data Type	Field Width	Usage
ID	Autonumber	Not applicable	Unique record identification number
Fname	Text	15 characters	Store first name
Lname	Text	20 characters	Store last name
Addr	Text	20 characters	Store address
City	Text	20 characters	Store city
St	Text	2 characters	Store state
Zip	Text	10 characters	Store zip code
Quantity	Number	Not applicable	Store quantity
RDCode	Text	1 character	Store a receipt/delivery code
RDDate	Date	Not applicable	Store date of receipt/delivery
RetCode	Text	1 character	Store a return code
RetDate	Date	Not applicable	Store a return date

Table 9-20 The RecDis Data

ID	Fname	Lname	Addr	City	St	Zip	Qnt.	Code	RDDate
1	Receipt	of Inventory					3000	r	4/1/99
2	Susan	Fortunato	2 Addison Rd.	Stockton	CA	95208	1	m	4/15/99
3	Bill	Jones	8 Feather Lane	W. Orange	NJ	07052	1	m	4/15/99
4	Diane	Smith	62 Oaklawn Rd.	Hewlet	NY	11557	2	m	4/15/99
5	Greg	Minor	818 Freemont Tr.	Florence	AZ	85232	1	m	4/15/99
6	Donna	Ende	16 Millhouse Rd.	Geneva	FL	32732	1	m	4/15/99
7	Jim	Bamson	22 Yale St.	Ann Arbor	MI	48106	3	m	4/15/99
8	Steve	Crowley	16 Maple St.	Springfield	MA	01101	1	m	4/15/99
9	Rhonda	Harrison	3 Chestnut St.	Harrison	NJ	07029	1	m	4/15/99
10	Rochelle	Brown	10 Tivoli Pl.	Springfield	OH	45501	1	m	4/15/99
11	Returned	to Vendor					300	t	4/17/99
12	Damaged	Inventory					125	d	4/17/99
13	Julia	McDonald	25 South St.	Hillsdale	NY	12529	1	m	4/17/99
14	Adjustment	to Inventory					30	o	4/17/99
15	Ronald	Dimol	18 Newman St.	Miami Beach	FL	33139	2	m	4/17/99
16	Loretta	Hartman	1 Ridgedale Ave.	St. Paul	MN	55101	2	m	4/17/99
17	Douglas	Evans	10 Pitman Pl.	Gunlock	TN	84733	1	m	4/17/99
18	Roberta	Lopez	18 2'nd St.	Madison	NJ	07940	5	w	4/17/99
19	Joe	Lesser	25 E. Palidino St.	Hollywood	FL	33022	1	m	4/17/99
20	Cash						1	w	4/17/99

In reviewing the current records in the RecDis file, first notice the last two columns, which list the RDCode and RDDate fields (the RD refers to Receipt and Disbursement). Valid codes for this field are listed in Table 9-21. These codes are used in the next Focus section to provide detailed reports on the exact disposition of inventory; including how many Mail In orders were fulfilled, how many Walk In orders were fulfilled, and how inventory was received and returned to the manufacturer.

Table 9-21 Valid RDCodes

Code	Meaning
m	A disbursement from inventory due to a Mail In order
w	A disbursement from inventory due to a Walk In order
r	A receipt into inventory from the disk manufacturer
t	A return to the vendor from inventory
d	Damaged inventory
o	Other inventory adjustment

With this preliminary understanding of the data that is stored for each transaction, we can now use the information presented in this chapter to connect our Rotech application to the Disktran database.

Connecting the Order-Entry Forms to a Database

The application's two order entry forms are the Mail In and Walk In forms. We will work with one form at a time, starting with the current Mail In form, which is shown in Figure 9-25. The first and only obvious change to this run time form is to make it look like Figure 9-26, where we have added a Label and Text box control for a date field.

As shown in Figure 9-26, the new Text box will contain a date when viewed by the user; the date presented will be the current ("today's") date. In addition to the two new visible run-time controls shown in this figure, we will also add an invisible Data control. Figure 9-27 shows how the Mail In form looks at design time, so that this Data control is visible. The relevant properties for the three new controls (Label, Text, and Data) are listed in Table 9-22.

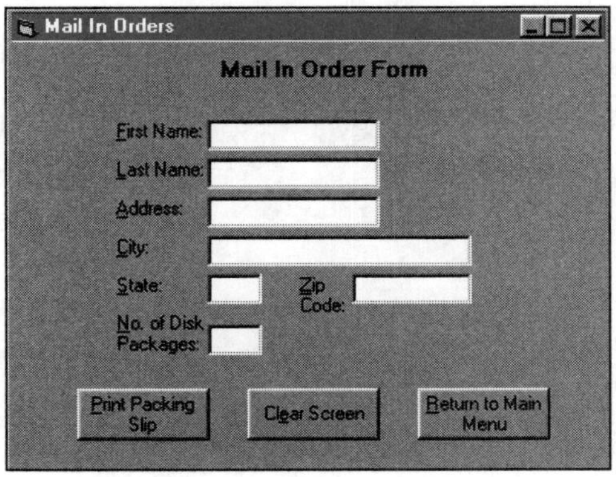

Figure 9-25
The Current Mail In Form

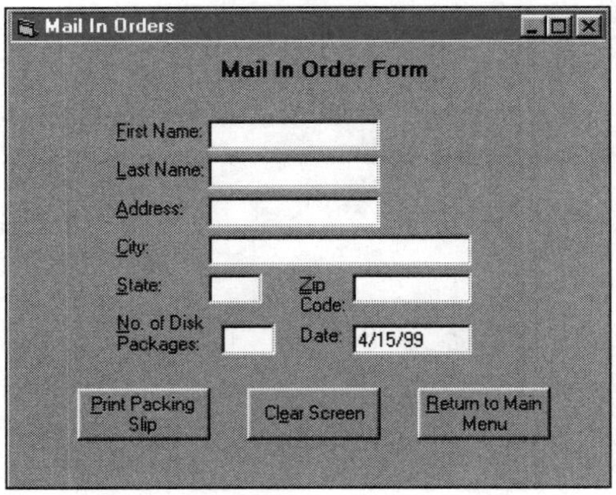

Figure 9-26
Adding a Date Input Capability

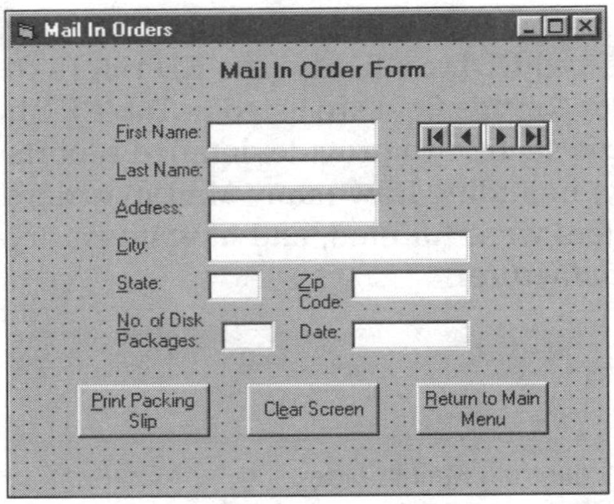

Figure 9-27
The Mail In Form at Design Time

Table 9-22	Additional Mail In Form Controls	
Object	**PropertySetting**	
Label	Name	lblDate
Text box	Name	txtDate
	Text	(Blank)
Data control	Name	datINV
	Caption	(Blank)
	DatabaseName	A:\Disktran.mdb
	RecordSource	RecDis
	RecordSetType	1-Dynaset
	Visible	False

Normally, after adding a Data control to a form, a number of Text box controls are bound to the Data control using each Text box's **DataSource** and **DataField** properties. In this particular case, however, we only want to use the Text boxes as input controls, and not to view and change data within existing transaction records. As such, we will not bind them to the Data control. In this manner, the only purpose for the Data control is to make the database table RecDis available to code on the form. It is in the code that we will capture the input data and write it to the database. Procedure Code 9-1 lists the total additional code required, both to initialize the current date into the added Text box and to write the transaction into the existing database table.

Procedure Code 9-1

```
Rem: Form-Level code to set the current date into txtDate
Private Sub Form_Load()
  txtDate.Text = Format(Now, "mm/dd/yy")
End Sub

Private Sub cmdPrint_Click()
  Rem: Add the following named constant at the top of the event code
  Rem: it provides the code for a mail-in disbursement from inventory

  Const strMAILINS As String = "m"

  Rem: Continue with the existing code
      .
      .
      .
      .

  Rem: Add the following section of code at the end of
  Rem: the event procedure, immediately before the End Sub statement

  'Now Save the data to the database
  'clear the buffer
  datINV.Recordset.AddNew
  'Load up the buffer
  datINV.Recordset("Fname") = txtFname
  datINV.Recordset("Lname") = txtLname
  datINV.Recordset("Addr") = txtAddr
  datINV.Recordset("City") = txtCity
  datINV.Recordset("St") = txtState
  datINV.Recordset("Zip") = txtZip
  datINV.Recordset("Quantity") = txtQuantity
```

```
    datINV.Recordset("RDCode") = strMAILINS
    datINV.Recordset("RDDATE") = txtDate
    'Write the record
    datINV.Recordset.Update 'write the record to the database
End Sub
```

In reviewing Procedure Code 9-1, notice that not much has been added to the existing code. The **Form_Load** event is used to initialize the added Text box with the current date. The code attached to the end of the existing `cmdPrint` button's **Click** event procedure simply sets the buffer values to those in the Text boxes, and then writes the data out using the **Update** command. Placing this code after the packing slip has been printed is the correct location, because it is at this point that all data has been validated and that the user has committed to having it printed. We are simply storing away data that has already been committed to a hard copy packing-slip printout.

Except for a few minor alterations, the same changes that we have made to the Mail In form must also be made to the Walk In form. Figure 9-28 shows the current Walk In form, while Figure 9-29 shows the new form as it will look at design time.

The three additional controls that we have added into the Walk In form have the properties listed in Table 9-23. Notice that these are the exact same properties as previously listed for the Mail In form in Table 9-22.

Table 9-23	Additional Walk In Form Controls	
Object	**Property**	**Setting**
Label	Name	lblDate
	Caption	Date:
Text box	Name	txtDate
	Text	(Blank)
Data control	Name	datINV
	Caption	(Blank)
	DatabaseName	A:\Disktran.mdb
	RecordSource	RecDis
	RecordSetType	1-Dynaset
	Visible	False

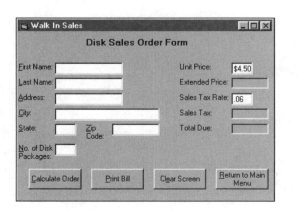

Figure 9-28
The Current Walk In Form

Figure 9-29
The Walk In Form at Design Time

Again, as with the Mail In form, we only want to use the Text boxes as input controls, and not for viewing or changing data in existing records. As such, we do not bind them to the Data control, but once again program the Data control to store transaction records into the RecDis table. Procedure Code 9-2 lists the additional code required.

Procedure Code 9-2

```
Rem: Form-Level code to set the current date into txtDate
Private Sub Form_Load()
  txtDate.Text = Format(Now, "mm/dd/yy")
End Sub

Private Sub cmdPrint_Click()
  Rem: Add the following named constant at the top of the event code
  Rem: it provides the code for a walk-in disbursement from inventory

  Const strWALKINS As String = "w"

  Rem: Continue with the existing code
        .
        .
        .
        .
        .
        .
  Rem: Add the following section of code at the end of
  Rem: the event procedure, immediately before the End Sub statement
  'Now Save the data to the database
  'clear the buffer
  datINV.Recordset.AddNew
  'Load up the buffer
  If Len(txtFname) > 0 Then
    datINV.Recordset("Fname") = txtFname
  End If
  If Len(txtLname) > 0 Then
    datINV.Recordset("Lname") = txtLname
  End If
  If Len(txtAddr) > 0 Then
    datINV.Recordset("Addr") = txtAddr
  End If
  If Len(txtCity) > 0 Then
    datINV.Recordset("City") = txtCity

  End If
  If Len(txtState) > 0 Then
    datINV.Recordset("St") = txtState
  End If
  If Len(txtZip) > 0 Then
    datINV.Recordset("Zip") = txtZip
  End If
  datINV.Recordset("Quantity") = txtQuantity
  datINV.Recordset("RDCode") = strWALKINS
  datINV.Recordset("RDDATE") = txtDate
  'Write the record
  datINV.Recordset.Update 'write the record to the database
End Sub
```

The only difference between Procedure Code 9-2 and that listed in Procedure Code 9-1 is the set of **If** statements to detect that we are not attempting to write out a zero-length string. Although this type of validation had been part of the Mail In form before we added the "store-to-table" code, no such validation existed in the Walk In form. It needs to be made now because an attempt to write a zero-length string into a database field results in a run-time error.

Auditing

The reason for not binding the Text box controls on both the Mail In and Walk In data entry forms concerns itself with auditing. An *audit* is an official examination and verification of accounts to ensure that they are in order. A general rule of auditing is that each and every transaction must be accounted for. Thus, once a transaction is made, it should never be deleted, and only altered when the alteration itself can be accounted for. Frequently, a second transaction is made that corrects an original record or the original record has extra fields that can be used to document the change. In this manner, a trail is always provided that can be followed to determine exactly what has happened and when it occurred.

For example, imagine that a dishonest employee sends free disks to friends using the Mail In form, and then goes in and deletes each record after the packing slip is printed. Permitting the same employee to delete records effectively erases all traces of the illegal transactions. It is for this reason that most commercial systems do not permit deleting any transaction that has been posted (stored) into a transactions database.

Clearly, the degree of transaction control provided for each system depends on the level of security required by both the user and the application itself. For smaller systems and companies with a few employees, security is usually not a prime concern. For our Rotech application we will provide an additional form that will allow a user to review and locate all past transactions, but not to delete any transactions. Of course, any record can still be altered if the user understands how to use Microsoft's Access database and the records have not been locked at the database level. Thus, the ultimate security for each database record depends on the security imposed on the database itself and the means of access to the data.

Adding an Inventory Receipt Form

Figure 9-30

The Rotech Project Explorer Window

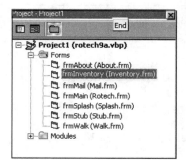

Connecting the existing Mail In and Walk In forms to our `Disktran` database permits us to store all disbursements from inventory. To record all deliveries into inventory we will create and add a new Inventory Receipt form to the project. Since we have added new forms in our two previous Focus sections, rather than once again listing the details of this procedure, we briefly review the necessary steps for adding a new form in this section's Programmers' Notes box. Following this procedure you should add a form named `frmInventory` and store this form in the file named `Invent.frm`. When this is done the Rotech Project Explorer Window will appear as shown in Figure 9-30.

The form that we want to provide is shown in Figure 9-31 (page 492). The relevant property values for this new form and its Trigger Task List (TTL) are given in Tables 9-24 (page 492) and 9-25 (page 493), respectively.

Procedure Code 9-3 provides the four event procedures that must be written, which correspond to the last four tasks listed in the form's TTL Table.

Figure 9-31

The Inventory Form

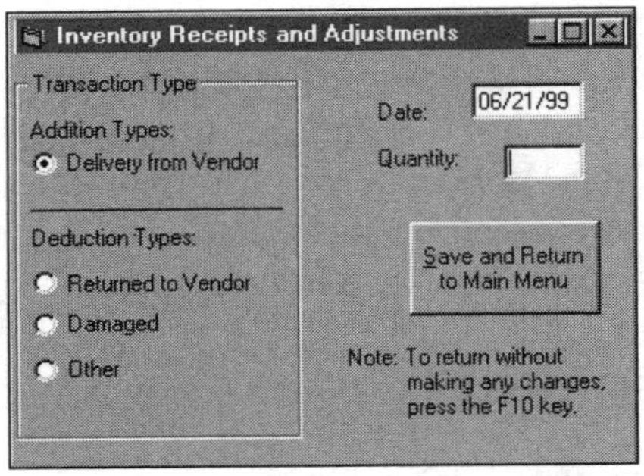

Table 9-24 The Inventory Form's Property Table

Object	Property	Setting
Form	Name	frmInventory
	Caption	Inventory Receipts and Adjustments
Frame	Name	frmType
	Caption	Transaction Type
Label	Name	lblAdd
	Caption	Addition Types:
Option box	Name	optInv1
	Caption	Delivery from Vendor
	Value	True
Line	Name	linInv
Label	Name	lblDeduct
	Caption	Deduction Types:
Option box	Name	optInv2
	Caption	Returned to Vendor
	Value	False
Option box	Name	optInv3
	Caption	Damaged
	Value	False
Option box	Name	optInv4
	Caption	Other
	Name	lbldate
	Caption	Date:
Text box	Name	txtdate
	Text	(Blank)
Label	Name	lblQuantity
	Caption	Quantity
Text box	Name	txtQuantity
	Text	(Blank)
	TabIndex	0
Label	Name	lblNote
	Caption	Note: To return without making any changes, press the F10 key.
Command button	Name	&Save and Return to Main Menu

PROGRAMMERS NOTES

Adding a New Form

To add a new form to an existing project, do the following:

Step 1: Either

a. Select the Add Form item from the Project menu, or

b. Press the Add Form button on the Standard Toolbar

Doing either of these two operations will bring up the Add Form dialog box.

Step 2: Select the Form icon under the Add Form dialog box's New tab.

- Doing this will cause a new form to be displayed and will add this new form to the Project Explorer Window.

- To switch between forms, simply click on the desired form in the Project Explorer Window.

Table 9-25 The Inventory Receipt Form's TTL Table

Form: Inventory Task	Trigger Object	Event
Obtain current date	txtDate	default or user entry
Obtain quantity	txtQuantity	user entry
Initialize date	Form	Load
Detect F10 key	Form	KeyDown
Validate quantity	txtQuantity	KeyPress
Write to database and return to Main Menu	cmdReturn	Click

Procedure Code 9-3

```
Private Sub Form_Load()
  txtDate.Text = Format(Now, "mm/dd/yy")
End Sub

Private Sub Form_KeyDown(KeyCode As Integer, Shift As Integer)
  If KeyCode = vbKeyF10 Then 'check for the F10 key
    KeyCode = 0
    Me.Hide
    frmMain.Show
  End If
End Sub

Private Sub txtQuantity_KeyPress(KeyAscii As Integer)
Const ENTER As Integer = 13 ' the ANSI value of the Enter key
  If KeyAscii = ENTER Then
    KeyAscii = 0
    cmdReturn.SetFocus
  ElseIf KeyAscii < Asc("0") Or KeyAscii > Asc("9") Then
    KeyAscii = 0
    Beep
    MsgBox "You can only enter a number here.", vbCritical, "Data Entry Error"
  End If
End Sub
```

continued

```
Private Sub cmdReturn_Click()
  Const strRECEIVE As String = "r"      ' code for receipt of inventory
  Const strRETURNED As String = "t"     ' code for returns to vendor
  Const strDAMAGED As String = "d"      ' code for damaged inventory
  Const strOTHER As String = "o"        ' code for other adjustments

  datINV.Recordset.AddNew  ' clear the copy buffer
  If optInv1.Value = True Then
    datINV.Recordset("Fname") = "Receipt"
    datINV.Recordset("Lname") = "of Inventory"
    datINV.Recordset("RDCode") = strRECEIVE
  ElseIf optInv2.Value = True Then
    datINV.Recordset("Fname") = "Returned"
    datINV.Recordset("Lname") = "to Vendor"
    datINV.Recordset("RDCode") = strRETURNED
  ElseIf optInv3.Value = True Then
    datINV.Recordset("Fname") = "Damaged"
    datINV.Recordset("Lname") = "Inventory"
    datINV.Recordset("RDCode") = strDAMAGED
  ElseIf optInv4.Value = True Then
    datINV.Recordset("Fname") = "Adjustment"
    datINV.Recordset("Lname") = "to Inventory"
    datINV.Recordset("RDCode") = strOTHER
  End If
  datINV.Recordset("Quantity") = txtQuantity
  datINV.Recordset("RDDate") = txtDate
  datINV.Recordset.Update

  Unload.Me
  frmMain.Show
  frmMain.Refresh
End Sub
```

The first three event codes listed in Procedure 3-1 have been used extensively within the Rotech project, and will not be commented upon. The last procedure is the one that is used to actually store the form's data into the Disktran database. The first task accomplished by this procedure is to assign the relevant codes (see Table 9-21) to named constants. Next, the code uses an **If-ElseIf** statement to determine which Option button has been checked. It is this part of the code that sets the values for the Fname, Lname, and RDCode fields. Finally, the Date and Quantity values are assigned to data fields and the complete record is written to the database table. At the end of the procedure the Inventory form is unloaded and the Main Menu form redisplayed. Since this new form is not intended to be used as extensively as the Order Entry forms, this choice of unloading and redisplay makes sense. If we were to stay on this form after each quantity was entered we would have to provide a separate Clear button, a separate Save button, and a separate Return button. We would also have to check each time that the Return button was pressed that the user actually wanted to directly return, without first saving the last entered values. All of this is rather unnecessary because of the form's intended usage, which is to enter an occasional receipt of inventory and return back to the Main Menu.

As the single Return button is used for both saving and returning, however, we do have to provide a means of return in case the user inadvertently displays this form and wants to get back to the main part of the system without saving any data. Here we can use the ⌜F10⌝ key that has been provided for each form. The general instruction to all users is "You can always get out of trouble by pressing the F10 key." Since this key is available, we simply make note of its use on the form. Even if you should want to provide a Return Without Saving key, you must be aware that a user could press this key by accident. Thus, the general rule for such keys is that if any saving of data might be required, you must provide a Return key with the type of "safety" code previously listed as Event Code 9-3 and the message previously shown in Figure 9-24. Pressing the ⌜F10⌝ key will not be done accidently, and so its use here makes good programming sense.

Exercises 9.6

(**Note:** The Rotech Systems project, at the stage of development begun in this section, can be found on the Student Disk in the rotech8 folder as project rotech8.vbp. The project, as it exists at the end of this section, can be found on the Student Disk in the rotech9 folder as project rotech9.vbp. If you are developing the system yourself, following the procedures given in this section, we suggest that you first copy all of the files in the rotech8 folder into the temp folder, and then work out of this latter folder. When you have finished your changes you can compare your results to the files in the rotech9 folder.)

1. a. Add the modifications to the Mail In form developed in this section to make your form look like Figure 9-26. Make sure to add the additional event code listed in Procedure Code 9-1.
   b. Test the modifications that you made in Exercise 1a to ensure that the modifications perform correctly.

2. a. Add the modifications to the Walk In form developed in this section so that the form looks like Figure 9-29. Make sure to add the additional event code listed in Procedure Code 9-2.
   b. Test the modifications that you made in Exercise 2a to ensure that the modification performs correctly.

3. a. Add a new form to the Rotech project and provide it with the properties listed in Table 9-24 and the event code listed in Procedure Code 9-3.
   b. Test the form added in Exercise 3a to ensure that all event codes operate correctly.

4. The current Rotech system has no means for either locating an existing record within the RedDis table or for browsing through the complete list of records. Rectify this by adding a new form to the project that permits locating records using a combination of a person's last name and city. Do not permit a user to alter any existing records from within your new form. Your new form should be accessed from the existing Mail In form and redisplay the Mail In form when the user is finished locating an existing record.

5. Modify the form created for Exercise 4 to permit entry of the return code value "a" for "address unknown", or "u" for refused shipment, when a disk package is returned by the postal delivery service for one of these reasons. This code should be stored in the existing record's RetCode field (see next to last field name in Table 9-19). Permit the user to also enter a RetDate value (last field listed

in Table 9-19) corresponding to when the return code was entered. If no date has been entered, the system should assign the current system (**Now**) date as the RetDate value.

6. a. **CASE STUDY**
      Make all necessary modifications to your selected project so that all of the data entry forms store each entered transaction (see project specifications at the end of Section 1.5). Additionally, add any new transaction forms that might be required by your application.
   b. Test that all modifications made to your project operate correctly.

9.7 ▶ Knowing About: Databases and the Application Wizard

The Application Wizard, introduced in Section 8.7, is especially useful for developing database applications.[6] This is because it both creates forms with data-bound controls for each selected database table and provides code for refreshing and updating RecordSets. In this section, we show the additional steps required to use the Application Wizard for creating database applications. In addition, the DBGrid control, a data-bound grid control that presents record information in a spreadsheet format, is described.

Recall from Section 8.7 that the basic Wizard dialogs used in creating an application are

- Introduction dialog
- Interface Type dialog (SDI, MDI, or Explorer)
- Menu dialog (File, Edit, View, etc.)
- Toolbar dialog
- Resources dialog
- Internet Connectivity dialog
- Standard Forms dialog (Login, Splash Screen, etc.)
- Data Access Forms dialog
- Finished dialog

For developing a database application, the only major change within this sequence is to use the Data Access Forms dialog to link to an existing database. As shown on Figure 9-32, this is accomplished by selecting the Create a New Form button on this dialog, and then providing information as to the name and type of database being accessed.

Pressing this button will produce a sequence of dialog boxes from which you specify the databases, tables, and fields that you want included into the current project. The first of these dialog boxes is shown in Figure 9-33. Selecting the default shown and pressing the Next button will display the dialog shown in Figure 9-34.

Since the database that we will be using was created using Microsoft's Access program, we select the Access option shown in Figure 9-34. When this is done, the next dialog permits us to specify the name of the database that we want to link into the project. In this sample application, as is seen

---

[6]The Application Wizard cannot be used to modify existing projects.

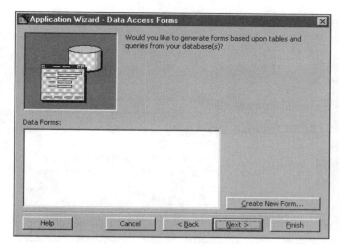

Figure 9-32
Using the Data Access Forms Dialog to Connect to a Database

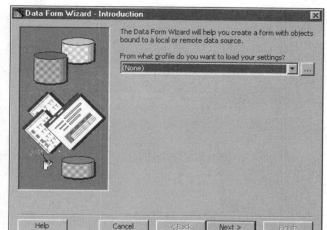

Figure 9-33
The Introduction Dialog

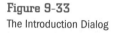

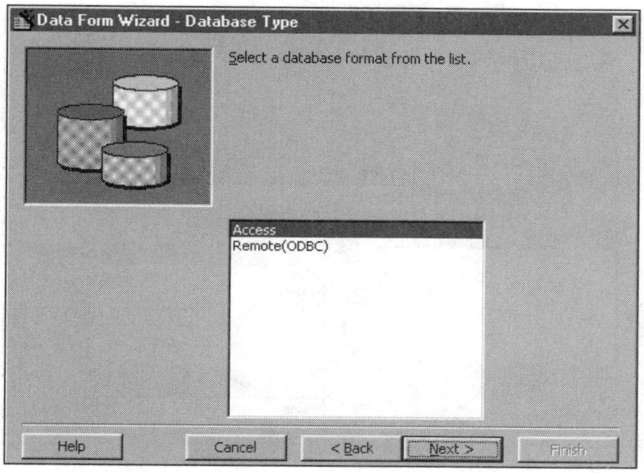

Figure 9-34
The Database Type Dialog

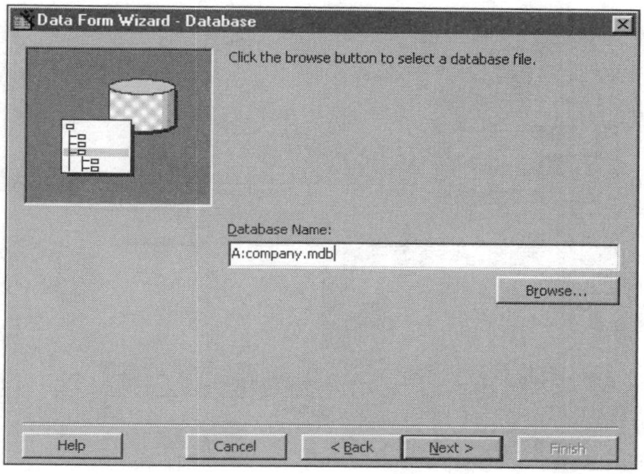

Figure 9-35
The Database Name Dialog

in Figure 9-35, we use this dialog to select the company.mdb database located on the A disk drive.

Once the connection to a specific database has been made, the App Wizard requests a name for the form it will build and link into the project that it will provide. As shown in Figure 9-36, we have named the form frmPhone and selected a single record layout, which permits viewing each record individually on the named form. After this form is completed, the next dialog, which is shown in Figure 9-37, requests information about the specific table from which the records will be displayed. For this dialog, as shown in Figure 9-37, we have used the drop-down list to select the PhoneBook table as our record source.

Once a record source has been selected, the available fields for this record source will be listed in the List box labeled Available Fields, which is located on the left side of the dialog. As shown in Figure 9-38, this List box now contains the fields that define each record in the PhoneBook table. By either double-clicking on individual desired fields or using the single right-facing arrowhead between the List boxes, selected fields are moved to the Selected Fields List box. (Clicking on the double right-facing arrowheads moves the complete list over. In a similar manner, the left-facing arrowheads

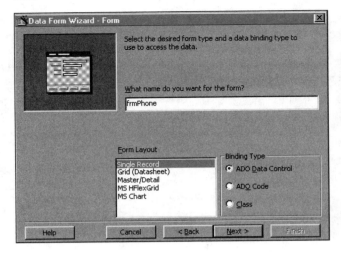

Figure 9-36
Naming the Form and Layout Type

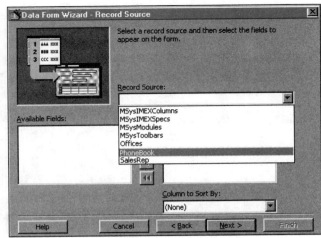

Figure 9-37
The Record Source Dialog

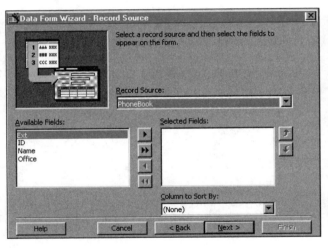

Figure 9-38
The Available Fields

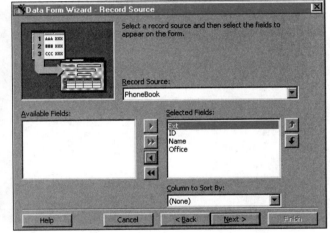

Figure 9-39
All Fields Selected

move items from the selected list back into the Available Fields list.) For our immediate purposes we have selected all of the fields using the double right-facing arrowhead, which produces the List shown in Figure 9-39.

After selecting the desired fields for display, the last dialog, which is shown in Figure 9-40, provides a selection of various buttons that can be added to the form that will be developed by the App Wizard (this is the frmPhone form previously shown in Figure 9-36). For purposes of illustration we will select all of the available button controls.

At this point in the procedure the Message box shown in Figure 9-41 will appear. By selecting the No button, you will be returned to the Data Access form shown in Figure 9-42. Notice that this is the same as Figure 9-32, except that the Data Forms List box now contains the name of the form that the App Wizard will create according to our specifications. You now have the option of creating another form or completing the application by pressing the Finish button.

Figure 9-43 illustrates the data form created by the Wizard when the View menu's PhoneBook option is selected from an executing application. As expected, this form is similar to the ones that we have created throughout this

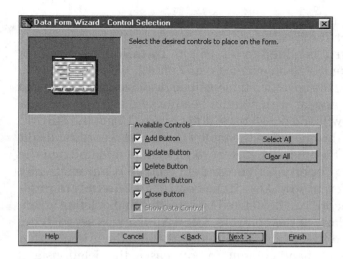

Figure 9-40
Selecting the Button Controls

Figure 9-41
The MessageBox Options

Figure 9-42
The Completed Data Access Dialog

Figure 9-43
The PhoneBook Table's Data Form

ID	Name	Ext	Office
1	Bronson, Bill	321	HM
2	Engle, Alan	234	HM
3	Dieter, Frank	289	F1
4	Dreskin, James	367	HM
5	Farrell, Mike	564	F1
7	Ford, Sue	641	F1
9	Gent, Hillary	325	HM
10	Grill, John	495	F1
11	Jones, Kay	464	F1
12	Jones, Mary	790	HM
14	Macleod, Jim	761	HM
15	Miller, Harriet	379	HM
21	O'Neil, Pat	856	F1
22	Schet, David	485	F1
23	Smith, Bill	251	F1
24	Smith, Dave	893	HM
26	Swan, Kurt	168	HM
27	Ward, Ann	726	F1
28	Williams, John	673	HM
30	Bass, Harriet	893	HM

Figure 9-44
A DBGrid Control View of a Table

chapter. Note, however, that the form also includes Command buttons for manipulating the table by adding, deleting, refreshing, and updating records.

Although we had selected single record layout for our form (see Figure 9-36), an alternate, and sometimes more useful, choice is the Grid (Database) layout. Selecting this option causes the **DBGrid** (short for data-bound grid) control to appear. This control, shown in Figure 9-44, displays the records in a table within the context of a spreadsheet view. Each row in the grid corresponds to a record, while each column corresponds to a field. Using this control, a user can move between records and fields using standard spreadsheet navigational methods.

In addition to being supplied by all database applications produced using the Application Wizard, the **DBGrid** control can also be manually placed on a form at design time. Figure 9-45 shows how the DBGrids icon appears within a Toolbox. The **DBGrid** control can be placed into a standard Toolbox by selecting it from the

Figure 9-45
The DBGrid Control Icon

Controls tab of the Project menu's Components option, or it can be accessed using the extended object Toolbox.

Once a DBGrid control is added to a form, its **DataSource** property must be set to bind the control to an existing data control. When this is done and the application is run, the specified table will be displayed in the DBGrid control. The control will appear with column headings taken from the data control's RecordSet and will add scroll bars, if necessary. Using the DBGrid control you can navigate through all of the table's fields and records and edit any field. Assuming that the underlying RecordSet can be updated and the control's **AllowUpdate** property is **True**, a field change is automatically made by moving to a different row. Also, if the control's **AllowDelete** property is set to **True**, any record can be deleted by selecting and deleting an entire row in the grid. Similarly, if the control's **AllowAddNew** is set to **True**, new records can be added to the table by entering them in the grid row that has an asterisk (*) in the left-hand column. In both cases, the deletions and additions will only be made if the underlying RecordSet is updatable.

Finally, in addition to being set at design time, individual cells within the grid can be selected and manipulated at run time. Specifically, each column has its own font, border, word-wrap, color, and other formatting attributes, and, at run time only, each cell can be individually located using the grid's **Row** and **Col** properties.

9.8 ▶ Common Programming Errors and Problems

The common errors and problems encountered when using Visual Basic to access and update database tables are:

1. Forgetting to use either a Dynaset- or Snapshot-type RecordSet type when using a structured query as the **RecordSource**.

2. Forgetting to use a Table-type RecordSet when using an indexed table.

3. Using a **Find** method on a non-sorted RecordSet. Although the **Find** will locate a record, due to the possible random ordering of records, the desired record can be missed.

4. Using a **Seek** method on a non-indexed RecordSet.

5. Forgetting to place a comma between the comparison expression and search criteria within a **Seek** method invocation.

6. Using the **AbsolutePosition** value to locate a record. Due to deletions and rebuilds, a record's position can change. A **Bookmark** should be used to retrieve a previously located record.

7. Not saving the last edit performed on a RecordSet. This occurs when the application is terminated before a movement button or movement method has been activated. When dealing with databases, an application's Exit button should always have a provision for saving the last edit.

9.9 ▶ Chapter Review

Key Terms

bound control	current record	database
browsing	data-aware control	DBMS
cardinality	Data control	Dynaset RecordSet

entities	record	structured query
field	relational database	Table RecordSet
Jet engine	relationships	update
navigating	Snapshot RecordSet	
organization	SQL	

Review

1. A *database* is defined as a collection of related data used by an organization, where an *organization* refers to any self-contained social unit, such as a company, university, hospital, or family.

2. A *relational database* is a database in which data is stored in tables.

3. Each row in a database table is referred to as a *record*, and each column is designated by a heading, referred to as a *field name*.

4. When records are ordered by the value of a particular field, the field is referred to as a *key field*.

5. An *index* is a special type of table that lists the position of another table's records in a key field order.

6. A structured query is a statement, written according to the rules of a language called Structured Query Language (SQL), that uniquely identifies a set of records from one or more tables. The set of records can be empty, if no records meet the selected criteria.

7. The basic syntax of an SQL Select command is

```
Select field-name(s) From table(s) Where condition(s) Order By field-name(s)
```

Formally, this statement consists of four clauses; a **Select** clause, a **From** clause, a **Where** clause and an **Order By** clause. The words **Select**, **From**, **Where**, and **Order By**, are all SQL keywords.

At a minimum, a structured query must contain both a **Select** and **From** clause; the **Select** clause specifies the fields that will be returned by the query, while the **From** clause specifies the table or tables whose records will be searched. In addition, if any restrictions are placed on the data to be selected, or if the selected information is to be presented in a specified order, a **Where** or **Order By** clause must be included. For example, in the statement

```
Select * From PhoneBook Order By Ext
```

the **Select** clause specifies that all fields are to be obtained, the **From** clause specifies that the fields are to come from the PhoneBook table, and the **Order** clause specifies that the RecordSet is to be constructed in increasing (ascending) order based on the values in the Ext field.

8. A database management system (DBMS) is a package of one or more computer programs designed to establish, maintain, and access a database.

9. The Microsoft Jet engine is a DBMS that is used by Visual Basic to open, locate records from, update, and close a database. When accessed by Visual Basic, the Jet engine creates a set of records, which is referred to as a *RecordSet*, from one or more database tables. Three types of RecordSets can be created: a Table-type, which uses an index for ordering the records, a Dynaset-type, which places records either in the order they are stored in their database table or are selected according to a

structured query, or a Snapshot-type, which is identical to a Dynaset-type except that the records are read-only (cannot be updated).

10. RecordSets can be created and accessed using a Data control. To use a Data control, at a minimum, the following three properties must be specified:

   - **DatabaseName**, which names the desired database and defines where it is located;
   - **RecordSource**, which names the table or structured query from which a RecordSet is created; and
   - **RecordsetType**, which defines the type of RecordSet that the Jet engine will create.

   The third property, **RecordsetType**, does not have to be explicitly set, because it uses a default Dynaset type.

11. The *current record* is the record in a RecordSet that is currently accessible by a Data control. Only one record can be the current record at any given time. This record can be changed by a Data control's movement buttons or by using a **Move** method in code. Moving around or changing the current record is referred to as *navigating* or *browsing* through a RecordSet.

12. A *bound control* can be a Text box, Label, Picture box, Image box, Check box, List box, Combo box, custom third-party control, or OLE container control. The control becomes a bound control by setting its **DataSource** property to the name of a Data control. The control is then made *data-aware* by setting its **DataField** property to a field name. Being data-aware means that the control has access to a field value contained in the current record.

13. The **Find** methods, which are used to locate specific records in either a Dynaset- and Snapshot-type RecordSet are listed in Table 9-26. The syntax for each of the **Find** methods is

   ```
   table.Recordset.Findmethod criteria
   ```

   where

   - *table* is the name of an existing Dynaset or Snapshot RecordSet;
   - *Findmethod* is one of the **Find** methods listed in Table 9-26;
   - *criteria* is a string expression used to locate the desired record. It is constructed in the same manner as a structured query, but without the **Where** keyword.

   For a **Find** command to work correctly, the RecordSet must be ordered by the search criteria being applied.

Table 9-26 The Find Methods

Method Name	Search Begins at:	Search to:
FindFirst	Beginning of RecordSet	End of RecordSet
FindLast	End of RecordSet	Beginning of RecordSet
FindNext	Current Record Position	End of RecordSet
FindPrevious	Current Record Position	Beginning of RecordSet

14. The **Seek** method is used to locate records in an indexed Table-type RecordSet. Specifically, the **Seek** method locates the first record in an indexed set that meets the specified criteria and makes that record the current record. The general syntax for the **Seek** method is

```
table.Seek comparison, value-1, value-2, . . . value-n
```

where

- *table* is the name of an existing Table-type RecordSet object;
- *comparison* is one of the string expressions "<", "<=", "=", ">=", or ">"; and
- *value-1, value-2, . . .* are one or more values corresponding to the underlying table's index setting.

15. To indicate whether or not a **Find** or **Seek** method was successful in locating a record, Visual Basic provides a **NoMatch** property. The value of this property is set to either **True** or **False** depending, respectively, on whether or not the **Find** or **Seek** method was successful in locating a record matching the given criteria.

16. **Move** methods, which are listed in Table 9-27, can be applied to a RecordSet to alter the current record. Each of these methods permit navigating through a RecordSet using code.

   Each of a Data control's movement buttons perform one of the equivalent **Move** methods listed in Table 9-27.

Table 9-27 The Move Methods

Name	Action	Example
MoveFirst	Make the first record in the RecordSet the current record.	datPhone.RecordSet.MoveFirst
MoveNext	Make the next record in the RecordSet the current record.	datPhone.RecordSet.MoveNext
MoveLast	Make the last record in the RecordSet the current record.	datPhone.RecordSet.MoveLast
MovePrevious	Make the prior record in the RecordSet the current record.	datPhone.RecordSet.MovePrevious

17. A Data control is programmed so that it will not move past either the first or last record in a RecordSet. When explicitly using a **Move** method, these same checks can be incorporated using the RecordSet properties named **EOF** and **BOF**, which stand *for End of File* and *Beginning of File*. The End of File (**EOF**) property is set to **True** only when the current record is positioned after the last record in a RecordSet. Similarly, the Beginning of File (**BOF**) is set to **True** only when the current record is positioned in front of the first record in a RecordSet. When either or these two property values is **True**, it means that the current record being pointed to is not valid.

18. *Programming a Data control* means writing code to alter the control's current record. A Data control is programmed using the **Find**, **Move**, and **Seek** methods. Additionally, a Data control can be programmed to update records in a RecordSet, where the term *update* refers to either adding, deleting, or editing records in both a RecordSet and its underlying database table. The update methods provided by Visual Basic for programming a Data control are listed in Table 9-28.

Table 9-28 Update Methods

Method Name	Description
AddNew	Creates a new record for both a Dynaset and Table-type RecordSet. This method sets all fields to Nulls, or any predefined default values. After the new record has been created and the fields edited, either an Update method or movement to another record (using either a movement method or the Data control's push buttons) must be used to make the changes permanent.
Delete	Deletes the current record in both an open Dynaset and Table-type RecordSet, and in the underlying database table.
Edit	Copies the current record from both a Dynaset and Table-type RecordSet to a copy buffer for subsequent editing.
Update	Saves the contents of the copy buffer to the specified Dynaset or Table RecordSet and the underlying database table.

Test Yourself—Short Answer

1. A database created with the Microsoft database engine and/or Access will have the extension _____.

2. If you want to prevent changes to your database but still allow the user to browse the database, you would set the _____ property to True.

3. **RecordSet** is a property of the _____ control.

4. Name the two properties that allow data-aware controls to be bound to a database.

5. A database where all of the data is stored in table form is a _____.

6. An index table is used to keep track of the record positions through the use of _____.

7. What processing would take place in a program with the statement datData1.Recordset.MoveNext?

8. What does the following statement do?

   datData1.Recordset.FindFirst = "State = 'CT'"

9. Write the code that will clear a data record on a database in preparation for creating a new record.

10. Write the code that would be needed to locate the first occurrence of a LastName of "Smith".

Programming Projects

Note: There is less direction given here as to the forms to be used and the way in which output is to be displayed than has been given in prior chapters. This is intentional and is meant to give you flexibility in designing your application.

1. This assignment is a modification to the Motel 8 project (Section 5.9, Ex. 7). The owner of Motel 8 has changed the pricing structure for a night's stay (to be described below). Additionally, he wants a daily report that categorizes and summarizes patron data for the previous night. Input to

the program will be records stored in an Access database table for which each record contains the following fields:

Room Number (integer)
Patron Name (20 characters)
Number of Adults (integer)
Number of Children

The name of the database, which is located on the Student Disk, is MOTEL.MBD and the table is PATRONS. Charges for a room are calculated using the following criteria:

If the number of adults is no more than two, the cost per adult is $30; otherwise the cost per adult is $25.

If the number of children is no more than two, the cost per child is $12; otherwise the cost per child is $10.

If the number of adults plus number of children is at least five, there is a 5% discount on the total charge.

There is a minimum charge per room of $50.

There is no state or local tax charged on the total cost. Also, there is no discount for multiple night stays by the same patron.

Output for the program should include the input plus adult charge, child charge, and total charge (after the discount, if applicable) for each room.

Your program should accumulate the number of adults, number of children, and total charge. Note that based upon the above criteria, the total charge for a room is not necessarily the sum of the adult charge plus the child charge. Use a function procedure to calculate room charge.

After the last record, print column totals (don't print totals for room numbers, adult charges, children charges, or discounts) for adult count, child count, and total charge.

As an optional addition to this problem, you might create a second table in the Access database and write the detail lines of your report to that table along with the appropriate date (using either the Date or Now function).

Sample Output:

Date: 5-10-99

```
                         MOTEL 8 DAILY REVENUE REPORT
ROOM  PATRON       ADULT   CHILD   ADULT   CHILD                   TOTAL
NMBR  NAME         COUNT   COUNT   CHARGE  CHARGE   DISCOUNT       CHARGE
-------------------------------------------------------------------------
1234  SMITH JOHN     2       0     60.00   00.00    00.00          60.00
1330  JONES JIM      2       3     60.00   30.00    04.50          85.50
1335  WILSON JOE     1       0     30.00   00.00    00.00          50.00
1400  KELLY BRIAN    1       2     30.00   24.00    00.00          54.00
-------------------------------------------------------------------------
                     6       5                                    249.50
```

2. This assignment is a modification to the State Utilities project (Section 5.9, Ex. 9). Using the original pricing structure, write the necessary code to produce a detail report with column totals.

Input to the program will be records stored in an Access database table for which each record contains the following fields:

```
CustomerID (integer)
CustomerName (text - 20 characters)
KWHUsed (integer)
```

The name of the database, which is located on the Student Disk, is UTILITY.MBD and the table is ACCOUNTS. For each record read, compute:

Base, undiscounted, untaxed bill amount
Discount amount
State utility tax amount
City utility tax amount
Total amount due

Also compute accumulated totals for each of these amounts. Your output should be in the form of a report that contains the data read for each record plus its corresponding calculated values (for each detail record). Format for the report could be similar to that used in Exercise 1 (this section).

Incorporate the code that you used in your original project solution that calculated the different charges into a sub procedure that can be called for each record read. Your program can send the number of KWH used to the sub procedure and it can return the five amounts listed above.

After having read all records and written all detail lines, write the appropriate accumulated totals at the bottom of their respective columns.

3. This assignment is a modification to the Texas Fence Company project (Section 7.9, Ex. 2). The company has asked you to expand the capabilities of your initial programming effort and write a program that will produce a list of necessary components that will be needed for the next day's fencing job. The necessary requirements for each fencing job are stored in an Access database table with each record containing the following fields:

```
Job number (integer)
Length (integer)
Width (integer)
Gates (integer)
```

The name of the database, which is located on the Student Disk, is FENCE.MBD and the table is JOBS. Output for the program should include a count for each of the following:

Connectors (integer)
Corner posts (integer)
Intermediate posts (integer)
Gate posts (integer)
Gate(s) (integer)
Fencing (integer)

Your program must read all records in the database table, compute the number of components needed for each job and accumulate totals for each component category. The output for this program is just the totals for each component category (number of connectors, number of corner posts, etc.).

Use a **Sub** procedure to calculate number of components for each category for each job (record read).

Additionally, you might offer the program user the chance to send the output to either the screen (with a form similar to the one used for the original project) or to the printer. You may also wish to create a second table for the database and write the fence component totals with the current date to that table.

Processing Visual Basic Data Files

A ny collection of data stored together under a common name on an external storage medium, such as a disk or tape, is referred to as a *file*. In the previous chapter we saw how to access database files that were under the control of a database management system. In this chapter we learn how to use files that are directly controlled by Visual Basic. The fundamentals of these files, and how they can be created and maintained by a Visual Basic application are presented. All files, no matter how they are maintained, permit an application to use data without the need for a user to enter it manually each time the application is executed. In addition, files provide the basis for sharing data between programs, so that the data output by one program can be input directly to another program.

10.1 Introduction to Visual Basic's File Types

A *file* is a collection of data that is stored together under a common name, usually on a disk, magnetic tape, or CD-ROM. For example, the Visual Basic project and form modules that you store on disk are examples of files. Each stored file is identified by file name, which is also referred to as the file's *external name*. This is the name of the file as it is known by the operating system, and as it is displayed when you open or save a file using the operating system.

Each computer operating system has its own specification as to the maximum number of characters permitted for an external file name. Table 10-1 lists these specifications for the most commonly used operating systems.

Table 10-1	Maximum Allowable File Name Characters
Operating System	**Maximum Length**
DOS, VMX, and Windows 3.1	8 characters plus an optional period and 3 character extension
Windows 95 and 98	255 characters
UNIX: Early Versions	14 characters
Current Versions	255 characters

When using the Windows 95 and 98 operating systems you should take advantage of the increased length specification to create descriptive file names within the context of a manageable length (generally considered to be no more than 12 to 14 characters). Very long file names should be avoided. Although such names can be extremely descriptive, they do take more time to type and are susceptible to typing errors.

Using the Windows 95 and 98 convention, the following are all valid file names:

balances.data	records	info.data
report.bond	prices.data	math.memo

File names should be chosen to indicate both the type of data in the file and the application for which it is used. Frequently, the initial characters are used to describe the data itself and an extension (the characters typed after a decimal point, which were limited to a maximum of three characters under DOS) are used to describe the application. For example, the Lotus 123 spreadsheet program automatically applies an extension .wk3 to all spreadsheet files, Microsoft's Word applies the extension .doc to its word processing files, while Corel's WordPerfect uses .wpx (where x is replaced by the version number). Visual Basic adds the extensions .frm and .vbp, respectively, to form and project files. When creating your own file names you should adhere to this practice. For example, the name prices.bond is appropriate in describing a file of prices used in a bond application.

On a fundamental level, the actual data stored in all files is nothing more than a series of related bytes. To access this data, a program must have some information as to what the bytes actually represent—characters, records, integers, etc. Depending on the type of data, various modes of access are appropriate. Specifically, Visual Basic directly provides three types of file access:

- Sequential,
- Random, and
- Binary.

The term *sequential access* refers to the fact that each item in the file must be accessed sequentially, one after another, starting from the beginning of the file. Thus, the fourth item in a file cannot be read or written until the previous three items have been read or written. Sequential access is appropriate for text files, where each stored character represents either a text or control character, such as a carriage return, that is stored using the ANSI code. This type of storage permits such files to be read as ordinary text.

Random access, which is also referred to as *direct access*, is appropriate for files that consist of a set of identical-length records. Typically, in using such files, you must first create a user-defined type to define the various fields making up a single record. Then, since each record in the file is the same length, you can directly access any record in the file by skipping over the fixed number of bytes that correspond to all of the records prior to the desired one. This permits accessing any specific record within the file without the need to read sequentially through prior records. Random-access files are stored using binary codes, but since each record has a well-defined fixed-length size, individual records can be conveniently and individually accessed.

In *binary-access*, no assumptions are made about either record sizes or data types. The data is simply read and written as pure binary information. The advantage to this approach is that binary files typically use less space than text files. The disadvantages, however, are that the file can no longer be visually inspected using a text-editing program and that the programmer must know exactly how the data was written to the file in order to read it correctly.

Exercises 10.1

1. a. Define the term *file*.
   b. Describe the difference between a file that is maintained by a database management system and the files directly supported in Visual Basic.

2. Describe the difference between a text and binary file.

3. List the three types of file access provided in Visual Basic.

4. a. An easy method of constructing a text file is to use the DOS `Copy` command. Use these steps to create a text file named `testfile`.

   Step 1: In Windows 95, open up a DOS window.
   Step 2: In the DOS window, type the command

   `copy con: testfile`

   (**Note:** `testfile` is the file's name. Any legitimate file name can be used instead.)

   Step 3: Enter any text that you want stored in the file. For example, enter the following text, pressing the (ENTER) key after each line is typed:

   ```
   Full many a gem of purest ray serene
      the dark unfathom'd oceans bear;
   Full many a flower is born to blush unseen,
      and waste its sweetness on the desert air.
   ```

   Step 4: Either press the (F6) function key or press the (CTRL) and (Z) keys together. This will terminate data entry and close the testfile file.

   b. To view the contents of any text file, the DOS `Type` command can be used. For example, to view the file named `testfile` created in Exercise 4a., enter the command `Type testfile` directly into a DOS window. In response to this command, the file's contents will be displayed. Using this command display the contents of the `testfile` file.

5. List three differences between sequential and random-access files.

10.2 File System Controls

Before a file can be accessed for either reading or writing, that file must be identified by name and location. In this context, location means specifying a drive, such as A:, C:, or D:, and a directory path. Clearly, the simplest method of providing this information is to permit the user to enter a full path name into a Text box and then use code to verify that a valid path has been provided. In an actual application, however, a Text box is typically included within a dialog box, which permits the rapid location of drive, directory, and file using Visual Basic controls. This is accomplished in one of two ways, both of which are presented in this section.

In the first method, we will use Visual Basic's file controls to create a custom-built dialog form. The second method makes use of a built-in Common Dialog control.

Creating a Custom Dialog Form

Figure 10-1

Visual Basic's File-System Controls

— Drive List Box

— File List Box

Directory List Box

Figure 10-1 illustrates the file-system controls provided by Visual Basic, which appear in the middle of the standard Toolbox. As shown, these consist of three controls that provide for extracting drive, directory, and file name information.

Figure 10-2 illustrates the interface for a Custom Dialog form that was created using the three file-system controls shown in Figure 10-1.

As is seen on Figure 10-2, the Drive list box is a drop-down box. What this means is that if the user clicks on the arrow provided in the box, a drop-down list of the drives connected to the system will be displayed. When a user clicks on a drive, it becomes the selected drive displayed in the Drive list box. The drive name itself is stored in the Drive box's **Drive** property. In a similar manner, the drive that appears when the box is first displayed can be set by assigning a suitable value to this property. For example, assuming the Drive box has been named drvSelect, the assignment statement

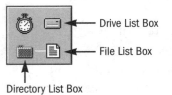

Figure 10-2

A Custom-Designed Dialog (Program 10-1's Interface)

```
drvSelect.Drive = "a:\"
```

sets the initial displayed drive to a:\.

Once a drive has been selected, it can be used to set the directory tree that is displayed in the Directory list box. This directory tree displays a directory structure, starting with the topmost directory, with all subdirectories suitably indented and the current directory highlighted. Each item in the directory tree is subsequently highlighted as the user moves up or down the list, and a vertical scroll bar is automatically provided to accommodate tree structures that do not fit within the confines of the box. The currently highlighted directory is contained in the Directory box's **Path** property. By default, this directory has a **ListIndex** property value of –1. The directory immediately above the highlighted directory has a **ListIndex** value of –2, the one above that has a value of –3, and so on. Similarly, the directory immediately below the highlighted directory has a **ListIndex** value of 0, the one below that has a value of 1, and so on. To ensure that the directory tree displayed in the Directory list box always corresponds to the drive selected in the Drive list box requires assigning the Drive box's **Drive** property to the Directory box's **Path** property. Assuming that the Drive and Directory list boxes have been given the names drvSelect and dirSelect, respectively, the following assignment statement, which is included within the Drive list box's **Change** event code, would be used:

```
dirSelect.Path = drvSelect.Drive
```

The last of the file-system controls, the File list box, displays a list of files for the path specified in the File list box's **Path** property. To ensure that this file list corresponds to the directory selected in the Directory list box requires assigning the Directory box's **Path** property to the File box's **Path** property. Assuming that the Directory and File list boxes have been given the names `dirSelect` and `filSelect`, respectively, the following assignment statement, which is included within the Directory list box's `Change()` event code, would be used:

```
filSelect.Path = drvSelect.Path
```

To display only a subset of files in the File list box, you can use its **Pattern** property. For example, and again assuming the File box has been named `filSelect`, the statement

```
filSelect.Pattern = "*.FRM; *.VBP"
```

causes only those files having an extension `.FRM` or `.VBP` to be displayed. Finally, the highlighted file name is automatically assigned to the File box's **FileName** property.

The interface illustrated in Figure 10-2 is used within the context of a complete program to display the file names within the selected drive and directory.

For this application the only required code is to assign the Directory box's path from within the Drive box, and to assign the File box's path from within the Directory box. This is accomplished using the Drive and Directory boxes' **Change** events, listed in Program 10-1's Event Code.

PROGRAMMERS NOTES

Creating Valid Path Names

In creating a full path name for use in an **Open** statement, a file name entered in a Text box is typically appended to a path supplied by a Directory List box. The path name in the Directory box is always a complete path name, such as C:\programs\vb5, with no final backslash. Thus, adding a file name to this path name requires inserting a backslash between the Directory box's **Path** property and the file's name. For example, if the Directory box is named `dirSelect` and the file's name is entered in a Text box named txtFile, a statement such as

```
filename = dirSelect.Path + "\" + txtFile.Text
```

can be used to assign the complete path name into the string variable named filename, which would then be followed by an **Open** statement for the variable filename. This solution, however, will fail if the current directory happens to be a root directory, such as c:\. Here, adding a backslash between the Directory path and the file's name makes the full path name c:\\file's name, which contains an extra backslash. What is required is an **If** statement that first checks the last character of the Directory box's path name. If this right-most character is not a backslash, one should be added; otherwise, a backslash character should not be added between the path and file name, as is done in the following code:

```
If Right$(dirSelect.Path,1) = "\" Then
  filename = dirSelect.Path + txtFile.Text
Else
  filename = dirSelect.Path + "\" + txtFile.Text
End If
```

Table 10-2 The Properties Table for Program 10-1

Object	Property	Setting
Form	Name	frmMain
	Caption	Program 10-1 A File Locator
Drive list box	Name	drvSelect
Directory list box	Name	dirSelect
File list box	Name	filSelect

Program 10-1's Event Code

```
Private Sub drvSelect_Change()
  dirSelect.Path = drvSelect.Drive
End Sub

Private Sub dirSelect_Change()
  filSelect.Path = dirSelect.Path
End Sub
```

Although the interface presented by Program 10-1 is useful for illustrating the relationship typically used for Drive, Directory, and File boxes, it limits the selection of file names to those already existing in a directory. In practice, we might need to open an entirely new file in which to store data or may find it easier simply to type in the name of an existing file without first going through each file-system list box. Both of these requirements are easily met by supplying a Text box in which the user can directly enter a file's name and location. The addition of a Text box to our custom-built file dialog is shown in Figure 10-3, the interface for Program 10-2.

In addition to making the assignments of drive and path that were made in Program 10-1, we have assigned the highlighted file name in the File list box as the Text box's **Text** property. Doing this permits the user either to select an existing file name from the file box or directly type in a file name into the Text box. The Text value is also cleared whenever the user changes either the Drive or Directory selections, as listed in Program 10-2's Event Code.

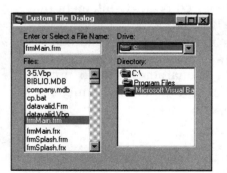

Figure 10-3

Program 10-2's Interface

Table 10-3 The Properties Table for Program 10-2

Object	Property	Setting
Form	Name	frmMain
	Caption	Custom File Dialog
Drive list box	Name	drvSelect
Directory list box	Name	dirSelect
File list box	Name	filSelect
Text box	Name	txtSelect
	Text	(Blank)

Program 10-2's Event Code

```
Private Sub dirSelect_Change()
  filSelect.Path = dirSelect.Path
  txtSelect.Text = ""
End Sub

Private Sub drvSelect_Change()
  dirSelect.Path = drvSelect.Drive
  txtSelect.Text = ""
End Sub

Private Sub filSelect_Click()
  txtSelect.Text = filSelect.filename
End Sub
```

In practice, the custom file dialog used in Program 10-2 would be displayed by a **cmdClick** event activated on an initial form, and the dialog itself would have an OK Command button to unload and hide itself and then return control to the calling form. Table 10-4 lists the various form-display tasks, the methods used to perform them, and examples for performing these functions.

Table 10-4   Loading, Displaying, and Hiding Forms

Task	How Task Is Accomplished	Example
Load a form into memory but not display it.	Use the **Load** statement.	`Load frmDialog`
Load and display a form.	Use the **Show** method.	`Show frmDialog`
Display a loaded form.	Use the **Show** method or set the form's **Visible** property to **True.**	`Show frmCustom`
Hide a form from view.	Use the **Hide** method, or set the form's Visible property to **False.**	`Hide frmCustom`
Hide a form from view and unload it from memory.	Use the **Unload** statement.	`Unload frmDialog`

Using a Common Dialog Control

An alternative to creating your own dialog boxes for entering file location information is to use Visual Basic's Common Dialog control. This control provides a choice of the following built-in dialog boxes to be displayed:

- Open dialog,
- Save As dialog,
- Color Selection dialog,
- Font Selection dialog,
- Print Selection dialog, and
- Help Window dialog.

As each of these dialogs are the same ones used within Windows 95 and 98, they are generally familiar to most users. For example, Figures 10-5 and 10-6 illustrate the Open and Save As dialog boxes. To include a Common

Figure 10-4
The CommonDialog Control Icon

Figure 10-5
The Open Common Dialog Box

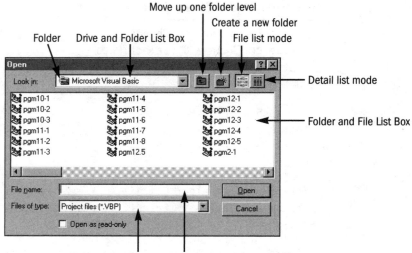

Figure 10-6
The Save As Common Dialog Box

dialog box within a form, use the CommonDialog icon (see Figure 10-4) from the toolbox, as you would any other control. Note, however, that this control is not a built-in control contained in the standard toolbox; rather, it is provided as an external .ocx file; to access it you must open a new project using the VB Professional Edition controls.[1]

As is seen in Figures 10-5 and 10-6, the Open and Save As dialogs are very similar, in that both provide the following components:

- Drive and Folders drop-down List box, where the user can select a drive and parent directory;

- Folder and File List box, where the user can select a current folder and file;

- File Name Text box, where the name of the selected file is displayed or where the user can enter a file name; and

- File Type List box, where the user can select the type of file to be displayed.

In addition, both dialogs provide a set of Command buttons for performing such functions as creating a new folder, moving up one folder level, switching between List and Detail modes, processing the selected file, or

---

[1] If the CommonDialog control icon is still not visible, make sure to select the Microsoft Common Dialog Control 6.0 on the Control tab, from within the Project menu's Component option.

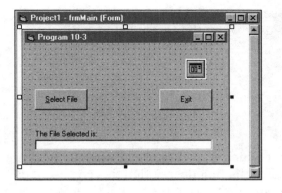

Figure 10-7
Program 10-3's Design-Time Interface

Method	Displayed Dialog	Example
ShowOpen	Open	cdlSample.ShowOpen
ShowSave	Save As	cdlSample.ShowSave
ShowColor	Color	cdlSample.ShowColor
ShowFont	Font	cdlSample.ShowFont
ShowPrinter	Print	cldSample.ShowPrinter
ShowHelp	Help	cdlSample.ShowHelp

Table 10-5 Common Dialog Selection Methods

canceling the dialog. Each of these functions is labeled with its corresponding button on Figure 10-5.

Once a CommonDialog control is placed on a form, the choice as to which dialog to activate is made at run time, using one of the methods listed in Table 10-5. For example, if the name of the CommonDialog control is cdlSample, the statement cdlSample.ShowOpen will cause an Open dialog to be displayed, while the statement cdlSample.ShowSave will cause a Save As dialog to appear.

Figure 10-7 illustrates the design-time interface for Program 10-3, which uses a CommonDialog control to obtain a user-entered file name and location. When the CommonDialog control is placed on a form it will automatically resize itself, and like a timer control, it becomes invisible at run time.

Program 10-3's Event Code

```
Private Sub cmdName_Click()
  picMessage.Cls
  cdlFile.Filter = "Project files (*.VBP)|*.VBP|All Files (*.*)|*.*"
  cdlFile.ShowOpen
  picMessage.Print cdlFile.filename
End Sub

Private Sub cmdExit_Click()
  Beep
  End
End Sub
```

In reviewing Program 10-3's event code, first notice the statement cdlfile.ShowOpen. This is the statement that causes the CommonDialog control to display an Open dialog box, similar to the one shown in Figure 10-5. In addition, the statement immediately above the call to show the Open dialog box is a statement that sets the CommonDialog's **Filter** property. This property can be set either at design time, using the Properties window, or at run time, as is done here. The string assigned to the **Filter** property specifies a list of file filters displayed in the dialog's Files of type: List box. The general syntax for setting this property is

control-name.**Filter** = "*description1|filter1|description2|filter2. . .*"

For example, the statement

```
cdlFile.Filter = "Project files (*.VBP)|*.VBP|All Files (*.*)|*.*"
```

used in Program 10-3 sets two descriptions and two corresponding conditions, which can be selected by a user when the Open dialog is displayed. The first description displayed is

```
Project files (*.VBP)
```

and the second description, which is displayed when the user activates the `Files of type:` drop-down list is

```
All Files (*.*)
```

The actual filters used to select which file types are displayed are contained within the filter conditions. For the first description this corresponds to the filter *.VBP, and for the second description the actual filter is *.*. In setting a condition, it is important to note that you should *not* include any spaces either before or after the symbol (|) used to separate descriptions and filter conditions.

Figure 10-8 illustrates a sample run using Program 10-3, where the user entered the name test.dat into the Open dialog's Filename: Text box.

In reviewing the output displayed by Program 10-3, it is important to note that the selected file, test.dat, has not been opened and may not even exist within the indicated folder. By pressing the Open dialog's Open Command button, the string entered into the `File name:` Text box is stored into the CommonDialog control's **FileName** property. It is this value that is subsequently displayed in Figure 10-8.

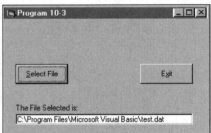

Figure 10-8
A Sample Output Produced by
Program 10-3

Table 10-6 The Properties Table for Program 10-3

Object	Property	Setting
Form	Name	frmMain
	Caption	Program 10-3
CommonDialog	Name	cdlFile
Command button	Name	cmdName
	Caption	&Select File
Command button	Name	cmdExit
	Caption	E&xit
Picture box	Name	picMessage
	Text	(Blank)
	TabStop	False

Exercises **10.2**

1. Enter and execute Program 10-1 on your computer.

2. Enter and execute Program 10-2 on your computer.

3. Write a Visual Basic program that uses an initial form to call the custom-designed dialog produced by the form used in Program 10-2. The call to the form containing the dialog should be invoked from a Command button on the initial form. In addition, the form containing the custom dialog box should contain a Command button with the caption OK that returns control to the calling form. The selected file name should then be displayed in a Picture box

contained on the initial form. Note that your program will consist of two forms.

④ Enter and execute Program 10-3 on your computer.

⑤ Write a Visual Basic program that uses an initial form to call an Open Command dialog. The call to the dialog box should be invoked from a Command button on the initial form. The selected file name should then be displayed in a Picture box contained on the initial form.

10.3 Sequential-Access Files

Within a Visual Basic program a file is referenced using a unit number, rather than the file's external file name. The unit number is a programmer-selected positive integer that corresponds to the file's name. The correspondence between unit number and file name is accomplished using an **Open** statement.

An **Open** statement is an executable statement that performs two tasks. First, opening a file establishes a physical communication link between the application and the data file. Since the specific details of this link are handled by the computer's operating system and are transparent to the program, the programmer normally need not consider them, except in one case. The single case is to ensure that the link has, in fact, been established.

From a programming perspective, the second purpose of opening a file is more relevant. Besides establishing the actual physical connection between an application and a file, the **Open** statement also equates the file's name to the integer unit number used by the application to reference the file. When a file is opened for sequential access, it is opened to perform one of the following operations:

- Output,
- Append, or
- Input.

To write to a file, it must be opened in either Output or Append modes. A file opened in Output mode creates a new file and makes it available for output. If a file exists with the same name as a file opened for output, the old file is erased. The general syntax of an **Open** statement that accomplishes this task is

```
Open filename For Output As #unit-number
```

For example, the statement

```
Open C:\programs\prices.data For Output As #1
```

creates and opens a file named `prices.data` in the `programs` directory of the C drive. It is now possible to write to that file. Once the file has been opened, the application accesses the file using the unit number (#1) while the computer saves the file under the name `prices.data`. As is seen in this example, a full path name can be used to designate the file, but it is not required. If the drive and directory information is omitted, the file is created in the current directory.

A file opened for appending can have data appended to its end. The general syntax of an **Open** statement that accomplishes this task is

> `Open` *filename* `For Append As` *#unit-number*

The difference between a file opened in Output mode and one opened in Append mode is in how existing files are used and where the data is physically stored in the file. In Output mode, a new file is always created and the data is written starting at the beginning of the file, while in Append mode the data is written starting at the end of an existing file. If the file, however, does not exist to begin with, the two modes produce identical results. For files opened in either Output or Append modes, the statements used to write data to the file are similar to the ones used for printing data on a form, and are described shortly.

A file opened in Input mode retrieves an existing file and makes its data available as input to an application. The general syntax of an **Open** statement that accomplishes this task is

> `Open` *filename* `For Input As` *#unit-number*

For example, the **Open** statement

```
Open C:\programs\prices.data For Input As #1
```

creates and opens a file named `prices.data` in the `programs` directory of the C drive and makes the data in the file available for input. Within the procedure opening the file, the file is read using the unit number (#1). Again, a full path name can be used to designate the file, but it is not required. If the drive and directory information is omitted, the file is assumed to exist in the current directory. The methods used to read data from a file are described shortly.

When opening a file for either input or output, good programming practice requires that you check that the connection has been established before attempting to use the file in any way. The check is made using an **On Error** statement. This statement tells the application what code to execute if an error occurs. Typically the **On Error** statement is used in code similar to the following, which attempts to open a file but reports an error message if the file was not successfully opened for input.

```
On Error GoTo FileError
Open cdlFile.filename For Input As #1
Rem:
Rem: Continue with normal file processing here
Rem:
Exit Sub
FileError: ' Control is only transferred here if there was an error
MsgBox "The File was not successfully opened!", vbExclamation, "File Error Notification"
Exit Sub
```

If an error occurs, control is transferred to the statement with the label `FileError`, which is a user-selected label that corresponds to Visual Basic's identifier rules. In this particular case a message box is displayed notifying the user of a file error, and the subsequent **Exit Sub** statement ends the procedure's execution. The first **Exit Sub** statement, immediately before the `FileError` label, permits the procedure to avoid executing the error-handling statements if no error occurred. Throughout the remainder of this chapter, we will include this type of error checking whenever a file is opened.

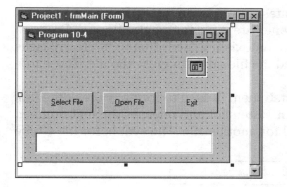

Figure 10-9
Program 10-4's Design-Time
Interface

Table 10-7 The Properties Table for Program 10-4

Object	Property	Setting
Form	Name	frmMain
	Caption	Program 10-4
Command button	Name	cmdName
	Caption	&Select File
Command button	Name	cmdOpen
	Caption	&Open File
Command button	Name	cmdExit
	Caption	E&xit
Common dialog	Name	cdlFile
Picture box	Name	picMessage
	TabStop	False

Program 10-4 illustrates the statements required to open a file in Read mode and includes an error-checking routine to ensure that a successful open was obtained. Except for the addition of the cmdOpen control, the interface and event code for this program is essentially identical to that used in Program 10-3. The code presented in the cmdOpen_Click() event uses an **Open** statement and an **On Error** statement to verify that a successful open was established, with an appropriate message displayed in a Picture box.

Program 10-4's Event Code

```
Private Sub cmdName_Click()
  picMessage.Cls
  cdlFile.Filter = "Data Files(*.dat)|*.dat|All Files (*.*)|*.*"
  cdlFile.ShowOpen
  picMessage.Print cdlFile.filename
End Sub

Private Sub cmdOpen_Click()
  Dim CR As String

  picMessage.Cls
  On Error GoTo FileError
  CR = Chr(13) ' carriage return character
  Open cdlFile.filename For Input As #1
  picMessage.Print "The file "; cdlFile.filename; CR; "  has been successfully opened."
  Exit Sub
FileError:
  picMessage.Print "The file was not successfully opened"; CR;
  picMessage.Print "Please check that the file currently exists."
End Sub

Private Sub cmdExit_Click()
  Beep
  End
End Sub
```

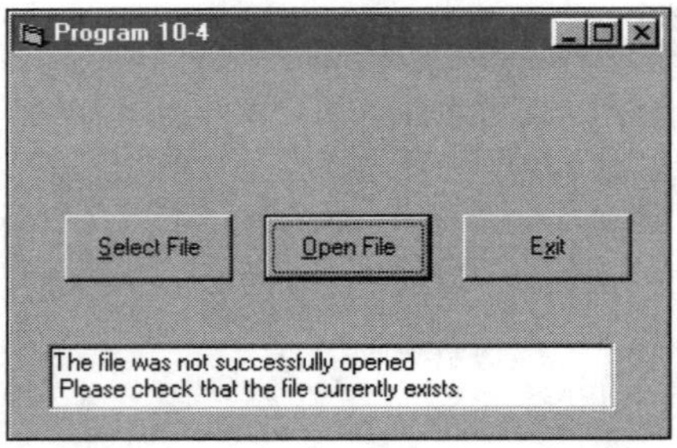

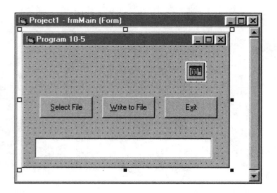

Figure 10-10
A Sample Output Produced by
Program 10-4

Figure 10-10 illustrates a sample run using Program 10-4 that attempted to open an nonexistent file for input. Although Program 10-4 can be used to open an existing file for input, it clearly lacks statements to either read the file's data or close the file. These topics are discussed next.

Formally, a **Close** statement is used to formally break the link established by the **Open** statement and releases the unit number, which can then be used for another file. The syntax for the **Close** statement is

```
Close unit-number list
```

where the unit-number list consists of one or more unit numbers that were assigned to the files when they were opened. If more than one unit number is provided in the **Close** statement, the unit numbers must be separated by commas.

Since all operating systems have a limit on the maximum number of files that can be opened at one time, closing files that are no longer needed makes good sense. In the absence of a specific **Close** statement, all open files existing at the end of normal program execution are automatically closed by the operating system.

When a file is closed, a special end-of-file (**EOF**) marker is automatically placed by the operating system after the last character in the file. This **EOF** character has a unique numerical code that has no equivalent representation as a printable character. This special numerical value, which is system dependent, ensures that the **EOF** character can never be confused with a valid character contained within the file. As we will see shortly, this **EOF** character can be used as a sentinel when reading data from a file.

Writing to a Sequential File

After a file is opened in either Output or Append modes, it can be written to using either a **Print #** or **Write #** statement and correctly referencing the file's unit number. The general form of a **Print #** statement is

```
Print #unit-number, List of comma separated expressions
```

For example, the statement

```
Print #1, price, txtAmt.Text, 36.25
```

causes the value of the variable named price, the contents of a Text box named txtAmt, and the number 36.25 to be written to a file previously opened as unit number 1. Notice that the **Print** statement used to write to a file is the same as that used to display values on the form, with the addition of a unit number that directs output to a specific file instead of a form.

Program 10-5's design-time interface is shown in Figure 10-11. The program illustrates using a **Print #** statement for writing data to an opened file. The properties table for Program 10-5 is identical to Program 10-4's, except for the form caption, which is now Program 10-5, and the cmdOpen control caption, which is now Write to File. The significant difference between Programs 10-4 and 10-5 is in the cmdOpen control's event code, which is listed below for Program 10-5. When this event code is executed, the user-entered

Figure 10-11
Program 10-5's Design-Time
Interface

PROGRAMMERS NOTES

Checking for a Successful Open and Error Trapping

It is important to check that the **Open** statement successfully established a connection between an application and an external file. This is because an **Open** is really a run-time request to the operating system that can fail for a variety of reasons. Chief among these reasons is a request to open an existing file for input that the operating system cannot locate. If the operating system cannot satisfy the open request, for whatever reason, you need to know about it and perform appropriate processing to avoid the inevitable abnormal program behavior or a subsequent program crash.

The most common method of checking for a successful connection is a fail code similar to the following:

```
On Error GoTo FileError
Open filename For Input As #1
Rem:
Rem: Continue with normal file processing here
Rem:
Exit Sub ' if there is no error, skip the error-code and exit the procedure
FileError: ' Control is only transferred here if there was an error
  MsgBox "The File was not successfully opened!", vbExclamation, "File Error Notification"
  Exit Sub
```

Intercepting errors that occur at run time, such as an **Open** error, is referred to as "trapping" an error. Trapping an error and then taking corrective action typically involves three steps—all visible in the previous code segment.

1. Enabling an error trap by telling the application where to branch when an error occurs. In Visual Basic this is accomplished by the **On Error** statement.

2. Writing an error-handling routine that appropriately responds to anticipated errors. Typically, such routines provide a user message.

3. Exiting the error-handling routine in a manner that affords the user a subsequent opportunity to correct the problem while the application is still executing.

---

file name is created by the operating system. After the file is opened, a **Print #** statement is used to write a single line to the file, which appears as follows:

```
Batteries        59.95            23
```

Program 10-5's cmdOpen_Click() Procedure

```
Private Sub cmdOpen_Click()
  Const description As String = "Batteries"
  Const price As Double = 59.95
  Const quantity As Double = 23
  Dim CR As String

  On Error GoTo FileError
  CR = Chr(13) ' carriage return character
  Open cdlFile.filename For Output As #1
  Print #1, description, price, quantity
  Close #1
  picMessage.Cls
  picMessage.Print "The file "; cdlFile.filename; CR; "   has been written."
  Exit Sub
FileError:
  picMessage.Print "The file was not successfully opened"; CR;
  picMessage.Print "Please check that the file currently exists."
End Sub
```

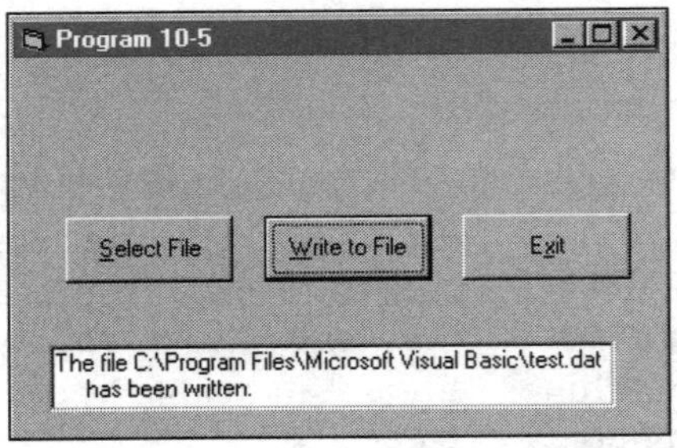

Figure 10-12
A Sample Run Using
Program 10-5

Figure 10-13
The File Created by
Program 10-5

66	97	116	116	101	114	105	101	115	32	32	32	32	32	32	53	57	46	57	53
B	a	t	t	e	r	I	e	s							5	9	.	9	5

32	32	32	32	32	32	32	32	32	50	51	32	13	10
									2	3		CR	LF

Figure 10-12 illustrates how Program 10-5's GUI looks upon completion of the output, assuming that the selected file was named test.dat. Now let's see how the actual data stored in this file looks.

For characters stored using the ANSI code, the file is physically stored as shown in Figure 10-13—as a sequence of 34 characters including blank spaces, a carriage return, and a line-feed character. For convenience, the character corresponding to each decimal code is listed below the code. A code of 32 represents the blank character, and the codes 13 and 10 represent a carriage return and line feed, respectively (see Appendix C). These are automatically placed at the end of each line produced by a **Print #** statement.

As illustrated in Program 10-5, writing to a file is essentially the same as writing to a form, except for the explicit designation of the file's unit number in the **Print #** statement. This means that all of the techniques that you have learned for creating output displays using a **Print** statement apply to file writes as well. For example, Event Procedure 10-1 illustrates storing data from an array into a file opened as unit number 3.

Event Procedure 10-1

```
Private Sub cmdOpen_Click()
  Dim result As Variant
  result = Array(16.25, 17.36, 15.75, 18.47, 19.51)
  Dim i As Integer

  Open cdlFile.filename For Output As #3
  For i = 0 To 4
    Print #3, i + 1, result(i)
  Next i
  Close #3
End Sub
```

When Event Procedure 10-1 is executed, the file name entered in the Common Dialog box named cdlFile is opened, and a **For** loop is used to invoke a **Print #** statement five times. Each time this statement is used, it prints one line to the file, which is automatically terminated with a carriage return and line-feed character. Thus, the written file consists of five lines, with each line containing two items. The file produced by this code, which we will assume has been written to a file named exper.dat, consists of the following data:

1	16.25
2	17.36
3	15.75
4	18.47
5	19.51

In addition to a **Print #** statement, Visual Basic also provides a **Write #** statement. This statement has the same syntax as the **Print #** statement, except that it puts quotation marks around each string expression that is written, and separates each written item with a comma.

Reading from a Sequential File

Once a sequential file has been created and written to, an **Input** statement can be used to read data from the file. The three types of **Input** statements available for reading data from a sequential file are

Statement	Description
Input #, variable list	Read data from a sequential file and assign the data to the variables in the variable list.
Line Input #, string-variable	Read a line from a sequential file and assign it to a string variable.
Input(n, #)	Read the next n characters from either a sequential or binary file.

For example, the statement

```
Input #2, A, B, C
```

causes three values to be read from the sequential file opened as unit number 2 into the variables A, B, and C.

Reading data from a sequential file requires that the programmer knows how the data was originally written to the file. This is necessary for correct "stripping" of the data from the file into appropriate variables for storage. Program 10-6 illustrates this by using an **Input #** statement to read the data in the exper.dat file created using Event Procedure 10-1.

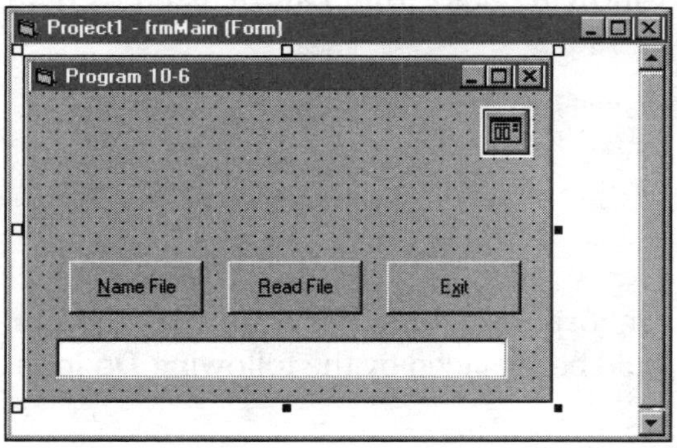

Figure 10-14
Program 10-6's Design-Time Interface

Table 10-8 Program 10-6's Properties Table

Object	Property	Setting
Form	Name	frmMain
	Caption	Program 10-6
Command button	Name	cmdName
	Caption	&Name File
Command button	Name	cmdOpen
	Caption	&Read File
Command button	Name	cmdExit
	Caption	E&xit
CommonDialog	Name	cdlFile
Picture box	Name	picMessage
	TabStop	False

Program 10-6's Event Code

```
Private Sub cmdName_Click()
  picMessage.Cls
  cdlFile.Filter = "Data Files(*.dat)|*.dat|All Files (*.*)|*.*"
  cdlFile.ShowOpen
  picMessage.Print cdlFile.filename
End Sub

Private Sub cmdOpen_Click()
  On Error GoTo FileError
  Dim i As Integer, n As Integer
  Dim value As Single
  Dim message As String

  Open cdlFile.filename For Input As #1
  For i = 1 To 5
    Input #1, n, value
    Print n, value
  Next i
  Close #1
  Exit Sub
FileError:
  message = "The file was not opened - please check that it exists."
  MsgBox message, vbExclamation, "File Error Notification"
End Sub

Private Sub cmdExit_Click()
  Beep
  End
End Sub
```

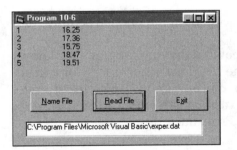

Figure 10-15

The Output Produced by Program 10-6

Program 10-6's **cmdOpen_Click** event reads the data from the opened file. Each time the file is read, an integer and a single-precision value are input to the program. Assuming Program 10-6 is used to read the exper.dat file created by Event Procedure 10-1, the display produced is illustrated on Figure 10-15.

In addition to using a **For** loop to read a specific number of lines, as is done in Program 10-6, the **EOF** marker appended to each file can be used as a sentinel value. When the **EOF** marker is used in this manner, the following algorithm can be used to read and display each line of the file:

> *Do Until the end-of-file has been reached*
>> *Read a line*
>> *Display a line*
> *Loop*

For example, if this algorithm is incorporated into Program 10-6, the **For** loop in the **cmdOpen_Click** event would be replaced by the following **Do** loop:

```
Do Until EOF(1)
  Input #1, n, value
  Print n, value
Loop
```

Using this **Do** loop within Program 10-6 produces the same output as that produced by the **For** loop's output previously illustrated on Figure 10-15. Notice that Program 10-6, no matter which loop algorithm is used, is effectively a line-by-line copying program. If we are not interested in extracting individual values from each line in the file, we can use a **Line Input #** statement in place of the **Input #** statement. For example, if we declare the variable lstring as a string variable, the following loop can also be used in Program 10-6 to produce the same output shown in Figure 10-15.

```
Do Until EOF(1)
  Line Input #1, lstring
  Print lstring
Loop
```

The **Line Input #** statement reads a line at a time, but does not include any carriage return or new line characters it encounters within its returned string. It simply considers these characters as delimiters that terminate input for the current line.

An alternative to using either the **Input #** or **Line Input #** statements is to use the **Input()** function. This function, which can be used for both sequential and binary files, returns a string, but requires the number of bytes that are to be read and included in the returned string. Unlike the **Line Input #** statement, however, the **Input** function returns all of the characters it reads, which includes carriage returns and new line characters.

To determine the size of a file, which can then be used as an argument to the **Input()** function, Visual Basic provides the **LOF()** and **FileLen()** functions, both of which return the size of file, in bytes, as a long integer. The difference between these functions is that the **LOF()** function returns the size of an open file, while the **FileLen()** function returns the size of an unopened file. For example, assuming the exper.dat file has been opened as unit number 1, the statement n = LOF(1) returns the total number of bytes in the file and assigns this value to the variable n. Using the **LOF()** function as an argument to the **Input()** function, the entire contents of a file opened as unit number 1 can be read using the statement lstring = Input(LOF(1), #1), where the variable lstring can be replaced by any user-declared string variable. Thus, the **For** loop in Program 10-6 can also be replaced by the code:

```
lstring = Input(LOF(1), #1)
Print lstring
```

In this code, the *complete* contents of file number 1 are input into the string variable named lstring.

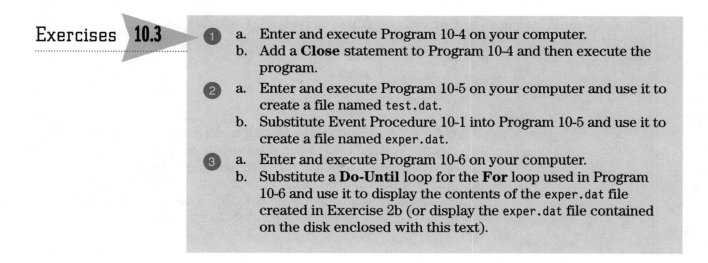

Exercises **10.3**

1. a. Enter and execute Program 10-4 on your computer.
    b. Add a **Close** statement to Program 10-4 and then execute the program.

2. a. Enter and execute Program 10-5 on your computer and use it to create a file named test.dat.
    b. Substitute Event Procedure 10-1 into Program 10-5 and use it to create a file named exper.dat.

3. a. Enter and execute Program 10-6 on your computer.
    b. Substitute a **Do-Until** loop for the **For** loop used in Program 10-6 and use it to display the contents of the exper.dat file created in Exercise 2b (or display the exper.dat file contained on the disk enclosed with this text).

④ Using the reference manuals provided with your computer's operating system, determine the maximum number of data files that can be open at the same time.

⑤ Would it be appropriate to call a saved Visual Basic form a file? Why or why not?

⑥ a. Write suitable **Open** statements to open each of the following files in Output mode: out_data, prices.dat, coupons, and file_1.

b. Write suitable **Open** statements to open each of the following files in Input mode: in_date, rates.dat, distance, and file_2.

⑦ Write individual **Open** statements to link the following external data file names to the given unit numbers.

External Name	Unit Number	Mode
coba.memo	1	Output
book.letter	1	Output
coupons.bond	2	Append
yield.bond	2	Append
prices.data	3	Input
rates.data	4	Input

⑧ Write **Close** statements for each of the files opened in Exercise 7.

⑨ a. Write a Visual Basic program that stores the following numbers into a file named results.dat: 16.25, 18.96, 22.34, 18.94, 17.42, 22.63.

b. Write a Visual Basic program to read the data in the results.dat file created in Exercise 9a and display the data. In addition, the program should compute and display the sum and average of the data. Using a hand calculation, check the sum and average displayed by your program.

⑩ a. Write a Visual Basic program that prompts the user to enter five numbers. As each number is entered, the program should write the numbers into a file named user.dat.

b. Write a Visual Basic program that reads the data in the user.dat file created in Exercise 10a and displays each individual number.

⑪ a. Create a file containing the following car numbers, number of miles driven, and number of gallons of gas used by each car:

Car No.	Miles Driven	Gallons Used
54	250	19
62	525	38
71	123	6
85	1,322	86
97	235	14

b. Write a Visual Basic program that reads the data in the file created in Exercise 11a and displays the car number, miles driven, gallons used, and the miles per gallon for each car. The output should also contain the total miles driven, total gallons used, and average miles per gallon for all the cars. These totals should be displayed at the end of the output display.

12 a. Create a file with the following data containing the part number, opening balance, number of items sold, and minimum stock required:

Part Number	Initial Amount	Quantity Sold	Minimum Amount
QA310	95	47	50
CM145	320	162	200
MS514	34	20	25
EN212	163	150	160

   b. Write a Visual Basic program to create an inventory report based on the data in the file created in Exercise 12a. The display should consist of the part number, current balance, and the amount necessary to bring the inventory to the minimum level.

13 a. Create a file containing the following data:

Identification Number	Rate	Hours
10031	6.00	40
10067	5.00	48
10083	6.50	35
10095	8.00	50

   b. Write a Visual Basic program that uses the information contained in the file created in Exercise 13a to produce the following pay report for each employee:

ID No.   Rate   Hours   Regular Pay   Overtime Pay   Gross Pay

Any hours worked above 40 hours are paid at time and a half. At the end of the individual output for each employee, the program should display the totals of the regular, overtime, and gross pay columns.

14 a. Store the following data into a file:

5 96 87 78 93 21 4 92 82 85 87 6 72 69 85 75 81 73

   b. Write a Visual Basic program to calculate and display the average of each group of numbers in the file created in Exercise 14a. The data is arranged in the file so that each group of numbers is preceded by the number of data items in the group. Thus, the first number in the file (5) indicates that the next five numbers should be grouped together. The number 4 indicates that the following four numbers are a group, and the 6 indicates that the last six numbers are a group. (**Hint:** Use a nested loop. The outer loop should terminate when the **EOF** marker is encountered.)

10.4 Random-Access Files[2]

The manner in which records in a file are written and retrieved is called *file access*. All of the files created so far have used *sequential access*, which means that each item in the file is accessed sequentially, one after another.

---

[2]This topic may be omitted on first reading without loss of subject continuity.

Thus, for example, the fourth item in a sequentially accessed file cannot be read without first reading the first three items in the file, the last item in the file cannot be read without first reading all of the previous items, and no item can be replaced without erasing all subsequent items. Due to this fact, updating a sequential-access file requires using a procedure in which a completely new file is created for each update. For those applications in which every record in a file must be updated, such as updating a monthly payroll file, sequential access conforms to the way the file must be updated and is not a restriction.

In some applications a direct access to each item in the file, where an individual item in the middle of the file can be retrieved, modified, and rewritten without reading or writing any other item, is preferable. *Random-access files*, which are also referred to as *direct-access files*, provide this capability. In this section we will see how to create and use such files. Note that the access method (sequential or random) refers to how data in the file are accessed and not to the codes used in storing the data. In point of fact, however, sequential files are stored by Visual Basic as text files, while random-access files are stored using the binary codes described in the next section.

In random-access files, the standard unit of storage is a record, where each record consists of one or more items. A record with only one field corresponds to any of Visual Basic's built-in data types, while a record with more than one field must be a user-defined type. Due to the record structure required when using random-access files, such files are typically used only for small amounts of data and simple applications; for large amounts of data and more complicated applications, the record structure inherent in the database methods presented in Chapter 8 would be used instead.

To illustrate the use of random-access files, consider the following application. All banks and financial institutions keep a table of official bank holidays, like Table 10-9, which is referred to as a Holiday Table. As shown in the table, some holidays, such as New Year's Day are always celebrated on the same day date, while others, such as President's Day are celebrated on different days, depending on the year. The importance of a Holiday Table is in computing settlement and maturity dates for financial instruments, such as stocks and bonds. Most stock and bond transactions must be settled within three working days, which excludes Saturdays, Sundays, and all holidays. Since there are algorithms for determining which dates fall on a weekend (for example, Zeller's algorithm described in Section 12.1,

Table 10-9 A Typical Bank Holiday Table

Holiday	Month	Day
New Year's Day	1	1
President's Day	2	Depends on year
Memorial Day	5	Depends on year
Independence Day	7	4
Labor Day	9	Depends on year
Columbus Day	10	Depends on year
Veterans' Day	11	Depends on year
Christmas Day	12	25

Exercise10) the specific dates for each weekend need not be stored separately. This is not the case for holidays, and hence the need for a specific table listing all the holiday dates.

A suitable user-defined record type for each entry in Table 10-9 is

```
Private Type HolidayRecord
   Description As String * 20
   Hdate As Date
End Type
```

Using a user-defined record type within the context of a complete application requires opening a file for random access, writing to and reading from the file, and closing the file. Table 10-10 lists the four statements Visual Basic provides for performing these operations on random-access files.

Table 10-10 Random-Access File Statements

Statement	Description	Example
Open	Open a file	`Open "Holiday.dat" For Random As #1 Len = Len(HolidayRecord)`
Close	Close a file	`Close #1`
Put #	Write a record	`Put #1, LastRecord, Holiday`
Get #	Read a record	`Get #1, LastRecord, Holiday`

The general syntax for an **Open** statement that opens a file for random access is

> `Open` *filename* `For Random As` *#unit-number* `Len` = *recordlength*

For example, the statement

```
Open "Holiday.dat" For Random As #1 Len = Len(HolidayRecord)
```

will open a file named `Holiday.dat` as a random-access file as unit number 1. The **Len =** expression in the **Open** statement specifies the size (i.e., length) of each stored record. Since each record is required to be of the same type, the length specification applies to all records in the file. If the specified length is less than an actual record's length, a run-time error is generated; if the specified length is greater than necessary, the record is stored with additional spaces to fill out the specified length. To make the length specification agree exactly with a record's size, the **Len( )** function can be used in the manner shown above.

Figure 10-16
Program 10-7's Design-Time Interface

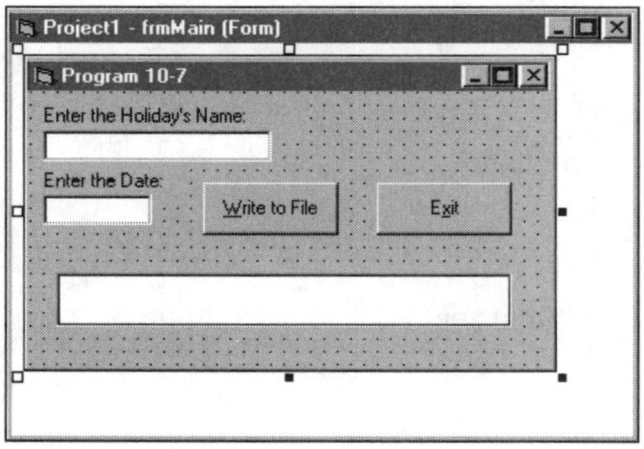

The file name used in the **Open** statement can be either a full pathname as a string literal enclosed in double quotes or as a string variable. If the path is omitted, the file is assumed to exist on the current directory. Finally, the expression `For Random`, which is the default for this form of the **Open** statement, can be omitted.

Once a file has been opened for random access, a **Put #** statement is required to write a record to the file and a **Get #** statement is used to read a record from the file. Program 10-7 illustrates using a **Put #** statement to store the holiday data listed in Table 10-9. The design-time interface for this program is shown in Figure 10-16.

Table 10-11 Program 10-7's Properties Table

Object	Property	Setting
Form	Name	frmMain
	Caption	Program 10-7
Text box	Name	txtDescrip
	Text	(Blank)
Text box	Name	txtDate
	Text	(Blank)
Command button	Name	cmdWrite
	Caption	&Write to File
Command button	Name	cmdExit
	Caption	E&xit
Picture box	Name	picMessage
	TabStop	False

Program 10-7's Event Code

General Declarations

```
Option Explicit
Rem: Define a Record Type
Private Type HolidayRecord
  Description As String * 20
  Hdate As Date
End Type

Rem: Declare a variable of the Record Type
Dim Holiday As HolidayRecord
Private Sub Form_Load()
  Const HolidayTable As String = "Holiday.dat"
  On Error GoTo FileError

  Open HolidayTable For Random As #1 Len = Len(Holiday)
  Exit Sub
FileError:
  MsgBox "The file " + HolidayTable + "was not opened.", vbExclamation
End Sub

Private Sub cmdWrite_Click()
  Static LastRecord As Integer

  Holiday.Description = txtDescrip.Text
  Holiday.Hdate = txtDate.Text
  Rem: Update the record number
  LastRecord = LastRecord + 1
  Rem: Write the record to the file
  Put #1, LastRecord, Holiday
  picMessage.Cls
  picMessage.Print "The record has been written."
End Sub

Private Sub txtDate_Click()
  picMessage.Cls
End Sub
```

```
Private Sub txtDescrip_GotFocus()
  picMessage.Cls
End Sub

Private Sub cmdExit_Click()
  Close #1
  Beep
  End
End Sub
```

In reviewing Program 10-7's event code initially, take a look at the General Declaration section. It is here that we define the record type used by the program and declare a variable to be of this type (if you are unfamiliar with user-defined data types, review Section 8.4). Next, notice that the Form_Load event procedure is used to open the file. Finally, notice the **Put #** statement within the cmdWrite_Click() event procedure. Prior to executing this statement, the procedure assigns the fields within the Holiday variable to the data entered into the two Text boxes. This procedure also updates the record number for the next record that is to be written, and stores this record number in the variable named LastRecord, where it is used to write the record into a file. **Put #** statements have the general syntax

```
Put #unit-number, record-position, variable-name
```

The record number in the **Put #** statement can be any integer expression that evaluates to a positive number. Since records in a random-access file are accessed by record number, applications that use random-access

---

PROGRAMMERS NOTES

A Way to Clearly Identify A File's Name and Location

During program development, test files are usually placed in the same directory as the program. Therefore, an expression such as Example 1 below causes no problems to the operating system. In production systems, however, it is not uncommon for data files to reside in one directory while program files reside in another. For this reason it is always a good idea to include the full path name of any file opened. For example, if the Holiday.dat file resides in the directory c:/test/files, the **Open** statement should include the full path name shown in Example 2 below. Then, no matter where the program is run from, the operating system will know where to locate the file.

Another important convention is to list all file names at the top of a program instead of embedding the names within the **Open** statement. This can easily be accomplished using a string variable to store each name, and placing this variable in the General Declarations section of the opening form. For example, if a declaration such as the one shown in Example 3 below is placed within the General Declarations section, it clearly lists both the name of the desired file and its location. Then, if some other file is to be tested, all that is required is a simple one-line change at the top of the program. Within an **Open** statement this string variable would appear as shown in Example 4 below.

Example 1: `Open Filename For Random As #1 Len = Len(HolidayRecord)`

Example 2: `Open "c:/test/files/Holiday.dat" For Random As #1 Len = Len(HolidayRecord)`

Example 3: `Const Filename As String = "c:\test\files\Holiday.dat"`

Example 4: `Open "Holiday.dat" For Random As #1 Len = Len(HolidayRecord)`

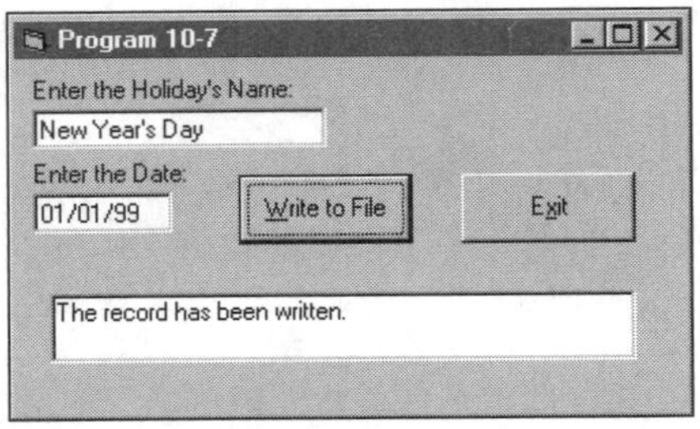

Figure 10-17
Using Program 10-7 to Write a
Record

files must contain a means of identifying each record's position in the file. If no record position is indicated, the record's contents will be written at the next available position; that is, the record is appended to the file. However, even if the record position is omitted, space must be indicated for it by separating the variable name from the unit number using two commas. In Program 10-7 the LastRecord variable is used to keep track of the current record position. Figure 10-17 illustrates how this program's run-time interface appears after a record has been entered and written.

The counterpart to the **Put #** is the **Get #** statement, which is used to read a record from a random-access file. The general syntax of this statement is

```
Get #unit-number, record-position, variable-name
```

In this statement, the unit-number is the number used in the **Open** statement to open the file. record-position is the record number of the record to be read and variable-name is the variable used to receive the contents of the record. If no record position is indicated, the next record in the file is read. However, as with the **Put #** statement, even if the record position is omitted, space must be indicated for it by separating the variable-name from the unit-number using two commas. Program 10-8 uses a **Get #** statement to read the records placed in the Holiday.dat file by Program 10-7. The design-time interface for Program 10-8 is shown in Figure 10-18.

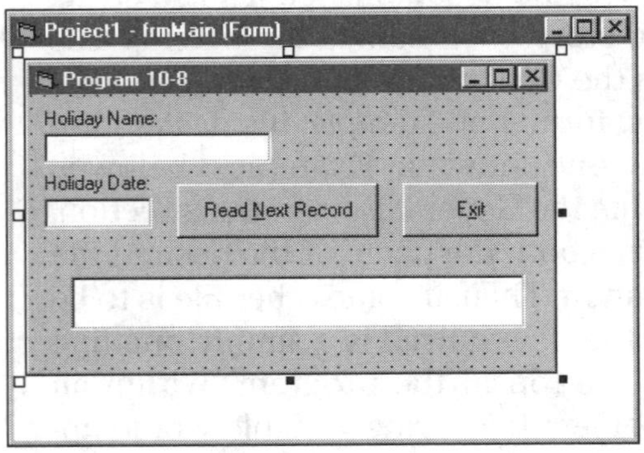

Figure 10-18
Program 10-8's Design-Time
Interface

Table 10-12	Program 10-8's Properties Table	
Object	**Property**	**Setting**
Form	Name	frmMain
	Caption	Program 10-8
Text box	Name	txtDescrip
	Text	(Blank)
Text box	Name	txtDate
	Text	(Blank)
Command button	Name	cmdNext
	Caption	Read &Next Record
Command button	Name	cmdExit
	Caption	E&xit
Picture box	Name	picMessage
	TabStop	False

Program 10-8's Event Code

```
Option Explicit

Rem: Define a Record Type
Private Type HolidayRecord
  Description As String * 20
  Hdate As Date
End Type

Rem: Declare a variable of the Record Type
Dim Holiday As HolidayRecord

Private Sub Form_Load()
  Const HolidayTable As String = "Holiday.dat"
  On Error GoTo FileError

  Open HolidayTable For Random As #1 Len = Len(Holiday)
  Exit Sub
FileError:
  MsgBox "The file " + HolidayTable + " was not opened.", vbExclamation
End Sub

Private Sub cmdNext_Click()
  Static LastRecord As Integer
  Dim records As Integer

  records = LOF(1) / Len(Holiday)
  picMessage.Cls
  picMessage.Print "There are"; records; "record in the file."

  Rem: Update the record number
  LastRecord = LastRecord + 1
  If LastRecord > records Then LastRecord = records
  Rem: Read the next record
  Get #1, LastRecord, Holiday
  txtDescrip.Text = Holiday.Description
  txtDate.Text = Holiday.Hdate
  picMessage.Print "This is record number"; LastRecord; "."
End Sub

Private Sub cmdExit_Click()
  Close #1
  Beep
  End
End Sub
```

Figure 10-19

Displaying the 4th Record in the File

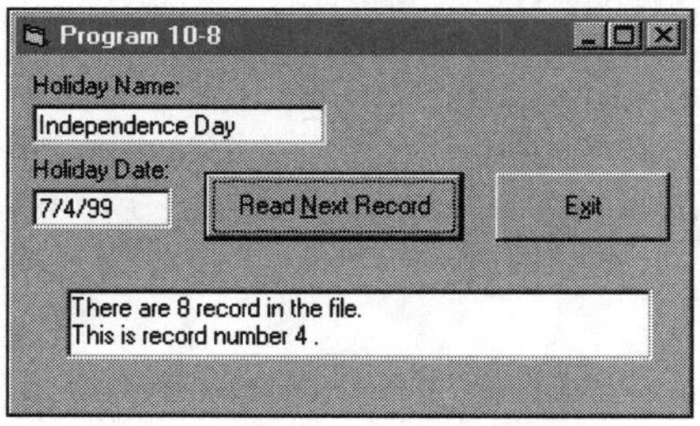

In reviewing Program 10-8's Event Code, the only really new items are contained within the **cmdNext_Click** event code. Here the **Click** event is used to execute a **Get #** statement to retrieve the next record in the file. As with Program 10-7, a variable named LastRecord is used to store the value of the next record to be read. Also, as with Program 10-7, the user-defined record type is declared in the General Declaration section of the program, and the file itself is opened when the form is loaded. The only remaining new feature is the calculation of the number of records, which is determined by dividing the total length of the file by the length of an individual record, and storing the result in the variable named records. A sample output displayed by Program 10-8 is shown in Figure 10-19.

Exercises 10.4

1. a. List the advantages of using a random-access file over a sequential file. What are the disadvantages?
   b. List two requirements in using a random-access file.
   c. Under what conditions would a database file be preferable to using a Visual Basic random-access file?

2. Enter and execute Program 10-7 on your computer.

3. Enter and execute Program 10-8 on your computer.

4. Modify Program 10-8 to include a Command button that can be used to read a previous record as well as the next record in the file.

5. A software distribution company is constantly opening and closing offices throughout the United States, Europe, and Asia. In its London office it maintains a file that contains an up-to-date listing of offices and their time zones. Currently the company's file contains the following data:

Paris	+1
London	0
New York	−5
Chicago	−6
Dallas	−7
San Francisco	−8
Honolulu	−10
Tokyo	+9

   The information in this file must be read each morning. It is then used by a program that automatically sends faxes to each office with the time adjusted to local time. For example, New York time is five hours behind London time and Tokyo is nine hours ahead of London time. Thus, when it is 12:00 noon in London, it is 7:00 a.m. in New York, and 9:00 p.m. in Tokyo. What management has asked you to do is write a Visual Basic program that can be used to create a random-access file for the current data.

6. Write a Visual Basic program that can be used to read and display the records created by the program written for Exercise 5. Your program should include a Command button for reading the next record in the file and a Command button for reading the previous record.

10.5 Binary-Access Files[3]

The last type of file access supported in Visual Basic is binary access. Unlike a sequential file, where each digit in a number is stored using its text (ANSI) code, in a binary-access file all numerical values are stored using the computer's internal binary code. For example, assuming that the computer stores integer numbers internally using 16 bits in the two's complement format described in Section 1.7, the decimal number 8 is represented as the binary

---

[3]This topic assumes that you are familiar with the computer storage concepts presented in Section 1.7.

number 0000 0000 0000 1000, the decimal number 12 as 0000 0000 0000 1100, and the decimal number 497 as 0000 0001 1111 0001. As hexadecimal numbers these numbers have the byte code 00 08, 00 0C, and 01 F1, respectively.

Since the external storage codes match the computer's internal storage representation, an advantage of using a binary format is that no intermediary conversions are required for storing or retrieving the data from the file. In addition, the resulting file usually requires less storage space than it would as a text file. For example, as text, the number 497 requires three bytes of storage consisting of the ANSI byte code sequence 34 39 37 (see Appendix C for these codes), while as a binary number it is stored using the two-byte sequence 01 F1. (For single-digit numbers, of course, the text format, which only requires one byte of storage, is smaller than the equivalent binary code.)

Like random-access files, the information in binary-access files is also accessed directly. The difference between the two file types, however, is that random-access files are organized as records, while binary-access files are organized by item. The same four statements used for opening, reading, writing, and closing random-access files are also used for binary-access files, with the main difference being that a byte position rather than a record position is used when reading and writing binary-access files. The general syntax for an **Open** statement, as it applies to a binary-access file is

> **Open** *filename* **For Binary** As *#unit-number*

For example, the statement

```
Open "bintest.dat" For Binary As #1
```

will open a file named `bintest.dat` as a binary-access file that is assigned unit number 1.

Notice that there is no **Len =** expression in the **Open** statement; if one is included it will be ignored. As always, the file name used in the **Open** statement can either be a full path name, as a string literal enclosed in double quotes, or a string variable. If the path is omitted, the file is assumed to exist on the current directory.

For writing data to a binary-access file, the **Put #** statement must be used. As it applies to binary files, this statement has the syntax

> **Put** *#unit-number,* byte-*position,* *expression*

In this statement `unit-number` is the number used in the **Open** statement to open the file, and `byte-position` is any integer expression that evaluates to a positive number. If no byte position is specified, the next unused byte position in the file is used (that is, data is appended to the file). However, if a byte position is omitted, a space for it still must be indicated by separating the unit number from the variable name using two commas.

For reading data from a binary-access file either a **Get #** statement or **Input( )** function can be used. The general syntax of the **Get #**, as it applies to binary-access files is

> **Get** *#unit-number,* byte-*position,* *variable-name*

Again, the `unit-number` is the number used in the **Open** statement to open the file, the `byte-position` is the position of the next item to be read, and the `variable-name` is the variable that is used to receive the contents of the item that will be read. If no byte position is specified, the next item in

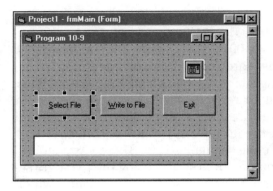

Figure 10-20

Program 10-9's Graphical User Interface

Table 10-13	Program 10-9's Properties Table	
Object	**Property**	**Setting**
Form	Name	frmMain
	Caption	Program 10-9
CommonDialog	Name	cdlFile
Command button	Name	cmdName
	Caption	&Select File
Command button	Name	cmdWrite
	Caption	&Write to File
Command button	Name	cmdExit
	Caption	E&xit
Picture box	Name	picMessage
	TabStop	False

the file is read. As with the corresponding **Put #** statement, if a byte position is not included, space for it must still be indicated by separating the unit number from the variable name using two commas.

Program 10-9 illustrates creating a binary file and writing three items to the file. The design-time interface for this program is shown in Figure 10-20.

Program 10-9's Event Code

```
Private Sub cmdName_Click()
  picMessage.Cls
  cdlFile.Filter = "Data Files(*.dat)|*.dat|All Files (*.*)|*.*"
  cdlFile.ShowOpen
  picMessage.Print cdlFile.filename
End Sub

Private Sub cmdWrite_Click()
  On Error GoTo FileError

  CR = Chr(13) ' carriage return character
  Open cdlFile.filename For Binary As #1
    Put #1, , 8
    Put #1, , 12
    Put #1, , 497
    Put #1, , "abcdef"
  Close #1
  picMessage.Cls
  picMessage.Print "The file "; cdlFile.filename; CR; "  has been written."
  Exit Sub
FileError:
  picMessage.Print "The file was not successfully opened"; CR;
  picMessage.Print "Please check that the file currently exists."
End Sub

Private Sub cmdExit_Click()
  Beep
  End
End Sub
```

00	08	00	0C	01	F1	61	62	63	64	65	66

Figure 10-21

The bintest.dat File as Stored by Program 10-9

Of the three event procedures used in Program 10-9, the **cmdName_Click** and **cmdExit_Click** event codes are identical to those used in earlier programs. The only new features in this program are the **Open** and **Put #** statements in the **cmdWrite_Click** event, as they relate to binary-access files. Notice that for each item written to the file, a separate **Put #** statement is required. Also notice that even though a specific byte position is not indicated in the **Put #** statements, a place for its position is reserved by placing two commas between the unit number and the expression value written to the file.

The binary file created by Program 10-9 is illustrated on Figure 10-21, which uses hexadecimal values to indicate the equivalent binary storage used for the file. As indicated in the figure, the file consists of twelve bytes, where the hexadecimal values correspond to the decimal values 8, 12, 497, and the characters a, b, c, d, e, and f.

Exercises 10.5

1. List the similarities and differences between binary- and random-access files.

2. Enter and execute Program 10-9 on your computer.

3. Write and execute a Visual Basic program that reads and displays the binary file created by Program 10-9.

4. a. Write and execute a Visual Basic program that writes the numbers 92.65, 88.72, 77.46, and 89.93 to a binary-access file name `result.bin`.

   b. Using the data in the `result.bin` file created in Exercise 4a., write a Visual Basic program that reads the file's data, determines the average of the four numbers read, and displays that average. Verify the output produced by your program by manually calculating the average of the four numbers.

5. a. Write and execute a Visual Basic program that creates a binary-access file named `grades.dat` and writes the following numbers to the file:

   100, 100, 100, 100
   100, 0, 100, 0
   86, 83, 89, 94
   78, 59, 77, 85
   89, 92, 81, 88

   b. Using the data in the `grades.dat` file created in Exercise 5a., write a Visual Basic program that reads the file's data, computes the average of each group of four numbers read, and displays the average.

10.6 Focus on Program Design and Implementation:

Creating Screen and Printer Reports

In this last Focus section we complete the Rotech application by providing a screen and hardcopy (printer) report. At this point the procedure for adding a new form into a project and then developing the form should be familiar to you. For a review, however, the steps are:

1. a. Add a new form to the project using either the <u>P</u>roject menu's Add <u>F</u>orm option or the Standard Toolbar's Add Form icon button.

   b. Supply the new form with a <u>R</u>eturn to Main Menu Command button, whose **Click** event consists of the following three lines of code:

```
Me.Hide
frmMain.Show
frmMain.Refresh  'This line is needed only if graphical
                 ' elements do not redisplay correctly
```

2. If the Main Menu has a Command button that is used to display an existing stub form, have this button display the new form; otherwise, add a Command button to the Main Menu to perform the display.

3. Develop the new form to perform its intended function.

Adding the New Report Form

Although we have added a number of new forms to the Rotech project, in this final Focus section we provide a last complete summary of the procedure. Specifically, to add a new form to our project, either select the Add Form item from the <u>P</u>roject menu, as shown in Figure 10-22, or press the Add Form button on the Standard Toolbar, as shown in Figure 10-23. Both of these choices will bring up the Add Form dialog shown in Figure 10-24, from which you should select the Form icon under the New tab. Once you have generated this new form, initially configure it with the objects and properties listed in Table 10-14.

At this stage you can link this new form into the Main Menu by making a few modifications to existing code on the Main Menu form and adding code to the cmdReturn button's **Click** event. Event Procedure 10-2 presents the new Return button's **Click** event code, while the black portions of Procedure Code 10-1 highlight the modifications made to the frmMain's existing code. As these are the standard types of changes that we have made throughout this Focus series for adding a new form, we will not comment on them further, except to note that Procedure Code 10-1 represents the final version of the mainmenu **Sub** procedure.

Figure 10-22
Adding a Second Form Using the Project Menu

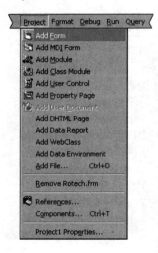

Figure 10-23
Adding a Second Form Using a Toolbar Button

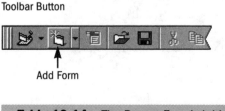

Add Form

Table 10-14	The Report Form's Initial Properties Table	
Object	**Property**	**Setting**
Form	Name	frmReport
	Caption	REPORTS SCREEN
Command button	Name	cmdReturn
	Caption	&Return to Main Menu

Figure 10-24
The Add Form Dialog Box

Event Procedure 10-2

```
Private Sub cmdReturn_Click()
  Me.Hide
  frmMain.Show
  frmMain.Refresh
End Sub
```

Procedure Code 10-1

```
Rem:(General) Declarations Section Code
Option Explicit
Rem: These constants are used to identify which button was pressed
Const intMAILBUTTON As Integer = 1
Const intWALKBUTTON As Integer = 2
Const intINVRECEIPTS As Integer = 3
Const intABOUT As Integer = 5
Const intREPORTS As Integer = 6
Const intEXITBUTTON As Integer = 7
Const intSTUB As Integer = 99

Private Sub cmdReports_Click()
    Call mainmenu(intREPORTS)
End Sub

Public Sub mainmenu(intFromButton As Integer)
  Me.Hide
  Select Case intFromButton
    Case intMAILBUTTON
      frmMail.KeyPreview = True
      frmMail.Show
      frmMail.Refresh
    Case intWALKBUTTON
      frmWalk.KeyPreview = True
      frmWalk.Show
      frmWalk.Refresh
    Case intINVRECEIPTS
      frmInvent.KeyPreview = True
      frmInvent.Show
      frmInvent.Refresh
    Case intREPORTS
      frmReports.KeyPreview = True
      frmReports.Show
      frmReports.Refresh
    Case intABOUT
      frmAbout.KeyPreview = True
      frmAbout.Show
      frmAbout.Refresh
    Case intSTUB
      frmStub.Show
      frmStub.Refresh
    Case intEXITBUTTON
      Beep
      End
  End Select
End Sub
```

Figure 10-25
The Completed Reports Form

Table 10-15 The Report Form's Property Table

Object	Property	Setting
Form	Name	frmReport
	Caption	REPORTS SCREEN
Frame	Name	frmScreen
	Caption	Screen reports
Command button	Name	cmdScreen1
	Caption	&1
Label	Name	lblScreen1
	Caption	Current Inventory
Frame	Name	frmScreen
	Caption	Screen reports
Command button	Name	cmdPrinter1
	Caption	&A
Label	Name	lblPrinter1
	Caption	Transactions Summnary
Command button	Name	cmdReturn
	Caption	&Return to Main Menu
DataControl	Name	datINV
	Caption	(blank)
	DatabaseName	A:\Disktran.mdb
	RecordSource	RecDis
	RecordsetTyype	1-Dynaset
	Visible	False

Table 10-16 The Report Form's TTL Table

Form: Report		Trigger
Task	Object	Event
Prepare screen report	cmdScreen1	Click
Prepare printer report	cmdReport1	Click
Return to Main Menu	cmdReturn	Click

Having added a new form and linked it into the Main Menu (Steps 1 and 2), it now remains to develop this form to perform its intended function (Step 3). Figure 10-25 illustrates how we want our report form to appear. For variety, we have labeled each Command button with a number or letter, and used labels to identify each button's usage. An alternative, and equally acceptable technique would be to make the buttons larger and use their **Caption** property for identification purposes.

Tables 10-15 and 10-16 provide the report form's properties and task list, respectively. One of the most important controls not visible in Figure 10-25 is the Data control, whose Visible property has been set to **False**. The sole purpose of this control is to provide access to the Disktran database table

RecDis, from which all of the reports will be constructed. Currently we will use this table to produce two reports; one for each of the first two Command buttons listed in the TTL table.

Creating a Screen Report

The screen report is intended to provide a quick summary of the number of disk packages available in inventory. Initially, this current inventory is determined using the following formula:

```
Current Inventory  =  Receipts
                      - (Returns + Damaged + Other Adjustments)
                      - (Mail-in Disbursals + Walk-in Sales)
```

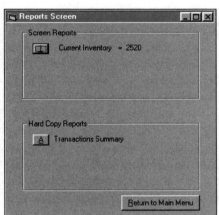

Figure 10-26
The Screen Report

Figure 10-26 illustrates how this report appears for the original data provided in the Disktran's RecDis table on the Student Disk (see Table 9-19).

The code used to produce the report shown in Figure 10-26 is listed in Procedure Code 10-2. In the **General Declarations** section the codes used for each category of inventory transaction (previously listed in Table 9-20) are given symbolic names. The real work in producing the report is then carried out in the **Click** event code. Within this event code, a single loop is constructed that is used to inspect each transaction record and either add or subtract the transaction amount, as appropriate, from a running total. After the loop is completed, the total within the variable intTotal is displayed as a label.

It should be noted that the method of calculating current inventory by cycling through each record, as is done in Procedure Code 10-2, only produces a report fairly quickly if the number of transactions is reasonably small (typically, under a few thousand records). As the number of transactions grows to where the calculation itself takes more than two or three seconds, a better method of computing the inventory is to do the addition or subtraction as each transaction is entered, using a current inventory value that is stored in a text file. A screen report of current inventory is then produced by simply reading and displaying the value previously calculated and stored in the text file. This method of producing the report is left as an exercise.

Procedure Code 10-2

```
Rem: These are the General Declaration statements
 Option Explicit
   Const strRECEIVE As String = "r"  ' code for receipt of inventory
   Const strRETURNED As String = "t" ' code for returns to vendor
   Const strDAMAGED As String = "d"  ' code for damaged inventory
   Const strOTHER As String = "o"    ' code for other adjustments
   Const strMAILINS As String = "m"  'code for a mail in disbursement
   Const strWALKINS As String = "w"  ' code for a walk in disbursement

Rem: This is the code that computes and displays the screen report

Private Sub cmdScreen1_Click()
   Dim intTotal As Integer

   intTotal = 0
   ' Move to first record and cycle through all records
   datINV.Recordset.MoveFirst
```

continued

```
                          Do While datINV.Recordset.EOF = False
                            If datINV.Recordset("RDCode") = strRECEIVE Then
                              intTotal = intTotal + datINV.Recordset("Quantity")
                            ElseIf datINV.Recordset("RDCode") = strRETURNED Then
                              intTotal = intTotal - datINV.Recordset("Quantity")
                            ElseIf datINV.Recordset("RDCode") = strDAMAGED Then
                              intTotal = intTotal - datINV.Recordset("Quantity")
                            ElseIf datINV.Recordset("RDCode") = strOTHER Then
                              intTotal = intTotal - datINV.Recordset("Quantity")
                            ElseIf datINV.Recordset("RDCode") = strMAILINS Then
                              intTotal = intTotal - datINV.Recordset("Quantity")
                            ElseIf datINV.Recordset("RDCode") = strWALKINS Then
                              intTotal = intTotal - datINV.Recordset("Quantity")
                            End If
                            datINV.Recordset.MoveNext
                          Loop
                            Beep
                            Beep
                            lblAmt.Caption = " = " & Str(intTotal)
                        End Sub
```

Creating a Printed Report

For extensive printed reports, a program such as the Data Report Designer described in Appendix H should be used. For simpler reports, however, we can use the **Print** command and direct the display to the printer. This is the approach we used in creating the simple packing slip developed in Section 4.4, and is the one we will use here.

Specifically the report that we want to produce is a detail of all transactions, a sample of which is shown in Figure 10-27. Notice that the final number presented in this report is the same as that provided by the screen report shown in Figure 10-26, but that the printed report provides more detail into how this value was calculated. This relationship between corresponding printed and screen reports should always hold: a printed report, while providing additional information, must always tally with any screen report that provides similar summary information.

The report shown in Figure 10-27 was produced using Procedure Code 10-3. Here, a number of variables are first dimensioned within the **General Declarations** section and subsequently used in the cmdPrinter1 button's **Click** event. The reason for making the declarations within the **General Declarations** section is that this set of variables will be used for a variety of additional reports (see Exercises) and since they are not used to pass data between procedures, it is safer and more efficient to make their declarations only once, at the form level.

The **While** loop within the **Click** event code listed in Procedure Code 10-3 is almost the same as that used in Procedure Code 10-2, except that the **If-ElseIf** statement separates out each individual receipt and disbursement type, rather than simply fold them into a general total. Each of these separate values is then printed using a **Printer.Print** statement.

In reviewing the **Click** event code, two further features should be noted. The first is the initialization of the variables that are declared in the **General Declaration** section. This initialization must be done within any

Figure 10-27
A Printed Report

```
Prepared: 4/17/99      (12:24 PM)

SUMMARY OF INVENTORY TRANSACTIONS
---------------------------------

Quantity Received :    3000
Less:
            Returned:    300
            Damaged :    125
            Other   :     30
                       -------
Net Into Inventory:    2545

Less:
            Mail-Ins:     19
            Walk-Ins:      6
                       =======
Current Inventory :    2520
```

procedure that requires these variables to be initialized, as assigning values to **Dim**ed variables cannot be done within a General Declarations section. Finally, notice the use of the @ formatting symbol within the Format function. This symbol is used to right-justify the displayed numbers, forcing the display to be aligned on the units values.

Procedure Code 10-3

```
Rem: These are the General Declaration statements
 Option Explicit
  Const strRECEIVE As String = "r"  ' code for receipt of inventory
  Const strRETURNED As String = "t" ' code for returns to vendor
  Const strDAMAGED As String = "d"  ' code for damaged inventory
  Const strOTHER As String = "o"    ' code for other adjustments
  Const strMAILINS As String = "m"  'code for a mail in disbursement
  Const strWALKINS As String = "w"  ' code for a walk in disbursement

  Dim intReceipts As Integer
  Dim intReturns As Integer
  Dim intDamaged As Integer
  Dim intOther As Integer
  Dim intMailins As Integer
  Dim intWalkins As Integer
  Dim intTotalIn As Integer
  Dim intAmount As Integer

Private Sub cmdPRINTER1_Click()

  intReceipts = 0
  intReturns = 0
  intDamaged = 0
  intOther = 0
  intMailins = 0
  intWalkins = 0
  intTotalIn = 0
  intAmount = 0
  ' Move to first record and cycle through all records
  datINV.Recordset.MoveFirst
  Do While datINV.Recordset.EOF = False
    If datINV.Recordset("RDCode") = strRECEIVE Then
      intReceipts = intReceipts + datINV.Recordset("Quantity")
    ElseIf datINV.Recordset("RDCode") = strRETURNED Then
      intReturns = intReturns + datINV.Recordset("Quantity")
    ElseIf datINV.Recordset("RDCode") = strDAMAGED Then
      intDamaged = intDamaged + datINV.Recordset("Quantity")
    ElseIf datINV.Recordset("RDCode") = strOTHER Then
      intOther = intOther + datINV.Recordset("Quantity")
    ElseIf datINV.Recordset("RDCode") = strMAILINS Then
      intMailins = intMailins + datINV.Recordset("Quantity")
    ElseIf datINV.Recordset("RDCode") = strWALKINS Then
      intWalkins = intWalkins + datINV.Recordset("Quantity")
    End If
    datINV.Recordset.MoveNext
  Loop
    ' Print the report
```

continued

```
            intTotalIn = intReceipts - (intReturns + intDamaged + intOther)
            intAmount = intTotalIn - (intMailins + intWalkins)
            Printer.Print
            Printer.Print
            Printer.Font = "Courier"
            Printer.FontSize = 12
            Printer.Print Spc(20); "Prepared: "; Format(Now, "mm/dd/yy");
            Printer.Print "   ("; Format(Now, "h:m AM/PM"); ")"
            Printer.Print
            Printer.Print
            Printer.Print Spc(20); "SUMMARY OF INVENTORY TRANSACTIONS"
            Printer.Print Spc(20); "--------------------------------"
            Printer.Print
            Printer.Print Spc(20); "Quantity Received : "; Format(intReceipts, "@@@@@@@")
            Printer.Print Spc(20); "Less:"
            Printer.Print Spc(20); "          Returned: "; Format(intReturns, "@@@@@@@")
            Printer.Print Spc(20); "          Damaged : "; Format(intDamaged, "@@@@@@@")
            Printer.Print Spc(20); "          Other   : "; Format(intOther, "@@@@@@@")
            Printer.Print Spc(20); "                  "; "-------"
            Printer.Print Spc(20); "Net Into Inventory: "; Format(intTotalIn, "@@@@@@@")
            Printer.Print
            Printer.Print Spc(20); "Less:"
            Printer.Print Spc(20); "          Mail-Ins: "; Format(intMailins, "@@@@@@@")
            Printer.Print Spc(20); "          Walk-Ins: "; Format(intWalkins, "@@@@@@@")
            Printer.Print Spc(20); "                  "; "======="

            Printer.Print Spc(20); "Current Inventory : "; Format(intAmount, "@@@@@@@")
            Printer.EndDoc
            Beep
            Beep
        End Sub
```

Exercises 10.6

(**Note:** The Rotech Systems project, at the stage of development begun in this section, can be found on the Student Disk in the rotech9 folder as project rotech9.vbp. The project, which includes both the screen and printer reports developed in this section, can be found on the Student Disk in the rotech10 folder as project rotech10.vbp. If you are developing the system yourself, following the procedures given in this section, we suggest that you first copy all of the files in the rotech9 folder into the temp folder, and then work out of this latter folder. When you have finished your changes you can compare your results to the files in the rotech10 folder.)

1. a. Add the screen report developed in this section to the Rotech project located in rotech9 folder.
   b. Test the screen report constructed in Exercise 1a to ensure that it correctly computes the current number of disks in inventory using the data in the RecDis table. This table is contained within the Disktran.mdb located on the Student Disk.
   c. Using Rotech's Mail In form, add a number of new transactions to the RecDis table, and then re-run the screen report constructed in Exercise 1a to verify that your program correctly accounts for the new transactions.

    d. Add the printer report developed in this section to the Rotech project.

    e. Test the printer report to verify that it correlates with the screen report produced for Exercise 1c.

(2) a. Add a screen report to the Rotech report screen that displays the total number of disk packages distributed due to mail-ins.

    b. Modify the screen report created for Exercise 2a to permit the user to specify a state designation. If the user enters the state designation XX, the report should display the total number of disk packages distributed to all of the states combined (this should be the same number reported in Exercise 2a).

(3) Add a screen report to the Rotech report screen developed in this section that displays the total number disk packages sold to walk-ins.

(4) a. The method used in producing the screen report shown in Figure 10-26 requires that each record in the transactions table be opened and inspected. Another method is to store the current inventory in a text file, and adjust this value as each transaction is entered. The screen report can then be provided by simply reading and displaying the value in this text file. For this part of the exercise, store the value 2520 into a text file (this is the current inventory amount corresponding to the records in the RecDis table), and create a screen report that opens the file, displays the number, and then closes the file.

    b. Modify the Walk In, Mail In, and Inventory Receipt and Disbursement forms so that each transaction entered into these forms correctly updates the text file created in Exercise 4a.

(5) Add a screen report to the Rotech report screen that displays the net number of disk packages added to inventory. The reported number should be the sum of packages received less the number of returned, damaged, or otherwise adjusted.

(6) Add a Printer report to the Rotech project that lists all of the Inventory receipts, including returns, damaged amounts, and other adjustments, by date.

(7) Add a Printer report to the Rotech project that lists all of the mail-in and walk-in disbursements, by date.

(8) Add a Printer report to the Rotech project that lists all of the states, in alphabetical order, to which mail-in disbursements were made, and the total mail-in disbursements made to each state. After the last state has been listed, the total number of walk-in disbursements should be listed.

(9) a. **CASE STUDY**
      Add at least one screen report to your selected project (see project specifications at the end of Section 1.5). The data for the report should be derived from a database table maintained by your application.

    b. Add at least one printer report to your selected project. Again, the data for the report should be derived from a database table maintained by your application.

10.7 Knowing About:

Creating ActiveX Controls Using the Interface Wizard

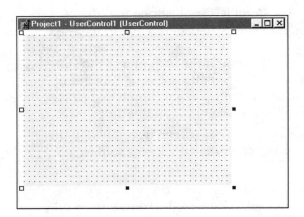

Figure 10-28
The UserControl Object

Constructing an ActiveX control is similar to constructing a Visual Basic application, except that in place of an initial form object upon which controls are placed, an initial UserControl object is used. For example, if you initiate a new project using the ActiveX Control icon rather than the Standard EXE icon, you will be presented with the UserControl object illustrated in Figure 10-28. The UserControl, which is the object upon which an ActiveX control is constructed, is similar in appearance to an initial form (see Figure 10-27).

Development Fundamentals

In developing an ActiveX control we will use almost the same techniques we have been using to create Visual Basic applications, except that we will be creating a component to be used in an application, rather than a complete application. Conveniently, at any point in the development of the ActiveX control, we can run it within the context of either a design-time or run-time application to see how it performs, similar to the way we can execute a Visual Basic application at any point in its development. A significant difference, as we will shortly see, is that the control can be executed directly on a design form, without running the form itself as a run-time application.

Like an initial form object onto which controls are placed, any standard Toolbox object, except the OLE container control (this object is described in Appendix F), and any other ActiveX control, can be placed onto a UserControl object. Controls placed on the UserControl object are referred to as *constituent controls*, and all of a constituent control's properties, events, and methods are available to us as developers of an ActiveX control. Once the control is developed, however, and placed in the Toolbox, a programmer using the control in a Visual Basic application will only have available the properties, events, and methods that we, as developers of the control, attach to it. Although a variety of events can be supplied with a control, two of the most important are the **Initialize** and **Resize** events. A programmer expects that any control placed on a form will be initialized correctly and can be resized using the standard sizing-handles.

With this as background, we are now ready to construct a working ActiveX control using the following steps:

Step 1. Initiate a project using the ActiveX Control icon.

Step 2. Place all desired constituent controls on the supplied UserControl object.

Step 3. Define an **Initialize** event that sets an initial state for each constituent control and a **Resize** event that resizes all constituent controls as the ActiveX control, as a whole, is resized.

Step 4. Invoke the Interface Wizard to add additional properties, events, and methods to the ActiveX control.

Step 5. Write any additional event code required by the ActiveX control.

At any stage in the development of an ActiveX control we can close the UserControl object, which automatically activates the control and places it in the current Toolbox. At that point we can add a standard EXE project to our ActiveX development project, place the ActiveX control on a design form, and test the current status and operation of the newly developed control. This design form, which is only created once, is added into the existing project following these steps:

Step A. Close the UserControl object's window (use the Close [X] button), which adds the object as an ActiveX control into the current Toolbox.

Step B. Add an EXE project that can be used to test the new ActiveX control. This is accomplished by using the A<u>d</u>d Project option from the <u>F</u>ile menu, and *not* by closing the current project and opening a New or Existing project.

These steps can performed at any time after development Steps 1 and 2 have been completed. Then the new control is tested by placing it on the design form in the same manner as any other control is placed on a design time form. Different results should be expected depending on at what stage in the development of the control it is tested. For example, if an ActiveX control is tested after Step 2, which is before a **Resize** event has been developed, the control itself can be resized when placed on the design-time form, but any constituent controls used in the control will remain the same size as they were when they were placed on the UserControl object. This is because we have not defined, in the **Resize** event, how these constituent controls should react to a resizing. We illustrate this effect next, as we develop a specific ActiveX control.

Constructing an ActiveX Control

To illustrate developing an ActiveX control, we will create and test a control that acts as a blinking strobe display. The constructed control consists of five rectangular bars that can be made to blink either from left to right or from right to left, depending on the state of a user-created property named **Direction**.

To begin constructing this specific control, use the Shape control and place a single rectangular shape onto the UserControl object previously shown in Figure 10-28. By definition, the Shape control is now a constituent control of the ActiveX control. Name this constituent Shape control shpStrobe and set the following properties: **Height** = 135 twips, **Width** = 495 twips, **FillStyle** = Solid, and **FillColor** set to Blue. Now copy and paste this shape four times, so that it appears as shown in Figure 10-29. When you are asked if you want to create a control array, answer Yes. Doing this will

Figure 10-29
The Strobe Control's Interface

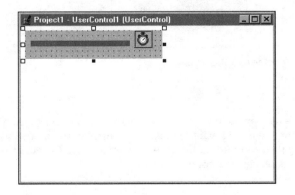

create five constituent controls named `shpStrobe(0)` to `shpStrobe(4)`. Also, as shown in the figure, add a Timer control named `tmrStrobe`.

At this stage let us test our control. To do so, first save and close the control. The control is closed by clicking on the **X** on the upper right-hand corner of the UserControl window. Notice that when the control is closed, its icon changes from grayed to active in the Toolbox.[4]

To test the control, we will need to create a design form onto which we can place our newly created (but, as yet, not completed) control. To do this,

- Save the UserControl object using either the Save or Save As option from the File menu;
- Close the UserControl object (see Step A, above);
- Add a standard EXE project using the Add Project option from the File menu (see Step B, above); and
- Add the ActiveX component from the Toolbox onto the newly created form. (Since the ActiveX component is in the Toolbox, it can be placed on the form in the same manner as any standard Toolbox object.)

After placing the ActiveX component on the design screen, notice the component's resizing capabilities. Although the outside dimensions of the ActiveX component can be altered using its sizing handles, since we have not provided the control with a **Resize** event, the internal constituent control shapes will not be resized as the control itself is expanded or contracted. Thus, we will now shift back to developing the control and provide it with a **Resize** event procedure that correctly modifies the shape of the control's internal shapes as the outer boundaries of the control are altered. We will also provide the control with an **Initialize** event procedure that causes the control to blink.

To create these event procedures, first click on the UserControl icon within the Project window shown in Figure 10-30. This will activate the UserControl design window. Once this window is active, double-click on the ActiveX control to bring up a Code window, and enter the code, including global declarations, listed in Procedure Code 10-4.

Figure 10-30
Creating a Test Environment

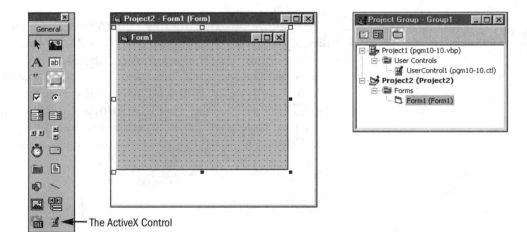

The ActiveX Control

---

[4]What is happening here is that the control itself changes from design mode to run mode. Note that you *do not* want to place the control in run mode by pressing either the F5 key or clicking the Start button, because this would place the entire project into run mode, which precludes placing the control on a form.

Procedure Code 10-4

```
Dim I As Integer
Const NumStrobes As Integer = 5

Private Sub UserControl_Initialize()
  Dim n As Integer
  For n = 0 To NumStrobes - 1
    shpStrobe(n).FillColor = vbBlue
  Next n
End Sub

Private Sub UserControl_Resize()
  Dim n As Integer
  Dim width As Integer

  Rem: determine the width of a single strobe
  width = Int(ScaleWidth / NumStrobes)
  Rem: Set the size and position of all the strobes
  For n = 0 To NumStrobes - 1
    shpStrobe(n).width = width
    shpStrobe(n).Height = ScaleHeight
    shpStrobe(n).Top = 0
    shpStrobe(n).Left = n * width
  Next n
End Sub
```

The **Initialize** event procedure is rather straightforward, in that it sets the fill color for each of the shpStrobe shapes to the symbolic constant **vbBlue**. The code for the **Resize** event is a bit more complicated. The first task accomplished by the **Resize** event code is to determine the width of one shpStrobe shape, so that all of the shpStrobe shapes will fit in the re-sized ActiveX control. The **ScaleWidth** and **ScaleHeight** properties refer to the ActiveX object. Thus, by dividing the **ScaleWidth** of the ActiveX control by the number of shpStrobe shapes, we have the correct width of each individual shpStrobe. The **For** loop then sets each shpStrobe element to the correct width and makes the height of each shpStrobe equal to the height of the ActiveX control itself. Finally, the top of each shpStrobe shape is aligned with the top of the ActiveX control, and the shapes are stacked, from left to right so that they align starting from the left side of the ActiveX control.

At this stage you can run the control and see that the internal shapes within it now resize correctly as the ActiveX control is resized. Do this by double-clicking on the Form icon shown in Figure 10-29, and resizing the control on the form. Notice that as the ActiveX control is resized, all of its constituent controls also change shape to conform to the new size.

Adding Properties and Events

At this stage we have an ActiveX component that has an initial color and can be resized but doesn't do very much. To complete its development we will need to add several custom properties and events. Specifically, we will add the three properties and single event listed in Table 10-17 on page 552.

In reviewing Table 10-17, notice that the ActiveX's **Interval** property is designated as "Mapped to Timer Interval." This means that the constituent timer's **Interval** property will be assigned to the ActiveX's **Interval** property. In a similar manner the ActiveX control's **Tick** event will be assigned

Table 10-17 Custom Properties and Events

Name	Type	Data Type	Initial Value
Blink	Property	Boolean	True
Direction	Property	Boolean	True
Interval	Property	Mapped to Timer interval	1000
Tick	Event	Mapped to Timer Tick event	

to the Timer's **Tick** event. To construct and correctly attach these properties and events to the ActiveX component we will use the Interface Wizard.

Installing the Wizard

The Interface Wizard, which was introduced with Version 5.0, is invoked by selecting the ActiveX Control Interface Wizard option from the Add-Ins menu. If this is the first time you are constructing an ActiveX component, however, this option may not have been installed and available. If this is the case, select the Add-In Manager option from the Add-Ins menu, as shown in

Figure 10-31
Invoking the Add-In Manger

Figure 10-31. Selecting this option will bring up the Add-In Manager dialog shown in Figure 10-32. Simply selecting the third item in this dialog and checking both the Loaded/Unloaded and Load on Startup boxes, as illustrated on the figure, and clicking the OK button will add the Wizard to the Add-Ins menu.

Using the Interface Wizard

Invoking the Interface Wizard is accomplished by selecting the ActiveX Control Interface Wizard option from the Add-Ins menu, as shown in Figure 10-33. This may be done to initially set an ActiveX component's initial properties, events, and methods, or to modify an existing ActiveX component currently on the UserControl.

Once the Wizard has been invoked, the initial Wizard dialog shown in Figure 10-34 is displayed. Click on the Next Command button to bring up the first "working" dialog, shown in Figure 10-35. This dialog is used to select from a set of predefined member properties, methods, and events. For

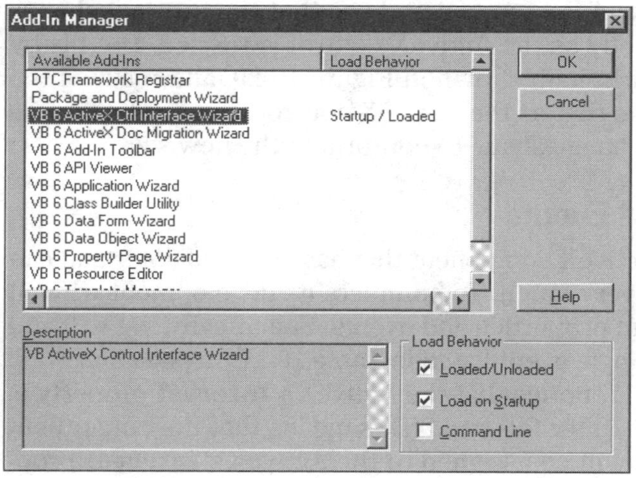

Figure 10-32
Activating the Interface Wizard

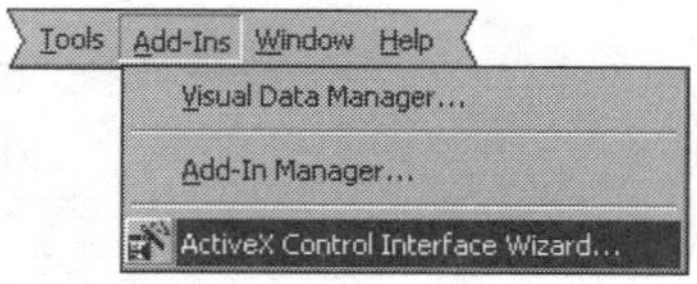

Figure 10-33
Invoking the Interface Wizard

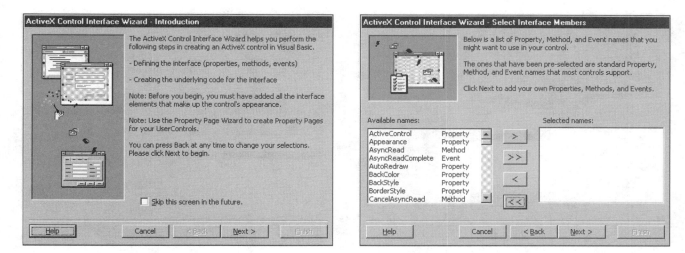

Figure 10-34
The Initial Interface Wizard Window

Figure 10-35
The First "Working" Interface Dialog

our particular purpose we will only use custom-designed members, so for now, simply click on the Next Command button, which brings up the dialog shown in Figure 10-36.

As we initially have no custom members for our ActiveX control, no members will be displayed in the List box area of this dialog. The procedure for adding new members is to click on the New button for each desired new member. Each time you click on this button, the Add Custom Member dialog, shown in Figure 10-37, is displayed. As illustrated on this figure, we have named a member Interval and have designated this member as a property by selecting this option from the Option buttons. Clicking the OK button will add this new member to the ActiveX control, and return you to the Create Custom Interface Members dialog as shown in Figure 10-36. The process of creating new members should be done four times, once for each member previously listed in Table 10-17. When this is accomplished, the Create Custom Interface Members dialog will appear as shown in Figure 10-38.

Having defined all of our custom members, we are now ready either to map them to constituent members or to set their initial values. To do this, once the dialog shown in Figure 10-38 is present, press the Next button.

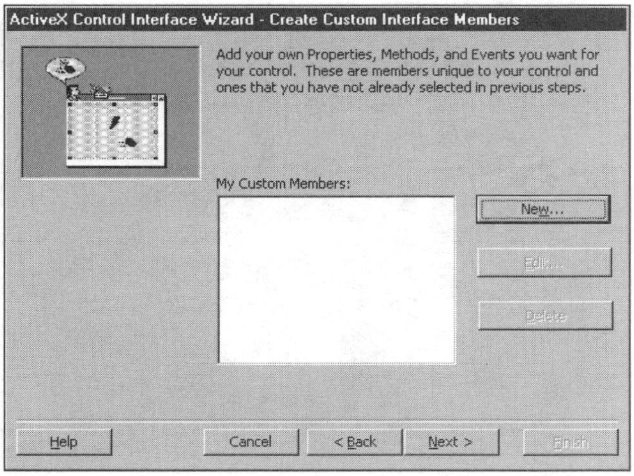

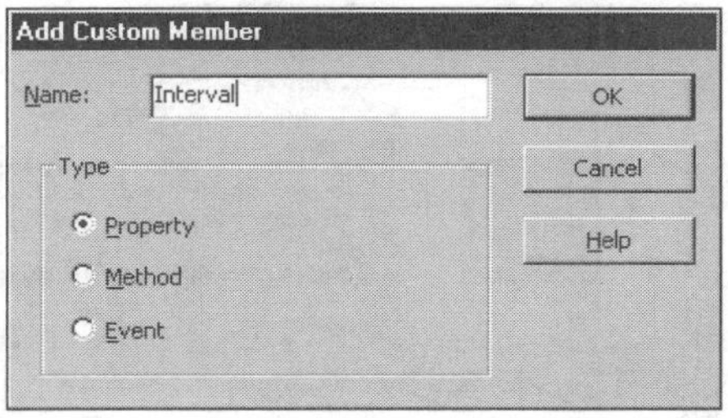

Figure 10-37
Add Custom Member Dialog

Figure 10-36
The Create Custom Interface Members Dialog

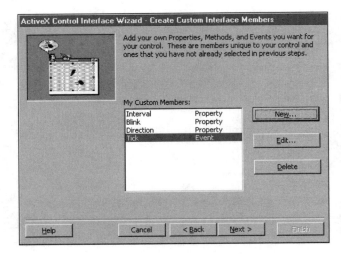

Figure 10-38
An ActiveX Control with Four Custom Members

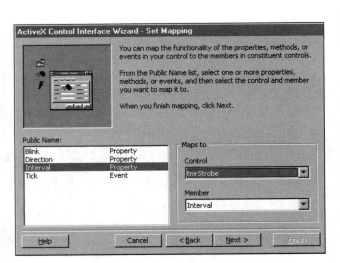

Figure 10-39
Mapping ActiveX Members to Constituent Control Members

Doing this will bring up the Set Mapping dialog shown in Figure 10-39. Use this dialog to map the **Interval** property to the constituent tmrStrobe **Interval** property, as shown, and also to map the **Tick** event to the tmrStobe's **Tick** event. Then press the Next button, which will bring up the Set Attributes dialog shown in Figure 10-40.

The Set Attributes dialog illustrated on Figure 10-40 is used to define the attributes of any unmapped ActiveX control members. As shown on this figure, the **Blink** and **Direction** property members are listed because they have not been mapped to any constituent controls. We will use this dialog to set the data types and initial values listed in Table 10-17. Once the attributes of both these properties have been defined, press the Next button, which will bring up the final Wizard dialog shown in Figure 10-41. When this last dialog is present, press the Finish button to complete the process.

At this point you will have the same ActiveX control previously shown on Figure 10-29, which contains the properties and event listed in Table 10-17. It only remains to add code to the **Timer** event to cause the control to blink in the desired manner. The required code is listed as Procedure Code 10-5. Included in this procedure are two variables, named m_Direction

Figure 10-40
Defining UnMapped Members

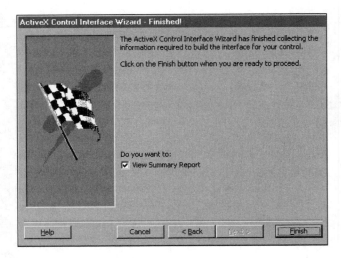

Figure 10-41
The Last Wizard Dialog

and m_Blink, which were automatically defined by the Wizard when the **Direction** and **Blink** properties where created.

Procedure Code 10-5

```
Dim m_Direction As Boolean
Dim m_Blink As Boolean
m_Direction = True
m_Blink = True

Private Sub tmrStrobe_Timer()
  If m_Blink = False Then Exit Sub
  shpStrobe(I).FillColor = vbBlue
  If m_Direction Then ' blinking from left to right
   If I = NumStrobes - 1 Then
     I = 0
   Else
     I = I + 1
   End If
  Else ' blinking from right to left
   If I = 0 Then
     I = NumStrobes - 1
   Else
     I = I - 1
   End If
  End If
  shpStrobe(I).FillColor = vbWhite
  RaiseEvent Tick
End Sub
```

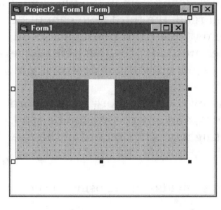

Figure 10-42
An Executing ActiveX Control

If you now test this ActiveX control by placing it on a design form, it will appear as shown in Figure 10-42. Notice that the control begins blinking from left to right when it is placed on the form. This is because the ActiveX control is active and we have set its initial properties to activate blinking in this direction. It may seem odd that the component is running at design time, but the object we have created is, in fact, a completed and active object once it is added to the Toolbox. By setting the control's **Blink** property to **False**, we can deactivate its initial blinking, both at design and run time. Also notice that for simplicity in describing how ActiveX controls are created, we have fixed the fill color of the constituent shpStrobe elements to blink between **vbWhite** and **vbBlue**. A more robust control would add two more properties to the ActiveX control that would permit the user to set the fill colors at design time.

10.8 Common Programming Errors

Four programming errors are common when using files:

1. Incorrect format of the **Open** statement.

2. Failure to construct a correct full path name when appending a file's name to its path for use in an **Open** statement.

3. Omitting the unit number when using the **Print**, **Put**, and **Get** statements. Programmers used to writing **Print** statements for output to a

form, where a specific unit number is not required, sometimes forget to include a unit number when accessing data files.

4. Using the **Put** and **Get** statements without including a starting record or byte position for random-access and binary-access files, respectively. Even though such file accesses do not require an explicit record or byte position, when the position is omitted, a double comma must be used as a placeholder for the starting position.

10.9 Chapter Review

Key Terms

binary-access file	external file name	random-access file
Close	file access	sequential-access file
data file	file organization	text file
direct-access file	**Open**	

Summary

1. A *data file* is any collection of data stored together under a common name.

2. The manner in which records are written to and read from a file is called the file's *access method*.

   a. In a *sequential-access file*, each record must be accessed in a sequential manner. This means that the second item in the file cannot be read until the first item has been read, the third item cannot be read until the first and second items have been read, and so on. Similarly, an item cannot be written until all previous items have been written and a item cannot be replaced without destroying all following items.

   b. In a *random-access file*, storage is by record, where each record consists of the same number of items, and any record can be read, written, or replaced without affecting any other record in the file. Each record in a random-access file is uniquely located by its position in the file.

   c. In a *binary-access file*, storage is by individual item, using the computer's internal binary code.

3. An **Open** statement is required to connect a file name to a unit number.

   a. For sequential files, the syntax for the **Open** statement is

   ```
   Open filename For Output As #unit-number
   ```

   b. For random-access files, the syntax for the **Open** statement is

   ```
   Open filename For Random As #unit-number Len = recordlength
   ```

   c. For binary-access files, the syntax for the **Open** statement is

   ```
   Open filename For Binary As #unit-number
   ```

4. a. Data is written to a sequential file using either a **Print #** or **Write #** statement. The syntax for the **Print #** statement is

```
Print #unit-number, List of comma separated expressions
```

Except for the keyword **Print**, a **Write #** statement uses the same syntax as the **Print #** statement. The **Write #** statement encloses each string in double quotes, and separates each written item with a comma.

b. Data is written to a random-access file using a **Put #** statement with the syntax

```
Put #unit-number, record-position, variable-name
```

If a record position is not included, the record will be placed after the current record. If the record position is omitted, its place must still be indicated by including two commas between the unit number and variable name.

c. Data is written to a binary-access file using a **Put #** statement with the syntax

```
Put #unit-number, byte-position, variable-name
```

If a byte position is not included, the record will be placed after the current item. If the byte position is omitted, its place must still be indicated by including two commas between the unit number and variable name.

5. a. Data is read from an existing sequential file using an **Input** statement. The three types of **Input** statements available for reading data from a sequential file are

Statement	Description
Input #, variable list	Read data from a sequential file and assign the data to the variables in the variable list.
Line Input #, string-variable	Read a line from a sequential file and assign it to a string variable.
Input(n, #)	Read the next n characters from either a sequential or binary file.

b. Data is read from a random-access file using a **Get #** statement with the syntax

```
Get #unit-number, record-position, variable-name
```

If a record position is not included, the record that is read is the next record after the current record. When omitting the record position, its place must still be indicated by including two commas between the unit number and variable name.

c. Data is read from a binary-access file using either an **Input( )** function or a **Get #** statement, having the syntax

```
Get #unit-number, byte-position, variable-name
```

If a byte position is not included, the item that is read is the next item after the current item. If the byte position is omitted, its place must still be indicated by including two commas between the unit number and variable name.

6. A **Close** statement is used to formally close a previously opened file and releases its unit number for further Program use. The general syntax of this statement is

```
Close #unit-number
```

Test Yourself—Short Answer

1. **Print #1** and **Write #1** will both cause a write to a disk for a sequential file. How are they different?

2. If a **mode** is not named in an **Open** statement, _____ is the default.

3. The manner in which records are written to and read from a file is called the file's _____.

4. When dealing with a binary access file, what does the 5 refer to in the statement Get #1, 5, inRec?

5. Explain what the following statement does:

```
Open "C:\mydata\lesson1\my.txt" for Output as #3
```

6. Write the code that will open a sequential file named testdata.txt to hold new data created during the execution of the program.

7. Write the code that will delete a file on the A drive called payfile.seq.

8. Write the code that will close all of the open files in your program.

9. Write the code to open a sequential file named "VBclass.seq" so records can be added to the end of the file.

10. If the three lines shown below are found in a sequential file, write the code for the **Input** statement to read the record. Make up any variable names that are needed.

```
"James Smith","113-90-2323",45000
"Mary Jones","123-45-6699",39000
"Karen Morris","118-22-0091",41000
```

Programming Projects

1. This assignment is a modification to the Motel 8 project (Section 9.9, Ex. 1). The owner of the motel has changed the pricing structure for a night's stay (to be described below). Additionally, he wants a daily report that categorizes and summarizes patron data for the previous night. Input to the program will be records stored in a BASIC sequential data file (comma delimited text file) for which each record contains the following fields:

    Room Number (integer)
    Patron Name (20 characters)
    Number of Adults (integer)
    Number of Children

The name of the file, which is located on the Student Disk, is MOTEL.TXT. Charges for a room are calculated using the following criteria:

If the number of adults is no more than two, the cost per adult is $30; otherwise the cost per adult is $25.

If the number of children is no more than two, the cost per child is $12; otherwise the cost per child is $10.

If the number of adults plus the number of children is at least five, there is a 5% discount on the total charge.

There is a minimum charge per room of $50.

There is no state or local tax charged on the total cost. Also, there is no discount for multiple night stays by the same patron.

Output for the program should include the input values, adult charge, child charge, and total charge (after the discount, if applicable) for each room. Your program should accumulate the number of adults, number of children, and total charge. Note that based upon the above criteria, the total charge for a room is not necessarily the sum of the adult charge plus the child charge. Use a function procedure to calculate the room charge. After the last record, print column totals (don't print totals for room numbers, adult charges, children charges, or discounts) for adult count, child count, and total charge.

As an optional addition to this problem, you might create a second sequential file and write the detail lines of your report to that file along with the appropriate date (using either the Date or Now function).

Sample Output:

```
Date: 5-10-99
                        MOTEL 8 DAILY REVENUE REPORT

ROOM  PATRON       ADULT   CHILD   ADULT   CHILD                  TOTAL
NMBR  NAME         COUNT   COUNT   CHARGE  CHARGE   DISCOUNT      CHARGE
---------------------------------------------------------------------
1234  SMITH JOHN   2       0       60.00   00.00    00.00         60.00
1330  JONES JIM    2       3       60.00   30.00    04.50         85.50
1335  WILSON JOE   1       0       30.00   00.00    00.00         50.00
1400  KELLY BRIAN  1       2       30.00   24.00    00.00         54.00
---------------------------------------------------------------------
                   6       5                                     249.50
```

2. This assignment is a modification to the State Utilities project (Section 5.9, Exercise 9). Using the original pricing structure, write the necessary code to produce a detail report with column totals. Input to the program will be records stored in a BASIC sequential data file (comma delimited text file) for which each record contains the following fields:

CustomerID (integer)
CustomerName (text – 20 characters)
KWHUsed (integer)

The name of the text file, which is located on the Student Disk, is UTILITY.TXT. For each record, (using the criteria from Exercise 5-9), compute:

Base, undiscounted, untaxed bill amount
Discount amount
State utility tax amount
City utility tax amount
Total amount due

Also compute accumulated totals for each of these amounts. Your output should be in the form of a report that contains the data read for each record plus its corresponding calculated values (for each detail record). Format for the report could be similar to that used in Exercise 1 (this section). Incorporate the code that you used in your original project solution that calculated the different charges into a **Sub** procedure that can be called for each record read. Your program can send the number of KWH used to the **Sub** procedure and it can return the five amounts listed above.

After having read all records and written all detail lines, write the appropriate accumulated totals at the bottom of their respective columns.

3. This assignment is a modification to the Texas Fence Company project (Section 7.9, Ex. 2). The company has asked you to expand the capabilities of your initial programming effort and write a program that will produce a list of necessary components that will be needed for the next day's fencing job. The necessary requirements for each fencing job are stored in a BASIC sequential data file (comma delimited text file) with each record containing the following fields:

> Job number (integer)
> Length (integer)
> Width (integer)
> Number of gates (integer)

The name of the text file, which is located on the Student Disk, is FENCE.TXT. Output for the program should include a count for each of the following:

> Connectors (integer)
> Corner posts (integer)
> Intermediate posts (integer)
> Gate posts (integer)
> Gate(s) (integer)
> Fencing (integer)

Your program must read all records in the data file, compute the number of components needed for each job and accumulate totals for each component category. The output for this program is just the totals for each component category. Use a **Sub** procedure to calculate the number of components for each category for each job (record read).

You might offer the program user the chance to send the output to either the screen (with a form similar to the one used for the original project) or to the printer. Additionally, you may wish to create a second file and write the fence component totals with the current date to that file.

Part Three
Additional Capabilities

Animation and Graphics

Included within the Toolbox is a set of controls that make the inclusion of graphics within an application quite simple. In this chapter we introduce these controls and show how they can be used to create animation effects. In addition, we show how you can control both the color and position of objects placed on the GUI. Finally, we introduce the graphical methods that can be used to create run-time lines, rectangles, and circles.

11.1 ▶ Animation

Animation consists of creating a moving image from one or more fixed figures. This effect can be produced in two ways.

Figure 11-1

Program 11-1's Graphical User Interface

In the first way, a sequential set of figures is displayed, one after another, in the same position on the screen. Each succeeding figure is slightly different from the previous one, creating the illusion of progressive motion. The key to producing this type of image, therefore, is to provide *both* a set of figures *and* a means of switching them, such that only one figure is visible at a time. For a very simple illustration of how this can be accomplished, consider the graphical user interface shown in Figure 11-1.

The image shown in Figure 11-1 actually consists of the three individual images shown in Figure 11-2 layered over each other. Two of these images have their **Visible** property set to **False** so they will not appear on the form at run time. The relevant properties for this interface are listed in Table 11-1 on page 564.

In reviewing the properties listed in Table 11-1, pay particular attention to the three Image controls. An Image control, like the Picture box control, can be used to load a picture file. Specifically, Visual Basic supports display of three types of images listed in Table 11-2 on page 564.

Figure 11-2

The Three Individual Images Used in Program 11-1

The three images used in Program 11-1 are provided with Visual Basic and are found in the directory /Common/Graphics/Icons/Traffic on the VB6.0 CDRom as Trffc10a.ico, Trffc10b.ico, and Trffc10c.ico. Notice that the **Visible** property of the first two images is set to **False** and only the third image's **Visible** property is set to **True**. This means that when the program is

563

Table 11-1 Program 11-1's Properties Table

Object	Property	Setting
Form	Name	frmMain
	Caption	Program 11-1
Image	Name	imgGreen
	Visible	False
	Picture	Trffc10a.ico
Image	Name	imgYellow
	Visible	False
	Picture	Trffc10b.ico
Image	Name	imgRed
	Caption	True
	Picture	Trffc10c.ico
Command button	Name	cmdLight
	Caption	&Change Light
Command button	Name	cmdExit
	Caption	E&xit

Table 11-2 Acceptable Visual Basic Image Formats

Format	Description
Bitmap	An image defined as a pattern of dots (pixels). These images can be manipulated using the Paint program provided in Microsoft Windows' Accessories group of programs. These files are stored with either a .BMP or .DIB extension.
Icon	A special type of bitmap file confined to a maximum size of 32 pixels by 32 pixels. They require much less storage space than a standard bitmap image. Icon files are stored with an .ICO extension.
Metafile	An image defined by a series of coded lines and shapes. Metafiles are stored with either a .WMF or .EMF extension and are referred to as "draw-type" images.

executed initially, only the Red-light image will be visible. Having provided a set of images, we still need a means of switching between each image to create an animation effect. This is provided by the cmdLight_Click event procedure listed in Program 11-1's procedure code.

Program 11-1's Procedure Code

```
Private Sub cmdLight_Click()
Rem: The light sequence is Red to Green to Yellow
  If imgRed.Visible = True Then
    imgRed.Visible = False
    imgGreen.Visible = True
  ElseIf imgGreen.Visible = True Then
    imgGreen.Visible = False
    imgYellow.Visible = True
  Else
    imgYellow.Visible = False
    imgRed.Visible = True
  End If
End Sub

Private Sub cmdExit_Click()
  Beep
  End
End Sub
```

Each time that the cmdLight button is pressed, the state of an image's **Visible** property is tested, starting with the Red-light image. If this image is visible, it is made invisible by setting its **Visible** property to **False** and the Green-light image is made visible; otherwise, the Green light's **Visible** property is tested. If the Green light is visible, it is made invisible by setting its

Visible property to **False** and the Yellow-light image is made visible; otherwise, the Yellow light is made invisible and the Red light is activated. Thus, the sequence in the **If-Else** statement produces the rotating sequence of lights from Red to Green to Yellow, with the speed of animation controlled by the speed with which the cmdLight button is pressed.

Creating a Moving Image

Program 11-1 creates an image that appears to change within a fixed image area. We can also create an image that not only changes but moves across the screen. To create this more complicated type of animation, we will not only need a set of images, but a means of moving the area in which the image is displayed.[1] In addition, instead of controlling the switching of images with a control button, we will automate the procedure using a Timer control. The two images we will use are Microsoft's BFLY1.BMP and BFLY2.BMP bitmap images. As shown in Figure 11-3, these images represent a butterfly with its wings open and with its wings closed.

Program 11-2's form is illustrated in Figure 11-4. As shown, this form consists of three images, a timer, and two control buttons.

First concentrate on the three images shown in Figure 11-4. The two images at the top of the form will have their **Visible** properties set to **False**, so they will not be visible at run time. The image at the bottom of the form will be visible and it is this image that we will move across the screen. Each time this image is moved, the displayed figure will be changed; this will be done by alternately loading the open- and closed-winged butterfly images into the moving Image control. The code that moves the image and loads it with one of the two fixed images is controlled by the Timer control.

A Timer control has only one event associated with it, which is called the **Timer** event. This event is automatically triggered by the Timer control at fixed intervals of time set by the timer's **Interval** property. For Program 11-2 we will set this property to 500, which means that the Timer event is activated every 500 milliseconds. Since there are 1000 milliseconds in one second, a setting of 500 means that the **Timer** event will trigger every half second. The timer is disabled by setting its **Enabled** property to **False**. By definition, timers are not visible at run time, so this particular timer will be

Figure 11-3
The BFLY1 and BFLY2 Bitmap Images

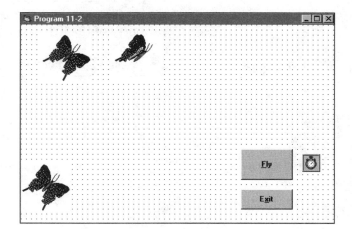

Figure 11-4
Program 11-2's Design-Time Form

---

[1] In this case, the set of figures can consist of a single figure since the movement is supplied by physically altering the position of the figure on the screen.

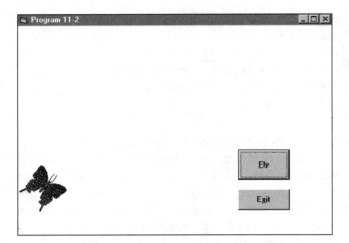

Figure 11-5
Program 11-2's Run-Time
Interface

Table 11-3	Program 11-2s Properties Table	
Object	**Property**	**Setting**
Form	Name	frmMain
	Caption	Program 11-2
	WindowState	2-Maximized
	BackColor	White (Palette Tab)
Image	Name	imgOpen
	Visible	False
	Picture	BFLY1.BMP
Image	Name	imgClosed
	Visible	False
	Picture	BFLY2.BMP
Image	Name	imgMove
	Visible	True
	Picture	BFLY1.BMP
Timer	Name	tmrMove
	Interval	500
	Enabled	False
Command button	Name	cmdFly
	Caption	&Fly
Command button	Name	cmdExit
	Caption	E&xit

both invisible and inactive when the program is executed. The properties table for Program 11-2 is listed in Table 11-3.

From a user's point of view, Program 11-2 will appear as shown in Figure 11-5 when the program is first executed. The visible butterfly image's movement is initiated and stopped by the cmdFly Command button. When this button is first pushed the cmdFly_Click event procedure sets the **Enabled** property of the Timer control to **True**, which starts the animation.

Program 11-2's Procedure Code

```
Private Sub cmdFly_Click()
  If tmrMove.Enabled = True Then
    tmrMove.Enabled = False
    cmdFly.Caption = "&Fly"
  Else
    tmrMove.Enabled = True
    cmdFly.Caption = "&Stop"
  End If
End Sub

Private Sub cmdExit_Click()
  Beep
  End
End Sub
```

```
Private Sub tmrMove_Timer()
  Static picstate As Boolean

  Beep
  imgMove.Move imgMove.Left + 20, imgMove.Top - 10
  If picstate = True Then
    imgMove.Picture = imgOpen.Picture
  Else
    imgMove.Picture = imgClosed.Picture
  End If
  picstate = Not picstate
End Sub
```

Notice that the `cmdFly_Click` procedure toggles the timer's **Enabled** property between **True** and **False**. Also notice that each time that the `cmdFly` button is pushed, its **Caption** property is changed. Thus, the sole purpose of this control is to allow the user to start and stop the timer. When the timer is enabled, it controls the butterfly's movement across the screen. To see how this is done, consider the `tmrMove_Timer` event code.

Whenever the **Timer** event code is activated, a **Move** method is executed. The syntax of this method is

```
objectname.Move horizontal-position, vertical-position, width, height
```

where *objectname* is the name of the object that is to be moved, *horizontal-position* is the position to place the left-hand side of the object, *vertical-position* is the position to place the top of the object, *width* is the object's width, and *height* is the object's height. The last two arguments, *width* and *height*, are optional and may be omitted. The unit of measurement for these four arguments is the *twip*, where there are 1440 twips to the inch. Thus, the statement contained in the `tmrMove_Timer` event code

```
imgMove.Move imgMove.Left + 20, imgMove.Top - 10
```

moves the imgMove object 20 twips to the right and 10 twips up from its current position. It also toggles the image loaded into the moving Image control based on the state of the `picstate` flag. This flag variable is declared as **Static** so that it retains its state between procedure calls. Finally, the value of the flag is also toggled at the end of each **Timer** event by setting it to its **Not** state. Thus, when the flag has a **True** value the **Not** operation will set it to **False**, and when it is **False**, the **Not** operation sets it to **True**.

Exercises 11.1

1. Enter and execute Program 11-1 on your computer.
2. Enter and execute Program 11-2 on your computer.
3. Modify Program 11-1 so that the switching of the light is controlled by a timer that activates its **Timer** event every quarter of a second.
4. a. Experiment with the **Move** method used in Program 11-2 to alter the motion of the butterfly across the screen.
   b. Modify Program 11-2 so that the butterfly moves across the screen starting at the top left-hand corner, and moves down toward the bottom right-hand corner of the screen.
5. Modify Program 11-2 to add two additional moving butterfly images.

6   Modify Program 11-2 so that the image restarts at the left-hand side of the screen once it moves off the right-hand side.

7   Locate the icon images of the plane and rocket on the VB6.0 CDRom. Use one of these icons to create an animated sequence. Include it in a working program.

11.2 Colors and Coordinates

Every object placed on a form has attributes of color and position. In this section, we describe how these fundamental attributes can be set at design time and how they can be altered at run time. We begin with the Color attribute.

Controlling Color

The two most obvious Color attributes of an object are its foreground and background colors. The foreground color determines the color of any displayed text or graphics, while the background color determines the color of the background. For example, the foreground color of this page is (mostly) black and its background color is white.

The vast majority of color monitors are of the RGB type, which means that they create their colors from combinations of Red, Green, and Blue. This color scheme is used in Visual Basic. Every color presented on the screen is defined by using three separate numbers, one for red, one for green, and one for blue.

Individually, the red, blue, and green components of a color are represented by a number between 0 and 255, which corresponds to a hexadecimal number between 0 and &HFF. The combined color is numerically represented as a long integer in the range 0 to 16,777,215. More conveniently, this is expressed as a hexadecimal number in the form &H00BBGGRR, where RR, GG, and BB represent the color's red, green, and blue content. For example, since pure white is created using full red, full green, and full blue, its numerical representation is "255 255 255", which is represented in hexadecimal as &H00FFFFFF. Here, the last set of two hexadecimal digits (FF) represents the red content of the number, the next-to-last set the green content, and the first set the blue content. Notice that the color value effectively specifies the relative intensity of red, green, and blue in the final color. The actual color displayed will depend on the color monitor used to display it.

At design time, the color code can be selected from the system's color palette or by typing in a numerical code in the designated property attribute, such as **ForeColor** and **BackColor**. At run time, the color code can be selected in one of four ways:

- By using the RGB function;
- By using the QBColor function, which selects one of 16 Microsoft QuickBasic™ colors;
- By using a system intrinsic constant listed in the Object Browser; or
- By entering a color value directly.

To get a clear understanding of the color codes, we will use the **RGB function**. This function permits us to set the color code by individually specifying the red, blue, and green content of the desired final color. The format of this function, which returns a long integer representing the RGB color value, is

RGB(*red, green, blue*)

where

- *Red* is a number in the range 0 to 255 that represents the color's red component,
- *Green* is a number in the range 0 to 255 that represents the color's green component, and
- *Blue* is a number in the range 0 to 255 that represents the color's blue component.

If a value greater than 255 is used for a color component, the number is assumed to be 255. Table 11-4 lists the red, green, and blue content of a few standard colors.

Table 11-4 RGB Color Values

Color	Red Content	Green Content	Blue Content
Black	0	0	0
Blue	0	0	255
Cyan	0	255	255
Green	0	255	0
Magenta	255	0	255
Red	255	0	0
Yellow	255	255	0
White	255	255	255

Program 11-3 can be used to determine the amount of red, green, and blue content in a color and the numerical value returned by the RGB function. This program uses horizontal scroll bars to select the individual intensity of each color component. The final color displayed in the Picture box is the color defined by the RGB function as the combination of all three components.

The advantage of using a Scroll Bar control is that the minimum and maximum values of the scroll can be set. In this case we will set the minimum and maximum values at 0 and 255, respectively, which represent the range of values accepted by the RGB function. Although we have used horizontal scroll bars, vertical scroll bars could have been used instead. As their names suggest, horizontal scroll bars scroll horizontally on the form, while vertical scroll bars scroll vertically. Figure 11-6 illustrates Program 11-3's design-time user interface.

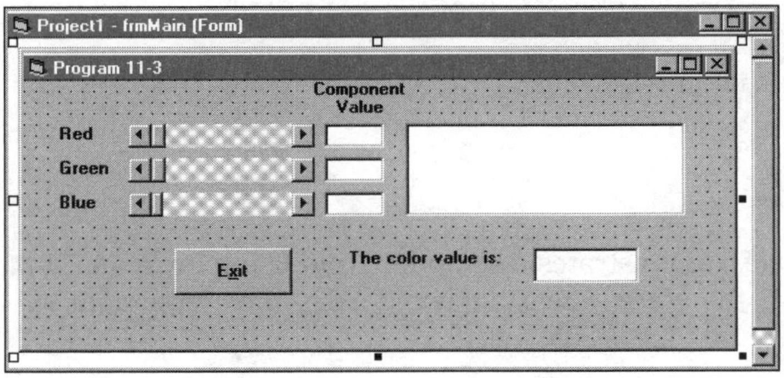

The central processing done by Program 11-3 is accomplished by the general procedure named docolor, which is listed within Program 11-3's procedural code. Notice that the docolor procedure clears all Picture boxes, calculates a new color value using the **RGB** function, and then displays all color

Figure 11-6
Program 11-3's Design-Time User Interface

values in their respective Picture boxes. This procedure is called by each horizontal scroll bar's **Scroll** and **Change** events. The reason for using two event procedures for each scroll bar is because the **Scroll** event is only activated as the thumb bar is moved, while the **Change** event is only activated by the arrow keys and the final placement of the thumb bar. Using both of these event procedures creates an output that is triggered, no matter how the user interacts with each scroll bar.

Program 11-3's Procedure Code

```
Rem: This is a [General] procedure
Private Sub docolor()
  Dim colorval As Long

  picRed.Cls
  picGreen.Cls
  picBlue.Cls
  picValue.Cls
  colorval = RGB(hsbRed.Value, hsbGreen.Value, hsbBlue.Value)
  picColor.BackColor = colorval
  picRed.Print hsbRed.Value
  picGreen.Print hsbGreen.Value
  picBlue.Print hsbBlue.Value
  picValue.Print colorval
End sub

Rem: Here are the event procedures
Private Sub hsbBlue_Change()
  docolor
End sub

Private Sub hsbBlue_Scroll()
  docolor
End sub

Private Sub hsbGreen_Change()
  docolor
End sub

Private Sub hsbGreen_Scroll()
  docolor
End sub

Private Sub hsbRed_Change()
  docolor
End sub

Private Sub hsbRed_Scroll()
  docolor
End sub

Private Sub cmdExit_Click()
  Beep
  End
End sub
```

Figure 11-7 on page 572 illustrates a sample output using Program 11-3. As listed in Table 11-4, the color blue is achieved using the component values red = 0, green = 0, and blue = 255.

Table 11-5   Program 11-3's Properties Table

Object	Property	Setting
Form	Name	frmMain
	Caption	Program 11-3
Horizontal scroll	Name	hsbRed
	Min	0
	Max	255
Horizontal scroll	Name	hsbGreen
	Min	0
	Max	255
Horizontal scroll	Name	hsbBlue
	Min	0
	max	255
Label	Name	lblRed
	Caption	Red
Label	Name	lblGreen
	Caption	Green
Label	Name	lblBlue
	Caption	Blue
Label	Name	lblValue
	Caption	Component Value
Label	Name	lblColor
	Caption	The color value is:
Picture box	Name	picRed
	TabStop	False
	BackColor	White (Palette tab)
Picture box	Name	picGreen
	TabStop	False
	BackColor	White (Palette tab)
Picture box	Name	picBlue
	TabStop	False
	BackColor	White (Palette tab)
Picture box	Name	picColor
	TabStop	False
	BackColor	White (Palette tab)
Picture box	Name	picValue
	TabStop	False
	BackColor	White (Palette tab)
Command button	Name	cmdExit
	Caption	E&xit

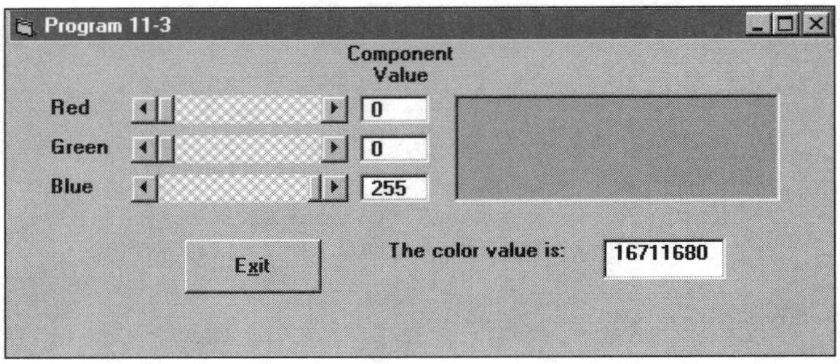

Figure 11-7

A Sample Output Using Program 11-3

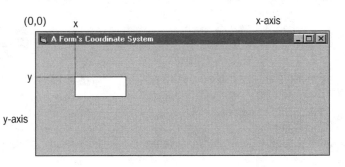

Figure 11-8

A Form's Coordinate System

(0,0)   x   x-axis

y

y-axis

Controlling Position

The position of each object placed on a form is defined by the position of its left-hand, top-corner point, as shown in Figure 11-8.

As illustrated in Figure 11-8, a form's coordinate system consists of a two-dimensional grid, with the origin of the form located at its top, left-hand corner. The horizontal line along the top of the form is referred to as the x-coordinate axis (or x-axis, for short),while the vertical line drawn down the side of the form is referred to as the y-coordinate axis (or y-axis, for short).

By default, each axis is marked in a fixed unit of length, called a *twip*, where there are 1440 twips to an inch. This measurement scale defines the size of an object when it is printed, while the actual distances displayed on the screen can vary due to the monitor's size.

Whenever an object is placed inside another object, the outer object is referred to as a *container*. Within each container, the same coordinate system is used. Thus, the default coordinate system for every container, including the form, starts with the origin of the coordinate system at the container's upper-left corner. The usefulness of this coordinate system, which is referred to as a Cartesian system, is that any point in a container can be located from the container's top left-hand corner (the origin) using two numbers, the point's x and y coordinate values.

Altering the Coordinate System

A container's complete coordinate system is defined by five properties: **ScaleMode**, **ScaleLeft**, **ScaleTop**, **ScaleWidth**, and **ScaleHeight**. By default the **ScaleMode** is set to 1, which defines the measurement scale to be in twips. Table 11-6 provides a complete list of **ScaleMode** values. Each of these measurement scales, except for **ScaleMode** values of 0 and 3, refers to the size of an object when it is printed and not how it will appear on the screen.

The **ScaleTop** and **ScaleLeft** properties define the coordinate of the top left-hand corner of each container. By default, each of these values is set to 0, which defines the origin of a container as the point (0, 0). The **ScaleWidth** and **ScaleHeight** define the *internal* width and height of the

Table 11-6 Available ScaleMode Property Values

Value	Description
0	User defined. This value is automatically set to 0 if any of the four other properties are user set.
1	Twips. This is the default setting. There are 1,440 twips to an inch.
2	Points. There are 72 points to an inch.
3	Pixels. The number of pixels per inch is monitor dependent.
4	Characters
5	Inches
6	Millimeters
7	Centimeters

container. These measurements do not include the border. All four of these property values can be either fractions or negative numbers. A negative setting for either the **ScaleWidth** or **ScaleHeight** properties simply reverses the respective coordinate axis orientation. Figure 11-9 illustrates the effects of the following property settings:

```
ScaleLeft = 100
ScaleTop = 200
ScaleWidth = 500
ScaleHeight = 300
```

In addition to setting individual scale property values, a custom scale can be designated using the **Scale** method. The syntax for this method is

objectname.**Scale** *(x1, y1)–(x2, y2)*

where *x1* and *y1* designate the settings of the **ScaleLeft** and **ScaleTop** properties. The difference between *x*-coordinate values designates the **ScaleWidth**, and the difference between *y*-coordinate values designates the **ScaleHeight**. As such, (*x1, y1*) designates the top-left corner coordinates of the object and (*x2, y2*) designates the bottom-right corner coordinates. For example, the coordinate system shown in Figure 11-9 could have been

Figure 11-9
A Scale from (100, 200) to (600, 500)

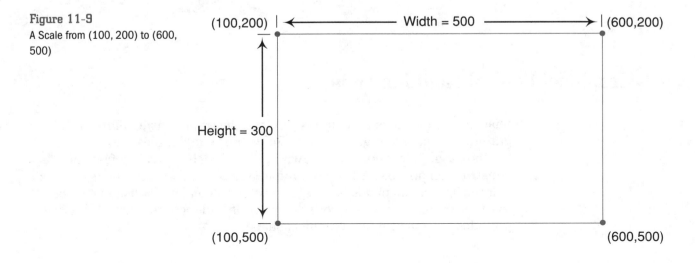

created using the statement `Scale (100, 200) -(600,500)`. Assuming that imgTest is contained in a form that uses this scale, the following statement will cause the image to be moved one-fifth of the way across and one-third of the way down the form.

```
imgTest.Move  imgTest.Left + 100, img.Top + 100
```

Alternatively, the effect of this single statement can be produced by setting each corner independently, using the two statements

```
imgTest.Left = imgTest.Left + 100
imgTest.Top = imgTest.Top + 100
```

Clearly, if an object is to be moved in both a horizontal and vertical direction, the **Move** method is more efficient than individually altering its **Left** and **Top** property values. However, if an object is to be moved in only one direction, its appropriate **Left** or **Top** property can be changed without recourse to the **Move** method.

Exercises **11.2**

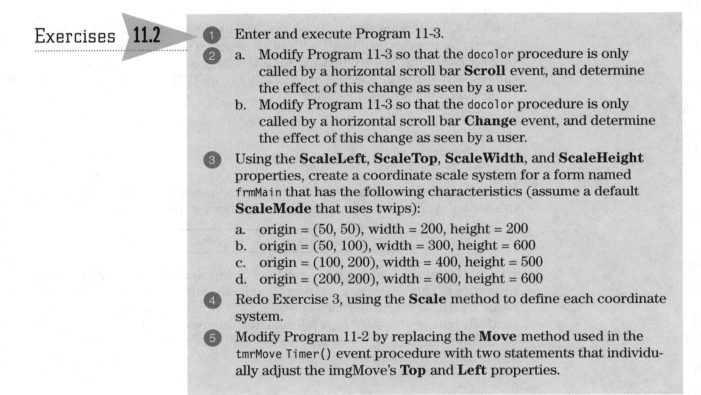

1. Enter and execute Program 11-3.

2. a. Modify Program 11-3 so that the `docolor` procedure is only called by a horizontal scroll bar **Scroll** event, and determine the effect of this change as seen by a user.
   b. Modify Program 11-3 so that the `docolor` procedure is only called by a horizontal scroll bar **Change** event, and determine the effect of this change as seen by a user.

3. Using the **ScaleLeft**, **ScaleTop**, **ScaleWidth**, and **ScaleHeight** properties, create a coordinate scale system for a form named `frmMain` that has the following characteristics (assume a default **ScaleMode** that uses twips):
   a. origin = (50, 50), width = 200, height = 200
   b. origin = (50, 100), width = 300, height = 600
   c. origin = (100, 200), width = 400, height = 500
   d. origin = (200, 200), width = 600, height = 600

4. Redo Exercise 3, using the **Scale** method to define each coordinate system.

5. Modify Program 11-2 by replacing the **Move** method used in the `tmrMove` `Timer()` event procedure with two statements that individually adjust the imgMove's **Top** and **Left** properties.

11.3 Graphical Controls and Methods

Shapes, such as lines and circles, can be constructed using either Toolbox graphical controls or graphical methods. For simple lines and circles, the Toolbox's graphical controls shown in Figure 11-10 provide a fast and easy construction approach. For creating more complex visual effects, such as painting individual pixels or creating arcs, graphical methods must be used. In this section, we present both the controls and methods that Visual Basic provides for constructing graphical shapes.

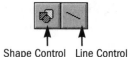

Shape Control   Line Control

Figure 11-10
The Line and Shape Controls

Figure 11-11
A Line Control

The Line and Shape Controls

Lines and shapes, such as rectangles and squares, can be used to help users focus on specific areas of the screen and group related data within a well-defined screen area. The Line and Shape controls are available directly from the Toolbox. Both of these controls are quite easy to use and create predefined images that can be resized as necessary.

If you double-click on the Line tool, a default line will be placed on the form. Each end of this line can be dragged to resize the line and place it in the desired position. Alternatively, by single-clicking on the Line control and then clicking and holding the mouse within a form or object, you will set one end of the line. The second end of the line is established by dragging the mouse to the desired point. No matter how a line is established, it can always be resized by moving either or both end points. You can also alter the line's width, color, and style using the line's Property window. Figure 11-11 illustrates typical Line controls.

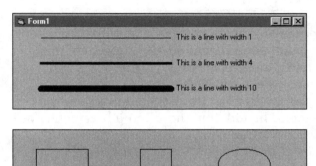

Figure 11-12
Shape Controls

Shape controls that can be constructed using the Toolbox's Shape tool are shown in Figure 11-12. Each of these shapes is constructed in the same manner. If you double-click on the Shape tool, a default Shape control will be placed on the form. Each end of this control can be dragged to resize it and the complete control can be moved to place it in its desired position. Alternatively, by single-clicking on the Shape control, then clicking and holding the mouse within a form or object, you can establish an image's initial size.

The default Shape control is a rectangle. To alter this default to one of the other shapes shown in Figure 11-12, activate the shape's Properties window and select the shape you desire in the List box provided for the **Shape** property (see Figure 11-13).

Two other very useful properties are provided for each Shape control: **FillStyle** and **FillColor**. The **FillStyle** provides a pattern that can be inserted into the shape, and ranges from a no-fill design (transparent), to a solid-fill design, to designs that consist of various combinations of lines and crosses. Figure 11-14 shows the List box options available for selecting a fill

Figure 11-13
Predefined Shape Options

Properties - Shape1	
Shape1 Shape	
Alphabetic	Categorized
BorderColor	■ &H80000008&
BorderStyle	1 - Solid
BorderWidth	1
DrawMode	13 - Copy Pen
FillColor	■ &H00000000&
FillStyle	1 - Transparent
Height	495
Index	
Left	1800
Shape	0 - Rectangle
Tag	0 - Rectangle
Top	1 - Square
Visible	2 - Oval
Width	3 - Circle
	4 - Rounded Rectan
	5 - Rounded Square

Shape
Returns/sets a value indicating the appearance of a control.

Figure 11-14
Predefined FillStyle Options

Properties - Shape1	
Shape1 Shape	
Alphabetic	Categorized
BackColor	□ &H80000005&
BackStyle	0 - Transparent
BorderColor	■ &H80000008&
BorderStyle	1 - Solid
BorderWidth	1
DrawMode	13 - Copy Pen
FillColor	■ &H00000000&
FillStyle	1 - Transparent
Height	0 - Solid
Index	1 - Transparent
Left	2 - Horizontal Line
Shape	3 - Vertical Line
Tag	4 - Upward Diagonal
Top	5 - Downward Diago
	6 - Cross
	7 - Diagonal Cross

FillStyle
Returns/sets the fill style of a shape.

design for the **FillStyle** property. The color of the fill design is determined by the **FillColor** property. For all fill patterns except solid, the **BackColor** will show through the selected pattern.

Plotting Points

To locate a specific point in a object and set its color, Visual Basic provides the **PSet** method. The general syntax of this method is

> *objectname*.**PSet Step***(x y), color*

where *(x, y)* are required coordinate points, *color* is an optional argument, and **Step** is an optional keyword. If **Step** is omitted, the x and y coordinates represent absolute values, while if the **Step** keyword is present, x and y are increments added to the current point's coordinate values. As is standard, if the object name is omitted, the method locates and paints a point on the form that contains this statement. In addition, the x and y parameters are single-precision values that can be any numeric expression yielding a single-precision value. In the absence of a color value, the designated point will be set to the form's foreground color.

As an example, using the **PSet** method, consider Program 11-4, whose interface is shown in Figure 11-15. Program 11-4 uses a Timer control, which is always invisible at run time and has only one event associated with it, the **Timer** event. This event is controlled by the timer's **Interval** and **Enabled** property settings. When the **Enabled** property is set to **True**, the interval setting, which is in units of milliseconds (there are 1000 milliseconds to a second), determines the time interval between **Timer** event activations. A timer is disabled when its **Enabled** property is set to **False**.

As indicated in Table 11-7, the Timer control is disabled initially. When it is enabled, it will have a timer interval of 100 milliseconds, which will activate its **Timer** event every one-tenth of a second. As indicated in Program 11-4's procedure code, the cmdShow_Click event is used to toggle the Timer control on and off. When activated, the **Timer** event calls the Confetti general procedure at 100 millisecond intervals. The Confetti procedure randomly sets both the red, green, and blue intensity values between 0 and 255 and the x and y coordinates of a point within the form's coordinate system. This action is provided by multiplying the returned value of the **Rnd** function,

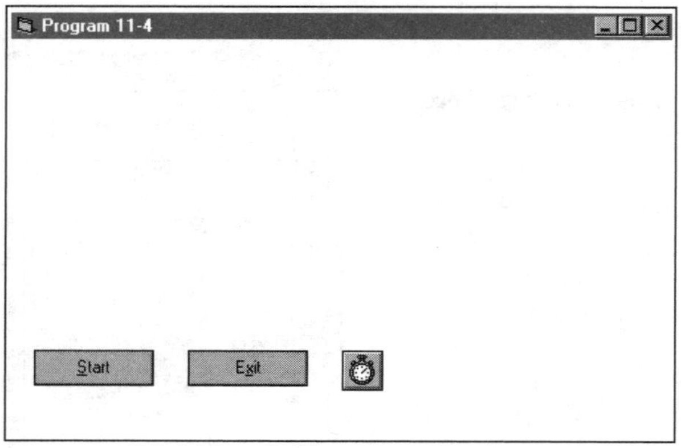

Figure 11-15
Program 11-4's Interface

Table 11-7	Program 11-4's Properties Table	
Object	**Property**	**Setting**
Form	Name	frmMain
	Caption	Program 11-4
	BackColor	White (Palette Tab)
Command button	Name	cmdShow
	Caption	&Start
Command button	Name	cmdExit
	Caption	E&xit
Timer	Name	tmrTime
	Enabled	False
	Interval	100

Figure 11-16
A Sample Output Produced by
Program 11-4

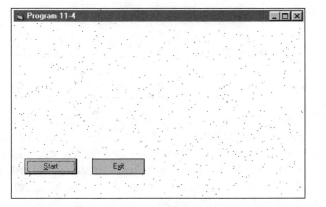

which is a value less than 1 but greater than or equal to 0, by appropriate scale factors. Finally, the Confetti function calls the **PSet** method to locate and paint the randomly selected point with the randomly selected color. Figure 11-16 shows how a sample run using Program 11-4 looks in black and white.

Program 11-4's Procedure Code

```
Private Sub cmdShow_Click()
  If cmdShow.Caption = "S&top" Then
     cmdShow.Caption = "&Start"
     tmrTime.Enabled = False
  Else
     cmdShow.Caption = "S&top"
     tmrTime.Enabled = True
  End If
End Sub


Private Sub cmdExit_Click()
  Beep
  End
End Sub


Private Sub tmrTime_Timer()
  Beep
  Call Confetti
End Sub


Rem: This is a [General] procedure
Public Sub Confetti()
  Dim red As Integer, green As Integer, blue As Integer
  Dim xcoord As Integer, ycoord As Integer

  red = 255 * Rnd
  green = 255 * Rnd
  blue = 255 * Rnd
  xcoord = ScaleWidth * Rnd
  ycoord = ScaleWidth * Rnd
  PSet (xcoord, ycoord), RGB(red, green, blue)
End Sub
```

Drawing Lines

To locate and draw a line between two coordinates, Visual Basic provides a **Line** method. The simplest syntax for this method is

```
objectname.Line (x1, y1)-(x2,y2), color
```

where *(x1, y1)* and *(x2, y2)* represent the desired line's end points, and *color* represents the desired line color. If the object name is omitted, the method locates and draws the line on the current form. Both the first set of coordinates and the color argument are optional. In the absence of a color value, the designated line is drawn in the object's foreground color, while if the first set of coordinates is omitted, the object's current *x* and *y* values are used as the starting drawing point.

The line constructed by the **Line** method includes the first point but not the point defined by the second set of coordinates. This is done to facilitate creating figures or sequences of lines drawn end to end. The last point in the sequence can always be colored using the **PSet** method. Each set of coordinates can be preceded by the **Step** keyword, which makes the individual coordinates incremental values that are relative to the current point. Finally, the *x* and *y* parameters are single-precision values that can be any numeric expression yielding a single-precision value.

Figure 11-17

A Sample Output of Program 11-5

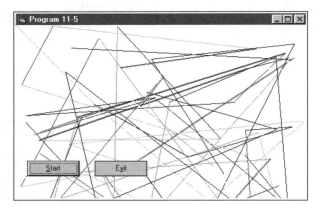

As an example using the **Line** method, we will change the call to **PSet** in Program 11-4 from

```
PSet (xcoord, ycoord), RGB(red, green, blue)
```

to the **Line** call

```
Line -(xcoord, ycoord), RGB(red, green, blue)
```

This form of the **Line** method constructs a line that starts at the current point, which has coordinates (CurrentX, CurrentY), and ends at coordinates (xcoord, ycoord).[2] The output of this program, named Program 11-5, will appear as shown in Figure 11-17.

Drawing Boxes

Although a box can be constructed by suitable placement of the four lines that define it, a simpler way is to append a B after the **Line** method's color argument. When this is done, Visual Basic considers each set of coordinates to represent opposite corners of a rectangle. For example, the statement

```
Line (300, 400) - Step(500, 1000), , B
```

produces a rectangle with opposite corners at the points (300, 400) and (800, 1400). Notice that when the color argument is omitted, two commas must be included before the B, which effectively creates a placeholder for the missing color argument. In this case the rectangle will be drawn in the current foreground color. In addition, the rectangle will be filled with the current **FillStyle**, which is typically transparent (that is, no fill). To create a solid fill, an F can be placed immediately after the B. For example, the statement

```
Line (300, 400) - Step(500, 1000), , BF
```

---

[2] The same effect can be obtained using the statement Line (CurrentX, CurrentY)-(xcoord, ycoord), RGB(red, green, yellow).

produces the same rectangle as previously, but fills it with a solid foreground color. The F argument can only be used in conjunction with the B argument; it cannot be used alone.

Drawing Circles

The **Circle** method is used to draw both circular and elliptical shapes. The required syntax for drawing circles is

```
objectname.Circle Step (x, y), radius, color
```

where the arguments (x, y), *radius*, and *color* define the circle's center point, radius, and color, respectively. As always, the object name, **Step**, and color arguments are optional. If the **Step** keyword is included, the (x, y) coordinates become incremental values that are added to the current point's coordinate values. Similarly, if the object name is omitted, the circle is drawn on the current form and, lacking a color argument, the current foreground color is used to draw the circle. The unit of measurement for the *radius* argument is always that of the horizontal scale. As an example, using the **Circle** method, the statement

```
Circle (3000, 4000), 2880
```

produces a circle with radius of 2880 twips (2 inches) whose center is the point (3000, 4000). Whether this circle will be visible on the form depends on the form's coordinate system. To ensure a visible circle, code such as the following should be used:

```
If ScaleLeft + ScaleWidth < ScaleTop + ScaleHeight then
    radius = (ScaleLeft + ScaleWidth) / 2
Else
    radius = (ScaleTop + ScaleHeight) / 2
Circle ((ScaleLeft + ScaleWidth) / 2, (ScaleTop + ScaleHeight) / 2), radius
```

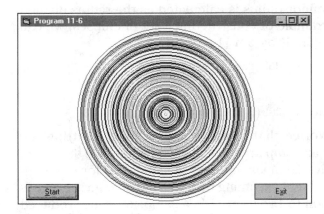

In this code, the circle is centered on the form and its radius is set to one-half of the form's smaller length or width dimension. Program 11-6 incorporates the essentials of this code into a general procedure named Confetti and, except for the placement of the Exit Command button, uses the same interface as that provided for Program 11-4. Thus, the only procedural code difference between Programs 11-4 and 11-6 is the Confetti procedure. Figure 11-18 illustrates a sample output created by Program 11-6.

Figure 11-18
A Sample Output Produced by
Program 11-6

Program 11-6's Procedure Code

```
Public Sub Confetti()
    Dim red As Integer, green As Integer, blue As Integer
    Dim xval As Single, yval As Single
    Dim radius As Single

    red = 255 * Rnd
    green = 255 * Rnd
    blue = 255 * Rnd

    xval = (ScaleLeft + ScaleWidth) / 2
    yval = (ScaleTop + ScaleHeight) / 2
```

continued

```
      If xval < yval Then
        radius = xval
      Else
        radius = yval
      End If
      radius = radius * Rnd
      Circle (xval, yval), radius, RGB(red, green, blue)
    End Sub
```

Drawing Ellipses and Arcs

An ellipse is defined by a major and minor axis, as shown in Figure 11-19. In Visual Basic, an ellipse is constructed using the **Circle** method and an aspect, where the aspect is the ratio of the ellipse's vertical to horizontal radii. Constructing an ellipse or arc requires using the following form of the **Circle** method's syntax:

```
objectname.Circle (x,y), radius, color, start, end, aspect
```

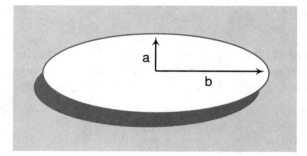

Figure 11-19
An Ellipse's Minor Radius a and Major Radius b

The last four arguments are all optional and are set to the default values **ForeColor**, 0 radians, 2 π radians, and 1, respectively. Specifically, the *start* and *end* arguments specify the beginning and ending positions of an arc, and *aspect* represents an ellipse's aspect ratio as a single-precision positive number. For a perfect circle, this argument must be 1.

When using the **Circle** method to construct an ellipse, the *radius* argument is always used to specify the major axis and is always specified in terms of the horizontal scale. Thus, if *aspect* is greater than 1, which means the vertical radius is greater than the horizontal radius, the radius is the major axis along the *y*-axis. In this case the minor radius is calculated as the radius divided by the aspect ratio. As an example of constructing a set of ellipses, we can simply change the **Circle** call in Program 11-6 from

```
Circle (xval, yval), radius, RGB(red, green, blue)
```

to the following **Circle** call

```
Circle (xval, yval), radius, RGB(red, green, blue), , , 1.5
```

Figure 11-20
A Sample Output Produced by Program 11-7

Notice that, even though we are omitting the *start* and *stop* arguments, we must include three successive commas to act as placeholders for the omitted values. Assuming that we also change the form's caption to Program 11-7, a sample output produced by the new program will appear as shown in Figure 11-20. As indicated in this figure, each ellipse is drawn in a vertical position, which is a result of the aspect ratio being greater than 1.

Finally, by using an aspect ratio that is less than 1, which means the vertical axis is less than the horizontal radius, the **Circle** method's radius argument will draw the major axis along the *x*-axis. The minor axis is then calculated as the radius length times the aspect ratio. Thus, if the statement

```
Circle (xval, yval), radius, RGB(red, green, blue), , , 0.5
```

Figure 11-21
A Sample Output Produced by
Program 11-8

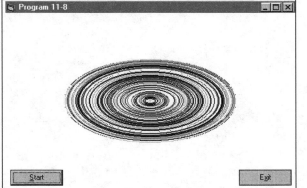

is substituted in the `Confetti` procedure called in Program 11-6 and the form's caption is changed to `Program 11-8`, the display produced by the new program will appear as shown in Figure 11-21.

Exercises **11.3**

1. Enter and execute Program 11-4 on your computer.

2. Enter and execute Program 11-5 on your computer.

3. Enter and execute Program 11-6 on your computer.

4. Using Program 11-4's interface, write a Visual Basic Program that constructs a triangle with vertices at the points (200, 400), (200, 1400), and (700, 1400). Use the **Line** method to construct the triangle.

5. a. Using Program 11-4's interface, write a Visual Basic Program that constructs a box with vertices at the points (200, 300), (1200, 300), and (1200, 700), and (200, 700). Use four calls to the **Line** method to construct each side of the box.

   b. Modify the program written for Exercise 5a to use the B option with the **Line** method. Thus, your program should make only one call to the **Line** method.

6. Modify Program 11-5 so that it produces a random series of randomly colored boxes.

7. Write a Visual Basic program that uses the following code to create the image shown in Figure 11-22.

Figure 11-22

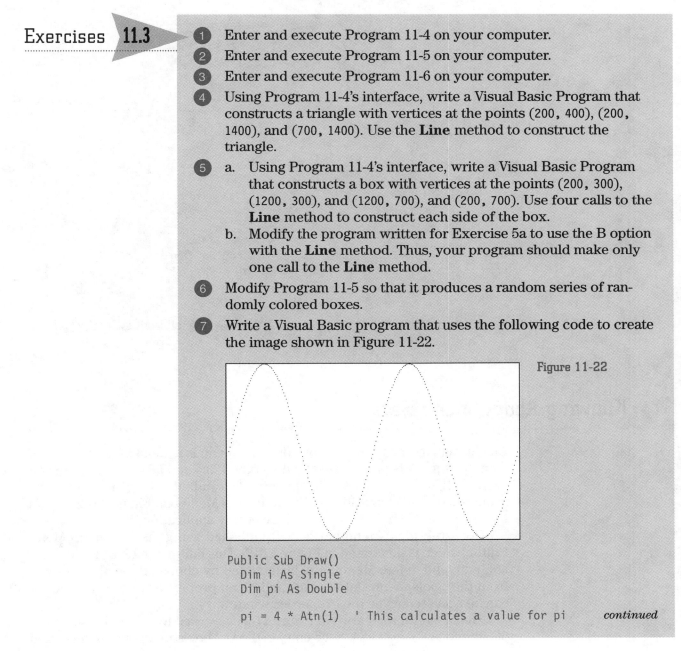

```
Public Sub Draw()
    Dim i As Single
    Dim pi As Double

    pi = 4 * Atn(1)   ' This calculates a value for pi
```

continued

```
      Scale (-2 * pi, 1)-(2 * pi, -1)

      For i = -2 * pi To 2 * pi Step 0.05
          PSet (i, Sin(i)), RGB(255 * Rnd, 255 * Rnd, 255 * Rnd)
      Next i
    End Sub
```

8 Modify the program written for Exercise 7 by changing the `Sin(i)` argument to `Cos(i)`.

9 Write a Visual Basic program that uses the following code to create the image shown in Figure 11-23.

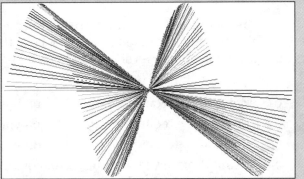

Figure 11-23

```
Public Sub Draw()
  Dim i As Single
  Dim pi As Double

  pi = 4 * Atn(1)   ' This calculates a value for pi

  Scale (-2 * pi, 1)-(2 * pi, -1)

  For i = -2 * pi To 2 * pi Step 0.05
     Line (0, 0)-(i, Sin(i)), RGB(255 * Rnd, 255 * Rnd, 255 * Rnd)
  Next i
End Sub
```

10 Modify the program written for Exercise 9 by changing the `Sin(i)` argument to `Cos(i)`.

11.4 Knowing About: Menu Bars

An alternative to a Command button main menu is a Menu bar. This type of menu was initially popularized by the Lotus 123® spreadsheet program and is currently used in almost all commercially available PC software. It is the same type of menu provided in Visual Basic's Menu bar. Figure 11-24 shows how such a menu might look for an inventory application.

Constructing a Menu bar is accomplished using Visual Basic's Menu Editor, which is illustrated in Figure 11-25. This editor, which is used to create, edit, and delete Menu bars, is activated by choosing the <u>M</u>enu Editor from the <u>T</u>ools menu. Additionally, all menu properties of existing menus can be accessed using the Properties window.

The Menu Editor shown in Figure 11-25 was used to create the Menu bar illustrated in Figure 11-24. Each entry in the List box corresponds to an option

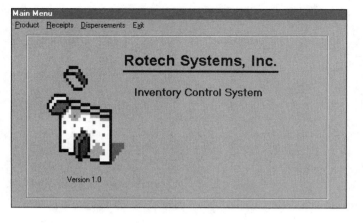

Figure 11-24
An Application with a Menu Bar

Figure 11-25
The Menu Editor

listed on the Menu bar. The ampersand (&) in front of a Menu option letter creates an access key, which permits the user to activate the menu option by pressing the ALT key and the designated letter.

In creating the Menu bar we named each item with the same name, mnuMain. What this does is to create a control array (see Section 8.3) in which each menu item shares common event procedures. It does require us, however, to assign index numbers to each item in the menu so that individual options can be uniquely identified. A requirement of assigning index numbers is that they be in increasing order for each option item added to the menu.

A distinct advantage of creating the menu options as a control array is that it simplifies our job of coding the menu, since we can use the menu control array's single **Click** event to determine which window to display next. The required code is listed as Procedure Code 11-1.

Although the menu bar that we have created has only one set of options, this is not a restriction of Visual Basic. Submenu items can be created by clicking the right-facing arrow on the Menu Editor (see Figure 11-25). This will indent the submenu item in the Menu Editor. Each indent level displayed in the editor is preceded by four dots (....) and can be removed by highlighting the desired item and clicking the Menu Editor's left-facing arrow. In addition, access keys can be assigned to each submenu item by placing an ampersand (&) symbol in front of the desired letter. Shortcut keys, which cause a menu item to be run immediately, can also be assigned to all menu options using the Menu Editor. Finally, a menu option that uses a hyphen (-) for its **Caption** property creates a separator bar between items at the appropriate indented level.

Procedure Code 11-1

```
Rem:(General) Declarations Section Code
Option Explicit
Rem: These constants correspond to the Index values
Rem: assigned to each menu option in the menu editor
Const ProdButton As Integer = 1
Const RecButton As Integer = 2
Const DispButton As Integer = 3
Const ExitButton As Integer = 4
```

continued

```
Private Sub mnuMain_Click(Index As Integer)
  Me.Hide
  Select Case Index
    Case ProdButton
      frmStub.Show
      frmStub.Refresh
    Case RecButton
      frmStub.Show
      frmStub.Refresh
    Case DispButton
      frmStub.Show
      frmStub.Refresh
    Case ExitButton
      Beep
      End
  End Select
End Sub
```

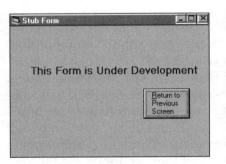

Figure 11-26
A Sample Stub Window

In reviewing Procedure Code's the `mnuMain_Click` procedure, notice that the first task it does is to hide the current Main Menu form, which is the form shown in Figure 11-24. A **Select Case** statement is then used to select the next form to be displayed depending on the value of the passed parameter. In each case, except when the Exit button is pressed, the same form, named `frmStub` is displayed. This form, which is illustrated in Figure 11-26, is used to test the operation of the menu and ensure that the display of the next form from the Menu bar, and the return to the Main Menu form is working correctly.

The reason for using both a **Show** and **Refresh** method in Procedure Code 11-1 is that, although the **Show** method automatically performs a load of the designated window, if the form's **AutoRefresh** property is set to **False**, all graphical elements on the form may not be displayed. Calling the **Refresh** method forces a redraw of all graphical elements on the form, which ensures a correct display.

The code for the stub window's return button's **Click** event is

```
Private Sub cmdReturn_Click()
  Me.Hide
  frmMain.Show
  frmMain.Refresh
End Sub
```

That is, the return button simply hides the current stub form and displays the initial `frmMain` window. The advantage of using a stub window is that it permits us to run a complete application that does not yet meet all of its final requirements. As each successive window is developed the call to the stub window can be replaced within the appropriate part of the **Select Case** statement. This incremental, or stepwise, refinement of the program is a standard development technique used by professional programmers.

11.5 Common Programming Errors and Problems

In constructing images and using color, the following problems can occur:

1. Using combinations of colors that are glaring and annoying to a user.

2. Drawing images at run time that do not fall within the boundaries of the desired container. Such images are invisible at run time.

3. Not realizing that the measurement system is relative to how the image will appear on a printer. The image's screen appearance depends on the screen's size.

4. Not getting the syntax correct for the method being used. Images should always be tested to see how they actually appear at run time. It is for this reason that the Line and Shape controls, which create their images at design time, are preferable. If you use graphical methods for creating runtime images, as you must for constructing arcs and painting individual pixels, make sure they are both visible and correct by seeing how they look at run time.

11.6 Chapter Review

Key Terms

animation	**ForeColor**	**ScaleLeft**
BackColor	icon	**Scale** method
bitmap	**Line** method	**ScaleMode**
Circle method	**Move** method	**ScaleTop**
Container	**PSet** method	**ScaleWidth**
FillColor	**RGB** function	twip
FillStyle	**ScaleHeight**	

Summary

1. Animation is produced by switching rapidly between two or more figures, each of which is slightly different, or by moving one or more images across the screen.

2. A bitmap image is defined as a pattern of dots (pixels).

3. An icon image is a special type of bitmap file that is confined to a maximum size of 32 pixels by 32 pixels.

4. RGB monitors produce colors by combining various intensities of red, green, and blue.

5. The RGB function returns a long integer in the range 0 to 16,777,215. The syntax of this function is

```
RGB(red, green, blue)
```

where each argument is a value between 0 and 255 that represents the intensity of the stated color.

6. Scroll bar controls can be either horizontal or vertical. Both types of scrolls include a thumb bar and arrow keys. When the thumb bar is placed at the left side of its scroll area for a horizontal scroll bar or at the bottom of its scroll area for a vertical scroll bar, the Scroll control's **Value** property is set to its **Minimum** property value. When positioned at the other end of the scroll area, the Scroll control's **Value** property is set to its **Maximum** property value.

7. A **Scroll** event is triggered by movement of the scroll's thumb bar.

8. A **Change** event is triggered by the final placement of the thumb bar or activation of the scroll's arrow keys.

9. A container is any object, including a form, onto which other objects are placed. A container's coordinate system is defined by its **ScaleMode**, **ScaleLeft**, **ScaleTop**, **ScaleWidth**, and **ScaleHeig**ht properties. The **ScaleMode** defines the measurement system, as listed in Table 11-6. By default, the measurement system is in twips, where there are 1440 twips to an inch, and refers to the size of an object when it is printed. The coordinate system's origin is defined as the point (**ScaleLeft, ScaleTop**), while the container's width and length are defined by its **ScaleWidth** and **ScaleHeight** properties.

10. An object's coordinate system can be set using the **Scale** method. The syntax for this method is

> *objectname.*`Scale` *(x1, y1)-(x2, y2)*

where *x1* and *y1* designate the settings of the **ScaleLeft** and **ScaleTop** properties. The difference between *x*-coordinate values designates the **ScaleWidth**, and the difference between *y*-coordinate values designates the **ScaleHeight**.

11. Custom lines and predefined rectangles and ovals can be created at design time using the toolbar's Line and Shape controls.

12. The **PSet** method can be used to locate a specific point and set its color. The general syntax of this method is

> *objectname.*`PSet Step`*(x y), color*

where *(x, y)* are required coordinate points, *color* is an optional argument, and **Step** is an optional keyword. If **Step** is omitted, the *x* and *y* coordinates represent absolute values, while if the **Step** keyword is present, *x* and *y* are increments added to the current point's coordinate values.

13. The **Line** method can be used to locate and draw a line between two points. The simplest syntax for this method is

> *objectname.*`Line` *(x1, y1)-(x2,y2), color*

where *(x1, y1)* and *(x2, y2)* represent the desired line's end points, and *color* represents the desired line color. If the first set of coordinates is omitted, the object's current *x* and *y* values are used as the starting drawing point.

In addition, each set of coordinates can be preceded by the **Step** keyword, which makes the individual coordinates incremental values relative to the current point. Each coordinate can be any numeric expression yielding a single-precision value.

14. A simple way to construct a rectangle is to append a B after the **Line** method's color argument. When this is done Visual Basic considers each set of coordinates to represent opposite corners of a rectangle.

15. The **Circle** method is used to draw both circular and elliptical shapes. The general syntax for this method is

> *objectname.*`Circle` *(x,y), radius, color, start, end, aspect*

where the arguments *(x, y)*, *radius*, and *color* define the circle's center point, radius, and color, respectively, the *start* and *end* arguments specify the beginning and ending positions of an arc, and *aspect* represents an ellipse's aspect ratio as a single-precision positive number. For a perfect circle this argument must be 1. The last four arguments are all optional and are set to the default values **ForeColor**, 0 radians, 2 π radians, and 1, respectively.

Test Yourself—Short Answer

1. The shape control offers six different shapes using the _____ property.

2. The statement `frmForm1.BackColor = RGB(0,0,0)` will produce a _____ background.

3. An object that can hold another object is called a _____.

4. The _____ line property sets a line's thickness.

5. Explain what the statement `imgImage1.Left = Image1.Left + 500` causes to happen.

6. Explain what the statement `Command1.Enabled = Not cmdCommand1.Enabled` causes to happen.

7. Explain what the statement `Circle(frmForm1.scaleWidth /2,frmForm1.scaleHeight /2), 1500` causes to happen.

8. Write the code that will change the **BackColor** of a from named `frmMain` to green. Use a Visual Basic named constant.

9. Write a statement that will cause a label's caption to toggle from visible to not visible to visible each time the statement is executed.

10. Write the run-time code that will place an existing Command button in the top-left corner of the form.

Programming Projects

1. For this project you will construct a set of circles of various colors, and keep track of some statistics on the circles drawn. The bulk of the code is attached to the "Add Circle" button shown in Figure 11-27. An executable example of this program can be found on the Student Disk as `circles.exe`.

Figure 11-27

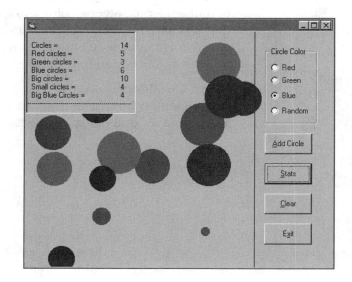

To complete this project you will need to understand the following

i.   The **If-Then-Else** statement.
ii. The **Circle** method, including the **FillColor** and **FillStyle** properties.
iii. Form level variables (to keep track of the circles drawn), that are declared in the General Declarations section.
iv. The **Cls** method.
v.   The **Rnd** function.

In addition to producing the shapes shown in Figure 11-27, you are required to keep track of the seven statistical categories listed in the figure.

For this exercise, a big circle is defined as any circle having a radius greater than 300. All circles drawn on the form should have a randomly set radius assigned by the statement:

```
radius = (Int(Rnd * 5) + 1) * 100
```

Hints:

a.   The form level variable declarations should look as follows:

```
Dim totalcircles as Integer
Dim numred as Integer
Dim numbigblue as Integer
```

b.   The algorithm for the Add Circle button is:

Generate a random radius value
Assign the circle's color
Save the circle size and color into the global counting variables
Generate a random position and draw the circle

c.   The algorithm for the Clear button is:

Clear the form
Reset the global counting variables

d.   The algorithm for the Stats button is:

Clear the form
Print the statistics
Reset the global counting variables

2. In this project you will use two sets of Option controls to permit a user to select a color and a shape, which can be either a square or circle. A Draw button then draws the shape on the form. A Draw 10 button draws five randomly colored squares and five randomly colored circles on the form.

Extra Challenge:
Use a Combo box, described in Appendix D to select a shape, and a Combo box to select a color.

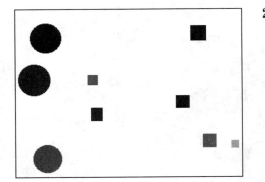

Figure 11-28

Introduction To Classes

12

In contrast to procedural programming, where software is organized by what it does to the data (its function), object-oriented programming organizes software as a collection of discrete objects that include both data and functional behavior.

As such, procedural programs are constructed as a sequence of transformations that convert input data into output data. In a well-constructed procedural program, each transformation is captured within an individual procedure, which in Visual Basic is coded as either a procedure or a function. The method for converting inputs to outputs is described by an algorithm. Thus, procedural code is frequently defined as an algorithm written in a programming language.

In object-oriented programming, the packaging of data and processing is handled in a much different manner. Both the data and the processing that can be applied to it are combined and packaged in a new unit called an *object.* Once suitable objects are defined, object-oriented programming is concerned with the interactions between objects. Notice that this way of thinking about code does not remove the necessity of understanding data and their related operations and algorithms. It simply binds the data and procedures in a new package, an object, and then concerns itself with the interactions between objects. One advantage to this approach is that once objects are defined for one application, they can be used, without reprogramming, in other applications.

Visual Basic Versions 4.0, 5.0, and 6.0 offer the ability to create user-defined objects. Central to this ability is the concept of an abstract, or programmer-defined, data type. In this chapter, we explore the implications of permitting programmers to define their own data types, and then present Visual Basic's mechanism for constructing abstract data types.

12.1 ▶ Classes and Class Modules

The programming environment has changed dramatically over the last few years with the emergence of mouse input, graphical-based color monitors, and the subsequent interest in Windows applications. Providing a graphical user interface (GUI), where a user can easily move around in even a single window, however, is a challenge using procedural code. Programming multiple and possibly overlapping windows on the same graphical screen increases the complexity enormously.

Unlike a pure procedural approach, however, an object-oriented approach fits well in graphical windowed environments, where each window can be specified as a self-contained rectangular object that can be moved and resized in relation to other objects on the screen. Within each window, other graphical objects, such as Check boxes, Option buttons, Labels, and Text boxes can easily be placed and moved.

Central to the creation of objects is the concept of abstraction and an abstract data type, which is simply a user-defined data type, as opposed to the built-in data types provided by all languages (such as integer and floating-point types), permitting a programmer to define new data types.

Abstract Data Types

To gain a clear understanding of what an abstract data type is, consider the following three built-in data types supplied in Visual Basic: Integers, Singles, and Strings. In using these data types, we typically declare one or more variables of the desired type, use them in their accepted ways, and avoid using them in ways that are not specified. Thus, for example, we would not use the subtraction operator on two strings. Since this operation makes no sense for strings, it is never defined, in any programming language, for such data. Thus, although we typically don't consider it, each data type consists of *both* a type of data, such as integer or single, *and* specific operational capabilities provided for each type.

In computer terminology, the combination of data and its associated operations is defined as a *data type*. That is, a data type defines *both* the types of data and the types of operations that can be performed on the data. Seen

---

PROGRAMMERS NOTES

Program and Class Libraries

The concept of a program library began with FORTRAN, which was the first commercial, high-level language, introduced in 1954. The FORTRAN library consisted of a group of completely tested and debugged mathematical routines provided with the compiler. Since that time, every programming language has provided its own library of functions. In Visual Basic, this library is referred to as the *intrinsic program library*, and includes functions such as **Format, Str, Val, Asc**, and **Rnd**. The advantage of library functions and procedures is that they enhance program development and design by providing code known to work correctly, without the need for additional testing and debugging.

With the introduction of object-oriented languages, the concept of a program library has been extended to include class libraries. A *class library* is a library of tested and debugged classes. Generally, the class is provided as either an executable (EXE) or dynamic linked library (DLL) module (see Appendix F) that cannot be changed by a user, but can be accessed and incorporated into a user's application.

One of the key practical features of class libraries is that they help realize the goal of code reuse. By providing tested and debugged code, consisting of both data and function members, class libraries furnish large sections of prewritten and reusable code ready for incorporation within new applications. This shifts the focus of writing application programs from the creation of new code to understanding how to use predefined objects and stitching them together in a cohesive way. A prime example is the visual object class—consisting of Check boxes, List boxes, Dialogs, Command buttons, and Option buttons—provided in Visual Basic.

in this light, the Integer data type, the Single data type, and the String data type provided in Visual Basic are all examples of *built-in* data types defined by a type of data and specific operational capabilities provided for initializing and manipulating the type. In a simplified form, this relationship can be described as

```
Data Type = Allowable Data + Operational Capabilities
```

Thus, the operations we have been using in Visual Basic are an inherent part of each of the data types we have been using. For each of these data types the designers of Visual Basic had to carefully consider, and then implement, specific operations.

To understand the importance of the operational capabilities provided by a programming language, let's take a moment to list some of those supplied with Visual Basic's built-in data types. The minimum set of the capabilities provided by Visual Basic's built-in data types is listed in Table 12-1.

Table 12-1   Required Data Type Capabilities

Capability	Example
Define one or more variables of the data type.	`Dim a As Integer`
Assign a value to a variable.	`a = 10`
Assign one variable's value to another variable.	`a = b`
Perform mathematical operations.	`a + b`
Perform relational operations.	`a > b`
Convert from one data type to another.	`a = 7.2`

Now let's see how all this relates to abstract data types (ADTs). By definition an *abstract data type* is simply a user-defined type that describes both a type of data and the operations that can be performed on it. Such data types are required when we wish to create objects more complex than simple integers and characters. When we create our own data types we must consider both the type of data we are creating and the capabilities we will provide to initialize and manipulate it.

As a specific example, assume we are programming an application that uses dates extensively and we wish to create our own Date data type independent of Visual Basic's built-in types. Clearly, from a data standpoint, a date must be capable of accessing and storing a month, day, and year designation. Although from an implementation standpoint there are a number of means of storing a date, from a user viewpoint the actual implementation is not relevant. For example, a date can be stored as three integers, one each for the month, day, and year. Alternatively, a single long integer in the form *yyyymmdd* can also be used. Using the long integer implementation the date 5/16/98 would be stored as the integer 19980516. For sorting dates, the long integer format is very attractive because the numerical sequence of the dates corresponds to their calendar sequence.

The method of internally structuring the date, unfortunately, supplies only a partial answer to our programming effort. We must still supply a set of operations that can be used with dates. Clearly, such operations could include assigning values to a date, subtracting two dates to determine the number of days between them, comparing two dates to determine which is earlier and which is later, and displaying a date in a form such as 6/3/96.

PROGRAMMERS NOTES

Procedural, Hybrid, and Pure Object-Oriented Languages

Most high-level programming languages can be categorized into one of three main categories: *procedural, hybrid,* or *object-oriented.* FOR-TRAN, which was the first commercially available, high-level programming language, is procedural. This makes sense because FOR-TRAN was designed to perform mathematical calculations using standard algebraic formulas. Formally, these formulas were described as algorithms and then the algorithms were coded using function and subroutine procedures. Other procedural languages that followed FORTRAN included BASIC, COBOL, Pascal, and C.

Currently there are only two "pure" object-oriented languages; Smalltalk and Eiffel. The first requirement of such a language is that it contain three specific features: *classes, inheritance,* and *polymorphism* (each of these features is described in this chapter). In addition to providing these features, however, an object-oriented language must always use classes. In a pure object-oriented language, all data types are constructed as classes, all data values are objects, and every operation can only be executed using a class member procedure or function. *It is impossible in a pure language not to use object-oriented features* throughout a program. This is not the case in a hybrid language.

In a hybrid language, such as Visual Basic Version 6.0, *it is impossible not to use elements of a procedural program.* This is because the use of any built-in data type or operation effectively violates the pure object-oriented paradigm. In addition, hybrid languages need not even provide inheritance and polymorphic features but they *must* provide classes. Languages that use classes but do not provide inheritance and polymorphic features are referred to as *object-based* rather than *object-oriented* languages. Although, starting with Version 4.0, Visual Basic permitted the construction of classes, as well as their use, Visual Basic still does not provide true inheritance features. Thus, Visual Basic is classified as an object-based language.

Notice that the details of how each operation works are dependent on how we choose to store a date (formally referred to as its data structure) and are only of interest to us as we develop each operation. For example, the implementation of comparing two dates will differ if we store a date using a single long integer as opposed to using separate integers for the month, day, and year.

The combination of the storage structure used for dates with a set of available operations appropriate to dates would then define an abstract Date data type. Once our Date type is developed, programmers who want to use it need never be concerned with *how* dates are stored or *how* the operations are performed. All they need to know is *what* each operation does and how to invoke it, which is as much as they know about Visual Basic's built-in operations. For example, we don't really care how the addition of two integers is performed but only that it is done correctly.

In Visual Basic an abstract data type is referred to as a *class.* Construction of a class is inherently easy and we already have all the necessary tools in variables and general procedures. What Visual Basic provides is a mechanism for packaging these two items together in a self-contained unit referred to as a *class module.* Let's see how this is done.

Class Construction

A class defines both data and procedures. This is usually accomplished by constructing a class in two parts, consisting of a data declaration section

PROGRAMMERS NOTES

Abstraction

Abstraction is a concept central to object-oriented programming. In its most general usage, an abstraction is simply an idea or term that identifies general qualities or characteristics of a group of objects, independent of any one specific object in the group. For example, consider the term *car*. As a term, this is an abstraction: it refers to a group of objects, each containing the characteristics associated with a car, such as a motor, passenger compartment, wheels, steering capabilities, brakes, etc. A particular car, such as "my car" or "your car," is not an abstraction. All are real objects classified as "type car" because they have the attributes associated with a car.

Although we use abstract concepts all the time, we tend not to think about them as such. For example, the words *tree*, *dog*, *cat*, *table*, and *chair* are all abstractions, just as *car* is. Each of these terms refers to a set of qualities possessed by a group of particular things. For each of these abstractions there are many individual trees, dogs, and cats; each of which conforms to the general characteristics associated with the abstract term. In programming we are much more careful to label appropriate terms as abstractions than we are in everyday life. You have already encountered a programming abstraction with data types.

Just as "my car" is a particular object of the more abstract "type car," a particular integer, "5," for example, is a specific object or instance of the more abstract "type integer," where an integer is a signed or unsigned number having no decimal point. Thus, each type—integer, character, and single—is considered an abstraction that defines a general type, of which specific examples can be observed. Such types, then, simply identify common qualities of each group and make it reasonable to speak of integer types, character types, and single types.

Having defined what we mean by a type, we can now create the definition of a data type. In programming terminology a *data type* consists of *both* an acceptable range of values of a particular type *and* a set of operations that can be applied to those values. Thus, the integer data type not only defines a range of acceptable integer values but also defines what operations can be applied to those values.

Although users of programming languages such as Visual Basic ordinarily assume that mathematical operations such as addition, subtraction, multiplication, and division will be supplied for integers, the designers of Visual Basic had to consider carefully what operations would be provided as part of the integer data type. For example, the designers of Visual Basic included an exponentiation operator, though this operation is not included in either the C or C++ languages (in which exponentiation is supplied as a library function).

The set of allowed values is more formally referred to as a data type's *domain*, and the following table lists the domain for Visual Basic's numeric data types.

Visual Basic's Numeric Data Types

Data Type	Domain
Byte	0 to 255
Integer	–32768 to +32767
Long	–2,147,483,648 to +2,147,483,647
Single	–3.402823E38 to –1.401298E-45
	+.401298E-45 to +3.402823E38
Double	–1.79769313486231E308 to –4.94065645841247E-324
	+4.94065645841247E-324 to +1.79769313486231E308

All of the data types listed in this table are part of the Visual Basic language. As such, they are formally referred to as *built-in, intrinsic,* or *primitive* data types (the three terms are synonymous). In contrast to built-in data types, Visual Basic permits programmers to create their own data types; that is, define a type of value with an associated domain and operations that can be performed on the acceptable values. Such user-defined data types are formally referred to as *abstract data types*. In Visual Basic abstract data types are called *classes*, and the ability to create classes is provided in Versions 4.0, 5.0, and 6.0.

```
Rem: Data Declaration Section
     Declaration of all variables
Rem: Methods Implementation Section
     Procedures and Functions that
     can be used on the above
     declared variables
```

Figure 12-1
Class Code Format

and a methods implementation section. As illustrated in Figure 12-1, the declaration section declares the data types of the class. The implementation section is then used to define the procedures and functions that will operate on this data.

First, notice that a class consists of code only. The variables, procedures, and functions provided in the declaration and implementation sections of the code are collectively referred to as *class members*. Individually, the variables are referred to as both *data members* and *instance variables* (the terms are synonymous), while the procedures and functions are referred to as *member methods*.

As a specific example of a class, consider the following definition of a class we have named CLDate.

The CLDate Class Code—Version 1

```
Rem: Data Declaration Section
Private Month As Integer
Private Day As Integer
Private Year As Integer

Rem: Methods Implementation Section
Public Sub setdate(mm As Integer, dd As Integer, yyyy As Integer)
  Month = mm
  Day = dd
  Year = yyyy
End Sub

Public Function showdate() As String
  showdate = Format(Month, "00") + "/" + Format(Day, "00") + "/" + Format(Year Mod 100, "00")
End Function
```

This class consists of both variable declarations and general procedure code. Notice that we have separated the declarations and remaining code into two sections—a declaration section and an implementation section. Both of these sections contain code you should be very familiar with.

The *declaration section* simply declares all variables that are to be members of the class. Although the initial capital letter is not required, it is conventionally used to designate a class data member. In this case the data members Month, Day, and Year are declared as integer variables. The keyword **Private** in each declaration defines the variable's access rights. The **Private** keyword specifies that the declared data member can only be accessed by using the procedures and functions defined in the *implementation section*. The purpose of the **Private** designation is specifically meant to enforce data security by requiring all access to private data members to go through member methods. This type of access, which restricts a user from seeing how the data is actually stored, is referred to as *data hiding*. Although a variable can be declared as **Public**, doing so permits any procedure or code that is not a part of the class module to access the variable.

Specifically, we have chosen to store a date using three integers: one for the month, day, and year, respectively. We will also always store the year as a four-digit number. Thus, for example, we will store the year 1998 as 1998 and not as 98. Making sure to store all years with their correct century designation will eliminate a multitude of problems that can crop up if only the last two digits, such as 98, are stored. For example, the number of years between 2002 and 1999 can be quickly calculated as 2002 − 1999 = 3 years, while this same answer is not so easily obtained if only the year values 02 and 99 are used. Additionally, we are sure of what the year 2000 refers to, while a two-digit value such as 00 could refer to either 1900 or 2000.[1]

The general procedures in the class have been declared as **Public**. This means that these class methods *can* be called from any code not in the class. In general, all class methods should be **Public**; as such, they furnish capabilities to manipulate the class variables from any code or form module outside of the class. For our class we have initially provided one procedure, named setdate, and one function, named showdate. These two methods have been written to permit assignment and display capabilities.

Specifically, the setdate procedure expects three integer parameters, mm, dd, and yyyy. The body of this procedure assigns the data members Month, Day, and Year with the values of its parameters. Finally, the last function header line in the implementation section defines a function named showdate. This function has no parameters and returns the values stored in Month, Day, and Year as a formatted string having the form mm/dd/yy. The single statement in this function, however, needs a little more explanation.

Although we have chosen to internally store all years as four-digit values that retain century information, users are accustomed to seeing dates where the year is represented as a two-digit value, such as 12/15/99. To display the last two digits of the year value, the expression year Mod 100 can be used. For example, if the year is 1999, the expression 1999 Mod 100 yields the value 99, and if the year is 2001, the expression 2001 Mod 100 yields the value 1. Formatting this value using a **Format** function with the "00" format string ensures that this latter value is displayed with a leading 0, as the string 01. We will shortly see how our class can be used within the context of a complete program. But first, we will have to code this class using a class module.

Creating a Class Module

Creating a class requires inserting a class module into a project and then adding the class's code to that module. The steps used to insert a class module are almost identical to those for inserting a code module. They are

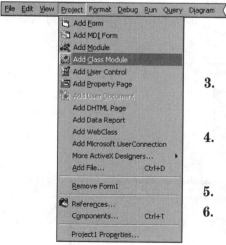

1. Open up either an existing or new project.
2. Choose the Add <u>C</u>lass Module option from the <u>P</u>roject menu (See Figure 12-2). Choosing this option will bring up the Add Class Module window shown in Figure 12-3 on page 596.
3. Select the Open Command button on the New tab (see Figure 12-3). Doing this will add a class module to the Project Explorer window, as shown in Figure 12-4 on page 596.
4. If the Properties window is not visible, make it so by either choosing the Properties <u>W</u>indow option from the <u>V</u>iew menu or pressing the F4 key.
5. Name the class in the Properties window.
6. Click on the Class Code window and in the (**General**) object's (**Declarations**) section enter the class's data member declarations.

Figure 12-2
The Add Class Module Option

---

[1] These problems are all included under the designation "The year 2000 problem."

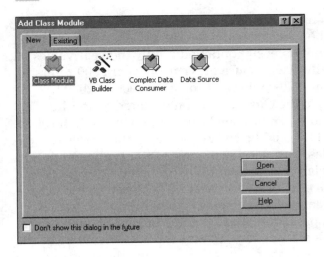

Figure 12-3
The Add Class Module Window

Figure 12-4
The Project Window
Containing a Class Module

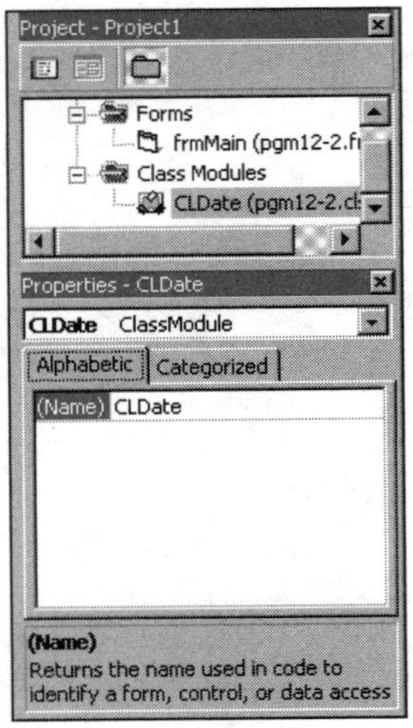

Figure 12-5
A Class Module Properties
Window

7. In the (**General**) object's (**Declarations**) section, type the header line for each class method and then complete the code in the template provided by Visual Basic.

Figure 12-5 shows the Project and Properties windows for a class that we have named CLDate (Step 5). By convention the first letter of a class name is capitalized. In this case we have chosen to capitalize the first three letters. You can always reactivate a class's Properties window at any time by pressing the F4 function key when the class module is active.

Figure 12-6 illustrates how the class's (**Declarations**) section will look, after you type in the data declarations. Notice that we have included the **Option Explicit** statement within this section so that all variables must be explicitly declared.

Figures 12-7 and 12-8 illustrate how the methods for the CLDate class will look when they have been entered in the class's Code window. Notice that, unlike a form module, which contains both a form and a Code window, a class module contains a Code window only.

Figure 12-6
The Declaration Section for the
CLDate Class

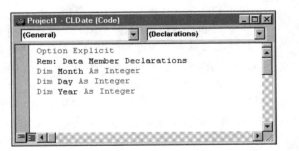

```
Option Explicit
Rem: Data Member Declarations
Dim Month As Integer
Dim Day As Integer
Dim Year As Integer
```

Figure 12-7
The setdate Procedure in the Code
Window

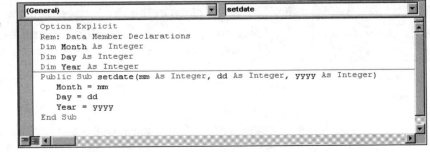

```
Option Explicit
Rem: Data Member Declarations
Dim Month As Integer
Dim Day As Integer
Dim Year As Integer
Public Sub setdate(mm As Integer, dd As Integer, yyyy As Integer)
    Month = mm
    Day = dd
    Year = yyyy
End Sub
```

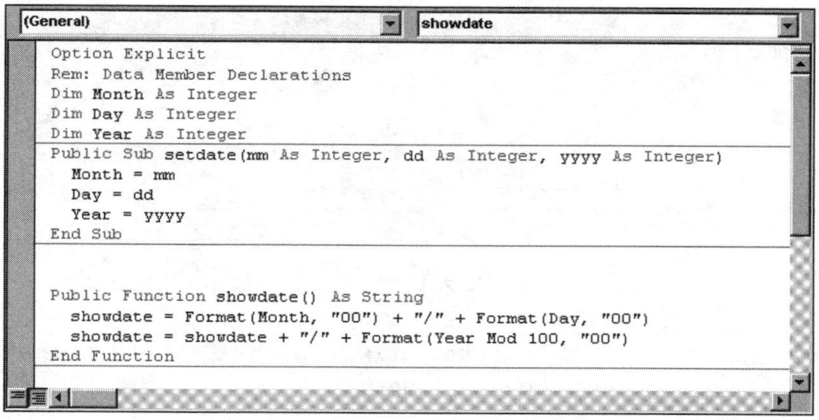

Figure 12-8

The showdate Procedure in the Code Window

```
(General)                              ▼   showdate                        ▼
    Option Explicit
    Rem: Data Member Declarations
    Dim Month As Integer
    Dim Day As Integer
    Dim Year As Integer
    Public Sub setdate(mm As Integer, dd As Integer, yyyy As Integer)
       Month = mm
       Day = dd
       Year = yyyy
    End Sub


    Public Function showdate() As String
       showdate = Format(Month, "00") + "/" + Format(Day, "00")
       showdate = showdate + "/" + Format(Year Mod 100, "00")
    End Function
```

Saving a Class Module

To save the module:

- Select the Save Option from the File's submenu, or
- Select the Save As option from the File's submenu, or
- Press the file icon on the Toolbar when the class module is active on the screen.

If you are using a class, your project will consist of at least two modules: a form module and a class module. To switch between modules you can double-click on the desired module within either the Project Explorer or Object Browser windows. The Project Explorer window is activated by

- Selecting Project Explorer from the View menu, or
- Pressing the CTRL+R keys.

The Object Browser window is activated by

- Selecting Object Browser from the View menu, OR
- Pressing the F2 function key.

Whichever module is active is the one that will be saved if you choose the Save option from the File menu. That is, when a form module is active the File's submenu will appear as shown in Figure 12-9a. Similarly, if a class module is active, the File's submenu will appear as shown in Figure 12-9b. As shown in this figure, class modules are saved with a .cls extension.

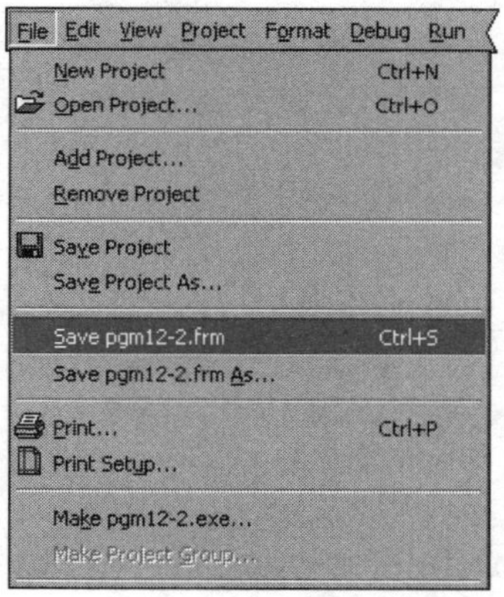

Note that this procedure saves only the class module—it does not save any other modules associated with an application. Be aware that if you are using a class in a program, your project will consist of at least two modules: a form module and a class module. *Both modules should be saved.* To save a form module, make sure it is active on the screen and repeat the steps you used to save the class module. As always, the project definition as a whole, which includes all modules, can be saved at any time using either the Save Project or Save Project As options of the File menu, or by pressing the file icon on the toolbar.

Figure 12-9a

The File SubMenu When a Form Module Is Active

```
File  Edit  View  Project  Format  Debug  Run
  New Project                      Ctrl+N
  Open Project...                  Ctrl+O
  Add Project...
  Remove Project
  Save Project
  Save Project As...
  Save pgm12-2.frm                 Ctrl+S
  Save pgm12-2.frm As...
  Print...                         Ctrl+P
  Print Setup...
  Make pgm12-2.exe...
  Make Project Group...
```

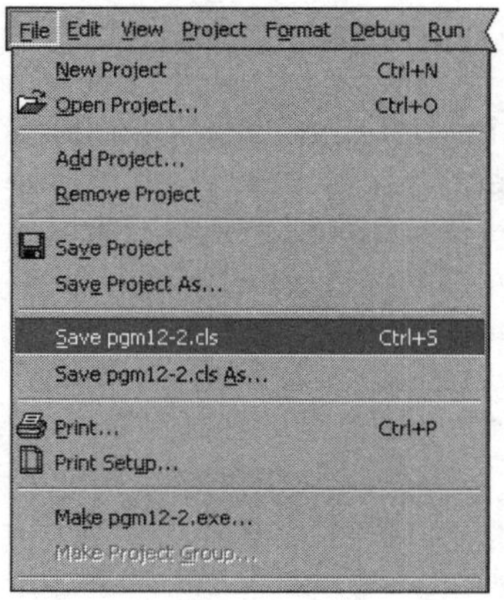

Figure 12-9b

The File SubMenu When a Class Module Is Active

```
File  Edit  View  Project  Format  Debug  Run
  New Project                      Ctrl+N
  Open Project...                  Ctrl+O
  Add Project...
  Remove Project
  Save Project
  Save Project As...
  Save pgm12-2.cls                 Ctrl+S
  Save pgm12-2.cls As...
  Print...                         Ctrl+P
  Print Setup...
  Make pgm12-2.exe...
  Make Project Group...
```

Using a Class

Once a class has been created, its public members can be used by any module within any project that includes the class module. For example, if we use the graphical interface shown in Figure 12-10 as Program 12-1's interface, enter the code listed as Program 12-1's procedure code, and insert

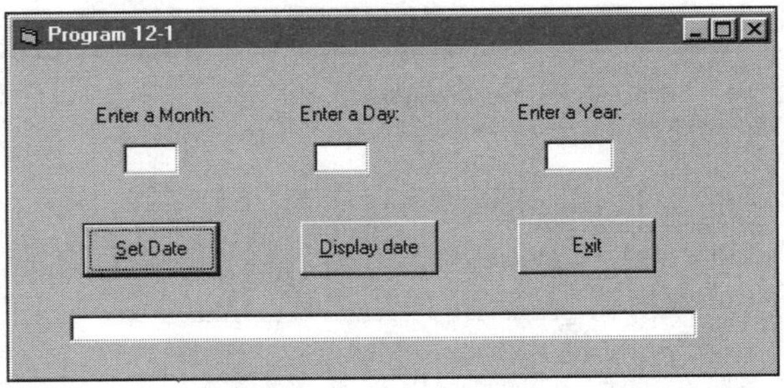

Figure 12-10
Program 12-1's Graphical User
Interface

the CLDate class into the project, we will have a completed application that
uses the CLDate class.

Program 12-1's Procedure Code

```
Rem: This is the code in the (Declarations) section
Option Explicit
Dim firstdate As New CLDate

Rem: This is the event code
Private Sub cmdDisplay_Click()
  picShow.Print "The date is "; firstdate.showdate()
End Sub

Private Sub cmdSet_Click()
  Dim mm As Integer, dd As Integer, yyyy As Integer

  picShow.Cls
  mm = Val(txtMonth.Text)
  dd = Val(txtDay.Text)
  yyyy = Val(txtYear.Text)
  Call firstdate.setdate(mm, dd, yyyy)
End Sub

Private Sub cmdExit_Click()
  Beep
  End
End Sub
```

In reviewing this code, realize that a class module only creates a data
type, *it does not create any variables or objects of this class type*. This is
true of all Visual Basic types, including the built-in types such as integers and
strings. Just as a variable of an integer type must be declared, variables of a
user-declared class must also be declared. Variables defined to be of a user-
declared class are referred to as objects, and objects are declared using the
New keyword. Thus, the second statement in the (**Declarations**) section is
a declaration statement that creates a new object of type CLDate class. Now
notice the syntax for referring to an object's method. This syntax is

```
object-name.method-name(arguments)
```

where *object-name* is the name of a specific object and *method-name* is the
name of one of the methods defined for the object's class. Since we have defined all class methods as **Public**, a statement such as Call firstdate.set-
date(mm,dd,yyyy) is valid inside an event procedure and is a call to the class's
setdate procedure. This statement tells the setdate procedure to operate on

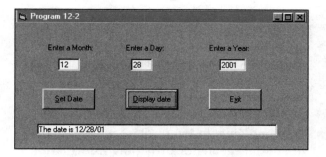

Figure 12-11
A Sample Output Using Program 12-1

Table 12-2 Program 12-1's Properties Table

Object	Property	Setting
Form	Name	frmMain
	Caption	Program 12-1
Label	Name	lblMonth
	Caption	Enter a Month:
Label	Name	lblDay
	Caption	Enter a Day:
Label	Name	lblRate
	Caption	Enter a Year:
Text box	Name	txtMonth
	Text	(Blank)
	BackColor	White (Palette Tab)
Text box	Name	txtDay
	Text	(Blank)
	BackColor	White (Palette Tab)
Text box	Name	txtYear
	Text	(Blank)
	BackColor	White (Palette Tab)
Command button	Name	cmdSet
	Caption	&Set
Command button	Name	cmdDisplay
	Caption	&Display
Command button	Name	cmdExit
	Caption	E&xit
Picture box	Name	picShow
	TabStop	False
	BackColor	White (Palette Tab)

the `firstdate` object with the arguments `mm`, `dd`, and `yyyy`. It is important to understand that, because all class data members were specified as **Private**, a statement such as `firstdate.Month = mm` is invalid from any procedure not on the class module. We are, therefore, forced to rely on member procedures to access data member values. For this same reason, a statement such as `picShow.Print firstdate` is invalid within the `cmdDisplay_Click` procedure, because the **Print** method does not know how to handle an object of class `CLDate`. Thus, we have supplied our class with a procedure that can be used to access and display an object's internal values. Figure 12-11 illustrates a sample run using Program 12-1.

Terminology

As there is sometimes confusion about the terms *class*, *object*, and other terminology associated with object-oriented programming, we will take a moment to clarify and review the terminology.

PROGRAMMERS NOTES

Interfaces, Implementations, and Information Hiding

The terms *interface, implementation,* and *information hiding* are used extensively in object-oriented programming literature. Each of these terms can be equated to specific parts of a class's declaration and implementation sections.

- An *interface* consists of the methods available to a programmer for using a class. Thus, a programmer should be provided with documentation as to the names and purpose of each class method, and how to correctly call it. As such, the interface should be all that is required to tell a programmer how to use the class.

- The *implementation* consists of all the information contained in a class module. It is how the class is constructed. This information should not be needed by a user of the class.

- The implementation or class module is the essential means of providing information hiding. In its most general context, *information hiding* refers to the principal that the internal construction of a class is not relevant to any programmer who wishes to use that class. That is, the implementation can and should be hidden from all class users, precisely to ensure that the class is not altered or compromised in any way. All a programmer need know to correctly use a class should be given in the interface information.

A *class* is a programmer-defined data type out of which objects can be created. *Objects* are created from classes; they have the same relationship to classes as variables do to Visual Basic's built-in data types. For example, in the declaration

```
Dim firstdate as Integer
```

firstdate is said to be a variable, while in Program 12-1's declaration

```
Dim firstdate as New CLDate
```

firstdate is said to be an object. If it helps you to think of an object as a variable, do so.

Objects are also referred to as *instances* of a class and the process of creating a new object is frequently referred to as an *instantiation* of the object. Each time a new object is instantiated (created), a new set of data members belonging to the object is created.[2] The particular values contained in these data members determines the object's *state.*

Seen in this way, a class can be thought of as a blueprint out of which particular instances (objects) can be created. Each instance (object) of a class will have its own set of particular values for the set of data members specified in the class's (**Declarations**) section.

Notice that a class also defines the operations permitted to be performed on an object's data members. Users of the object need to know *what* these operations can do and how to activate them through function calls, but unless run time or space implications are relevant, they do not need to know *how* the operation is done. The actual implementation details of an object's operations are contained in the implementation section, which can be hidden from the user. Other names for the operations defined in a class implementation section are *procedures, functions, services, method*s, and *behavior.* We will use these terms interchangeably throughout this chapter.

---

[2] Note that only one set of class methods is created. These methods are shared among objects.

PROGRAMMERS NOTES

Values and Identities

Apart from any behavior supplied to an object, a characteristic feature that objects share with variables is that they always have a unique identity. It is an object's identity that permits distinguishing one object from another. This is not true of a value, such as the number 5, because all occurrences of 5 are indistinguishable from one another. As such, values are not considered as objects in object-oriented programming languages such as Visual Basic.

Another distinguishing feature between an object and a value is that a value can never be a container whose value can change, while an object clearly can. A value is simply an entity that stands for itself.

Now consider a string such as "Chicago". As a string, this is a value. However, since *Chicago* could also be a specific and identifiable object of type *City*, the context in which the name is used is important. Notice that when the string "Chicago" is assigned to an object's Name attribute, it reverts to being a value.

Exercises 12.1

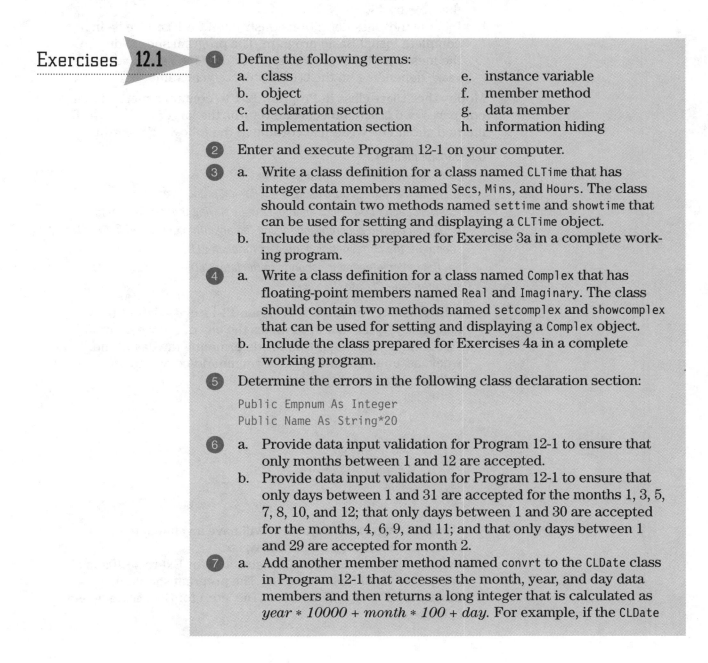

1. Define the following terms:
   a. class
   b. object
   c. declaration section
   d. implementation section
   e. instance variable
   f. member method
   g. data member
   h. information hiding

2. Enter and execute Program 12-1 on your computer.

3. a. Write a class definition for a class named CLTime that has integer data members named Secs, Mins, and Hours. The class should contain two methods named settime and showtime that can be used for setting and displaying a CLTime object.
   b. Include the class prepared for Exercise 3a in a complete working program.

4. a. Write a class definition for a class named Complex that has floating-point members named Real and Imaginary. The class should contain two methods named setcomplex and showcomplex that can be used for setting and displaying a Complex object.
   b. Include the class prepared for Exercises 4a in a complete working program.

5. Determine the errors in the following class declaration section:

```
Public Empnum As Integer
Public Name As String*20
```

6. a. Provide data input validation for Program 12-1 to ensure that only months between 1 and 12 are accepted.
   b. Provide data input validation for Program 12-1 to ensure that only days between 1 and 31 are accepted for the months 1, 3, 5, 7, 8, 10, and 12; that only days between 1 and 30 are accepted for the months, 4, 6, 9, and 11; and that only days between 1 and 29 are accepted for month 2.

7. a. Add another member method named convrt to the CLDate class in Program 12-1 that accesses the month, year, and day data members and then returns a long integer that is calculated as *year * 10000 + month * 100 + day*. For example, if the CLDate

is 4/1/1996, the returned value is 19960401. (Dates in this form are useful when performing sorts, because placing the numbers in numerical order automatically places the corresponding `CLDates` in chronological order.)

   b. Include the modified `CLDate` class constructed for Exercise 7a in a complete Visual Basic program.

8. a. Add an additional member method to Program 12-1's class definition named `leapyr` that returns a 1 when the year is a leap year and a 0 when it is not a leap year. A leap year is any year that is evenly divisible by 4 but not evenly divisible by 100, with the exception that all years evenly divisible by 400 are leap years. For example, the year 1996 is a leap year because it is evenly divisible by 4 and not evenly divisible by 100. The year 2000 will be a leap year because it is evenly divisible by 400.

   b. Include the class definition constructed for Exercise 8a in a complete Visual Basic program. The program should display the message "The year is a leap year" or "The year is not a leap year" depending on the `CLDate` object's year value.

9. Modify the `CLDate` class in Program 12-1 to contain a method that compares two `CLDate` objects and returns the larger of the two. The method should be written according to the following algorithm:

Comparison method
   Accept two CLDate values as arguments
   Determine the later CLDate using the following procedure:
      Convert each CLDate into an integer value having the form yymmdd.
         Which can be accomplished using the algorithm described in Exercise 7.
      Compare the corresponding integers for each CLDate.
         The larger integer corresponds to the later CLDate.
   Return the later CLDate

10. a. Add a member method to Program 12-1's class definition named `DayofWeek` that determines the day of the week for any `CLDate` object. An algorithm for determining the day of the week, assuming a date of the form mm/dd/ccyy, known as Zeller's algorithm, is the following:

```
if mm is less than 2
  mm = mm + 12
  ccyy = ccyy - 1
Endif
Set T = dd + Int(26*(mm + 1)/10) + yy + Int( yy/4) + Int(cc/4) - 2 * cc
Set DayofWeek = T Mod 7
If DayofWeek is less than 0 then DayofWeek = DayofWeek + 1
```

      Using this algorithm `DayofWeek` will have a value of 0 if the `CLDate` is a Saturday, 1 if a Sunday, etc.

   b. Include the class definition constructed for Exercise 10a in a complete Visual Basic program. The program should display the name of the day (Sun, Mon, Tue, etc.) for the `CLDate` object being tested.

12.2 Initializing and Terminating Events

For each class, Visual Basic permits two event procedures: **Initialize** and **Terminate**. The first time a line of code that refers to a class object is executed, memory is allocated for the object and a class initialization event occurs. The header line for this event procedure is

```
Private Sub Class_Initialize()
```

Any code that is placed in this event procedure is executed once, when the object is created, prior to the execution of any other method. As indicated by the event procedure's header line, it accepts no parameters. To access this procedure, select the **Initialize** procedure in the class's Code window Class object, as shown in Figure 12-12. The Class object is always listed under the Class object in the Code window.

As an example, consider the following **Initialize** event code added to our CLDate class:

```
Private Sub Class_Initialize()
  Month = 1
  Day = 1
  Year = 2001
  MsgBox ("*** A CLDate object has being initialized ***")
End Sub
```

When any CLDate object is created, this Initialize event code is automatically called. For example, if we create a CLDate object named firstdate, the data members of this object will be initialized to

```
firstdate.Month = 1
firstdate.Day = 1
firstdate.Year = 2001
```

In addition, we have included a Message box display within the **Initialize** event code so you can see when the event procedure is actually called. Program 12-2, which uses the same form module as Program 12-1, can be used to test this **Initialize** event. When Program 12-2 is run, the Message box does not immediately appear. However, if the cmdDisplay button is the first button pushed, it will execute a line of code that refers to firstdate. As this is the first time this object is referenced, it is created and the **Initialize** event procedure is called, resulting in the display shown in Figure 12-13.

The intended purpose of the **Initialize** event procedure is to initialize a new object's data members. Although this event procedure can be used to perform other tasks when it is called, its use should generally be restricted to performing data member initialization. In other programming languages, the procedure used to initialize an object's member variables when an object

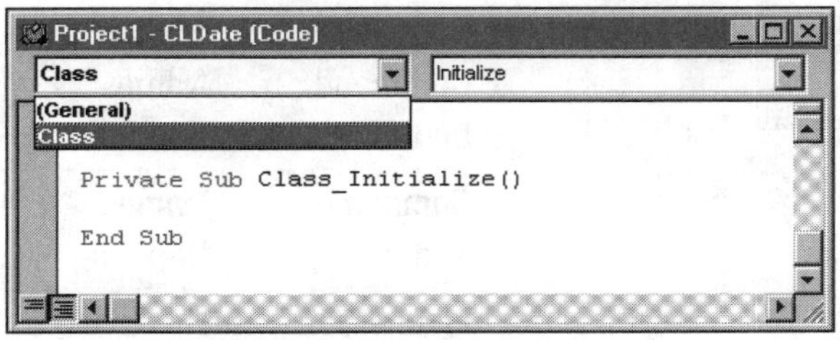

Figure 12-12
The Initialize Event in the Code Window

Figure 12-13
The Activation of the Initialize Event

Figure 12-14
An Example of a Terminate Event
Procedure

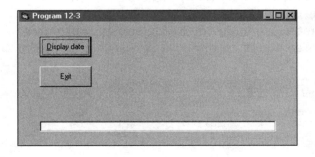

is created, is referred to as a *constructor*. As such, the **Initialize** event procedure is effectively Visual Basic's constructor procedure.

The counterpart to the **Initialize** event is the **Terminate** event. This event procedure is automatically called whenever an object goes out of existence, and is meant to "clean up" any undesirable effects that might be left by the object. The header line for this event procedure, which can be found in the class's Code window for the Class object is

```
Private Sub Class_Terminate()
```

As this header indicates, the **Terminate** event procedure takes no parameters and returns no value. For purposes of illustrating when this event procedure is triggered, we have added the following **Terminate** event procedure to the CLDate class used by Program 12-2.

```
Private Sub Class_Terminate()
  MsgBox ("*** A CLDate object is going out of existence ***")
End Sub
```

When you close an executing version of Program 12-2, the Message box shown in Figure 12-14 will appear.

Arrays of Objects

The importance of the **Initialize** event procedure becomes evident when arrays of objects are created. Since the **Initialize** event is called each time an object is created, this event provides an elegant way of initializing all objects to the same state.

Declaring an array of objects is the same as declaring an array of any built-in type. For example, the declaration

```
Option Base 1
Const NUMELS As Integer = 5
Dim adate(NUMELS) As New CLDate
```

can be used to create five objects, named adate(1) to adate(5), respectively. Member methods for each of these objects are called by listing the object name followed by a dot (.) and the desired method. An example using an array of objects of type CLDate is provided by Program 12-3.

Figure 12-15
The Interface for Program 12-3

Table 12-3	The Properties Table for Program 12-3	
Object	**Property**	**Setting**
Form	Name	frmMain
	Caption	Program 12-3
Command button	Name	cmdDisplay
	Caption	&Display
Command button	Name	cmdExit
	Caption	E&xit
Picture box	Name	picShow
	TabStop	False
	BackColor	White (Palette Tab)

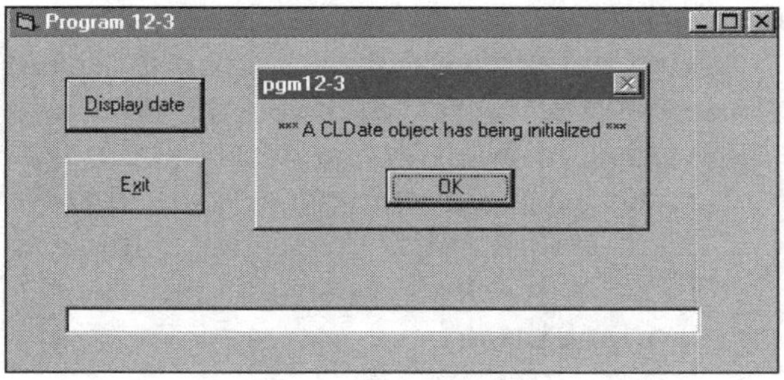

Figure 12-16
A Sample Output Using Program 12-3

Program 12-3's Procedure Code

```
Rem: This is the code in the (declarations) section
Option Explicit
Option Base 1
Const NUMELS As Integer = 5
Dim adate(NUMELS) As New CLDate

Rem: This is the event code
Private Sub cmdDisplay_Click()
  Dim i As Integer
  For i = 1 To NUMELS
    picShow.Print "The date is "; adate(i).showdate()
  Next i
End Sub

Private Sub cmdExit_Click()
  Beep
  End
End Sub
```

When the <u>D</u>isplay Command button is pushed for the first time, five adate objects will be created. Figure 12-16 illustrates how the interface will look at run time as each object is created.

Exercises 12.2

1. Enter and execute Program 12-1 on your computer.

2. Enter and execute Program 12-2 on your computer.

3. a. Construct a class named CLTime that has integer data members named Secs, Mins, and Hours. The class should contain two methods named settime and showtime that can be used for setting and displaying a CLTime object and include an **Initialize** event that initializes all data members to 0.

   b. Include the class constructed in Exercise 3a in a complete working program.

4. a. Write a class named Complex that has floating-point members named Real and Imaginary. The class should contain two methods named setcomplex and showcomplex that can be used for setting and displaying a Complex object and include an **Initialize** event that initializes all data members to 0.

   b. Include the class constructed in Exercise 4a in a complete working program.

5. a. Construct a class named CLCircle that has integer data members named Xcenter and Ycenter and a floating-point data

member named `Radius`. The class should contain two methods named `setradius` and `setcenter` to set the radius and center values, respectively, and two methods named `showradius` and `showcenter` to display these values. The class should also include an **Initialize** event that initializes all data members to 1.

   b. Include the class constructed in Exercise 5a in a complete working program.

6. a. Construct a class named `System` that has string data members named `Computer`, `Printer`, and `Screen`, each capable of holding 30 characters, and floating-point data members named `Comp_price`, `Print_price`, and `Scrn_price`. The class should include an **Initialize** event procedure that initializes all strings to the NULL value and all numeric values to 0. Include methods that permit a programmer to both set and display member values.

   b. Include the class constructed in Exercise 6a in a complete working program.

7. a. Construct a class named `Student` consisting of an integer student identification number, an array of five floating-point grades, and an integer representing the total number of grades entered. The **Initialize** event for this class should initialize all `Student` data members to zero. Included in the class should be member procedures to (1) enter a student ID number, (2) enter a single test grade and update the total number of grades entered, and (3) compute an average grade and display the student ID followed by the average grade.

   b. Include the class constructed in Exercise 7a within the context of a complete program. Your program should declare two objects of type `Student` and accept and display data for the two objects to verify operation of the member procedures.

12.3 ▶ Access Procedures Let and Get

An *access procedure*, which is frequently referred to simply as an *accessor*, is any member method that accesses a class's private data members. For example, the procedure `showdate` in the `CLDate` class is an access procedure. Such procedures are extremely important because they provide the only public means of access to a class's data members.

When constructing a class, it is important to provide a complete set of access procedures. Each access procedure does not have to return a data member's exact value, but it should return a useful representation of the value. For example, assume that a date such as 12/25/98 is stored as a long integer member variable in the form 1982512. Although an accessor procedure could display this value, a more useful representation would typically be either 12/25/98, or December 25, 1998.

Besides being used for output, accessors can also provide a means of data input. For example, the `setdate` procedure in the `CLDate` class is an example of an input access procedure. Although the **Initialize** and **Terminate** procedures also access a class's private data members, as event procedures these two are not formally classified as accessors.

Accessor procedures are considered so important that Visual Basic provides three procedures specifically designed for access purposes, referred to as **Property** procedures. The two most commonly used of these **Property** procedures are listed in Table 12-4.

Table 12-4	Visual Basic's Property Procedures	
Name	**Description**	**Usage**
Property Get	Read a data member's value.	variable = objectname.procedure()
Property Let	Assign a data member's value.	objectname.procedure = expression

As an example of constructing property **Get** and **Let** procedures, consider the CLDate class that we have been using throughout this chapter. For convenience, this class's data member declaration section is repeated below:

```
Rem: The CLDate class data declaration section
Private Month As Integer
Private Day As Integer
Private Year As Integer
```

For this class we will construct three property **Let** and **Get** procedures, one pair for each data member. For the Month data member, a suitable pair of procedures is

```
Property Let accessMonth(mm As Integer)
  Month = mm
End Property

Property Get accessMonth() As Integer
  accessMonth = Month
End Property
```

The first item to notice about these two procedures is that they both share the same name, which is typical but not required. The second item to notice is that the **Get** procedure *always* takes one less parameter than its related **Let** procedure. Here the **Let** procedure takes one parameter that is assigned to the Month data member and the related **Get** procedure returns the value of this data member. This brings up the third item required by a related pair of **Let** and **Get** procedures: the data type of the **Get** procedure *must be* the same as the data type of the last parameter in the related **Let** procedure. Our last version of the CLDate class, with **Property Let** and **Get** procedures for all data members, is listed as Version 3 below:

The CLDate Class—Version 3

```
Option Explicit
Private Month As Integer
Private Day As Integer
Private Year As Integer

Property Let accessMonth(mm As Integer)
  Month = mm
End Property

Property Get accessMonth() As Integer
  accessMonth = Month
End Property
```

continued

```
Property Let accessDay(dd As Integer)
  Day = dd
End Property

Property Get accessDay() As Integer
  accessDay = Day
End Property

Property Let accessYear(yy As Integer)
Rem: Make sure that Year is between 00 and 99
  If yy < 1000 Then
    MsgBox("Enter a 4-digit Year")
  Else
    Year = yyyy
  End If
End Property

Property Get accessYear() As Integer
  accessYear = Year
End Property

Private Sub Class_Initialize()
  Month = 1
  Day = 1
  Year = 2001
End Sub
```

Except for the **Property Let** procedure for the Year data member, all of the **Let** and **Get** procedures are straightforward variations of the accessMonth procedures. The **Property Let** procedure for the Year data member includes additional processing to ensure that the final assigned value is a four-digit year.

Program 12-4 uses this version of the CLDate class within a complete application. The interface for this program is shown in Figure 12-17.

Program 12-4's Procedure Code

```
Option Explicit
Dim firstdate As New CLDate

Private Sub cmdDDay_Click()
  picShow.Cls
  picShow.Print "The Day has been set to"; firstdate.accessDay()
End Sub

Private Sub cmdDMonth_Click()
  picShow.Cls
  picShow.Print "The Month has been set to"; firstdate.accessMonth()
End Sub

Private Sub cmdDYear_Click()
  picShow.Cls
  picShow.Print "The Year has been set to"; firstdate.accessYear()
End Sub

Private Sub cmdExit_Click()
  Beep
  End
End Sub
```

continued on page 610

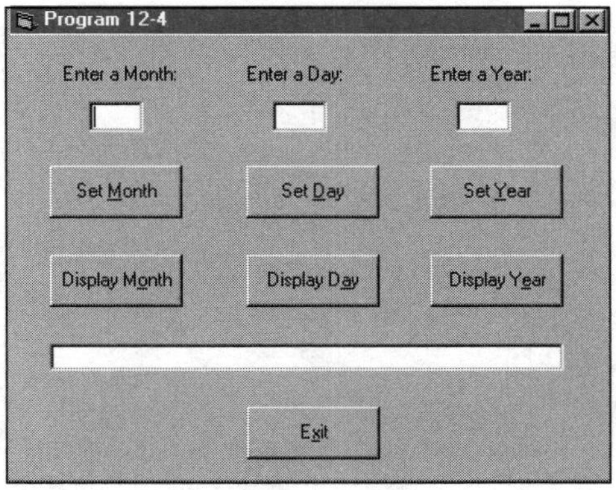

Figure 12-17
Program 12-4's Interface

Table 12-5 Program 12-4's Properties Table

Object	Property	Setting
Form	Name	frmMain
	Caption	Program 12-4
Label	Name	lblMonth
	Caption	Enter a Month:
Label	Name	lblDay
	Caption	Enter a Day:
Label	Name	lblRate
	Caption	Enter a Year:
Text box	Name	txtMonth
	Text	(Blank)
	BackColor	White (Palette Tab)
Text box	Name	txtDay
	Text	(Blank)
	BackColor	White (Palette Tab)
Text box	Name	txtYear
	Text	(Blank)
	BackColor	White (Palette Tab)
Command button	Name	cmdSMonth
	Caption	Set &Month
Command button	Name	cmdSDay
	Caption	Set &Day
Command button	Name	cmdSYear
	Caption	Set &Year
Command button	Name	cmdDMonth
	Caption	Display M&onth
Command button	Name	cmdDDay
	Caption	Display D&ay
Command button	Name	cmdDYear
	Caption	Display Y&ear
Command button	Name	cmdExit
	Caption	E&xit
Picture box	Name	picShow
	TabStop	False
	BackColor	White (Palette Tab)

```
                    Private Sub cmdSDay_Click()
                      firstdate.accessDay = Val(txtDay.Text)
                    End Sub

                    Private Sub cmdSMonth_Click()
                      firstdate.accessMonth = Val(txtMonth.Text)
                    End Sub

                    Private Sub cmdSYear_Click()
                      firstdate.accessYear = Val(txtYear.Text)
                    End Sub

                    Private Sub txtDay_GotFocus()
                      picShow.Cls
                    End Sub

                    Private Sub txtMonth_GotFocus()
                      picShow.Cls
                    End Sub

                    Private Sub txtYear_GotFocus()
                      picShow.Cls
                    End Sub
```

It is worthwhile noting in Program 12-4's procedure code that the actual calls to both **Let** and **Get Property** procedures do not use a conventional **Call** statement. Rather, these procedures are called following the syntax listed in Table 12-5 on page 609.

Exercises **12.3**

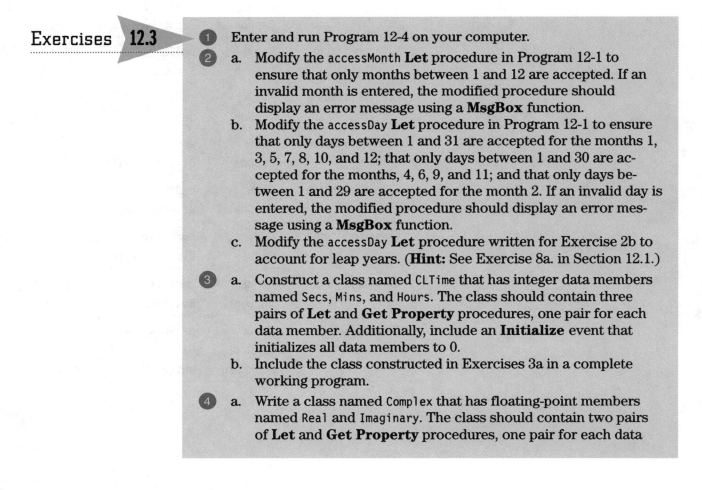

1. Enter and run Program 12-4 on your computer.
2. a. Modify the accessMonth **Let** procedure in Program 12-1 to ensure that only months between 1 and 12 are accepted. If an invalid month is entered, the modified procedure should display an error message using a **MsgBox** function.
   b. Modify the accessDay **Let** procedure in Program 12-1 to ensure that only days between 1 and 31 are accepted for the months 1, 3, 5, 7, 8, 10, and 12; that only days between 1 and 30 are accepted for the months, 4, 6, 9, and 11; and that only days between 1 and 29 are accepted for the month 2. If an invalid day is entered, the modified procedure should display an error message using a **MsgBox** function.
   c. Modify the accessDay **Let** procedure written for Exercise 2b to account for leap years. (**Hint:** See Exercise 8a. in Section 12.1.)
3. a. Construct a class named CLTime that has integer data members named Secs, Mins, and Hours. The class should contain three pairs of **Let** and **Get Property** procedures, one pair for each data member. Additionally, include an **Initialize** event that initializes all data members to 0.
   b. Include the class constructed in Exercises 3a in a complete working program.
4. a. Write a class named Complex that has floating-point members named Real and Imaginary. The class should contain two pairs of **Let** and **Get Property** procedures, one pair for each data

member. Additionally, include an **Initialize** event that initializes all data members to 0.

    b. Include the class constructed in Exercise 4a in a complete working program.

5 a. Construct a class named CLCircle that has integer data members named Xcenter and Ycenter and a floating-point data member named Radius. The class should contain two methods named setradius and setcenter to set the radius and center values, respectively, and two methods named showradius and showcenter to display these values. Additionally, the class should include an **Initialize** event that initializes all data members to 1.

    b. Include the class constructed in Exercise 5a in a complete working program.

12.4 ▸ An Example: Constructing an Elevator Object

Now that we have an understanding of how classes are constructed and the terminology used in describing them, let us apply this knowledge to a particular application. In this application we simulate the operation of an elevator. We assume that the elevator can travel between the first and fifteenth floors of a building and that the location of the elevator must be known at all times.

For this application the location of the elevator corresponds to its current floor position and is represented by an integer variable ranging between 1 and 15. The value of this variable, which we will name Curfloor, for current floor, effectively represents the current state of the elevator. An **Initialize** event procedure will set the initial floor position when a new elevator is put into service, and a request function will change the elevator's position (state) to a new floor. Putting an elevator in service is accomplished by declaring a single class instance an object of type Elevator, while

---

PROGRAMMERS NOTES

Encapsulation, Inheritance, and Polymorphism

An object-based language is one in which data and operations can be incorporated together in such a way that data values can be isolated and accessed through the specified class functions. The ability to bind the data members with operations in a single unit is referred to as *encapsulation*. In Visual Basic encapsulation is provided by its class capability.

For a language to be classified as object-oriented it must also provide inheritance and polymorphism. *Inheritance* is the capability to derive one class from another. A derived class is a completely new data type that incorporates all the data members and member functions of the original class with any new data and function members unique to itself. The class used as the basis for the derived type is referred to as the *base* or *parent* class and the derived data type is referred to as the *derived* or *child* class.

Polymorphism permits the same method name to invoke one operation in objects of a parent class and a different operation in objects of a derived class.

requesting a new floor position is equivalent to pushing an elevator button. To accomplish this, a suitable class definition is

```
Rem: Class Elevator

Rem: Data Declaration Section
Const MAXFLOOR As Integer = 15
Private Curfloor As Integer

Rem: Methods Implementation Section
Public Sub request(newfloor As Integer)
  If newfloor < 1 Or newfloor > MAXFLOOR Then
    frmMain.picError.Print "An invalid floor has been selected"
  ElseIf newfloor > Curfloor Then
    frmMain.picFloor.Print "Starting at floor"; Curfloor
    Do While newfloor > Curfloor
      Curfloor = Curfloor + 1
      frmMain.picFloor.Print "Going Up - now at floor"; Curfloor
    Loop
    frmMain.picFloor.Print "Stopping at floor"; Curfloor
  ElseIf newfloor < Curfloor Then
    frmMain.picFloor.Print "Starting at floor"; Curfloor
    Do While newfloor < Curfloor
      Curfloor = Curfloor - 1
      frmMain.picFloor.Print "Going Up - now at floor"; Curfloor
    Loop
    frmMain.picFloor.Print "Stopping at floor"; Curfloor
  End If
End Sub

Rem: Initialize Event Code
Private Sub Class_Initialize()
  Curfloor = 1
End Sub
```

Notice that we have declared one data member, Curfloor, and implemented one method and an initializing event procedure. The data member, Curfloor is used to store the current floor position of the elevator. As a private data member, it can only be accessed through member procedures and functions. The single member procedure named request defines the external services provided by each Elevator object and the **Initialize** procedure is used to initialize the starting floor position of each Elevator type object. The **Initialize** procedure is straightforward. Whenever an Elevator object is first accessed it is initialized to the first floor.

The request procedure defined in the implementation section is more complicated and provides the class's primary service; it is used to alter the position of the elevator. Essentially this procedure consists of an **If-Else** statement having three parts: (1) if an incorrect service is requested, an error message is displayed; (2) if a floor above the current position is selected, the elevator is moved up; and (3) if a floor below the current position is selected, the elevator is moved down. For movement up or down, the procedure uses a **Do/While** loop to increment the position one floor at a time, and reports the elevator's movement to a picFloor Picture box object located on frmMain. It is worth noting two points with respect to the notation used here.

First, since the picFloor control is not on the current class module (class modules cannot contain visual objects), the complete designation for where the object resides must be given. Hence the full name of the object, frmMain.picFloor, must precede the **Print** method name. This is the standard

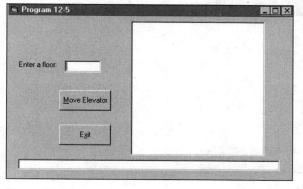

Figure 12-18
Program 12-5's Interface

Table 12-6	Program 12-5's Properties Table	
Object	**Property**	**Setting**
Form	Name	frmMain
	Caption	Program 12-5
Label	Name	lblFloor
	Caption	Enter a floor:
Text box	Name	txtFloor
	Text	(Blank)
	BackColor	White (Palette Tab)
Command button	Name	cmdFloor
	Caption	&Move Elevator
Command button	Name	cmdExit
	Caption	E&xit
Picture box	Name	picFloor
	TabStop	False
	BackColor	White (Palette Tab)
Picture box	Name	picError
	TabStop	False
	BackColor	White (Palette Tab)

way of having code on one module access objects and methods defined on a different module. Next, the request method is over ambitious precisely because it references an object not contained within the class. Theoretically, a class should be self-contained and not require any object outside of the class for it to be executed correctly. In Exercise 4 we explore how to reconstruct this class to adhere to this requirement.

Program 12-5 includes this class in a working program. The interface for this program is shown in Figure 12-18.

Program 12-5's Procedure Code

```
Option Explicit
Private a As New Elevator

Private Sub txtFloor_GotFocus()
  picError.Cls
End Sub

Private Sub cmdFloor_Click()
  picFloor.Cls
  a.request (Val(txtFloor.Text))
End Sub

Private Sub cmdExit_Click()
  Beep
  End
End Sub
```

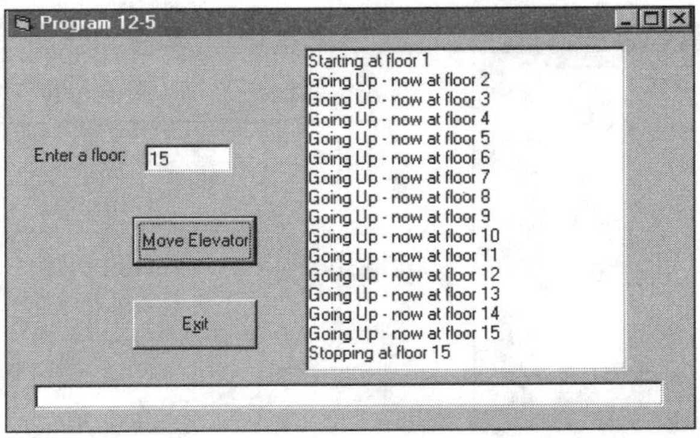

Figure 12-19
A Sample Run Using
Program 12-5

Program 12-5's procedure code is extremely simple, precisely because all the work in moving the elevator is contained within the class's request method. Notice that this method is called in the standard way by placing a period and an object's name before the method's name. A sample run using Program 12-5 is illustrated in Figure 12-19.

The basic requirements of object-oriented programming are evident in even as simple a program as Program 12-5. Before a form module can be written, a useful class must be constructed. This is typical of programs that use objects. For such programs, the design process is front-loaded with the requirement that careful consideration of the class—its declaration and implementation—be given. Code contained in the implementation section effectively removes code that would otherwise be part of a form's responsibility. Thus, any program that uses the object does not have to repeat the implementation details within its form's procedures. Rather, the form's procedures are only concerned with sending arguments to its objects to activate them appropriately. The details of how the object responds to the arguments and how the state of the object is retained are hidden within the class construction.

Exercises 12.4

1. Enter Program 12-5 in your computer and execute it.

2. Modify Program 12-5 to put a second elevator in service. Have this second elevator move to the twelfth floor and then move to the fifth floor.

3. Verify that the **Initialize** event procedure in Program 12-5 is called by adding a message within it that is displayed each time a new object is created. Run your program to ensure its operation.

4. The Elevator class violates pure class construction rules because one of its methods accesses an object that is not in the class. Modify the Elevator class to remove this violation. To do so, provide the class with a procedure named oneup and onedown, which add and subtract 1, to and from the current value of Curfloor. Then modify the cmdMove_Click procedure to incorporate an **If-Else** similar to the one used in request.

5. a. Modify the CLDate class used in Program 12-4 to include a nextDay procedure that increments a date by one day. Test your procedure to ensure that it correctly increments days into a new month and into a new year.

b. Modify the `CLDate` class used in Program 12-4 to include a `priorDay` function that decrements a date by one day. Test your function to ensure that it correctly decrements days into a prior month and into a prior year.

6 a. In Exercise 3 of the previous section, you were asked to construct a `CLTime` class. For this class include a `tick` procedure that increments the time by one second. Test your procedure to ensure that it correctly increments into a new minute and a new hour.

   b. Modify the `Time` class written for Exercise 6a to include a `detick` procedure that decrements the time by one second. Test your procedure to ensure that it correctly decrements time into a prior hour and into a prior minute.

7 a Construct a class that can be used to represent an employee of a company. Each employee is defined by an integer ID number, a name consisting of no more than 30 characters, a floating-point pay rate, and the maximum number of hours the employee should work each week. The services provided by the class should be the ability to enter data for a new employee, the ability to change data for a new employee, and the ability to display the existing data for a new employee.

   b. Include the class definition created for Exercise 7a in a working Visual Basic program that asks the user to enter data for three employees and displays the entered data.

   c. Modify the program written for Exercise 7b to include a menu that offers the user the following choices:

      1. Add an Employee.
      2. Modify Employee data.
      3. Delete an Employee.
      4. Exit this menu.

   The program should be able to initiate appropriate action to implement a user's choice.

8 a. Construct a class that can be used to represent types of food. A type of food is classified as basic or prepared. Basic foods are further classified as either Dairy, Meat, Fruit, Vegetable, or Grain. The services provided by the class should be the ability to enter data for a new food, the ability to change data for a new food, and the ability to display the existing data for a new food.

   b. Include the class definition created for Exercise 8a in a working Visual Basic program that asks the user to enter data for four food items and displays the entered data.

   c. Modify the program written for Exercise 8b to include a menu that offers the user the following choices:

      1. Add a Food item.
      2. Modify a Food item.
      3. Delete a Food item.
      4. Exit this menu.

   In response to a choice, the program should initiate appropriate action to implement the choice.

12.5 ▶ Knowing About: Insides and Outsides

Just as the concept of an algorithm is central to procedures, the concept of encapsulation is central to objects. In this section we present this encapsulation concept using an inside-outside analogy, which should help your understanding of what object-oriented programming is all about.

In programming terms, an object's attributes are described by data, such as the length and width of a rectangle, and the operations that can be applied to the attributes are described by procedures and functions.

As a practical example of this, assume that we will be writing a program that can deal a hand of cards. From an object-oriented approach, one of the objects we must model is clearly a deck of cards. For our purposes, the attribute of interest for the card deck is that it contains 52 cards, consisting of four suits (hearts, diamonds, spades, and clubs), with each suit consisting of thirteen pip values (ace to ten, Jack, Queen, and King).

Now consider the behavior of our deck of cards, which consists of the operations that can be applied to the deck. At a minimum we will want the ability to shuffle the deck and deal single cards. Let's now see how this simple example relates to encapsulation using an inside-outside concept.

A useful visualization of the inside-outside concept is to consider an object as a boiled egg, as shown in Figure 12-20. Notice that the egg consists of three parts: a very inside yolk, a less inside white surrounding the yolk, and an outside shell, which is the only part of the egg visible to the world.

In terms of our boiled egg model, the attributes and behavior of an object correspond to the yolk and white, respectively, which are inside the egg. The innermost protected area of an object, its data attributes, can be compared to the egg yolk. Surrounding the data attributes, as an egg's white surrounds its yolk, are the operations we choose to incorporate within an object. Finally, in this analogy, the interface to the outside world, the shell, represents how a user gets to invoke the object's internal procedures.

The egg model, with its eggshell interface separating the inside of the egg from the outside, is useful precisely because it so clearly depicts the separation between what should be contained inside an object and what should be seen from the outside. This separation forms an essential element in object-oriented programming. Let's see why this is so.

From an inside-outside perspective, an object's data attributes, the selected algorithms for controlling operations, and the ways these algorithms are actually implemented are always inside issues, hidden from the view of

Figure 12-20
The Boiled Egg Object Model

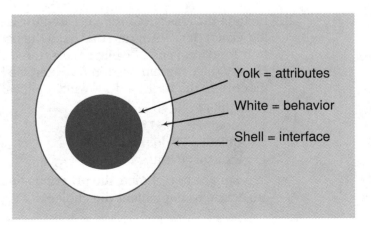

Yolk = attributes

White = behavior

Shell = interface

object users. On the other hand, the way a user or another object can actually activate an inside procedure, is an outside issue.

Now let's apply this concept to our card deck example. First, consider how we might represent cards in the deck. Any of the following attributes (and there are others) could be used to represent a card:

1. Two integer variables, one representing a suit (a number from 1 to 4) and one representing a value (a number from 1 to 13).

2. One character value and one integer value: the character represents a card's suit and the integer represents a card's value.

3. One integer variable having a value from 0 to 51: the expression **Int** (number / 13 + 1) provides a number from 1 to 4, which represents the suit, and the expression (number Mod 13 + 1) represents a card value from 1 to 13.

Whichever one we decide on, however, is not relevant to the outside. The specific way we choose to represent a card is an inside issue to be decided by the designer of the deck object. From the outside, all that is of concern is that we have access to a deck consisting of 52 cards having the necessary suits and pip values.

The same is true for the operations we decide to provide as part of our card deck object. Consider just the shuffling for now.

There are a number of algorithms for producing a shuffled deck. For example, we could use Visual Basic's random number function, **Rnd**, or create our own random number generator. Again, the selected algorithm is an inside issue to be determined by the designer of the deck. The specifics of which algorithm is selected and how it is applied to the attributes we have chosen for each card in the deck are not relevant from the object's outside. For purposes of illustration, assume that we decide to use Visual Basic's **Rnd** function to produce a randomly shuffled deck.

If we use the first attribute set previously given, each card in a shuffled deck is produced using **Rnd** at least twice; once to create a random number from 1 to 4 for the suit, and then again to create a random number from 1 to 13 for the card's pip value. This sequence must be done to construct 52 different attribute sets, with no duplicates allowed.

If, on the other hand, we use the second attribute set previously given, a shuffled deck can be produced in exactly the same fashion as above, with one modification: the first random number (from 1 to 4) must be changed into a character to represent the suit.

Finally, if we use the third representation for a card, we need to use **Rnd** once for each card, to produce 52 random numbers from 0 to 51, with no duplicates allowed.

The important point here is that the selection of an algorithm and how it will be applied to an object's attributes are implementation issues and *implementation issues are always inside issues*. A user of the card deck, who is outside, does not need to know how the shuffling is done. All the user of the deck must know is how to produce a shuffled deck. In practice, this means that the user is supplied with sufficient information to correctly invoke the shuffle function. This corresponds to the interface, or outer shell of the egg.

Abstraction and Encapsulation

The distinction between insides and outsides relates directly to the concepts of abstraction and encapsulation. Abstraction means concentrating on what an object is and does, before making any decisions about how the object will be implemented. Thus, abstractly, we define a deck and the operations we want to provide. (Clearly, if our abstraction is to be useful, it had better capture the attributes and operations of a real-world deck.) Once we have decided on the attributes and operations, we can actually implement them.

Encapsulation means separating and hiding the implementation details of the chosen abstract attributes and behavior from outside users of the object. The external side of an object should provide only the necessary interface to users of the object for activating internal procedures. Imposing a strict inside-outside discipline when creating objects is really another way of saying that the object successfully encapsulates all implementation details. In our deck-of-cards example, encapsulation means that users need never know how we have internally modeled the deck or how an operation, such as shuffling, is performed; they only need to know how to activate the given operations.

Code Reuse and Extensibility

A direct advantage of an inside-outside object approach is that it encourages both code reuse and extensibility. This is a result of having all interactions between objects centered on the outside interface and hiding all implementation details within the object's inside.

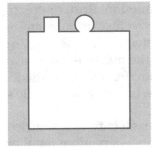

Figure 12-21
Using an Object's Interface

For example, consider the object shown in Figure 12-21. Here, any of the two object's operations can be activated by correctly stimulating either the circle or square on the outside. In practice the stimulation is simply a method call. We have used a circle and square to emphasize that two different methods are provided for outside use. In our card deck example, activation of one method might produce a shuffled deck, while activation of the other method might result in a card suit and pip value being returned from the object.

Now assume that we want to alter the implementation of an existing operation or add more functionality to our object. *As long as the existing outside interface is maintained, the internal implementation of any and all operations can be changed without the user ever being aware that a change took place.* This is a result of encapsulating the attribute data and operations within an object.

In addition, as long as the interface to existing operations is not changed, new operations can be added as they are needed. From the outside world, it looks like all that is being added is another function call accessing the inside attributes and modifying them in a new way.

12.6 Common Programming Errors

The more common programming errors initially associated with the construction and use of classes are

1. Failing to make data members **Private**.
2. Failing to make member methods **Public**.
3. Failing to include an appropriate **Initialize** event procedure.
4. Using a **Call** statement to access the **Let** and **Get Property** procedures.

12.7 Chapter Review

Key Terms

abstract data type	data members	instantiation
class	data type	intrinsic program library
class library	declaration section	member methods
class members	implementation section	object
constructor	inheritance	polymorphism

Summary

1. A *class* is a programmer-defined data type. *Objects* of a class may be defined and have the same relationship to their class as variables do to Visual Basic's built-in data types.

2. A class definition consists of a declaration and implementation section. The most common form of a class definition is

```
Rem: Data Declaration Section
     Declaration of all variables
Rem: Methods Implementation Section
     Procedures and Functions that
     can be used on the above
     declared variables
```

   The variables, procedures, and functions declared in the class declaration section are collectively referred to as *class members*. The variables are individually referred to as class *data members* and the procedures and functions as class *member methods*.

3. The keywords **Private** and **Public** are formally referred to as *access specifiers*, because they specify the access permitted to the class's variables and procedures. The **Private** keyword specifies that a class member is private to the class and can only be accessed by member methods. The **Public** keyword specifies that a class member may be accessed from outside the class. Generally, all data members should be specified as **Private** and all member methods as **Public**. This ensures that variables declared as **Private** within the Data Declaration section can only be accessed through member methods, and that the member methods are available and can be called from outside the class.

4. Objects are created using the **New** keyword. For example, if CLDate is the name of a class, the statement

```
Dim firstdate As New CLDate
```

   declares firstdate as an object of type CLDate.

5. Visual Basic provides two event procedures for classes: **Initialize** and **Terminate**. The **Initialize** event procedure is automatically called when an object is first referenced. Its purpose is to initialize each created object. The **Terminate** event procedure is called when an object goes out of scope.

6. An *access procedure* is any member method that accesses a class's private data members. Two access procedures provided by Visual Basic are the **Let** and **Get Property** procedures. The purpose of the **Get** procedure is to read a data member's value, while the **Let** procedure is used to

assign a value to a data member. Typically, **Let** and **Get** procedures are used in pairs that share a common property name. The **Get Property** procedure is called using the syntax

```
variable = objectname.procedure()
```

while the **Let** property procedure is called using the syntax

```
objectname.procedure = expression
```

Test Yourself–Short Answer

1. In an object-oriented language, the data and the procedures are bound together in the _____.
2. A data type is defined as a combination of data and the _____.
3. An abstract data type is more frequently called a _____.
4. In what type of module would you find a class definition?
5. A Class module consists only of code and is broken down into two sections, the _____ section and the _____ section.
6. The filename extension for a class module is _____.
7. A class module creates a user-declared class which is referred to as an _____.
8. The keyword that is used to declare an object is _____.
9. When an object is created from a class, it is referred to as an _____, which gives the class instantiation.
10. Another word for instantiated is _____.

Programming Projects

1. Using **Property Get** and **Let** procedures (see Program 12-4) create a class named CLName and the form shown in Figure 12-22 that permit the following operations:

   a. Assign a value to a CLName object's FirstName member (**Property Let** procedure).

   b. Assign a value to a CLName object's LastName member (**Property Let** procedure).

   c. Read a value from a CLName object's FirstName member (**Property Get** procedure).

   d. Read a value from a CLName object's LastName member (**Property Get** procedure).

   e. Read values from both FirstName and LastName members and concatenate the two together with a space embedded between the names (equivalent to the showdate() method in Program 12-1 in the chapter).

   The First Name and Last Name should be stored in such a way that the first letter of each name is capitalized and the remaining letters of the name are stored in lowercase. The **Property Let** procedures should handle this conversion. (**Hint:** Use the **UCASE**, **LCASE**, and **MID** functions to build the strings for first and last name in the **Let** procedures.) You might create a function to perform the conversion.

Figure 12-22
Form for Exercise 1

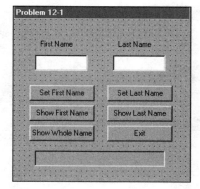

Clicking the form's "Show Whole Name" Command button should call (and display) a method in the class module that joins the first and last names together (e.g., Tommy Melbourne).

2. The following is the repeated description of the Motel 8 project initially described in Section 3.8, Exercise 8:

   A night's stay at Motel 8 costs $30 per adult and $10 per child. There is no discount for multiple nights stay. Additionally, there is a 5% state and local tax that is computed on the sum of the nightly charges.

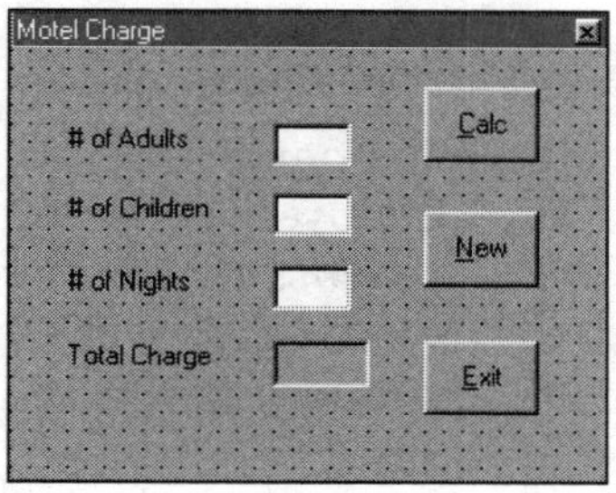

Figure 12-23
Form for Exercise 2

For this description, and using a form like that shown in Figure 12-23, create a class module `CLMotel8` that permits the following operations:

a. Assign a value to a `CNMotel8` object's `Adults` member (**Property Let** procedure).

b. Assign a value to a `CNMotel8` object's `Children` member (**Property Let** procedure).

c. Assign a value to a `CNMotel8` object's `Nights` member (**Property Let** procedure).

d. Read a value that returns the computed charge for a stay at the Motel 8 based upon the values in the `Adults`, `Children`, and `Nights` members (similar to the `showdate()` method in Program 12-1 in this chapter).

Your code can execute the class module's **Property Let** procedures for number of adults, number of children, and number of nights and the class method (`showcharge()`) when the Calc command button is clicked. Pressing the New command button can call the Class **Initialize** event. You should set the `Adults`, `Children`, and `Nights` properties to 0 (in the class module). Additionally, blank all text boxes.

3. All hourly employees at Acme Ltd. are paid time and a half for all hours worked over 40. Create an employee class (`CLEmployee`) that has the following properties:

   ```
   FirstName
   LastName
   HoursWorked
   HourlyRate
   BasePay
   OvertimePay
   GrossTotalPay
   ```

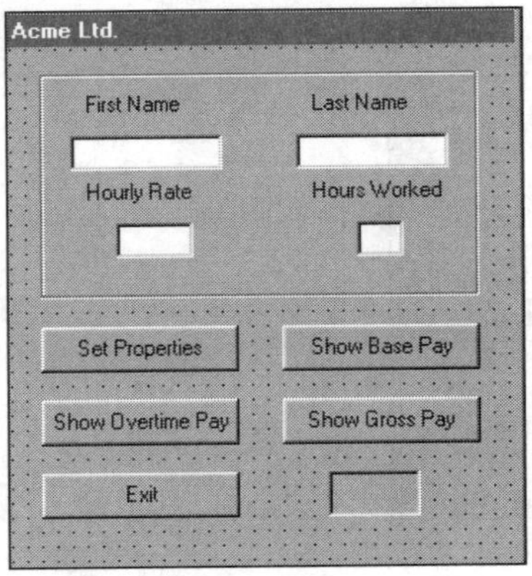

Figure 12-24
Form for Exercise 3

Your project should use a form like that shown in Figure 12-24. It should also create **Property Let** procedures in the class module that permit direct assignment of object properties First Name through Hourly Rate, and assign to the remaining object properties, values based upon the following rules:

a. Base Pay is calculated by multiplying hours worked (up to a maximum of 40) times hourly rate.

b. Overtime Pay is calculated by multiplying hours worked in excess of 40 times hourly rate time 1.5.

c. Gross Total Pay is the sum of Base Pay and Overtime Pay.

The Set Properties command button should call the **Property Let** procedures for the current instance (object) of class CLEmployee (and compute values for the Base Pay, Overtime Pay, and Gross Total Pay properties). Additionally, the Base Pay, Overtime Pay, and Gross Total Pay command buttons should display the appropriate values in the picture control (by calling the class module's **Property Get** procedures).

Keywords

Abs	DoEvents	LBound	Rnd
And	Double	LCase	Second
Array	Else	Let	Seek
Asc	End	Like	Select Case
Atn	EOF	Line Input #	Sin
Beep	Eqv	LOF	Single
Boolean	Erase	Log	Sgn
Byte	Err	Long	Sqr
Call	Error	Loop	Static
CBool	Exit	Me	Stop
CByte	Exp	Minute	Str
CCur	FileLen	Month	String
CDate	Fix	New	Sub
CDbl	For	Next	Switch
CDec	For Each	Not	Tab
Choose	Format	Now	Tan
Chr	Function	Object	Then
CInt	Get	Oct	Time
Clear	GoSub	On	Timer
CLng	GoTo	On Error	TimeSerial
Close	Hex	Open	TimeValue
Const	Hour	Option Base	TypeName
Cos	If	Option Explicit	Ubound
CSng	Imp	Or	Ucase
CStr	Input	Print	Val
Currency	Input #	Print #	Variant
CVErr	Int	Private	VarType
Date	Integer	Property Get	Weekday
DateAdd	Is	Property Let	Wend
DateDiff	IsArray	Property Set	While
DatePart	IsDate	Public	With
DateSerial	IsEmpty	Put	Write #
DateValue	IsError	Raise	Xor
Day	IsMissing	Randomize	Year
Deftype	IsNull	ReDim	
Dim	IsNumeric	Reset	
Do	IsObject	Return	

Standard Control Object Prefixes

Control	Prefix	Example
Form	frm	frmMain
Check box	chk	chkOpenFile
Combo box	cbo	cboFileName
Data-bound combo box	dbc	dbcRecord
Command button	cmd	cmdAverage
Data	dat	datCompany
Directory list box	dir	dirSelect
Drive list box	drv	drvChoice
File list box	fil	filName
Frame	fra	fraCity
Grid	grd	grdSalary
Data-bound grid	dbg	dbgSalary
Horizontal scroll bar	hsb	hsbColor
Image	img	imgBfly
Label	lbl	lblGrade
Line	lin	linStraight
List box	lst	lstPhones
Data-bound list box	dbl	dblPhones
Menu	mnu	mnuChoices
Ole container	ole	oleObject
Option button	opt	optChannel
Picture box	pic	picBfly
Shape	shp	shpSquare
Test box	txt	txtGrade
Timer	tmr	tmrDelay
Vertical scroll bar	vsb	vsbColor

Supported ANSI Character Set

Value	Symbol	Value	Symbol	Value	Symbol	Value	Symbol
0	**	30	**	60	<	90	Z
1	**	31	**	61	=	91	[
2	**	32	(space)	62	>	92	\
3	**	33	!	63	?	93	]
4	**	34	"	64	@	94	^
5	**	35	#	65	A	95	_
6	**	36	$	66	B	96	'
7	**	37	%	67	C	97	a
8	***	38	&	68	D	98	b
9	***	39	'	69	E	99	c
10	***	40	(	70	F	100	d
11	**	41	)	71	G	101	e
12	**	42	*	72	H	102	f
13	***	43	+	73	I	103	g
14	**	44	,	74	J	104	h
15	**	45	-	75	K	105	i
16	**	46	.	76	L	106	j
17	**	47	/	77	M	107	k
18	**	48	0	78	N	108	l
19	**	49	1	79	O	109	m
20	**	50	2	80	P	110	n
21	**	51	3	81	Q	111	o
22	**	52	4	82	R	112	p
23	**	53	5	83	S	113	q
24	**	54	6	84	T	114	r
25	**	55	7	85	U	115	s
26	**	56	8	86	V	116	t
27	**	57	9	87	W	117	u
28	**	58	:	88	X	118	v
29	**	59	;	89	Y	119	w

** These characters are not supported by Microsoft Windows.

*** Values 8, 9, 10, and 13 convert to a backspace, tab, linefeed, and carriage return character, respectively.

Value	Symbol	Value	Symbol	Value	Symbol	Value	Symbol
120	x	154	**	188	_	222	_
121	y	155	**	189	_	223	ß
122	z	156	**	190	_	224	à
123	{	157	**	191	¿	225	á
124	|	158	**	192	À	226	â
125	}	159	**	193	Á	227	ã
126	~	160	(space)	194	Â	228	ä
127	**	161	¡	195	Ã	229	å
128	**	162	¢	196	Ä	230	æ
129	**	163	£	197	Å	231	ç
130	**	164	¤	198	Æ	232	è
131	**	165	¥	199	Ç	233	é
132	**	166	¦	200	È	234	ê
133	**	167	§	201	É	235	ë
134	**	168	¨	202	Ê	236	ì
135	**	169	©	203	Ë	237	í
136	**	170	ª	204	Ì	238	î
137	**	171	«	205	Í	239	ï
138	**	172	¬	206	Î	240	∂
139	**	173	–	207	Ï	241	ñ
140	**	174	®	208	_	242	ò
141	**	175	¯	209	Ñ	243	ó
142	**	176	°	210	Ò	244	ô
143	**	177	±	211	Ó	245	õ
144	**	178	2	212	Ô	246	ö
145	'	179	3	213	Õ	247	÷
146	'	180	´	214	Ö	248	ø
147	**	181	µ	215	x	249	ù
148	**	182	¶	216	Ø	250	ú
149	**	183	·	217	Ù	251	û
150	**	184	,	218	Ú	252	ü
151	**	185	1	219	Û	253	y
152	**	186	º	220	Ü	254	_
153	**	187	»	221	Y	255	ÿ

** These characters are not supported by Microsoft Windows.

Additional Controls

In this appendix we present two of the remaining three controls provided in the standard Toolbox that have not been previously described: the List box and Combo box. The third control, which is the OLE container control, is presented in Appendix F.

If we categorize the standard Toolbox controls into two tiers, the controls presented in Part I (Command button, Text box, Label control, etc.) would be classified as tier one controls, because the vast majority of Visual Basic applications use them. Using this categorization, the remaining controls, including the List and Combo boxes, would be placed within the second tier of controls, in that they are extremely useful and important controls, but are not as widely or commonly used as the tier one controls.

The List Box Control

Figure D-1
The List Box Control

The List box control, whose Toolbox icon is shown in Figure D-1, is extremely useful for presenting a small list of items, such as might be obtained from a file, array, or user-input. At design time, the properties commonly set for a List box by programmers are those listed in Table D-1.

Table D-1		
Property Name	**Value(s)**	**Description**
Columns	0 (default)	Single column with vertical scrolling.
	1	Single column with horizontal scrolling.
	>1	Multi-column with horizontal scrolling.
Sorted	True	Items are added in alphabetical order.
	False (default)	Items are not added in alphabetical order.
MultiSelect	0 (default)	Only a single item in the box can be highlighted.
	1	A Mouse click or Spacebar selects and deselects additional items in the box.
	2	The selection and deselection of items in the box can be made using a SHIFT+Click or SHIFT+arrow keys. In addition, a CTRL+Click selects and deselects list items.

At run time, List boxes provide a number of additional properties that are not available at design time. The most useful of these run-time properties are listed in Table D-2. For example, if we have a List box named `lstItem`, the value of the expression `lstItem.ListCount` is the number of items in the current list.

Table D-2	Commonly Used Run-Time List Box Properties
Property Name	**Description**
List	A string array in which each element is a list item.
ListIndex	The integer index value of the currently selected item.
ListCount	The number of items in the list.
Selected	The Boolean value (True or False) indicating if an item is selected.
Text	The value of the currently highlighted item.

Within a List box, each item is uniquely identified by an integer index value ranging from 0, which corresponds to the first list item, to the value ListCount–1, which corresponds to the last list item. Thus, for a List box named `lstItem`, the value of the property

```
lstItem.List(lstItem.ListIndex)
```

is the item currently highlighted in the List box. As an alternative, this value can also be referenced as

```
lstItem.Text
```

Finally, a List box provides a number of methods, the most commonly used of which are listed in Table D-3.

Table D-3	Commonly Used List Box Methods
Method	**Description**
AddItem	Add an item to the list displayed in the List box.
RemoveItem	Remove an item from the list displayed in the List box.
Clear	Remove all items from the list displayed in the List box.
NewIndex	The index value of the most recently added item.

The general syntax for adding an item to a list is

```
ListBox-Name.AddItem string
```

For example, if we have a List box named `lstItem` and a Text box named `txtItem`, the statement

```
lstItem.AddItem txtItem.Text
```

causes the string contained in the Text box to be added to the list displayed in the List box. If the List box's **Sorted** property is **True**, the added item is inserted in alphabetical order within the existing list; otherwise, the item is appended to the end of the list. In a similar manner the general syntax for removing an item from the list is

```
ListBox-Name.RemoveItem index-number
```

For example, the statement

```
lstItem.RemoveItem lstItem.ListIndex
```

causes the currently highlighted value in the list to be removed. Finally, the general syntax required to clear the list of all items is

```
ListBox-Name.Clear
```

Table D-4	Program D_1's Properties Table	
Object	**Property**	**Setting**
Form	Name	frmMain
	Caption	List Box Application
List box	Name	lstIem
	Sorted	True
Text box	Name	txtItem
	Text	(Blank)
Picture box	Name	picItem
	TabStop	False
Command button	Name	cmdAdd
	Caption	&Add
	TabStop	False
Command button	Name	cmdRemove
	Caption	&Remove
	TabStop	False
Command button	Name	cmdlear
	Caption	&Clear All
	TabStop	False
Command button	Name	cmdExit
	Caption	E&xit
	TabStop	False

Thus, the statement `lstItem.Clear` would cause all items in the List box named `lstItem` to be removed, which would also set the value of `lstItem.ListCount` to 0.

Program D-1, whose design-time interface is shown in Figure D-2, illustrates a typical list handling application.

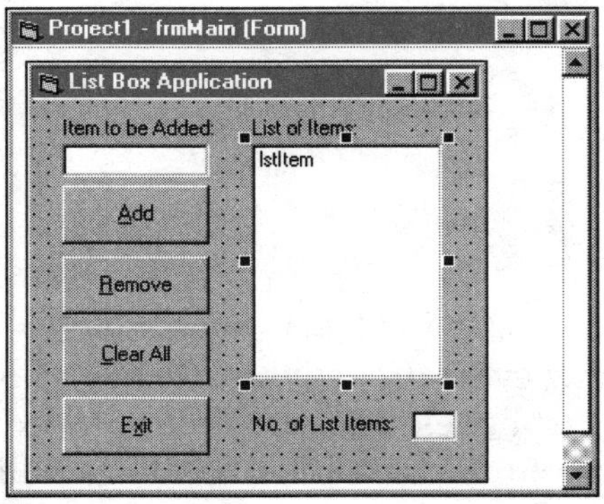

Figure D-2
Program D-1's Design-Time
Interface

Program D-1's Event Code

```
Private Sub Form_Load()
  lstItem.AddItem "Zebra"
  lstItem.AddItem "Lion"
  lstItem.AddItem "Antelope"
  lstItem.AddItem "Monkey"
  lstItem.AddItem "Dog"
  lstItem.AddItem "Cat"
  picItem.Print lstItem.ListCount
  picItem.Refresh
End Sub

Private Sub cmdAdd_Click()
  If Len(txtItem.Text) > 0 Then
    lstItem.AddItem txtItem.Text
    txtItem.Text = ""    ' Clear text box
    txtItem.SetFocus
    picItem.Cls
    picItem.Print lstItem.ListCount
    picItem.Refresh
  Else
    Beep
  End If
End Sub

Private Sub cmdRemove_Click()
  Dim itemno As Integer

  itemno = lstItem.ListIndex
  If itemno >= 0 Then
    lstItem.RemoveItem itemno
    picItem.Cls
    picItem.Print lstItem.ListCount
    picItem.Refresh
  Else
    Beep
  End If
  txtItem.SetFocus
End Sub

Private Sub cmdClear_Click()
  lstItem.Clear
  txtItem.SetFocus
  picItem.Cls
  picItem.Print lstItem.ListCount
  picItem.Refresh
End Sub

Private Sub cmdExit_Click()
  Beep
  End
End Sub
```

Except for the cmdExit_Click() event, which we have used throughout the text, the remaining event procedures use methods and properties specifically applicable to List boxes. The first event procedure, which is the Form_Load event code, uses the **AddItem** method to initialize the list. As a List box's contents cannot be set at design time, the Form_Load event is typically used to initialize a list, as is done in Program D-1. Since the List box's **Sorted** property was set to **True** at design time, the list will appear in the alphabetical order shown in Figure D-3. Notice also that the count displayed in the Picture box is obtained using the **ListCount** property's value.

The cmdAdd_Click event procedure first determines that the Text box contains a string by checking for a string length greater than zero. If such a string is present in the Text box it is added to the list, and the new **ListCount** value is displayed. In a similar manner, the cmdRemove_Click event procedure first determines that an item has actually been selected from the list before the **RemoveItem** method is invoked. Finally, the cmdClear_Click event procedure invokes the **Clear** method to clear all items from the list. In each of these event codes the focus is reset back to the Text box in preparation for another item to be added to the list.

Figure D-3
Program D-1's Initial Run-Time
Interface

The Combo Box Control

Figure D-4
The Combo Box Control

A Combo box control can be considered as a List box control that includes a Text box. Therefore, you should be familiar with the List box control as a prerequisite to understanding a Combo box. The difference in usage between the List box and Combo box is that a List box should be used when the list of choices presented to a user is to be limited, while a Combo box, with one exception, should be used to provide a list of *suggested* choices, to which the user can enter an item that is not on the list.

Additionally, since the list of choices presented in a Combo box is, with one exception, only displayed as a drop-down list when the user clicks on the box's down-facing arrowhead, a Combo box can save a considerable amount of space on a form. Figure D-5 (on page 632) illustrates the three available types of Combo boxes, each of which is described in Table D-5.

Like a List box, all three Combo box types have a **Sorted** property and **AddItem** and **RemoveItem** methods for adding and removing items from the list. Additionally, there is a **Style** property for setting the Combo box's

Table D-5	Available Combo Box Types	
Type	**Name**	**Description**
Style 0	Drop-down Combo box	By either clicking on the down-facing arrowhead or pressing the ALT+↓ when the box has the focus, a Text box and a drop-down list is presented. A user can enter an item in the Text box by either selecting it from the list or by directly typing into the Text box. The entered item does not have to be in the list.
Style 1	Simple	The complete list is displayed at run time only if the box has been made large enough at design time; otherwise, a vertical scroll bar is automatically displayed. As with the Style 0 box, an item can be entered in the Text box by either selecting it from the list or by directly typing into the Text box. The entered item does not have to be in the list.
Style 2	Drop-down List box	This is essentially a List box, whose items are displayed only when the down-facing arrow is clicked. As such, a user cannot type into the Text box, but can only select an item in the list.

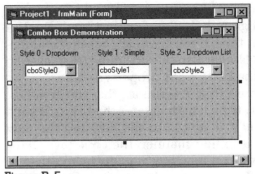

Figure D-5
The Three Types of Combo Boxes
As They Appear at Design Time

Figure D-6
The Combo Boxes at Run-Time

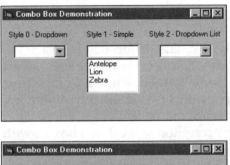

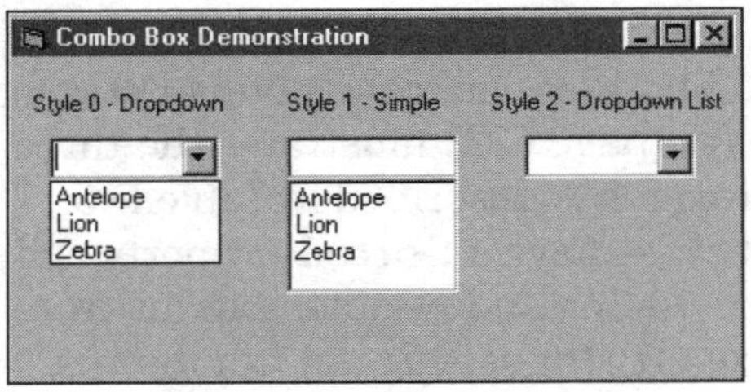

Figure D-7
Activation of the Style 0
Combo Box

type. For example, assuming the three Combo boxes shown in Figure D-5 are named cboStyle0, cboStyle1, and cboStyle2, respectively, the following Form_Load event code can be used to create the same list for each box.

```
Private Sub Form_Load()
    cboStyle0.Text = ""
    cboStyle0.AddItem "Zebra"
    cboStyle0.AddItem "Lion"
    cboStyle0.AddItem "Antelope"
    cboStyle1.Text = ""
    cboStyle1.AddItem "Zebra"
    cboStyle1.AddItem "Lion"
    cboStyle1.AddItem "Antelope"
    cboStyle2.AddItem "Zebra"
    cboStyle2.AddItem "Lion"
    cboStyle2.AddItem "Antelope"
End Sub
```

Assuming that the **Sorted** property for each box has been set to **True**, Figure D-6 shows how each Combo box appears at run time. As is seen in this figure, the lists *do not* initially appear in either the Style 0 and Style 2 boxes; the lists will appear in these boxes when the down-facing arrows are clicked. Note, however, that the Style 1 box is the exception to this drop-down format. The list appears in a Style 1 Combo box as it would in a normal List box, and in this case is in alphabetical order because the **Sorted** property has been set to **True**.

Figure D-7 shows how the list appears when the down arrow is clicked on the Style 0 Combo box. If a user clicks on any item in the list, the selected item will automatically appear in the Text box; alternatively, any item, whether it is in the list or not, can be directly typed into the Text box.

Figure D-8 shows what happens when an item in the Style 1 Combo box is selected. As shown, the selected item is automatically displayed in the Text box. As with the Style 0 box, a user can also enter any item, whether it is in the list or not, directly into the Text box.

Finally, Figure D-9 shows the selection of an item from an activated Style 2 list. As with Style 0, this list is activated by clicking on the down-facing arrowhead. Unlike the Style 0 list, however, a user may not type into the Text box because only items in the list can be selected. Thus, a Style 2 Combo box is effectively a List box presented as a drop-down list.

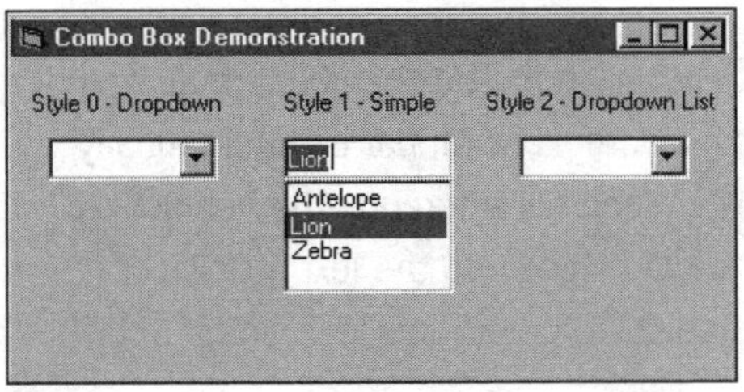

Figure D-8
Selection of a Style 1 List Item

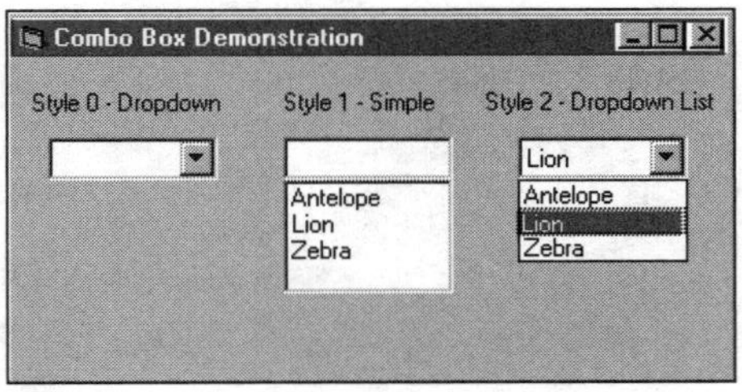

Figure D-9
Selection of a Style 2 List Item

MsgBox Constants

Table E-1 MsgBox Arguments

Constant	Value	Description
vbOKOnly	0	Display OK button only (default).
vbOKCancel	1	Display OK and Cancel buttons.
vbAbortRetryIgnore	2	Display Abort, Retry, and Ignore buttons.
vbYesNoCancel	3	Display Yes, No, and Cancel buttons.
vbYesNo	4	Display Yes and No buttons.
vbRetryCancel	5	Display Retry and Cancel buttons.
vbCritical	16	Display Critical image.
vbQuestion	32	Display Query image.
vbExclamation	48	Display Exclamation image.
vbInformation	64	Display Information image.
vbDefaultButton1	0	The first button is the default (default).
vbDefaultButton2	256	The second button is the default.
vbDefaultButton3	512	The third button is the default.
vbApplicationModal	0	Present an application modal message box (default).
vbSystemModal	4096	Present a system modal message box.

Table E-2 MsgBox Return Values

Constant	Value	Description
vbOK	1	The OK button was pressed.
vbCancel	2	The Cancel button was pressed.
vbAbort	3	The Abort button was pressed.
vbRetry	4	The Retry button was pressed.
vbIgnore	5	The Ignore button was pressed.
vbYes	6	The Yes button was pressed.
vbNo	7	The No button was pressed.

OLE and ActiveX

Prior to Version 5.0, the term OLE, which is an acronym for Object Linking and Embedding, was used in the following three related, but distinct contexts:

1. OLE Container Control—this is the control found on the standard Toolbox, which is sometimes simply referred to as the OLE Control. This control is used to either embed or link an object from another application, such as an Excel spreadsheet, into a Visual Basic application. A Visual Basic application that uses this control is referred to as a *container application*[1]. In Version 6.0 the term OLE retains this same meaning.

2. OLE Custom Controls—these are controls that are not part of the standard Toolbox's built-in controls, but are stored as separate files having either a .vbx or .ocx filename extension. A number of these controls come with Visual Basic and additional custom controls can either be purchased as third-party controls or created from within Visual Basic.[2] Custom controls can be added to the standard Toolbox using the procedure described later in this section. In Version 5.0 these custom controls became, and are now known as, ActiveX controls.

3. OLE Automation—this defines a process in which an object is shared between client and server applications. Specifically, a Visual Basic application, which is known as the *client* application, is permitted to create objects from, and use methods that are part of another application's class. The class definition is contained within a second Visual Basic application known as the *server* application. The server application can either be an OLE DLL, which becomes dynamically linked to the client application, or an OLE EXE, which is a separate executable program. In versions 5.0 and 6.0, OLE DLLs are known as ActiveX DLLs and OLE EXEs are known as ActiveX EXEs.

Thus, in Version 6.0, the term ActiveX refers to a set of components that previously where referred to as OLE custom controls and OLE automation. Additionally, ActiveX components also include a new set of components, referred to as ActiveX documents. These documents are Visual Basic applications for the Internet, and exist in both DLL and EXE forms.

At its most fundamental level, an ActiveX component, be it a control, DLL, EXE, DLL document, or EXE document is simply a unit of executable code that can be created or purchased. All such components can be used and extended by any programming environment that supports the ActiveX specification. This means that an ActiveX component created in Visual

---

[1] More formally, a container application is one that can display another application's objects.

[2] The Learning, Professional, and Enterprise editions provide eight, twenty, and twenty-one custom controls, respectively.

Basic, for example, can be used and extended within a C++ environment that supports the ActiveX technology. In the remaining sections of this appendix we expand on the three types of OLE and ActiveX uses listed above.

Using the OLE Container Control

Figure F-1
The OLE Container Control

The OLE container control, which is shown in Figure F-1, permits you to either link or embed an object into your current Visual Basic application. For example, suppose you have an existing Excel spreadsheet that you want to include within a Visual Basic application. If you link this spreadsheet into your application, both your application and Excel can access and modify the spreadsheet's data. What happens here is that *only one copy* of the spreadsheet is saved, and both applications can retrieve, modify, and save the file. From an operational viewpoint, the Visual Basic application contains a placeholder, or reference to the spreadsheet. When you double-click on the Visual Basic OLE control from within a running Visual Basic application, Excel is activated. In this context Excel becomes a server application running as an OLE EXE, while your Visual Basic application becomes the client application. Linking is extremely useful in maintaining one set of data that can be accessed from several applications.

In contrast to linking, you can tell the OLE container control to embed an object, such as a spreadsheet. In this case, an actual copy, or image, of the spreadsheet is stored as part of your application. Here, no other application has access to the data in the embedded object. As you might imagine, embedded objects can greatly increase the size of your Visual Basic files.

When you add an OLE control to your Visual Basic application, the OLE Dialog window shown in Figure F-2 will appear (you can always activate this dialog by clicking the right mouse button when the container control is active). As shown in Figure F-2, we have selected a Microsoft Excel Spreadsheet as the Object Type. By clicking the Create from File radio button, the dialog shown in Figure F-3 will appear.[3]

In Figure F-3 we have designated the spreadsheet with the full path name `C:\Program File\Microsoft Visual Basic\test1.xls` and also checked the Display As Icon Check box. Checking this box means that an icon of Excel will appear in the OLE container control rather than the spreadsheet.

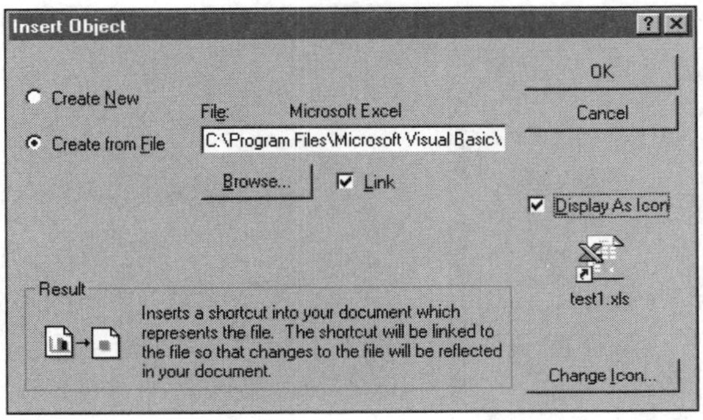

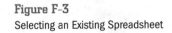

Figure F-2
The Initial OLE Container Dialog

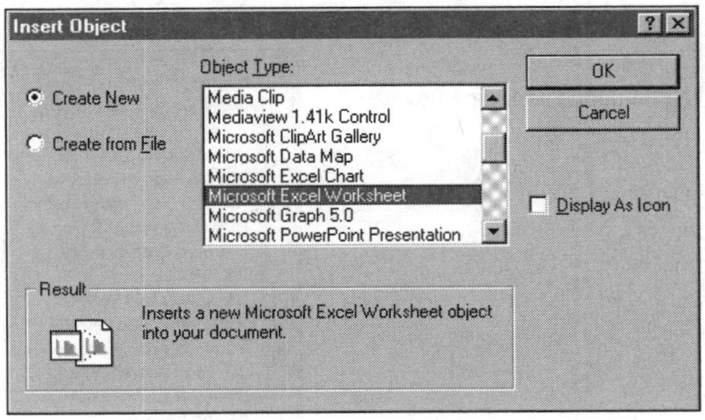

Figure F-3
Selecting an Existing Spreadsheet

---

[3] To have the application create a new spreadsheet, and not use an existing one, you would click the Create New Option Button. This creates an embedded file automatically.

To activate the spreadsheet at run time, the user simply double-clicks the icon rather than double-clicking a displayed portion of the spreadsheet. Finally, notice that Link check box has been checked. This creates the spreadsheet as a linked object; if this box is not checked the spreadsheet would be inserted as an embedded object.

ActiveX Controls

An ActiveX control is simply an external control object, similar in function to the built-in controls found in the standard Visual Basic Toolbox. Creating an ActiveX control involves a similar process as creating a Visual Basic application, in that a UserControl object is displayed, which is almost identical to a form object, on which the control is then constructed. There are three related ways that this UserControl object can be used to create an ActiveX control:

● Create a completely new control from scratch.

● Assemble a new control from a combination of existing controls.

● Enhance an existing control.

Section 10.7 shows how Visual Basic's Interactive Wizard can be used to assemble a new control from existing controls. When you want to use an existing ActiveX control in an application, you must first add the control to the Toolbox. This is accomplished by first selecting the Components item from the Projects menu, which will bring up the Components dialog box shown in Figure F-4. To add an ActiveX control from the displayed list, select the Check box to the left of the desired control's name. When the OK Command button is subsequently clicked, all of the selected controls will appear in the Toolbox.

ActiveX DLLs and EXEs

Prior to Version 5.0, the term OLE automation was used to describe the process whereby one application, referred to as the *client application*, both accessed objects created from another application's class, and used methods and properties of the defining class. In versions 5.0 and 6.0, the term

Figure F-4
The Components Dialog Box

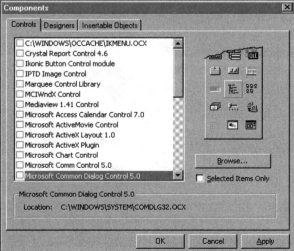

ActiveX has replaced the phrase OLE Automation; however, the underlying operation implied by both terms is identical.

The application that provides the objects, methods, and properties used by the client application is referred to as a *server application*, or server, for short. Servers come in two varieties, as dynamic linked libraries, which are referred to as DLLs, or as stand-alone executable programs, which are referred to as EXEs. The differences in these two types of programs is how they link with a client application.

An ActiveX EXE always runs as a separate process from the client application that uses it. For example, the spreadsheet program Excel is an ActiveX EXE. This means that another program, the client program, can effectively make a call to Excel to manipulate a linked spreadsheet object. When this is done, an executing version of Excel is initiated, which runs as a separate process from the client application. Because they execute as a distinct program, outside of the process in which the client program is executing, ActiveX EXEs are referred to as *out-of-process* servers.

In contrast to EXE servers, an ActiveX DLL becomes dynamically linked into a client application, so that the DLL runs within the same process as the client during run time. For this reason, DLL's are frequently referred to as *in-process* servers. Since a call to an in-process server does not require the "firing up" of a separate server application, accessing a DLL can be considerably faster than accessing an EXE.

Creating an Executable Application

Once you have completed your program design and development, you can create an executable version of it, including an icon that can be used to launch the program, by selecting the Make Project.exe . . . submenu item from the File menu. Using this selection will provide you with the dialog shown in Figure G-1. The Save in: box shown in this figure is where you enter the directory folder in which the executable version of the program will be created and saved. As with all Save-In dialog boxes, you can use the arrow provided in the dialog to display a drop-down list, and select a storage folder by navigating through the list.

Figure G-1
Creating an Executable File

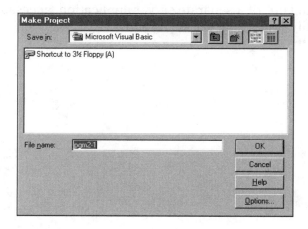

The Data Report Designer[1]

The Data Report Designer utility is a new feature introduced with Version 6.0. Crystal Reports, which used to be shipped with Versions 4 and 5, is no longer bundled with Visual Basic. In this section, we show how to create reports using the new report design utility.

Before creating a report, you must first create a Data Environment, a Connection, and a Command object. You also need to add the necessary designer components to your Visual Basic setup. To do this, select Components from the Project menu, and click on the Designers tab. Make sure the Data Environment and Data Report items are checked as shown in Figure H-1.

Figure H-1

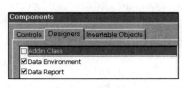

Editing the Main Form

Before creating each of the reports, we will start by editing the startup form that launches the reports. To provide a specific example, we will use the Biblio database provided with Version 6.0 and the sample form shown in Figure H-2. Notice that this form has been provided with six Command buttons for each of the report types, plus an Exit command button.

For the form shown in Figure H-2, we will provide the following event procedures:

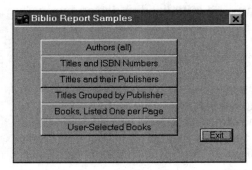

Figure H-2

```
Private Sub cmdAuthors_Click()
    rptAuthors.Show
End Sub

Private Sub cmdTitles_Click()
    rptTitles.Show
End Sub

Private Sub cmdTitlesAndPublishers_Click()
    rptTitlesAndPublishers.Show
End Sub

Private Sub cmdPublisherGrp_Click()
    rptPublisherGrp.Show
End Sub

Private Sub cmdBooks_Click()
    rptBooks.Show
End Sub
```

continued

---

[1]The material in this appendix is taken from *Advanced Visual Basic 6*, by Kip Irvine, published by Scott/Jones, Inc. Permission to use this material was graciously granted by both the author and publisher.

```
Private Sub cmdUserSelected_Click()
Rem: The frmSelectBooks form must be shown modelessly
Rem: because it will in turn show the data report
Rm: window modelessly.
    frmSelectBooks.Show vbModeless
End Sub

Private Sub cmdExit_Click()
    Unload Me
End Sub
```

The ReportDesigner Toolbox

Before getting involved in creating the reports, let's take a look at the report designer toolbox, which is shown in Figure H-3 and contains six controls that may be placed directly on a report. The specific report design controls appear when you are designing a report, if you click on the DataReport command button:

Figure H-3

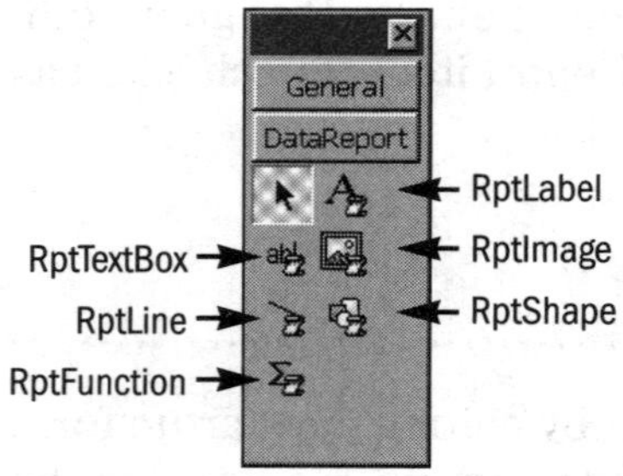

A RptLabel control may contain any characters, and is usually used to display a field name or title. An RptTextBox control must be linked to one of the fields in a Command object, typically a database or query field. It works much the same was as a label that has bound to a data control on a Visual Basic form. An RptImage control can hold a graphic such as an icon or bitmap. The RptLine and RptShape controls display lines and a variety of shapes on the report. An RptFunction control can be configured to automatically calculate a sum, average, count, minimum value, or maximum value.

DataReport Properties

Table H-1 on page 641 describes the unique DataReport properties. The Data-Member and DataSource properties must be initialized in design mode, unless you plan to create an ADO object at run time and attach it to the report.

Avoiding Errors

If you set the DataMember property in design mode to an existing Command object and later rename the Command object, you must remember to correct the DataMember property in the report. Similarly, if you alter the attached Command object by renaming columns or changing the selection of columns, any attached reports will not work until the individual report text box properties are fixed. This is a common source of run-time errors. Some of the more common error messages are shown in Table H-2 on page 641.

Viewing and Printing Reports

A number of different run-time methods are available for DataReport objects, shown in Table H-3 on page 641.

When a data report is shown, printed, or exported, there are at least two separate steps that Visual Basic must go through:

● Query: An SQL query is sent to the data provider. In our examples, the provider is a Jet Database.

Table H-1 DataReport Properties

Property	Description
Caption	Text that appears in the report window title bar.
DataMember	The name of the Command object providing data to the report. If the Command object contains child commands, those commands also provide data for the report.
DataSource	The name of the DataEnvironment object containing the Connection object that generates this report.
GridX, GridY	Specifies the horizontal divisions of the alignment grid in design mode. Controls will automatically snap to these grid lines. Larger values for GridX and GridY give you more precise control over the positions of controls.
Margins: TopMargin, BottomMargin, LeftMargin, RightMargin	Sizes of report margins, measured in Twips. For reports displayed on the screen, left and top margins of 600 Twips seem to work well. For output to a printer, the default value of 1440 Twips is appropriate.
ReportWidth	The width of all sections of the report, in Twips.
Title	The title of the report, which shows up when exporting to HTML and when using the Insert Control command to place a report title in the report heading or page heading area.

Table H-2 Data Report Error Messages

Error Message	Explanation
"DataField <command>.<field> not found."	Either the DataMember property or the DataField property of a RptTextBox object in the report is incorrect. The DataMember property must contain the name of a Command object, and the DataField property must contain the name of a field within a Command object.
"Failed getting rowset(s) from current data source."	The report's DataMember property does not contain the name of a Command object in the DataEnvironment named by the report's DataSource property.
"Invalid data source."	The report's DataSource property does not contain the name of a DataEnvironment object.

Table H-3 DataReport Object Methods

Method	Description
ExportReport	Export the report to either HTML (for Web pages) or plain text.
Hide	Hide a report window.
PrintReport	Print the report on the default printer.
Refresh	Immediately update a report window.
Show	Display the report in a modeless window. If this command is issued from a form, the form must also be shown modelessly. This command requires at least one printer to have been installed on the computer.

- Processing: The data retrieved by the query is processed by Visual Basic, creating the report in a temporary file. You can monitor the progress of this step by writing code in the report form's **ProcessingTimeout** event procedure.

  A third step is also required if the report is either printed or exported to a file:

- Printing/Exporting: The report is printed on the printer or exported to either a plain text or HTML file. This step is asynchronous, allowing the Visual Basic program to continue doing other event processing. The report is generated as a background process. You can write code in the report form's **AsyncProgress** event procedure to monitor the progress of this step.

The following events occur, in order, when a report is generated:

1. **Initialize:** Occurs after the query has completed.
2. **Resize:** Occurs when the report window is displayed and when the window is resized or moved.
3. **Activate:** Occurs when the report window becomes the active window.
4. **ProcessingTimeout:** Occurs approximately once per second, beginning when the query has completed, and ending when the report has been completely generated.
5. **Deactivate:** (optional) Occurs if another window has become the active window.
6. **QueryClose:** Occurs just before the report window is closed.
7. **Terminate:** Occurs when all references to the DataReport have been released.

A DataReport has a Code window that can be accessed by double-clicking on the report in design mode. Any of the seven events just listed can be automatically given an event handler procedure. We can use this to our advantage, for instance, when a report takes a long time to create by showing the progress and allowing the user to cancel the remaining part of the report.

Displaying the Report's Progress

If you write code in the report's **ProcessingTimeout** event handler procedure, you can display progress information for the user, and you can cancel a Show, PrintReport, or ExportReport operation that is taking too long. In the example shown in Figure H-4, we display a ProgressBar control on the program's main form that provides a visual cue to the user that the report is being generated:

Figure H-4

Of course, we don't know how many pages the report will contain, so if the progress bar fills up, we can clear it and begin filling it again. We also provide a Cancel button so the user can stop generating the report and see only the pages generated so far. The following code, placed in the **ProcessingTimeout** event handler of the report window, updates the progress and checks to see if the user has clicked on the Cancel button.

```
Private Sub DataReport_ProcessingTimeout(ByVal Seconds As Long, _
   Cancel As Boolean, ByVal JobType As _
   MSDataReportLib.AsyncTypeConstants, _
   ByVal Cookie As Long)

' Update the progress bar on frmMain.
   With frmMain.prgShow
      .Value = (.Value + (.Max / 20)) Mod .Max
   End With
   frmMain.SetFocus    'bring frmMain to the front
   DoEvents            'allow frmMain to be repainted

' Check to see if the user has cancelled the report.
   Cancel = frmMain.CancelReport
End Sub
```

Setting the **Cancel** property to **True** automatically stops further report generation. The techniques shown here for canceling the report can be applied to any program that uses the report designer. We must call the **DoEvents** method when switching focus to another form within a procedure. Without **DoEvents**, the form getting the focus in our example is not repainted until the report is completely finished.

In the **Initialize** event handler of the report form, we make the progress bar and Cancel button visible on **frmMain**, and initialize its public Cancel-Report variable to **False**.

```
Private Sub DataReport_Initialize()
   With frmMain
      .CancelReport = False
      .cmdCancel.Visible = True
      .prgShow.Visible = True     'enable progress bar
      .prgShow.Value = 0
   End With
End Sub
```

In the **QueryClose** event handler of the report form, we hide the progress bar and Cancel button on frmMain.

```
Private Sub DataReport_QueryClose(Cancel As Integer, _
   CloseMode As Integer)
   With frmMain
      .prgShow.Visible = False
      .cmdCancel.Visible = False
   End With
End Sub
```

In frmMain, when the user clicks on the Cancel button, we set the public CancelReport variable to **True**.

```
(Public CancelReport As Boolean)

Private Sub cmdCancel_Click()
   CancelReport = True
End Sub
```

Author Table Example

In the first few examples, we will use the Biblio.mdb database shipped along with Visual Basic. Biblio contains several tables relating to books and publishers:

- Authors: ID numbers, names, and birth dates of book authors.
- Publishers: Names and addresses of publishers.
- Titles: Detailed information about individual books, including their ISBN number, title, publisher ID, and year published.
- TitleAuthor: A table that binds ISBN numbers to author ID numbers.

Creating a Data Environment

The first step is to create a data environment and a connection to the Biblio database.

1. Create a new project, selecting the project type as *Data Project*.
2. Double-click on DataEnvronment1 to open the Data Environment window. Right-click on Connection1, rename it to Biblio, right-click again, and select Properties. Click on the Provider tab and select "Microsoft Jet 3.51 OLE DB Provider."
3. Click on the Connection tab, and locate the Biblio.mdb database. By default, this file is installed in the `C:\Program Files\Microsoft Visual Studio\VB98\Biblio.mdb`, but the file might be located somewhere else on your computer. Close the properties page.
4. Right-click on the Biblio connection and select **Add Command**. Rename the command to Authors.
5. Right-click on the Authors command and select **Properties**. Under the General tab, set the database object to Table and the object name to Authors.

Creating a Data Report

After you have created a Data Environment, a Connection, and a Command object, you can create a new Data Report and attach it to the data environment. If you created a data project when Visual Basic first started up, you already have a single empty report object called DataReport1. Here are a series of steps to follow:

1. From the Project window, double-click on DataReport1 to open the Report Designer window. Press F4 to bring up its Properties windows and set the following values:

Property	Value
Name	rptAuthors
Caption	All Authors
DataSource	DataEnvironment1
DataMember	Authors
Title	Listing of the Author Table

2. Using the mouse, drag the Authors command object into the Detail area of the report. Click the mouse in the report area to deselect all the fields that were just pasted in.

3. Rearrange the text boxes and their labels with the mouse, placing the field labels in the Page Header area, and moving the report Text boxes into a horizontal line in the Detail area.

4. Select all of the field labels in the heading area, press F4 to display the Properties window, and set the font to bold.

5. Next, you're going to add a title, date, and page number to the Page Header area. In the ToolBox window, click on the tab labeled **Data-Report** to expose the data report tools. Select the tool called RptLabel and drag a rectangle in the report header area. Set its **Caption** property to "Complete Listing of the Authors Table". Set its font to 10 point bold.

6. Right-click inside the Page Header area, and select Insert Control, Current Page Number. The symbol %p should appear in the header area. Insert another control into the header area, this time a Label. Set its caption to "Page". Insert another control, called "Current Date (Short Format)". It will appear as %d in the header area. Your report should now appear as shown in Figure H-5.

7. Bring up the main form (called frmMain) and insert a Command button. Set its caption to "All Authors Report" and place the following code in its click event procedure:

```
rptAuthors.Show   'display the report on the screen
```

Make sure frmMain is the Project startup form, and run the program. Click on the Command button, and wait about 10 seconds for the report to generate itself. Figure H-6 provides a sample of the output.

Figure H-5

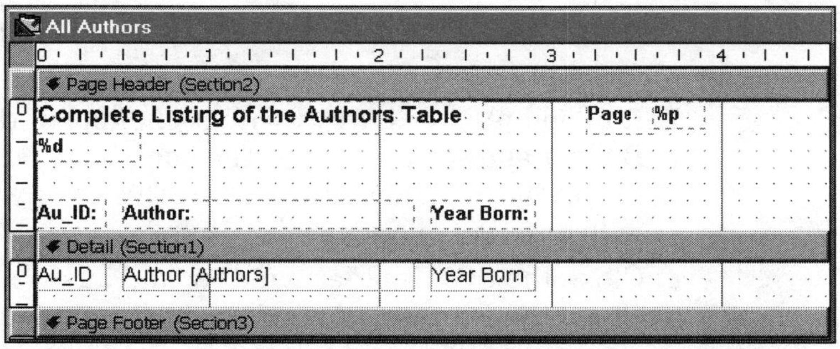

Figure H-6

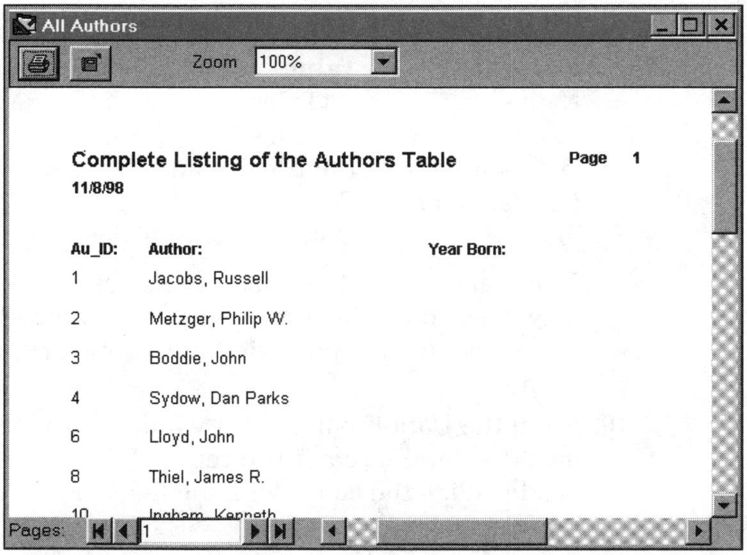

Building a Report Using SQL

Next, let's build a report using the Titles table, using the SQL Query Designer. A primary advantage to using SQL is that it gives us the ability to sort and select rows from one or more tables. Each detail line of the report will contain a book title, the year it was published, and the book's ISBN number. The report will be sorted by the book title. You can build this report step-by-step:

1. Create a new Command object: In the Data Project window, right-click on Biblio (a connection object), and select Add Command. Rename the command to Titles.

2. Attach the Titles table to the new Command object: Right-click on the Titles command and select Properties. In the General tab of the Properties window, select SQL Statement, and click on the SQL Builder button.

3. When the SQL Builder window opens, look for another window that just appeared, called the Data View window. In this window, expand the tree until the Titles table name appears.

4. Drag the Titles table from the Data View window into the upper portion of the SQL Builder window. Place checks next to the Title, Year Published, and ISBN fields. You should see these field names appear in the grid area.

5. In the grid area of the SQL Builder, click in the Sort Order column of the row corresponding to the Title field. Select '1' for this field, indicating that the primary sort field will be Title.

6. The following SQL statement should appear in the SQL Builder window:

```
SELECT Title, 'Year Published', ISBN FROM Titles
ORDER BY Title
```

7. Run and test the query by right-clicking in the upper pane of the SQL Builder and selecting Run. The query data will appear in the lower portion of the SQL Builder window. (This gives you a chance to experiment with different queries.)

8. Close the SQL Builder window and answer Yes when asked to save. Close the Properties window. In the Project window, right-click the Designers folder, and select Add, Data Report.

9. Set the following report properties:

Property	Value
Name	rptTitles
Caption	rptTitles
DataSource	DataEnvironment1
DataMember	Titles
Title	Listing of Book Titles

Tip: Sometimes, after you have selected specific areas of a report, you may want to display the Properties window for the report itself. To do this, click on the report window's caption bar and press F4 to display its properties.

10. From the Data Environment window, drag the Titles Command object into the detail area of the report. Move the field labels into the page header, align the labels with the fields. Place a report line control on the report in the page header.

Figure H-7

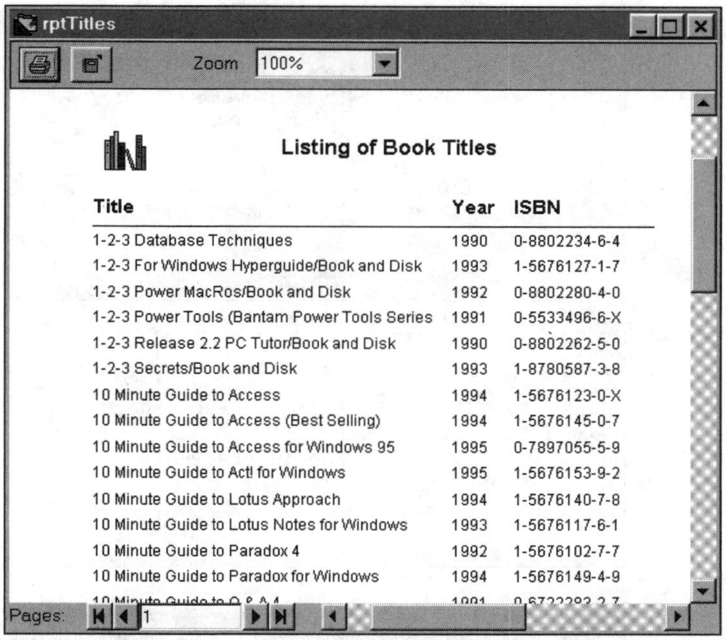

11. To add a heading to the report, right-click inside the page header area, and select Insert Control, Report Title. Drag the dotted rectangle to the right, making it larger. Set its font to 10 points bold. Set its alignment to centered.

12. Select the report image control from the Toolbox and place a copy in the Page Heading area. Select the image, press F4 to display its Properties window, and set its Picture property to an icon from your computer's hard drive.

13. Place another Command button on frmMain, double-click on it, and add a program code statement that will show the report called rptTitles. Run and test the program. Figure H-7 provides a sample of the report display.

You can always customize this report by adding a date and time, a page footing, page number, and so on. You can also place shapes such as circles and rectangles on the report.

Joining the Titles and Publishers Tables

Let's create a table that joins the Titles and Publishers tables so we can view each book title and its publisher name. Create a Command object containing a query that joins the Titles and Publishers tables. Its attributes are shown here:

Property	Value
Name	TitlesAndPublishers
Connection	Biblio
SQL Statement	SELECT DISTINCT Titles.Title, Publishers.Name FROM Titles, Publishers WHERE Titles.PubID = Publishers.PubID AND (Titles.Title < 'C') ORDER BY Titles.Title

Each book title is joined to its publisher name, the titles are sorted alphabetically, and only titles starting with an ASCII character lower than 'C' are displayed. Figure H-8 provides a sample of the Query Designer window:

Figure H-8

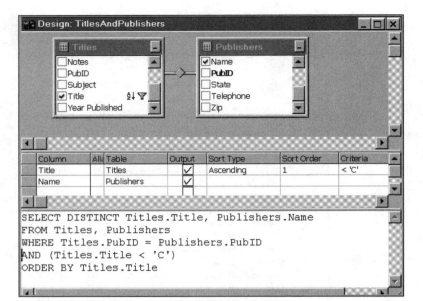

Figure H-9

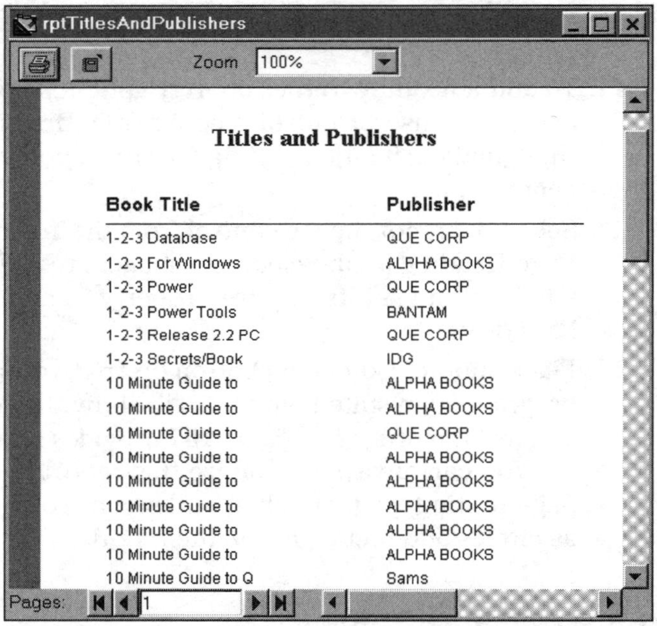

Create a new report called rptTitlesAndPublishers, connect it to the TitlesAndPublishers command, and drag the title and publisher fields into the report, and add a nice title. Here are the report properties:

Property	Value
Name	rptTitlesAndPublishers
Caption	rptTitlesAndPublishers
DataSource	DataEnvironment1
DataMember	TitlesAndPublishers
Title	Titles and Publishers

Figure H-9 provides a sample of the output:

Adding a Footer with a Counter

Let's add one more feature to this report, which will be a report footer containing a count of the number of books in the table. Right-click anywhere in

Figure H-10

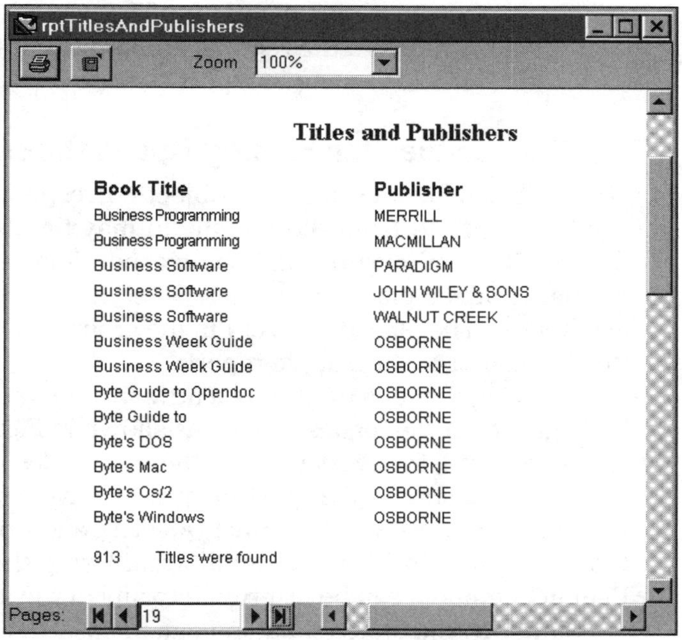

the Report Designer window and select "Show Report Header/Footer". Right-click in the Report Footer area, and select Insert Control, Function. This will place a rptFunction object in the footer area. Press F4 to display its properties window and set the following values:

Property	Value
Name	rfnTitleCount
DataField	Title
DataMember	TitlesAndPublishers
Functiontype	rptFuncRCnt (counter)

Place a label in the report footer just to the right of the counter with its caption set to "Titles were found." Run the program, display the report, and go to the last page where you should be able to view the counter, as shown in Figure H-10.

Reports with Groups

The DataEnvironment designer allows Command objects to be combined in hierarchical relationships. Such relationships make it easy to create record groups in reports. For example, if you wanted to track company sales grouped by cities within counties, County would be the parent command and City would be the child command, as shown in Figure H-11.

What is needed, then, is a way of relating a command hierarchy to sections of reports. The lowest level command (in this case, City) corresponds

Figure H-11

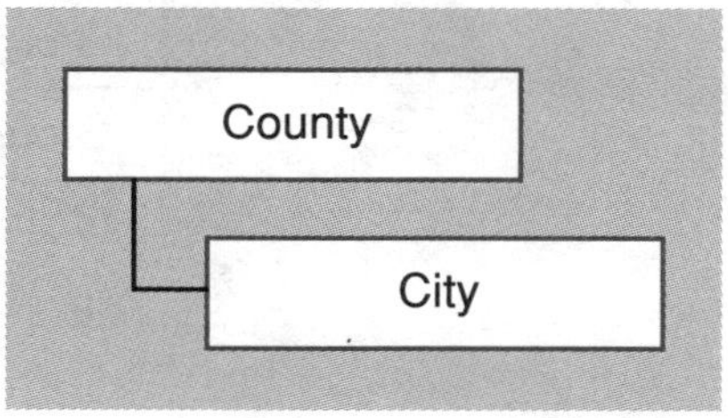

Group Header (County) – 1
Detail (City) – 2
Group Footer (County) – 1

Figure H-12

to the report detail line. The parent command (County) corresponds to the report's group header and footer sections. Figure H-12 is a sample report structure, showing levels 1 and 2.

Rules for Placing RptTextBox Controls

When a Command object corresponds to a report section, any field from the command may be placed in the report (as an RptTextBox) in its corresponding section on the report. Also, the field may be placed at a lower level. A field from the Authors table, for example, can be placed at level 1 in the group header or footer, or at level 2 in the detail area of the sample report.

Carrying the idea of groups a little farther, let's also include Region and State groups at the highest levels. As shown in Figure H-13, for every Region, for every State, for every County, there are sales within a City.

The corresponding report must now have separate group headers and footers for Region (level 1), State (level 2), and County (level 3). Meanwhile, City (level 4) is still in the detail area. Using the rules stated earlier, the Region command can be inserted into any of the areas shown in Figure H14.

Similarly, the State command can be inserted into levels 2, 3, and 4. The County command can be inserted into levels 3 and 4. The City command can only be inserted into level 4.

Example: Creating a Publishers–Titles Hierarchy

Let's use the principles shown in this section to create a simple command hierarchy that involves the Publishers and Titles tables from the Biblio database. To try this, first insert a command called Publishers and attach it to the Publishers table in the database. Then right-click on the Publishers command and insert a child command. Rename the child command to Titles and attach it to the Titles table in the database. Before closing the Properties window for the Titles command, click on the Relation tab. Click on the Add button to relate the Titles command to its parent object, Publishers, as shown in Figure H-15.

By default, the Properties window tries to connect two tables using a field by the same name. If no two such fields exist, you can still select specific field names before clicking on the Add button. Notice also that the "Relate to a Parent Command Object" check box must be checked.

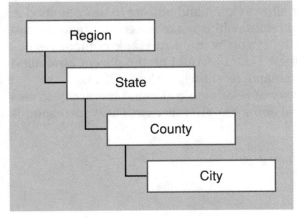

Figure H-13

Group Header (Region) – 1
Group Header (State) – 2
Group Header (County) – 3
Detail (City) – 4
Group Footer (County) – 3
Group Footer (State) – 2
Group Footer (Region) – 1

Figure H-14

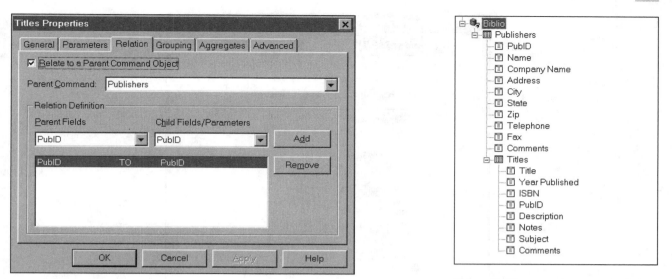

Figure H-15

Figure H-16

After closing the Properties window for Titles, the data environment window, which is shown in Figure H-16, will display the parent-child relationship of Publishers and Titles.

In the DataReport designer, set the **DataSource** property to your data environment name, and set the **DataMember** property to the parent command name, Publishers. Right-click on the report and select "Add Group Header/Footer." For the moment, we will turn off the Report Header and Page Header options. Notice that, as shown in Figure H-17, Publisher fields have been placed in the group header and footer, and Title fields have been placed in the detail section:

Figure H-17

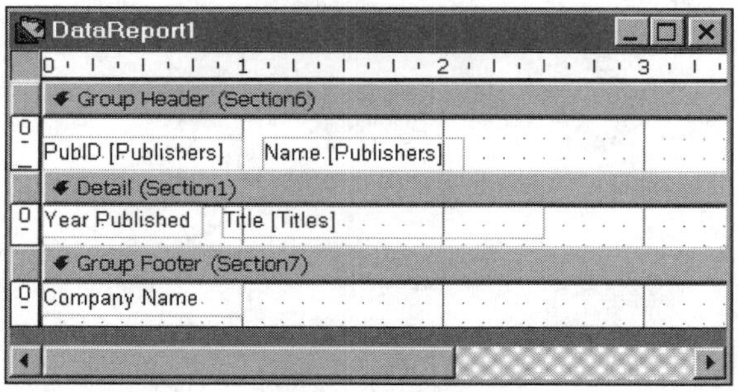

As an experiment, try to place a Title field in the group header section. The mouse pointer changes to a "not-permitted" icon (circle with diagonal line), and you cannot insert the field.

Tip: Always set the **DataSource** and **DataField** properties before adding fields to a report. Otherwise, the report designer will not prevent you from inserting fields in the wrong report sections. This causes a run-time error later when you try to show the report.

Other Types of Reports

Sometimes, it is advantageous to display a single record on each page of a report. Let's try this, using the Titles table from the Biblio database. Create a command called "Books" and attach the following SQL query that selects books published since 1998 with a price less than $30:

```
SELECT * FROM titles
  WHERE (Val(Description) < 30.00)
  AND (Val(Description) > 0)
  AND 'Year Published' > 1998
  ORDER BY Title
```

Figure H-18

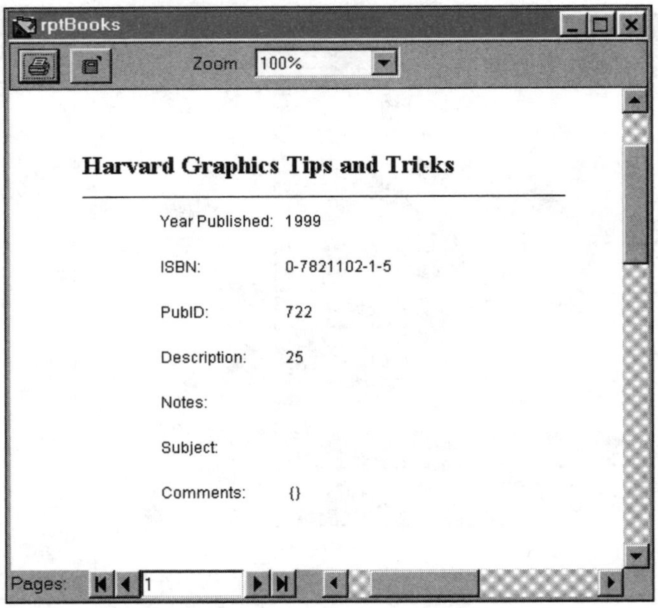

Create a report, call it rptBooks, and attach it to the Books query. Drag the Command object into the detail line area. Assign a large font to the book's Title property. In the Detail area of the report, set the **ForcePageBreak** property to rptPageBreakAfter. This tells the report to insert a page break after each book. Figure H-18 illustrates a sample of the first page of the output:

Glossary

Accelerator key: Any key sequence that initiates an action by pressing the ALT key and a designated letter. An accelerator key is created by preceding the designated letter with an ampersand (&) in an object's **Caption** property. Also referred to as a hot-key sequence.

Access key: Any key sequence that permits a user to open a menu or shift focus to a control by pressing the ALT key and a designated letter. The access key is always underlined.

Application: A collection of visual objects and procedural code that constitutes a complete program. Synonymous with the terms *program* and *project*.

Argument: A value or expression that is passed into a subprogram (subroutine, procedure, or function).

Array: A group of variables, all of the same type, that share a common name. Individual variables that comprise the array are referred to as array elements. Each array element is distinguished from another by its position in the array, which is designated by an integer value known as an index number.

Bitmap: A rectangular arrangement of dots, arranged to make a picture. Also referred to as a raster.

Bookmark: A system-generated string identifying the current record contained in a RecordSet object's **Bookmark** property.

Boolean expression: An expression that evaluates to either **True** or **False**.

Bound controls: Controls that can be linked to database fields and are used to display the values in the fields they are linked to. Also referred to as data-aware controls, they include Check boxes, Image, Label, Text box, and Picture box controls.

Break mode: Temporary suspension of program execution in the development environment. In Break mode, you can examine, debug, reset, step through, or continue program execution. You enter Break mode when you

- Encounter a break point during program execution;
- Press CTRL+BREAK during program execution;
- Encounter a **Stop** statement or run-time error during program execution;
- Add a **Break When True** watch expression. Execution stops when the value of the watch changes and evaluates to **True**; or
- Add a **Break When Changed** watch expression. Execution stops when the value of the watch changes.

Breakpoint: A selected program line at which execution automatically stops. Breakpoints are not saved with your code.

Built-in: A data type, object type, function, or subroutine that comes with the Visual Basic language. Built-in data types are also referred to as primitive types.

Call: A request to execute a procedure. When the procedure is completed, control returns to the statement immediately following the statement making the call.

Call stack dialog: Lists the procedure calls in an application that have been started but are not yet completed. Available only in Break mode.

Check box: A control that permits a user to make one or more selections by placing a check mark next to the desired item.

Code: Procedural instructions that are used to produce a result.

Code window: The window in which code is written and displayed.

Collection: An object that contains a set of related objects. An object's position in the collection can change whenever a change occurs in the collection; therefore, the position of any specific object in the collection may vary.

Combo box control: A control that is a combination of a List box and Text box control.

Command button: A control that is used to initiate an event procedure when it is clicked.

Comment: A remark used to document code. A comment is designated by the keyword **Rem** placed at the start of a line, or any text placed after an apostrophe. Remarks are non-executable code.

Compile time: The period during which source code is translated to executable code.

Control: An object that can be placed on a form with its own set of recognized properties, methods, and events. Controls are used to receive user input, display output, and trigger event procedures. Most controls can be manipulated using methods. In addition, some controls are interactive, which means that they are responsive to user actions, while other controls are static, which means that they are accessible only through code.

Control array: A group of controls that share a common name, type, and common event procedures. Each control in the array has a unique index number that can be used to determine which control recognizes an event.

Copy buffer: A location created by the Microsoft Jet database engine for the contents of a record that is open for editing. The Edit method copies the current record to the copy buffer; the AddNew method clears the buffer for a new record and sets all default values; and the Update method saves the data from the copy buffer to the database, replacing the current record or inserting the new record. Any statement that resets or moves the current record pointer, such as the **MoveNext** method, discards the copy buffer's contents.

Constant: A value that cannot change during program execution. It can be either a string constant, a number, or a symbolic constant.

Current record: The record in a RecordSet that is available for modification or examination. The **Move** methods can be used to reposition the current record in a RecordSet. In addition, for dynaset- or snapshot-type RecordSets, the **Find** methods may be used. For table-type RecordSets, the **Seek** method can be used.

Data control: A control that incorporates the Microsoft Jet engine for accessing databases and is used to view database records in connection with bound controls.

Data type: The characteristic of a variable that determines what kind of data it can hold. Data types include Byte, Boolean, Integer, Long, Currency, Single, Double, Date, String, Object, Variant (the default), and user-defined types, as well as specific types of objects.

Debug: To locate and eliminate errors in a program.

Declaration statement: A statement used to declare variables and constants.

Design time: The time during which an application is constructed within the development environment by adding controls, setting control or form properties, and so on.

Development environment: A set of software, presented as a unified environment, in which the software developer can efficiently work. Microsoft Visual Basic is an example of a development environment.

Dialog box: A box that requests user input. A modal dialog requires input before an application can continue, while a modeless box permits shifting the focus from the box and allows an application to continue without the box being closed.

Directory List box: A control that displays available directories on the current disk drive.

DLL: Dynamic Link Library; a file having the extension .DLL used to hold procedures that are dynamically linked into an application.

Drive List box: A control that displays available disk drives.

Drop-down: A list that is displayed in a drop-down fashion by either the clicking of a down-facing arrowhead or the action of an accelerator key.

Dynaset: A temporary set of data records selected from one or more database tables.

Embedded object: An object created in one application and then embedded in a second application. All of the data associated with the embedded object is copied to and contained within the embedding application.

EOF: End-of-file. A condition that evaluates to **True** when the end of a sequential file or the end of a RecordSet object has been reached.

Error trapping: Detecting an error and invoking code when the designated error occurs.

Event: Any user or system action to which an object responds.

Event procedure: A **Sub** procedure that is attached to an object and initiated by an event.

Event driven program: A program that executes code based on user- and system-initiated events.

EXE: A stand-alone application that is executed as an individual process. Also refers to controls that are built-in to Visual Basic and are displayed in the standard Toolbox.

Expression: A syntactically correct arrangement of constants, variables, operators, functions, and subroutines that evaluates to a single value.

Field: A single item that represents an attribute or entity of a database record.

File List box: A control that displays a list of file names that match the value set in the **Pattern** property.

Focus: The state that defines the currently active control. A control can receive focus by being tabbed to, clicked on, selected by access keys, or designated by program code.

Form: Forms are containers for controls. At run time, a form becomes either a window or dialog box. Forms can be of two types, MDI or SDI.

Form-level: A variable, declared in the **(General) Declarations** section, that is accessible by all procedures on the form.

Format: The specification for how data will be displayed.

Frame: A control used to contain other controls. Typically used to provide containers for Option button controls in which each Option button group provides a separate set of options.

Function: A general procedure that directly returns a single value.

(General) Declarations section: The section of a code module that is used to declare module-level variables and symbolic constants.

General procedure: A user-defined procedure that can be either a **Sub** or **Function** procedure.

Graphical User Interface: GUI. The graphical portion of a program that is visually presented to a user for interaction with the procedural code.

Grid control: A control having rows and columns that is used to display data in a similar manner to a spreadsheet.

Handle: A small square on a control that is visible at design time and can be used to resize the control. Also referred to as a sizing handle.

Horizontal scroll bar: A control that uses a horizontal scroll bar to set a numerical value. One end of the control corresponds to a minimum value, while the opposite end corresponds to a maximum value.

Image box control: A control used to hold a graphic, text, or other control. Although an Image box supports fewer properties than a Picture box control, it repaints faster and pictures can be stretched to fit the control's size.

Immediate window: A Debug window that is active during Break mode, and can be used to immediately evaluate an expression or determine the value of a variable.

Index: When used with a table-type RecordSet, the current index determines the order is which data records are returned to the RecordSet.

Instant Watch: A debug feature that permits determining the value of an expression or variable.

Key field: One or more combined fields on which records in a database are organized and searched.

Keyword: A word that has a special meaning in Visual Basic. Unrestricted keywords may be used as identifiers, but doing so precludes their use for the feature normally associated with them as keywords. Restricted keywords may only be used for their intended purpose.

Line control: A control that is used to produce a straight line on a Graphical User Interface.

Linked object: An object created in one application that is linked to a second application. When an object is linked, a reference to the object is inserted into the second application, rather than the actual object. Unlike an embedded object, a linked object's data is stored in and managed by the application that created it.

List box: A control that displays a list of items from which one or more may be selected.

Local scope: The scope of a symbolic constant or variable in which visibility is limited to the declaring procedure.

Logic error: An error that causes an erroneous, unexpected, or unintentional result due to a flaw in the program's logic.

Logical operator: The **And**, **Or**, and **Not** operators used to construct compound relational expressions.

Message box: A dialog box that displays a message and one or more options that must be selected before an application can continue execution.

Method: A procedure that is connected to an object. The method is invoked by providing an object name, followed by a period, followed by the method's name.

Microsoft Jet database engine: A database management system that retrieves data from, and stores data into, user- and system-databases. The Jet engine can be thought of as a data manager component from which other data access systems, such as Visual Basic and Microsoft Access are built.

Modal dialog box: A dialog box that requires input from a user, and must be closed before an application can continue.

Modeless dialog box: A dialog box where focus can be shifted from the box, and one in which an application can continue without the box being closed.

Module: A set of declarations followed by procedures. May be a form module, a code module, or a class module. Each module is stored as a separate file.

Module level: Code and variables that are only available to procedures within the module.

Multiple Document Interface (MDI): An application that can support multiple windows from one application instance. An MDI application consists of a main window that contains internal windows referred to as child windows. The main window and its child windows can all be visible at the same time.

Numeric expression: Any expression that evaluates to a number. Elements of the expression can include keywords, variables, constants, operators, and subroutine calls.

OLE object: Object Linking and Embedding. An object that can be transferred and shared between applications, either by linking or embedding.

One-to-many relationship: An association between two tables in which the primary key value of each record in the primary table corresponds to the value in the matching field or fields of a number of records (or no record) in the related table.

Option button control: A control that permits selection of a single item from a group of items. If additional sets of options are required, a Frame control is used to contain the additional Option controls.

Parameter: A variable used by a procedure whose value is initialized outside of the procedure and transferred to the procedure when the procedure is called.

Pass by Reference: A transfer of data to a procedure in which the procedure has access to the memory location of the argument being passed. This permits the procedure to alter the value of the argument.

Pass by Value: A transfer of data to a procedure in which a copy of an argument's value is passed to the procedure.

Picture box control: A control used to hold a graphic, text, or other control. Although a Picture box supports more properties than an Image box control, it repaints slower and pictures cannot be stretched to fit the control's size.

Primary key: One or more fields whose value or values uniquely identify each record in a table. A table can have only one primary key.

Procedure: A named sequence of statements executed as a unit. **Function**, **Property**, and **Sub** are types of procedures. A procedure name is always defined at the module level. All executable code must be contained in a procedure. Procedures cannot be nested within other procedures.

Procedure template: An empty procedure that consists only of a header line and either an **End Sub** or **End Function** statement.

Project: The collection of elements that constitute an application.

Project window: A window that displays all of the forms, modules, and elements that comprise a project. Also referred to as the Project Resource window.

Property: A named attribute of an object. Properties define object characteristics, such as size, color, screen location, and the state of an object, such as **Enabled** or **Disabled**.

Public scope: The scope that permits a procedure or variable to be called from all project modules.

Quick Watch dialog: Displays the current value of a variable, property, or watch expression. Only available in Break mode.

Random-access file: A file in which all records are fixed-length, and records may be read or written in any order.

Record: A group of related fields.

RecordCount: A method that returns the number of records accessed in a RecordSet.

RecordSet: The current set of records associated with a data control.

Run time: The time during which a program is executing.

Scope: Defines the availability of a variable, procedure, or object, which is referred to as its visibility. For example, a variable declared as **Public** is available to all procedures in all modules in a project, unless the **Option Private** module is in effect. When the **Option Private** module is in effect, the module itself is private and, therefore, not visible to other projects. Variables declared in a procedure are visible only within the procedure and lose their value between calls unless they are declared as **Static**.

Single Document Interface (SDI): An application that supports a single visible document at a time. SDI applications can contain multiple windows, but only one can be visible at a time.

Sizing handle: A small square on a control that is visible at design time and can be used to resize the control.

Snapshot: A RecordSet that is read-only and cannot be updated.

SQL statement: An expression that defines a Structured Query Language (SQL) command, such as **Select**, **Update**, or **Delete**, and includes clauses such as **Where** and **Order By**. SQL statements are typically used in queries.

Static variable: A variable whose value is retained between procedure calls.

String expression: Any expression that evaluates to a sequence of contiguous characters. Elements of the expression can include a function that returns a string, a string literal, a string constant, a string variable, a string variant, or a function that returns a string variant.

Sub procedure: A procedure that only returns values through its parameter list.

Symbolic constant: A constant that has been named using the **Const** keyword.

Syntax: The set of rules for formulating grammatically correct language statements.

Text box control: A control used for data entry and display.

Timer control: A control used to automatically execute an event at a specified interval of time.

Toolbar: A set of icons, referred to as buttons, that are used as shortcuts for menu options.

Toolbox: A window containing controls that can be placed on a form at design time.

Transaction: A series of changes made to a database's data and structure. The beginning of a transaction starts with a **Begin Trans** statement, transactions are committed using a **Commit Trans** statement, and all changes made since the last **Begin Trans** statement can be undone using a **RollBack** statement.

Twip: A unit of measurement that is equivalent to 1/20 of a point and 1/1440 of an inch.

Variable: A named location containing data that can be modified during program execution. Each variable has a name that uniquely identifies it within its scope. Variable names must begin with an alphabetic character, must be unique within the same scope, cannot be longer than 255 characters, and cannot contain an embedded period or type-declaration character. Variables declared in a procedure are visible only within the procedure and lose their value between calls unless they are declared as **Static**.

Vertical scroll bar: A control that uses a vertical scroll bar to set a numerical value. One end of the control corresponds to a minimum value, while the opposite end corresponds to a maximum value.

Watch expression: A user-defined expression that enables observation of a variable's or expression's behavior during program execution. Watch expressions appear in the Watch debug window and are automatically updated when Break mode is entered. The Watch window displays the value of an expression within a given context, and is not saved with a project's code.

Solutions and Source Code

The source code to all of the programs contained in this text are stored in the file named srcode.zip, which is included on the disk provided with this text, and is a compressed file. To uncompress this file, first copy both the srcode.zip and unzip.exe files, both of which are on the diskette, to your hard disk. Then change directories to the directory where these two files have been copied, and issue the command unzip srcode.

For example, assuming that you want the final, uncompressed, source code files to reside in an existing directory named vbprogs on your C drive, and that the diskette is currently on the A drive, the following series of DOS commands can be used:

```
C:>cd \vbprogs
C:\vbprogs> copy a:srcode.zip
C:\vbprogs> copy a:unzip.exe
C:\vbprogs> unzip srcode
C:\vbprogs> del srcode.exe
C:\vbprogs> del unzip.exe
```

Solutions

Chapter 1

....

Exercises 1.1

1 a. A first-generation language, which is also referred to as a machine language, consists of a sequence of instructions that is represented in binary numbers. Such languages are machine dependent.

b. A second-generation language is a machine-dependent language that uses symbols for operations and labels for data locations. Such languages are also referred to as assembly languages.

c. A third-generation language, which is also referred to as a high-level language uses symbols for both operations and data locations. Such languages, which include BASIC, Pascal, and C are not machine dependent.

d. A fourth-generation language is a high-level language in which visual objects are provided for use without the need to construct them from procedural code or the ability to retrieve and format data does not require the writing of any procedural code.

e. A high-level language is a programming language that uses instructions that resemble a written language, such as English, and can be translated to run on a variety of computer types.

f. A low-level language is a programming language that uses instructions that are directly tied to one type of computer. They consist of machine-level and assembly languages.

g. A machine language contains the binary codes that can be executed by a computer. Such languages are frequently referred to as executables.

h. An assembly language permits symbolic names to be used for mathematical operations and memory addresses. Assembly languages are low-level.

i. An assembler is a program that translates an assembly language program into machine code.

j. An interpreter is a program that translates individual source program statements, one at a time, into executable statements. Each statement is executed immediately after translation.

k. A compiler is a program that is used to translate a high-level source program as a complete unit before any one statement is actually executed.

l. An object is a programming element that is defined by a state, which defines how the object appears, and a behavior, which defines how the object reacts to external inputs.

m. An event is any user or system action to which an object responds.

n. A graphical user interface is the graphical portion of a program that is visually presented to a user for interaction with the program.

o. A procedure-oriented language has instructions that are used to create procedures, where a procedure is a logically consistent set of instructions that produce a specific result.

p. An object-oriented language permits the construction of objects, that can be manipulated and displayed. Such languages are gaining increasing usage in graphical-oriented programs.

3 a. Low-level languages use instructions that are directly tied to one computer and generally execute at the fastest level possible. High-level languages are portable, but must be compiled into a low-level language before it can be executed.

b. A procedure-oriented language uses instructions to create procedures, which are self-contained units that manipulate input values to produce resulting outputs. An object-oriented language permits the construction of objects, such as rectangles, that can be manipulated and displayed. Typically object-oriented languages are used for producing programs that have a graphical component.

5 a. A 4GL language must provide the ability to access and format information without the need to explicitly write any procedural code.

b. No.

Exercises 1.2

1 a. Clearly define the problem—To ensure that the problem is clearly understood, including what inputs will be given and what outputs are required.

Develop a solution—Define an appropriate set of steps, called an algorithm, to solve the problem.

Code the solution—Write the program by translating the solution into a source program.

Test and correct the program—Test the completed computer program to ensure that it does provide a solution to the problem.

b. Documentation—Provide adequate user documentation for people who will use the program and programmer documentation for people who will have to maintain the program.

Maintenance—Keep the solution up to date by making modifications required wither due to changes in requirements or because errors are found during program execution.

3 If Phase I is 40% of the total effort, then coding represents 20% of 40% = (.2)*(.4) = .08 = 8% of the total effort.

5 A fixed fee is a good choice if you have experience in exactly what is wanted, or are selling an existing program to a new client, or both you and the client are in total agreement as to what will be produced; otherwise, it is generally a bad choice for both parties. On the positive side is that you do know how much you will receive for your work and the client knows how much they will have to pay. The disadvantage is that unless you both are very clear as to what will be produced, you may end up doing double and triple the amount of work contracted for very little if any additional funding. This occurs because after the client sees the program, new features immediately present themselves. You, as a programmer, may claim these are additional features, while the client may claim them as normal features that you should have incorporated as part of a useful program. No matter how the issue is resolved, generally, one or both sides may feel they have been deceived.

Exercises 1.3

1 A form module contains a form object, objects that are displayed on the form, and procedural code.

3 Form and standard modules both can contain procedural code.

5 a. Clicking on the Command button

b. Double-clicking on the Command button.

7 Input the length and width
Calculate the area
Output the area

9 a. Input Daily Billing Data
Prepare Daily Invoices
Print Daily Invoices
Select Past Invoices
Print Selected Invoices

b. A modify invoices module is needed to correct errors in data that has been input previously. This module would interact with all of the other modules so as to automatically correct all stored data, produce updated reports, and leave an audit trail.

c. An audit trail is required for both internal and external security. It provides a method of easily tracking changes and repayments, prevents fraud, and is useful in preparing documented proof of all changes for management, customers, and required Federal and State oversight agencies.

Exercises 1.4

1 a. One possible solution:

Make sure the car is parked, the engine is off, and the key is out of the ignition switch
Go to the trunk
Put the correct key into the trunk
Open the trunk
Remove the spare tire and the jack
Put the jack under the car . . . and so on

b. Go to a phone
Remove the handset from the phone
Wait for the dial tone
Take out the correct change for the call
Put the correct change into the phone
Dial the number

   c. Arrive at the store
      Walk through the door
      Go to the bread aisle
      Select the desired bread
      Go to the cashier
      Pay for the bread and leave

   d. Prepare the turkey
      Preheat the oven
      Open the oven door
      Put the turkey in the oven
      Close the oven door
      Wait the appropriate time for the turkey to cook

3 Step 1: Pour the contents of the first cup into the third cup
Step 2: Rinse out the first cup
Step 3: Pour the contents of the second cup into the first cup
Step 4: Rinse out the second cup
Step 5: Pour the contents of the third cup into the second cup

5 Step 1: Compare the first number with the second number and use the smallest of these numbers for the next step.

Step 2: Compare the smallest number found in step 1 with the third number. The smallest of these two numbers is the smallest of all three numbers.

7 a. Step 1: Compare the first name in the list with the name JONES. If the names match, stop the search; else go to step 2.

     Step 2: Compare the next name in the list with the name JONES. If the names match, stop the search; else repeat this step.

Chapter 1—Self Test

1 Program

2 Examples are Fortran, COBOL, Pascal, C, C++, Visual Basic

3 machine code

4 interpreted

5 compiled

Chapter 2

Exercises 2.1

1 Object-based visual part and a procedural-based language part.

3 The Toolbox provides a standard set of visual objects that forms the basis of the visual part of an application.

5 A window.

Exercises 2.2

1 Design time designates the phase during which an application is designed and developed. Run time designates the phase during which an application is executing.

3 The **Name** and **Caption** properties.

5 Create the graphical user interface (GUI)
Set the properties of each object on the interface
Write the code

7 A form has 50 design-time properties.

9 The caption within the Title bar indicates the mode.

Exercises 2.3

1 a. Event procedure: A procedure that is attached to an object and initiated by an event.

    b. Dialog box: A box that requires user input.

    c. Method: A procedure that is connected to an object.

    d. Header line: The first line of a procedure.

    e. Argument: Data that is passed into a procedure.

    f. Template: An empty procedure that consists of a header line and a statement.

3 a.
```
Private Sub cmdButton1_Click()
    Private Sub cmdButton2_Click()
```

    b. The provided template is

```
Private Sub cmdButton1_Click()

End Sub
```

5 The required event procedure should appear as

```
Private Sub Form_Click()
  Print "your name in here"
  Print "your street address in here"
  Print "your city, state, and zip code in here"
End Sub
```

Exercises 2.4

1 A Command button has 17 event procedures associated with it.

3 A **Label** has a **Caption** property but does not have a **TabStop** property.

5 By inserting an ampersand symbol (&) before one of the letters in the caption.

Exercises 2.5

1 a. There are 17 events associated with a Command button

    b. Click
DragDrop
DragOver
GotFocus
KeyDown
KeyPress
KeyUp
LostFocus
MouseDown
MouseMove
MouseUp
OLECompleteDrag
OLEDragDrop

continued

> OLEDragOver
> OLEGiveFeedback
> OLESetData
> OLEStartDrag

❸ a. There are 17 events associated with a **Label**

❺ a. Command button's **Click** event

b. Command button's **LostFocus** event

c. Text box's **GotFocus** event

d. Text box's **LostFocus** event

❼ a. `txtTest.Text = "Welcome to Visual Basic"`

b. `txtTest.Text = "Now is the time"`

c. `txtTest.Text = "12345"`

d. `txtTest.Text = "4 * 5 is 20"`

e. `txtTest.Text = "Vacation is Near"`

Chapter 2—Self Test

❶ design time

❷ graphical user interface

❸ object-based visual part and procedural-based language part

❹ window

❺ context-sensitive menu

❻ Create a graphical user interface, set the properties of each object on the interface, and write the code.

❼ The **Caption** property will be shown on the interface, while the name property will not.

❽ `Text1.Text = ""`

❾ `Form1.Cls`

❿ `txtWelcome.text = "Welcome to Visual Basic"`

Chapter 3

....

Exercises 3.1

❶ a. Single or Double

b. Integer

c. Single or Double

d. Integer

e. Single or Double

f. String

❷ 634000
195.162
83.95
.00295
.0004623

❸ 1.26E2
6.5623E2
3.42695E3

4.8932E3
3.21E-1
1.23E-2
6.789E-3

7 a. $3 + 4 * 6 = 3 + 24$
$= 27$

b. $3 * 4 / 6 + 6 = 12 / 6 + 6$
$= 2 + 6$
$= 8$

c. $2 * 3 / 12 * 8 / 4 = 6 / 12 * 8 / 4$
$= 0.5 * 8 / 4$
$= 4 / 4$
$= 1$

d. $10 * (1 + 7.3 * 3) = 10 * (1 + 21.9)$
$= 10 * 22.9$
$= 229$

e. $20 - 2 / 6 + 3 = 20 - 0.33 + 3$
$= 19.67 + 3$
$= 22.67$

f. $20 - 2 / (6 + 3) = 20 - 2 / 9$
$= 20 - 0.22$
$= 19.78$

g. $(20 - 2) / 6 + 3 = 18 / 6 + 3$
$= 3 + 3$
$= 6$

h. $(20 - 2) / (6 + 3) = 18 / 9$
$= 2$

Exercises 3.2

1 The following are not valid:

12345 does not begin with a letter
Print is a reserved word
$total does not begin with a letter
new bal cannot contain a space
9ab6 does not begin with a letter
sum.of contains a special character

3 a. `Dim count As Integer`

b. `Dim grade As Single`

c. `Dim yield As Double`

5 a. `Dim firstnum As Integer, secnum As Single`

b. `Dim speed As Single, distance As Double`

c. `Dim years As Integer, yield As Single, maturity As String*8`

Exercises 3.3

1 $c = 2 * 3.1416 * 3.3$

3 $celsius = 5 / 9 * (fahrenheit - 32)$

5 $lengthInches = 2.54 * lengthCentimeters$

7 The first integer displayed is 4
The second integer displayed is 4

9 The sum is 0
The sum is 26.27
The final sum is 28.238

11 a. Private Sub Form_Click()

```
    width = 15 <-- missing declaration for all variables
    area = length * width <-- missing assignment for length
    Print "The area is"; area
End Sub
```

b. Private Sub Form_Click()

```
    Dim length As Integer, width As Integer, area As Integer

    area = length * width <-- this should come after
    the assignment of values
    length = 20
    width = 15
    Print "The area is"; area
        <-- Missing End Sub statement
```

c. Private Sub Form_Click()

```
    Dim length As Integer, width As Integer, area As Integer

    length = 20
    width = 15
    length * width = area   <-- incorrect assignment statement
    Print "The area is; area
End Sub
```

Exercises 3.4

1 The name of the desired intrinsic function,
What the intrinsic function does,
The type of data required by the intrinsic function, and
The data type of the result returned by the intrinsic function

3 a. Sqr(6.37)

b. Sqr(x − y)

c. Sqr(a^2 − b^2)

5 a. 0

b. 0

c. 123

d. 123.4

e. 123.5

f. 123

Chapter 3—Self Test

1 An example is a + b

2 An example is x = 89

3 There are many; some examples are beep, print, for, next, do, loop, if.

4 A variable is a name you give to a memory area that can hold various values assigned to it. Only one value, however, can be held at a time.

⑤ 255 characters or less
no space permitted
must start with alphabetic letter
Visual Basic keyword may not be used
arithmetic operators are not permitted
special Visual Basic operators and data type characters are not permitted

⑥ `Dim PayAmt As Single   'or As double or currency`

⑦ `Dim DeptName as string * 14`

⑧ `Option Explicit`

⑨ `Dim busRiders as Byte ' there will never be a negative number`
`                      ' and as a bus can't hold more`
`                      ' than 255 riders a byte can be used`

⑩ `Sum = 78 + 2`

Chapter 4

Exercises 4.1

❶ a. `test = InputBox("Enter a grade", "Input dialog", "0")`

   b. `test = InputBox("Enter a temperature", "Data Analysis", "98.6")`

   c. `test = InputBox("Enter a Name", "Mail List Application")`

   d. `test = InputBox("Enter a price", "Pricing Application")`

❸ The required event procedure is

```
Private Sub cmdTax_Click()
  Dim amount As Single
  Dim salestax As Single

  amount = InputBox("Enter the amount of the bill")
  salestax = 0.06 * amount
  picShow.Print salestax
End Sub
```

Exercises 4.2

❶ The display produced is

$155.99
155.99
155.986
15.60%
1.56E+02
155.99
Yes
True

❸ The correct syntax for these function calls are

   a. `Format(5, "##")`

   b. `Format(56829, "#####")`

   c. `Format(526.768, "###")`

   d. `Format(526.78, "##.##")`

Exercises 4.3

1 The modified procedure is

```
Private Sub Form_Click()
   Const PI As Single = 3.1416
   Dim radius As Single, area As Single
   Dim circumference As Single

   radius = InputBox("Enter a radius:", "Input Dialog", "0")
   circumference = 2 * PI * radius
   area = PI * radius ^ 2
   Print "The circumference of the circle is "; circumference
   Print "The area of the circle is "; area
End Sub
```

3 The modified procedure is

```
Private Sub Form_Click()
   Const FACTOR As Single = 5 / 9
   Dim fahren As Single, celsius As Single

   fahren = InputBox("Enter a temperature in degrees _
      Fahrenheit", , "0")
   celsius = FACTOR * (fahren - 32)
   Print "The equivalent Celsius temperature is "; celsius
End Sub
```

Chapter 4—Self Test

1 With a monospaced font, each letter takes up the same amount of space. The letter "W" requires the same space as the letter "I". With a proportional font, the amount of space taken on the screen or line, depends on the letter itself.

2 The print zone for a proportional font is the width of 14 average character widths, and for a monospaced font it is 14 columns.

3 It will move the cursor over 5 spaces from its current position.

4 The **InputBox** function returns a variant data type. The **InputBox$** returns a string.

5 By using certain characters, it is possible to create almost any format for dates, numerics, and strings. Also available are 4 different sections so you can handle positive, negative, and zero values differently.

6 2345, 218, 0, and 0

7 `Print Text1.Text; Text2.Text; Text3.Text`

The values found in each of the text boxes will be printed right next to each other. No space has been allowed between them.

8 `PicShow.currentx = 100`
`PicShow.currenty = 200`

9 `Printer.NewPage`

10

Number	Result	Code
22345	$22,345.00	Format(22345, "currency")
5.26	005.2600	Format(5.26, "000.0000")
5.26	5.26E+00	Format(5.26, "scientific")

Chapter 5

Exercises 5.1

1 a. Check box because it is a Yes/No selection

b. Option buttons because it is really a choice between two different types of transmissions. It could, however, be constructed using a Check box with the No choice corresponding to the default transmission type.

c. Option buttons

d. Check box

e. Option buttons

f. Check box

g. Option buttons

h. Option buttons

3 b. A check box can always be replaced by two Command buttons, where one button selects the choice and one button deselects the choice. Therefore, any choice that can be represented as a selection between two alternatives states is best presented using a check box. Command buttons are more useful in initiating actions, such as Begin Processing and End Processing.

Exercises 5.2

1 a. True

b. True

c. True

d. True

e. True

f. True

g. True

3 a. $a = 5$
   $5 = 5$ is True

b. $b * d = c * c$
   $2 * 5 = 4 * 4$
   $10 = 16$ is False

c. d Mod b * c > 5 Or c Mod b * d < 7
   $(((d \text{ Mod } b) * c) > 5)$ Or $(((c \text{ Mod } b) * d) < 7)$
   $(((5 \text{ Mod } 2) * 4) > 5)$ Or $(((4 \text{ Mod } 2) * 5) < 7)$
   $((1 * 4) > 5)$ Or $((0 * 5) < 7)$
   $(4 > 5)$ Or $(0 < 7)$
   0 Or 1 is True

5 The expression being tested is whether True is considered greater than or equal to **False**. Thus, the statement Print True >= False will display a **False**. This means that **True** is considered as less than **False** in Visual Basic.

Exercises 5.3

1 a.
```
If (angle = 90) Then
    Print "The angle is a right angle";
Else
    Print "The angle is not a right angle";
End If
```

b.
```
If (temperature > 100) Then
    Print "above the boiling point of water";
Else
    Print "below the boiling point of water";
End If
```

c.
```
If (number > 0) Then
    possum = possum + number
Else
    negsum = negsum + number
End If
```

d.
```
If (slope < 0.5) Then
    flag = 0
Else
    flag = 1
End If
```

e.
```
If ((num1 - num2) < 0.001) Then
    approx = 0
Else
    approx = (num1 - num2) / 2.0
End If
```

f.
```
If ((temp1 - temp2) > 2.3) Then
    error = (temp1 - temp2) * factor
End If
```

g.
```
If ((x > y) && (z < 20)) Then
    p = InputBox("Enter a value for p")
End If
```

h.
```
If ((distance > 20) And (distance < 35)) Then
    time = InputBox("Enter a value for time")
End If
```

3 Assuming the name of the Picture box is **picShow**, the procedural code is

```
Dim num1 As Single, num2 As Single

num1 = InputBox("Enter a value for the first number", , "0")
num2 = InputBox("Enter a value for the second number", , "0")
picShow.Cls

If num1 > num2 Then
    picShow.Print "The first number is greater"
Else
    picShow.Print "The first number is smaller"
End If
```

If the two numbers entered are equal, the **Else** statement will be executed, and the message "The first number is smaller" is displayed.

5 a.
```
Private Sub Form_Click()
  Dim grade As Single

    grade = InputBox("Enter the grade", , "0")
    If grade >= 70 Then
      Print "A passing grade"
    Else
      Print "A failing grade"
    End If
  End Sub
```

b. At least three runs should be made: one input under 70.0, one at 70.0, and one over 70.0. Another run, if necessary, might be made for some unexpected input, such as "seventy."

Exercises 5.4

1 The required changes must be made in the **LostFocus** event code. The modified **LostFocus** event code is

```
Private Sub txtMcode_LostFocus()
  Dim Marcode As String

    Marcode = txtMcode.Text

    If Marcode = "M" Or Marcode = "m" Then
      picBox.Print "Individual is married."
    ElseIf Marcode = "S" Or Marcode = "s" Then
      picBox.Print "Individual is single."
    ElseIf Marcode = "D" Or Marcode = "d" Then
      picBox.Print "Individual is divorced."
    ElseIf Marcode = "W" Or Marcode = "w" Then
      picBox.Print "Individual is widowed."
    Else
      picBox.Print "An invalid code was entered."
    End If
  End Sub
```

3
```
Private Sub Form_Click()
  Dim angle As Single

  angle = InputBox("Enter the angle", , "0")
  If angle < 90 Then
    Print "The angle is acute."
  ElseIf angle = 90 Then
    Print "The angle is a right angle"
  ElseIf angle > 90 Then
    Print "The angle is obtuse"
  End If
End Sub
```

5
```
Private Sub Form_Click()
  Dim grade As Single
  Dim letter As String

  grade = InputBox("Enter the student's numerical grade", , "0")
```

continued

```
        If (grade >= 90) Then
          letter = "A"
        ElseIf (grade >= 80) Then
          letter = "B"
        ElseIf (grade >= 70) Then
          letter = "C"
        ElseIf (grade >= 60) Then
          letter = "D"
        Else
          letter = "F"
        End If
        Print "The student receives a grade of "; letter
      End Sub
```

Notice that an **If-Then-ElseIf** chain is used. If simple **If** statements were used, a grade entered as 75.5, for example, would be assigned a 'C' because it was greater than 60.0. But, the grade would then be reassigned to 'D' because it is also greater than 60.0.

7 a. Yes.

   b. Program 5-6 is a better program because fewer calculations would typically be made. For example, If 45000 was entered for MonthlySales in Program 5-6, the first **If** statement is executed and found to be false. The first **Else-If** statement is then executed, found to be true, and further execution of the chain stops. This is not true for the Exercise program. Here, all **If** statements are executed, regardless of which has a true condition. Program 5-6 also requires fewer comparisons, using simpler relational expressions.

Exercises 5.5

1
```
Select Case let_grad
   Case "A"
      Print "The numerical grade is between 90 and 100"
   Case "B"
      Print "The numerical grade is between 80 and 89.9"
   Case "C"
      Print "The numerical grade is between 70 and 79.9"
   Case "D"
      Print "How are you going to explain this one"
   Case Else
      Print "Of course I had nothing to do with the grade."
      Print "It must have been the professor's fault."
End Select
```

3
```
Select Case code
   Case 1
      Print "360 Kilobyte Drive (5 1/2 inch)"
   Case 2:
      Print "1.2 Megabyte Drive (5 1/2 inch)"
   Case 3:
      Print "722 Kilobyte Drive (3 1/4 inch)"
   Case 4:
      Print "1.4 Megabyte Drive (3 1/4 inch)"
End Select
```

Chapter 5—Self Test

1 `End Select`

2 A gray check box is not disabled as one would expect. Once it is clicked, the gray area is eliminated and the box becomes unchecked.

3 desk checking

4 All 5 of the check boxes can be true at the same time. Only 1 of the option buttons can be true at the same time.

5
```
Select Case myNum
   Case 1, 7, 15
      myNum = myNum + 100
   Case 2, 9, 21
      myNum = myNum + 150
   Case 3, 6, 13
      myNum = myNum + 200
   Case Else
      Print "Can't find it"
End Select
```

Chapter 6

Exercises 6.2

1
```
Private Sub Form_Click
   Dim count As Integer

   count = 2   ' initialize count
   Do While count <= 10
     Print count;
     count = count + 2  ' increment count
   Loop
End Sub
```

3 a.   21 items are displayed, which are the integers from 1 to 21

c.   21 items are displayed, which are the integers from 0 to 20

5
```
Private Sub Form_Click()
   Dim pcount As Integer, count As Integer

   count = 0
   Do While count <= 9
     pcount = count
     Do While pcount > 0
       Print "  ";
       pcount = pcount - 1
     Loop
     Print count
     count = count + 1
   Loop
End Sub
```

7
```
Private Sub Form_Click()
   Dim feet As Integer
   Dim meters As Single

   Font = "Courier" ' force a fixed spaced font
   Print "FEET   METERS"
   Print "----   ------"
   feet = 3

   Do While (feet <= 30)
     meters = feet / 3.28
     Print Format(feet, "00"); "       ";
     Print Format(meters, "00.00")
     feet = feet + 3
   Loop
End Sub
```

9
```
Private Sub Form_Click()
     Dim Time As Single, miles As Single

     Font = "Courier" ' force a fixed spaced font
     Print "TIME     MILES"
     Print "----     ------"
     Time = 0.5

     Do While (Time <= 4)
       miles = 55 * Time
       Print Format(Time, "0.0"); "       ";
       Print Format(miles, "000.00")
       Time = Time + 0.5
     Loop
   End Sub
```

Exercises 6.3

1 a.
```
Dim n as Integer
n = 33
Do While n >= 3
  Print n; "   ";
  n = n - 3
Loop
```

b.
```
Dim n As String
n = "Z"
Do While n >= "A"
  Print n; "   ";
  n = Chr(Asc(n) - 1)
Loop
```

3 See below.

```
Private Sub cndRun_Click()
  Dim maxnums As Integer
  Dim count As Integer
  Dim num As Single
  Dim total As Single
```

```
    Cls
    maxnums = InputBox("Please type in the total number of data values to be added", , "0")
    count = 1
    total = 0
    Do While count <= maxnums
      num = InputBox("Enter a number", "Input Dialog", "0")
      total = total + num
      Print "The number entered is"; num
      Print "The total is now"; total
      count = count + 1
    Loop
    Print "The final total is"; total
End Sub
```

5 a. See below.

```
Private Sub Form_Click()
  Dim cels As Single, fahr As Single
  Dim start As Single, final As Single
  Dim incr As Single

  start = InputBox("Enter the starting temperature in degrees Celsius", , "0")
  final = InputBox("Enter the ending temperature in degrees Celsius", , "0")
  incr = InputBox("Now enter the increment between conversions", , "1")

  cels = start
  Font = "Courier" ' force a fixed space font
  Print "Celsius     Fahrenheit"
  Print "---------------------"
  Do While (cels <= final)
    fahr = (9# / 5#) * cels + 32#
    Print Format(cels, "00.00"); "          ";
    Print Format(fahr, "00.00")
    cels = cels + incr
  Loop
End Sub
```

Exercises 6.4

1 a. For I = 1 To 20

b. For count = 1 To 20 Step 2

c. For J = 1 To 100 Step 5

d. For count = 20 To 1 Step -1

e. For count = 20 To 1 Step -2

f. For count = 1.0 To 16.2 Step 0.2

g. For xcnt = 20.0 To 10.0 Step -0.5

3 a. 55

b. 1024

c. 75

d. −5

e. 40320

f. 0.03125

❺ 20
16
12
8
4
0

❼ The only change that needs to be made is to change the **For** statement in the event procedure to

```
For num = 10 To 1 Step -1
```

Exercises 6.5

❶
```
Private Sub Form_Click()
  Const EXPERS As Integer = 4
  Const RESULTS As Integer = 6
  Dim i As Integer, j As Integer
  Dim total As Single
  Dim average As Single, data As Single

  For i = 1 To EXPERS
    Print "Enter "; RESULTS; " results for experiment No."; i
    total = 0
    For j = 1 To RESULTS
      data = InputBox("Enter a result", , "0")
      total = total + data
    Next j
    average = total / RESULTS
    Print "   The average for experiment No."; i; "is"; average
  Next I
End Sub
```

❸ a.
```
Private Sub Form_Click()
    Const BOWLERS As Integer = 5
    Const GAMES As Integer = 3
    Dim bowler As Integer, game As Integer
    Dim score As Single
    Dim plyr_tot As Single, plyr_avg As Single
    Dim message As String

    For bowler = 1 To BOWLERS
      plyr_tot = 0
      For game = 1 To GAMES
        message = "Enter the score for bowler " + Str(bowler)
        message = message + " and game " + Str(game)
        score = InputBox(message, , "0")
        plyr_tot = plyr_tot + score
      Next game
      plyr_avg = plyr_tot / GAMES
      Print "   The average for bowler"; bowler; "is"; plyr_avg
    Next bowler
  End Sub
```

```
b.  Private Sub Form_Click()
        Const BOWLERS As Integer = 2
        Const GAMES As Integer = 3
        Dim bowler As Integer, game As Integer
        Dim score As Single
        Dim plyr_tot As Single, plyr_avg As Single
        Dim team_tot As Single
        Dim message As String

        For bowler = 1 To BOWLERS
          plyr_tot = 0
          team_tot = 0
          For game = 1 To GAMES
            message = "Enter the score for bowler " + Str(bowler)
            message = message + " and game " + Str(game)
            score = InputBox(message, , "0")
            plyr_tot = plyr_tot + score
          Next game
          team_tot = team_tot + plyr_tot
          plyr_avg = plyr_tot / GAMES
          Print "   The average for bowler"; bowler; "is"; plyr_avg
        Next bowler
        team_avg = team_tot / (BOWLERS * GAMES)
        Print "The average for the whole team is"; team_avg
    End Sub
```

5
```
Private Sub Form_Click()
    Const SMALLDIF As Single = 0.00001
    Dim x As Single, y As Single, z As Single

    Cls
    Font = "Courier" 'set fixed space font
    Print "x   z        y   "
    Print "--  --   -------"
    For x = 1# To 5#
      For z = 2# To 10#
        Print Format(x, "00"); "   ";
        Print Format(z, "00"); "   ";
        If Abs(x - z) > SMALLDIF Then
          y = x * z / (x - z)
          Print Format(y, "000.00")
        Else
          Print "Value Undefined"
        End If
      Next z
    Next x
End Sub
```

7
```
Private Sub Form_Click()
    Dim dependents As Integer
    Dim salary As Long
    Dim deducations As Single

    Cls
    Font = "Courier"
```

continued

```
     Print "                |<---------------------- Deducti";
     Print "ons ------------------------>|"
     Print " Salary    |  0          1          2       ";
     Print "  3        4          5    |"
     Print "--------   --------   --------   --------   ";
     Print "--------   --------   --------"
  For salary = 10000 To 50000 Step 10000
    Print salary; "   ";
    For dependents = 0 To 5
      deductions = dependents * 500 + 0.05 * (50000 - salary)
      Print "     "; Format(deductions, "00000");
    Next dependents
    Print ' start a new line
  Next salary
End Sub
```

Exercises 6.6

1 a.
```
Private Sub Form_Click()
   Const LOWGRADE As Integer = 0
   Const HIGHGRADE As Integer = 100
   Dim grade As Integer
   Do
      grade = InputBox("Enter a grade", , "-1")
   Loop Until (grade >= LOWGRADE And grade <= HIGHGRADE)
   Print "The grade entered is"; grade
End Sub
```

Note: A default grade of –1 is used to ensure that the user must enter a valid grade to exit the loop. A more appropriate approach would be to display a message alerting the user when an invalid grade has been entered. This can be accomplished by the following code:

```
Private Sub Form_Click()
   Const LOWGRADE As Integer = 0
   Const HIGHGRADE As Integer = 100
   Dim grade As Integer
   Dim message As String

   message = "Enter a grade"
   Do
      grade = InputBox(message, , "-1")
      If (grade < LOWGRADE Or grade > HIGHGRADE) Then
         message = "Invalid grade - please reenter a valid grade"
      End If
   Loop Until (grade >= LOWGRADE And grade <= HIGHGRADE)
   Print "The grade entered is"; grade
End Sub
```
b.
```
Private Sub Form_Click()
   Const LOWGRADE As Integer = 0
   Const HIGHGRADE As Integer = 100
   Const SENTINEL As Integer = 999
   Dim grade As Integer
   Dim message As String
```

```
            message = "Enter a grade"
            Do
               grade = InputBox(message, , "-1")
               If grade = SENTINEL Then
                  Exit Do
               ElseIf (grade < LOWGRADE Or grade > HIGHGRADE) Then
                  message = "Invalid grade - please reenter a valid grade"
               End If
            Loop Until (grade >= LOWGRADE And grade <= HIGHGRADE)
            Print "The grade entered is"; grade
         End Sub

   c.    Private Sub Form_Click()
            Const LOWGRADE As Integer = 0
            Const HIGHGRADE As Integer = 100
            Const BADTRIES As Integer = 5
            Dim grade As Integer
            Dim message As String

            message = "Enter a grade"
            badgrades = 0
            Do
               grade = InputBox(message, , "-1")
               If (grade < LOWGRADE Or grade > HIGHGRADE) Then
                  message = "Invalid grade - please reenter a valid grade"
                  badgrades = badgrades + 1
                  If (badgrades = BADTRIES) Then
                     Exit Do
                  End If
               End If
            Loop Until (grade >= LOWGRADE And grade <= HIGHGRADE)
            Print "The grade entered is"; grade
         End Sub
```

3 a.
```
      Private Sub Form_Click()
         Dim num As Long, digit As Integer

         Cls
         num = InputBox("Enter a positive integer", , "0")
         Print "The digits reversed are:";
         Do
            digit = num Mod 10
            num = num / 10
            Print digit;
         Loop While num > 0
      End Sub
```

Chapter 6—Self Test

1 loop

2 sentinel

3 The counter X will be incremented by 5 on each pass.

4 i.   A repetitive statement that defines the boundaries containing the repeating section of code and controls whether or not that code will be executed.

ii. A condition that needs to be evaluated.

iii. A statement that initially sets the condition

iv. A statement that modifies the condition to allow the repetitions to stop

5 A pretest loop will test the condition before any action takes place. In a posttest loop, the statements within the loop will be executed at least once before the test is made.

Chapter 7

Exercises 7.1

1 a. `Factorial()` expects to receive one integer value.

b. `Price()` expects to receive one integer and two single-precision values, in that order.

c. An integer and two double-precision values, in that order, must be passed to `Yield()`.

d. A boolean value character and two double-precision values, in that order, must be passed to `Interest()`.

e. Two single-precision values, in that order, must be passed to `Total()`.

f. Two integers, two strings, and one single-precision value, in that order, are expected by `Roi()`.

g. Two integers and two boolean values, in that order, are expected by `Get_val()`.

3 a. Both the `Check()` procedure and a procedure that can be used to call it are listed below

```
Public Sub Check(num1 As Integer, num2 As Single, num3 As Double)
    Print "The integer is " num1
    Print "The single-precision number is" num2
    Print "The double-precision number is" num3
End Sub

Private Sub Form_Click()
    Dim first As Integer
    Dim second As Single
    Dim third As Double

    first = InputBox("Enter an integer", , "0")
    second = InputBox("Enter a single-precision number", , "0")
    third = InputBox("Enter a double-precision number", , "0")
    Call Check(first, second, third)
End Sub
```

5 a. Both the `Mult()` procedure and a procedure that can be used to call it are listed below

```
Public Sub Mult(num1 As Single, num2 As Single)
    Print "The product of these numbers is"; num1 * num2
End Sub
```

```
Private Sub Form_Click()
  Dim first As Single
  Dim second As Single

  first = InputBox("Enter a number", , "0")
  second = InputBox("Enter another number", , "0")
  Call Mult(first, second)
End Sub
```

Exercises 7.2

1 Both the Find_abs() procedure and a procedure that can be used to call it are listed below

```
Public Sub Find_abs(num As Double, val As Double)
  If (num < 0) Then
    val = -num
  Else
    val = num
  End If
End Sub


Private Sub Form_Click()
  Dim firstnum As Double, absval As Double

  firstnum = InputBox("Enter a number", , "0")
  Call Find_abs(firstnum, absval) ' the procedure is called here

  Print "The absolute value of the entered number is "; absval
End Sub
```

3 Both the Findmax() procedure and a procedure that can be used to call it are listed below

```
Public Sub Findmax(x As Single, y As Single, max As Single)
  If (x >= y) Then   'find the maximum number
    max = x
  Else
    max = y
  End If
End Sub


Private Sub Form_Click()
  Dim firstnum As Single
  Dim secnum As Single
  Dim maxnum As Single

  firstnum = InputBox("Enter a number", , "0")
  secnum = InputBox("Great! Please enter a second number", , "0")
  Call FindMax(firstnum, secnum, maxnum) ' the procedure is called here

  Print "The maximum of the two numbers is "; maxnum
End Sub
```

5 a. Both the `Totsec()` procedure and a procedure that can be used to call it are listed below

```
Public Sub Totsec(hh As Integer, mm As Integer, ss As Integer, total As Integer)
  total = 60 * (60 * hh + mm) + ss
End Sub

Private Sub Form_Click()
  Dim hours As Integer, mins As Integer
  Dim secs As Integer, tsecs As Integer

  hours = InputBox("Enter the hours", , "0")
  mins = InputBox("Enter the minutes", , "0")
  secs = InputBox("Enter the seconds", , "0")
  Call Totsec(hours, mins, secs, tsecs) ' the procedure is called here

  Print "The total seconds is "; tsecs
End Sub
```

Exercises 7.3

1 a. `IntToSingle()` expects to receive one integer value and it returns a single-precision value.

b. `Volts()` expects to receive two single-precision values, and returns a single-precision value.

c. A boolean and a single-precision value, in that order, must be passed to `Power()`. The function returns a double-precision value.

d. A boolean and a double-precision value, in that order, must be passed to `Flag()`. The function returns a boolean value.

e. Two double-precision values must be passed to `Energy()`. The function returns a double-precision value.

f. Three single-precision values and one integer value, in that order, are expected by `Roi()`. The function returns an integer value.

g. An integer and string value, in that order, are expected by `Getval()`. The function returns a double-precision value.

h. The function `Locase()` expects to receive a single string value and returns a string value.

3 Both the `CelToFar()` function and a procedure that can be used to call it are listed below

```
Public Function CelToFar(temp As Single) As Single
  CelToFar = 9/5 * temp + 32
End Function

Private Sub Form_Click()
  Dim celsius As Single
  Dim fahrenheit As Single

  celsius = InputBox("Enter a Celsius temperature", , "0")
  fahrenheit = CelToFar(celsius) ' the function is called here

  Print "The equivalent Fahrenheit temperature is "; fahrenheit
End Sub
```

5 Both the `Absdif()` function and a procedure that can be used to call it are listed below

```
Public Function Absdif(x As Single, y As Single) As Single
  Absdif = Abs(y - x)
End Function

Private Sub Form_Click()
  Dim firstnum As Single
  Dim secnum As Single

  firstnum = InputBox("Enter a number", , "0")
  secnum = InputBox("Enter a second number", , "0")
  difference = Absdif(firstnum, secnum)   ' the function is called here

  Print "The absolute difference between these numbers is"; difference
End Sub
```

Exercises 7.4

1 The scope of a variable tells where the variable is recognized in the program and can be used within an expression. If, for example, a variable is declared within a procedure, it is local and use is limited to the body of the procedure.

3 a. Private procedure-level variables can only be used within the procedure that they are declared. Such variables are referred to as local variables.

b. Public procedure-level variables are not permitted.

5 Even though both procedures used the same variable and parameter names there is no problem. Each of these variables and parameters are local to their respective procedures; thus, the `Form_Click()` event procedure only has access to its declared variables n and sum, and the `Accumulate()` function only has access to its n parameter and sum variable. That is, four distinct memory locations are created.

b. The output displayed is: The sum of the numbers entered is 40

c. The declaration for sum within Accumulate should be changed to

```
Static sum As Single
```

Exercises 7.5

1 The required function and a procedure that can be used to call it are listed below:

```
Private Sub Form_Click()
  Dim n As Integer

  n = InputBox("Enter a positive integer", , "0")
  result = Fibon(n - 1) ' the series starts with term 0, not 1
  Print "Term"; n; "of the Fibonacci sequence is "; result
End Sub

Public Function Fibon(n As Integer) As Long
  If (n < 2) Then
    Fibon = n
  Else
    Fibon = Fibon(n - 1) + Fibon(n - 2)
  End If
End Function
```

3 The required function and a procedure that can be used to call it are listed below:

```
Private Sub Form_Click()
   Dim x As Integer, n As Integer
   Dim result As Long

   x = InputBox("Enter the value of x", , "0")
   n = InputBox("Enter the value of n", , "0")
   result = XToTheN(x, n)
   Print x; "raised to the power"; n; "is"; result
End Sub

Public Function XToTheN(x As Integer, n As Integer) As Long
   If (n = 0) Then
     XToTheN = 1
   Else
     XToTheN = x * XToTheN(x, n - 1)
   End If
End Function
```

5 The required function and a procedure that can be used to call it are listed below:

```
Public Function nTerm(a As Integer, d As Integer, n As Integer)
As Integer
   If (n = 1) Then
     nTerm = a
   Else
     nTerm = d + nTerm(a, d, n - 1)
   End If
End Function

Private Sub Form_Click()
   Dim a As Integer, d As Integer
   Dim n As Integer, term As Integer

   n = InputBox("Enter the desired term", , "0")
   a = InputBox("Enter the first term", , "0")
   d = InputBox("Enter the common difference", , "0")

   term = nTerm(a, d, n)
   Print "Term"; n; "of the sequence is"; term
End Sub
```

Chapter 7–Self Test

1 a. form, b. standard basic, and c. class modules

2 The public designation allows the procedure to be called from any form or any module in the application. The private designation restricts the use of the **Sub** procedure to being called from the module in which the procedure resides.

3 argument list

4 x and z can be changed, but not y; because y is passed by value it cannot be changed, while x and z are passed by reference so they can be changed.

⑤ Arguments passed by reference can be changed by the **Sub** procedure or by the function. The actual location of the variable is passed. When passing by value, the contents of the variable is passed so it may be used, but the original value remains the same.

⑥ Hat

⑦ 7

⑧ 12

⑨ `Call message(msg, num)`

⑩
```
Public Sub Mine(price As Single)
Call Mine(dollar)
```

Chapter 8

Exercises 8.1

① a. `Dim grades(100) As Single`

b. `Dim temp(50) As Single`

c. `Dim code(30) As String*1`

d. `Dim year(100) As Integer`

e. `Dim velocity(32) As Single`

f. `Dim distance(1000) As Single`

g. `Dim code_num(6) As Integer`

③ a.
```
grade(1) = InputBox("Enter a value",,"0")
grade(3) = InputBox("Enter a value",,"0")
grade(7) = InputBox("Enter a value",,"0")
```

b.
```
message = "Enter a value for grade("
For i = 1 To 20
  message = message + Str(i) + " )"
  grade(i) = InputBox(message, , "0")
Next i
```

⑤ a. a(1) a(2) a(3) a(4) a(5)

b. a(1) a(3) a(5)

c. b(3) b(4) b(5) b(6) b(7) b(8) b(9) b(10)

d. b(3) b(6) b(9) b(12)

e. c(2) c(4) c(6) c(8) c(10)

⑦
```
Private Sub Form_Click()
  Const Numels As Integer = 8
  Dim fmax(Numels) As Single
  Dim sum As Single
  Dim message As String
  Dim i As Integer

  sum = 0
  For i = 1 To Numels
    message = "Enter a value for element no."
    message = message + Str(i)
    fmax(i) = InputBox(message, , "0")
    sum = sum + fmax(i)
  Next i
```

continued

```
        Print "The array elements are:"
        For i = 1 To Numels
            Print fmax(i)
        Next i
        Print "The average of these numbers is:"; sum / Numels
    End Sub
```

9
```
Private Sub Form_Click()
    Const NUMELS As Integer = 5
    Dim grades(NUMELS) As Single
    Dim deviation(NUMELS) As Single
    Dim sum As Single
    Dim message As String
    Dim i As Integer

    sum = 0
    For i = 1 To NUMELS
        message = "Enter a value for element no."
        message = message + Str(i)
        grades(i) = InputBox(message, , "0")
        sum = sum + grades(i)
    Next i
    average = sum / NUMELS

    Rem: Here is where the deviations are calculated and displayed
    For i = 1 To NUMELS
        deviation(i) = grades(i) - average
        Print Format(grades(i), "###.##"), Format(deviation(i), "###.##")
    Next i
End Sub
```

Exercises 8.2

1

```
Private Sub Form_Click()
    Const NUMELS As Integer = 5
    Dim temp(5) As Integer
    Dim minimum As Integer

    temp(1) = 2
    temp(2) = 18
    temp(3) = 1
    temp(4) = 27
    temp(5) = 6
    Call Fmin(temp, NUMELS, minimum)
    Print "The minimum value is"; minimum
End Sub

Public Sub Fmin(vals() As Integer, final As Integer, minval As Integer)
    Dim i As Integer

    minval = vals(1)
    For i = 2 To final
        If minval > vals(i) Then minval = vals(i)
    Next i
End Sub
```

3
```
Private Sub Form_Click()
    Const NUMELS As Integer = 5
    Dim price(NUMELS) As Single
    Dim quantity(NUMELS) As Single
    Dim amount(NUMELS) As Single
    Dim i As Integer

    price(1) = 10.62
    price(2) = 14.89
    price(3) = 13.21
    price(4) = 16.55
    price(5) = 18.62

    quantity(1) = 4
    quantity(2) = 8.5
    quantity(3) = 6
    quantity(4) = 7.35
    quantity(5) = 9

    For i = 1 To NUMELS
      amount(i) = price(i) * quantity(i)
      Print price(i), quantity(i), amount(i)
    Next i
End Sub
```

5 a. `Dim nums(6,10) As Integer`

  b. `Dim nums(2,5) As Integer`

  c. `Dim codes(7,12) As String*1`

  d. `Dim codes(15,7) As String*1`

  e. `Dim vals(10,25) As Single`

  f. `Dim vals(16,8) As Single`

7 The procedural code for adding equivalent elements of the two arrays is

```
For i = 1 To ROWS
  For j = 1 To COLS
    result(i,j) = first(i,j) + second(i, j)
  Next j
Next i
```

Exercises 8.4

1 a.
```
Type Student
    idnum As Long
    credits As integer
    gpa As Single
End Type
```

  b.
```
Type Student
    name As String*40    ' the length of the string is arbitrary
    Born As BirthDate     ' within realistic limits
    credits As Integer
    gpa As Single
End Type
```

c. Type Mailing
```
    name As String*40     ' the length of the strings are arbitrary
    street As String*80   ' within realistic limits
    city As String *40
    state As String *2
    zip As String*9
  End Type
```

d. Type Stock
```
    name As String *40    ' the length of the string is arbitrary
    price As Single       ' within realistic limits
    date as String*8      ' Assumes a date in the form mm/dd/yy
  End Type
```

e.
```
Type Inventory
  part_no As Integer
  description As String* 50   ' the length of the string is arbitrary
  quant As Integer            ' within realistic limits
  reorder As Integer
End Type
```

3
```
Option Explicit
Private Type CurrentDate
  month As Integer
  day As Integer
  year As Integer
End Type

Private Sub Form_Click()
  Dim num As Integer
  Dim someday As CurrentDate

  someday.month = InputBox("Enter the month", , "1")
  someday.day = InputBox("Enter the day", , "1")
  someday.year = InputBox("Enter the year", , "98")

  Print "The date entered is"; someday.month; "/";
  Print someday.day; "/"; someday.year
End Sub
```

5
```
Option Explicit
Private Type CurrentTime
  hours As Integer
  mins As Integer
End Type

Public Sub newtime(hh As Integer, mm As Integer)
  If mm < 58 Then
    mm = mm + 1
  ElseIf hh < 12 Then
    hh = hh + 1
    mm = 0
  Else
    hh = 1
    mm = 0
  End If
End Sub
```

```
                    Private Sub Form_Click()
                        Dim num As Integer
                        Dim now As CurrentTime

                        now.hours = InputBox("Enter the hour", , "1")
                        now.mins = InputBox("Enter the minute", , "1")

                        Call newtime(now.hours, now.mins)
                        Print "The time, one minute later is ";
                        Print Format(now.hours, "00"); ":";
                        Print Format(now.mins, "00")
                    End Sub
```

7 a. `Dim students(100) As Student   ' the array name is arbitrary`

b. `Dim students(100) As Student   ' the array name is arbitrary`

c. `Dim list(100) As Mailing       ' the array name is arbitrary`

d. `Dim stocks(100) As Stock       ' the array name is arbitrary`

e. `Dim parts(100) As Inventory    ' the array name is arbitrary`

Exercises 8.5

1 The **Form_Click** event should be appear as follows:

```
Private Sub Form_Click()
  Const numel As Integer = 100
  Dim nums(numel) As Single
  Dim i As Integer, moves As Integer

  Randomize
  For i = 1 To numel
    nums(i) = Int(1 + (100 * Rnd)) ' Generate random value between 1 and 100
  Next i

  moves = selectionSort(nums, numel)

  Cls
  Print "The sorted list, in ascending order, is:"
  For i = 1 To numel
    Print "  "; nums(i);
  Next i
  Print
  Print moves; " moves were made to sort this list"
End Sub
```

3 A `swap()` function appropriate to the selection and bubble sort presented in this section is

```
          Public Sub swap(num1 As Variant, num2 As Variant, min As Integer)
              Dim temp As Integer

              temp = num1
              num1 = min
              num2 = temp
          End Sub
```

The following illustrates how the `selectionSort()` would be modified to call `swap()`

```
Public Function selectionSort(num As Variant, numel As Integer) As
Integer
  Dim i As Integer, j As Integer
  Dim min As Integer, minidx As Integer
  Dim temp As Integer, moves As Integer

  moves = 0
  For i = 1 To (numel - 1)
    min = num(i)        ' assume minimum is the first array element
    minidx = i          ' index of minimum element
    For j = i + 1 To numel
      If num(j) < min Then   ' if we've located a lower value
        min = num(j)         ' capture it
        minidx = j
      End If
    Next j
    If min < num(i) Then
      Call swap(num(i), num(minidx), min) ' here is the call to swap()
      moves = moves + 1
    End If
  Next i
  selectionSort = moves  ' return the number of moves
End Function
```

Chapter 8—Self Test

1 index

2 Lbound

3 The **Option Base** statement allows a programmer to set the base for an array at 1 instead of the default 0. It is placed in a form module's General Declarations section.

4 A fixed array is declared with a specific size. A dynamic array is declared with no explicit size and the size may vary throughout the program

5 index

6 This **Dim** statement declares an array with the starting index of 5 and the upper index of 10 in which all elements will be integers.

7 `Dim aintQuantities(10) As Integer  ' assumes Option Base 1`

8 `Dim afltPrices(10) As Single  ' assumes Option Base 1`

9 `Dim astrMessages(10) as String * 15  ' assumes Option Base 1`

10 `Dim aintPartNums(4,5) As Integer  ' assumes Option Base 1`

Chapter 9

Exercises 9.1

1 a. A table is a logical grouping of related information arranged in rows and columns. Each row in a table corresponds to a record, and each column corresponds to a field.

    b. A record consists of a related set of fields.

    c. A field consists of a single item of information.

3 a. The record for Mike Farrell would be displayed.

    b. The record for James Dreskin would be displayed.

    c. The record for Bill Bronson would be displayed.

    d. Ascending (i.e., increasing) order.

5 A Publisher is consists of zero or more Titles.
A Title is related to exactly one Publisher.
A Title can have one or more Authors.
An Author can be associated with one or more Titles.

7 a. Since the last record listed in Table 9-1 has an ID of 30 and there are only 20 records currently in the table, we know that at least 10 records were deleted. The IDs of the deleted records are 6, 8, 13, 16, 17, 18, 19, 20, 25, and 29. From the table itself, we have no way of knowing if any records after the last displayed record were deleted.

    b. Since the last assigned ID number in Table 9-2 is 10 and all ID numbers are accounted for, we know that none of the first 10 records have been deleted. From the table itself, we have no way of knowing if any records after the last displayed record were deleted.

Exercises 9.2

1 **DatabaseName**, **RecordSource**, and **RecordsetType**. The **RecordsetType** property does not have to be explicitly set because it has a default value of Dynaset.

3 a. A bound control is any control whose **DataSource** property is the name of a Data control. This means that the control will have access to a data field value in the current record identified by the Data control. The field that the control is bound to must be specified as the control's **DataField** property.

    b. Text box, Label, Picture box, Image, Check box, List box, Combo box, OLE container control, and custom third-party controls.

    c. **DataSource** and **DataField** properties.

7 a. The statement

```
datPhone.Caption = datPhone.Recordset("ID")
```

      should be placed in both the `Form_Load` and `datPhone_Reposition` event procedures in place of the existing statements that set the datPhone.Caption property.

    b. The statements setting the datPhone.Caption property in both the `Form_Load` and `datPhone_Reposition` event procedures should either be commented out or removed.

Exercises 9.3

1 b. The four clauses are: Select, From, Where, and Order By

    c. The Select and From clauses must be present.

3 a. `Select * From Publishers Where City = 'New York'`

    b. `Select * From Publishers Where State = 'NY'`

    c. `Select * From Publishers Where City = 'New York' And State = 'NY'`

> d.   Select * From Publishers Where Name >= 'A' And Name < 'B'
>
> e.   Select * From Publishers Where Zip >= '07000' and Zip <= '07999'

Exercises 9.4

3 a.   `datPhone.Recordset.FindFirst "Office = 'F1' "`

b.   `datPhone.Recordset.FindNext "Office = 'F1' "`

c.   `datPhone.Recordset.FindLast "Office = 'F1' "`

d.   `datPhone.Recrodset.FindPrevious "office = 'F1' "`

5 a.   The current record is the record in a RecordSet that is available for modification or examination and is the record whose fields are currently displayed in all bound controls.

b.   There can only be one current record for each Data control.

7 a.   `datPub.Recordset.MoveFirst`

b.   `datPub.Recordset.MoveNext`

c.   `datPub.Recordset.MoveLast`

d.   `datPub.Recordset.MovePrevious`

Exercises 9.5

1 a.   Programming a Data control means writing procedural code to alter the control's current record, as opposed to using the control's movement buttons.

b.   The four methods that can be used to program a Data control are the **AddNew**, **Delete**, **Edit**, and **Update** methods.

3   Changes made to a current record are saved when one of the Data control's movement buttons are pushed or an **Update** method has been invoked. This assumes that the proper permissions have been set that allow changes to be made to a RecordSet.

Chapter 9—Self Test

1 mdb

2 The **ReadOnly** property

3 Data control

4 The **DataSource** property and **DataField** property

5 relational database

6 pointers

7 The next record becomes the active record in the database.

8 The database table identified with the `datData1` Data control will be searched to find the first record with the contents of CT in the state field.

9 `Data1.Recordset.AddNew`

10 `Data1.Recordset.FindFirst   "LastName = 'Smith'"`

Chapter 10

....

Exercises 10.1

1 a.   A file is a collection of data that is stored together under a common name on an external storage medium.

b. Files maintained by a database management system consist of records, each of which has the same format. Files maintained directly by Visual Basic need not have this format.

3 Sequential, random, and binary access.

5 Sequential files store numbers as a sequence of ANSI codes, while random-access files store numbers as binary numbers. Random access files must consist of records that have the same length. Items within a random access file can be accessed directly, without the need to sequentially read all prior records in the file.

Exercises 10.3

5 Anything stored on disk is referred to as a file. The two major divisions of files are data files and executable (application) files. Although source code files are sometimes called program files, strictly speaking they are data files used by a compiler or interpreter program. A compiled Visual Basic program is an example of an executable file.

7
```
Open "coba.memo" For Output As #1
Open "book.letter" For Output As #1
Open "coupons.bond" For Append As #2
Open "yield.bond" For Append As #2
Open "prices.data" For Input As #3
Open "rates.data" For Input As #4
```

Exercises 10.4

1 a. One advantage of using a random access file over a sequential file is that any record in the random access file can be read and written without the need to sequentially access all prior records. Another advantage is that individual records can be updated in place, without the need to construct a new file. A disadvantage to random access files is that they store numbers in a non-ANSI binary format that cannot be accessed by simple text editors. A second disadvantage is that they generally require construction of a user-defined record type within the procedural code used to access them, making them slightly more complex from a programming standpoint.

b. Two requirements are that each record in the file be of the same length and that the stored data be in a non-ANSI binary format.

c. When dealing with large numbers of records it is more advantageous to store that data as a database file and let a DBMS, such as the Jet Engine (described in Chapter 9), handle the data access.

Exercises 10.5

2 Random access and binary files are similar in that both store data in a non-ANSI binary format. They are also similar in that the data in each file type can be accessed directly. They differ in that random access files are organized on a record level, where each record in the file must be of the same length, while binary files are organized on a byte position basis.

Chapter 10—Self Test

1 Print #1 will write an entire line to the sequential file. The various fields would not be distinguishable. This is generally used for writing a report line to a disk. Write #1 will cause individually named fields to be written with comma delimiters. Numeric fields are written without double quotes while text fields are written with double quotes.

2 random

3 access method

4 The 5 refers to the byte position to be read

5 A file called my.txt will be created on the hard drive. The program will use the unit number 3 in all references to this file.

6 Open "a:\testdata.txt" for Output as #1

7 Kill "a:\payfile.seq"

8 Close

9 Open "VBclass.seq" For Append as # 1

10 Input #1, fullName, socsec, salary

Chapter 11

Exercises 11.2

3 a. ScaleLeft = 50
        ScaleTop = 50
        ScaleWidth = 200
        ScaleHeight = 200

   b. ScaleLeft = 50
        ScaleTop = 100
        ScaleWidth = 300
        ScaleHeight = 600

   c. ScaleLeft = 100
        ScaleTop = 200
        ScaleWidth = 400
        ScaleHeight = 500

   d. ScaleLeft = 200
        ScaleTop = 200
        ScaleWidth = 600
        ScaleHeight = 600

Chapter 11—Self Test

1 Shape

2 black

3 container

4 Borderwidth

5 The image1 will be moved 500 twips to the right.

6 This acts as a toggle switch, if Command1.Enabled is true, it will be changed to false. If it is false, it will be changed to true.

7 This will produce 1 circle that has a radius of 1500 twips. The center of the circle is in the center of the usable portion of the form.

⑧ `Form1.BackColor = vbGreen`

⑨ `Label1.Visible = Not Label1.Visible`

⑩ `Command1.Top = 0`
`Command1.Left = 0`

Chapter 12

Exercises 12.1

① a. A class is a programmer defined data type. The class specifies both the types of data and the types of operations that may be performed on the data.

b. An object is a specific instance of a class.

c. The declaration section declares the data types of a class.

d. The implementation section defines the class's functions.

e. An instance variable is another name for a class data member.

f. A member method is a procedure or function defined in the class implementation section.

g. A data member is a variable declared in the class declaration section.

h. Information hiding refers to the principle that the internal construction and implementation of a class can be hidden from a user of the class.

③ a. The class declaration and implementations are

```
Option Explicit
Rem: Data Member Declarations
Dim Secs As Integer
Dim Mins As Integer
Dim Hours As Integer
Public Sub settime(ss As Integer, mm As Integer, hh As Integer)
  Secs = ss
  Mins = mm
  Hours = hh
End Sub

Public Function showtime() As String
  showtime = Format(Hours,"00") + ":" + Format(Mins,"00") + ":"
            + Format(Secs, "00")
End Function
```

⑤ Both data members should be declared as **Private** to ensure that they only can be accessed using member procedures and functions.

Exercises 12.2

③ a. The class declaration and implementations are

```
Option Explicit
Rem: Data Member Declarations
Dim Secs As Integer
Dim Mins As Integer
Dim Hours As Integer
```

continued

```
Public Sub settime(ss As Integer, mm As Integer, hh As Integer)
  Secs = ss
  Mins = mm
  Hours = hh
End Sub

Public Function showtime() As String
  showtime = Format(Hours,"00") + ":" + Format(Mins,"00") + ":"
           + Format(Secs, "00")
End Function

Private Sub Class_Initialize()
  Secs = 0
  Mins = 0
  Hours = 0
End Sub
```

5 a. The class declaration and implementations are

```
Option Explicit
Rem: Data Member Declarations
Dim XCenter As Integer
Dim YCenter As Integer
Dim Radius As Single

Public Sub setcenter(x As Integer, y As Integer)
  XCenter = x
  YCenter = y
End Sub

Public Sub setradius(r As Single)
  Radius = r
End Sub

Public Function showcenter() As String
  showcenter = "(" + Str(XCenter) + "," + Str(YCenter) + ")"
End Function

Public Function showradius() As String
  showradius = Str(Radius)
End Function

Private Sub Class_Initialize()
  XCenter = 1
  YCenter = 1
  Radius = 1
End Sub
```

Exercises 12.3

3 a. The class declaration and implementations are

```
Option Explicit
Rem: Data Member Declarations
Dim Secs As Integer
Dim Mins As Integer
Dim Hours As Integer

Property Let accessSecs(ss As Integer)
  Secs = ss
End Property
```

```
Property Get accessSecs() As Integer
  accessSecs = Secs
End Property

Property Let accessMins(mm As Integer)
  Mins = mm
End Property

Property Get accessMins() As Integer
  accessMins = Mins
End Property

Property Let accessHours(hh As Integer)
  Hours = hh
End Property

Property Get accessHours() As Integer
  accessHours = Hours
End Property

Private Sub Class_Initialize()
  Secs = 0
  Mins = 0
  Hours = 0
End Sub
```

5 **a.** **The class declaration and implementations are**

```
Option Explicit
Rem: Data Member Declarations
Dim XCenter As Integer
Dim YCenter As Integer
Dim Radius As Single

Property Let accessXCenter(x As Integer)
  XCenter = x
End Property

Property Get accessXCenter() As Integer
  accessXCenter = XCenter
End Property

Property Let accessYCenter(y As Integer)
  YCenter = y
End Property

Property Get accessYCenter() As Integer
  accessYCenter = YCenter
End Property

Property Let accessRadius(r As Single)
  Radius = r
End Property

Property Get accessRadius() As Single
  accessRadius = Radius
End Property

Private Sub Class_Initialize()
  XCenter = 1
  YCenter = 1
  Radius = 1
End Sub
```

Chapter 12—Self Test

1. object
2. types of operations that can be performed on the data
3. class
4. class module
5. Declaration section and the Methods Implementation section
6. cls
7. abstract data type
8. New
9. instance
10. created

Index